CANAAN,

AS DIVIDED AMONG

THE TWELVE TRIBES.

English Miles

0   10   20   40

The Cities of Refuge are
underlined thus **Golan**

A SCRIPTURE MANUAL

Directed to the Interpretation of Biblical Revelation

BY THE

REV. JOHN-MARY SIMON, O.S.M.

Bachelor of Sacred Theology

05888

VOLUME I

General Introduction to the Sacred Scriptures

and

Special Introductions to the Books of the Old Testament

SECOND REVISED EDITION

NEW YORK

JOSEPH F. WAGNER, INC.

LONDON: B. HERDER

𝕹𝖎𝖍𝖎𝖑 𝕺𝖇𝖘𝖙𝖆𝖙:

P.-M. CONDON, O.S.M., S.T.M.
Censor Deputatus ex parte Ordinis

𝕴𝖒𝖕𝖗𝖎𝖒𝖎 𝕻𝖔𝖙𝖊𝖘𝖙:

P.-M. BROSNAHAN, O.S.M., S.T.B.
Prior Provincialis

𝕹𝖎𝖍𝖎𝖑 𝕺𝖇𝖘𝖙𝖆𝖙:

ARTHUR J. SCANLAN, S.T.D.
Censor Librorum

𝕴𝖒𝖕𝖗𝖎𝖒𝖆𝖙𝖚𝖗:

✠ PATRICK CARDINAL HAYES
Archbishop, New York

NEW YORK, FEAST OF THE MOST HOLY ROSARY
October 7, 1924

MARIÆ
SALVTI INFIRMORVM

DOMINE DEUS MEUS, olim inardesco meditari in lege Tua, et in ea Tibi confiteri scientiam et imperitiam meam. . . . Sacrificem Tibi famulatum cogitationis et linguæ meæ, et da quod offeram Tibi,—inops enim et pauper sum. . . . Sint castæ deliciæ meæ Scripturæ Tuæ! Neque enim frustra scribi voluisti tot paginarum opaca secreta: aut non habent illæ silvæ cervos suos, recipientes se in eas, et resumentes, ambulantes et pascentes, recumbentes et ruminantes? . . . Vide Pater, aspice et approba. Et placeat in conspectu misericordiæ Tuæ invenire me gratiam ante Te, ut aperiantur, mihi pulsanti interiora sermonum tuorum!

—Confessiones, XI: ii

FOREWORD

Of old the Hebrews—whose whole history prefigured the Church—when they stood upon the outer ramparts of Jerusalem defending their holy city against the onslaught of the heathen Assyrian and Babylonian, keeping their eyes perforce upon the maneuvers of their enemies, turned their backs for the time being on the Temple of Solomon, whose glories were none the less the real inspiration of their valiant defense. Yet, when the hostile armies again receded from their fierce but unsuccessful attempts to breach the walls, providentially impregnable, the tribes of Israel once more turn their faces toward the Temple to gaze upon the beauty of its structure.

Thus has it been with the members of the everlasting spiritual Kingdom of Heaven, the Church, who are inhabitants of the new great City of God, and the defenders of its fair Temple of Revelation, the Sacred Scriptures. Whilst "the Gentiles raged, and the peoples schemed out vain devisings" (Ps. 2:1) whereby to undermine the very foundations of Christian revelation, the watchmen upon the City's walls turned all their efforts towards frustrating the attacks made upon the authenticity and historicity of the Sacred Scriptures, and little leisure was left to enjoy in reflective study the intimate sweetness of God's written word. Hence the majority of Catholic books on the Bible composed during the historic cycle just closing have been apologetic and critical in tone, intent rather upon establishing the existence of a written revelation than upon conning over that revelation itself. Excellent authors have of necessity been occupied rather with establishing the veracity and extension of the Scriptures than with explaining the content of their divine message.

But keen observers of the succession of historic vicissitudes may note that the violent tide of assaults on these points has reached its crisis, and is again tending toward the ebb. Vainly once more have "the kings of earth stood up, and the princes met together, against the Lord and against His anointed" (Ps. 2:2), arraying their armies of hypercritical devisings. Once more He that dwelleth in Heaven

v

hath laughed at them when they strove to destroy His sacred word, and the Lord derided those who would have overthrown the divine character of His holy Book. The mighty attacks made in the 19th century under the guise of Biblical Criticism have succeeded only in demonstrating how unshakable is the substantially supernatural quality of the Sacred Scriptures.

Those adversaries who, like Saul of Tarsus, were the most learned and sincere, and therefore the most keen and searching in their investigations, scripturists and critics who could and did apply every test of objective scientific scrutiny to the authenticity and integrity of the Old and New Testament documents, have one by one, sometimes gradually, often reluctantly, come to acknowledge that what the Church has ever claimed for the Sacred Books in their natural order, their authenticity, substantial integrity, and consequent credibility, was not to be denied. Nay, the very stones which the archeologist's pick turned up to build a foundation for his hostile preconceptions have indeed cried out in testimony to the historical truth of God's written word. Therefore it may now be said that reputable and really scientific critics or investigators have almost all ceased to deny the objective and historic value of the Bible.

The net result of the last century's controversies in regard to the Scriptures is this: certain qualities and functions ascribed to the Bible by the exaggerations of the 16th century innovators have been rather drastically ruled out; but the substantial authenticity and veracity of the Sacred Scriptures, ever claimed for them by the Church as a preliminary of their supernatural character, have remained undisproved, nay, have been brought out more emphatically by keen searchlights of investigations focussed upon them. Now, more than ever, "the words of the Lord" appear as "true words,—as silver fire-tested, purged from dross, seven times refined" (Ps. 11: 7). Hence also the man-in-the-street, Christianity at large, believes as firmly as ever in the supernatural character of the Bible, and is perhaps in even better position than formerly it was to interpret its message.

* * * * * * *

The present work means to recognize and take advantage of the last mentioned facts. So, instead of filling these pages with sham-battles over the ground so successfully defended by predecessors in the field of Scripture study, the author would encourage the use of the spoils of victory. He aims at being concerned with the con-

tent of Sacred Scripture itself rather than with the writings of its
enemies. His treatment plans to be exegetic rather than critical.

To facilitate entrance into the rich treasure house of God's inspired Book, so that the student may exclaim with the Psalmist:
"I will rejoice at Thy Word, as one who hath found great spoil"
(Ps. 118:162), is the primary object of this work. It is offered
specially to those to whom the custody and study of the Scriptures
have been primarily entrusted: the clergy. "Moses wrote this law
and delivered it to the priests . . . and he commanded them: Thou
shalt read the words of this law before all Israel, . . . that hearing
they may learn, and revere the Lord your God" (Deut. 31:9-13).
"Attend unto reading," said St. Paul first of all, writing Timothy
(I Tim. 4:13), referring, of course, to the Scriptures, and then he
continues: "to exhortation and to doctrine," as if insinuating that
the latter functions of the priest's work would flow effectually from
the first. Of old this duty was emphasized for a decadent period
by the last of the prophets: "The lips of the priest shall keep
wisdom, and the law shall be sought at his mouth, because he is the
messenger of the Lord of Hosts" (Mal. 2:7). And it is precisely
for the mass of the people, who form the woof of the mighty fabric
of the Church—who, by the way, are little interested in the academic
bickerings of the coterie of chronic critics in specialist periodicals—
that the priest is commissioned to explain the Scriptures, so that
indeed "the expounding of Thy words giveth light, and granteth
understanding to the little ones" (Ps. 118:130), whereas "the
wicked have told me fables, but not Thy law" (ibid., 85).

However, the method of this work is not exclusively exegetical.
The author has embodied statements of the more important difficulties that have been raised in modern biblical controversies and
has indicated the lines of their solution, whilst referring the student to earlier and more competent authorities for detailed technical
discussion.

The plan generally adopted here in the treatment of a Sacred
Book is the following: to give the author and date, and note outstanding textual features; to outline the political or social background, and point out the special occasion or purpose of composition; to sketch the arrangement and divisions; to indicate the
thought-content in the divers sense-planes; and finally, to note
any peculiar difficulties or points of special interest.

The order of Scripture study exemplified need not necessarily
be followed in class work. It may frequently be advisable, especially in seminaries where the biblical course begins during phi-

losophy, to start directly with some Sacred Book more familiar or more interesting to the student, such as the Pentateuch or the Old Testament historical section, and to postpone at least some parts of the General Introduction until later years of theology.

In connection with each article of the present work certain sections of biblical text are proposed for reading. These texts may have at times only an indirect or secondary bearing on the topic under discussion, although usually they comprise the more important or more striking parts of the Book under consideration. In any case, if their perusal is insisted upon as part of the class work, students can scarcely help making some acquaintance with the actual text of the Bible, and this superficial acquaintance will eventually develop, it is hoped, into familiarity and love. The English version of the Scripture citations is not always that of the current Douay-Challoner editions. Sometimes it is made directly from the original. Again, a passage may be given with interpolated expansions bringing out the sense, in order to eliminate a lengthy commentary that would otherwise be necessary. Passages of particular interest are, as far as convenient, given preferential treatments under the headings of their respective Books. But many passages will also be found touched upon elsewhere throughout the work. All are grouped together for easy references in the Index of Scripture Passages.

May Mary, of whom it is written that she "kept all these words, pondering them in her heart" (Luke 2: 19), and whose *Magnificat* shows her spirit steeped in the majestic cadences of the Old Testament, be a guide and light to all students of God's written word, by inspiration both divine and human, as is the Incarnate Word, of which she was truly the Mother! May every priest especially deserve the praise addressed by St. Paul to Timothy: "From thy infancy thou hast known the holy scriptures", whereby "the man of God may be made perfect, equipped for every good work" (II Tim. 3: 15, 17). For, what things soever were written, were "written, that you may believe that Jesus is the Christ, the Son of God, and that, believing, you may have life in His name" (John 20: 31).

THE AUTHOR.

ASSUMPTION PRIORY,
WELBY-AT-DENVER, COLO.,
Nativity of Our Lady, 1924.

COMMENDATIONS BY CARDINAL GASQUET AND
CARDINAL LÉPICIER

The *Scripture Manual* of Fr. John Simon, O.S.M., is a real addition to the many helps to students who are beginning their Scripture studies, and it is a handy book of reference for those who want to refresh their minds in regard to any of the questions about the Bible which are treated of in its pages, and in regard to matters about which queries are constantly put to a priest.

For example, one of the earliest points about which a student of the Sacred Writings will desire to have clear information is: the meaning and extent of Inspiration. This difficult question, as it seems to me, is treated by Fr. Simon in a clear and masterly manner; he gives all that it is needful to know on the subject, and his book contains a summary of what is taught by the Church in that matter. The treatment of the Canon of Holy Scripture, that is: The Books which the Church has declared to be part of the inspired Writings, is equally satisfactory.

A useful and most important section, especially in these days, deals with the creation of the world, and of man. The warning that the author gives from St. Thomas should be remembered by all students. He writes: "When reading the Mosaic cosmogony one should primarily keep in mind the comment of St. Thomas: 'In regard to the beginning of the world, something belongs to the substance of the Faith, namely: that it was created. But as to the manner and order in which it was created, such questions only accidentally, in so far as Scripture relates them, have to do with the Faith. Various holy writers have explained them in different manners.' It should be borne in mind also in regard to the six days of creation that in composing this section the writer of Genesis did not intend to display in detail the interrelationship and make-up of the material world and to explain the complete order of its coming into being in the technical terminology of a science text-book, but rather to give the Chosen People a popular but correct account in everyday speech that would be accommodated to the language and capacity of men of those days."

I am not called upon to pass a critical judgment on this book. That has been done by the theologians to whom it has been submitted. But, having read the volume, I certainly congratulate Fr. Simon upon having produced a very useful manual. And I earnestly beg God's blessing upon him and upon all those who will make use of his labors. A. CARD. GASQUET.

ROME, SAN CALLISTO IN TRASTEVERE
May 9th, 1926

Cardinal Lépicier, who until his appointment as Apostolic Visitor to the Indies, was a Consultor of the Biblical Commission, wrote the following letter to the author upon receipt of the "Scripture Manual."

My dear Fr. Simon:

Your book "A Scripture Manual" reached me here in the course of my apostolic visitations. Though pressed with work on all sides and with hardly time "to eat bread," I at once set perusing your most interesting volume. The affection I bear you and the paramount importance of the subject urged me to undertake this task, a task of love. And I will not tarry congratulating you on the success of your labors in this portion of the vast Scriptural field. There may, perhaps, be variances of opinion on secondary points; but, on the whole, I must say that you have struck the true note on many a vexed question, and that I consider your work a most valuable contribution towards the study of the Sacred Scriptures.

While the attitude you take on the more debated points shows that you are fully conversant with the latest researches, the cautious way in which you meet some modern unwarranted hypotheses convinces the reader of the care you have, not to depart from either the explicit teaching of the Church or that more recondite fountain of truth which is ecclesiastical tradition. I therefore gladly bless your efforts in the hope that you will soon give us the other volume which you implicitly promise.

Believe me, dear Fr. Simon,

Yours sincerely in Xto,

FR. ALEXIS HENRY M. LÉPICIER, O.S.M.

Visitor Apostolic to India.

PONDICHERY, FEAST OF ST. JOHN CHRYSOSTOM, 1925.

Dear Father Simon:

It gives me great pleasure to approve of your proposal to publish a re-print of your book, "A Scripture Manual."

A small work on Holy Scripture that has been so well received and praised by such an authority as His Eminence Cardinal Gasquet is certainly deserving of recommendation.

I am confident that it will not only prove useful to Ecclesiastical Students, but that it will become a very acceptable help to Teachers and Scholars alike in many of our Catholic High Schools and Secondary Schools in English-speaking countries.

May God bless you and grant that your studies of Holy Writ may redound to His greater honor and glory and to the welfare of souls.

Yours sincerely in Christ,

AUSTIN MOORE, O.S.M.

Prior General.

3121 JACKSON BOULEVARD, CHICAGO
November 9th, 1926

CONTENTS

FIRST PART

CONTENTS

CONTENTS xiii

FIFTH PART

THE PROPHETICAL BOOKS............................ 317

Art. 1. THE BOOK OF ISAIAS 323
    DECISIONS OF THE BIBLICAL COMMISSION............. 331
  2. THE BOOK OF JEREMIAS; THE LAMENTATIONS........ 332
  3. THE BOOK OF BARUCH 338
  4. THE BOOK OF EZECHIEL 340
  5. THE BOOK OF DANIEL 345
  6. THE TWELVE MINOR PROPHETS...................... 352

SIXTH PART

THE POETICAL BOOKS................................ 373

Art. 1. THE BOOK OF JOB 377
  2. THE PSALMS 387
    DECISIONS OF THE BIBLICAL COMMISSION............. 397
  3. THE CANTICLE OF CANTICLES....................... 399

SEVENTH PART

THE SAPIENTIAL BOOKS 407

Art. 1. THE BOOK OF PROVERBS 410
  2. THE BOOK OF ECCLESIASTES 414
  3. THE BOOK OF WISDOM 419
  4. THE BOOK OF ECCLESIASTICUS 423

APPENDIX. A DIGEST OF THE ENCYCLICAL "SPIRITUS
  PARACLITUS" 431

INDEX OF SUBJECTS, PROPER NAMES, PLACES, ETC......... 447

INDEX OF SCRIPTURE PASSAGES, QUOTED, COMMENTED, OR
  REFERRED TO.. 453

COMPARATIVE LIST OF THE TITLES OF BIBLICAL BOOKS.... 457

MAPS:
  CANAAN, AS DIVIDED AMONG THE TWELVE TRIBES......*Frontispiece*
  ANCIENT JERUSALEM.............................Opp. page 135
  THE TEMPLE OF JERUSALEM AT THE TIME OF CHRIST...Opp. page 142
  JOURNEYINGS OF THE CHILDREN OF ISRAEL...........Opp. page 232

A SCRIPTURE MANUAL

FIRST PART

GENERAL INTRODUCTION

Avete il vecchio e il nuovo Testamento,
E il Pastor della Chiesa, che vi guida:
Questo vi basti a vostro salvamento.
    Se mala cupidigia altro vi grida,
Uomini siate, e non pecore matte.
Dante, Parad. V, 76-80.

FIRST PART

GENERAL INTRODUCTION TO THE SACRED SCRIPTURES

PROLEGOMENA

1. Bible Unique in World's Literature.—Literature, the expression of thought in writing, is the supreme permanent product of the human mind, the highest form of earthly art. God, whose "delights are to be with the children of men" (Prov. 8:31), so much so that "He was seen upon earth and conversed" with them (Bar. 3:38), as if not content with sculpturing the tremendous sweeps of the everlasting hills and clothing in delicate hues the lilies of the field, deigned likewise to produce a masterpiece of the essentially human art of expressing ideas in language. This, the literary *opus ad extra* of the Divinity, is contained in the Sacred Scriptures, called the world over "the Bible," the Book *par excellence.*

As in His providential ruling of the universe, God generally operates through secondary agencies,[1] such as angels, men, and even creatures of lower orders, so in the composition of the Sacred Scriptures He made use of the coöperation of men as His instrumental agents. The manner of employment of these writer-agents or hagiographers[2] was such that the resultant work truly belongs within the realm of the world's

---

[1] "Habet autem hoc naturalis ordo divinitus institutus, ut quælibet causa primo operetur in id quod est sibi propinquius, et per illud operetur in alia magis remota, . . . et ipse Deus primo illuminat substantias sibi magis propinquas, per quas illuminat magis remotas" (*Summa,* 3a, q. 56, a. 1, c.).

[2] This term (derived from ἄγιος and γράφω and equivalent to "writers of sacred things") may well be used to designate specifically the human instruments God employed in the composition of the Bible, being authorized by St. Jerome (Prologue to Kings), St. Thomas (*Summa,* 2a 2æ, q. 174, a. 2, ad 3um) and the Encylical *Providentissimus* of Leo XIII. However, it has sometimes been applied to the writers of lives of the Saints.

1

literature [3] whilst at the same time it far transcends the latter by reason of its unique characteristic of Divine authorship. Hence, though the essentially Divine origin of the Sacred Scriptures must primarily be insisted upon, yet the fact of the true co-authorship of the hagiographers is likewise clearly to be borne in mind, else a correct valuation of the Bible and its proper understanding and use will not be attained.

2. Bible Paralleled with Incarnation.—In this characteristic double phase the communication of God's *written word* to men may easily be compared to that other, supreme, communication of the Divinity whereby God's *personal* "Word became flesh and dwelt among us" (John 1:14), assuming human nature in such a manner that the resultant Individual, Christ, was at the same time divine and human, true God and true man. [4] And just as neglect of clear recognition and distinction of His Divine and human natures has led to manifold misapprehension of the Person and function of Christ, so lack of realization of the double authorship, Divine and human, operative in the composition of the Sacred Scriptures, has ever been a basic cause of misunderstanding in regard to the status and function of the Bible.

As the union of the Divine and the human nature in Christ—with the result that human acts had Divine efficiency—was brought about by the Incarnation, so the combination of Divine and human authorship in the Sacred Scriptures—whereby human language affords expression to Divine ideas—was accomplished by the process of *Inspiration*. This is the unique characteristic which sets the Bible apart from and above all the rest of literature: it is θεόπνευστος, "inspired by God" (II Tim. 3:16). The fact of its being inspired may, in Scholastic phrase, be considered as the *forma* of Sacred Scripture, the soul which vivifies the body of the language content that may be called the *materia*.

[3] Thus the Bible is legitimately included within the scope of such works as Baumgartner's *Weltliteraturgeschichte* (I, pp. 3–53 and 143–157).

[4] "Perfectus Deus, perfectus homo . . . qui, licet Deus sit et homo, non duo tamen, sed unus est, Christus . . . non conversione divinitatis in carnem, sed assumptione humanitatis in Deum" (Athanasian Creed).

CHAPTER I

INSPIRATION

Art. 1: NATURE OF INSPIRATION

Texts: II Tim. 3:16; II Pet. 1:21; *also* Job 32:8.

3. The process of God's influence upon the hagiographers being a supernaturalization of human faculties and functions, is truly a *gratia,*—grace being naught else but a sublimation of man's natural life into the supernatural plane, [1] a participation by adoption in the very life of the Divinity. [2] Being given rather for acts of utility to the Church at large than for the habitual holiness of the recipient, it is a *gratia gratis data,* [3] a *charisma.* [4] Hence a state of personal sanctity is not thereby necessarily implied in the hagiographer. [5]

4. Definition and Explanation.—*Inspiration* means, on the part of God, *a positive supernatural influx on the mind of man, whereby the latter's understanding is illumined and his will determined to express such things and such only as God wishes to have written.* [6] This supernatural influx is primarily

---

[1] "The grace of God, life everlasting" (Rom. 6:23).

[2] "Being justified by grace we may be heirs according to the hope of life everlasting" (Tit. 3:7), and having "received the spirit of adoption of sons . . . we are the sons of God, and if sons, heirs also; heirs indeed of God, and joint heirs with Christ" (Rom. 8:15b, 16b, 17a). See *Summa,* 1a 2æ, q. 110, a. 3, c., and a. 4, c., and q. 112, a. 1, c., and many other places.

[3] *Summa,* 2a 2æ, q. 171, and q. 172, a. 2, 2°.

[4] "There are diversities of graces . . . : to another (is given) prophecy" (I Cor. 12:4, 10b).

[5] *Summa,* 2a 2æ, q. 172, a. 4. Thus, *e.g.,* the fact that Solomon sinned does not militate against his writing inspired works. Note, however, that the hagiographers generally are qualified as "holy men of God" (II Pet. 1:21b).

[6] "By supernatural power (God) so moved and impelled them (the hagiographers) to write—He was so present to them—that the things which He ordered, and those only, they, first, rightly understood,

3

positive, that is: the idea, or *verbum mentale,* of the truth to be written—although the latter may already previously have been within the hagiographer's purview of knowledge through his own experience or study, or from the information furnished by others (including written records) [7]—is conceived and expressed through God's special impulse moving the hagiographer's faculties in this function.[8]   Thus the hagiographer is but an instrumental agent, a secondary cause, a *movens motus,* in the operation of composing an inspired writing, God Himself being the primary cause.

The interoperation of God and the hagiographer in the process of inspiration may be analyzed in the words of St. Thomas.   "In revelatione prophetica [inspiration] movetur mens prophetæ [hagiographer] sicut instrumentum deficiens respectu principalis agentis".[9] Hence, "effectus [in this case, the Bible] non assimilatur instrumento sed principali agenti" [that is, the Sacred Scriptures having as their primary author God, belong essentially to the supernatural order], since principalis quidem causa operatur per virtutem suæ formæ, cui assimilatur effectus . . . causa vero instrumentalis non agit per virtutem suæ formæ, sed solum per motum quo movetur a principali agenti",[10] even though in this coöperation "instrumentum . . . habet actionem propriam quæ competit ei secundum propriam formam." [11]   Therefore "auctor principalis Scripturæ Sacræ est Spiritus Sanctus [12] . . . homo autem fuit auctor instrumentalis." [13]

then willed faithfully to write down, and finally expressed in apt words and with infallible truth'' (Encyclical *Providentissimus*).   The insufficiency of theories of ''subsequent adoption'' or mere ''freedom from dogmatic and moral error'' and the like, to constitute real inspiration, is evident from the above pronouncement of the Church.

[7] ''Qui hagiographa conscripserunt . . . loquebantur frequentius de his quæ humana ratione cognosci possunt, non quasi ex persona Dei, sed ex persona propria, cum adiutorio tamen divini luminis'' (*Summa*, 2a 2æ, q. 174, a. 2, ad 3um; also *ibid.*, q. 171, a. 3).

[8] ''Motus mentis propheticæ non est secundum virtutem propriam, sed secundum virtutem superioris influxus'' (*Summa*, 2a 2æ, q. 173, a. 3, ad 3um).

[9] *Summa*, 2a 2æ, q. 173, a. 4, c.

[10] *Summa*, 3a, q. 72, a. 1, c.

[11] *Ibid.*, ad 2um.

[12] Whilst, of course, inspiration, like God's other *opera ad extra,* is common to the Three Divine Persons, nevertheless this work is commonly ascribed more especially to the Holy Spirit (Acts 1: 16; 28: 25; Heb. 10: 15-16), because movement of the will is particularly the function of love, and the Holy Ghost is essentially by His relationship divine Self-Love in the Trinity.   This basic idea is well carried out in the etymologic relationship of *spiritus* and *inspiratio,* and in the idealogic of πνεύμα and φέρειν (II Pet. 1: 21).

[13] *Quodlibet.*, VII, a. 14, ad 5um.

In short: authorship essentially implies being the originator of the complete product of intellectual action, the idea formulated in a proposition. But God, by virtue of inspiration, gave the original impulse to the conception and expression of the ideas contained in the Sacred Scriptures. Therefore by inspiration God is the primary and principal author of the Bible.

5. Contingently implied in inspiration are two other charismatic subsidiary graces: the negative one of *infallibility* [14] and the positive one of *revelation*. Through the former the hagiographer is prevented from erring either by wrongly expressing inspired ideas, or by interlarding his own or others' ideas as inspired. Through the latter are made known, either by infused ideas or in vision, truths which are either beyond the purview of the hagiographer's own knowledge or altogether beyond the ken of human intellect. Whilst inspiration is continually operative in the composition of the Sacred Writings, these complementary or assistant graces come into action only at times when the hagiographer would otherwise either err or be bereft of necessary knowledge.

Infallibility.—Hagiographic infallibility is of wider comprehension than papal, since the latter extends only to *res fidei et morum*, whilst the former must necessarily be coextensive with the broad scope of inspiration itself. For the inspired Books include (often incidentally and as by-products) truths of the historical and scientific orders, whose conception and expression being also primarily of Divine origin, must be kept free from error equally with *res fidei et morum*. However, the functioning of biblical infallibility (concomitantly with inspiration) is to be restricted to the *autographa* or writings original with the hagiographers,[15] and is not to be conceived of as inhibiting the merely stylistic peculiarities of the periods, circumstances and persons of the latter. It should be borne in mind that the function of infallibility is simply to prevent propositional errors, negative, not to engender perfection of expression.

Revelation.—Just as the function of biblical infallibility is underrated by admitting the presence of propositional errors or of non-inspired *obiter dicta* in the Sacred Scriptures, so the action of revelation is exaggerated by extending it to every page of the Bible or by identifying it with inspiration. For, revelation, in its strict sense, is necessary only for the communication of truths which

[14] The futility of trying to reduce the whole nature of inspiration to this negative assistance becomes apparent when it is realized that the Pope is never considered to be the *author* of the propositions upon which he may pronounce infallibly.
[15] See No. 14.

transcend the natural powers of the human mind.[16]   Such are:
events of the prehistoric past or remote future, divine positive laws,
supernatural mysteries, like the Trinity. Its operation is not confined to hagiographers. Moreover, revealed truths are to be found
also outside the Sacred Scriptures, and not at all indicated, or only
barely suggested, therein, such as: that God is the primary author
of the whole Bible, the Immaculate Conception of Our Lady. Again,
private revelations have been vouchsafed at various times subsequent
to the close of public revelation with the death of the Apostles.
A case in point is the revelation of the Sacred Heart devotion to
St. Margaret Mary Alacoque.   Hence, a given book may contain
revealed truths, yet not be inspired, that is, have God for its author
and be privileged with infallibility. On the other hand, an inspired
book need not be entirely, or even at all, revealed.

Cases of this may be verified from the statements of the hagiographers themselves. Thus, St. Luke states that "having diligently
attained to all things" he wrote "according as they have delivered
who from the beginning were eyewitnesses and ministers" (Luke
1: 2-3). And the writer of II Machabees admits in his preface that
"in undertaking (that) work of abridging (the five books of Jason
of Cyrene) we have taken in hand no easy task, yea rather a business full of watchin and sweat" (II Mach. 2: 26). The translator
of Ecclesiasticus likewise witnesses that its writer composed it on
the base of "a diligent reading of the law, and the prophets, and
the other books, that were delivered to us from our fathers" (Prologue of Ecclus.).

6. Hagiographers' Coöperation.—Being a grace, inspiration does not inhibit the functioning of human faculties, but
rather perfects it; for, grace acts according to and not against
nature.[17] Now, the hagiographers were men having understanding, free-will, and all the divers characteristics of personal habits, associations, and language which in sum go to
make up the human individual. Though some of them may
at times have been in abnormal, ecstatic condition, especially
when receiving visionary revelations, nevertheless, such condition is not postulated for the actual composition of the
Sacred Writings.[18] Under the influence of inspiration the
hagiographers operated in the composition of the Bible freely
and with the utilization of their respective faculties, habits,

[16] ''Prophetica cognitio est eorum quæ naturaliter excedunt humanam
cognitionem . . . ;prophetia simpliciter dicta non potest esse a natura,
sed solum ex revelatione divina'' (Summa, 2a 2æ, q. 172, a. 1, c.).

[17] See Summa, 1a, q. 1, a. 8, ad 2um, and q. 2, a. 2, ad 1um.

[18] Hence the work of the hagiographers may not be compared to
automatic writing or to the literary productions of a tranced medium
whose faculties may be possessed by an alien personality.

associations, language, according to the ordinary processes of human nature in the work of composition, *citra errorem.* Thus in their allusions, metaphors, and language the hagiographers unmistakably left upon their product the imprint of their own mentality, times, and associations, just as other authors do upon ordinary works of literature.

So intimate, indeed, was the coöperation of the hagiographers with God in the composition of the Bible, that they may truly, though in a secondary plane, be called the authors of the inspired works which issued from their pens. For although the primary impulse in inspired composition is supernatural, nevertheless, the operation of the human faculties (being moved, as is God's way, according to their nature) is such that it parallels the ordinary processes of authorship. Consequently, from the human standpoint, the hagiographers are truly entitled to be called authors, or at least, co-authors of their respective works, as is ordinarily done by scripturists.

Hence, also, the hagiographer may be imaged, not so much as a pen in the hand of God, blindly tracing letters under His guidance, but rather as an amanuensis or secretary, with this superiority: that the hagiographer himself may also under the *afflatus* of inspiration conceive the propositions to be enunciated and elaborate their expression, *citra errorem.* For, God, unlike men dictating to a secretary, does not have to use words to impart His ideas to the writer.[19]

This interoperation of the Divine and human authors seems to be indicated in the latent simile of the text of II Pet. 1:21, which emphasizes that the hagiographers spoke " ὑπὸ πνεύματος ἁγίου φερόμενοι: borne onward by the Holy Ghost (as ships before the wind; see Acts 27:15, 17)". Now, a sailing vessel's progress on its course is certainly primarily due to the wind propelling it; nevertheless, the will and intellect of the mariners must equally coöperate with the power of nature to insure proper navigation.

Etymologically the use of the word "inspiration" may be traced to II Tim. 3:16: "Every sacred-writing, being *God-inspired,* θεόπνευστος, serves both for teaching and argumentation etc.", where the adjective used refers elsewhere to the heathens' idea of their

---

19 Thus ''dictatio'' the expression frequently used in dogmatic declarations regarding inspiration—according to Billot, ''consistit in interiore motione seu instinctu ad concipiendas mentaliter sententias et propositiones quas principalis auctor in libro esse vult, easque sic conceptas scripto consignandum'' (*De inspiratione,* p. 44).

seers being breathed upon by the divinity at periods of oracular
activity.[20]

Art. 2: FACT OF INSPIRATION [21]

Texts: Gal. 1: 11-12; I Tit. 2: 13; Exod. 34: 27.

7. Inspiration Not Demonstrable from Internal Evidence.
—That amidst the mass of the world's literature of all times
and regions certain books should have God as their primary
author can not be demonstrated conclusively from such writings themselves, although their unmatched beauty of diction,
sublime moral character, and hoary antiquity might lead men
to surmise for such volumes some extraordinary origin, and
to treasure their teaching of religion and morality beyond
that of all others. The reason is that acts of God in the supernatural plane proceeding from the free will (not from necessity of essence) of the Divinity, having consequently no
necessary connection with the natural order, can not become
known of themselves to the human intellect, whose unaided
powers do not transcend the natural order. Now inspiration
(the act whereby God freely becomes the author of certain
writings) is precisely such an act of the Divinity in the supernatural plane, having no necessary causal connection linking
it with the natural order. Hence, the inspiration or Divine
authorship of any book is not definitely demonstrable from
internal evidence of the writings themselves. Like other free
acts of the supernatural order (for example: the Incarnation,
or justification) it can become known and be demonstrated for
certain *only by external evidence,* that is: by revelation from
God declaring His authorship of such writings.

Now, the Church being the only supernatural organization
upon earth, custodian, therefore, of the deposit of revelation,
and, as the Mystical Body of Christ, the authoritative agency

---

[20] In *Pseudo-Phocyl.*, 121.

[21] The fact of the inspiration of the Sacred Scriptures is funda-
mentally assumed by biblical science, just as any other science assumes,
but does not demonstrate, its own basic principles. To prove the
inspired character of the Bible, then, is properly the function of fundamental theology, and not of biblical introduction. Hence this article
must be considered supplemental.

of communication between God and men in supernatural matters, it is from her official declarations that the fact of the inspiration, or Divine authorship, of the Sacred Scriptures can be established. The following are excerpts from such declarations.

8. Church's Declarations of Bible's Inspiration.—From the symbol of faith proposed by Leo IX (died 1054) to Peter III, Patriarch of Antioch, which even to-day is embodied in the test-examination for any bishop about to be consecrated: "I believe also that God, the Lord Almighty, is the one Author of the Old and New Testaments, of the (writings of the) Law and the Prophets and the Apostles".—From the Bull *Cantate Domino* of Eugene IV at the Council of Florence (July 6th, 1439): "The Holy Roman Church . . . professes that one and the same God is Author of the Old and the New Testament, of the Law and the Prophets and the Gospel, since, by the inspiration of the same Holy Ghost, the Saints of both Testaments spoke".—The Council of Trent (Sess. IV) declares that it "receives and venerates . . . with equally pious affection . . . all the Books of both the Old and the New Testament, since one God is the author of both".—From the Council of the Vatican (*De revel.*, can. 4): "If any one shall not receive the complete Books of Sacred Scripture with all their parts as enumerated by the Council of Trent, as holy and canonical, or denies that they are divinely inspired, let him be anathema!"—From the Encyclical *Providentissimus* of Leo XIII: "All the books which the Church receives as sacred and canonical are written wholly and entirely, with all their parts, at the dictation of the Holy Ghost".—The Syllabus *Lamentabili* of Pius X condemns, among others, the following proposition as erroneous: "Those who believe that God is really the Author of the Sacred Scriptures display excessive simplicity or ignorance".

Certain passages of the Bible—once the Church has guaranteed their inerrancy—likewise secondarily establish the fact of inspiration. Thus many of the prophetical Books have prefixed a statement that their content was written at God's order. See Is. 1:2; Jer. 1:2, 4; Ezech. 1:3, etc. The inspiration of the Old Testament as a whole is established by II Pet. 1:21 and II Tim. 3:16.

Isaias and Jeremias are vouched for by Acts 28:25 and Heb. 10:15-16; the Psalms by Matt. 22:43 and Acts 1:16. Of the New Testament, I Tim. 5:18 cites, as Scripture, Luke 10:7; the Epistles of St. Paul are put on a par with the rest of Scripture by II Pet. 3:15-16.

Art. 3: EXTENT OF INSPIRATION

Texts: Apoc. 22:19; Luke 11:52; II Cor. 3:6; I Mach. 12:9.

9. Precisely to what extent in the process of inspiration the supernatural absorbed the natural and God influenced the hagiographer, is a matter of the supernatural plane and consequently can not be defined from internal evidence alone. But, insistent and clear as are the declarations of revelation regarding the *fact* of inspiration, yet no detailed pronouncements have been given as to its exact extent in the above sense. The Church contents herself with warning that "it is absolutely wrong and forbidden . . . to narrow inspiration to certain parts only of Holy Scripture" (Encycl. *Providentissimus*), and with condemning the proposition that "Divine inspiration is not to be so extended to the whole of Sacred Scripture as to render its parts all and single immune from all error" (Syllabus *Lamentabili*, Prop. 11). She leaves open the question as to just to what extent certain phases of the complete product of inspiration may be more particularly traced to the hagiographers as God's instrumental agents. This warning of the Church was directed toward the error of those exegetes who, during the strong reaction movement of the 19th century from the Reformation's exaggerated sentimental worship of the Bible by Protestants, in deference to rationalistic criticism, thinking by yielding a little they might save much, began to limit the inspiration of the Bible according to the Socinian theory, restricting it to those parts only which treated directly of faith and morals.

10. Inspiration Must Extend to Propositions.—It is an established fact that God is the author of the Bible, of each and all of its parts. Whilst this fact does not imply verbal intervention, *it does demand that God be the responsible Author of each and every logical proposition in the auto-*

grapha, whether such propositions be expressed or implied,[22] and whether they be of the historical, moral, theological, or scientific order.[23] The terminus of inspiration (as of ordinary human authorship) is essentially the *complete unit of rational thinking;* and this is naught else but the proposition, or *iudicium* of the logicians, consisting of a subject and a predicate which affirms or denies something of that subject. Out of such propositions, elaborated in manifold ways, yet ever resolvable into simple elementary propositions, all literature is built up. According to whose mind the propositions primarily proceeded from, the true authorship of a book is determined.

Words being but arbitrary signs of concepts which are fractional parts of the proposition, and having no rational value outside a proposition, are not the terminus of the formal act of the intellect.

Thus, the *Confessions* of St. Augustine translated into French or English or any other tongue, must, insofar as the translator has done his work without error, still be ascribed to St. Augustine as author. Because, though all the words may have been changed, nevertheless the translation faithfully represents and contains the original propositions conceived and enunciated by St. Augustine. To the translator must be truly ascribed the new set of words, but the original author alone is responsible for the ideas contained in the translation.

11. Inspiration Need Not Extend to Words.—Whether or not God, besides making the hagiographers conceive the ideas, made them also use the very words and constructions which are found in the original texts, can not be determined for certain without revelation, as such a fact belongs to the free supernatural order. The Church has no formal pronouncement in the matter. But the following considerations seem to point to the view that inspiration did not extend, at

[22] An implied proposition is one only partially expressed, generally contained in a grammatically subordinate part of a sentence. Thus the opening sentence of II Kings 3: 1, "Now there was a long war between the House of Saul and the House of David", contains, besides the expressed proposition, also the implied one: "The war between the House of Saul and the House of David was long".

[23] So-called "obiter dicta", statements apparently made in passing, or of interest to the hagiographer alone, such as Tob. 11: 9, can not be excluded from the compass of inspiration.

least always, to choice of the very words in which the thoughts were expressed.

(a) God when acting through secondary agencies, generally does so with a utilization of the latter's own proper powers. (b) But a characteristic function of man is to express thought in words. Therefore it may be presumed that God would leave this function to the hagiographer, only safeguarding His instrument against error by the negative assistance of infallibility. (c) That this was actually the case seems to be indicated by the diversity of language and style so evident in the Sacred Scriptures, a diversity at the same time characteristically befitting the times and personalities of the respective hagiographers. (d) If inspiration were verbal, this phase would be of benefit to and could be appreciated by those only who might peruse the *autographa* or faultless copies thereof, and the vast majority of men, who are acquainted with the Scriptures only through translations in vulgar tongues, would appear to be missing some of the inspired quality of the original,—*quod apparet inconveniens.*

12. **Translators, Redactors, etc., Not Inspired.**—Inspiration meaning essentially Divine authorship of a book through the instrumental use of hagiographers, to claim that it be operative in translators, redactors, editors, copyists of the Sacred Texts, is a gratuitous assertion and at the same time a misnomer.[24] St. Jerome was the first to ridicule a kindred statement when made in connection with the Septuagint version: "Nescio quis primus auctor septuaginta cellulas Alexandriæ mendacio suo extruxerit quibus divisi eadem scriptitarent [interpretes]. . . . Aliud est enim vatem, aliud esse interpretem. Ibi Spiritus ventura prædicit; hic eruditio et verborum copia ea quæ intelligit transfert."—The senseless extremes into which the Protestant Reformation fell in its worship of the Bible, may be gathered from the Swiss "Consensus" of 1675, which claimed inspiration even for the 6th century vowel points of the Hebrew text: "In specie, hebraicus Veteris Testamenti codex quam ex traditione ecclesiæ iudaïcæ accepimus, tum quoad consonas, tum quoad vocalia seu puncta, *theópneustos*".[25]

[24] It is to be hoped that a future edition of *The Catholic Encyclopedia* will eliminate or change the following sentence in the article ''Psalms'': ''We incline to the opinion that God inspired the meanings of the psalms as originally written, and in like manner inspired every redactor who gathered and edited the songs of Israel until the last inspired redactor set them together in their present form''.

[25] *Art. 2,*—quoted by Reuss, *Histoire du canon des écritures saintes,* p. 295 (Strassbourg, 1863); may be seen also in Vigouroux, *Introduction,* p. 457 (1900).

13. Citations and Documents.—The Sacred Writings frequently quote the words of persons other than God or the hagiographer. Examples of such citations are: the words of the Apostle and of the bystanders during Peter's denial of Christ (Mark 14: 66-71); the letter of the Samaritans to Artaxerxes (I Esd. 4: 11-16). Such citations, when made explicitly and without indication that the hagiographer is adopting their wording simply as the expression of his own propositions, can not be considered inspired by the very fact of quotation,[26] except in the sense that the Holy Ghost vouches for the accuracy of the quotation. Consequently they may contain propositional errors.

On the other hand the use of uninspired sources and documents by hagiographers in the composition of their works,—such as the five books of Jason of Cyrene (II Mach. 2: 24) or the Book of Acts of the Kings of Juda (IV Kings 20: 20; 21: 25, etc.)—does not in any way militate against the inspired character of the resultant work. For, in such cases the propositions of these sources or documents are so assimilated and approved by the hagiographer's mind that they become his own. Possible errors, therefore, of the original documents, can not find their way into the hagiographic work.

Implicit or *tacit citations* of non-inspired sources (which, as citations, would not be divinely guarded from propositional errors) are not to be assumed just to untangle some historic difficulty. Such an explanation may legitimately be used only when it can be proved by solid arguments that the hagiographer (*a*) is really citing from another person or document, and (*b*) at the same time neither approves nor makes the other's propositions his own, so that the hagiographer can not be considered as speaking in his own name.[27]

14. Autographs Alone Directly Inspired.—The declarations of the Church offering no information to the contrary from revelation, it may reasonably be assumed that the Written Word of God, once it had been supernaturally composed

---

[26] Neither do citations from other books or references to them in an inspired work, imply that such other works were inspired. Evident examples are St. Paul's quotations from the heathen writers Epimenides (Tit. 1: 12) and Aratus (Acts 17: 28). Neither does the allusion to the Book of Henoch in Jude 1: 9 make that apocryphal work canonical.

[27] *Biblical Commission*, 13 Feb., 1905; see Appendix.

by inspiration, was thereupon left subject to the ordinary
vicissitudes of works of literature among men, just as the
consubstantial Word of God, becoming incarnate, shared the
usual vicissitudes of human kind, so that indeed He "removed
from Himself [all external glory and appearance of Divinity],
taking on a slave's form, being made in the likeness of men,
and in all appearance found as a man" (Philip. 2:7). It is
not denied, however, that God by His ordinary providence
thenceforth preserved His inspired Word from destruction or
formal corruption during the course of ages. But such action
of Providence in regard to the transmission of the Sacred
Text is certainly not to be identified with the grace of inspiration. To speak accurately, then, only the original writings of the hagiographers under the influence of inspiration,
the *autographa* which have all long ago disappeared, can be
considered directly inspired. Subsequent copies and versions
may be called inspired insofar as they reproduce with substantial accuracy the propositions originally expressed under
inspiration in the autographs.

15. Material Errors in Present Texts.—Human skill is
and always has been quite adequate to preserve the *substantial* correctness of public or official documents and even of
works of minor import in literature,[28]—else there would be
neither history nor classics. It was not fitting, then, that God
should work a continuous miracle to preserve the texts and
versions of Sacred Scripture from every material error of
copyists, redactors, editors and translators. For, the Bible,
whilst in its formal element essentially inspired or divine,
is equally on its material side a human document transmitted
in a human way. Hence in almost each succeeding copy or
version there have appeared material variations, additions,
omissions, and other errors which form the base of many
legitimate critical difficulties. But these lie upon the Written

---

[28] Even in this present age of high perfection in typographical art,
stenographers, linotypers, printers, yea even proofreaders, do not leave
the pages of books and documents absolutely free of errors. But no
sane man on that account denies the validity or authenticity of such
documents of books. *Bonus etiam aliquando dormitat Homerus,* said
the ancients, yet they never considered that a reason for rejecting the
Iliad as a model of Greek composition.

Word of God as the dust of Galilee's roads upon the garments of the Word Incarnate, proving real humanness, but at no time effective to destroy or even to cloak the essential Divinity beneath. For this reason, then, in the face of scriptural difficulties one does well to follow the practice of St. Augustine: "When in the pages of Sacred Writ I come upon something that seems contrary to the truth, I do not doubt but that the text is faulty, or that the translator did not strike the right meaning, or simply that I do not understand".[29]

As the most ancient manuscripts were written without any separation of words or punctuation (*scriptio continua*), a translator or editor might at times misdivide and thus misgroup the letters. Thus a Septuagint reading of I Kings 3:13 was "that his sons reviled the Lord", instead of the present King James version: "that his sons made themselves vile". Dividing differently, in like manner, Judges 15:19 reads: "The Lord clave a hollow place in Lehi".

Copies were frequently made by several scribes at the reading or dictation of one; then a word having a similar sound but different spelling and meaning from that read from the codex, might be written down in haste. Thus *lô* "unto him" sounds like *l'o* "not" and was probably written for the latter in IV Kings 8:10, where one should read: "Go, say: 'Thou shalt not recover!'" instead of the present: "Go, say unto him: 'Thou shalt recover!'" Sometimes, perhaps through illegibility, words or even whole *stichoi* or lines became lost. Thus in I Kings 13:1, "Saul was a child of *one* year", the italicized number is entirely wanting and marked as such by the Masoretes. In Ps. 22:4, before "Thy rod and staff . . ." the metrical construction and sense show the loss of one hemistich. Occasionally *homoioteleuton,* identity of words at the beginning or the end of a line, caused the scribe's eye to miss an entire *stichos.* To such an error is due the absence of the third Beatitude: MAKARIOIOIKΛAIONTES in Luke 6:21 of the *Codex Bezæ* (D).

An interesting combination of mistakes is to be found in the Septuagint translation of IV Kings 8:9, where that version reads: "Thy son, the son of Adar, the king of Syria" instead of the present: "Thy son Benadad the king of Syria". The Greek translator separated the first part of the proper name, *ben,* and translated it as the common noun "son". In what remained, *adad,* he confused the final *daleth* with *resh,* these two letters being most similar in the square script of Hebrew, and thus evolved the word "Adar".

[29] *Epist. ad Hieron.* 82:3 (P. L., 33:277). Compare also his *Contra Faustum,* XI, 5: "Ibi [in sacris litteris] si quod velut absurdum movet, non licet dicere: auctor huius libri non tenuit veritatem sed aut codex mendosus est, aut interpres erravit, aut tu non intelligis" (P. L., 42:249).

In the face of these facts the Church, whilst ever jealously insisting on the essentially Divine authorship of the Sacred Scriptures and their consequent freedom from any formal propositional error, has likewise been ever zealously watchful of the purity and integrity of the text, and has at all times encouraged the work of scripturists to purge it of the accidental material imperfections that have crept in during the course of ages.

16. Parallel between Eucharist and Bible.—In conclusion, the idea of the true nature and function of inspiration—which heretofore has been illustrated by comparisons with the Incarnation,— may be further brought into clear relief by noting a parallel that may be drawn between it and that earthly continuation of the Incarnation which is the Eucharist. Such a parallel will be evident at least for the faithful intimates of the operations whereby God "disposeth all things sweetly" (Wis. 8:1), so that His acts in the world interweave and mesh into wondrous patterns of beauty.

The Bible, the Written Word of God, *par excellence* the Bread of His doctrine, which, being broken by explanation "giveth understanding to the little ones" (Ps. 118:130), nourishes the minds of the elect, is like to that other Divine Bread, the Eucharist, in which the Incarnate Word of God is given to men for the strengthening of their souls. And, though the Eucharist is in substance the Divine Body and Blood of Christ, nevertheless It preserves in Its accidents (which are real) the normal characteristics of the bread and wine as they came from the hands of men before the Consecration. These accidents, then, vary with the materials, the workmen, the instruments of preparation, yet never is there any variation in the Divinity which is hidden beneath. In like manner Sacred Writ also, whilst in each and every proposition of its logical substance it is Divine, God's own thought, yet, being expressed in human words it perfectly preserves the accidents of language and style which were the hagiographer's at the time of inspiration. In both the Eucharist and the Scriptures the accidents may be affected by vicissitudes of time and place, but the substantial Divinity ever remains concealed beneath, discernible to the eye of Faith alone.

CHAPTER II

CANONICS

17. Of equal import with having the correct idea of the nature and extent of Inspiration, is it to know just *which Books* of the world's vast literature *are inspired*. These Books have at divers times been enumerated in lists called "canons",[1] whence such Books are also called "canonical". Of these lists or canons some are official and authoritative, others are those of private persons, generally, however, reflecting the acceptance of the community. Moreover a canon may be either a formal pronouncement, or it may be constituted by the universal acceptance of some definite collection of Books. As St. Vincent of Lerins says: "In ipsa catholica ecclesia magnopere curandum est: ut id teneamus quod ubique, quod semper, quod ab omnibus, creditum est; hoc est etenim vere proprieque catholicum" (*Commonit.*, c. 2).

18. Church Alone Can Establish Canon.—As the inspired character of any given book is not determinable for certain from internal criteria,[2] because this fact belongs essentially and exclusively to the supernatural plane, which transcends the powers of unaided reason, the *declaration as to which Books are inspired,* or canonical, *belongs* in the last instance *to the Church,* which is the divinely constituted intermediary between the natural and the supernatural orders.

But the Church broadly has declared that a certain collection of Books, primarily divided into two groups called the Old and the New Testament respectively, are inspired of God.[3] Of these two groups, the Old Testament came into

[1] From κανών in the sense of "standard or norm"; hence it is equivalent to "rule of faith" here.

[2] See No. 7 above.

[3] See No. 8 above.—There is not here a vicious circle, as if the Church were used to prove the divinity of the Bible, and the Bible as inspired to vindicate the supernatural character of the Church. For,

being and use before the establishment of the Church. Hence she received and accepted its canonical listing from her legitimate predecessor, the Synagogue, as held by that organization before its supernatural and authoritative powers became void. The individual Books comprised in each of these two main groups are considered below.

Art. 1: OLD TESTAMENT CANON

Texts: Deut. 17:18; 31:9; Jos. 24:26a; Prov. 25:1; Dan. 9:2; II Esd. 8:1, 18; 9:3; I Mach. 159-60; 12:9; II Mach. 2:13-15; Luke 24:44.

19. The texts alleged above give, in broad outlines and implications, evidence as to which books were considered by the Synagogue as inspired. To these texts should be added the statement of the Prologue of Ecclesiasticus to the effect that the translator's grandfather had read "the law, the prophets, and other books, that were delivered to us from our fathers". Two others passages therein testify to the existence of an acknowledged collection consisting of "the law, the prophets, and the rest of the books".

Likewise of value is the testimony of Josephus (about A.D. 100), although it must be kept in mind that this author reflects the mind of Jewry when it had already been stripped of supernatural authority and become hostile to the Church and all its works. "Only prophets . . . have written the original and earliest accounts of things, as they learned them of God Himself by inspiration; and others have written what hath happened in their own times, and that in a very distinct manner also. [No. 8] For we have not an innumerable multitude of books among us, disagreeing from and contradicting one another, but only twenty-two books, which contain the records of all the past times, which are justly believed to be divine. And of them, five belong to Moses, which contain his laws and the traditions of the origin of mankind till his death. . . . But as to the time from the death of Moses till the reign of Artaxerxes . . . the prophets who were after Moses wrote

leaving aside altogether its supernatural aspect and demonstrative value, the Bible may be utilized in the same manner as any purely human collection of sources or documents witnessing to facts of the world's history. Thus merely as a human historical source of evidence the Bible taken in conjunction with other sources demonstrates that God revealed a supernatural order to men, and established the Church as the formal organization of the order with human kind.

down what was done in their times in thirteen books. The remaining four books contain hymns to God, and precepts for the conduct of human life. It is true our history hath been written since Artaxerxes very particularly, but hath not been esteemed of the like authority with the former by our forefathers, because there hath not been an exact succession of prophets since that time" (*Contra Apion*, I, Nos. 7-8).[4]

20. Ancient Grouping of Sacred Books.—In order to evaluate these testimonies properly, the ancient terminology and method of grouping the Sacred Books must be taken into consideration. Already in the 3rd century B.C. the whole Bible was divided by the Jews into three large sections: I, the *Thora,* or law,[5] comprising the five Books of Moses; II, the *Nebyim,* or Prophets, including besides strictly prophetical works in the modern sense, also historical works, such as Kings; III, the *Kethubim,* the Rest, or Others (called also David or Psalms, from its most distinguished part), which embraced chiefly poetical and gnomic compositions, but likewise minor historical works which had been accepted after the groups of the Law and the Prophets had already been closed. Whilst the content of all three groups was considered equally canonical and as such used indiscriminately in the public readings, nevertheless especial veneration attached to the Books which were more antique.

Moreover it must be remembered that in ancient times several Books at present considered distinct were grouped as single volumes. Thus the present two Books each of Samuel, Kings, and Chronicles, once formed respectively single volumes. Judges originally seems to have been joined to Ruth; Jeremias included the Lamentations and Baruch; Esdras and Nehemias were one.

These considerations help to explain the number (thirteen) of

[4] Data on the O. T. canon derived from the Talmud are not very illuminating. *Baba bathra* discusses the canon; on f. 14b it is noted that the recording of Cant., Eccles., and Is. was fostered by King Ezechias. The comments of the Mishna, it must be remembered, were written long after Christ, and are frequently colored by hostility to the Church.

[5] Originally Josue may have been grouped with the Pentateuch, as seems suggested by the mutilated Jos. which the Samaritans seem to have known. Sometimes, however, the designation "law" seems to be used for the whole Old Testament, as in John 12: 34.

books assigned by Josephus to the *Nebyim*, although it can not now be determined just which books he included. For the abnormally low figure (four) assigned to the third group, the *Kethubim*, it must be noted that Josephus' figures had to fit into the artificial total of "twenty-two" (corresponding to the number of letters in the Hebrew alphabet). Moreover in his day the Pharisaic party's narrowing of the canon to exclude works composed in a foreign tongue or outside the limits of Palestine had already begun. In his closing sentence Josephus himself admits the existence of other books than those of his enumeration, which had canonical claim, even whilst he disparages them.

21. Alexandrine or Septuagint Canon.—But the full detailed canon of the Old Testament as generally accepted by the Synagogue at the time that the Church was established, is witnessed to unmistakably by the Books comprised in the Septuagint or Greek version.[6] This collection, reflecting the authentic unbiased acceptance of universal Jewry (and not of one sect or group alone, as did the much later Palestinian selection) includes all the Books enumerated in the adjoined conspectus, although the order may vary slightly in different MSS.

The Old Testament Canon

The *Thora, Nómos,* or **Law (Moses)**	Genesis Exodus Leviticus Numbers Deuteronomy	*Alluded to in following texts:* Deut. 17:18; 31:9
....		II Esd. 8:1, 18; 9:3 Jos. 24:26a
The *Nebyim, Prophêtai,* or **Prophets,**	Josue Judges and Ruth I, II Kings	
"Earlier Prophets"	III, IV Kings	
"Later Prophets"	Isaias Jeremias, Lamentations and *Baruch Ezechiel	Dan. 9:2
	Osee, Joel, Amos, Abdias, J o n a s, Micheas, Nahum, Habacuc, Sophonias, Aggeus, Zacharias, Malachias	Acts 28:23

[6] See No. 55 below.

· ·

The *Kethubim, Tà Loipà,* **or other books, called also** "The Psalms," or "David," or *Hagiographa*	Psalms Proverbs Job Canticles *Wisdom *Ecclesiasticus Ecclesiastes	Prov. 25:1
(Books excluded from present Hebrew Bible as deuterocanonical, a r e marked with an asterisk.*)	Daniel I, II Paralipomenon I, II Esdras *Tobias *Judith Esther *I Machabees *II Machabees	II Mac. 2:13 Prologue of Ecclus. II Mac. 2:14 Luke 24:44

22. Protocanonical and Deuterocanonical.—Whilst the Septuagint collection of Sacred Books was ever accepted by the Church as the official canon of the Old Testament, still the fact that later Jewry by contraction of its ancient canon excluded seven Books (Baruch, Tobias, Judith, I and II Machabees, Ecclesiasticus or Sirach, and Wisdom) and portions of two others (Esther 10:4 to 16:24, and Dan. 3:24-90; 13; 14) caused some confusion. Because of this confusion, fostered by Jewish anti-Christian propaganda, some ecclesiastical writers,[7] from the 3rd century on, seem at times to hesitate regarding the full canonicity of the Books and parts omitted from the Hebrew Bible,—which were later called *"deuterocanonical".*[8] But even these men, although they

[7] St. Cyril of Jerusalem, *Catech.,* IV, 35 (Migne, 23:497); St. Gregory Nazianzen, *Carm.,* I, i, 12 (36:474); St. Athanasius, *Epist.* 39 (26:1177), etc. The disparaging attitude of St. Jerome, the great ancient scripturist, in his *Prologus galeatus* (48:556) may be laid to his exaggerated enthusiasm for the Hebrew text, and to the pronounced Jewish influences connected with his early biblical studies. Many of the Eastern writers of the Antiochian school came more under the influence of Jewish propaganda in this matter. Subsequent writers, down into the Middle Ages, based their opinions largely on the authority of the preceding.

[8] That is "belonging to the canon in a secondary manner", as opposed to "protocanonical", which was reserved for Books common to both Septuagint and Hebrew. These two terms seem to have been used first by Sixtus of Sienna (1520–1569) in his *Bibliotheca sancta,* I, No. 1, p. 2 (ed. Cologne, 1626).

theoretically held that these Books could not be used to establish dogmatic points in controversies, nevertheless in practice themselves cited them as inspired Scripture in their works.[9] There was no definite dogmatic decision by the Church concerning the matter,[10] until the 16th century Reformers directly denied the inspired character of the "deuterocanonical" works, and pinned their faith in the Old Testament to the Masoretic text alone as fixed about the 6th century after Christ, with the absurd results noted above (No. 12). Then the Church, through the Council of Trent, issued its decree declaring once and for all that the "deuterocanonical" works were in inspiration on a par with all the other Books of the Canon, thereby formally adopting for the Old Testament the older Alexandrine, or Septuagint, canon, which she had held in practice from the very beginning, and rejecting the later, Palestinian, canon as incomplete. The followers of the Reformers, however, have preferred to adhere to this newer, mutilated, canon, and Protestant Bibles to this day entirely omit the seven Books and odd parts called "deuterocanonical" from their versions of the Old Testament.

23. From the critical standpoint the correctness of the Church's choice in adopting the broader Alexandrian rather than the narrower Palestinian canon, may be vindicated from the following considerations, which tend largely to show that *the Alexandrian was* before the time of Christ *also the canon of the Palestinian Jews.*

(*a*) The Sacred Books which the Alexandrian translators and editors included in their Scripture collection compiled for the Jewish colony in Egypt must have been acceptable to it. Because between Jerusalem and Alexandria there was continual communication, and Jerusalem, being the motherland, could and would certainly have censured any unwarranted religious innovations in Alexandria. But Pales-

---

[9] Thus, St. Cyril cites Baruch as a "prophet" in *Catech.*, XI, 15 (Migne 33: 710); St. Athanasius, Wisdom as "scripture" in *Orat. contra gentes*, XI (25: 23); St. Jerome, Ecclesiasticus as "sacred scripture" in *Com. in Is.*, III, 15 (24: 67); and others in like manner.

[10] The "Decretal of Pope Gelasius" (492-496) enumerated the Books "received [in any manner] by the universal Catholic Church".

tine did not reject the Alexandrian canon till about the year 100 after Christ, at the earliest.

(b) From the *Letter of Aristeas* [11] and the *Letter of the Palestinian Jews* (II Mach. 2 : 14-15), one may deduce that the pre-Christian Palestinian Synagogue itself furnished Alexandria with most of the material for the Septuagint version. Again, an isolated Jewish sect of Upper Egypt (Abyssinia), the Falashas, dating from before the Christian era, uses an Ethiopic Old Testament which also contains all the "deutero-canonical" Books.[12]

(c) The Septuagint version is used almost exclusively in the writings of the New Testament, showing that during Christ's time or shortly after it was in full repute in Palestine. Moreover, almost a hundred passages in the New Testament have been shown to be quotations from or allusions to "deuterocanonical" texts.[13]

(d) In the Talmud Ecclesiasticus is mentioned as Scripture with the Law and the Prophets, about the 4th century.[14] Baruch was read in the synagogues as late as the 3rd century.[15]

By accepting the Greek versions of the Old Testament rather than the Hebrew text as it was edited about a century after Christ, the Church provided rather a superior text and better readings of the Old Law, because the Septuagint version was based in its translations upon much more ancient MSS. than were available for the present standard Hebrew Bible. Moreover, in a few places this later Hebrew text seems to have been deliberately tampered with, in order to discredit Christianity (e. g.: Ps. 109: 3; 21: 17).

24. The present Hebrew (so-called Palestinian) canon seems to date from not earlier than the famous Jewish synagogue of Jabneh or Jamnia, where the leaders of the then defunct Synagogue (after the fall of Jerusalem) assembled and, among other matters, decreed that Ecclesiastes and Canticles belonged to the *Hagiographa.* By that time the

---

[11] Josephus, *Antiquities*, XII, ii, 11, 13.

[12] Trumpp, *Göttingische gelehrte Anzeigen*, 30th Jan., 1878, p. 132.

[13] Thus James 1: 19 witnesses to Ecclus. 5: 11; 4:29; I Cor. 2: 10 to Judith 8: 14; Heb. 11: 34–35 to II Mach. 6: 18; 7: 42; Rom. 1: 20–32 to Wisdom 13–15; Heb. 1: 3 to Wisdom 7: 26, etc. The allusions can be best appreciated by comparison in the Greek text.

[14] *Kamma*, 92b; also *Sabbath*, c. 1; *Edayoth*, V, 3.

[15] Eusebius, *Hist. eccl.*, VI, 25 (Migne, 20: 581).

Pharisaic party was in full control of Jewish national and religious life. Hence, according to their exaggerated principle of non-communication with the *goyim,* the Gentiles, they seem to have ruthlessly cast out of their canon of Sacred Writ all such Books or editions which had originally been written in a foreign tongue or upon foreign soil,[16] or which did not seem to conform strictly to the Law of Moses as interpreted by themselves. Therefore the present Old Testament series of the Jews and Protestants might in fact be called the Pharisaic canon.[16b]

Art. 2: NEW TESTAMENT CANON

Texts: II Pet. 3: 16; 1: 19; John 20: 31; Rom. 15: 4; I John 5: 3; Apoc. 22: 3.

25. Origin of N. T. Writings.—Whilst the Old Testament was ready at hand to the nascent Church, in the Septuagint collection, the new Scriptures had yet to make their appearance, for Christ Himself had left behind no written page. As most of the ancient hagiographers had been Prophets, so the writers of the New Testament were either Apostles or their immediate disciples.

[16] To breathe the air of a non-Palestinian country was, according to the latter Jews, legally defiling. See Josephus, *Contra Apion,* II, 25, *ad finem.*

[16b] This last is openly admitted by Max Margolis in his *Hebrew Scriptures in the Making* (Jewish Publication Society of America, 1922, pp. 87–91): ". . . That brings us down to the years immediately preceding and following the destruction of Jerusalem in the year 70. It was then that Pharisaism made ready to take over the sole leadership of the nation. . . . A stricter view was taken of the Canon . . . that body of near-scriptural writings which had hovered on the borderland . . . was resolutely pushed aside and put without . . . at the memorable session at Jabneh about 90 of the common era, when Gamaliel was deposed and Eleazar ben Azariah made head of the school. . . . The closing of the Canon by the excluding act which segregated the Apocrypha was the work of Pharisaism triumphant.'' Thus was the first false Canon established by those who refused to follow Christ and His Church. And this clearly post-Christian and erroneous norm was subsequently, when the 16th century ''Reformers'' similarly broke away from Christ's Church, adopted as the Canon of Protestant Bible versions,—despite the fact that Christ Himself had long ago warned His disciples to ''beware of the leaven of the Pharisees and Sadducees'', *i.e.,* of their specific doctrines (Matt. 16: 6, 12).

The Apostles wrote when particular local or personal conditions caused them to do so. Only a few of their works were from the outset intended for general use, such as the Epistles to the Colossians and Galatians, and the first Epistle of Peter. In the churches where the apostolic writings had been composed (St. Mark's Gospel in Rome), or to which they were addressed, and whither they had been brought by trustworthy messengers, it was the custom to read them at public worship. If then one or another Christian church expressed a desire to possess also some particular book of apostolic authorship, a copy was made and dispatched. No work was accepted as apostolic unless it had evidence for its authenticity from the church where it had been written, or to which it was addressed. If no such evidence were forthcoming, the book was not considered authentic, even though it professed to be written by an Apostle.[17]

Therefore not every Christian congregation can originally have possessed every book written by the Apostles. The multiplication and diffusion of the apostolic writings was hindered by well-grounded suspicions of their authenticity, by the poverty of the majority of Christians, by the difficulties of traveling and of transport, as well as by the danger of persecution. The collections of books must have varied at first, and must have remained so for a longer or shorter time, according to circumstances.

26. Some of the apostolic writings were, however, collected and circulated almost everywhere comparatively soon, so that, as far as is known, there was never any doubt as to their authenticity. These were: the four Gospels, the Acts, thirteen Epistles of St. Paul, the first Epistle of St. Peter, and the first of St. John. Papias and St. Ignatius Martyr witness to the existence of a collection which probably comprised these Books.[18] Thus during the first part of the 2nd century the greater and more important Books of the New Testament were already well known. But the Epistle to the Hebrews, the second Epistle of Peter, the second and third of John, those of James and Jude, and the Apocalypse, were known indeed

---

[17] Ireneus, *Adv. hær.*, III, iv, 1; Tertullian, *Adv. Marcion.*, IV, 5.
[18] Papias, in Eusebius, *Hist. eccl.*, III, 39: 4; Ignatius, in *Epist. ad Philadelphenses*, 5: 12, and 9.

to some congregations from the very beginning, but only later found general acceptation. For convenience in discussion these seven Books may be termed the "deuterocanonical works of the New Testament".[19] After the 4th century the full canon was accepted in all parts of the universal Church.

The New Testament Canon

The Gospels	Matthew
	Mark
	Luke
	John

....

	Acts
The "Apostle"	
	Romans
	I Corinthians
	II Corinthians
	Galatians
	Ephesians
	Philippians
	Colossians
	I Thessalonians
	II Thessalonians
	I Timothy
	II Timothy
(Books concerning which there was some hesitation till the 4th century are marked with an asterisk*.)	Titus
	Philemon
	*Hebrews
	I Peter
	*II Peter
	I John
	*II John
	*III John
	*James
	*Jude
	*Apocalypse

27. History of the N. T. Canon.—Setting aside references to the New Testament Books (including at least some of those

---

[19] To these "deuterocanonical" N. T. Books may be added the following parts of the Gospels, omitted in some MSS.: Mark 16: 9–20; Luke 22: 43–44; John 7: 53 to 8: 11.

later in dispute), to be found in the earliest Fathers,[20] a formal collection or canon may be traced in existence already in the latter half of the 2nd century, commonly held in Asia Minor, Gaul, at Alexandria, and in Western Africa, as attested by St. Ireneus, Clement of Alexandria, and Tertullian.[21]

For the Roman Church the testimony of the *Muratorian Fragment* is at hand.[22] Dating from about 170 (Zahn 210), probably originally written in Greek, but now reproduced in faulty and obscure Latin, it gives a formal canon, which lists all the present Books of the New Testament, except James and I and II Peter (if it be admitted that Hebrews is understood by "ad Alexandrinos"). Jude and two Johannine Epistles are put in a "deuterocanonical" category. One Epistle of St. John is mentioned in connection with the latter's Gospel.

For the 3rd century the *Codex Claramontanus* (D²) gives the full canon (except Philippians and Thessalonians, omitted by copyist's error). Hebrews is designated by the term *Barnabæ Epistola,* as some ancient writers [22] attributed it to the Apostle Barnabas.[23]

At the close of the 3rd century (about 267–338) the fullest account of the books of the New Testament is given by the ecclesiastical writer Eusebius. In his *Historia ecclesiastica* (III, 26) he gives the names of all the books which in his time

---

[20] In his edition of the Apostolic Fathers, Funk has counted 68 allusions to the New Testament in the Epistle of Barnabas, 158 in the first Epistle written by Clement of Rome to the Corinthians, 79 in the second Epistle, 53 in the letters of Ignatius, 68 in those of Polycarp. and 29 in the Epistle to Diognetus.

[21] Ireneus, *Adv. hær.*, III, xi, 7; Eusebius, *Hist. eccl.*, VI, 14; see also Origen (185–254), *Hom. 7 in Josue.*

[22] See text in Appendix. This catalogue is named after the Italian scientist who discovered it in the Ambrosian Library at Milan in 1740. It is mutilated at the beginning and the end. The fact that the author mentions the publication of the *Pastor Hermæ* "nuperrime temporibus nostris" during the pontificate of "Pius," (who can only have been Pius I, 142–157), enables the date of the writing to be fixed quite accurately.

[23] Thus Tertullian, *De pudicitia*, xx (Migne, 2: 1021). Some modern scripturists have conjectured that St. Barnabas may have been St. Paul's secretary in the composition of Hebrews. There is little probability to this opinion.

were regarded as being of apostolic origin, and he classifies
them thus: (*a*) those universally acknowledged as genuine
(ὁμολογούμενα); (*b*) those decidedly not genuine or of heretical
origin (παντελῶς νόθα); and (*c*) those whose authenticity is
contested.

Under the heading (*a*) he places the four Gospels, the
Acts, 14 Epistles of St. Paul, first of St. Peter and first
of St. John, and (though with some hesitation) the Apocalypse. Under (*b*) the Shepherd of Hermas, the Apocalypse
of St. Peter, etc., and under (*c*) the Epistle of St. James, that
of St. Jude, the second Epistle of St. Peter, and the second
and third of St. John.

In 363 the Council of Laodicea, after forbidding the reading of apocryphal books in the churches (Can. LIX), gives
a catalogue of the Old and New Testaments which omits only
the Apocalypse (Can. LX).

In Africa the Councils of Hippo (393) and Carthage
(397), of which St. Augustine was the leading mind, have
the full canon, as has also the Itala version.

At Rome Pope Damasus (366–384), Pope Innocent I (in
405), Pope St. Gelasius I (492–496), Pope St. Hormisdas
(514–524), all witness to the use of the traditional canon.

The canons of the ancient Abyssinian (Ethiopian) and
Armenian churches, for both the Old and the New Testament,
are identical with the present Latin canon. The Armenians
must have had a complete translation of the Bible from the
5th century. Whilst the ancient Syrian version (Peshito)
omitted the four "Catholic" Epistles and the Apocalypse,
the greatest Syrian authority, St. Ephrem (died about 373)
recognized as inspired all the present canonical Books.

Thus the current of ecclesiastical tradition regarding the canon
of Scripture flowed on, growing more and more definite with the
process of time and study. The first rejection of it came from the
16th century Reformers, some of whom rejected also the "deuterocanonical" Books of the New Testament, and especially disputed
sections of the Gospels. The decree of Trent on the Canon was
directed primarily against their errors.

28. Council of Trent Regarding "Parts".—Whilst but
repeating the traditional lists of the Old and New Testament

Books, as preserved in the Vulgate version, the Council of Trent laid emphasis on the inspiration also of every "part" of the Sacred Scripture.[24] By the word *partes* the Fathers of the Council *did not* have in mind *all the words and phrases* of Sacred Writ, but only the "deuterocanonical" sections whose canonicity was then being attacked or denied. At the most a *pars* would have to be understood of a passage of such length that its omission would rightly make a book be considered incomplete: a short verse or mere phrase would be called rather a *particula* than a *pars* of a composition.[25]

Art. 3: APOCRYPHAL WORKS

Texts: Deut. 18:20; Luke 16:31; II Tim. 2:16a; Matt. 24:4-5.

29. Origin, Nature and Value.—Apocryphal works are such as either falsely claim to be of supernatural origin and value, or were for a time esteemed by some to have such a character. The name is borrowed from the religious books of the heathen, which were carefully kept secret ($\dot{\alpha}\pi\acute{o}\kappa\rho\upsilon\phi$os = concealed). The Christians seem to have regarded all books falsely claiming to be inspired with the same sort of horror as the secret religious writings of the heathen. They are divided into Old Testament and New Testament *apocrypha*, according as their authorship or subject matter allies them to either of those groups respectively.

As for the apocryphal works in vogue with the Jews before the time of Christ, when not simply books of magic, attributed to Abraham, Moses or Solomon, they were chiefly concerned with the coming of the Messias and the end of the world (generally considered concurrent). The later Machabean times

---

[24] "Si quis autem libros ipsos *integros cum omnibus suis partibus*, prout in Ecclesia catholica legi consueverunt et in veteri vulgata Latina editione habentur, pro sacris et canonicis non susceperit . . . , anathema sit" (Sess. IV). See the entire decree in Appendix.

[25] See Lebel, S.J., in *La Nouvelle France*, pp. 159-174 (Québec, avril 1917). Franzelin, somewhat differently, was of the opinion that "ad *partes* declaratas canonicas pertinere imprimis loca omnia . . . quæ per se *testimonia ac præsidia* continent ad *confirmanda dogmata et instaurandos* in Ecclesia *mores*" (*De script. sacra*, p. 475, ed. 1870).

were rather prolific in such writings, which strove to raise the spirits of the Jews, then being galled to exasperation beneath the yoke of the Gentiles, by visions of a world-conquering Messias. Such works fostered many false or exaggerated opinions, which had to be corrected in Christ's time: one such was the belief in the proximity of the Parousia of the Messias in power. On the other hand, the better class of these writings may contain some stray passage of revealed truth as preserved in the ancient traditions of the Jews.[26] At times a study of their thought and language throws light on passages of true Scripture, by showing the mental background of the hagiographer.

30. Of entirely different purpose are the New Testament *apocrypha*. Masquerading under the cloak of apostolic authorship, they were frequently the compositions of heretics who thus sought to bolster their position with Scripture. Indeed, even the members of the Church at times incorporated their controversial arguments in such works. Sometimes, however, they are mere harmless and rather naïve records of pious legends or romances.[27] These works, too, are useful insofar as they may preserve some truths of tradition, but more especially as bearing witness unconsciously to the beliefs of Christians and their adversaries in their respective periods.

31. Among the *Apocryphal Writings of the Old Testament* mention should be made more particularly of: (*a*) *The Book of Henoch*, written by Jews in the second century before Christ;[28] (*b*) *The Psalms of Solomon,* a collection of 18 psalms, that have been preserved in Greek, but were composed in Hebrew by pious Jews in the second century before Christ; (*c*) *The Third and Fourth books of Esdras;* the third was written before Christ, but the fourth about A.D. 100;

---

26 A case of this may be the passage of Henoch, 1, 9, which seems to be alluded to in Jude 1: 14–15.

27 According to the looser methods of ancient (and especially Oriental) literary procedure, the placing of names of Apostles, etc., at the head of writings, was not always done with the intention of deceit. For, these characters were at times assumed only as literary vehicles for giving expression to personal philosophizing or romancing.

28 The complete text exists only in Ethiopian, edited by Dillmann in 1853. An imperfect Greek text was found at Akhmim in Upper Egypt.

(d) *The Prayer of King Manasses,* date unknown. The last-mentioned two books—(c) and (d)—were formerly often regarded as canonical, and so are appended to official editions of the Vulgate. To these may be added: (e) *The Book of Jubilees* or *Little Genesis* (not to be confused with the Apocalypse of Moses), written in Palestine by a Jew before the destruction of the Temple, to strengthen the faith of the Israelites by recalling their history; (f) *The Ascension* or *Vision of Isaias,* in Ethiopian, of the Christian era, incorporating the legend of the martyrdom of Isaias by sawing, under King Manasses; (g) lastly the heterogeneous collection of pagan, Jewish, and Christian elements in the *Sibylline Books.*[29]

32. *The Apocryphal Books of the New Testament* are very numerous. They fall into two classes: (a) those written in support of heresies, and (b) harmless legends and similar works.

(a) To the apocryphal books of the first kind belong:

(1) The *Gospel according to the Hebrews,* used by the Nazarenes and Ebionites, two sects of Christian Jews. The common opinion of antiquity was that this book was the Hebrew original of St. Matthew's Gospel which had suffered many alterations. This view was not shared by the sects mentioned, nor is it by modern critics. (2) The *Gospel and Apocalypse of Peter,* works with Docetic tendencies, written probably in Syria in the second century. A fragment of the Gospel was discovered in 1892 by Bouriant (see Zahm, *Das Petrusevangelium,* Erl. and Lpz., 1893). (3) The *Gospel of Marcion,* a mutilated version of St. Luke, dating from the second century. The *Gospel of Basilides* seems to have been a similar work.

33. (b) Among the legends and similar works, which are very numerous, may be mentioned:

(1) *The Protoevangelium of James,* brother of the Lord.

---

[29] Collections of Apocrypha: Fabricius, *Codex pseud-epigraphus, V. T.,* and *Codex apocryphus, N. T.* (Hamburg, 1703–1723); Thilo, *Codex apocryphus, N. T.* (Leipzig, 1832); Tischendorf, *Evangelia apocrypha* (Leipzig, ed. 2, 1876); *Acta Apost. apocr.* (Leipzig, 1851); *Apocalypses apocr.* (Leipzig, 1866); Hilgenfeld, *Novum Test. extra canonem receptum* (Leipzig, 1866).

The greater part of this book is concerned with Mary, the Mother of Christ, and the Wise Men from the East. The story is told in a simple and dignified manner, and it must be very ancient, as Origen was acquainted with it. (2) *The Gospel of Nicodemus*, extant both in Greek and Latin, a very dignified account of Christ's Passion, was highly esteemed and widely known in the Middle Ages. (3) The *Acta Pilati*, a collection of written documents and reports concerning Our Lord's Passion. (4) The letter written by King Abgar of Osroëne to Christ, and His reply to it. This correspondence can not be regarded as genuine, for the first Christian King of that district was Abgar VIII, who only ascended the throne in A.D. 176. (5) The *Didache*, or "teaching of the Twelve" Apostles, written in Syria or Palestine, and discovered in Constantinople in 1884. It is quoted by many of the Fathers, and was often used in ancient times for the instruction of catechumens, but as it does not possess any apostolic credentials, Eusebius (*Hist. eccl.*, III, 52) classes it among the ἀντιλεγόμενα. It is important on account of its high antiquity, for it probably dates from the first century. It contains 16 chapters in Greek. (6) The *Sayings of Jesus*, very recently discovered, and belonging probably to the third century. At first it was suggested that these were a part of the λόγια κυρίου, which, according to Papias, formed the groundwork of the Gospel of St. Matthew; but this view is not tenable. (7) Of considerable importance also is the recently discovered *Epistola Apostolorum*.[30]

[30] See the articles by Schumacher in *The Homiletic and Pastoral Review* (New York), from May, 1922, onward. Discovered by Carl Schmidt at Cairo as a Coptic MS. on papyrus (1895), the *Epistola Apostolorum* was finally edited with many additions and emendations, by him in 1919 (*Gespräche Jesu mit seinen Jüngern nach der Auferstehung: Ein katholisch-apostolisches Sendschreiben des 2ten Jahrhunderts, Leipzig*). To its early date (before A.D. 180) must be added the fact that it records with most interesting detail the ecclesiastical tradition of the 2nd century regarding the canon of the Scriptures, the *regula fidei*, Christology, eschatology, the spreading of heresies, etc. The work is an anti-gnostic circular epistle of an author or of authors who are writing in the name of orthodoxy. Particularly illuminating light is thrown on the *Descensus ad inferos*.

CHAPTER III

BIBLICAL LANGUAGE

Art. 1: LITERARY ASPECTS OF THE BIBLE

Texts: Ps. 118:25; Hab. 2:2; Deut. 30:11-14; Tit. 2:11-12a.

34. Bible's Style Characteristics.—Notwithstanding that sublime, unique, and withal basic characteristic of being of Divine authorship, which lifts it far above the plane of all merely human writings, the Bible comes also within the scope of literature, and is to be studied and appreciated as such. For, just as the Son of God in the Incarnation deigned to lower Himself "a little less than the angels" (Ps. 8:6) and to assume the limitations of human nature, so the Holy Spirit in Inspiration likewise poured the hot-surging flood of His exalted message into the fragile molds of man's speech, leaving clearly impressed upon it the peculiarities of style of each hagiographer and his time.

Morphological analysis, then, of the Sacred Writings is quite useful. For, a clear grasp of the outer, literary, accidents of any document, is an efficient guide to the appreciation and attainment of the inner substance and spirit; and any person who "recognizes that God has been pleased to put His revelation of Himself in the form of literature, must surely go on to see that its literary form is a thing worthy of study".[1]

35. Semitic Mentality is Keynote.—But as the Bible was compiled during the wide expanse of almost two millennia of history, through the instrumentality of many persons, who treated on divers topics, it would seem incongruous to speak of a common style for such a conglomerate. The fact is, how-

[1] Moulton, *Bible as Literature,* p. iv.

33

ever, that the thought and language characteristics of almost
all the hagiographers may be reduced to the common denomi-
nator of Semitic mentality.[2] For, almost every page of the
Scriptures bears witness that its propositions have passed
through a non-Aryan mind.

Indeed there is an abyss of modal difference between the
thought-methods and consequent expression-forms of the East
and the West, particularly of the Semitic and Aryan races.
Hence it becomes almost imperative for one who would appreciate the delicate *nuances* of Scripture language to be well
acquainted with at least one Semitic language. For, those
who know only their mother tongue, or have studied none
but Indo-European languages, will with difficulty realize the
differences which separate Semitic from Aryan thought-forms.
Such a person is easily liable to attempt to project the Western or Indo-European mentality into the entirely different
thought atmosphere of the East.

36. Semitic Mind Unanalytic.—Whilst the mental processes of the Indo-European, Aryan, races tend towards the
analytic, delighting to take apart ideas and to examine into
their constituent elements, the Semites prefer synthesis, to
combine or fuse together fragments of thought into broad principles or truths. That is perhaps why the West is the home
of philosophy (and rationalism); and the East, of poetry,
mysticism,—and religion.

The Aryan mind revels in numbers, division, enumeration,—
thoroughly analytic processes. The Hindu mythological chronolo-
gies of the *Vishnu-Purâna* divide time and divinities into such dizzy
immensities that this page could not contain the ciphers of their
calculations (see Baumgartner, *Weltliteraturgeschichte*, II, p. 10).[3]
The Semite, on the other hand, confines himself to a modest
"seventy times seven" (Matt. 18:22), or, at the most, indulges in

---

[2] Moreover later scripture writers frequently, consciously or unconsciously, imitate the style of earlier hagiographers, or at least are
saturated with the ideas and even expressions of their predecessors.

[3] Compare the Aryan trend toward the analytic in the ancient Hindu
Pançatantra, where the Ass of the fable enumerates the basic principles
of music, recounting "seven tones and three octaves and 21 intervals,
and three quantities and *tempi*, . . . three sorts of pauses, six methods,
nine keys, 24 shadings, and 40 conditions" (Baumgartner, *Weltliteraturgeschichte*, II, p. 210). Not even modern technique goes into such
detail.

vague "thousands of thousands" and "ten times a hundred thousand", figures never intended to suggest analytic approximation.

This lack of analysis, as a psychological characteristic of biblical composition, manifests itself in various ways. Thus, there is *defective recognition* or at least *expression* of the finer shadings of emotion or passion. Semitic mentality does not distinguish between hatred, dislike, aversion, on the one hand, or between love, attraction, preference, on the other. Frequently the two extreme terms alone are used. Thus in Malachy (1:2-3) God says: "Jacob I have loved, but Esau I have hated", and in the New Testament Christ seems to command His followers to "hate" father, mother, wife, and child, —instead of simply insisting on giving God's service the preference in all matters (Luke 14:26).

Again, the Jew of old gave little consideration to secondary causes, but easily referred all activity in the world to God as the First Cause. Whatever in any way at all may be traced to God, He is said simply and entirely to "will". No distinction is made between modalities of the Divine will: to wish, desire, permit, command, invite, counsel, give occasion, not to hinder or prevent,—all these are referred to the Divine will by almost identical expression, without any intention at all of thereby reflecting on the wisdom and sanctity of the Divinity.

To the unanalytic tendency of the Semitic mind must be traced also the general *use of concrete or circumlocutory* terms for the expression of the abstract, or of the finer psychic functions or distinctions. Thus, the body is *sarx;* the soul and life itself are designated as the "flesh", *basâr, néfesh*. "They are dead who sought the *soul* of the child", the angel says to Joseph (Matt. 2:20). The evangelists never write that Christ gave sight to the blind, hearing to the deaf, movement to the paralyzed, but rather that "the blind see, the deaf hear, the lame walk" (Matt. 11:5). Again, to "see" is frequently used to express the functions of other senses than sight: in Isaias the idol carver says: "Aha! I am warm, I have *seen* the fire" (Is. 44:16); and Christ Himself, on entering the house of Jaïrus, "*saw* the noise" (Mark 5:38).

This same Semitic characteristic manifests itself in *anthropomorphism*, that is, in speaking of God in terms of man. The hagiographers appear to ascribe to the Supreme Being, who is pure Spirit, not only a human body and lineaments,[4] but also human emotions and actions. Thus, before the Deluge, "seeing the wickedness of men . . . it repented" God "that He had made man upon the earth" (Gen. 6:6). But, after the Flood, God "smelled a sweet savor" (Gen. 8:21), as Noe offered sacrifice. In Exodus (24:10) it is said that Moses and others "saw the God of Israel, and under His feet as it were a work of sapphire stone",—a passage changed by the Septuagint translator to read: ". . . saw the place where the God of Israel stood", in order not to seem absurd in the eyes of Hellenistic philosophy. The Decalogue is written on two stone tablets "by the finger of God" (Deut. 9:10; Exod. 31:18).

37. Parallelism.—What the language of Sacred Scripture may lack in analytic expression, is abundantly made up for by its two other (likewise intensely Semitic) characteristics: Parallelism and Symbolism.

Of Parallelism [5] there are several kinds. The most common is that in which an *idea* is simply *repeated in other terms*, giving synonymic amplification. An example may be taken from the description of the Leviathan in Job (41:10-12, 19):

> Out of his mouth go forth lamps   like torches of lighted fire;
> Out of his nostrils goeth smoke   as out of a pot heated and boiling;
> His breath kindleth coals   and a flame goeth forth from his maw.
>
> .   .   .   .
>
> For he shall esteem iron as straw   and brass as rotten wood.
> The bowman shall not make him to flee   and slingstones are to him stubble.

[4] Not understanding this peculiarity of anthropomorphism of the Scripture, the theocratic sect of the Latter-Day Saints (Mormons) has made it one of its cardinal doctrines that God the Father has a real "body, parts, and passions".

[5] This peculiarity of Parallelism marks also ancient Babylonian and newer Arabic literature.

The next most common form of Parallelism is by *antithetic contrast,* exemplified in the following:

> A fool uttereth all in his mind:
>> a wise man deferreth and keepeth it till afterwards
>> (Prov. 29:11).

> Better is the poor man's fare under a roof of boards
>> than sumptuous cheer abroad in another's house (Ecclus.
>> 29:28).

Lastly there is Parallelism by a subtly *rhythmic concatenation* of thoughts which do not necessarily have synonymic or antithetic relation. The thought-cadences of this parallelism may be heard in almost all biblical writings as soon as these rise above the plane of mere history. A random example may be taken from Abraham's blessing of Isaac (Gen. 27: 28-29):

> God give thee of the dew of heaven
>> and fatness of the earth and abundance of corn and wine.
>
> Let peoples serve thee   and tribes worship thee.
> Be thou lord of thy brethren
>> and let thy mother's sons bow down to thee.
> Cursed be he that curseth thee,
>> and let him that blesseth thee be filled with blessings!

38. Symbolism.—Where Western poetry rests mainly upon imagery, the poetry of the East adds to the imagery symbolism. Elusive of definition, symbolism may be described as *the marshalling in one plane of thought of figures and expressions which* (by a kind of sublimated parallelism) *designate persons, things, and actions in a different,* usually higher, spiritual, *plane,* sometimes dividing even into a third thought-stratum or plane. The figures and allusions employed may be incongruous among themselves, and even incompatible with pleasing pictorial effect to Western minds. Still their use is most powerful and expressive. The symbolic style is most frequently to be found in the Prophets and the Canticle of Canticles: the Parables of the New Testament are in a manner allied to it. The selection given below is the eulogy of the Spouse by the Bridegroom in Canticles (4:1-4):

How beautiful art thou, my love, how beautiful art thou!
Thou hast doves' eyes, besides what is hid by thy veil.
Thy hair is as flocks of goats that come up from Mount
    Galaad;
Thy teeth are as flocks of sheep that have been shorn, coming
    up from the washing,—
All with twins, and there is none barren among them.
Thy lips are as scarlet ribbon, and thy speech comely.
Thy cheeks are as a piece of pomegranate, besides that which
    is hid by thy veil.
Thy neck is as the Tower of David, builded with bulwarks;
Upon it hang a thousand bucklers, all shields of mighty men.

39. Providential Fitness of Bible Language.—In the choice of Hebrew thought forms for the communication of so much of supernatural revelation one may recognize the wisdom of the sweetly disposing hand of Divine Providence. For, because of their simplicity, almost primitive, the propositions enshrined in them suffer little loss, in the hands of a skillful translator, when rendered into another tongue. In fact, no book has been found so amenable to translation as the Bible. Many even of the stylistic peculiarities of the originals may be happily reproduced in Western speech, without detracting from the readableness of the translation, a privilege not enjoyed by other classic productions of the world's literature. In fact, the more famous versions of the Bible, the Latin Vulgate, and the English Douay-Rheims and King James, are themselves generally considered quite exceptional in correctness and beauty of diction.

40. Scripture Language Essentially Human.—But, first and last, in reading the Bible it must always be remembered that Scripture language is not something esoteric, or set high above all the frailties of mankind, but is essentially human language, which consequently must be interpreted as such. "Est enim consuetum in scripturis", says St. Thomas, "ut divina per modum humanorum tradantur".[6] Its terminology, except in a few isolated instances, is not even that of the scientist; it is the terminology used and understood best by the common folk, the plainest, simplest kind of human language. The statement of the sublimest moral and theological

---

[6] *Contra gentiles*, IV, c. 23, ad 3 um.

doctrine is made, not with the intricate and abstruse technicalities of theologians, but in straightforward everyday speech that will bring the content of the message to the understanding of shepherds and fishermen, of the poor and unlettered, who were indeed to "have the gospel preached to them" (Matt. 11:5). And because men have presumptuously imagined that "by searching" in narrow, blind pride of intellect they might find out God, the sense of His revelation of Himself has been "hidden from the wise and prudent and revealed to the little ones" (Matt. 11:25).

"It is clearly necessary from the beginning to the end of time, that God's way of revealing Himself to His creatures should be a *simple* way which *all* those creatures may understand. Whether taught or untaught, whether of mean capacity or enlarged, it is necessary that communion with their Creator be possible to all. . . . In order to render this communion possible, the Deity has stooped from His throne, and has not only, in the person of the Son, taken upon Him the veil of our human *flesh,* but, in the person of the Father [better: of the Spirit], has taken upon Him the veil of our human *thoughts,* and permitted us, by His own spoken authority, to conceive Him simply and clearly as a loving Father and Friend, a being to be walked with and reasoned with; to be moved by our entreaties, angered by our rebellion, alienated by our coldness; pleased by our love, and glorified by our labor; and finally to be beheld in immediate and active presence in all the powers and changes of creation. This conception of God, which is the child's, is evidently the only one which can be universal, and therefore the only one which *for us* can be true. The moment that in our pride of heart we refuse to accept the condescension of the Almighty, and desire Him, instead of stooping to hold our hands, to rise up before us into His glory,—we hoping that by standing on a grain of dust or two of human knowledge higher than our fellows, we may behold the Creator as He rises,—God takes us at our word: He goes forth upon the ways which are not our ways; and He retires into the thoughts which are not our thoughts; and we are left alone. And presently we say in our vain hearts: 'There is no God!'" (Ruskin, *Modern Painters,* IV, p. 82; Everyman's ed.).

Art. 2: THE BIBLICAL LANGUAGES

Texts: Is. 19:18; IV Kings 18:26; II Mach. 7:27a; Acts 21:37c; 22:2.

41. Holy Scripture was written partly in Hebrew, partly in Aramaic (Western, called formerly Chaldee), and partly in Greek. The greater part of the Old Testament was both composed and preserved in Hebrew. Portions of I Esdras (4:8—6:18; 7:12-26), about half of Daniel (2:4—7:28), and a doubtful verse of Jeremias (10:11), are written in Aramaic. Judith, Tobias, Baruch, Ecclesiasticus, I Machabees, and parts of Daniel (3:24-90; 13 and 14) and of Esther (10—16) were originally written in either Hebrew or Aramaic, but have been preserved for the most part only in Greek translation.[7] Wisdom and II Machabees, and all of the New Testament (but Matthew—whose Aramaic original is lost) were written in Greek.

42. Hebrew.—Hebrew is one of the large group of languages spoken in Western Asia by Assyrians, Phenicians, Arabs, Jews, Ethiopians, and other peoples. The language group is commonly known as the Semitic, because the majority of the nations speaking such tongues could trace their ancestry to Sem, although some (Phenicians and Ethiopians) were in fact descended from Cham.

While an inflecting language, Hebrew (as all Semitic tongues), differently from the Indo-European languages, indicates the logico-grammatical relationships of its elements chiefly by changes of vowels within the words themselves, rather than by auxiliaries or additions, as do Western inflected languages. Hence also originally only the consonants were written, the varying vowel sounds with their important grammatical and categorical connotations being left to be supplied by the reader. Thus *DBR* may be read *DaBáR*, ''word or thing''; *DiBéR*, ''he said''; *DeBeR*, ''death or pestilence''; *DoBéR*, ''pasture'', according to the context. Hebrew has a very restricted and simple vocabulary (of scarcely 500 roots) and does not lend itself to periodic or other intricate expression. Both its terminology and its construction are so primitive as to be almost crude. Adjectives and adverbs are scarce; general and abstract terms, rare. A single word, particularly if a verb, may have a variety of meanings which in Western speech are expressed by quite distinct words.

[7] Of Ecclesiasticus, however, a great part of the lost Hebrew original has recently been discovered.

Thus, *qôl* may signify the "voice" of a man, the "cry" of an animal, or the "noise" of the wind or other inanimate things. Resulting difficulties in understanding and translating the Old Testament writings correctly may be readily surmised.

Unchangeableness, conservatism, being a characteristic of Semitic peoples, it is not surprising that only comparatively slight modifications may be noted in the Hebrew language throughout the almost two thousand years of its life. Nevertheless three periods may be distinguished in Hebrew literature: (*a*) the Mosaic period, marked by archaisms to be noted in the Pentateuch; (*b*) the period of the Kings, from Samuel to the Captivity, reaching its zenith in the writings of David and Solomon and of their times; (*c*) the period of the Captivity, a time of literary decadence, when foreign expressions, chiefly Aramaic, entered the language from the Babylonian environment in which Israel then found itself. At Christ's time Hebrew was already practically a dead language in Judea; and the Old Testament writings, when read in the synagogues, had to be interpreted in Aramaic for the people. (See also II Esd. 8:8-9).

43. Aramaic or Chaldee.—Through invasions, and most of all during the Babylonian captivity, the Jews adopted the Aramaic tongue, spoken in Northern Mesopotamia. It also is a Semitic language and closely allied to Hebrew. As Western Aramaic, or Syro-Chaldaic, this was the speech of Christ and the Palestinians of His time.[8] Afterwards it continued for a time in Jewish literature in the Targumim and the Palestinian Talmud. Eastern, or Babylonian, Aramaic, in which the Babylonian Talmud was written, has continued in Christian literature as Syriac.

Modern Yiddish, although written with Hebrew letters, is not a derivative of either Hebrew or Aramaic, but rather, in both vocabulary and construction, is a conglomerate of corrupt German and Polish with stray expressions traceable to Hebrew. Spanish Jews, moreover, have a different tongue.

44. Greek.—The Greek of the New Testament writings, and of the Septuagint version of the Old Testament, is not

[8] Aramaic expressions have been transliterated in the New Testament: *talitha qumi* (Mark 5:41), *kepha* (John 1:42), *abba* (Mark 14:36; Rom. 8:15). In His death cry, however, Christ seems to have quoted Ps. 21:2 in Hebrew, since He was misunderstood by the bystanders (Matt. 27:46-47).

to be identified with the classic language of Homer or Xenophon. It is called κοινὴ διάλεκτος, that is: the common or vulgar speech, being not Hellenic so much as Hellenistic Greek, as it was first spoken in the phalanges of Alexander's world-conquering armies. With those same armies and with the traders and colonists that came in their wake it had, during the three centuries preceding Christ, taken root along every caravan road upon land, and become the *bèche de mer* of every port upon the Mediterranean sea.

It was lacking indeed in the delicate flectional *nuances* of the ancient Attic, upon which it was based; it was blunt, and rudely disregarded niceties of grammar; [9] it gave new meanings to words of the old classic tongue; [10] it lent itself with facility to the formation of new words and compounds, [11] and readily absorbed terms from all languages. It was, therefore, fresh, virile, clear, readily adaptable to the newest topics and, above all, understood by most men from the Black Sea even to the coasts of Spain.

When this Hellenistic Greek was employed to express the ideas of Jews, as at Alexandria, the superimposed hebraistic words and constructions added a decidedly Semitic atmosphere. Moreover, at Christ's time already the Roman conquest of Greece and the world had left its traces upon this absorbent tongue in the presence of such purely Latin elements as συμβούλιον λαβεῖν, *consilium capere* (Matt. 12:14); πραιτώριον, *prætorium* (John 18:28); κῆνσος, *census* (Matt. 17:24 Greek).

This, then, was the language chosen by God wherein He would in writing incorporate His Son's message, to be the first instrument for spreading the revealed truth of both the

---

[9] Thus it uses ἔρχεσθαι with the infinitive: ἤλθομεν προσκυνῆσαι, "we are come to worship" (Matt. 2:2); the infinitive frequently with τοῦ, as: οὐ μακρυνεῖς τοῦ ποιῆσαι, "thou will not hesitate about doing" (Judith 2:13); ἵνα and ὅταν are often followed by the indicative (John 17:3; Mark 11:25).

[10] Thus εὐχαριστεῖν means "to give thanks" (Wis. 18:2); παῤῥησία, "constancy" (Wis. 5:1); σχολή, "school" (Acts 19:9).

[11] Thus ἀλλοφυλισμός means "following foreign customs" (II Mac. 4:13); γῦρος, "circle" (Ecclus. 24:8 [5]); φυλακίζειν, "to imprison" (Wis. 18:4).

Old and New Testaments far and wide, even beyond the confines of Jewry. Yet, outside the Bible at present it can be studied only in papyrus fragments and *ostraka* preserved in the sand heaps covering ancient Jewish colonies in Egypt.

CHAPTER IV

ORIGINAL TEXTS OF THE BIBLE

Art. 1 : THE HEBREW TEXT

Texts: Deut. 10 : 4; 27 : 2–3; 31 : 9; 24, 26; 1 Esd. 7 : 6, 11.

45. First Script Old Phenician.—The setting down in writing of the oldest section of the Bible, the Pentateuch, took place some time before 1200 B.C. along the route of the exodus on the way from Egypt to Palestine. Yet it is not unlikely that already Abraham, on leaving his homeland in southern Mesopotamia, brought along precious documents inscribed in cuneiform on clay tablets recording traditions of God's primitive revelation.[1] That these would be treasured, and that the ancestral mode of writing would be applied to the gradually developing Hebrew tongue, is not improbable.[2] But there is no proof that Moses used cuneiform for the composition of the Pentateuch. Nor is there any evidence that the Hebrews first learned writing in Egypt, and not even a theory that Egyptian hieratic was the script of Moses or his secretaries.

On the other hand, recent discoveries have shown that the alphabetic Phenician script, perfectly accommodated to writ-

---

[1] Trace of a cuneiform original may perhaps be seen in the odd *nà wanad* (=''vagus et profugus'') of Gen. 4: 12b, 14, derived perhaps from an Assyrian original *nu'u û nidu*, whence would come a justification for the Hebrew ''land of Nod'' (Greek: *Naïd*) of Gen. 4: 16b, which on the etymology of a Sumerian original *Nidu* would very conformably mean ''that [region which is] at the end [of the world],'' or, in modern parlance, ''No-man's-land'' (*Proceedings of Soc. of Bibl. Archeology*, vol. 38, p. 6; Jan. 19, 1916).

[2] The Tel el-Amarna tablets, making up a library of the reports of Syrian governors to their Egyptian overlords and giving the correspondence of the kings of Babylon, Ashur, Mitanni and of the land of the Hittites with the Pharaohs of about 1400 B.C., witness to the use of cuneiform in Palestine before the time of Moses. At Boghaz Keui in Angora Winckler unearthed Babylonian tablets dealing with Ramses II, 19th dynasty, who reigned about 1290–1220 B.C.

ing Hebrew, was in use in Palestine and adjacent countries
at least as early as Moses' time. On the very road of the
exodus Flinders Petrie found the Sinai inscriptions, of about
1500 B.C.[3] At Byblos, the ancient Gebal, on the north coast
of Palestine, the Ahiram sarcophagus inscription [4] shows that
in the 13th century B.C. Phenician writing had such fixedness
and ease of form that the old Semitic alphabet must have
already been in use for centuries earlier. All probabilities,
therefore, point to the Pentateuch's having been composed
in ancient Phenician alphabetic characters, and there is no
longer any justification for hypotheses that substantial errors
crept into the Mosaic work by transmission through several
diverse systems of writing. After the 10th century—Moabite
stele set by Mesa about 853; Siloam conduit inscription about
701, etc.—Phenician characters are found quite commonly on
the monuments, inscriptions and coins of Palestine,[5] even till
as late as the Machabees. The Samaritan Pentateuch, dating
from the First Captivity, has always preserved the early
Aramaic characters, still practically identical with Phenician
writing in the 8th century.

46. Assyrian or Square Script.—Rabbinic tradition [6]
ascribes the adoption of the "square" script, in which the
Hebrew text is at present preserved, to the time of the Captivity, and specifically to Esdras and the college of scribes of
which he is considered the founder. For this reason also the
characters were called "Assyrian." Archeological evidence,
however, does not trace their use in Jerusalem until the 2nd

---

[3] On these only a little over a dozen of "Old Sinaitic" characters
have been recognized, derived according to Grimme from the hiero-
glyphic and hieratic. In the longest inscription the "foreman of the
miners and superintendent of the temple" has without adequate base
been identified with Moses. See *Biblica*, March, 1925, pp. 26–49, and
Homiletic and Pastoral Review, February, 1926.

[4] See *Revue Biblique*, April, 1925, pp. 161–193.

[5] See Vigouroux, *Manuel biblique*, I, pp. 159, 162.

[6] Origen records this: "Narrant Esdram in captivitate alios
ipsis characteres loco priorum tradidisse" (*Selecta in Psalm.*, I, 2;
Migne, 12: 1103). Esdras may be taken collectively for the school of
scribes.

and 1st centuries B.C.   Hence it is most probable that the
Septuagint translation of the Pentateuch was made from a
text written in Phenician or Aramaic letters.   But by
Christ's time the square script seems to have been in common
use, since He speaks of the tiny *yod* and the delicate
distinctive flourishes of certain letters, which are still characteristic of the square script (Matt. 5:18).

47. Masoretic Fixation of Text.—Masoretes is the name
given to the long-continued group of Jewish scholars who,
after the time of Christ, looked to the preservation of the
text of the Sacred Books retained as canonical by the Jews.
They seem to have begun their labors shortly after the fall
of Jerusalem, and continued their care until as late as the
11th century.   Their object was to safeguard the integrity
of the Hebrew text by conserving its traditional reading as
handed down from of old.   They did this by laying down
elaborate rules for the copyists, noting anomalies of writing,
and counting the very letters of the text.   The beginning of
their revision or rather edition seems to have had for base
but a single manuscript which was used for correcting others
and for multiplying copies.

The minute details which the Masorah notes with punctilious
scrupulosity vouch for the general fidelity of the Jews in conserving
the Sacred Text unchanged.   Even the "smaller Masorah" accompanying the text in ordinary Hebrew Bibles, at the end of each
Book, counts the verses therein and notes the middle point, and
remarks such insignificant abnormalities as that the *Aleph* in the
first word of Leviticus is written a little smaller than elsewhere.
The "great Masorah" patiently recounts that the phrase *wayomér
Elohím*, "and God said", occurs twenty-five times in Holy Writ,
yôm sheni, "the second day" (Gen. 1:8c), but once; the letter
Beth, 38,218 times.[7]

48. One of the greatest services rendered by the Masoretes is the elaboration of the system of *vowel-points* and other
diacritical marks whereby the traditional reading of the
basic purely consonantal text is assured.   For, originally
only the consonants of the words were written (as is the case
with most Semitic languages), and the readers skill and tradi-

---

[7] Haneberg, *Geschichte der biblischen Offenbarung*, p. 756 (Ratisbon, 1863).

tion had to supply the vowels, as is the case even to-day in the official book-rolls used in the synagogues. The Masoretes crystallized the traditional vowel and accentual reading by little points and marks placed below, above, and within the original consonants. And the general conformity of the Masoretic reading with that of St. Jerome in the 4th century after Christ, and with that of the Septuagint before Christ, is most remarkable.

The Masoretes have likewise recorded a considerable number of emendations in the Hebrew Bible. These are the *qeri* (=that which is to be read), indicated in the text by a little circle over a word, which latter is *kethib* (=that which is written). The *qeri* are given at the foot of the text: they consist of real grammatical emendations (correct or incorrect), or merely of euphemisms to be employed instead of objectionable terms, in public reading. The holy name of God, similarly, was considered too sacred to be profaned by frequent pronunciation; thus *Ádonai* (=lord) is generally suggested to replace it. Now whenever a variant word was written in the margin as *qeri*, the vowel-points of the suggested word are affixed to the *kethib* word in the text itself. For the Sacred Name, occurring so frequently, the *qeri* annotation was omitted, but the vowels of *Ádonai* continued to be annexed to *YHWH*,—whence through ignorant reading came the word "Jehova" instead of the real pronunciation of "Yahweh".

49. Hebrew MSS.—Hebrew MSS. hitherto discovered are not very old or numerous. Perhaps this may be explained by the fact that texts of the Scripture, after they had become worn in the service of the synagogue readers, were laid away to decay in the *genizah*, being considered too sacred to be preserved for any common use. Thus there is scarcely any pre-Masoretic material, from which alone a fresh text might be constructed.

Aside from a parchment MS. of the Pentateuch written in 735 in Samaritan (Phenician) characters, which was reported found at Cairo in February, 1903, only one single MS., containing the prophetical Books, has been discovered to go back to 916.[8] A Crimean edition of the whole Hebrew Bible, dating from 1009, was deposited in Petrograd. The Pentateuch in the British Museum (No. 4445) belongs to the 9th or 10th century.

[8] See * Strack, *Prophetarum posteriorum codex Babylonicus Petropolitanus* (St. Petersburg, 1876).

Obtainable and useful *critical editions* of the Masoretic text are: *Kennicott's, in two folio volumes (Oxford, 1776-80), which considers only the consonants; De Rossi's *Variæ lectiones Veteris Test.* (Parma, 1784-88); *Haupt and others of the destructive school brought out the curious "Rainbow Bible" (Leipzig, 1893), wherein conjectured "genuine" and "spurious" passages are marked by being printed in different colors.

Art. 2: THE GREEK TEXT

Texts: II John 1:12; III John 1:13; II Cor. 3:3; II Tim. 4:13c.

50. Originals on Papyrus Lost.—Aside from Wisdom and II Machabees, the study of the Greek originals is concerned entirely with the New Testament. The Greek Books of the Bible came into existence at a less remote period than the Hebrew Books, but nevertheless the originals, and earliest copies of them also, have long been lost. The originals were no longer extant in the third century, as is plain from the writings of Origen, Clement of Alexandria and Tertullian,[9] who complain of difficulties occurring in their copies of the Bible, and of their having to take pains to discover the correct text by comparing parallel passages and other means. Had the originals still existed, it would have been quite simple for these writers to consult them, or to employ others to do so.

The early loss of the originals is probably due to want of durability in the Egyptian vegetable paper,[10] which was universally used for writing purposes in the time of our Lord and the Apostles. Many manuscripts perished, too, during the persecutions of the Christians. In spite of all this, however, an attempt to ascertain the correct text is much easier in the case of the Greek Books than in that of the Hebrew,

[9] Reference is occasionally made to Tertullian, *De præscript.*, c. 35, where he states that the Apostles' *authenticæ* still existed in his time at Corinth, Philippi, etc. The word, however, does not mean the Apostles' autograph writings, but only the Greek text as distinguished from the Latin translation.

[10] Papyrus was made of the inner layers of the reed of that name, which were laid across each other, to the requisite size, moistened with Nile water (which served as a glue or size), pressed and then dried, and marketed in bundles.

because of the availability of Greek MSS. dating from the early centuries.

51. Ancient Method of Writing Books.—All the ancient Greek MSS. of the Bible that have hitherto been discovered are in book form (*codices*), made of folded signatures joined at the back; continuous rolls (*volumina*) have not so far been found. All, except *Codex Q Paul,* are written on parchment.[11] It was only after the Crusades that paper made of linen gradually came into use.

The ancient MSS., despite the admirable skill of the monastic copyists who frequently embellished their pages with marvelous decorations and even miniatures in blue and carmine and gold, lacked many helpful details of the printed art, which make any book so easily intelligible at the present day. For, first of all, the ancients did not distinguish between small letters and capitals, and until the 10th century they always wrote with what are called *uncials* or *majuscules, i.e.,* the letters resembled the present capitals and were not connected with one another. *Minuscules* came into use only in the 10th century, and thus all the oldest manuscripts are uncials.[12] Moreover, ancient writers did not divide their words, and employed no punctuation or accents. In order, however, to make it easier for the reader to survey the whole, they did not write all the way across, but each page of parchment was divided into three or four columns. After the 5th century the stichometric mode of writing came into use, in which as much of the text was written on one line as was to be read in one breath; this was called a στίχος.[13] Later on, in order to economize space on the costly material, the end of each στίχος was marked with a dot or a little stroke, and the writing was continued in the same line. This was the

---

[11] The word *parchment* is derived from Pergamus, in Asia Minor, where the art of preparing writing material from the skins of animals was particularly well understood. Parchment was costly, but it had the advantage of being durable, so that when it was used the great trouble and expense of frequently copying the Sacred books were avoided and the risk of originating mistakes was diminished. Vegetable paper is less durable, and the results of using it had been unsatisfactory.

[12] *Literæ unciales,* literally, letters measuring an inch. *Literæ majusculæ, minusculæ,* large, small letters.

[13] στίχος = arrangement, row, member, division.

origin of punctuation. Greek accents came into general use only after the 7th century. In some manuscripts, both profane and biblical, it is possible to see that the accents have been added by a later hand, and were not inserted by the original writer. The text began to be divided into words in the 9th century.

Other graphic divisions or indications are much later. Thus Cardinal Stephen Langton (died 1228) was the first to divide the Bible into chapters, approximately according to content. But frequently the present chapter divisions do not accord with the logical parts or groups of the Books as originally composed. A little later the Dominican Cardinal Hugh de St-Cher, whilst compiling the first verbal concordance, subdivided each chapter into seven parts, marked in the margin by the letters a, b, c, d, e, f, g. Older editions of the missal and breviary still cite Scripture according to this system. The present enumeration of verses in the chapters was first introduced by Robert Etienne (Stephanus), a printer of Paris, in 1551. Its purpose is to facilitate citing a given passage, rather than logically to elucidate the text, for in fact it often obscures the sense.

The manuscripts are often only fragments, written on parchment that has been used to bind other books. Sometimes the Bible text has been obliterated, and other works copied on the same sheets of parchment. Such remains are called *codices rescripti*, or *palimpsests*. When the sheets have been used in this way, they have often been separated and fastened together again in different order.

Παλιμψηστός = rubbed off again ($ψάω$ = to wipe, rub). The original writing was wiped or rubbed off, and the parchment then smoothed with pumice stone to make it fit for use again. The old writing is sometimes still legible, but again it has to be revived by means of chemicals. Often it remains illegible, and occasionally the chemicals employed injure the parchment and the writing with it.

For the sake of brevity, uncial manuscripts are generally designated by Greek and Latin capital letters, and recently Hebrew letters have also been used; minuscule manuscripts are numbered. Indices are added to the capital letters to distinguish the manuscripts. Thus J is a palimpsest from Palestine, now in Petrograd; J^b is a manuscript in the British Museum; 51 is a minuscule manuscript in Oxford; 422 to 430 are minuscules at Munich. To the books of *pericopæ* also Arabic numbers are assigned, as *Evl.* 45 in Vienna (a book of the Gospels).

52. Greek MSS.—Greek MSS. of the Bible comprise not only the Books originally written in Greek, but frequently

also the Septuagint version of the Old Testament. The following are the more important:

(*a*) The *Codex Vaticanus*, B. It is in the Vatican Library in Rome. It contains the whole of the Old and New Testaments, with some very small omissions. It is written in three columns and came probably from Egypt, dating from about the time of the First Council of Nicæa (325).

Several printed editions of this manuscript have appeared, but they are not all free from mistakes. The Old Testament was printed in Rome in 1587, by order of Sixtus V. August Mai published the whole codex in 1858, and Vercellone brought out a more accurate edition in 1881 in Rome.

The New Testament was published by Loch at Ratisbon in 1862, and by Tischendorf at Leipzig in 1867. An edition of the New Testament, reproduced by photolithography, was brought out by Cozza-Luzi in Rome, 1889, and a similar edition of the Old Testament in 1890.

(*b*) The *Codex Sinaiticus*, designated ℵ by its discoverer. It was found by Constantine Tischendorf on February 4, 1859, in St. Catherine's monastery on Mount Sinai. It contains almost the whole of the Old and New Testaments in Greek, and is written in four columns. This codex, like the preceding, belongs probably to the fourth century. It is now in Petrograd.

Tischendorf believes this manuscript to be older than the Vatican Codex, but others doubt its being so old. It was printed at St. Petersburg in 1862; and the New Testament was published separately by Tischendorf at Leipzig in 1863, under the title, *Novum Testamentum Sinaiticum*.

(*c*) The *Codex Alexandrinus*, A, in the British Museum in London. It was found on Mount Athos and given to King Charles I of England in 1628 by the Patriarch Cyrillus Lucaris. It dates from the fifth century.

A printed edition of the Old Testament, by Baber, appeared in 1816-1828; one of the New Testament by Cowper, in London, 1860. The missing portions have been supplied from R. Stephanus. A photolithographic reproduction of this important codex has existed since 1883.

(*d*) *Codex C,* also called *Regius* or *Parisiensis,* or *Ephræmi rescriptus,* belongs to the same period. It is in the National Library in Paris.

Originally it contained the whole Old and New Testaments, but in the tenth or eleventh century the writing was obliterated, and the parchment used for a copy of some works of St. Ephrem the Syrian. Much of what was written first has in this way become illegible. About two hundred leaves are left, containing the greater part of the New Testament. It was printed by Tischendorf in 1843 and 1845.

(*e*) *Codex s. Matthæi Dublinensis rescriptus, Z.* This contains the greater part of St. Matthew's Gospel, and serves to fill up the voids in other manuscripts. It resembles C, and seems to belong to the same period.

As the name suggests, it is now in Dublin, and was printed there in 1801.

The following manuscripts are stichometric:

(*f*) *Codex Bezæ* or *Cantabrigiensis,* D, belongs probably to the sixth century. It was found in a monastery in Lyons, and came into the possession of Theodore Beza, one of the Reformers, who presented it in 1581 to the University of Cambridge.

This manuscript differs from the other texts in a very remarkable way. As it was found at Lyons, and exactly agrees with the quotations made by St. Irenæus from the Bible, it seems to be based upon a copy belonging to this bishop (177-202). It was printed by Scrivener in 1864.

(*g*) *Codex Laudianus,* E, contains the Acts of the Apostles. It is named after the English Archbishop William Laud, to whom it belonged in the seventeenth century. It dates probably from the sixth century, and is now at Oxford.

(*h*) *Codex Claramontanus,* D^2, belongs to the sixth century, and contains the Pauline epistles. It is now in Paris, and was printed by Tischendorf at Leipzig in 1852. It was brought from the North of Africa, and contains a list of the canonical books (see No. 27).

(*i*) *Codex Rossanensis,* Σ, found at Rossano in Calabria. It belongs to the sixth century and contains St. Matthew's and St. Mark's Gospels.

This codex was discovered in 1879. It is also called *Codex purpureus,* because the parchment leaves are dyed purple, and the letters are written in gold and silver. It is of artistic and liturgical importance on account of the miniatures in it. Another purple codex of the sixth century, containing a large portion of St. Matthew's Gospel, and agreeing in its text precisely with Σ, was discovered recently at Sinope in Pontus and placed in the National Library in Paris.

53. Critical Editions.—Editions of the Greek Books of the Bible, and indeed elaborate polyglots of the whole Scripture, appeared rapidly after the invention of printing. The most famous polyglot is the *Complutensis,* brought out by Cardinal Ximénez at Alcalá in Spain.[14] Soon after Erasmus and Robert Etienne (Stephanus) published the New Testament in Greek (1546). The Elzevir editions, published at Leyden, Holland, despite many defects held the honored position of *textus receptus* for almost 200 years.

In the period immediately following the invention of printing, whenever a Bible was to be produced the first manuscript that came to hand was printed; and the more the Bibles were distributed the more did they seem to differ. The spirit of rivalry, however, constrained scholars to have recourse to older and more numerous manuscripts, and thus in course of time many old manuscripts were brought to light and used.

Later editors made greater and more successful efforts to reproduce the Greek text as nearly as possible in its primitive purity. Their interest centered, of course, on the New Testament writings. Thus Lachman, with the aid of about eight important Greek MSS., and of the Itala, strove to restore the text as it had stood in the 4th century (published 1850). Tischendorf utilized also other translations and quo-

---

[14] It appeared in 1520 in six folio volumes, the first four containing the Old Testament in Hebrew, Greek, and Latin, in three columns, together with the Targum of the Pentateuch accompanied by a Latin translation. The fifth volume contained the New Testament in Greek and Latin (Vulgate). Volume six comprised dictionaries and various tables.

tations in the Fathers, hoping to attain a 2nd century text (published 1887, 1890). Tregelles' apparatus was even more elaborate (published 1857–1879). Griesbach, Weiss (1900), and von Soden (1903) have likewise accomplished noteworthy work in the field of text restoration. As an illustration of some of the methods employed in these researches, the basic system of Westcott and Hort (1881–1882) is here given.

Hort primarily grouped all the available text material of the New Testament into four classes:

I. *Antiochian* (Syrian); characterized by combining words that appear in two or more of the other groups; is a later and less reliable text,—reproduced in the Greek *textus receptus,* and in the King James and earlier English versions.

II. *Western;* characterized by "free amplification of text", insertions and omissions (hence rated low in approach to original); followed by the Syriac [15] and Itala and, to a large extent, the Vulgate. (Recent discoveries, however, have increased respect for the Western text.)

III. *Alexandrian;* found chiefly in writings of the Fathers, which originated in Alexandria.

IV. *Neutral;* for the most part without peculiarities noticeable in the other groups; followed by Sinaiticus and Vatican (Aleph and B) MSS.; held by Westcott and Hort to be nearest original; represented in the Revised English versions.

It will be noted that the determining voice need not necessarily be that of the oldest MSS.; Westcott and Hort follow largely Sixtus V's principle of resting the decision upon early quotations.

[15] But the Syriac discovered in 1892 contains no additions.

CHAPTER V

VERSIONS OF THE BIBLE

54. Translations of the Books of the Bible from their original tongue into another language are of importance not only as aids in interpreting the meaning, but also for reconstructing the original; for, translations give evidence as to how the text was read by the translator. However, not all versions are of equal value. As a rule, those made from the original surpass those made from another translation in importance and authority; literal translations deserve consideration more than free; and, above all, the old translations have more weight than later ones. Hence particular importance is attached to such as were made before the seventh century.

Early translations are fairly numerous. There are several Greek and Aramaic translations (of the Old Testament); a Samaritan version (of the Pentateuch), some Syriac, several Arabic, one Armenian, one Persian, some Egyptian (Coptic), one Ethiopian, one Slavonic, one Georgian, one Gothic, several Latin, and fragments of an Anglo-Saxon version.

The most important are the Greek, Syriac and Latin translations.

Art. 1: THE SEPTUAGINT VERSION

Texts: Judg. 1: 35; II Esd. 8: 9, 13; II Mac. 1: 36; I Cor. 12:10f.

55. Origin of the Name.—The earliest Greek translation's name of "Septuagint" (= the Seventy, LXX) is traceable to an elaborate legend preserved in Josephus [1] and Eusebius.[2] The fact probably is that this translation was made by Jews

[1] *Ant.*, XII, ii, 1–13; *Contra Apion*, II, 4.
[2] *Præpar. evang.*, VIII, 2–5.

in Alexandria to supply an existing need, as the Egyptian Jews (refugees, some of them, from the time of the Assyrian invasions, others, from the conquest of Alexander) mostly did not understand Hebrew.   That a bibliophile Ptolemy in the literary city of Alexandria should evince great interest in and even aid a translation of the Jews' Sacred Books is not excluded, but rather to be expected, in view of the preferred position held by the large Jewish colony of that city.   The very persistence of the name *Septuagint*, and the fact that the anniversary of the edition was celebrated later as a feast day in Alexandria and as a fast day in Jerusalem, give a certain probability to the legend, elaborated, perhaps, later to make the idea of a translation of the Scriptures into a Gentile tongue palatable to Palestinian Jews.

According to the Talmud (*Sopherim*, I, 7) the translation of the Pentateuch was finished on the 8th *Tébeth* (about Jan. 1st), and this day was to be considered as unfortunate for Israel as the day on which the golden calf was cast by Aaron (Exod. 32: 4). *Taanith* (fol. 50, 1) claims that a three days' darkness ensued upon the translation of the Bible into Greek.   After Christ's time the Jews became intensely hostile to the Greek version, whose irrefutable evidences were urged against them most effectively by the Christians.   But, despite bitter hostility, the Talmud of Jerusalem (*Megillah*, fol. 6) and the Babylonian Talmud (*Megillah*, fol. 9) can find only thirteen and fifteen passages respectively, wherein they accuse the Greek translators of having altered the text.

The legend itself purports to be based upon a letter written by Aristeas, an official at the Egyptian court, to his brother Philocrates, in which Aristeas says that Demetrius Phalereus, chief librarian at the royal library at Alexandria, advised his master, King Ptolemy Philadelphus, to add the Jewish law to the treasures in his library. The king was pleased with the advice, and in order to procure the Book of the Law, he set 200,000 Jews at liberty, and then sent some men, amongst whom was Aristeas himself, with costly presents to Jerusalem, in order to fetch the book from the high priest.   The latter not only gave the book to the envoys, but sent seventy-two learned Jews to Egypt to translate the *Thora*.   They were received honorably, and sent with Demetrius Phalereus to the neighboring island of Pharos, where they worked at their translation undisturbed.   According to the story, each man was shut up alone in a cell, and made a translation by himself, but when all the results were compared, they were found to be exactly the same.

From the evidence available, one may conclude to the following: A Greek translation of the Pentateuch, so uniform as to appear the product of a single expert hand, was made in Alexandria probably as early as Ptolemy Lagos I (323–285)—rather than under his son Ptolemy Philadelphus (285–247), who banished Demetrius Phalereus, the librarian of Aristeas' letter, soon after his accession (Clement of Alexandria, *Stromata*, I, 22). The other sacred Books of the Jews were likewise subsequently translated into Greek in Egypt by various persons, so that a complete version of the Old Testament was available to Jew and Gentile certainly not later than 130 B.C., and probably even a century earlier, for the three great divisions of the Hebrew Bible were known in Greek to the translator of Ecclesiasticus (*Prologue* to Ecclus.).

56. Characteristics of the Septuagint.—Outside the Pentateuch (whose translator seems to have been an expert, and whose texts were probably in better condition) the version is quite uneven, clearly betraying divers hands at work.

The Pentateuch is best translated, and next in order of merit are the Books of Josue, Judges, Ruth, Chronicles and Proverbs. Less to be commended is the translation of the four books of Kings, and of Esdras, Nehemias and Esther. Ecclesiastes is translated too literally, Job too arbitrarily. The Psalms and the prophetic writings are unsatisfactory, and the worst translation is that of the Book of Daniel, for which reason the Church did not admit the Septuagint version of this prophet, but a later rendering by Theodotion, into the Canon.

The translation in general is faithful, and often slavishly literal. But the influence of Hellenistic philosophical thought is already seen in the toning down of anthropomorphisms (see No. 36) and other expressions of the original that might offend the rationalistic and esthetic Greeks.[3] Wutz's theory is that the Septuagint translation was not made from a text written in Hebrew characters, whether ancient or square, but from a transcription or transliteration of the Hebrew into Greek letters[4] for the convenience of Jews living in the *diaspora*.

[3] See the Greek of Gen. 15:4; Deut. 23:14; 28:30, for examples.

[4] Thus, in Ps. 36:20, by assuming a misreading of ΜΕΖΛΑΡΧΕΛΕΜ for ΛΛΕΖΛΑΡΧΕΛΕΜ (ΛΛ for Μ) one would get the original "Yahweh's *strutting* enemies vanish like smoke."

57. *Differences between the Septuagint* reading and the present *Hebrew text* are generally explainable in favor of the Septuagint, but they seem to indicate a certain fluidity of text, which disappears by the time of Onkelos (1st century after Christ). In the Pentateuch the divergences of the Septuagint from the present Hebrew are generally supported by the pre-Masoretic text of the Samaritan Pentateuch. Moreover, for the Pentateuch, variants arise from different reading of original Semitic characters; in the later portions, from confusion of square letters (see No. 15); in all the Books, from the substitution of different vowels to the consonantal text, and from the ordinary errors of translators and copyists.[5] The occasional *plus* of the Septuagint as compared with the present Masoretic text, whilst at times composed of true accretions from tradition, more often only evinces a hypercritical paring down of the Hebrew text by later Jewry.

58. Its History and Ancient Editions.—That the use of the Septuagint was not confined to the Jews of Alexandria and Egypt, but extended even to the homeland of Palestine, is shown especially by the numerous citations in the New Testament which are made according to this version rather than the Hebrew original.[6] Philo used it throughout his writings, and Josephus paid it honor in his favorable account of its origin.[7] It was even read in the synagogues,[8] and the text was surely used in the assemblies "of the Libertines, and of the Cyrenians, and of the Alexandrians" at Jerusalem (Acts 6:9).

In the Church, of course, the Septuagint was always highly esteemed, the very canon of the Old Testament being based upon its redaction (see Nos. 21-23). Many old translations, such as the Itala, the Coptic, the Ethiopian, and the Armenian, were made from the early Greek version.

[5] Thus in Gen. 4:22 ΘΟΒΕΛΚΑΙΝ, ''Tubalcain'' was divided into θόβελ καὶ ἦν; through carelessness the ταφείς of Gen. 15:15 became τραφείς; ὠφείλησα of Jer. 15:10, ὠφέλησα, etc.
[6] Thus Matt. 4:10 (Deut. 6:13); 21:5 (Zach. 9:9); Heb. 11:21 (Gen. 47:31); Acts 8:33 (Is. 53:8); I Pet. 2:6 (Is. 28:16); Heb. 10:5 (Ps. 39:7); Heb. 10:38 (Hab. 2:4); Acts 7:14 (Gen. 46:28); Heb. 11:5 (Gen. 5:24), etc.
[7] *Ant.*, XII, ii, 1-13.
[8] *Megillah* (Jerus.), 16.

59. Ancient revisions of the Alexandrian text were undertaken by Lucian the Martyr, at Antioch (312), and the Egyptian Hesychius (311), also a martyr. But by far the most noteworthy was the earlier (231) monumental work of the *Hexapla,* compiled at Cesarea in Palestine by the great scripturist, Origen. His system of arrangement was the following:

He divided the rolls of manuscript into six columns, or, in dealing with some books of the Bible, into seven, eight or even nine. In the first he wrote the Hebrew text in Hebrew letters; in the second the same text in Greek characters; in the third the literal translation, viz., that of Aquilas; in the fourth that of Symmachus; in the fifth the Septuagint version, and in the sixth that of Theodotion. In the case of some books other columns were added, containing the *quinta, sexta* and *septima,* so that these parts of the whole may be called *heptapla, octapla* and *enneapla* respectively. In the fifth column, containing the Septuagint, Origen inserted definite marks, intended to show exactly the relation between that version and the original. If he found something added in the LXX that was absent in the Hebrew text, he marked it with an obelus—∸, signifying that it ought to be omitted; if he detected something left out, he supplied it, generally from Theodotion, marking it with an asterisk * and naming the source whence he had taken what was missing. A metobelus (∕) marked the end of the passage to which the other marks applied.

It is probably to the juxtaposition of these various Greek versions in the Hexapla that are due many of the changes, inversions, corrections, and doublets to be found in the Septuagint versions now, particularly in Proverbs and Jeremias (also Is. 7:16; Hab. 3:2; Joel 1:8).

Art. 2: MINOR ANCIENT VERSIONS

Texts: Luke 11:52; 16:29; 24:27, 45.

60. The Targumim.—As the Hebrew tongue fell into desuetude among the Jews of Palestine, it gradually became

necessary for the selections to be read publicly in the synagogues to be translated for the benefit of the assembly. The
reader, therefore, after perusing a section, gave a vulgar
version thereof in Aramaic, at the same time inserting explanations and glosses from tradition. Later these verbal translations, or rather paraphrases, were written down, forming
the *Targumim.* These translations, similarly to the Septuagint, tone down the anthropomorphisms of the original, and
sometimes change the figurative language of the original into
the underlying literal sense. They are very valuable for the
understanding of the Old Testament, as they frequently
record the reading and interpretation in use before Christ.

The more important Targumim are those of Onkelos (a
proselyte, probably of Palestine, during 1st century after
Christ) on the Pentateuch; that of Jonathan (a disciple of
Hillel, according to the Talmud, hence a possible contemporary of Christ) on the "earlier and later Prophets" (see No.
21); that of "pseudo-Jonathan" on the Pentateuch (about
middle of 7th century).

61. Later Greek Translations.—*Aquila* of Pontus, at first
a convert to Christianity, was later expelled from the Church
on account of superstition, and went over to Judaism, during the times of the emperor Hadrian. His version (now
lost, with the exception of a few fragments) was slavishly
literal, bristling with solecisms, and was intended to aid the
Jews in their controversies with the Christians.

Theodotion, an Ebionite from Ephesus (before 160), retained the Septuagint text whenever, in his opinion, it gave
a correct rendering of the Hebrew, and made a fresh translation only when the Septuagint appeared quite misleading.
The Vulgate contains Dan. 3 : 24-90; 13; 14 translated from
this version.

Symmachus, also a renegade to Judaism (about 192–211),
put forth a version which was freer and clearer than the preceding ones, and probably taken as model by St. Jerome for
his own works.

62. Syriac Versions: The Peshito.—The Syrian Church,
the first community of Gentile Christians, possessed various

translations of the Bible, of which the most important is that
known as the Peshito version. It is certainly not the work
of one man. The New Testament alone may have been done
by one writer. As the Syrian Church is one of the oldest, the
Syriac version of the New Testament must belong to quite
the early part of the 2nd century, and the uniformity of the
language points to its being the work of one translator. The
Books of the Old Testament, at least the protocanonical, had
existed in Syriac before this time, for in the New Testament
Peshito quotations are made from the Old Testament Peshito,
hence the latter must have been written in the 1st century;
it was translated from the Hebrew text, and is probably the
work of several persons, as its language has not the same
uniformity and evenness as that of the New Testament
Peshito.

In 1858 Cureton, an Englishman, published some fragments of
a Syriac text of the Gospels that is older than the Peshito in its
present form. In 1892, in the monastery on Sinai, a palimpsest
manuscript of the Gospels in Syriac was discovered that appears
to be still older than Cureton's text. This *Codex Sinaiticus Syrus*
is called Lewis Codex after the lady who discovered it, Mrs. Smith-
Lewis, an Englishwoman. It was photographed *in situ,* and published at Cambridge in 1894, under the title *The Four Gospels in
Syriac, transcribed from the Sinaitic Palimpsest.* It was followed
by *A Translation of the Four Gospels,* by Smith-Lewis (London,
1894, 8vo).

63. Old Latin Versions and the Itala.—Greek was comparatively little known in the Roman province of Africa;
hence it has been well conjectured that the first Latin translations of the Sacred Books appeared there, to serve the
ritual and devotional needs of early Christian communities.[9]
These Old Latin versions were made from uncorrected pre-
Hexaplar Greek texts, perhaps as early as the year 150.
Being very literal they clearly reflect the Greek text and
construction of their times, and are therefore of great im-

[9] Sts. Augustine and Jerome both complained of the variety of
biblical versions current in their time. Thus, the former states that
"qui Scripturas ex hebræa lingua in græcam verterunt numerari possunt, latini autem interpretes nullo modo" (*De doct. christiana,* II, 16;
Migne, 34: 43). Writing to Pope Damasus, St. Jerome says: "Si
enim latinis exemplaribus fides est adhibenda, respondeant quibus; tot
enim sunt exemplaria (= recensions) pæne quot codices" (*Epist.* 18).

portance in reconstructing the original. In the Old Latin versions there are still available the Psalms, Esther, Job, the Pentateuch, and some smaller Books, as well as the New Testament.[10]

The old Latin version is marked by pre-Augustan archaisms, which would be more likely to survive in the remote province of Africa: thus, deponents are found with passive meaning, as "consolor", "hortor" in II Cor. 1:6; Ps. 118:52; Luke 17:25; "ministrari" in Matt. 20:28; Mark 10:45; II Cor. 8:19, 20; II Pet. 1:II; the ending -ibo is used for futures of the fourth conjugation (Ps. 59:8); "nubentur"[11] (Matt. 22:30); compounds with "super-" in Luke 6:38; 10:35; II Cor. 5:4; 16:15; verbs ending in "-ifico", in Ps. 36:42; 43:22; Rom. 7:4.

Amid the variety of Latin versions current early in the 5th century, St. Augustine expresses his preference for an edition which he calls *itala*[12] *interpretatio*. Remembering that St. Augustine was converted to Christianity at Milan, it has been conjectured that the African Doctor brought back with him a biblical text in use in the Lombard plain, which was more exact in translation and clearer in Latinity than the texts then in use in Africa. Whether the *Itala* recension depended upon an African archetype, or had an independent origin, is a moot question among critics. It is clear, however, that the appelation *Itala* should not be used as a blanket name for all the pre-Hieronymian Latin versions.

Art. 3: THE VULGATE VERSION

Texts: Eph. 6:17b; Jer. 23:29; Is. 55:10-11.

64. St. Jerome and His Work.—When the variety of Latin versions of the Sacred Scriptures in use in the Church was threatening to issue in hopeless confusion; when the hos-

---

[10] See Drum in *Ecclesiastical Review*, July, 1918 and Sept., 1918.

[11] Nonius remarks: ''Nubere, *veteres*, non solum mulieres sed etiam viros dicebant''. Consult Wiseman's *Essay on 1 John 5:7*.

[12] Bentley conjectured that here for *itala* one should read *illa;* Potter urged *usitata* as a substitute, emendations which are quite gratuitous and useless except insofar as they show what certain ''higher'' critics might have written had they been in St. Augustine's position.

tile Jews, and sometimes heretics, were beginning to taunt their Christian adversaries in controversy, with not having texts conformable to the Hebrew originals, Providence raised up that greatest of scriptural scholars, St. Jerome. He was born at Stridon in Dalmatia, in 329, and named Eusebius Hieronymus. After a brilliant career as a lecturer at Rome, he withdrew from the world to Bethlehem, where he began the study of Hebrew at the age of forty-five. Under the tutoring of a number of Jews, and at no little expense, he acquired a marvelous mastery of this tongue. This in conjunction with his rhetorical proficiency in Latin and skill in Greek, fitted him eminently for the work he was to accomplish. The saintly Roman ladies gathered in religious community about his retreat at Bethlehem were, no doubt, of great assistance in transcribing the MSS. and other secretarial work which his labors entailed.

His first extensive scriptural work was a revision of the New Testament Itala, upon excellent Greek MSS., at the request of Pope Damasus. This was followed shortly by a revision of the Psalter after the Septuagint, later known as the *Psalterium Romanum*.[13] For this there was later substituted in the Church at large the *Psalterium Gallicanum*, likewise a revision by St. Jerome upon the base of the Septuagint, but approaching more closely to the Hebrew than the previous one. This Psalter is still retained in the Vulgate, instead of the Hebrew translation of St. Jerome.

From 390 to 405 the chief labor of the great scripturist was the translation of the Hebrew and Aramaic texts of the Old Testament into Latin. For this purpose he copied with his own hand the Hebrew rolls then in use in the Bethlehem synagogue; he traveled all through Palestine, in order to have first-hand knowledge of biblical geography; he continually compared the Greek translations of the Septuagint, Aquila, Theodotion, and Symmachus, as well as the Hexapla of Origen; lastly, for enlightenment on passages of special

---

13 This text of the Psalter is still used in the breviary of the Chapter of St. Peter's at Rome; also in the Roman Missal, and in the version of Ps. 92 read in the Roman Breviary on the feast of Epiphany.

difficulty, he consulted learned scripturists among the Jews. The sum of St. Jerome's monumental labor of revision and translation of the Scriptures constitutes the bulk of the great Latin version of the Bible known later as the Vulgate.

The Vulgate consists of the following parts: (*a*) the proto-canonical Books of the Old Testament (with the exception of the Psalms) according to St. Jerome's translation from the Hebrew or Aramaic, (*b*) the deuterocanonical Books of Tobias and Judith, also translated by him directly from the same languages; [14] (*c*) the Psalms, from the *Itala,* but revised twice by St. Jerome in accordance with the Septuagint; (*d*) the deuterocanonical Books of the Old Testament (with the exception of Tobias and Judith), as taken from the *Itala,* and not revised by St. Jerome (Baruch, I and II Machabees, Ecclesiasticus, Wisdom); [14] (*e*) the whole of the New Testament is taken from the *Itala,* but modified by St. Jerome's revision mentioned above.

65. Characteristics and Value of the Vulgate.—St. Jerome's obsession for the *hebraica veritas* made him adhere scrupulously to the text before him, with the result that his translation is most faithful to the Hebrew original. Aside from obscure and disputable passages, the places where he has missed the real meaning of the original are extremely rare.[15] Yet his translation is by no means servile, but rather strives to render the propositions of the Hebrew into not only intelligible but even somewhat elegant Latin. To this end he at times adapted purely classical allusions and expressions.[16] Lastly, with a very prudent conservatism, St. Jerome strove to preserve as far as might be the language of the Itala, which had become familiar to the ears of the faithful through centuries of use in the liturgical readings and chant; hence many hebraisms of the Septuagint, through the Old Itala, have passed into the Vulgate.

The Vulgate, as embodying the labors of St. Jerome, is undoubtedly the best of the ancient translations of the Bible.

[14] Esther 10: 4 to 16: 24, St. Jerome translated from the Septuagint, and Dan. 3:24–90 to end of 14, from the Greek of Theodotion.
[15] Thus Gen. 14: 5 renders בָּהֶם, *be-Ham,* as "cum eis" instead of "at Ham".
[16] Thus Prov. 26: 8: *acervus Mercurii;* IV Kings 21: 6: *aruspices;* Is. 34: 14; *lamia, onocentauri;* Jer. 50: 39: *fauni,* etc.

It is not a haphazard but a scientific work, in which the author was aided not only by his own keen critical instinct, but by his lengthy and studious preparation in biblical philology and archeology, and by the early MSS. he had at his disposal. Its basic correctness and reliability,[17] then, made St. Jerome's compilation stand the fire test of abundant criticism at its origin, to emerge as the *vulgata*, or common, popular version of every people of Europe.

66. Vulgate in Middle Ages.—But the Vulgate likewise was not free from the influences that had tended to make the older Latin versions unsatisfactory. In the course of time frequent copying and the many corrections attempted by various owners or copyists led to great diversity of text in the copies of the Latin Bibles. Most of the variant readings are due to familiarity with the Old Itala, and the liturgy especially was not without influence upon the text. Charlemagne employed his learned chancellor, Alcuin, in revising the text of the Vulgate, probably in accordance with the oldest manuscripts obtainable (801). In the eleventh century the great scholar, Lanfranc (1089), undertook a new emendation, and his text was long considered as the standard for copyists.

From the 12th century onwards the so-called *Correctoria* came into use, to secure as far as possible the accuracy of the text. They originated with Stephen Harding, Abbot of Cîteaux (1134). He corrected a manuscript of the Bible in accordance with a very old Latin copy, using at the same time the Hebrew and the Greek texts. The revised version thus produced was thenceforth the standard text for the whole Cistercian Order. Other Orders and learned bodies followed Stephen Harding, and every community desired in a similar way to procure for itself a standard copy of the Bible. The standard copy of the Vulgate used by the University of Paris was very frequently copied, but as it was by no means free from mistakes, theologians from the 13th century onwards collected various readings, adding notes to say which had the best claim to preference. These various readings were written on the broad margins of the Bible texts, and a text containing them, or even a copy of the *apparatus criticus* without the text, was called a *correctorium*. Many such *correctoria* are preserved in various libraries.

Towards the close of the Middle Ages two things exerted great influence upon the Latin text; the study of classical literature and the invention of printing.

[17] The following are the words of Tischendorf, one of the greatest modern biblical editors and critics: ''Illæ [variantes lectiones ex plurimis græcis codicibus collectæ] non modo non nocent scripturarum sensui quoad fidem et mores, sed ei maiorem lucem afferunt, *et latinam vulgatam ab omni vindicant convicio.* Hodie enim constat non vulgatam latinam, sed editionem græcam [Robert Stephani, 1550] vitiosam esse''. Admonitio (ed. Novi Test.), Parisiis, 1847.

The increase of classical studies had the result that in many places people tried to "improve" the traditional text on classical lines, because St. Jerome's language did not savor of Cicero. Moreover, many wished to make the Latin text conform more closely to the Greek or Hebrew. Alterations of both these kinds could be made only at the cost of sacrificing the uniformity and purity of the text.

The introduction of the art of printing had similar effects. The first book ever printed was the Latin Bible (Mayence, 1450). By the year 1500 over one hundred different editions of the Bible had been printed and were in circulation. In bringing out the earliest editions, there was no thought of textual criticism, and any manuscript that came to hand was printed. As competition increased, however, recourse was had to Hebrew and Greek texts. The more numerous these aids were, and the more various their sources, the greater and more striking were the diversities in the Latin text.

To these were superadded, at the time of the Reformation, variations introduced by enemies of the Church and of everything traditional, who would wrest even the Scriptures to their own destruction. It was high time, then, that the Church should once more take action to safeguard the purity of the Sacred Text under the form in which it chiefly was familiar to common folk. Hence the action of the Council of Trent [18] declaring the Vulgate to be an authentic version, recognized by the Church as containing the inspired Word of God, and making it the official or standard text for official or public use in the Western or Latin rite.

67. Council of Trent on the Vulgate.

—One can not help marveling at the prudent, yet clearly discriminating, action of the Fathers of the Council of Trent in thus selecting the Vulgate version as the official Latin edition of the Bible sanctioned by the Church. They did not thereby condemn, even tacitly, all the other versions,[19] much less did they intend to

---

[18] "Sancta synodus declarat, ut hæc ipsa vetus et vulgata editio, quæ longo tot sæculorum usu in ipsa ecclesia probata est, in publicis lectionibus, disputationibus, prædicationibus et expositionibus pro authentica habeatur et ut nemo illam reiicere audeat vel præsumat" (Sess. IV). See full decree in Appendix.

[19] Merkle-Ehses, *Acta Conc. Trid.*, p. 65.—The Church recognizes several authentic Bible texts, original or translated, such as the Hebrew, the Greek, the Latin Vulgate, the Syriac Peshito, the Coptic, the Armenian, the Slavonian; and all these, with the exception of the Hebrew, are at the same time official for public use in the liturgy, etc., of the respective rites. The whole question of Trent and the Vulgate is extensively and excellently treated by Grannan in his *General Introduction*, vol. I, pp. 138-185 (Herder, 1921).

disparage in any manner the Hebrew and Greek originals from which the Vulgate itself had been derived. They simply wished to appoint for Christians of the Western or Latin rite, from among the multitude of Latin versions then current, one standard text which reproduced the Hebrew and Greek originals with substantial correctness.

From the correspondence and minutes of the Council in regard to the Vulgate, one may conclude that the dogmatic authority conferred on that redaction by the Council is not so much positive as negative, simply implying that the Vulgate version is *free from any error in faith or morals.* As far as conformity with the originals is concerned, the words of the Council certainly imply that the Vulgate is *substantially conformable* to the originals; this conformity need not necessarily be *critical,* vouching for the genuineness and correct translation of every detail, but it must be at least *doctrinal,* consisting in the fact that the Vulgate version contains no dogmatic or moral passage contrary to doctrine revealed by God, as recorded either in Scripture or tradition. The Vulgate was not by that decree declared to be infallible, absolutely free from error, in matters other than faith and morals.[20] In fact, the same Council of Trent acknowledged the presence of textual errors in the Vulgate,[21] by ordering that a carefully revised and corrected edition be prepared as soon as possible,—a task which was finally accomplished under Sixtus V and Clement VIII (1590–1598). Since that time no Latin Scripture editions may be published without the special permission of the Holy See.

The work of preparing a new edition of the Vulgate, as conformable as possible to the text as it issued from the pen of St. Jerome, was entrusted by Pius X in 1907 to the Benedictines of St. Anselm's, Rome.

[20] See Léon Lebel in *La Nouvelle-France,* avril 1917, pp. 159–174.
[21] Compare the letter of Card. Rampolla of April 30, 1907: ''Già i Padri del Concilio di Trento, pur riconoscendo la Volgata quale edizione autentica per gli usi pubblici della Chiesa, non ne dissimularono le imperfezioni, onde espressero il voto che con ogni diligenza venisse sottomessa ad un esame minutissimo e ridotta a forma più definitivamente conforme ai testi originali'' (*Acta Sanctæ Sedis,* XL, p. 446).

Art. 4: ENGLISH VERSIONS

Texts: II Tim. 4: 3-4; Jer. 8: 8-9; II Pet. 1: 19.

68. Anglo-Saxon, Wyclif, and Tyndale Versions.—The earliest English or Anglo-Saxon versions, such as Caedmon's (670), Venerable Bede's (735), Alfred the Great's (901) and Aelfric's (10th century) have survived only in fragments. St. Bede's seems to have comprised the whole Bible, but the others contained but portions, such as the Psalms or the Gospels, and were at times rather paraphrases.

John Wyclif is generally believed to have done the New Testament of a Bible, afterwards revised by Purvey (1388). But Gasquet holds that the Wyclif Bible was originally the work of the bishops of the pre-Reformation English church.[22] Of greater importance (because of its subsequent influence on the King James version) is Tyndale's Bible (Pentateuch, Jonas, New Testament), the earliest English version to be made from the Greek. Other non-Catholic versions of this period were: Coverdale's (1535), made from Luther's German and the Vulgate Latin; the Cranmer or "Great Bible", a later edition of the above, from which the Psalms in the Anglican Book of Common Prayer are taken; the "Geneva Bible" (1557–1560), having a strongly Calvinistic or Presbyterian bias; and the "Bishops' Bible" of 1568. None of these versions lays claim to special value or interest.

69. The Original Douay Version.—Various faulty and biased Protestant versions having appeared in England with the opening there of the Reformation, a group of Catholic scripturists, formerly of the Oxford faculty but in exile at the Catholic university founded in 1562 at Douay, in Flanders, France,[23] resolved to produce an English version worthy of the Church. The result of their labors was the Douay

---

[22] *Old English Bible and Other Essays* (London, 1897); see also
* Kenyon, *Our Bible and the Ancient Monuments.*

[23] The university was transferred from Douay to Rheims in 1578, and returned to Douay in 1593. All the work of translation was done at Rheims, probably, but the Old Testament was published at Douay in 1609–1610.

version,[24] the New Testament of which, after delay owing to lack of means, was published in 1582,[25] thus antedating by nearly thirty years the King James version, with the appearance of which the publication of the Old Testament of the Douay practically coincided.

The actual translation was done chiefly by Dr. Gregory Martin,[26] formerly of St. John's College, Oxford, "an excellent linguist, exactly read and versed in the Sacred Scriptures", who moreover "went beyond all his time in humane literature". His assistants, Doctors Allen (later Cardinal), Bristow, Reynolds, Worthington, also formerly professors or fellows at Oxford, wrote the annotations and marginal notes and revised the work. For the base of their labor these divines wisely chose the Latin Vulgate instead of the uncritical Greek *textus receptus* then current, continually, however, taking note of the original Greek and Hebrew. The result was a version in somewhat cumbersome English, enriched with latinisms, above all really scholarly and accurate. The following sample from the original first edition is taken from Psalm 21:

> 2. God my God haue respect to me: why hast thou forsaken me? far from my saluation are the wordes of my sinnes.
>
> 3. My God I shal crie by day, and thou wilt not heare: and by night, and not for follie unto me.
>
> 4. But thou dwellest in the holie place, the prayse of Israel.
>
> 5. In thee our fathers haue hoped: they hoped, and thou didst deliuer them.
>
> 6. They cried to thee, and were saued: they hoped in thee, and were not confounded.

[24] See Cardinal Newman, *History of the Rheims and Douay Version of Holy Scripture* (1859) in his *Tracts Theological and Ecclesiastical;* consult also Drum in *Ecclesiastical Review,* March, 1919, pp. 330–337.

[25] This was during the reign of Queen Elizabeth, at a time when Shakespeare was probably eighteen years of age.

[26] "No English translator ever had a more exquisite perception of the exact value of words; when he found no word in the language to express perfectly the thought of the original, he coined a word". Thus most correctly did he render the verb of Ps. 39: 7: "eares thou hast perfited to me" = *aures autem perfecisti mihi,* which Challoner made easier to read but incorrect by changing it to "thou hast pierced ears for me". See Sheahan in *Ecclesiastical Review,* Nov., 1920, pp. 519–530.

7. But I am a worme and no man: a reproach of men and outcast of the people.

8. All that see me haue scorned me: they haue spoken with the lippes, and wagged the head.

70. The King James or "Authorized" Version.—When the Catholic version of the Bible was already well on its way, in 1604, at a conference between representatives of the Church of England men (Episcopalians) and the non-Conformists (Puritans) a version without notes on the base of the Hebrew and Greek texts was projected. King James I was particularly insistent on the omission of the notes in the Geneva Bible. Fifty-four men, leading biblical scholars of the day, were appointed to do the work, being divided into six groups, working at Westminster, Oxford, and Cambridge. It took two years and nine months to complete the task, the work issuing from press in 1611. Despite the words "Appointed to be read in the Churches" on the title page (whence the name *Authorized* Version) "there is no evidence to show that any authority, civil or ecclesiastical, ever formally approved the work for such a purpose".[27] In elegance of diction, stateliness of language, this version is almost unsurpassed, but dogmatic interests were, in some cases, allowed to bias the translation; and the Calvinism of one party and the Episcopalianism of the other were both represented at the expense of accuracy (*Smith, *Bible Dictionary*, article: Version). Moreover, since the parts translated from the Greek were based upon the very imperfect reading of the *textus receptus,* the publication later on of the Codex Vaticanus, etc., and the labors of textual critics brought into glaring relief the numerous inaccuracies of the original King James version.

Hence a revision was determined upon in 1870, commissions appointed both in England and America, and the results published in 1881–1885. The "deuterocanonical" Books of the Old Testament were now omitted altogether. But the resultant Revised Version, aside from this, was a decided improvement over the old King James as far as accuracy, correctness of translation, is concerned. Hence it also ap-

27 Grannan, *General Introduction to the Bible,* vol. I, p. 191.

proaches much closer to the Vulgate and modern Douay, in whose favor many of the changes and corrections were made. The newest "Revised Revision" (1901) of the English Protestant Bible in both text and margin approaches yet more closely to the readings always maintained by the Vulgate.

Examples of Vulgate (Douay) translations adopted by Revised version: Matt. 6:13; 19:17; Luke 10:42; 11:2-4; 22:43-44; John 1:18; 3:13; 7:8; Acts 11:20; I Cor. 11:27; 13:3; Apoc. 12:18; also, without marginal comment, Acts 16:7; I John 2:23. The Protestant version is still inferior to the Vulgate in its rendition of Ps. 24:6; Matt. 11:19; Luke 5:5; 24:26; Acts 4:13; Rom. 5:7; II Cor. 10:1-2; I Tim. 3:2; 5:4; 6:7; Philem. 1:12; Apoc. 15:6. Based on the Greek, it dissents from the Vulgate also in Matt. 27:35; Mark 7:19; John 5:3-4; 7:53-58; 11:10-16; Acts 8:37; 15:34; I Cor. 11:24; 15:51; I Thess. 2:7; Jam. 4:4; I Pet. 1:2; 3:15; I John 5:7; 8:18, etc. See the * Gould Prize Essays on *Roman Catholic and Protestant Bibles Compared* (Scribner's, 1908).

71. Challoner's Revisions of the Douay Version.

—Long before the King James version was revised, between 1749 and 1777, Dr. Challoner, then Vicar Apostolic of the London District, desirous of satisfying the needs of his people for a Bible in readable English, with notes suitable to the times, got out several editions of the Old and of the New Testament, based on the fifth edition (1738) of the original Rheims-Douay. Most of these editions, moreover, differed from each other, as Dr. Challoner made new emendations without calling attention thereto in either preface or margin. So extensive were the modifications made that Cardinals Wiseman and Newman both consider his work a new translation rather than a mere revision of the Douay. The Challoner-Douay version is the one at present generally used by Catholics in English-speaking countries.[28]

[28] The editions of the Douay-Challoner version current in America at the present time are most unattractive to readers and reflect little honor on their publishers. In fact, they barely escape the prohibition of Canon 1391, by printing here and there a few antiquated polemical or exegetical notes: explanations from the Fathers are practically lacking. The exceedingly brief anonymous preface contains statements which, if not erroneous, yet do not well convey the teaching of the Church to the faithful. Perhaps it is time to take action on the suggestion of S. C. Propaganda (24 Jan. 1868) recorded in the appendix to Acts of the II Plenary Council of Baltimore (p. CXXXIXX).

Whilst Challoner's work has modernized the Douay, yet his thoroughgoing changes are to be deplored in so far as they have removed so many picturesque and vigorous archaisms, and especially the inversions of the Latin. Compare his version of Heb. 13: 9 with the Rheims: "With various and strange doctrines be not led away".   In John 2: 4b his insertion of "that" or "it" does not translate the idiom and at the same time gives to English ears an impression disparaging to Our Lady; in Apoc. 14: 6 one still reads the inserted article, "having *the* eternal gospel," which has misled for decades the members of the Latter Day Saints into maintaining a second giving of public revelation to earth, as distinct from the gospel of Christ.

CHAPTER VI

SENSES OF SACRED SCRIPTURE

Art. 1: DISTINCTION OF BIBLICAL SENSES

Texts: Ecclus. 32:19; II Cor. 3:6; 4:3-4; Acts 18:24-25.

72. The purpose of any writing is to preserve and convey to others the ideas of its author; the object of the reader is to grasp just what the author intended to mean; and the *real meaning* of any writing is just the sense in which the *author intended his words* to be taken and understood. Words being but arbitrary or conventional signs of ideas, the very nature and function of language as the chief means of human intercourse demand that normally but a single idea or sense be assigned to a given word or group of words. An indeterminable variety of meanings, or meanings not recognized by common agreement of the community, attached to one and the same word or expression, would lead to ambiguity and frustrate the purpose of language. Hence the Bible also can have but one primary meaning beneath the letter of its language, that is: a sense which is appreciable by any person of sound mind, in the natural order, in the same manner as the sense of the author of any other writing may be discerned.

73. One Primary Inspired Sense.—The sense of any writing expressing the real primary intent of the author is generally called *literal*. This may be expressed in its own proper terms without any deviation from the grammatical and lexicographic acception, and may then be named the *precise* literal sense. If the sense of the author is expressed in terms modified from the normal, or in the terms of ideas altogether diverse, there is a superficial *metaphorical* or figurative sense enveloping the precise literal one, which like the shell of a nut must be cracked and rejected before the meat of real meaning can be enjoyed. Figurative language is especially familiar to Orientals, particularly the Semitic peoples, who use it to supplement for the lack of abstract and universal terms in their speech; hence its frequent occurence in the Bible. The following are characteristic examples:

> Stand therefore, having your loins girt about with truth, and having on the breastplate of justice, and your feet shod with the preparation of the gospel of peace (Eph. 6:14-15).
> Behold the sovereign Lord of Hosts shall break the earthen vessel with terror, and the tall of stature shall be cut down, and the lofty shall be lowered. And the thickets of the forest shall be cut down with iron, and Libanus with its high ones shall fall. And there shall come forth a rod out of the root of Jesse, and a flower shall rise up out of his root (Is. 10:33-34; 11:1).

The primary sense, whether expressed precisely or metaphorically, must be attained as the base of any ulterior expansion of meaning, and it alone has an absolute and universally conclusive argumentative value in the establishment of dogmatic truths.[1]

74. Several Inspired Secondary Senses.—Although a primary literal meaning is *alone valid as controversial proof for all men*, whether acknowledging the supernatural order or not, nevertheless the Divine Author of Sacred Scripture can not be denied the power to lay also beneath the same text, besides the above-mentioned primary sense, one or more secondary literal or truly inspired senses designating verities of the supernatural order, and appreciable by such as already admit the unlimited scope of the supernatural order. Thus God who controls not only words but also the actual persons, things, actions, for which words stand, can at will so dispose the former that they themselves will typify or represent a parallel set of persons, things, actions entirely diverse in time and place, yet preserving the same essential

---

[1] Lépicier, *De Deo Uno*, p. 99, commenting on St. Thomas: ''Ex solo litterali sensu posse trahi argumentum, quia nihil sub spirituali sensu continetur fidei necessarium, quod Scriptura per litteralem sensum alicubi manifeste non tradat'' (1a, q. 1, a. 10).

relationships in proportion. Moreover, when the text of the Sacred Scriptures was composed it was certainly known to the Holy Spirit what meanings (not repugnant, of course, to the principles of faith) conformable to the signification of the primary sense, really expansions and particular symbolic applications of the latter, might be drawn therefrom, and consequently the Holy Spirit *could* [2] intend and authorize these secondary senses, thereby making them truly His and inspired. For every sense that the author intends to be conveyed by a text is the true sense of that text, though there may be an order of intent among the various senses, and although not all the senses may be equally appreciable by every person.

75. The various senses which have been found in Sacred Scripture may be classified as follows:

Senses of the Bible	Primary (Literal)	One only, though this may be expressed metaphorically; appreciable universally, hence argumentatively valid for establishing dogmatic declarations
	Secondary (Spiritual)	Typical: Messianic = of Christ on earth / Ecclesiastic = of the Church [3] / Eschatologic = of the End of the World
		Accommodated (Mystical): Allegorically, to persons or things / Tropologically, to conduct, morals / Anagogically, to the future life

To illustrate: Jerusalem, in primary literal sense, signifies the chief city of Palestine (as in Mark 11:1); metaphorically it stands for the inhabitants of that city (Matt. 23:37). Typical senses are such as are indicated not by the words themselves, but by the things the words stand for. Where

---

[2] Whether the Holy Ghost actually did intend these secondary senses, and consequently, whether they are inspired, is a moot question amongst scripturists. No. 78 below gives the writer's opinion with supporting reasons.

[3] "Ipsum vero corpus Christi et ea quæ in ipso sunt gesta, sunt figura corporis Christi mystici, et eorum quæ in ipso gerunter. . . . Ea quæ ad litteram de ipso Christo capite dicuntur, possunt exponi et allegorice, referendo ad corpus eius mysticum; et moraliter, referendo ad actus nostros qui secundum ipsum debent reformari; et anagogice, in quantum in Christo est nobis iter gloriæ demonstratum" (*Quodlibet.*, VII, a, 5, ad 5um).

Old Testament texts foreshadow vicissitudes in the period of Christ's personal presence upon earth, they are types in the Messianic sense. Thus the brazen serpent reared in the desert by Moses (Num. 1: 9) is a type of Christ raised upon His cross (John 3: 14) ; similarly the prohibition of breaking the bones of the paschal lamb (Exod. 12: 46) foreshadowed the sparing of Christ's Body from the mutilation inflicted upon the thieves (John 19: 36). When the parallel in the Old Testament applies rather to the Mystical Body of Christ, the Kingdom of God, which is the Church, the sense may be said to be ecclesiastic. Thus David's kingdom is a type of Christ's reign in His Church (Luke 1: 32) ; and in Gal. 4: 22-31, by very intricate symbolism, St. Paul finds the New Testament, the Church, and its members, to be typified by Sara, Jerusalem, and Isaac, whilst Agar, Mt. Sinai, and Ismael are representative of the Old Covenant and of the obsolete and rejected ceremonial obligations of the dethroned Synagogue. Lastly, in the eschatologic [4] sense, the destruction of Jerusalem, as prophesied by Daniel and Christ Himself (Dan. 9: 27 and elsewhere; Matt. 24: 2-31 in parts) is a fit figure of the destruction of the world and the punishment of the wicked at Christ's Second Coming in judgment.

76. The typical and the accommodated senses often overlap and intermingle, so that a clear distinction between them is not to be drawn. Nevertheless, the accommodated sense may be said to be the application of the *wording* of a text (congruently by some proportion with its literal meaning) to other persons, things, or events, rather than of the *types* signified by the words. Thus St. Paul (Heb. 13: 2) argues to reliance upon God's providence from Yahweh's words to Josue, urging the latter to enter the Promised Land (Jos. 1: 5): "I will not leave thee, neither will I forsake thee" (tropological). The same Apostle (Rom. 10: 17) uses the words of the Psalmist (Ps. 18: 5), speaking of the universe showing forth the handiwork of God, to express the world-

---

[4] From ἔσχατος, final, furthest. This term is used particularly in connection with the general judgment or end of the world, but may also refer to death, heaven, hell, or all the four last things.

wise preaching of the gospel by the ministers of the faith; again (Rom. 10:8) he applies Yahweh's words to the effect that the Law of the Old Covenant was easily intelligible (Deut. 30:11-14), to the truths of faith of the New Dispensation (allegorical). St. John (Apoc. 21:2) uses Jerusalem as a term for the beatitude of Heaven (anagogic).

The Church continually makes use of the secondary senses of Scripture in the liturgy. Thus the language of the "Wisdom sections" of Ecclesiasticus (24) and Wisdom (6-8) have ever been found fitly applicable to the Blessed Virgin; the Messianic longings and promises of Isaias are still used in the Advent Office in preparation for Christmas. And the teachers and preachers of the church have always freely employed the secondary senses as "profitable to teach, reprove, correct, instruct in justice" (II Tim. 3:16). But it is not every passage of Holy Scripture that contains a mystical sense. Clement of Alexandria, Origen and the Alexandrian exegetical writers in general went too far in this respect, and tried to extract a mystical sense from almost every passage in the Bible. To some extent St. Ambrose and St. Gregory the Great did the same. The school of Antioch, the chief representative of which was St. John Chrysostom, did not go to such extravagant length.—What kind of mystical meaning can be discovered in sentences such as: "Thou shalt love the Lord thy God", "Thou shalt not kill", etc.? In the same way it would be wrong to assume that any passage in Holy Scripture possesses only a mystical, and not a literal meaning.

Art. 2: SECONDARY SENSES INSPIRED

Texts: Rom. 15:4; I Cor. 10:6, 11.

77. Plural Literal Sense Maintained.—Whilst all scripturists strenuously maintain the inspiration of the literal (primary) sense, and at the same time admit the presence of spiritual (secondary) senses, yet whether these secondary senses are likewise actually inspired by the Holy Ghost is a much mooted question. By and large, the opinions of theologians incline to a negative answer,[5] perhaps chiefly in order to safeguard the controversially demonstrative force of the primary sense. However, such great Doctors of the Church as St. Augustine and St. Thomas seem to have recog-

---

[5] Gigot, *General Introduction*, p. 203; Cornély, *Comp. Introduct.*, III, c. 1; Vasquez, *Summa*, I, i, 10, Disp. 17:3.

nized beneath the one text of Sacred Scripture a plural literal sense, in other words, more than one sense *intended by the Divine Author* and, therefore, also inspired. Among recent authors the positive opinion is upheld by Lépicier (*De Deo Uno*, pp. 100-106), and Assuad (*Polysema sunt sacra biblia*).

Seisenberger allows an inspired secondary sense "when the Church has pronounced in favor of the mystical interpretation of some passage, or when the Holy Scripture or the consensus of the Fathers unmistakably requires a mystical explanation" and goes on to say that "in these circumstances the mystical meaning constitutes valid evidence, as it is then clear that the Holy Ghost has intended . . . a mystical meaning".

St. Augustine writes: "So when one says: 'Moses meant as I do;' and another: 'Nay, but as I do,' I suppose that I speak more reverently: 'Why not rather as both, if both be true?' And if there be a third and a fourth, yea if any other seeth any other truth in those words, why may not He be believed to have seen all these things, through whom the One God hath tempered the Holy Scripture to the sense of many, who should see therein things true but divers? . . . Were I to indite anything to have supreme authority, I should prefer so to write that any truth that might be apprehended on these matters, might be conveyed in my words, rather than set down my own meaning so clearly as to exclude the rest, which not being false could not offend me" (*Confessions*, XII, 31; see also *De doctr. christ.*, III, 27).

St. Thomas expresses his opinion as follows: "Hoc enim ad dignitatem divinæ Scripturæ pertinet, ut sub una littera multos sensus contineat, ut sic et diversis intellectibus hominum conveniat, et unusquisque miretur se in divina Scriptura posse invenire veritatem quam mente conceperit. . . . Unde si etiam aliqua vera ab expositoribus sacræ Scripturæ litteræ aptentur, quæ auctor [=hagiographus] non intelligit, non est dubium quin Spiritus Sanctus intellexerit. . . . Unde omnis veritas quae salva litteræ circumstantia, potest divinæ Scripturæ aptari, est eius sensus" (*De potentia*, a. 1; see also 1a, q. 1, a. 10).

78. That the Divine Author of Sacred Scripture actually did intend more than one sense to be conveyed by the same biblical text (at least in places), or, in other words, that the secondary or spiritual (mystical) senses are also inspired, seems evident from the following considerations:

(1) By the autexegesis of Scripture. In certain places [6]

[6] John 2:17 (Ps. 68:10); 15:25 (Ps. 24:19); Acts 1:20 (Ps. 68:26; 108:8); 23:5 (Ex. 22:28); Rom. 2:24 (Ezech. 36:20), etc. All the texts quoted in Nos. 75 and 76 as examples are likewise Scriptural accommodations.

the Divine Author of the whole Bible cites His own words
of an earlier pronouncement in a sense not identical with,
but only analogous to, the sense which was expressed by these
same words at their first recording,—and this secondary,
*spiritual, sense is often explicitly quoted with the stereotyped
formula indicating a divinely inspired meaning,* as "it is
written". If the Holy Ghost Himself quotes Scripture passages in a spiritual sense as inspired, it would appear that
He originally intended more than one meaning to be conveyed by the letter of the text.

(2) In the case of Canticles the Church has ever insisted
that the spiritual sense (based upon a literal expressed in
elaborate metaphor), is that primarily intended by the Holy
Spirit, therefore inspired.

(3) St. Paul plainly vouches for a secondary inspired
sense in the Old Testament when he declares that the vicissitudes of Israel "were done in a figure of us" and that "all
these things happened to them [the Jews] in figure: and they
are *written as a warning for us* who live in the concluding
period of time" (I Cor. 10:6, 11).

(4) Moreover the abundant use of spiritual or accommodated senses of Scripture by the Church in her liturgy and
homiletics can scarcely be considered as mere happy punning,
but rather would seem to imply that she considers such senses
to be positively authorized by God.

Besides it would seem congruent with the infinite power,
wisdom,[7] and kindness of God and with the particular and
special love which He extends to each and every man, that
the message of His Book should not be confined to the time
and place of the hagiographers and their first readers, and
have only a universal or historical sense, but rather that all
men in all times and places, nay even each individual for his
own private edification, should be able by proper and pious
effort to draw from the Sacred Text lessons fitting and useful

[7] "For, Wisdom is more active than all active things, and reacheth
everywhere . . . and, being but one, she can [nevertheless]do all things;
and remaining in herself the same, she reneweth all things, and in every
generation communicating herself to saintly souls, she trains friends of
God and prophets" (Wis. 7:24a, 27 Greek).

for his life and work. Such a view would seem to broaden
and sublimate the concept of the function of Sacred Scripture to harmonize with the wondrous magnificence of God's
other dealings with men, and best of all to accord with St.
Paul's dictum that *"what things soever* were written, were
written for our learning, that through patience and the comfort of the Scriptures we might have hope" (Rom. 15:4).

To define the spiritual, or accommodated, sense as "that which
was not intended by the Holy Ghost" is a misnomer, for there can
be no true sense of any writing, which does not express the ideas
intended to be conveyed by the author. Hence the spiritual (accommodated, mystical) sense would better be described as that which
was intended by the Holy Ghost, not indeed primarily, but secondarily. It is not the obvious one, accessible to all, but it is that
deeper, intimate meaning which is valid at least for those who can
read the Sacred Text according to the principles of the supernatural
order.

But, maintaining that the secondary senses of the Bible were
intended by the Holy Spirit does not imply that they were intended
or even known to the respective hagiographers at the time of composition, as St. Augustine and St. Thomas seem to insinuate. Moreover, when suggesting that each of the faithful may draw from the
Bible meanings of individual personal use and benefit which are
inspired, it is understood that the reading and interpretation of the
Bible should be in accord with the general principles of faith and
at the same time be at least analogously conformable to the primary
literal meaning. Mere punning or similarity of words can not be
the base of an inspired sense. Thus the Vulgate "Confessio et
magnificentia opus eius" (Ps. 110:3) can not be applied to the
sacrament of Penance. In the vineyard of an Italian monastery
a beautiful statue of Our Lady was erected with this apparently
fitting inscription from the Canticles on the pedestal: "Posuerunt
me Custodem in Vineis" (Cant. 1:5). But a visitor, looking up
the full text, found it not so appropriate. St. Francis de Sales
rightly corrected the Bishop of Belley on one occasion when the
latter whilst preaching applied to the contagious danger of bad
company the words of the Psalmist: "And with the perverse thou
wilt be perverted" (Ps. 17:27), which in reality applied to the
judgment dealings of God with the wicked.

CHAPTER VII

INTERPRETATION OF THE BIBLE

79. In whatsoever language the Sacred Scriptures may be translated, their true sense is ever the same, being nought else than the meaning attached by God, the prime Author, to the language used. Yet this very language, being human and conventional, does not always spontaneously as it were manifest the true sense in each individual portion of the text; rather the directing hand of a sure guide and scientific directive norms must be invoked by him who would attain the true meaning. Hermeneutics,[1] or the science of the interpretation of the Bible, expounds the principles and rules according to which the true sense of Holy Scripture, both in its human and in its divine aspect, can be ascertained. Hermeneutics bears to exegesis[2] the relations of theory to practice,—exegesis being concerned with the actual explanation of a given text.

Art. 1: WHO IS THE AUTHORITATIVE INTER-PRETER OF THE BIBLE?

Texts: Luke 24:27, 45; Acts 8:26-35.

80. Bible Not Its Own Interpreter.—Sacred Scripture is written in human language, paralleling in this respect any book or document current among men. Now, *language symbols,* whether of sound or of writing, are but *conventional*

---

[1] The name ''hermeneutics'' (ἑρμηνευτική *sc.* τέχνη) comes from ἑρμηνεύειν, to interpret, to expound, and designates the art of making plain a writer's meaning.

[2] Name derived from ἐξάγω, to lead or bring out [the true sense].

81

signs used by certain groups of men to designate certain ideas. They are not the ideas themselves, nor is there even any *necessary* or natural connection between the spoken or written word and the idea, whereby the reader or hearer might always *infallibly* grasp exactly the meaning intended by the author to be conveyed by his words, which alone is the true sense.

These shortcomings of language by which men's true minds are essentially isolated from each other are scarcely noticeable in the ordinary intercourse of neighbors and acquaintances, for their long association and contact with the same everyday matters makes Mr. *A* and Mrs. *B* attach practically identical significations to the word "X", or the expression "XYZ". The chances of the attached meanings or ideas not being identical (and consequently the chances of misinterpretation of a writing) increase exactly in proportion as *A* and *B*, users of the word "X" or the expression "XYZ", are separated by distance, nationality, race, customs, habits, business, and time. Then if *A* be an hagiographer, living about three thousand years ago, racially a Semite, amidst Oriental surroundings, given to meditation and study of the supernatural, and *B* be a modern American schoolgirl materialistically inclined, with mind occupied almost entirely with the latest frivolities of the season, the chances that the latter will be incapable of correctly interpreting the language of the former must certainly be raised to the *n*th power.

Now, Sacred Scripture is not in one whit exempt from the interpretative shortcomings inherent in language in general,—and it has superadded others arising from the fact that its Divine Author strives therein to express and make intelligible to men ideas and revelations of the *supernatural* order so sublime and transcendent as to be almost incapable of expression by human speech, which is essentially "of the earth, earthy" (I Cor. 15:47).[3] One can not therefore maintain with reason that the Bible is self-interpretative, that it should in this matter be privileged uniquely beyond other books and documents. And if the Bible is not self-interpretative, its *true* sense or meaning need not *necessarily* be apparent to everyone who reads it. Hence the *private opinion* or judgment which the individual arrives at as to what the

---

[3] "If I have spoken to you earthly things, and you believe not; how will you believe, if I shall speak to you heavenly things?" (John 3:12).

meaning of a Scripture passage is, without other guidance than his own reasoning power and the nude text, *is not infallible.*

Human society for its own welfare has never recognized the validity of private interpretation in matters affecting the public weal. Thus, if ever self-interpretativeness might be presumed in writings, it should certainly be verified in the case of laws and wills. These should indeed be composed with such clarity that "he who reads might run through it" (Hab. 2:2) and yet understand. Nevertheless the interpretation of the true sense of laws and wills is never left to the judgment of private individuals, but is reserved to the decision of the courts. And if such be the procedure of sound reason in purely earthly affairs, it seems in truth absurd to claim, as did the 16th century Reformers, that any one at all may correctly interpret the majestic moral code laid down by God in the Sacred Scriptures, the sublime legacy of revealed truths left by Him to the world in the Old and the New Testament.

81. Church alone Infallible Interpreter of Scripture.— In an absolute sense, only the author of a given writing can make known the interpretation thereof which will be infallibly correct. For, the author alone knows just what ideas he intended to express and convey by his word-signs. But God is the primary and principal Author of Sacred Scripture; therefore He alone can interpret the true meaning of the Bible. But for His public and general supernatural dealings with men God has established as His official agency and mediator the Church, which is nought else than the "Mystical Body of Christ",[4] the God-Man, delegated with the essential powers to continue His functions throughout the ages. As God the Father had authorized and sent His Only-Begotten Son Christ the God-Man to be the teacher of men for supernatural truth, so in turn Christ authorized and sent His Church (John 20:21),[5] so that he who hears and receives the teaching of the Church, hears and receives the teaching of the God-Man Himself (Luke 10:16), and on that account "the Church of the living God" in her function of interpreting unto men God's own written word, is "the pillar and ground of truth" (I Tim. 3:15).

[4] See Col. 1:18; Eph. 4:12–16; Col. 3:15; I Cor. 10:17; 12:12–13, 28; Col. 1:24; Rom. 12:4–5.
[5] See also Matt. 10:40; 28:16; 18–20.

82. The theory whereby any man may read the bare text of
Scripture and, without consultation of any authority whatsoever,
arrive infallibly at the true meaning every time, is absurd as maintaining the equal truthfulness of contradictory opinions which must
invariably result from such a procedure. It may go further than
this and be unjust also, if the private opinion or interpretation of
one man regarding a Scripture passage is to be foisted upon another,
who, under the above theory, has a perfect right to claim that his
own personal judgment is as correct as that of the other man.

Moreover the Bible itself declares that "no exposition of Scripture is made by private interpretation" (II Pet. 1: 20),[6] because
the fact of its supernatural composition (since "the holy men of
God spoke inspired by the Holy Ghost") necessarily demands a
supernatural interpreter. Again, Holy Writ itself again and
again witnesses that, though the Apostles were well versed in the
text of the Old Law, nevertheless at various times they failed to
grasp certain of the Master's allusions to the ancient prophecies.[7]
And indeed after the Resurrection one of the perfecting graces
given our Lord's disciples was the opening of the true sense and
significance of Scripture to their minds (see Luke 24: 27, 32, 45).

Man's correct attitude toward the interpretation of the Bible
is suggested by the conduct of the treasurer of Queen Candace, as
related in the Acts (8: 26-35). The pious treasurer returning from
Jerusalem in his carriage was intently perusing a copy of Isaias.
Surely if private interpretation were ever operative, it would have
been made manifest in such a case. Yet, to the deacon Philip's
question: "Thinkest thou that thou understandest what thou read-
est?" the treasurer answered frankly: "And how can I, unless some
man show me". Whereupon Philip, being invited into the carriage,
as minister or mouthpiece of the Church, began to expound unto
him the Scriptures.

Of course, when the Scriptures are used, not as writings
inspired by God, but simply as human historical documents
emanating from the hagiographers, and when the sense sought
is merely the natural import of the language, then it is sufficient for the proper interpretation of the Bible for it to be
made in accordance with the usual strict principles of logic
and historical criticism which are applied by courts and ex-
perts to other historical documents and writings.[8] It is in

[6] The first "prophecy" in this text means properly an "explanation
of Scripture", in which sense the word is used in Rom. 12: 1; I Cor.
12: 12–14; I Thess. 5: 20, etc. This is confirmed by the use of the word
ἐπιλύσεως in connection, the latter meaning "an unfolding, solving, un-
ravelling".

[7] See John 20: 9; Mark 9:31; Luke 18:34; 9:45; 24:25.

[8] The treatment of the Bible for special circumstances outlined here,
is not to be confused with that condemned in the Syllabus *Lamentabili*

such manner that the Bible must be used in discussion with those who are not yet convinced of its divine character, or of the existence of a Church commissioned by God to be the organization of the supernatural order among men.

Art. 2: PRINCIPLES OF HERMENEUTICS

Texts: Ps. 118: 34, 47, 97, 105, 130, 162; Luke 24: 32.

83. Negative Principle to Prevent Error.—Being the divinely constituted custodian and interpreter of Holy Writ, the Church, ever encouraging the activity of the human intellect within the limits of its powers, has laid down for the interpretation of the Bible but a single principle, which joins absolute prevention of error with the broadest liberty for critical research. For, this *basic rule is* not positive but *negative,* being content to warn against wrong roads which would "lead to destruction" (Matt. 7:13), whilst leaving open to the utmost exertion of human ingenuity every avenue of investigation that may indeed "lead unto life" and the true senses of Sacred Scripture. This canon for the interpretation of the Bible, in practical use from the very beginning —being but an expansion or clarification of the Apostolic rule: "Understanding this first [i.e., as a fundamental principle], that no prophecy [= correct sense; see No. 82, Note 1] of Scripture is made by private interpretation [i.e., without God's authorization]" (II Pet. 1:20)—was thus formulated at the Council of Trent (Sess. IV):

The holy synod declares that no one relying on his own judgment shall dare to wrest Holy Scripture in accordance with his opinion, contrary to that which our holy Mother the Church held and still holds, for to her does it belong to decide upon the true meaning and interpretation of Holy Scripture; nor shall any one dare to expound the same Holy Scripture in a way contrary to the unanimous decision of the Fathers.

(Prop. 12): "The exegete, if he wishes to apply himself usefully to biblical studies, must first of all put aside all preconceived opinions concerning the supernatural origin of the Sacred Scriptures, and interpret it not otherwise than other merely human documents" (*Congr. Inquis.*, July 3rd, 1907).

Three points are emphasized by this decree (which was later renewed by the Vatican Council [9] with the specification that it applies particularly to "matters of faith and morals"):

(1) The exegete may not interpret Holy Scripture according to his own subjective judgment alone. Personal opinion is not to be considered the standard for designating the true sense of the Bible, for, private judgment is fallible, but the Church as Christ's Mystical Body is infallible.

(2) The exegete may not adopt as correct an interpretation *at variance with the doctrines of the Church,* but must reject it as false, for the Holy Ghost can not contradict Himself by revealing to the Church one sense and inspiring the Scriptures with another quite opposed thereto.

(3) The exegete may not pronounce an interpretation to be correct that is *contrary* to the *unanimis consensus Patrum.* For unanimous agreement of the Fathers on an interpretation in matters of faith and morals, whilst not constituting a dogma of the Church, nevertheless is an undoubted sign of Apostolic tradition which borders upon defined doctrine.

84. The Church herself has *formally* interpreted by her infallible authority the true sense of comparatively few passages of Scripture. This has been done either (*a*) *negatively,* by condemning a false sense, as when the Fifth Ecumenical Council condemned the figurative sense in which Theodore of Mopsuestia interpreted John 20:22: "Receive ye the Holy Ghost"; or when the Council of Trent condemned the sense in which John 20:23 would mean: to receive only the power to preach the Gospel (Sess. XIV, c. 3); or (*b*) *positively,* by declaring the true meaning: for example, the Council of Trent defined that the words of Christ: "This is my Body" (Luke 22:19, etc.) meant that Our Lord became really and substantially present under the appearances of bread and wine (Sess. XII, c. 1. See also Sess. XIV, cc. 1-4 and James 5:14). Indirectly, however, the Church has pointed out the

---

9 "Nos, idem decretum renovantes, hanc illius esse mentem declaramus, ut in rebus fidei et morum, ad ædificationem doctrinæ Christianæ pertinentium, is pro vero sensu Sacræ Scripturæ habendus sit, quem tenuit ac tenet Sancta Mater Ecclesia, cuius est iudicare de vero sensu et interpretatione Scripturarum Sanctarum, atque ideo nemini licere contra hunc sensum, aut etiam contra unanimem consensum Patrum, ipsam Scripturam Sanctam interpretari" (*Conc. Vat.*, Sess. III, c. 2).

correct meaning of many passages by the use she has made of them in her definitions of revealed doctrines, adducing them to demonstrate that the truths defined are actually revealed. For instance, the Vatican Council used the words of Christ to Peter: "I have prayed for thee that thy faith fail not" (Luke 22:32) to prove the infallibility of the Pope.

Of course, antecedently to any textual explanation, the exegete, in conformity with the teaching of the Church in regard to the infallibility (inerrancy) of the Scriptures, can not ascribe to the inspired Writings any formal moral, dogmatic, scientific, or historic error, all such being incompatible with Divine Authorship (see No. 15). But the Sacred Text has never been guaranteed by the Church to be free from all material defects and mistakes.

Moral considerations must also be kept in view. Whoever wishes to comprehend the meaning of Holy Scripture must have a good intention and moral purity, for "wisdom will not enter into a malicious soul, nor dwell in a body subject to sins" (Wis. 1:4), and he must also have humility, for "where humility is, there also is wisdom" (Prov. 11:2). Reading and study of the sacred books are no less necessary. Lastly, but not least, one must pray for understanding, as St. Augustine said: "Quod est præcipuum et maxime necessarium, orent ut intelligant" (*De doctrina christiana*, III, 37). What is more beautiful than his prayer for light to understand the Scriptures, as given in his *Confessions* (XI, 2). Any reader of the Bible would do well to accommodate to himself for this purpose the prayer of the Wise man:

"God of my fathers and Lord of mercy, who hast made all things with Thy Word, . . . give me Wisdom that sitteth with Thee upon Thy throne!

"Cast me not off from among Thy children, for, I am Thy servant and the son of Thy handmaid,—a weak man, of brief time, and falling short in understanding judgments and laws.

"For even if one be perfect in knowledge among the children of men, yet if Thy Wisdom be not with him, he shall be nothing regarded.

"Send her, therefore, out of Thy holy heaven, and from the throne of Thy majesty, that being present to me she may labor with me, that I may know what is acceptable to Thee.

"For, she knoweth and understandeth all things, and shall lead me soberly in my works, and shall preserve me by her power. And so shall my works be acceptable.

"For, who among men knoweth the counsel of God? or who can think what the will of God is? The thoughts of mortals are timid, and our counsels uncertain.

"For, the corruptible body is a load upon the soul, and the earthly habitation presseth down the mind that museth upon many things. And hardly do we guess aright at things that are upon the earth, and with difficulty do we find the things that are before us.

"But the things that are in heaven who shall search out? And who shall know Thy thought?—except Thou give Wisdom, and send Thy Holy Spirit from above, that so the ways of them that are upon earth may be corrected, and men may learn the things that please Thee"!

(Wis. 9:1-18.)

85. Common Critical Principles as Applied to Scripture. —Safeguarded by the above principle, the student of the Sacred Scriptures proceeds to apply to his text the rules and methods commonly employed by sane science in the historical and critical investigation of books or documents, to determine their true sense. For, the language of the Bible being human, the determination of the true sense expressed thereby must —the safeguarding principle of the Church being assumed— follow the ordinary procedure of human ingenuity in such matters. This procedure, with its special application to the Bible, may be summarized under the following heading or rules:

(1) The student of Sacred Scripture will read its text *in accordance with the usual laws of logic, grammar, and rhetoric,* with particular regard to the idioms of the language in which it was originally composed.

The latter implies bearing in mind the Semitic characteristics of biblical literature in general (see Nos. 35-38 above), as well as the peculiarities of the original Hebrew or Greek (see Nos. 42-44), and even of the version language.

(2) He will carefully take into consideration the *author, time, place, purpose, plan, manner, and addressees* of the composition in question.

This is what is comprised by "higher biblical criticism" in its best sense, employing *both internal and external evidence* in its research of the origin and history of a biblical composition. It pays special attention likewise to *historic background. Internal* evidence is such as may be deduced from the text of the Bible itself; *external* evidence is such as may be adduced from other historic documents, from archeology, in short from all reliable sources outside the Bible, including of course the tradition of the

Church. The false "higher criticism" "pretends to judge the origin, integrity, and authority of each Book from internal indications alone", whilst "it is clear, on the other hand, that in historical questions, such as the origin and handing down of writings, the witness of history is of primary importance, and that historical investigation should be made with the utmost diligence; and that in this manner internal evidence is seldom of great value, except as confirmation" (Encyc. *Providentissimus Deus*).

(3) He will examine the passage studied, in *connection with its own immediate context*, and in comparison with *illustrative* or *parallel passages* elsewhere in the Bible.

Of supreme import is the *autexegesis* of Holy Writ, that is: when the Bible, citing or alluding to its own words in another passage, indicates in what sense they were previously uttered and understood. Hence the usefulness of familiarity with the whole of Sacred Scripture, whereof one part or passage explains another perhaps widely distant and apparently unrelated.

In case of language obscurity at least, and always in controversially important matters:

(4) The student of Sacred Scripture will *consult the original texts*, ancient versions, and also any parallel language evidence outside the Bible.

(5) He will examine, when necessary, the *critical reading* of the text in the light of ancient MSS. and other paleographic evidence.

This is properly "textual criticism". In this connection it may be remarked that an obscure or difficult reading is not for that reason alone to be rejected in favor of a more obvious or simple one. For, editors and copyists were always prone to substitute familiar and apparently more intelligible terms in place of strange or difficult expressions. If after diligent critical research the obscurity can not be cleared up, and a scribal error seems pointed to by probable cause, a reasonable textual emendation may be indicated. However, one should be most chary lest such changes should be mere subjective conjectures, reflecting rather what the critic would have the text say than what the author really intended.

In cases of *antilogies* [10] or of theologic, moral, philosophic, scientific or historic *difficulties:*

[10] This term, from ἀντὶ λόγος, is applied to passages of the Bible that apparently clash or contradict one another, such as Num. 25:9 and I Cor. 10:8; Matt. 27:44 (Mark 15:32c) and Luke 23:39–43.

(6) The student of Sacred Scripture will always *assume* what *faith or reason indicates* to be the proper sense intended by the Holy Ghost, and with this assumption as a guide further research in either textual (Rules 4 and 5) or higher criticism (Rule 2) will generally provide a solution or satisfactory harmonization.

In the case of difficulties raised by rationalists and other opponents of the supernatural order, it is well to remember that the propositions which these men adduce as proven *facts,* are frequently only tentative *theories,* if not mere assertions, which can not successfully militate against established verities. Frequently indeed modern pseudo-scientists and hypercritics, instead of facing a biblical text as it stands, with its consectaries, endeavor by "critical" cutting and manipulating to fit it to the Procrustean beds of their theories, which are often more fanciful than rational. Thus, in such cases it is best first of all to search carefully the factual and logical bases of such statements, whose falsity may often be patently exposed by pointing out the glaring absurdities to which they frequently lead. Above all, whilst giving due regard to a non-Catholic critic's erudition, the Catholic exegete, being in secure possession of infallible truth, should never be cowed by the mere sound of a name which may be trumpeted from the housetops of the unthinking during a brief season of popularity. As for others, non-professional scripturists, they are generally but exegetical cobblers deserving only of pity or ridicule for amateurishly dabbling in matters far beyond their lasts.

(7) Lastly, the student of Sacred Scripture should have sufficient common sense to recognize his own limitations as well as the fallibility of critical art, and courage to confess ignorance when for the nonce the solution of some difficulty happens to elude him. He should read the Bible *objectively,* and not strive to wrest its words to fit preconceived subjective opinions. He should never dare to bound the sense of Scripture by his own capacity for knowledge.

Art. 3: REQUISITES AND AIDS FOR BIBLE STUDY

Texts: Jer. 15:16; II Tim. 3:15; Prov. 24:13-14.

86. Equipment of the Scripturist.—No science, perhaps, makes such arduous demands upon its incumbents as the study of Sacred Scripture. Besides being thoroughly grounded in philosophy and theology, the scripturist must have ample knowledge of archeology, ancient history, and philology, and likewise should be well posted in the natural sciences. He must have a working acquaintance with Latin, Greek, and Hebrew. Other Semitic tongues, such as Arabic or Syriac, will be of great assistance. Of modern tongues, English, German, and French, at least, are imperative in order that he may avail himself of books and articles published in those languages. His reading must range from the ancient Fathers to the newest disquisitions in the technical biblical and archeological periodicals. For, whilst the inspired truth of the Bible, like the doctrine of the Church, remains ever unchanged, yet study and discussion bring about a continual evolution or development of its understanding on the part of men. The labor of the scripturist is indeed formidable, but his pleasure therein is proportionate, because he soon realizes that "he who is learned in the Word, acquireth good things" (Prov. 16:20), and therefore he gives up all else "to understand the Word of prudence and to receive the instruction of doctrine, justice, judgment, and equity" (Prov. 1:3).

87. Suggestions for the Scripture Student.—One who is desirous of becoming better acquainted with God's written Word should first of all read the *whole Bible* through rapidly, so as to have a general notion of its contents. Next he will take up some *one Book* that appeals more especially to him, to concentrate upon its deeper study. It is characteristic of the Sacred Writ, that, being all from the same primary Author, it is permeated throughout by the same Spirit, and thus a thorough grasp of any one part will lead to the comprehension of the whole. At this stage it is well to consult a *special Introduction* to the book under consideration, which will make plain its *object, thought-plan,* and other useful circumstances.

Then the *text itself* should be taken up in detail, with a view to utilizing the results either for preaching, meditation, elucidation of dogma or morals, apologetics, or the defense and exposition of the Scripture itself. Here a common fault is: reading the Bible in small morsels, whereby one misses the broader lessons and relationships of its pages. The reader should peruse a logical section at least, without regard to the largely arbitrary chapter and verse divisions of the Stephanus system (see No. 51, note 3). Then he should stop and *reflect on the text*, asking himself questions like the following: What is the significance of this? its connection with the rest? with dogma and morals? with life and men? What message did the Holy Spirit intend to convey by these words? by these events and combinations of circumstances?

For aid in this process the reader may consult *commentaries* upon the *literal sense* (primary). Homiletic and ascetic commentaries are to be eschewed for the time being, as they are generally occupied largely with the spiritual (secondary) senses, which themselves must always be based upon the primary or literal.

The results of one's reflections and reading had best be *noted down* preferably upon the margin of the Bible itself.[11] It is well also to underscore and otherwise mark the text as one's needs and proclivities suggest. A Bible thus personally annotated will with age and use become an ever richer and dearer treasure to its possessor.

88. Aids to Research.—For convenience in referring to the various texts the student should have a *polyglot Bible* containing the original Greek and Hebrew texts together with at least the Vulgate version, in parallel columns, so that the eye may at a glance pass from one language to the other.[12] Textual critical notes and

[11] It is to be hoped that a publisher may some day be found to put out a Vulgate or Douay version printed with all the refinements of modern editing and typography, giving logical chapter and paragraph divisions, distinguishing prose and poetry, putting in more summaries and notes really explanatory of the text, and leaving ample margins or, better still, blank pages for the reader's personal annotations. For the King James version (American revisioin) *Moulton has done exemplary work along these lines in his *Modern Reader's Bible*.

[12] The most practical polyglot available to Catholic students is perhaps Vigouroux, *Sainte bible polyglotte* (8 vols. octavo, Paris, 1900–09). It contains the Masoretic Hebrew with *qeri;* the Greek *textus receptus* with the variants of the more important MSS. and editors; the Vulgate version accompanied by copious cross-references; Glaire's excellent modern French translation; abundant critical and explanatory footnotes in French; several maps, and numerous practically useful illustrations drawn from archeological finds, all excellently printed.

variants are generally included in such works. The use of a polyglot, it may be noted, is an unconscious aid to familiarity with its divers languages. Ample *dictionaries* are of course a prime necessity. Next a *verbal concordance* is of the greatest assistance not only in finding desired passages of the Bible, but also for comparing the value of the same word in various passages and Books.[13] Subject concordances are useful for their grouping of various passages bearing on a common topic; they generally give prominence to the spiritual senses also.[14] A large, clear map of the Holy Land is invaluable for visualizing the territory in which the biblical scenes were enacted.[15]

89. Pontifical Biblical Commission and its Institute at Rome.—The cyclic break-up of Protestantism at the close of its four hundred year period has been marked by extreme and violent reaction against the original rabid Reformation shibboleths of "faith and the Bible alone".

This reaction from the early principles of Protestantism may be well illustrated by the following statements of F. J. Peabody, former Dean of the Harvard Divinity School: "With admirable prudence the Roman Catholic system has always guarded the Bible from the uninstructed study of the laity, maintaining that Scripture, though holy, must be interpreted by a Holy Church. Protestantism, on the other hand, has encouraged a supreme confidence in the printed word. The Bible has been very generally accepted, not merely as a medium for the word of God, but as that word itself; inerrant, conclusive, accessible to all who can read, mark, learn, and inwardly digest. . . . As one reflects on this . . ., it seems surprising that so unstable a support of faith should have remained so long undisturbed. An infallible Book is much more difficult to guarantee than an infallible Church. Unchangeable as an institution may be affirmed to be, there is always room for re-definition and expansion, through the action of some Council or Pope or Conference; but a book is always the same; and a closed book shuts

---

[13] There is no verbal concordance of the Douay version; concordances by Catholic scripturists are generally based upon the Vulgate; one of the best is Dutripon's (in folio, Paris, 1838), which is very comprehensive. For the Greek text of the New Testament, *Wigram's *Englishman's Greek Concordance,* giving the Greek words and all passages in which they occur according to the King James version, is quite helpful (Harper, New York, 1855). *Cruden's large verbal concordances in English are of course based upon the King James also. Other Vulgate concordances are those of de Raze (17th ed., Gabalda, Paris); Peultier (Lethielleux, Paris); Coornaert (Beyart, Bruges).

[14] In this connection the compact but compendious *Divine Armory of Holy Scripture* by Kenelm Vaughan (New York, 1894) can be highly recommended.

[15] A cheap aid is *Rand, McNally's *Bible Atlas* (Chicago), being a "Manual of Biblical Geography and History".

out a changing world. For many generations of Protestantism the
Book was a sufficient guide; one might open its pages at random
and obey the first command that met the eye. But the Nemesis
which Biblical literalism invited could not be forever delayed, and
it has been reserved for the present time to follow the logic of
literalism to its limit" (*Yale Review*, Jan., 1923. pp. 327-328).

Faith, which at first was declared sufficient, without good
works, unto salvation, has now been replaced by paternalistic
exaggeration of humanitarian philanthropy. The Bible has
been relegated by its erstwhile fanatic upholders to the realm
of myths and fairy tales. The last progeny of the 16th century Reformers wrenched at the bonds which bound them to
the two supporting pillars of the false temple of Protestantism, and tumbled the latter in suicidal destruction upon the
heads of its own devotees.

Having destroyed the four hundred year old illusions of
the followers of Luther and Calvin, rationalistic investigators
endeavored at the close of the 19th and the opening of the
20th centuries to shake in the same manner the age-old verities of the Kingdom of God upon earth, the Church. The
destructive criticism of the Tübingen school, of Delitzsch,
Renan, Wellhausen, Jülicher, Haupt, and their numerous
imitators, was opposed by Catholic exegetes like Hummelauer,
Kaulen, Vigouroux, Maas, and Drum. Pope Leo XIII during
his lengthy pontificate especially encouraged the revival of
biblical studies in the Church, and crystallized this activity
in the establishment of the Pontifical Biblical Commission
and its accompanying Institute.

90. The Pontifical Biblical Commission is composed of a
group of Cardinals with decisive vote, who depend upon the
counsel of about 40 eminent scripturists and theologians of
all schools and nationalities. This Commission studies and
discusses biblical questions of the day, and from time to time
issues pronouncements thereon, bearing the approval of the
Pope. These pronouncements, whilst not infallible, are nevertheless practical directive norms to be received and adhered
to in conscience as disciplinary safeguards with which the
Church protects her treasure of written revelation.

The Biblical Commission was founded in 1902, by the Apostolic Letter *Vigilantiæ studiique memores* (*Acta Sanctæ Sedis,* xxxv, p. 234). The decisions of this Commission are given in the Appendices.

The authority of the Biblical Commission is made clear in the Motu Proprio *Præstantia scripturæ sacræ* of Pius X (Nov. 18th, 1907, in *Acta Sanctæ Sedis,* xi, p. 723): "Declaramus in præsens expresseque præcipimus, universos omnes conscientiæ obstringi officio sententiis Pontificalis Consilii de Re Biblica, sive quæ adhuc sunt emissæ sive quæ posthac edentur, perinde ac decretis Sacrarum Congregationum pertinentibus ad doctrinam, probatisque a Pontifice, se subiiciendi; nec posse notam tum detractæ obedientiæ tum temeritatis devitare aut culpa propterea vacare gravi quotquot verbis scriptisque sententias has tales impugnent; idque præter scandalum, quo offendant, ceteraque quibus in causa esse coram Deo possint, aliis, aut plurimum, temere in his errateque pronunciatis".

Connected with the Biblical Commission is an Institute for Scripture studies, giving intensive postgraduate courses along all lines of biblical research, and conferring special degrees of Licentiate and Doctor in Sacred Scripture. The professors in this Institute are specialists in their respective branches, and chosen from various nationalities. A library, archeological museum, and special publications complete the facilities of this school.

Thus it is, in the words of the Encyclical *Providentissimus Deus* (Leo XIII, Nov. 18th, 1893):

"that the watchful eye of the Church shines forth conspicuously. By admirable laws and regulations, she has shown herself solicitous that 'the celestial treasure of the sacred books, so bountifully bestowed upon man by the Holy Spirit, should not lie neglected'.[16] She has prescribed that a considerable portion of them shall be read and piously reflected upon by all her ministers in the daily office of the sacred psalmody. She has ordered that in cathedral churches, in monasteries, and in other convents in which study can conveniently be pursued, they shall be expounded and interpreted by capable men; and she has strictly commanded that her children shall be fed with the saving words of the Gospel at least on Sundays and solemn feasts.[17] Moreover, it is owing to the wisdom and exertions of the Church that there has always been continued, from century to century, that cultivation of Holy Scripture which has been so remarkable and has borne such ample fruit."

[16] *Conc. Trid.,* Sess. V, de reformatione, 1.
[17] *Ibid.,* 1, 2.

APPENDIX

ECCLESIASTICAL TEXTS AND DOCUMENTS

Encyclical "Providentissimus Deus" [1]

The God of all providence, who in the adorable designs of His love at first elevated the human race to the participation of the divine nature, and afterwards delivered it from universal guilt and ruin, restoring it to its primitive dignity, has, in consequence, bestowed upon man a splendid gift and safeguard—making known to him, by supernatural means, the hidden mysteries of His divinity, His wisdom and His mercy. For although in divine revelation there are contained some things which are not beyond the reach of unassisted reason, and which are made the objects of such revelation in order "that all may come to know them with facility, certainty, and safety from error, yet not on this account can supernatural revelation be said to be absolutely necessary; it is only necessary because God has ordained man to a supernatural end".[2] This supernatural revelation, according to the belief of the universal Church, is contained both in unwritten tradition and in written books, which are, therefore, called sacred and canonical because, "being written under the inspiration of the Holy Ghost, they have God for their author, and as such have been delivered to the Church".[3] This belief has been perpetually held and professed by the Church in regard to the Books of both Testaments; and there are well-known documents of the gravest kind, coming down to us from the earliest times, which proclaim that God, who spoke first by the prophets, then by His own mouth, and lastly by the apostles, composed also the canonical Scriptures,[4] and that these are His own oracles and words [5]—a Letter written by our Heavenly Father and transmitted by the sacred writers to the human race in its pilgrimage so far from its heavenly country.[6] If, then, such and so great is the excellence and dignity of the Scriptures, that God Himself has composed them, and that they treat of God's marvelous mysteries, counsels and works, it follows that the branch of sacred

---

[1] Leo XIII, Nov. 18, 1893.

[2] *Conc. Vat.*, Sess. III, c. 2, de rev.

[3] *Ibid.*

[4] St. Augustine, *De civ. Dei*, XI, iii.

[5] St. Clement of Rome, I *ad Cor.*, 45; St. Polycarp, *ad Phil.*, 7; St. Ireneus, *Contra hær.*, II, xxviii, 2.

[6] St. Chrysostom, *In Gen. hom.* ii, 2; St. Augustine, *In ps. xxx, serm.* 2, 1; St. Gregory the Great, *Ad Theo. ep.* iv, 31.

theology which is concerned with the defense and elucidation of these divine books must be excellent and useful in the highest degree.

The Intention of the Holy Father

Now We, who by the help of God, and not without fruit, have by frequent Letters and exhortation endeavored to promote other branches of study which seem capable of advancing the glory of God and contributing to the salvation of souls, have for a long time cherished the desire to give an impulse to the noble science of Holy Scripture, and to impart to Scripture study a direction suitable to the needs of the present day. The solicitude of the apostolic office naturally urges, and even compels us, not only to desire that this grand source of Catholic revelation should be made safely and abundantly accessible to the flock of Jesus Christ, but also not to suffer any attempt to defile or corrupt it, either on the part of those who impiously or openly assail the Scriptures, or of those who are led astray into fallacious and imprudent novelties. We are not ignorant, indeed, Venerable Brethren, that there are not a few Catholics, men of talent and learning, who do devote themselves with ardor to the defense of the sacred writings and to making them known and better understood. But whilst giving to these the commendation they deserve, We cannot but earnestly exhort others also, from whose skill and piety and learning We have a right to expect good results, to give themselves to the same most praiseworthy work. It is Our wish and fervent desire to see an increase in the number of the approved and persevering laborers in the cause of Holy Scripture; and more especially that those whom divine grace has called to Holy Orders should, day by day, as their state demands, display greater diligence and industry in reading, meditating, and explaining it.

Benefit of Bible Study

A. *In General*

Among the reasons for which the Holy Scripture is so worthy of commendation—in addition to its own excellence and to the homage which we owe to God's Word—the chief of all is, the innumerable benefits of which it is the source, according to the infallible testimony of the Holy Ghost Himself, who says: *All Scripture inspired of God is profitable to teach, to reprove, to correct, to instruct in justice: that the man of God may be perfect, furnished to every good work.*[7] That such was the purpose of God in giving the Scripture to men is shown by the example of Christ our Lord and of His apostles. For He Himself who "obtained authority by miracles, merited belief by authority, and by belief

[7] II Tim. 3: 16–17.

drew to himself the multitude" [8] was accustomed, in the exercise of His divine mission, to appeal to the Scriptures. He uses them at times to prove that He is sent by God, and is God Himself. From them He cites instructions for His disciples and confirmation of His doctrine. He vindicates them from the calumnies of objectors; He quotes them against Sadducees and Pharisees and retorts from them upon Satan himself when he dares to tempt Him. At the close of His life His utterances are from the Holy Scripture, and it is the Scripture that He expounds to His disciples after His resurrection, until He ascends to the glory of His Father. Faithful to His precepts, the apostles, although He Himself granted *signs and wonders to be done by their hands*,[9] nevertheless used with the greatest effect the sacred writings, in order to persuade the nations everywhere of the wisdom of Christianity, to conquer the obstinacy of the Jews, and to suppress the outbreak of heresy. This is plainly seen in their discourses, especially in those of St. Peter; these were often little less than a series of citations from the Old Testament making in the strongest manner for the new dispensation. We find the same things in the Gospels of St. Matthew and St. John and in the Catholic Epistles; and, most remarkable of all, in the words of him who "boasts that he learned the law at the feet of Gamaliel, in order that, being armed with spiritual weapons, he might afterwards say with confidence, 'the arms of our warfare are not carnal but mighty unto God' ".[10] Let all, therefore, especially the novices of the ecclesiastical army, understand how deeply the sacred books should be esteemed, and with what earnestness and reverence they should approach this great arsenal of heavenly arms. For those whose duty it is to handle Catholic doctrine before the learned or the unlearned will nowhere find more ample matter or more abundant exhortation, whether on the subject of God, the supreme Good and the all-perfect Being, or the works which display His glory and His love. Nowhere is there anything more full or more express on the subject of the Saviour of the world than is to be found in the whole range of the Bible. As St. Jerome says, *to be ignorant of the Scripture is not to know Christ*.[11] In its pages His image stands out, living and breathing; diffusing everywhere around consolation in trouble, encouragement to virtue, and attraction to the love of God. And as to the Church, her institutions, her nature, her office and her gifts, we find in Holy Scripture so many references and so many ready and convincing arguments that, as St. Jerome again most truly says, "A man who is well grounded in the testimonies of the Scripture is the bulwark of the Church".[12] And if we come to morality and discipline, an apostolic man finds in the sacred writings abundant and excellent assistance; most holy precepts, gentle and strong exhortation, splen-

[8] St. Augustine, *De util. credendi*, xiv, 32.
[9] Acts 14: 3.
[10] St. Jerome, *Ad Paulinam de studio Script.*, ep. liii, 3.
[11] *In Isaiam*, prologue.
[12] *Ibid.*, liv, 12.

did examples of every virtue, and finally the promise of eternal
reward and the threat of eternal punishment, uttered in terms of
solemn import, in God's name and in God's own words.

B. *For the Pulpit Orator*

And it is this peculiar and singular power of Holy Scripture,
arising from the inspiration of the Holy Ghost, which gives authority to the sacred orator, fills him with apostolic liberty of
speech, and communicates force and power to his eloquence. For
those who infuse into their efforts the spirit and strength of the
Word of God speak *not in word only, but in power also, and in
the Holy Ghost, and in much fullness.*[13] Hence, those preachers
are foolish and improvident who, in speaking of religion and pro-
claiming the things of God, use no words but those of human science
and human prudence, trusting to their own reasonings rather than
to those of God. Their discourses may be brilliant and fine, but
they must be feeble and they must be cold, for they are without the
fire of the utterance of God [14] and they must fall far short of that
mighty power which the speech of God possesses: *for the Word of
God is living and effectual, and more piercing than any two-edged
sword; and reaching unto the division of the soul and the spirit.*[15]
But, indeed, those who have a right to speak are agreed that there
is in the Holy Scripture an eloquence that is wonderfully varied
and rich and worthy of great themes. This St. Augustine thoroughly understood and has abundantly set forth.[16] This, also, is
confirmed by the best preachers of all ages, who have gratefully
acknowledged that they owed their repute chiefly to the assiduous
use of the Bible, and to devout meditation on its pages.

The Holy Fathers well knew all this by practical experience,
and they never cease to extol the sacred Scriptures and its fruits.
In innumerable passages of their writings we find them applying
to it such phrases as *an inexhaustible treasury of heavenly doctrine,*[17] or *an overflowing fountain of salvation,*[18] or putting it
before us as fertile pastures and beautiful gardens in which the
flock of the Lord is marvelously refreshed and delighted.[19] Let us
listen to the words of St. Jerome, in his Epistle to Nepotian: "Often
read the divine Scriptures; yea, let holy reading be always in thy
hand; study that which thou thyself must preach. . . . Let the speech
of the priest be ever seasoned with Scriptural reading".[20] St. Greg-

---

[13] I Thess. 1: 5.
[14] Jer. 23: 29.
[15] Heb. 4: 12.
[16] *De doct. christ.*, IV, 6, 7.
[17] St. Chrysostom, *In Gen. hom.* xxi, 2; *hom.* lx, 3; St. Augustine,
De disc. christ., ii.
[18] St. Athanasius, *Epist. fest.*, xxxix.
[19] St. Augustine, *Serm.* xxvi, 24; St. Ambrose, *In ps. cxviii, serm.*
xix, 2.
[20] St. Jerome, *De vita cleric. ad Nepot.*

ory the Great, than whom no one has more admirably described the pastoral office, writes in the same sense. "Those," he says, "who are zealous in the work of preaching must never cease the study of the written Word of God".[21] St. Augustine, however, warns us that "vainly does the preacher utter the Word of God exteriorly unless he listens to it interiorly"; [22] and St. Gregory instructs sacred orators "first to find in Holy Scripture the knowledge of themselves, and then carry it to others, lest in reproving others they forget themselves".[23] Admonitions such as these had, indeed, been uttered long before by the apostolic voice which had learned its lesson from Christ Himself, who "began to do and teach". It was not to Timothy alone, but to the whole order of the clergy, that the command was addressed: *Take heed to thyself and to doctrine; be earnest in them. For in doing this thou shalt both save thyself and them that hear thee.*[24] For the saving and for the perfection of ourselves and of others there is at hand the very best of help in the Holy Scriptures, as the Book of Psalms, among others, so constantly insists; but those only will find it who bring to this divine reading not only docility and attention but also piety and an innocent life. For the sacred Scripture is not like other books. Dictated by the Holy Ghost, it contains things of the deepest importance, which in many instances are most difficult and obscure. To understand and explain such things there is always required the "coming" [25] of the same Holy Spirit; that is to say, His light and His grace; and these, as the royal psalmist so frequently insists, are to be sought by humble prayer and guided by holiness of life.

The Solicitude of the Church

It is in this that the watchful eye of the Church shines forth conspicuously. By admirable laws and regulations, she has shown herself solicitous that "the celestial treasure of the sacred books, so bountifully bestowed upon man by the Holy Spirit, should not lie neglected".[26] She has prescribed that a considerable portion of them shall be read and piously reflected upon by all her ministers in the daily office of the sacred psalmody. She has ordered that in cathedral churches, in monasteries, and in other organizations in which study can be conveniently pursued, they shall be expounded and interpreted by capable men; and she has strictly commanded that her children be fed with the saving words of the Gospel at least on Sundays and solemn feasts.[27] Moreover, it is owing to the wisdom and exertions of the Church that there has always been

---

[21] St. Gregory the Great, *Regul. past.*, ii, 11 (al. 22); *Moral.*, XVII, xxvi (al. xiv).
[22] St. Augustine, *Serm.* clxxix, 1.
[23] St. Gregory the Great, *Regul. past.*, iii, 24 (al. 14).
[24] I Tim. 4: 16.
[25] St. Jerome, *In Mic.*, i, 10.
[26] *Con. Trid.*, Sess. V, decret. de reform. 1.
[27] *Ibid.*, 1, 2.

continued, from century to century, that cultivation of Holy Scripture which has been so remarkable and has borne such ample fruit.

A. *In the Early Times*

And here, in order to strengthen Our teaching and Our exhortations, it is well to recall how, from the beginning of Christianity, all who have been renowned for holiness of life and sacred learning have given their deep and constant attention to Holy Scripture. If we consider the immediate disciples of the apostles, St. Clement of Rome, St. Ignatius of Antioch, St. Polycarp,—or the apologists, such as St. Justin and St. Irenæus,—we find that in their letters and books, whether in defense of the Catholic faith or in its commendation, they drew faith, strength, and unction from the Word of God. When there arose, in various sees, catechetical and theological schools, of which the most celebrated were those of Alexandria and of Antioch, there was little taught in those schools but what was contained in the reading, the interpretation, and the defense of the divine written word. From them came forth numbers of Fathers and writers whose laborious studies and admirable writings have justly merited for the three following centuries the appellation of the golden age of biblical exegesis. In the Eastern Church the greatest name of all is Origen—a man remarkable alike for penetration of genius and persevering labor; from whose numerous works and his great *Hexapla* almost all have drawn who came after him. Others who have widened the field of this science may also be named as especially eminent; thus, Alexandria could boast of St. Clement and St. Cyril; Palestine, of Eusebius and the other St. Cyril; Cappadocia, of St. Basil the Great and the two Gregories, of Nazianzus and Nyssa; Antioch, of St. John Chrysostom, in whom the science of Scripture was rivaled by the splendor of his eloquence. In the Western Church there are as many names as great: Tertullian, St. Cyprian, St. Hilary, St. Ambrose, St. Leo the Great, St. Gregory the Great; most famous of all, St. Augustine and St. Jerome, of whom the former was so marvelously acute in penetrating the sense of God's Word and so fertile in the use that he made of it for the promotion of the Catholic truth, and the latter has received from the Church, by reason of his preeminent knowledge of Scripture and his labors in promoting its use, the name of the "great Doctor".[28]

B. *In the Middle Ages*

From this period down to the eleventh century, although biblical studies did not flourish with the same vigor and the same fruitfulness as before, yet they did flourish, and principally by the instrumentality of the clergy. It was their care and solicitude that selected the best and most useful things that the ancients had left,

[28] See the Collect on his feast, Sept. 30th.

arranged them in order, and published them with additions of their own—as did St. Isidore of Seville, Venerable Bede, and Alcuin, among the most prominent; it was they who illustrated the sacred pages with "glosses" or short commentaries, as we see in Walafrid Strabo and St. Anselm of Laon, or expended fresh labor in securing their integrity, as did St. Peter Damian and Blessed Lanfranc. In the twelfth century many took up, with great success, the allegorical exposition of Scripture. In this kind, St. Bernard is preeminent; and his writings, it may be said, are Scripture all through. With the age of the scholastics came fresh and welcome progress in the study of the Bible. That the scholastics were solicitous about the genuineness of the Latin version is evident from the *Correctoria Biblica*, or list of emendations, which they have left. But they expended their labors and industry chiefly on interpretation and explanation. To them we owe the accurate and clear distinction, such as had not been given before, of the various senses of the sacred words; the assignment of the value of each "sense" in theology; the division of books into parts, and the summaries of the various parts; the investigation of the objects of the writers; the demonstration of the connection of sentence with sentence, and clause with clause; all of which is calculated to throw much light on the more obscure passages of the sacred volume. The valuable work of the scholastics in Holy Scripture is seen in their theological treatises and in their Scripture commentaries; and in this respect the greatest name among them all is St. Thomas Aquinas.

When Our predecessor, Clement V, established chairs of Oriental literature in the Roman College and in the principal universities of Europe, Catholics began to make more accurate investigation on the original text of the Bible as well as on the Latin version. The revival amongst us of Greek learning, and, much more, the happy invention of the art of printing, gave a strong impetus to biblical studies. In a brief space of time, innumerable editions, especially of the Vulgate, poured from the press and were diffused throughout the Catholic world; so honored and loved was Holy Scripture during that very period against which the enemies of the Church direct their calumnies.

C. *In Modern Times*

Nor must we forget how many learned men there were, chiefly among the religious orders, who did excellent work for the Bible between the Council of Vienna and that of Trent; men who, by the employment of modern means and appliances, and by the tribute of their own genius and learning, not only added to the rich store of ancient times but prepared the way for the succeeding century, the century which followed the Council of Trent, when it almost seemed that the great age of the Fathers had returned. For it is well known, and We recall it with pleasure, that Our predecessors, from Pius IV to Clement VIII, caused to be prepared the celebrated editions of the Vulgate and the Septuagint, which, having been published by the command and authority of Sixtus V, and of the same Clement, are now in common use. At this time, moreover, were carefully brought out various other ancient versions of the Bible, and the Polyglots of Antwerp and of Paris, most important for the investigation of the true meaning of the text; nor is there any one book of either Testament which did not find more than one expositor, nor any grave question which did not profitably exercise the ability of many inquirers, among whom there are not a few—more especially of those who made most use of the Fathers— who have acquired great reputation. From that time downwards the labor and solicitude of Catholics have never been wanting; for, as time went on, eminent scholars have carried on biblical studies with success, and have defended Holy Scripture against rationalism with the same weapons of philology and kindred sciences with which it had been attacked. The calm and fair consideration of what has been said will clearly show that the Church has never failed in taking due measures to bring the Scriptures within reach of her children, and that she has ever held fast and exercised profitably that guardianship conferred upon her by Almighty God for the protection and glory of His Holy Word; so that she has never required, nor does she now require, any stimulation from without.

Rules for the Present Time

We must now, Venerable Brethren, as Our purpose demands, impart to you such counsels as seem best suited for carrying on successfully the study of biblical science.

But first it must be clearly understood whom we have to oppose and contend against, and what are their tactics and their arms. In earlier times the contest was chiefly with those who, relying on private judgment and repudiating the divine traditions and teaching office of the Church, held the Scriptures to be the one source of revelation and the final appeal in matters of faith. Now we have to meet the rationalists, true children and inheritors of the older heretics, who, trusting in their turn to their own way of thinking, have rejected even the scraps and remnants of Christian belief which had been handed down to them. They deny that there is any such thing as revelation or inspiration, or Holy Scripture at all; they see, instead, only the forgeries and falsehoods of men; they set down the Scripture narratives as stupid fables and lying stories: the prophecies and oracles of God are to them either predictions made up after the event or forecasts formed by the light of nature; the miracles and wonders of God's power are not what they are said to be, but the startling effects of natural law, or else mere tricks and myths; and the apostolic gospels and writings are not the work of the apostles at all. These detestable errors, whereby they think they destroy the truth of the divine books, are obtruded on the world as the peremptory pronouncements of a newly invented *free science;* a science, however, which is so far from final that they are perpetually modifying and supplementing it. And there are some of them who, notwithstanding their impious opinions and utterances about God, and Christ, the Gospels and the rest of Holy Scripture, would fain be considered both theologians and Christians and men of the Gospel, and who attempt to disguise by such honorable names their rashness and their pride. To them we must add not a few professors of other sciences who approve their views and give them assistance, and are urged to attack the Bible by a similar intolerance of revelation. And it is deplorable to see these attacks growing every day more numerous and more severe. It is sometimes men of learning and judgment who are assailed; but these have little difficulty in defending themselves from evil consequences. The efforts and arts of the enemy are chiefly directed against the more ignorant masses of the people. They diffuse their deadly poison by means of books, pamphlets, and newspapers; they spread it by addresses and by conversation; they are found everywhere; and they are in possession of numerous schools, taken by violence from the Church, in which, by ridicule and scurrilous jesting, they pervert the credulous and unformed minds of the young to the contempt of Holy Scripture. Should not these things, Venerable Brethren, stir up and set on fire the heart of every pastor, so that to this *knowledge, falsely so-called*,[29] may be opposed the ancient and true science which the Church, through the apostles, has received from Christ, and that Holy Scriptures may find the champions that are needed in so momentous a battle?

Let our first care, then, be to see that in seminaries and academical institutions the study of Holy Scripture is placed on such a footing as its own importance and the circumstances of the time demand. With this view, the first thing which requires attention is the wise choice of professors. Teachers of Sacred Scripture are not to be appointed at haphazard out of the crowd; but they must be men whose character and fitness are proved by their love of, and their long familiarity with, the Bible, and by suitable learning and study.

It is a matter of equal importance to provide in time for a continuous succession of such teachers; and it will be well, wherever this can be done, to select young men of good promise who have successfully accomplished their theological course, and to set them apart exclusively for Holy Scripture, affording them facilities for full and complete studies. Professors thus chosen and thus prepared may enter with confidence on the task that is appointed for them; and that they may carry out their work well and profitably, let them take heed to the instructions We now proceed to give.

INTRODUCTION

At the commencement of a course of Holy Scripture, let the professor strive earnestly to form the judgment of the young beginners so as to train them equally to defend the sacred writings and to penetrate their meaning. This is the object of the treatise which is called "Introduction". Here the student is taught how

[29] I Tim. 4: 20.

to prove the integrity and authority of the Bible, how to investigate and ascertain its true sense, and how to meet and refute objections. It is needless to insist upon the importance of making these preliminary studies in an orderly and thorough fashion, with the accompaniment and assistance of theology; for the whole subsequent course must rest on the foundation thus laid and make use of the light thus acquired.

INTERPRETATION

Next, the teacher will turn his attention to that more fruitful division of Scripture science which has to do with interpretation, wherein is imparted the method of using the Word of God for the advantage of religion and piety. We recognize, without hesitation, that neither the extent of the matter nor the time at disposal allows each single book of the Bible to be separately gone through. But the teaching should result in a definite and ascertained method of interpretation—and, therefore, the professor should equally avoid the mistake of giving a mere taste of every book, and of dwelling at too great a length on the part of one book. If most schools can not do what is done in large institutions—take the students through the whole of one or two books continuously and with a certain development—yet at least those parts which are selected should be treated with suitable fullness, in such a way that the students may learn from the sample that is put before them to love and use the remainder of the sacred book during the whole of their lives. The professor, following the tradition of antiquity, will make use of the Vulgate as his text; for the Council of Trent decreed that "in public lectures, disputations, preaching, and exposition",[30] the Vulgate is the "authentic" version; and this is the existing custom of the Church. At the same time, the other versions, which Christian antiquity has approved, should not be neglected, more especially the more ancient MSS. For, although the meaning of the Hebrew and Greek is substantially rendered by the Vulgate, nevertheless wherever there may be ambiguity or want of clearness, the "examination of older tongues",[31] to quote St. Augustine, will be useful and advantageous. But in this matter we need hardly say that the greatest prudence is required, for the "office of a commentator", as St. Jerome says, "is to set forth not what he himself would prefer but what his author says".[32] The question of "reading" having been, when necessary, carefully discussed, the next thing is to investigate and expound the meaning. And the first counsel to be given is this: that the more our adversaries contend to the contrary, so much the more solicitously should we adhere to the received and approved canons of interpretation. Hence, whilst weighing the meaning of words, the connection of ideas, the parallelism of passages, and the like, we should by all means make use

[30] Sess. IV, decret. de edit. et usu Sacr. Librorum.
[31] *De doctrina christiana*, iii, 4.
[32] *Ad Pammachium*.

of such illustrations as can be drawn from opposite erudition of an external sort; but this should be done with caution, so as not to bestow on questions of this kind more labor and time than are spent on the sacred books themselves, and not to overload the minds of the students with a mass of information that will be rather a hindrance than a help.

The professor may now safely pass on to the use of Scripture in matters of theology. On this head it must be observed that, in addition to the usual reasons which make ancient writings more or less difficult to understand, there are some which are peculiar to the Bible. For the language of the Bible is employed to express, under the inspiration of the Holy Ghost, many things which are beyond the power and scope of the reason of man—that is to say, divine mysteries and all that is related to them. There is sometimes in such passages a fullness and a hidden depth of meaning which the letter hardly expresses and which the laws of interpretation hardly warrant. Moreover, the literal sense itself frequently admits other senses, adopted to illustrate dogma or to confirm morality.

SENSUS, QUEM TENET ECCLESIA

Wherefore, it must be recognized that the sacred writings are wrapped in a certain religious obscurity, and that no one can enter into their interior without a guide; [33] God so disposing, as the Holy Fathers commonly teach, in order that men may investigate them with greater ardor and earnestness, and that what is attained with difficulty may sink more deeply into the mind and heart, and, most of all, that they may understand that God has delivered the Holy Scripture to the Church, and that in reading and making use of His Word they must follow the Church as their guide and their teacher. St. Ireneus long since laid down that where the *charismata* of God were, there the truth was to be learned, and the Holy Scripture was safely interpreted by those who had the apostolic succession.[34] His teaching and that of other holy Fathers is taken up by the Council of the Vatican, which in renewing the decree of Trent declared its "mind" to be this—that "in things of faith and morals, belonging to the building up of Christian doctrine, that it is to be considered the true sense of Holy Scripture, which has been held and is held by our Holy Mother the Church, whose place is to judge of the true sense and interpretation of the Scriptures; and, therefore, that it is permitted to no one to interpret Holy Scripture against such sense or also against the unanimous agreement of the Fathers".[35]

[33] St. Jerome, *Ad Paulinam de studio Script.* ep. liii, 4.
[34] *Contra hæreses*, IV, 26, 5.
[35] Sess. III, c. 2, de rev.; see *Conc. Trid.*, Sess. IV, decret. de edit. et usu Sacr. Librorum.

No Restraint

By this most wise decree the Church by no means prevents or restrains the pursuit of biblical science, but rather protects it from error, and largely assists its real progress. A wide field is still left open to the private student, in which his hermeneutical skill may display itself with signal effect and to the advantage of the Church. On the one hand, in those passages of Holy Scripture which have not as yet received a certain and definite interpretation, such labors may, in the benignant providence of God, prepare for and bring to maturity the judgment of the Church; on the other, in passages already defined, the private student may do work equally valuable, either by setting them forth more clearly to the flock or more skillfully to the scholars, or by defending them more powerfully from hostile attack. Wherefore the first and dearest object of the Catholic commentator should be to interpret those passages which have received an authentic interpretation either from the sacred writers themselves, under the inspiration of the Holy Ghost (as in many places of the New Testament), or from the Church, under the assistance of the same Holy Spirit, whether by her solemn judgment or by her ordinary and universal *magisterium* [36]—to interpret these passages in that identical sense, and to prove by all the resources of science that sound hermeneutical laws admit of no other interpretation. In the other passages the analogy of faith should be followed, and Catholic doctrine, as authoritatively proposed by the Church, should be held as the supreme law; for, seeing that the same God is the author both of the sacred books and of the doctrine committed to the Church, it is clearly impossible that any teaching can, by legitimate means, be extracted from the former which shall, in any respect, be at variance with the latter. Hence it follows that all interpretation is foolish or false which either makes the sacred writers disagree one with another, or is opposed to the doctrine of the Church.

Commentaries of the Fathers

The professor of Holy Scripture, therefore, amongst other recommendations, must be well acquainted with the whole circle of theology and deeply read in the commentaries of the holy Fathers and Doctors, and in other interpreters of mark.[37] This is inculcated by St. Jerome, and still more frequently by St. Augustine, who thus justly complains: "If there is no branch of teaching, however humble and easy to learn, which does not require a master, what can be a greater sign of rashness and pride than to refuse to study the books of the divine mysteries by the help of those who have interpreted them?" (*De util. cred.*, xvii. 35.) The other Fathers have said the same, and have confirmed it by their example,

[36] *Conc. Vaticanum*, Sess. III, c. 2, de fide.
[37] *Con. Vat.*, Sess. III, c. 2, de fide.

for they "endeavored to acquire the understanding of the Holy Scriptures not by their own lights and ideas but from the writing and authority of the ancients, who, in their turn, as we know, received the rule of interpretation in direct line from the apostles" (Rufinus, *Hist. eccl.* li 9.). The holy Fathers "to whom, after the apostles, the Church owes its growth—who have planted, watered, built, governed, and cherished it" (St. Aug., *Contra Julian.*, ii. 10. 37); the holy Fathers, We say, are of supreme authority, whenever they all interpret in one and the same manner any text of the Bible, as pertaining to the doctrine of faith and morals; for their unanimity clearly evinces that such interpretation has come down from the apostles as a matter of Catholic faith. The opinion of the Fathers is also of very great weight when they treat of these matters in their capacity of Doctors unofficially; not only because they excel in their knowledge of revealed doctrine and in their acquaintance with many things which are useful in understanding the apostolic books, but because they are men of eminent sanctity and of ardent zeal for the truth, on whom God has bestowed a more ample measure of His light. Wherefore the expositor should make it his duty to follow their footsteps with all reverence, and to use their labors with intelligent appreciation.

But he must not on that account consider that it is forbidden, when just cause exists, to push inquiry and exposition beyond what the Fathers have done; provided he carefully observes the rule so wisely laid down by St. Augustine—not to depart from the literal and obvious sense, except only when reason makes it untenabl or necessity requires (*De Gen. ad litt.*, lviii. c. 7, 13); a rule to which it is the more necessary to adhere strictly in these times, when the thirst for novelty and the unrestrained freedom of thought make the danger of error most real and proximate. Neither should those passages be neglected which the Fathers have understood in an allegorical or figurative sense, more especially when such interpretation is justified by the literal, and when it rests on the authority of many. For this method of interpretation has been received by the Church from the apostles, and has been approved by her own practice, as the holy Liturgy attests; although it is true that the holy Fathers did not thereby pretend directly to demonstrate dogmas of faith, but used it as a means of promoting virtue and piety, such as, by their own experience, they knew to be most valuable.

OTHER INTERPRETERS

The authority of other Church interpreters is not so great; but the study of Scripture has always continued to advance in the Church, and, therefore, these commentaries also have their own honorable place, and are serviceable in many ways for the refutation of assailants and the explanation of difficulties. But it is most unbecoming to pass by, in ignorance or contempt, the excellent work which Catholics have left in abundance, and to have recourse to the work of non-Catholics—and to seek in them, to the detriment of sound doctrine and often to the peril of faith, the explanation of passages on which Catholics long ago have successfully employed their talent and their labor. For although the studies of non-Catholics, used with prudence, may sometimes be of use to the Catholic student, he should, nevertheless, bear well in mind—as the Fathers also teach in numerous passages [38]—that the sense of Holy Scripture can nowhere be found incorrupt outside the Church, and cannot be expected to be found in writers who, being without the true faith, only know the bark of sacred Scripture, and never attain its pith.

THE PLACE OF SCRIPTURE RESEARCH AMONG THEOLOGICAL STUDIES

Most desirable is it, and most essential, that the whole teaching of theology should be pervaded and animated by the use of the divine Word of God. That is what the Fathers and the greatest theologians of all ages havè desired and reduced to practice. It is chiefly out of the sacred writings that they endeavored to proclaim and establish the Articles of Faith and the truths therewith connected, and it was in them, together with divine tradition, that they found the refutation of heretical error, and the reasonableness, the true meaning, and the mutual relation of the truths of Catholicism. Nor will any one wonder at this who considers that the sacred books hold such an eminent position among the sources of revelation that without their assiduous study and use theology can not be placed on a true footing, or treated as its dignity demands. For although it is right and proper that students in academies and schools should be chiefly exercised in acquiring a scientific knowledge of dogma, by means of reasoning from the Articles of Faith to their consequences, according to the rules of approved and sound philosophy—nevertheless the judicious and instructed theologian will by no means pass by that method of doctrinal demonstration which draws its proof from the authority of the Bible; "for theology does not receive her first principles from any other science, but immediately from God by revelation. And, therefore, she does not receive of other sciences as from a superior, but uses them as her inferiors or handmaids".[39] It is this view of doctrinal teaching which is laid down and recommended by the prince of theologians, St. Thomas of Aquin;[40] who moreover shows—such being the essential character of Christian theology—how she can defend her own principles against attack: "If the adversary," he says, "do but grant any portion of the divine revelation, we have an argument against him; thus, against a heretic we can employ Scripture authority, and against those who deny one article we can use another. But

---

[38] Cf. Clement of Alexandria, *Strom.* VII, xvi; Origen, *De prin.*, iv, 8; *In Levit. hom.* 48; Tertullian, *De præscript,* xv *ss.;* St. Hilary of Poitiers, *In Matt.*, 13, 1.

[39] St. Gregory the Great, *Moral.*, XX, ix (al. xi).

[40] *Summa*, 1a, q. 1, a. 5, ad 2um.

if our opponent reject divine revelation entirely, there is no way left to prove the Articles of Faith by reasoning; we can only solve the difficulties which are raised against them".[41]   Care must be taken, then, that beginners approach the study of the Bible well prepared and equipped; otherwise, just hopes will be frustrated, or, perchance, what is worse, they will unthinkingly risk the danger of error, falling an easy prey to the sophisms and labored erudition of the rationalists.   The best preparation will be a conscientious application to philosophy and theology under the guidance of St. Thomas of Aquin, and a thorough training therein—as We Ourselves have elsewhere pointed out and directed.   By this means, both in biblical studies and in that part of theology which is called *positive,* they will pursue the right path and make satisfactory progress.

AUTHORITY OF THE BIBLE

To prove, to expound, to illustrate Catholic doctrine by the legitimate and skillful interpretation of the Bible is much; but there is a second part of the subject of equal importance and equal difficulty—the maintenance in the strongest possible way of its full authority.   This cannot be done completely or satisfactorily except by means of the living and proper *magisterium* of the Church.   The Church, by reason of her wonderful propagation, her distinguished sanctity, and inexhaustible fecundity in good, her Catholic unity, and her unshaken stability, is herself a great and perpetual motive of credibility, and an unassailable testimony to her own divine mission.[42]   But, since the divine and infallible *magisterium* of the Church rests also on Holy Scripture, the first thing to be done is to vindicate the trustworthiness of sacred records, at least as human documents, from which can be clearly proved, as from primitive and authentic testimony, the divinity and the mission of Christ our Lord, the institution of a hierarchical Church and the primacy of Peter and his successors.

DEFENDERS OF THE BIBLE

It is most desirable, therefore, that there should be numerous members of the clergy well prepared to enter on a contest of this nature, and to repulse hostile assaults, chiefly trusting in the armor of God recommended by the Apostle,[43] but also not unaccustomed to modern methods of attack.   This is beautifully alluded to by St. John Chrysostom, when describing the duties of priests: "We must use every endeavor that the 'Word of God may dwell in us' abundantly'; [44] not merely for one kind of fight must we be prepared—for the contest is many-sided and the enemy is of every

41 *Ibid.,* a. 8.
42 *Con. Vat.,* Sess. III, c. 2, de fide.
43 Eph. 6: 13 *ss.*
44 See Col. 3: 16.

sort; and they do not all use the same weapons nor make their onset in the same way. Wherefore it is needful that the man who has to contend against all should be acquainted with the engines and the arts of all—that he should be at once archer and slinger, commandant and officer, general and private soldier, foot-soldier and horseman, skilled in sea-fight and in siege; for unless he knows every trick and turn of war, the devil is well able, if only a single door be left open, to get in his fierce bands and carry off the sheep".[45] The sophisms of the enemy and his manifold arts of attack we have already touched upon. Let us now say a word of advice on the means of defense.

MEANS OF DEFENSE

A. *Ancient Languages*

The first means is the study of the Oriental languages and of the art of criticism. These two acquirements are in these days held in high estimation, and, therefore, the clergy, by making themselves fully acquainted with them as time and place may demand, will the better be able to discharge their office with becoming credit; for they must make themselves *all to all*,[46] always *ready to satisfy every one that asketh them a reason for the hope that is in them*.[47] Hence it is most proper that professors of sacred Scripture and theologians should master those tongues in which the sacred books were originally written; and it would be well that Church students also should cultivate them, more especially those who aspire to academic degrees. And endeavors should be made to establish in all academic institutions—as has already been laudably done in many —chairs of the other ancient languages, especially the Semitic, and of subjects connected therewith, for the benefit, principally, of those who are intended to profess sacred literature.

B. *Criticism*

These latter, with a similar object in view, should make themselves well and thoroughly acquainted with the art of true criticism. There has arisen, to the great detriment of religion, an inept method, dignified by the name of the "higher criticism", which pretends to judge the origin, integrity and authority of each book from internal indications alone. It is clear, on the other hand, that in historical questions, such as the origin and handing down of writings, the witness of history is of primary importance, and that historical investigation should be made with the utmost care; and that in this manner internal evidence is seldom of great value, except as confirmation. To look upon it in any other light will be to open the

---

[45] *De sacerdotio*, IV, 4.
[46] I Cor. 9: 22.
[47] I Pet. 3: 15.

door to many evil consequences. It will make the enemies of religion much more bold and confident in attacking and mangling the sacred books; and this vaunted "higher criticism" will resolve itself into the reflection of the bias and the prejudice of the critics. It will not throw on the Scripture the light which is sought, or prove of any advantage to doctrine; it will only give rise to disagreement and dissension, those sure notes of error which the critics in question so plentifully exhibit in their own persons; and seeing that most of them are tainted with false philosophy and rationalism, it must lead to the elimination from the sacred writings of all prophecy and miracle, and of everything else that is outside the natural order.

C. *Natural Sciences*

In the second place, we have to contend against those who, making an evil use of physical science, minutely scrutinize the sacred book in order to detect the writers in a mistake, and to take occasion to vilify its contents. Attacks of this kind, bearing as they do on matters of sensible experience, are peculiarly dangerous to the masses, and also to the young who are beginning their literary studies; for the young, if they lose their reverence for the Holy Scripture on one or more points, are easily led to give up believing in it altogether. It need not be pointed out how the nature of science, just as it is so admirably adapted to show forth the glory of the Great Creator, provided it is taught as it should be, may, if it be perversely imparted to the youthful intelligence, prove most fatal in destroying the principles of true philosophy and in the corruption of morality. Hence, to the professor of Sacred Scripture a knowledge of natural science will be of very great assistance in detecting such attacks on the sacred books, and in refuting them. There can never, indeed, be any real discrepancy between the theologian and the physicist, as long as each confines himself within his own lines, and both are careful, as St. Augustine warns us, "not to make rash assertions, or to assert what is not known as known".[48] If dissension should arise between them, here is the rule also laid down by St. Augustine, for the theologian: "Whatever they can really demonstrate to be true of physical nature we must show to be capable of reconciliation with our Scriptures; and whatever they assert in their treatises which is contrary to these Scriptures of ours, that is to Catholic faith, we must either prove it as well as we can to be entirely false, or at all events we must, without the smallest hesitation, believe it to be so".[49] To understand how just is the rule here formulated we must remember, first, that the sacred writers, or, to speak more accurately, the Holy Ghost "who spoke by them, did not intend to teach men these things [that is to say, the essential nature of the things of the visible universe], things

[48] *In Gen. op. imperf.*, ix, 30.
[49] *De Gen. ad litt.*, i, 21, 41.

in no way profitable unto salvation".[50] Hence they did not seek to penetrate the secrets of nature, but rather described and dealt with things in more or less figurative language, or in terms which were commonly used at the time, and which in many instances are in daily use at this day, even by the most eminent men of science. Ordinary speech primarily and properly describes what comes under the senses; and somewhat in the same way the sacred writers—as the Angelic Doctor also reminds us—"went by what sensibly appeared",[51] or put down what God, speaking to men, signified, in the way men could understand and were accustomed to.

The unshrinking defense of the Holy Scripture, however, does not require that we should equally uphold all the opinions which each of the Fathers or the more recent interpreters have put forth in explaining it; for it may be that, in commenting on passages where physical matters occur, they have sometimes expressed the ideas of their own times, and thus made statements which in these days have been abandoned as incorrect. Hence, in their interpretations, we must carefully note what they laid down as belonging to faith, or as intimately connected with faith—what they are unanimous in. For "in those things which do not come under the obligation of faith, the saints were at liberty to hold divergent opinions, just as we ourselves are",[52] according to the saying of St. Thomas. And in another place he says most admirably: "When philosophers are agreed upon a point, and it is not contrary to our faith, it is safer, in my opinion, neither to lay down such a point as a dogma of faith, even though it is perhaps so presented by the philosophers, nor to reject it as against faith, lest we thus give to the wise of this world an occasion of despising our faith".[53] The Catholic interpreter, although he should show that those facts of natural science which investigators affirm to be now quite certain are not contrary to the Scripture rightly explained, must, nevertheless, always bear in mind that much which has been held and proved as certain has afterwards been called in question and rejected. And if writers on physics travel outside the boundaries of their own branch, and carry their erroneous teaching into the domain of philosophy, let them be handed over to philosophers for refutation.

D. *History*

The principles here laid down will apply to cognate sciences, and especially to history. It is a lamentable fact that there are many who with great labor carry out and publish investigations on the monuments of antiquity, the manners and institutions of nations, and other illustrative subjects, and whose chief purpose in all this is to find mistakes in the sacred writings and so to shake

[50] St. Augustine, *ibid.*, ii, 9, 20.
[51] *Summa*, 1a, q. 80, a. 1, ad 3um.
[52] *In* II *Sent.*, dist., q. 1, a. 3.
[53] *Opusc.* X.

and weaken their authority. Some of these writers display not
only extreme hostility but the greatest unfairness; in their eyes a
profane book or ancient document is accepted without hesitation,
whilst the Scripture, if they only find in it a suspicion of error,
is set down with the slightest possible discussion as quite untrust-
worthy. It is true, no doubt, that copyists have made mistakes in
the text of the Bible; this question, when it arises, should be carefully considered on its merits, and the fact not too easily admitted,
but only in those passages where the proof is clear. It may also
happen that the sense of a passage remains ambiguous, and in this
case good hermeneutical methods will greatly assist in clearing up
the obscurity.

INSPIRATION

But it is absolutely wrong and forbidden either to narrow inspiration to certain parts only of Holy Scripture or to admit that
the sacred writer has erred. For the system of those who, in order
to rid themselves of those difficulties, do not hesitate to concede
that divine inspiration regards the things of faith and morals, and
nothing beyond, because (as they wrongly think) in a question of
the truth or falsehood of a passage we should consider not so much
what God has said as the reason and purpose which He had in
mind when saying it—this system can not be tolerated. For all the
books which the Church receives as sacred and canonical are written
wholly and entirely, with all their parts, at the dictation of the
Holy Ghost; and so far is it from being possible that any error
can co-exist with inspiration, that inspiration not only is essentially
incompatible with error, but excludes and rejects it as absolutely
and necessarily as it is impossible that God Himself, the Supreme
Truth, can utter that which is not true. This is the ancient and
unchanging faith of the Church, solemnly defined in the Councils
of Florence and of Trent, and finally confirmed and more expressly
formulated by the Council of the Vatican. These are the words of
the last: "The books of the Old and New Testament, whole and
entire, with all their parts, as enumerated by the decree of the same
Council (Trent) and in the ancient Latin Vulgate, are to be received as sacred and canonical. And the Church holds them as
sacred and canonical not because, having been composed by human
industry, they were afterwards approved by her authority, nor only
because they contain revelation without error, but because, having
been written under the inspiration of the Holy Ghost, they have
God for their author".[54] Hence, because the Holy Ghost employs
men as His instruments, we can not, therefore, say that it was
these inspired instruments who, perchance, have fallen into error,
and not the primary author. For, by supernatural power, He so
moved and impelled them to write—He was so present to them—
that the things which He ordered, and those only, they first, rightly
understood, then willed faithfully to write down, and finally ex-

54 Sess. III, c. 2, de revel.

pressed in apt words and with infallible truth. Otherwise, it could not be said that He was the author of the entire Scripture. Such has always been the persuasion of the Fathers. "Therefore," says St. Augustine, "since they wrote the things which He showed and uttered to them, it can not be pretended that He is not the writer; for His members executed what their head dictated".[55] And St. Gregory the Great thus pronounces: "Most superfluous it is to inquire who wrote these things—we loyally believe the Holy Ghost to be the author of the Book. He wrote it who dictated it for writing; He wrote it who inspired its execution".[56]

It follows that those who maintain that an error is possible in any genuine passage of the sacred writings either pervert the Catholic notion of inspiration or make God the author of such error. And so emphatically were all the Fathers and Doctors agreed that the divine writings, as left by the hagiographers, are free from all error, that they labored earnestly, with no less skill than reverence, to reconcile with each other those numerous passages which seem at variance—the very passages which in a great measure have been taken up by the "higher criticism"; for they were unanimous in laying it down that those writings, in their entirety and in all their parts were equally from the *afflatus* of Almighty God, and that God, speaking by the sacred writers, could not set down anything that was not true. The words of St. Augustine to St. Jerome may sum up what they taught: "On my own part I confess to your charity that it is only to those books of Scripture which are now called canonical that I have learned to pay such honor and reverence as to believe most firmly that none of their writers has fallen into any error. And if in these books I meet anything which seems contrary to truth I shall not hesitate to conclude either that the text is faulty, or that the translator has not expressed the meaning of the passage, or that I myself do not understand".[57]

CATHOLIC SCHOLARS

But to undertake fully and perfectly, and with all the weapons of the best science, the defense of the Holy Bible is far more than can be looked for from the exertions of commentators and theologians alone. It is an enterprise in which we have a right to expect the co-operation of all those Catholics who have acquired reputation in any branch of learning whatever. As in the past, so at the present time, the Church is never without the graceful support of her accomplished children; may their service to the Faith grow and increase! For there is nothing which We believe to be more needful than that truth should find defenders more powerful and more numerous than the enemies it has to face; nor is there anything which is better calculated to impress the masses with

[55] *De Consensu evangel.*, 1, 1, c. 35.
[56] *Præf. in Job*, n. 2.
[57] Ep. 77, 1, and elsewhere frequently.

respect for truth than to see it boldly proclaimed by learned and distinguished men. Moreover, the bitter tongues of objectors will be silenced, or at least they will not dare to insist so shamelessly that faith is the enemy of science, when they see that scientific men of eminence in their profession show towards faith the most marked honor and respect. Seeing, then, that those can do so much for the advantage of religion on whom the goodness of Almighty God has bestowed, together with the grace of the faith, great natural talent, let such men, in this bitter conflict of which the Holy Scripture is the object, select each of them the branch of study most suitable to his circumstances, and endeavor to excel therein, and thus be prepared to repulse with credit and distinction the assaults on the Word of God. And it is Our pleasing duty to give deserved praise to a work which certain Catholics have taken up—that is to say, the formation of societies and the contribution of considerable sums of money for the purpose of supplying students and learned men with every kind of help and assistance in carrying out complete studies. Truly an excellent fashion of investing money, and well suited to the times in which we live! The less hope of public patronage there is for Catholic study, the more ready and the more abundant should be the liberality of private persons—those to whom God has given riches thus willingly making use of their means to safeguard the treasure of His revealed doctrine.

CAUTION IN DOUBT

In order that all these endeavors and exertions may really prove advantageous to the cause of the Bible, let scholars keep steadfastly to the principles which We have in this Letter laid down. Let them loyally hold that God, the Creator and Ruler of all things, is also the Author of the Scriptures—and that, therefore, nothing can be proved either by physical science or archeology which can really contradict the Scriptures. If, then, apparent contradiction be met with, every effort should be made to remove it. Judicious theologians and commentators should be consulted as to what is the true or most probable meaning of the passage in discussion, and hostile arguments should be carefully weighed. Even if the difficulty is after all not cleared up and the discrepancy seems to remain, the contest must not be abandoned; truth cannot contradict truth, and we may be sure that some mistake has been made either in the interpretation of the sacred words or in the polemical discussion itself; and if no such mistake can be detected, we must then suspend judgment for the time being. There have been objections without number perseveringly directed against the Scripture for many a long year, which have been proved to be futile and are now never heard of; and not infrequently interpretations have been placed on certain passages of Scripture (not belonging to the rule of faith or morals) which have been rectified by more careful investigations. As time goes on, mistaken views die and disappear;

but *truth remaineth and groweth stronger forever and ever.*[58] Wherefore, as no one should be so presumptuous as to think that he understands the whole of the Scripture, in which St. Augustine himself confessed that there was more that he did not know than that he knew,[59] so, if he should come on anything that seems incapable of solution, he must take to heart the cautious rule of the same holy doctor: "It is better even to be oppressed by unknown but useful signs than to interpret them uselessly, and thus to throw off the yoke only to be caught in the trap of error".[60]

As to those who pursue the subsidiary studies of which We have spoken, if they honestly and modestly follow the counsels We have given—if by their pen and their voice they make their studies profitable against the enemies of truth, and useful in saving the young from the loss of their faith—they may justly congratulate themselves on their worthy service to the sacred writings, and on affording to Catholicism that assistance which the Church has a right to expect from the piety and learning of her children.

Conclusion

Such, Venerable Brethren, are the admonitions and the instructions which, by the help of God, We have thought it well, at the present moment, to offer to you on the study of Holy Scripture. It will now be your province to see that what We have said be observed and put in practice with all due reverence and exactness; that so We may prove our gratitude to God for the communication to man of the words of His wisdom, and that all the good results so much to be desired may be realized, especially as they affect the training of the students of the Church, which is our own great solicitude and the Church's hope. Exert yourself with willing alacrity, and use your authority and your persuasion in order that these studies may be held in just regard and may flourish in seminaries and in educational institutions which are under your jurisdiction. Let them flourish in completeness and in happy success, under the direction of the Church, in accordance with the salutary teaching and example of the holy Fathers, and the laudable traditions of antiquity; and, as time goes on, let them be widened and extended as the interests and glory of truth may require—the interests of that Catholic truth which comes from above, the never-failing source of man's salvation. Finally, We admonish with paternal love all students and ministers of the Church always to approach the sacred writings with reverence and piety; for it is impossible to attain to the profitable understanding thereof unless the arrogance of "earthly" science be laid aside, and there be excited in the heart the holy desire for that wisdom "which is from above". In this way the intelligence which is once admitted to these sacred

---

[58] III Esdras 4: 38.
[59] *Ad Januar.* ep. lv, 21.
[60] *De doctr. christiana,* III, 9, 18.

studies, and thereby illuminated and strengthened, will acquire a marvelous facility in detecting and avoiding the fallacies of human science, and in gathering and using for eternal salvation all that is valuable and precious; whilst, at the same time, the heart will grow warm, and will strive, with ardent longing, to advance in virtue and in divine love. *Blessed are they who examine His testimonies; they shall seek Him with their whole heart.*[61]

And now, filled with hope in the divine assistance, and trusting to your pastoral solicitude—as a pledge of heavenly grace, and a sign of Our special good-will—to you all, and to the clergy, and to the whole flock intrusted to you, We lovingly impart in Our Lord the Apostolic Benediction.

Propositions from the Syllabus "Lamentabili" [62]

With truly lamentable results, our age, intolerant of all check in its investigations of the ultimate causes of things, not unfrequently follows what is new in such a way as to reject the legacy, as it were, of the human race, and thus falls into the most grievous errors. These errors will be all the more pernicious when they affect sacred disciplines, the interpretation of the Sacred Scripture, the principal mysteries of the faith. It is to be greatly deplored that among Catholics also not a few writers are to be found who, crossing the boundaries fixed by the Fathers and by the Church herself, seek out, on the plea of higher intelligence and in the name of historical considerations, that progress of dogmas which is in reality the corruption of the same.

But lest errors of this kind, which are being daily spread among the faithful, should strike root in their minds and corrupt the purity of the faith, it has pleased His Holiness Pius X, by Divine Providence Pope, that the chief among them should be noted and condemned through the office of this Holy Roman and Universal Inquisition.

Wherefore, after a most diligent investigation, and after having taken the opinion of the Reverend Consultors, the Most Eminent and Reverend Lords Cardinals, the general Inquisitors in matters of faith and morals, decided that *the following propositions are to be condemned and proscribed, as they are, by this general Decree, condemned and proscribed:*

1. The ecclesiastical law, which prescribes that books regarding the Divine Scriptures are subject to previous censorship, does not extend to critical scholars or students of the scientific exegesis of the Old and New Testament.

2. The Church's interpretation of the Sacred Books is not indeed to be condemned, but it is subject to the more accurate judgment and to the correction of the exegetes.

[61] Ps. 118: 2.

[62] Errors condemned by the S. Congregation of the Inquisition, July 3rd, 1907.

3. From the ecclesiastical judgments and censures passed against free and more scientific (*cultiorem*) exegesis, it may be gathered that the faith proposed by the Church contradicts history and that the Catholic dogmas can not be reconciled with the true origins of the Christian religion.

4. The *magisterium* of the Church can not, even through dogmatic definitions, determine the genuine sense of the Sacred Scriptures.

5. Since in the deposit of the faith only revealed truths are contained, under no respect does it appertain to the Church to pass judgment concerning the assertions of human sciences.

*　　*　　*

9. Those who believe that God is really the author of the Sacred Scripture display excessive simplicity or ignorance.

10. The inspiration of the books of the Old Testament consists in the fact that the Israelite writers have handed down religious doctrines under a peculiar aspect, either little or not at all known to the Gentiles.

11. Divine inspiration is not to be so extended to the whole of Sacred Scriptures that it renders its parts, all and single, immune from all error.

12. The exegete, if he wishes to apply himself usefully to Biblical studies, must first of all put aside all preconceived opinions concerning the supernatural origin of the Sacred Scripture, and interpret it not otherwise than other merely human documents.

13. The evangelists themselves and the Christians of the second and third generation arranged (*digesserunt*) artificially the evangelical parables, and in this way gave an explanation of the scanty fruit of the preaching of Christ among the Jews.

14. In a great many narrations the evangelists reported not so much things that are true as things which even though false they judged to be more profitable for their readers.

15. The Gospels until the time the canon was defined and constituted were increased by additions and corrections; hence in them there remained of the doctrine of Christ only a faint and uncertain trace.

16. The narrations of John are not properly history, but the mystical contemplation of the Gospel; the discourses contained in his Gospel are theological meditations, devoid of historical truth concerning the mystery of salvation.

17. The Fourth Gospel exaggerated miracles not only that the wonderful might stand out but also that they might become more suitable for signifying the work and the glory of the Word incarnate.

18. John claims for himself the quality of a witness concerning Christ; but in reality he is only a distinguished witness of the Christian life, or of the life of Christ in the Church, at the close of the first century.

19. Heterodox exegetes have expressed the true sense of the Scriptures more faithfully than Catholic exegetes.

*　　*　　*

23. Opposition may and actually does exist between the facts which are narrated in Scripture and the dogmas of the Church which rest on them; so that the critic may reject as false facts which the Church holds as most certain.

*   *

30. In all the evangelical texts the name *Son of God* is equivalent only to Messias, and does not at all signify that Christ is the true and natural Son of God.

31. The doctrine concerning Christ taught by Paul, John, the Councils of Nicea, Ephesus and Chalcedon, is not that which Jesus taught, but that which the Christian conscience conceived concerning Jesus.

32. It is not possible to reconcile the natural sense of the Gospel texts with the sense taught by our theologians concerning the conscience and the infallible knowledge of Jesus Christ.

*   *   *

63. The Church shows itself unequal to the task of efficaciously maintaining evangelical ethics, because it obstinately adheres to immutable doctrines which cannot be reconciled with modern progress.

64. The progress of science involves a remodeling (*ut reformentur*) of the conceptions of Christian doctrine concerning God, Creation, Revelation, the Person of the Incarnate Word, Redemption.

65. Modern Catholicism can not be reconciled with true science unless it be transformed into a non-dogmatic Christianity, that is into a broad and liberal Protestantism.

And on the following Thursday, the fourth day of the same month and year, an accurate report of all this having been made to Our Most Holy Lord Pope Pius X, His Holiness approved and confirmed the Decree of the Most Eminent Fathers, and ordered that the propositions above enumerated, all and several, be held by all as condemned and proscribed.

> PETER PALOMBELLI,
> *Notary of the H. R. U. I.*

The Canon of Muratori [63]

. . . quibus tamen interfuit et ita posuit.

Tertio evangelii librum secundum Lucam. Lucas, iste medicus, post ascensum Christi, cum eum Paulus quasi ut iuris studiosum secundum [secum?] adsumpsisset, nomine suo ex opinione con-

---

[63] This text, discovered by the Italian savant Muratori in the Ambrosian Library at Milan in 1740, was written, perhaps originally in Greek, at Rome in the second half of the 2nd century. Pope Pius I, the brother of Hermas who had "nuperrime temporibus nostris" written the *Pastor*, occupied the Pontifical chair about 142–146. (See Tregelles, *Canon Muratorianus*.)

scripsit. Dominum tamen nec ipse vidit in carne. Et idem, prout assequi potuit, ita et a nativitate Iohannis incipit dicere.

Quarti evangeliorum Iohannes ex discipulis. Cohortantibus condiscipulis et episcopis suis dixit: "Conieiunate mihi hodie triduo, et quid cuique fuerit revelatum, alterutrum nobis enarremus". Eadem nocte revelatum Andreæ ex apostolis, ut recognoscentibus cunctis Iohannes suo nomine cuncta describeret. Et ideo, licet varia singulis Evangeliorum libris principia doceantur, nihil tamen differt credentium fidei, cum uno ac principali spiritu declarata sint in omnibus omnia, de nativitate, de passione, de resurrectione, de conversatione cum discipulis suis ac de genuino eius adventu, primo in humilitate despectus, quod fuit, secundo [in] potestate regali . . . præclarum, quod futurum est. Quid ergo mirum si Iohannes tam constanter singula etiam in epistolis suis proferat, dicens in semetipsum: "Quæ vidimus oculis nostris et auribus audivimus et manus nostræ palpaverunt, hæc scripsimus vobis". Sic enim non solem visorem, sed et auditorem, sed et scriptorem omnium mirabilium Domini per ordinem profitetur.

Acta autem omnium Apostolorum sub uno libro scripta sunt. Lucas optime Theophile comprendit quia sub præsentia eius singula gerebantur, sicuti et semote passionem Petri evidenter declarat, sed et profectionem Pauli ab Urbe ad Spaniam proficiscentis.

Epistulæ autem Pauli, quæ, a loco vel ex qua causa directæ sint, volentibus intelligere ipsæ declarant. Primum omnium Corinthiis schismæ hæreses interdicens deinceps Galatis circumcisionem, Romanis autem ordinem Scripturarum, sed et principium earum esse Christum intimans, prolexius scripsit, de quibus singulis necesse est ab nobis disputari.

Cum ipse beatus Apostolus Paulus, sequens prædecessoris sui Iohanni ordinem, nonnisi nominatim septem ecclesiis scribat ordine tali: Ad Corinthios prima, ad Efesios secunda, ad Philippenses tertia, ad Colossenses quarta, ad Galatas quinta, ad Thessalonicenses sexta, ad Romanos septima. Verum Corinthiis et Thessalonicensibus licet pro correptione iteretur: una tamen per omnem orbem terræ Ecclesia diffusa esse dignoscitur. Et Iohannes enim in Apocalypsi, licet septem Ecclesiis scribat, tamen omnibus dicit.

Verum ad Philemonem unam, et ad Titum unam, et ad Timothæum duas pro affectu et dilectione; in honore tamen Ecclesiæ catholicæ, in ordinatione ecclesiasticæ disciplinæ sanctificatæ sunt.

Fertur etiam ad Laodicenses, alia ad Alexandrinos. Pauli nomine finctæ ad hæresem Marcionis, et alia plura, quæ in catholicam Ecclesiam recipi non potest. Fel enim cum melle misceri non congruit.

Epistola sane Iudæ et super scripti Ioannis duas in catholica habentur, et [ut] Sapientia ab amicis Salomonis in honore ipsius scripta.

Apocalypsem etiam Ioannis et Petri tantum recipimus, quam quidam ex nostris legi in Ecclesia nolunt.

Pastorem vero nuperrime temporibus nostris in Urbe Roma Herma conscripsit, sedente cathedra Urbis Romæ Ecclesiæ Pio episcopo fratre eius. Et ideo legi eum quidem oportet, se publicare vero in Ecclesia populo neque inter Profetas completum numero, neque inter Apostolos in finem temporum potest.

Arsinoi autem seu Valentini vel Miltiadis nihil in totum recipimus. Quin etiam novum psalmorum librum Marcioni conscripserunt. Una cum Basilide Asianum Catafrygum constitutorum . . .

Canon of Pope Damasus

This was originally drawn up at a Roman synod under Pope Damasus (366-384), the patron of St. Jerome, about 374. It is also called "Decretum Gelasianum", from the name of Pope Gelasius I (492-496). Baruch is not mentioned, as that Book was classed with Jeremias. In 393 the same canon was repeated by the Council of Hippo, and by Pope Innocent I in his "Epist. ad Exuperium", who, however, has "Ioannis Apostoli [epistolæ] tres".

Nunc vero de Scripturis divinis agendum est, quid universalis catholica recipiat Ecclesia vel quid vitare debeat. Incipit ordo Veteris Testamenti. Genesis liber I. Exodi liber I. Levitici liber I. Numeri liber I. Deuteronomii liber I. Iesu Nave liber I. Iudicum liber I. Ruth liber I. Regum libri IV. Paralipomenon libri II. Psalmorum CL liber I. Salomonis libri III. Proverbia liber I. Ecclesiastes liber I. Cantica Canticorum liber I. Item Sapientiæ liber I. Ecclesiasticus liber I. Item ordo prophetarum. Isaiæ liber I. Ieremiæ liber I, cum Chinoth, id est, Lamentationibus suis. Ezechielis liber I. Daniheli liber I. Oseæ liber I. Amos liber I. Michææ liber I. Ioel liber I. Abdiæ liber I. Ionæ liber I. Naum liber I. Abbacuc liber I. Sophoniæ liber I. Aggæi liber I. Zachariæ liber I. Malachiæ liber I. Idem ordo historiarum. Iob liber I, ab aliis omissus. Tobiæ liber I. Hesdræ libri II. Hester liber I. Iudith liber I. Machabæorum libri II.

Item ordo Scripturarum Novi et æterni Testamenti, quem catholica sancta Romana suscipit et veneratur Ecclesia: id est Evangeliorum libri IV, secundum Matthæum liber I, secundum Marcum liber I, secundum Lucam liber I, secundum Iohannem liber I. Item Actuum Apostolorum liber I. Epistolæ Pauli Apostoli numero XIV: ad Romanos epistola I, ad Corinthios epistolæ II, ad Ephesios epistola I, ad Thessalonicenses epistolæ II, ad Galatas epistola I, ad Phillipenses epistola I, ad Colossenses epistola I, ad Timotheum epistolæ II, ad Titum epistola I, ad Philemonem epistola I, ad Hebræos epistola I. Item Apocalypsis Iohannis liber I. Item canonicæ epistolæ numero VII: Petri Apostoli epistolæ II, Iacobi epistola I, Iohannis Apostoli epistola I, alterius Iohannis presbyteri epistolæ II, Iudæ Zelotis epistola I. Explicit canon novi Testamenti.

Canon of the Council of Trent

Sacrorum vero Librorum indicem huic decreto (de Canonicis Scripturis) adscribendum censuit, ne cui dubitatio suboriri possit,

quinam sint, qui ab ipsa Synodo suscipiuntur. Sunt vero infra-
scripti Testamenti Veteris: Quinque Moysi, id est, Genesis, Exodus,
Leviticus, Numeri, Deuteronomium; Iosue, Iudicum, Ruth; quatuor
Regum; duo Paralipomenon; Esdræ primus, et secundus, qui dicitur
Nehemias; Tobias, Iudith, Esther, Iob, Psalterium Davidicum cen-
tum quinquaginta Psalmorum, Parabolæ, Ecclesiastes, Canticum
Canticorum, Sapientia, Ecclesiasticus, Isaias, Ieremias cum Baruch,
Ezechiel, Daniel; duodecim prophetæ minores, id est, Osea, Ioël,
Amos, Abdias, Ionas, Michæas, Nahum, Habacuc, Sophonias,
Aggæus, Zacharias, Malachias; duo Machabæorum, primus et secun-
dus. Testamenti Novi: Quatuor Evangelia secundum Matthæum,
Marcum, Lucam et Ioannem; Actus Apostolorum a Luca Evan-
gelista conscripti; quatuordecim Epistolæ Pauli Apostoli: ad
Romanos, duæ ad Corinthios, ad Galatas, ad Ephesios, ad Philippenses, ad Colossenses, duæ ad Thessalonicenses, duæ ad Timotheum,
ad Titum, ad Philemonem, ad Hebræos; Petri Apostoli duæ;
Ioannis Apostoli tres; Iacobi Apostoli una; Iudæ Apostoli una; et
Apocalypsis Ioannis Apostoli. Si quis autem libros ipsos integros,
cum omnibus suis partibus, prout in Ecclesia catholica legi consueverunt, et in veteri vulgata Latina editione habentur, pro sacris et
canonicis non susceperit, et traditiones prædictas, sciens et prudens,
contempserit, anathema sit (Sess. IV, De canonicis scripturis
decret.).

Vatican Council on Inspiration

Supernaturalis revelatio, secundum universalis Ecclesiæ fidem,
a Sancta Tridentina Synodo declaratam, continetur in libris scriptis
et sine scripto traditionibus, quæ ipsius Christi ore ab Apostolis
acceptæ, aut ab ipsis Apostolis Spiritu Sancto dictante, quasi per
manus traditæ ad nos usque pervenerunt. Qui quidem Veteris et
Novi Testamenti libri, integri cum omnibus suis partibus, prout in
eiusdem Concilii decreto recensentur, et in veteri vulgata latina
editione habentur, pro sacris et canonicis suscipiendi sunt. Eos
vero Ecclesia pro sacris et canonicis habet, non ideo quod sola
humana industria concinnati, sua deinde auctoritate sint approbati:
nec ideo dumtaxat, quod revelationem sine errore contineant; sed
propterea quod, Spiritu Sancto inspirante conscripti, Deum habent
auctorem, atque ut tales ipsi Ecclesiæ traditi sunt (Sess. III, Const.
dogm., ap. II).

Decisions of the Biblical Commission
Declaratio
*de additione variarum lectionum in editionibus versionis vulgate
novi et veteris testamenti*

In Præfatione ad Lectorem editionis Clementinæ versionis vulgatæ Sacrarum Scripturarum legitur:

"Porro in hac editione nihil non canonicum . . . nullæ ad marginem concordantiæ (quæ posthac inibi apponi non prohibentur)
nullæ notæ, nullæ variæ lectiones, nullæ denique præfationes . . .

Sed sicut Apostolica Sedes industriam eorum non damnat, qui concordantias locorum, varias lectiones, præfationes S. Hieronymi et alia id genus in aliis editionibus inseruerunt; ita quoque non prohibet, quin, alio genere characteris, in hac ipsa Vaticana editione eiusmodi adiumenta pro studiosorum commoditate atque utilitate in posterum adiiciantur; ita tamen, ut lectiones variæ ad marginem ipsius textus minime adnotentur".

Quum autem sint qui putent ultimis hisce verbis prohiberi additionem variarum lectionum non solum in margine laterali, verum etiam in inferiore seu ad calcem textus, quæsitum est a pontificia Commissione Biblica: utrum liceat in editionibus versionis Vulgatæ tam Novi quam Veteris Testamenti lectiones varias aliave huiusmodi studiosorum adiumenta ad calcem textus adiicere?

Re examinata, Pontificia Commissio Biblica respondit: Affirmative (*Acta Apostolicæ Sedis*, XIV, p. 27).

Circa Citationes Implicitas in Sacra Scriptura contentas

Utrum ad enodandas difficultates quæ occurrunt in nonnullis Sacræ Scripturæ textibus, qui facta historica referre videntur, liceat Exegetæ catholico asserere agi in his de citatione tacita vel implicita documenti ab auctore non inspirato conscripti, cuius adserta omnia auctor inspiratus minime adprobare vel sua facere intendit, quæque ideo ab errore immunia haberi non possunt?

Prædicta Commissio respondendum censuit:

Negative, excepto casu in quo, salvis sensu ac iudicio ecclesiæ solidis argumentis probetur: *primo* hagiographum alterius dicta vel documenta revera citare; et *secundo* eadem nec probare, nec sua facere, ita ut iure censeatur non proprio nomine loqui.

Die autem 13 Februarii 1905 Ssmus referente me infrascripto Consultore ab Actis, prædictum responsam adprobavit atque publici iuris fieri mandavit. Fr. David Fleming, O.F.M. Cons. ab Actis.

De Narrationibus Specietenus tantum Historicis in Sacræ Scripturæ libris qui pro historicis habentur

Proposito sequenti dubio Consilium Pontificium pro studiis de re biblica provehendis respondendum censuit prout sequitur:

Dubium—Utrum admitti possit tamquam principium rectæ exegeseos sententia quæ tenet Sacræ Scripturæ libros, qui pro historicis habentur, sive totaliter, sive ex parte, non historiam proprie dictam et obiective veram quandoque narrare, sed speciem tantum historiæ præ se ferre ad aliquid significandum a proprie litterali seu historicam verborum significatione alienum? *Resp.* Negative, excepto tamen casu, non facile nec temere admittendo, in quo, Ecclesiæ sensu non refugante, eiusque salvo iudicio, solidis argumentis probetur hagiographum non verum et proprie dictam historiam tradere, sed, sub specie et forma historiæ, parabolam, allegoriam, vel sensum aliquem a proprie litterali seu historica verborum significatione remotum proponere.—Die autem 23 Iunii 1905 in audientia ambobus Rmis Consultoribus ab Actis benigne concessa, Sanctissimus prædicta Responsum ratum habuit ac publici iuris fieri mandavit.

SECOND PART

BIBLICAL ARCHEOLOGY

(after Dr. Michael Seisenberger)

"Neque vero ullam puto digniorem disputationis nostræ confabulationem fore, quam si de Scripturis sermocinemur inter nos".
Pope Damasus to St. Jerome, in Ep. "Dormientem te".

NOTE

The text of this Part has been adapted from that of the like-named section in Dr. Michael Seisenberger's "Practical Handbook for the Study of the Bible," published in 1911 by Joseph F. Wagner, Inc., New York.

BIBLICAL ARCHEOLOGY

PROLEGOMENA

91. Monotheism Precedes Polytheism.—In the history of antiquity one everywhere meets with the worship of God. But, as the Deity is worshiped differently in different places, it has been assumed by modern students of religion that polytheism was the original, and that monotheism was a later development, as generally what is imperfect precedes what is perfect, the latter developing from the former. This opinion is, however, erroneous. In the lives of nations, as of individuals, there may be a falling away from good to bad. Polytheism is a degeneration of the earliest religion of mankind, and hints of this decay are given plainly enough in the stories of a golden age, stories that are of almost universal occurrence among all nations, and therefore certainly contain a grain of historical truth. Moreover, according to a generally accepted axiom, the plural of a thing presupposes a singular.

True it is, unfortunately, that the ancient nations generally worshiped several gods. But, amidst the plurality of deities, there is a glimmer of the original idea of one true God. Even the name of this one God exists in similar forms among many nations. *El* of the Israelites is the same as *Ilu* of the Babylonians and Assyrians, *Allah* of the Arabs and *Alloho* of the Syrians. In the Turin *Book of the Dead,* that goes back to nearly 3000 years before Christ and supplies us with the earliest recorded doctrines of the Egyptians, is found this passage: "There is One most Holy Creator of the world in its fullness. He sees as you see, hears as you hear, stands as you stand. Suffer me to praise the Architect, who hath made the fullness of the universe; who caused all things on the earth and beyond the world to come into being in due time, who hath fashioned them for me". But when Moses lived there were eight elementary deities recognized by this

127

ancient and highly civilized nation. In Babylonia originally one, and only one, local deity was honored in each town, but a plurality of gods was recognized from the time when the various districts were united into one monarchy; and the deities were all classed together in the same way as the towns and people. The same thing happened in Rome; and this is how polytheism originated.

92. Causes of Polytheism.—No nation of either ancient or modern times, no matter how primitive, has ever been found to be entirely devoid of some religious beliefs and practices. Atheism and crass materialism have always appealed only to individuals, never to peoples. However, it is an equally undeniable truth that among most nations the worship of the one true God perished, and that even among the most civilized peoples religious worship was perverted. The former fact can be explained only by accepting a very early revelation, which was never completely forgotten, but in remote times was more fresh in men's minds. The latter has several causes:

(1) Man can not and will not live without God. His religious feelings need satisfaction, and whenever, in consequence of human transgression, the true God is no longer recognized, man seeks his god in the stars, in thunder and lightning, in wood and stone. (2) True religion at all periods has required strict control of the passions. Heathen religions, on the contrary, have taken the sensual inclinations of mankind under their protection, and thus have won ready acceptance. (3) Demoniacal influences have played their part. The fallen angels wished to be equal with God, and, having failed in this attempt in Heaven, they tried to win divine honors for themselves on earth. Just as the devil contributed to the sin of the first human beings, so he has promoted the errors of mankind in later periods.

The Israelites themselves, although they were the Chosen People, again and again fell into idolatry, sacrificing "to devils and not to God" (Ps. 95:5).[1] A fatal cause for them

---

[1] According to the Hebrew words this passage means literally "they sacrificed to the destroyers" (from שׁוּד = שָׁדַד, to attack violently,

was the example of their Canaanite neighbors, whose naturalistic heathen worship had very great attractions. During
the time of the kings many rulers even of Israel set an evil
example. Those of the Northern Kingdom especially had
strong political grounds for fostering idolatry. If their
people had no religious interest in the Temple at Jerusalem,
there would be less probability of their giving allegiance to
the Davidic line (IV Kings 12:27).

93. Worship of the Stars.—Possibly the earliest form of
degeneration undergone by the original monotheism of revelation, was the worship of the heavenly bodies, known as Saba-
ism (from צבא = host of the heavenly bodies). It occurred
occasionally among the Israelites. Deut. 17:3 set the penalty
of death for its practice. Job (31:26-28) declared his freedom from such sin:

> If my heart was ever mysteriously enticed,
> And my hand touched my lips to waft a kiss,
> When I saw the moon shining brightly
> Or the moon growing luminous—
> That too would have been a grave sin.

Ezechiel (8:16-17) indicates that sunworshipers faced the
east, holding a branch before their eyes. As if in opposition
to any solar cult the Temple faced the setting of the sun.

94. Worship of Images.—The reason for the stringent
prohibition of Exod. 20:4 was the ever-present danger of
idolatry that prevailed generally. Especially in Egypt the
Israelites had witnessed idolatrous worship, and hence in the
wilderness they attempted to worship the true God under the
form of a golden calf; just as the Egyptians worshiped the
deity under the form of a bull. The same thing occurred in
the schismatic kingdom of Samaria. Jeroboam I, who had
lived in Egypt in his youth, caused two golden calves to be
made, one to stand in Dan, and the other in Bethel, as representations of Yahweh (IV Kings 12:29). The prophets
vigorously opposed this design, and denounced it as being

to ruin). The Septuagint translated ἔθυσαν δαιμολοις and understood
thereby the gods of the heathen, who, in contrast to the true God, could
bring nothing but disaster. This is possible only if they are self-con-
scious beings, hostile to God, viz. evil spirits.

idolatrous (Amos 3:14; 5:5; Osee 4:15; 8:5). Other images of gods were the *teraphim,* little domestic deities, mentioned as early as the times of the Patriarchs and Judges (Gen. 31:18; Judges 17:5; 18:31).

The prohibition referred only to figures intended to represent the true God or other deities, for in Lev. 26:1, it has the addition "to worship it". Figures having no religious significance were not prohibited; cherubim were set up near the Ark of the Covenant and brazen cattle near the laver in the Temple. At a later period the Jews extended the prohibition to all figures, and would not even allow the Roman soldiers to enter Jerusalem with eagles on their standards. This aversion on the part of the Jews passed on to Islam. It is well known that Leo III, the Isaurian, encouraged iconoclasm among the Christians, in his anxiety to conciliate Jews and Mohametans.

95. Canaanite Deities.—The chief god common to all Canaanite or Phenician peoples was Baal or Bel (הַבַּעֲל, Chald. בְּעֵל, abbreviated בֵּל; in the cuneiform inscriptions Bil), *i.e.,* the Lord, and especially the husband. He was honored as personifying the procreative and propagating principle in nature, but he was also thought of as a natural force tending both to preserve and to destroy. His worship varied at different periods and in different places. Therefore there were several Baals (I Cor. 8:5, κύριοι πολλοί). Babylon seems to have been the original home of this cultus.[2]

In Holy Scripture there is mention of (*a*) Baal-berith = the Baal of the covenant. A temple in Sichem was dedicated under this name; (*b*) Baal-šemeš = Baal as sun-god; (*c*) Baal-zebub (Beelzebub) = Baal of the flies. Under this name he was worshiped in Accaron, a city of the Philistines. He was believed to have power to bring swarms of destructive flies and to remove them again. The Israelites in later times, who detested idolatry, gave this name to the chief of the devils, and, through the similarity in sound, they seem often to have called him Beelsebul, *i.e.,* lord of the dwelling, because he chose human bodies as his habitation, for the name is given in this form in the Gospels. There were originally no figures of Baal, but stone *matseboth,* phallic emblems, were erected on the *bâmoth* or "high places". Connected with these seem to have taken

[2] After the introduction of polytheism the name Baal was used to designate the chief of the gods, as were the names Zeus and Jupiter. Here, too, a trace of the primitive monotheism remains. The frequently mentioned name Marduk (in the Bible Merodak or Merodach) was only another expression for Bel. Marduk was primarily the god worshiped at Babel.

place also infant sacrifices, as charred bones of children have been found in nearby buried urns.

96. The chief female deity of the Canaanites was Aštoreth (Greek Αστάρτη). She represented the female principle in nature, or nature itself as conceiving and bringing forth ever new forms of life. There were originally no real statues of this deity, but wooden columns, called *Ašerim* or *Ašeroth,* marked her cultus. They stood on mountains and hills, or among trees with thick foliage, for which reason the Septuagint and Vulgate translate the word *Ašera* by "wood" or "grove." They generally were placed near the altars to Baal, but were shaped differently from the stone pillars dedicated to that god. Astarte was subsequently often represented as a cow, or as a woman with a cow's head, or with a human head and cow's horns. The worship of this goddess was very obscene; men and women gave themselves up to obscenity in her honor. She had persons specially dedicated to her, *gedešim* and *gedešot* (Gen. 38:15). Astarte is to be identified with Baaltis or Beltis of the Babylonians (also called Bilit or Mylitta), also with Ištar of the Assyrians, with the Syrian goddess Anaitis, with the Greek Aphrodite and the Roman Venus. On account of her cow's horns the western nations sometimes honored her as Luna or Juno, as the horns suggested a crescent moon. The Israelites very early adopted her worship, as may be seen from Judges 2:13; 10:6; II Kings 3:4; 12:10.

97. The worship of Thammuz seems to have been connected with the service of Baal, and had its chief seat in the Phenician town of Biblos. This cultus, too, spread from Phenicia to the west, first to Cyprus and then to Greece, where the god was known as Adonis = my Lord. Under the Jewish kings his worship was introduced into Jerusalem, for Ezechiel says that the women in the Temple mourned over Adonis (Ezech. 8:14). The idea underlying this cultus is the expression of sorrow for the decay and death of the powers of nature in the autumn, and of joy over their re-awakening, as soon as the sun turns again to the north. In spring, therefore, there was a joyful festival and in late autumn a time of mourning, when women especially gave themselves up to sorrow and lamentation over the loss of Adonis.

The two Philistine deities, Dagon and Derketo (Gr. 'Αταργάτις), bore some resemblance to Baal and Astarte. Both were represented with the bodies of fish, and human heads and hands. Dagon, the male deity, symbolized water and the procreative forces of nature, which are rendered active by means of water. The female deity, Derketo, is supposed to represent the power of the earth to absorb moisture, and as a result to produce living things. The name Dagon is to be connected with *dag* = a fish.

98. Assyrian and Babylonian Deities.—The god Moloch (= king), also called Milkom or Malkom, is often mentioned in Holy Scripture, and was honored in Western Asia as early as the time of Moses. In Leviticus 18:21 the Israelites are warned against him. He is generally spoken of as the false god of the Moabites, but Chamos (= ruler), the god of the Ammonites, is identical with him (Num. 21:29; Judges 11:24; III Kings 11:5); and Orotal (= God's fire) mentioned by Herodotus as the fire-god of the Edomites may also be regarded as the same deity. To please his heathen wives, Solomon built shrines to him on the Mount of Olives (III Kings 11:7 and 33), but they were intended only for the king's wives and for foreigners in general. The Israelites, however, themselves worshiped Moloch in the valley of Hinnom, south of Jerusalem. Holy Scripture records also (IV Kings 17:31) that the colonists from the Euphrates, who settled in Samaria after the downfall of the Northern Kingdom, offered children in sacrifice to their national god Moloch, whom they called Adramelech (= splendor of the king) or Anamalech (King Anu). This fact shows that the cultus of Moloch, like that of Baal, was introduced from Assyria and Babylonia. It was intended to emphasize one special aspect of the worship of Baal, viz. the honoring of the destructive and, therefore, fearful forces of nature. That Moloch was well known in Assyria appears from inscriptions on monuments that still exist, on which the name Anamalech (King Anu) very frequently occurs.

Diodorus Siculus describes the statue of this god at Carthage as follows: "There was a brazen statue of Kronos, in human shape, stretching its hands upwards and somewhat sloping, so that children, laid upon them, rolled down and fell into its throat, which was full of fire". Raschi (Jarchi), the rabbinical commentator, says on Jer. 7:31: "Moloch was made of brass and heated from below. The hands were stretched out and glowed with heat, and the child was laid upon them and burned up, shrieking all the while; but the sacrificing priests made a noise with kettledrums, so that the father could not hear its cries".

99. Sources of Biblical Archeology.—Holy Writ itself furnishes the greater part of the information concerning Hebrew and allied antiquities. But almost every book or article written about the archeological discoveries of either Egypt, Mesopotamia, or Palestine itself, throws a ray of light upon obscure passages or allusions of Sacred Scripture. Outside the Bible the greatest amount (though not necessarily the most valuable portion) of biblical archeological data is to be found in the writings of Philo, of Josephus Flavius, and in the Talmud.

Philo was born in Alexandria in 25 B.C. He was the son of a Jewish priest, lived in Alexandria and received there a comprehensive Greek education. He employed the knowledge thus acquired in writing books intended to defend and expound Judaism for the benefit of pagan readers. His chief works are: *The Life of Moses; The Creation; The Decalogue; Circumcision; Sacrifices.*

The writings of Josephus, who bore the Roman cognomen Flavius, are still more important. He, too, was the son of a Jewish priest, and was born in Jerusalem in A.D. 37. His works, written in Rome, far from Palestine, and after the destruction of Jerusalem, are nevertheless most valuable, especially for the later period, of which the Bible does not give much account. They are: *History of the Jewish War,* in seven books; *Jewish Antiquities,* in twenty books; two books against the Sophist Apion, and the history of his own life.

In the *Antiquities,* XVIII, iii, 3, Josephus speaks of Christ, in whom he did not himself believe. The passage is as follows: "At this time lived Jesus, a wise man, if indeed we may call him a man; for he was a worker of miracles and a teacher to those who gladly receive the truth. He had many followers, both Jews and Gentiles, and was regarded as the Messias. In consequence of the envy of our rulers he was condemned by Pilate to be crucified. Nevertheless those who had formerly loved him remained loyal to him, for he showed himself to them alive again on the third day. This and many other wonderful things had been foretold concerning him in the writings of the prophets, and hitherto the sect of Christians, taking its name from him, has not ceased to exist". Many critics have pronounced this passage to be a forgery, but it bears tokens of being genuine.

100. The Talmud is, for the Jews, by far the most important book after the Bible;[3] it consists of two parts, the Mishna and the Gemara. The first part, which forms the Talmud strictly so called, is the Mishna (from *šana,* to repeat, hence it is the repetition of the Law). This is in Hebrew,[4] and contains a collection of the earliest Jewish traditions, written down at the end of the 2nd or at the beginning of the 3rd century by Rabbi Juda Hakkadosch, who was head of the school at Tiberias, in order to preserve them from being forgotten or tampered with.[5] Explanations were added later, and these form the second part of the Talmud, viz. the Gemara (from *gamar,* Aramaic *gemar,* to complete, hence conclusion, completion). This part is in Aramaic and falls into two portions, the Jerusalem and the Babylonian. The former originated, like the Mishna, in the school at Tiberias, and was compiled by Rabbi Jochanan (189–279). It is in the West Aramaic dialect. The Babylonian Gemara is much longer and is in East Aramaic, a dialect akin to the Syrian. It was brought from Babylon, where there had always been many Jews, ever since the Captivity, and where they had famous schools. It was written in the 5th and 6th centuries, and was the joint work of several Rabbis (Asche, Jose, etc.).

[3] In this connection may be quoted a sentence from the introduction to an English translation of eighteen treatises from the Mishna: ''We find the holy pages of the Pentateuch, the Prophets, and the Hagiography open for . . . instruction, comfort, and consolation; and the same free access should be given to pages containing so large a portion of the Oral Law, *which also claims a divine origin*'' (Sola and Raphall, *The Mishna;* London, 1845).

[4] That is, in modern Hebrew, which bears the same relation to biblical Hebrew as is borne by the Latin of medieval scholars to that of the Roman classical authors.

[5] Rabbi Juda divided his writings into six sections (*sedarim,* arrangements): viz. (1) *seder ser'im* = seed section, containing all relating to husbandry, i. e. explanations of the laws regarding it; (2) *seder mo'ed* = of festivals (Sabbath, Pasch, Day of Atonement, etc.); (3) *seder naschim* = of women, marriage laws; (4) *seder nesigin* = of injuries (damage to property, compensation, trials, etc.); (5) *seder qodaschim* = of holy things (regulations for sacrifice); (6) *seder theharoth* = purifications (Levitical uncleanliness, ablutions, bathing, etc.). The Gemara also, both in the Palestine and in the Babylonian portions, shows the same division into sections.

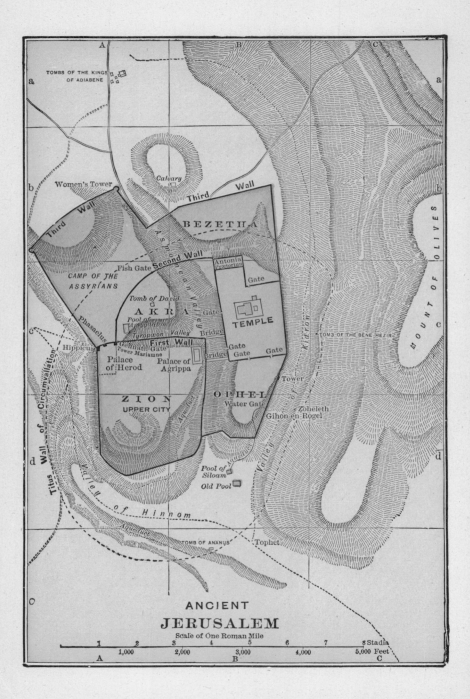

TOMBS OF THE KINGS
OF ADIABENE

Calvary

Third Wall

Women's Tower

BEZETHA

Third Wall

Fish Gate Second Wall

Antonia
Pretorium

Gate

CAMP OF THE
ASSYRIANS

Tomb of David

AKRA

Gate

TEMPLE

Pool of
Hezekiah

Tyropœon Valley

Bridge

Phasaelus

First Wall

Tower Mariamne

Gate Bridge Gate Gate Gate

Hippicus

Palace
of Herod

Palace of
Agrippa

Tower

ZION
UPPER CITY

OPHEL
Water Gate

TOMB OF THE BENE HEZIR

Zoheleth
Gihon en-Rogel

Titus Wall of Circumvallation

Valley of Hinnom

Pool of
Siloam

Old Pool

MOUNT OF OLIVES

Kidron

Valley

TOMB OF ANANUS Tophet

Aqueduct

ANCIENT
JERUSALEM
Scale of One Roman Mile

1   2   3   4   5   6   7   8 Stadia

1,000   2,000   3,000   4,000   5,000 Feet

Art. 1: THE TABERNACLE AND ITS FURNISHINGS

Texts: Exod. 25:8; 27:21.

101. The Tabernacle.—At God's command Moses employed skillful workmen to erect a tent temple on Sinai, according to the plan revealed to him by God. This was called the Dwelling (*miškan*) or Tabernacle.[6] This tent was entered from the east and was divided into two parts, the Holy and the Most Holy places. It formed a long quadrangle, and its length (interior) was 30 cubits,[7] its breadth 10 cubits and its height 10 cubits; it was made of a wooden framework, composed of 48 strong planks [8] or beams of acacia wood.[9] Each plank was covered with gold, and measured 10 cubits in length and 1½ in breadth. This wooden frame surrounded the interior on three sides, but on the fourth side were columns and a curtain. The two side walls contained 20 planks each, the shorter end wall only 8. Each plank must have been a cubit in thickness, so that the two at the ends of the shorter wall were flush with those at the ends of the long walls.[10] At the lower end of each plank were two projections [11] which fitted into silver sockets, and on the outer

[6] In the Vulgate it is called *tabernaculum fœderis* or *tabernaculum testimonii*. In the Septuagint, σκηνή τοῦ μαρτυρίου; in the Hebrew Bible, "Tent of the Agreement, Tent of the Testimony, Dwelling of the Testimony".

[7] An ell or cubit is the length from the point of the middle finger to the elbow = six handbreadths or two spans; about half a yard.

[8] The Hebrew קְרָשִׁים (from קֶרֶשׁ, to cut off) is generally translated planks. The word, however, only signifies something cut or hewn of wood, as in Ezech. 27:6. In the Septuagint it is rendered στῦλοι, pillars. The Vulgate has (less accurately) *tabulæ*. The word might be translated beams or uprights.

[9] Hebrew, "wood of šittim". This is the plural of *šittah* = the genuine acacia, *Mimosa nilotica*. The tree grew to a considerable size and its wood was very durable and at the same time very light. This wood was to be used because the acacia was the only tree that throve in the valleys of Sinai.

[10] The transport of such solid wooden pillars from one encampment to another must have caused great difficulty, though there was not so much hurry as in our day and in our countries. According to Num. 7:4, etc., the heavier articles were laid on wagons drawn by oxen.

[11] As beams measuring 1½ cubits in breadth were perhaps difficult to obtain, it may be assumed that each consisted of two parts, firmly fastened together—the "two projections" seem to suggest this. Accord-

side were strong golden rings, five on each beam, through which were passed the gilded bars that kept all the planks in place, and so kept the whole erection together. On the front side stood five gilded pillars of acacia wood with artistic capitals. These pillars rested on brazen sockets and supported a curtain, through which the Tabernacle was entered. The curtain was arranged thus: At the top of the pillars were golden hooks holding up gilded rods to which the curtain was fastened. In the inside was another curtain dividing the Tabernacle into two parts, the Holy and the Most Holy Places. It hung down from four gilded pillars, resting on silver sockets. The inner portion, which was the Most Holy Place, measured 10 cubits in length, breadth and height; the Holy Place had the same breadth and height, but was 20 cubits in length.

The bare earth formed the floor, nor had the Tabernacle any wooden roof, the place of which was taken by coverings stretched over the framework. These coverings were four in number.

The lowest covering was the most magnificent. It consisted (Exod. 26:1, etc.) of ten cloths or curtains of white linen, fine but strong, prepared in such a way that on the white ground cherubim could be artistically worked with thread of a violet, dark red and bright red color. Each of the ten curtains was 28 cubits long and 4 wide, and they were joined together in two sets of five, so as to form two large curtains each measuring 28 by 20 cubits, and the whole covering that they formed together was 40 cubits long and 28 wide. Each of the two at the end of the curtains had 50 violet loops, placed opposite to one another, and fastened together by means of 50 golden pins, which gripped them on either side. This covering was arranged over the holy Tabernacle so that the joint down the middle lay precisely above the inner curtain. It must therefore have hung down 8 cubits on the two long sides (north and south) and 9 cubits at the back, behind the Most Holy Place. It was probably fastened down to the earth by means of pegs.[12]

ing to the reports of missionaries, however, even at the present time the acacia furnishes very substantial wood for building purposes in China.

[12] If the planks were each 1 cubit in thickness, the covering could not have hung down more than 8 cubits, rather than 9, at the west end. That it hung outside is very probable, as this was, and still is, the usual arrangement for tents, and moreover there would have had to be some special means of securing it on the inner side, and no such thing is mentioned. The pegs (or pins) and cords of the Tabernacle are referred to in Exod. 27: 19; 35: 18; 38: 20 and 31. The space thus formed under

The second covering was less precious. It was woven of goats' hair, and was composed not of 10, but of 11 pieces, each of which was 30 cubits long and 4 wide. Its total extent, therefore, was 30 by 44 cubits. It, too, consisted of two parts, the front one being made of 6 pieces and the back one of only 5. These two parts were fastened together by means of 50 loops and 50 brass clasps, so as to form one whole. The part consisting of 5 pieces was spread over the Most Holy Place, and that of 6 pieces over the Holy Place. One piece hung over, and this was folded back and doubled on the front of the Tabernacle, to gain more solidity, so that it measured only 2 cubits, and projected for a space of 1 cubit, so as to form a kind of shelter over the entrance. At the other end of the tent this covering extended 1 cubit beyond the former, and this was the case also at the sides, so that the second covering was a protection to the innermost one, stretching 1 cubit beyond it in all directions. The fastenings, where the two halves were joined together, cannot apparently have been exactly above the entrance to the Most Holy Place, but about half a yard behind it.

The two outer coverings are mentioned in Holy Scripture, but are not fully described. The lower one of these, *i.e.*, the third covering, consisted of rams' skins dyed red,[13] the upper, or fourth covering, of *tahaš* skins.[14] The *tahaš* was probably the sea-cow found in the Red Sea, and now called manati; some authorities, however, believe that the badger is meant, as *tahaš* = to penetrate, creep in; and the badger lives in holes in the earth. The innermost appears to have been intended chiefly as an ornament; the others served as protections against dust and storms.

The two curtains separating the Holy and Most Holy Places formed each a square, measuring 10 cubits in each direction. They were made of the same materials as the first or innermost covering, but whereas the inner curtain also bore pictures of cherubim, the outer one had none, but was only embroidered in colors.

102. Court and Furniture of Tabernacle.—The Tabernacle just described was surrounded by a large court or yard whose outlines were marked by a fence or wall of linen curtains. The sacred tent was erected probably nearer the western end. Within this enclosure and in front of the Tabernacle were set the altar of burnt offerings and the brazen laver for cleansings.

---

the coverings could be used for the storage of utensils and as a sleeping place (I Kings 3: 3).

[13] Vulgate, *de pellibus arietum rubricatis;* Septuagint, δέρματα κριῶν ἠρυθροδανωμένα.

[14] In the Septuagint the name is given as δέρματα ὑακίνθινα; in the Vulgate, *ianthinæ pelles* = violet-colored hides.

The altar of holocausts (Exod. 27:1-8; 38:1, etc.) consisted of a framework of acacia wood, 5 cubits in length and breadth and 3 cubits in height. The frame was hollow and was filled up with earth and stones, so that the latter formed the altar proper. The wooden sides were covered with brass, and provided at the corners with four brazen horns. Halfway up the altar ran a projecting ledge about a cubit in breadth, having at its outer edge a copper grating or network resting on the ground; brass rings were attached to the four corners. This ledge served for the priests to stand on, so that they might more easily perform their duties at the top of the altar. The fire on this altar, which consumed the victims, was never allowed quite to die out (Lev. 6:9, 12, 13): "This is the perpetual fire which shall never go out on the altar".

The brazen laver, made of metal mirrors, stood between this altar and the Tabernacle, a little to the south. It is not clearly described in Holy Scripture, but, on the analogy of the great basin in the Temple, one may imagine it to have been shaped like a cauldron, and of considerable size. Probably there were openings and taps at the sides for letting out the water when necessary, as it was used for washing the priests' hands and feet, whenever they entered the Tabernacle, and also to cleanse the flesh of the sacrifice, and the sacrificial vessels and garments if they happened to be stained. There was below the laver a base of brass to receive the water that flowed out of it (*ken*).

The correct explanation of the words in Exod. 38:8 is doubtful: The Septuagint renders them: καὶ ἐποίησε τὸν λουτῆρα τὸν χαλκοῦν καὶ τὴν βάσιν αὐτοῦ χαλκῆν ἐκ τῶν κατόπτρων τῶν νηστευσασῶν, αἱ ἐνήστευσαν παρὰ τῆς θύρας τῆς σκηνῆς τοῦ μαρτυρίου. Vulgate: *Fecit et labrum æneum cum basi sua de speculis mulierum, quæ excubabant in ostio tabernaculi.* It seems certain that the word צבאת denotes women who took some kind of part in the service of the Tabernacle. The Hebrew מַרְאָה, and κάτοπτρον, mean, not figure, but mirror. It is more likely that women are referred to, who lived austere lives near the Tabernacle, and sometimes were employed there, perhaps in baking, and in making the priests' garments. See II Mach. 3:19, where, in the account of the plundering of the Temple, mention is made of "shut up" virgins (αἱ κατακλεῖστοι τῶν παρθένων) who sought by their prayers to avert the sacrilege. The Septuagint translators must have been guided by some tradition, when they rendered the

Hebrew ב (= by, by means of, with) by ἐκ, and אָבָא by νηστεύω (= to fast, abstain). The sons of Heli were said to have sinned by behaving in an unseemly way towards such women (I Kings 2:22). Jephte seems to have placed his daughter among these women in consequence of his vow (Judges 11:31). The mirrors belonging to such persons might have been attached to the laver, in order that the priests could always see whether their clothes and faces were properly clean; but this would probably have been stated in the Hebrew in a separate clause. It is most likely that these women offered their metal mirrors as the material out of which the laver was made. This is the Vulgate interpretation.

103. In the Holy Place, the larger, front portion of the Tabernacle there stood the seven-branched candelabrum, the table for the showbread, and the altar of incense.

The golden candlestick stood sideways on the south side of the Holy Place. It was of beaten work of the finest gold (therefore not massive), and it had seven branches, the one in the middle rising straight up, and the others being in pairs on either side of it. The central shaft rested upon a pedestal called *yarek* (= hip or loin); the name seems to have been selected because there were probably feet lower down, whilst the upper part suggested a body with outstretched arms. On the branches were ornaments like the cup of a flower, consisting of a knob and a blossom. These were placed on the central shaft below the points where the arms branched off, and also at the place where the shaft joined its pedestal. Moreover, each side branch bore three such ornaments, so that there were twenty-two in all. At the upper ends were lamps, but these did not actually form part of the candlestick, and only rested on the seven branches. In shape they probably resembled the ordinary lamps of antiquity; that is to say, they were oval, having at one end a projecting wick and at the other a handle by which they could be carried. At the ends of the seven arms were slight depressions to hold them. The lamps cast their light inwards, towards the "side of the Countenance" on the north. Every morning they had to be taken down to be cleaned, and then were replaced. It is uncertain whether the lamps burned constantly, day and night. Josephus (*Ant.*, VI, iii, 9) agrees with the Rabbis in saying that by day only three were alight, but at night all seven. While Lev. 24:4 states that they were *always* (*tamid*) to be burning, it probably only means that the light ought never quite to be extinguished. The purest olive oil was burned in these lamps. As accessories are mentioned (Exod. 25:38) golden tongs (probably snuffers) and dishes to hold the snuffers and wicks.

104. The table of the bread of proposition or showbread (Exod. 25:23-30) stood on the north side of the sanctuary, opposite the candlestick. It was of acacia wood, measuring 2 cubits long, 1 cubit wide and 1½ cubits high, completely covered with sheets of gold. At the top was a projecting ledge of gold (*misgereth* = enclosure) as wide as a man's hand, so that the surface of the table lay below it, and round about this margin ran a golden garland. To the legs of the table four rings were fastened, through which rods could be passed, so that it might be carried. The rods also were of acacia wood, overlaid with gold. Upon the table lay always twelve thin loaves [15] of the finest wheat flour; they were arranged in two rows of six, and according to Josephus Flavius they were unleavened. The Hebrew text calls them ''loaves of the Countenance''; the Authorized Version has ''showbread''. Every Sabbath they were taken away and replaced by fresh ones; and the priests ate the stale bread within the sanctuary. At this ceremony the incense near the loaves was burned (perhaps on the altar of incense). The loaves were carried in on (probably two) shallow dishes and set in order; the incense was placed in little bowls. Wine also was brought in (perhaps only on the Sabbath) in special jugs, poured into bowls and then offered as libations, being thrown out on the ground. All these accessories were of pure gold.

The altar of incense (Exod. 30:1, etc.; 27:25, etc.) occupied a position in the middle before the inner curtain. It was four-cornered and made of acacia wood, measuring 2 cubits in height and 1 cubit in length and breadth. It had

[15] The number refers to the twelve tribes of Israel, and the offering placed before the Face of God testified that they owed their bread to the Lord's goodness.

a so-called "roof" (*gag*), *i.e.*, a raised edge ran all round the flat upper surface, and a golden garland was fastened to the edge, as in the table of the showbread. Below the garland were two golden rings on each side, through which staves were passed for carrying the altar. Horns were fastened to the four corners. The whole was overlaid with gold. Incense was offered on this altar daily, both morning and evening.

The ritual of this incense sacrifice was as follows. A priest took some glowing charcoal from the altar of holocausts and carried it in a golden vessel into the Tabernacle, whilst another carried the incense. The first priest scattered the charcoal on the altar, and the second laid the incense upon it. Meanwhile the people stood in the court, engaged in prayer, and then they received the priest's blessing. The incense consisted of four ingredients, which were called collectively *sammim*, sweet perfumes. It had to be salted, and had to be clean and holy, *i.e.*, some salt was strewn over it, as over everything offered in sacrifice; it was not to contain any foreign ingredients, and after it was mixed, was to be used only in the sanctuary. It was forbidden, under penalty of death, to use incense mixed in this particular way for any profane purpose.

105. In the Holy of Holies, the smaller rear room of the Tabernacle partitioned off by the great curtain, stood the Ark of the Covenant. It was a chest of acacia wood, covered with gold both inside and outside. Its length was 2½ cubits, its breadth and height 1½ cubits. Round the middle of it ran a garland of pure gold. At the four corners were golden rings, through which gilded rods were passed to enable the ark to be carried; these rods were never to be removed. Inside the ark was nothing but the two stone tables, on which the Ten Commandments were inscribed (Exod. 26:16; Deut. 10:4, 5). According to Hebrews 9:4, beside the holy ark were kept Aaron's rod and a vessel of manna.[16] In Deuter-

---

[16] In Heb. 9:4 the reading is ἐν ᾗ (κιβωτῷ), which is generally translated "*in* which [ark]". But ἐν, like the Latin *in*, also means near, beside. In Exod. 16:33 all that is said of the vessel of manna is that it was לִפְנֵי יְהֹוָה = before the Lord; Sept. ἐναντίον τοῦ θεοῦ. In Num. 17:35 (Vulg. 17:10) Aaron's rod is commanded to be carried into the Tabernacle for safe keeping. At the time of Solomon, according to III Kings 8:9 and II Par. 9:10, there were only the two tables of the law in the ark, but it is possible that for a time the vessel of manna and Aaron's rod, probably cut short, were kept in it also.

onomy, 31:25, etc., it is said that the Book of the Law also lay beside the ark. Moses commanded the Levites to "take this book and put it at the side of the Ark of the Covenant" (מִצַּד אֲרוֹן, ἐκ πλαγίων τῆς κιβωτοῦ, Vulgate, *in latere arcæ*). The book was, as it were, the commentary upon the Decalogue.

Over the ark was the *Kapporeth,* or cover of pure gold. It was by no means intended merely to close the ark, but had a far higher purpose. This is implied by the fact that it was of solid gold, whilst the ark was only of wood overlaid with sheets of gold, and also by the command that the Kapporeth should be as long and as broad as the ark (Exod. 25:27),—if it were only a cover, this would be a matter of course. Its true destination is suggested by the Holy of Holies being called the house of the Kapporeth. The word *kapporeth* may indeed mean "covering", but it may equally well be translated "place of atonement".[17] The Kapporeth may be explained as God's resting-place. At either end of it, and inseparable from it, was a cherub of beaten gold, undoubtedly in human form, but with wings, which were stretched inwards over the ark. The space between the two cherubim on the Kapporeth was considered to be God's abode on earth. It was therefore called the *Šekina,* dwelling. From this spot God made answer to Moses and other leaders of the people, when they consulted Him on important matters.[18]

Art. 2: THE TEMPLE AND ITS APPURTENANCES

Texts: III Kings 6-8; II Par. 3-5; Ez. 40-42.

106. Solomon's Temple.—As long as the people of Israel were wandering in the Wilderness, the Tabernacle and all its furniture and utensils were carried by the Levites (Num. 4) from one encampment to another.

The Tabernacle stood within the camp. In Exod. 33:7, etc., one reads that Moses erected a "tabernacle of the covenant" outside the camp. This may be explained in the following way: On account of their rebellious spirit the Israelites were not permitted to be in

---

[17] The name comes from *kaphar,* to cover; *kapper* = to atone, propitiate. On the Day of Atonement every year the solemn ceremony of atonement had to be performed here.

[18] Exod. 25:22: "Thence will I give orders, and will speak to thee over the propitiatory, and from the midst of the two cherubims, which shall be upon the ark of the testimony, all things which I will command the children of Israel by thee". See Num. 7:89; Deut. 5:7; I Kings 3:3.

NORTH

THE TEMPLE OF JERUSALEM AT THE TIME OF CHRIST

(RESTORATION BY DE VOGÜE)

God's immediate neighborhood, but later (Exod. 40) the holy Tabernacle was erected inside the camp, and the tribe of Levi was placed nearest to it, the other tribes were further away, three on each side of it. To the east was the tribe of Juda, and to the left of Juda was Issachar, and to the right Zabulon; to the south was Ruben with Simeon and Gad; to the west Ephraim with Manasses and Benjamin; and to the north Dan with Aser and Nephtali.

After the Israelites had taken possession of the Promised Land, the Tabernacle was erected in various places. It stood for a long time at Silo, then at Nobe, and later still at Gabaon. Meantime the ark had been separated from it, and during a war had passed into the possession of the Philistines, but they voluntarily restored it, and it was kept for a time in a private house, and then was placed by David in a specially erected tent [19] on Mount Sion, whence it was transferred to the new Temple.

When the Israelites took Jerusalem from the Jebusites and obtained complete possession of the city, it was proposed to build a temple to the Lord on Mount Moria, perhaps = אמוריא = Land of the Amorites, according to the same plan as the Tabernacle.[20] King David collected a great quantity of materials for this purpose (I Par. 29: 2), and gave them and the designs that he had prepared to his son Solomon, who faithfully carried out his father's wishes. He began to build the Temple in the fourth year of his reign, and completed it in seven years (III Kings 6).

The surface of Mount Moria proved to be too small for the Temple, so huge walls were built up on the eastern side and the space between them and the hill was filled up with earth, and thus a sufficiently large site was obtained.

The stone and the cedar and cypress wood all came from Lebanon, as Solomon had made an agreement for this purpose with Hiram, King of Tyre, who supplied also some

[19] This was no longer the Tabernacle made by Moses, but a new tent, probably made in the same fashion as the Mosaic Tabernacle which remained in Gabaon, having possibly become damaged in course of time. Solomon had it solemnly removed and brought into the new Temple, where it was most likely kept in the upper story above the Holy of Holies. Allusions to it occur in III Kings 3: 4; I Par. 21: 29; II Mach. 2: 4, 5.

[20] In Wisdom 9: 8 the Temple is called μίμημα σκηνῆς ἁγίας.

workmen well trained in their art. Solomon gave Hiram in return the products of his country, especially grain, oil and wine.

Like the Tabernacle, its model, the Temple was divided into a house and a court.

107. The Temple proper, called the House (*habbayith*), was built of hewn stone, and measured 60 cubits in length, 20 in breadth, and 30 in height;—these are the inside measurements, not including the thickness of the walls. It had a flat roof. The interior was divided into the Holy Place and the Holy of Holies. The former was 40 cubits long, 20 broad and 30 high; the latter was 20 cubits in length, breadth and height, as the other 10 cubits, deducted from the total height of the building, formed an upper chamber. The masonry was covered on the inside with wooden panels; these were not smooth, but were carved with figures of cherubim, palms, gourds and opening blossoms. Over these very thin plates of gold were fastened with golden nails, so that the carved figures showed through the gold with which they were covered. It is probable that some beams of wood were built into the masonry. The ceiling and the floor were also covered with wood and sheets of gold, but no figures were carved upon them.

A door of sycamore wood with five corners,[21] in the middle of the partition wall, formed the entrance to the Holy of Holies. It was 6 cubits in width (Ezech. 41:3) and was in two parts; they, like the walls, were covered with gilded carvings, and turned on golden hinges. Both halves of the door were usually open, but it was not possible to see into the Holy of Holies, as a curtain of the same kind as that which hung formerly in the Tabernacle (II Par. 3:14) shut off all view. The Holy Place was entered by folding doors of cypress wood, but they folded back in two pieces on each side, and were ornamented like the doors of the Holy of Holies. In front of the house of the Temple was a porch 10 cubits in depth, and running along the whole breadth of the building (20 cubits). In the porch stood two thick

---

[21] That is to say, a square running up into a fifth point at the top.

columns, one known as Jakin and the other as Boaz. They were hollow, cast of brass, measuring 12 cubits in circumference and 18 in height, and on the top of each was a capital specially cast, 5 cubits high, so that the columns and capitals together measured 23 cubits, and this may have been the height of the porch.[22]

All round the outside of the Temple, except at the east or front, ran an annex (*yazua* = spread out) containing three tiers of chambers for the things used in the Temple worship and for storage of supplies. The beams supporting these stories rested on rebatements in the Temple wall at each story; the beams were not built into the wall. As the thickness of the Temple wall diminished by a cubit at each story, the chambers in the annex varied in width. The house of the Temple itself, being 30 cubits high, rose considerably above it, and in the upper part of the wall on either side were windows, latticed openings intended to admit air rather than light. The Holy Place was lighted with lamps, but the Holy of Holies was totally dark. Doors on the north and south sides (Ezech. 41: 11) formed the entrances to the lowest story in the annex, and a winding staircase, beginning close to the door, led up to the apartments above.

Around the House of the Temple was the Inner Court, for the use of the priests. It was enclosed by a wall of hewn stone, covered with cedar wood, and, according to II Par. 7: 3, this court (and probably the other also) was paved with stones.

The Outer or Great Court for the people seems to have surrounded the Inner Court on all four sides, and it was certainly also enclosed by a wall, as it had gateways with folding doors. Jeremias 36: 10 speaks of the Inner Court as the Upper; it was therefore on higher ground than that of the people, and it is most likely that the house of the Temple, following the form of Mount Moria, occupied the highest part of the hill, and was raised above the court of the priests.

108. Furnishings of the Temple.—In the Holy of Holies stood the Ark of the Covenant. Apparently no new one was made, but Moses' ark with the Kapporeth and the two cherubim upon it was transferred to the Temple (III Kings 8: 1;

---

[22] These tall, hollow brass pillars with chains and pendants swinging from the capitals may have acted as two massive chimes, giving forth melodious, bell-like sounds as the pendant "pomegranates" were stirred by the wind (see II Par. 3: 15–17; 4: 12–14; Jer. 52: 17, 20–23). Heathen antiquity makes occasional mention of such pillar-chimes, which were often used for oracular purposes (Eusebius, *Præf. evang.*, IX, 34, and *Hist. eccl.*, IX, 7; Josephus, *Ant.*, VIII, v, 3; Pliny, XXXVI, 13, 91).

II Par. 5:22).[23] Near the ark, however, were stationed two large cherubim, figures of angels in human form, made of sycamore wood overlaid with gold, keeping watch over it. Each figure was 10 cubits high and had wings each 5 cubits long. One wing was stretched out backwards and touched the wall; the other was lifted forwards so as to meet the corresponding wing of the other cherub above the Kapporeth. The figures stood upright, with their faces turned towards the entrance (II Par. 3:13). The staves for carrying the ark, that were never removed, projected so that their ends could be recognized through the curtain (III Kings 8:8).

In the Holy Place stood: (a) The Altar of Incense near the curtain; it was of cedar wood overlaid with gold. (b) Ten golden candlesticks, bearing seven lamps each; the candlesticks were arranged five along the north and south walls respectively. (c) Ten tables of showbread, five on each side.

In the Inner Court were: (a) The brazen altar of holocausts, 20 cubits in length and breadth and 10 cubits in height. In design it resembled that of Moses, and was filled up inside with earth and stones. It probably had several projecting ledges, on the uppermost of which the officiating priests stood. It must also have had steps, at least on the east side, as may be inferred from Ezechiel 43:17, "and its steps turned towards the east". (b) The brazen sea or laver was a great round basin of water, 5 cubits high and 10 cubits in diameter at the top. It was cast of brass of the thickness of a man's hand and had an edge curving outwards, beneath which were two rows of gourds as ornamentation. The laver contained 2000 *bath*, *i.e.*, about 360 hectoliters of water. It rested on twelve brazen bulls, three of which looked towards each quarter of the heavens, and presumably they stood on a brazen base. The water could probably be drawn off as required, by means of taps. It was used for washing the hands and feet, and also the flesh of the victims. There must have been some sort of aqueduct. Near the altar on the

---

23 As at this time the ark contained only the two tables of the law, it seems probable that Aaron's rod and the vessel of manna and the Book of the Law were kept, with Moses' Tabernacle, in the room above the Holy of Holies.

147

north and south sides were ten brazen stands with brazen
basins upon them, intended for the reception of the flesh of
the victims. These stands were four-cornered boxes, 40 cubits square at the top and 3 cubits in height. Under each
were four wheels, so that they could be moved to and fro
when required, and convey the flesh to the laver and the
altar. On the sides of these stands were biblical figures,—
oxen, lions, and cherubim. The basins on them contained
each 4 *bath* (about 9 hectoliters) and were removable. These
stands and basins were not used either in the Tabernacle or
in the second Temple.

109. Solomon's Temple stood from about 1004 to 588 B.C., when
it was destroyed by the Babylonians. In its place the Jews returning from the Captivity raised the second or Zorobabel's Temple,
completed in 515 B.C. This was larger in extent than Solomon's,
but not nearly so magnificent, on account of the poverty of the
Israelites. Moreover, the chief treasure of the earlier Temple, the
Ark of the Covenant, was missing, and the Holy of Holies was
empty. According to II Mach. 2:4, 5, the prophet Jeremias in 588
"commanded that the tabernacle and the ark should accompany
him, till he came forth to the mountain (Nebo) . . . and when Jeremias came thither he found a hollow cave: and he carried in
thither the tabernacle, and the ark, and the altar of incense, and
so stopped the door". But afterwards the place could not be found
(*l. c.*, 6, 7). Where the ark should have stood, a stone was placed,
on which the high priest set the censer on the Day of Atonement.
In the Holy Place was the altar of incense, a golden candlestick
and a table for the showbread; in the court was an altar of holocausts built of stone; and a laver stood between the altar and the
porch, somewhat to the south (Ecclus. 50:3). The Court of the
Priests was surrounded by the larger Court of the People. In
consequence of many costly offerings being made, this Temple gradually became more magnificent, and the Temple tax of half a shekel
(about 30 cents), demanded yearly of every Jew, even in foreign
countries, supplied funds for its decoration.

In the second century B.C., Antiochus Epiphanes plundered and
laid waste the Temple, and desecrated it by the worship of false
gods. Judas Machabæus, after driving out the Syrians, repaired
the buildings, as far as they had been injured, caused some of the
furniture to be replaced by new, and had the Temple reconsecrated.
This was the origin of the feast of the Encænia or Dedication
(ἐγκαίνια, John 10:22). At this time strong fortifications were
added to the Temple, but nevertheless it was again taken by
the Romans under Pompey (64 B.C.), and also by Herod the Great,
who by the aid of Roman troops captured Jerusalem (37 B.C.) and
stormed the Temple.

110. Herod's Temple.—Herod the Great showed his passion for building, and at the same time conciliated the Jews, by enlarging and altering the Temple, although he did not actually rebuild it. The reason why he did not undertake to build an entirely new Temple, which would perhaps have been less costly, was, as many think, because the prophet Aggeus (2:10) foretold that the second Temple should excel Solomon's in glory. Herod's Temple is always spoken of as the second, never as the third.

Work on the Temple began in 20 B.C., and in a year and a half the whole house of the Temple had been transformed; all the building being done by priests and Levites, after the materials had been prepared and arranged for them. The courts were finished in ten years, but work on the surrounding buildings was still going on during Christ's lifetime, and even later.

In the form that it now assumed the Temple area measured a stade, or 500 cubits, in each direction.[24] It was laid out in terraces, so that one court was on a higher level than the other, and the Temple itself occupied the top of the hill. It could therefore be seen from all parts of the city and also from a great distance, and presented a magnificent appearance.

The outermost court was that of the Gentiles. It was surrounded by a high wall with several gates; it contained several halls, and was paved with colored stones. It ran round all the other buildings, enclosing them on all four sides. This huge court was generally filled with a crowd of people, and goods were sold in it as if it had been a market place. It was twice cleansed by Christ from this desecration.

Within it, and on higher grounds, being reached by 14 steps, was the Court of the People, also surrounded by a wall, on which were notices in Greek and Latin, warning the Gentiles on pain of death to go no farther. On the east side this court was entered by Nicanor's Gate, which was very

[24] 1 stade = 1/40 geographical mile; so 4 stades = 1/10 mile = 742 meters (nearly half an English mile). The Talmud contains an account of this Temple (tract *Middoth*); see also Josephus, *Ant.*, XV, 11, and *Bell. Jud.*, V, 5.

large and magnificent,[25] and which is called the Beautiful Gate in Acts 3:2 and 10, and the Brazen Gate by Josephus. Besides this gate there were several others on the north and south sides, leading into the Court of the People, one on each side into the Court of the Women and three into the Court of the Men, for this court was divided into a square and somewhat lower court assigned to the women, and a higher court for the men; the former lay nearest to Nicanor's Gate.

On the same level as the Court of the Men was the Court of the Levites, separated from it only by a low fence. In it was the great altar of holocausts, 15 cubits high and, at its lowest projection, 40–50 cubits broad; somewhat to the south was the huge laver.

The house of the Temple was situated on rather higher ground. It was built of immense blocks of white marble, and was richly gilded both inside and outside, and had larger dimensions than the earlier Temple. It consisted of a magnificent porch (100 cubits high, 100 broad and 20 deep); the Holy Place (40 cubits long, 20 broad and 40 high) and the Holy of Holies (20 cubits long, 20 broad and 40 high). The Holy of Holies was empty; the Holy Place contained the altar of incense, one golden candlestick and one table for showbread. At the sides, as in Solomon's Temple, there were three stories containing small rooms. The roof was a low gable, with gilded spikes on the gable.

Such was the Temple where Christ taught and worked miracles. Beholding it, He foretold its speedy destruction, and that no stone would be left upon another. This prophecy was fulfilled in the year 70.

At the time of Nehemias [26] the Samaritans built themselves a temple on Mount Garizim, near Sichem. It was destroyed by the Jewish king John Hyrcanus in 129 B.C. The colony of Jewish Mercenaries garrisoning Elefantine during the Achaemenid period also had a Yahweh temple there,[27] though other gods seem also to have

[25] This Nicanor is not to be identified with the Syrian General Nicanor, mentioned in the books of Machabees; it was an Alexandrian Jew who had this gate built.

[26] See John 4:19. Josephus is in error when (*Ant.*, VI, viii, 2) he says that this Temple was built in the time of Alexander the Great.

[27] See introduction to Book of Esdras, below.

been venerated there. Onias the high priest also built a temple at Leontopolis [28] (about 70 miles north of Cairo) in Egypt, when so many of the Jews during the Syrian wars of the Seleucid era fled from the persecutions of Antiochus. This was destroyed by the Romans under Vespasian. These temples were considered schismatical and illegitimate by the Jews of Palestine.

Synagogues, which date only from after the Captivity, were not considered substitutes for the Temple, but simply houses of assembly and prayer. The law was read and commented upon there, even during Christ's time, but sacrifices were never offered. This use of synagogues has continued to the present day. They are only meeting houses, without priest, liturgy, or sacrifice, like the "churches" (originally and properly called "meeting houses" only) of the Protestants. The only requisites for the establishment of a synagogue are: (1) a cupboard for books on the side of the building towards Jerusalem, in which the parchment rolls of the Holy Scripture are stored; (2) a lectern—the synagogue being especially the place where instruction is given in the law, and those learned in Scripture are required to expound it; (3) seats for the congregation, the sexes being separated, the front row of seats being reserved for those learned in the law; (4) one or more candlesticks to give solemn light on important festivals. To keep order a ruler of the synagogue was appointed; he was assisted by a college of elders, and by a minister who had to attend to the opening, closing and cleaning of the building.

Art. 3: THE PRIESTS AND LEVITES

Texts: Exod. 29:1-39; Lev. 8; Num. 3:41-4.

111. Position and Function.—After the Hebrews quitted Egypt the firstborn son of every family was dedicated to God (Num. 8:17; 3:13). Subsequently the command was given that, instead of the firstborn sons, all the males of a whole tribe should be in a peculiar way God's property and look after His service (Num. 3:41). This was the tribe of Levi, to which Moses belonged. The reason for this change was probably that the setting apart of the firstborn would have caused excessive disturbances in the maintenance of families; however (Num. 3:47), in order that the original custom should not be forgotten, every firstborn son had to

[28] See *The Temple of Onias at Leontopolis*, by Hugh Pope, O.P., in *Irish Theological Quarterly* (Oct., 1908), pp. 417–424.

be redeemed by the payment of a sum fixed by the priest, but not exceeding 5 shekels.

The task of the tribe of Levi was generally to preserve and continue the work of Moses. The Levites had to keep the Law of Moses free from all falsification;[29] they themselves had to observe its precepts most strictly and instruct the people.

Unlike the other tribes, the Levites received no land as their property in Palestine. God alone was to be their portion. "Levi hath no part nor possession with his brethren, because the Lord Himself is his possession" (Deut. 10:9). There were, however, forty-eight places assigned to them as dwellings in the midst of the other tribes; a list of these is given in Josue 21:9-40. Besides these they had pasture ground for their cattle, but no land for cultivation. These forty-eight places were by no means the property of the Levites, who only lived there amidst the other inhabitants.

The tribe of Levi had, however, a sufficient income, at least if the law was faithfully observed. To the Levites belonged all tithes, *i.e.*, the tenth part of all the yearly produce of the fields and gardens, and of all cattle and sheep; and in addition the first fruits, *i.e.*, the first produce of all the fields and gardens, the firstborn of all animals, and the sums paid for the redemption of the firstborn sons. They had also definite shares of all sacrifices.

The duty of attending to the actual worship of God was imposed upon one particular family, viz., the descendants of Aaron. Aaron himself and the firstborn of his family in each generation were the high priests, all his other direct descendants formed the priesthood, and the whole tribe was subject to them. This division of his family corresponds with that of the sanctuary. The high priest had to serve in the Holy of Holies; the priests attended to all the ceremonies in the Holy Place, whilst the Levites were required to help the priests only in the court.

112. The Levites.—Levi, the forefather of the sacerdotal tribe, had three sons, Gerson, Cahath and Merari, so the tribe

---

29 The book of the Law was kept in the Holy of Holies, but there can be no doubt that copies existed for the use of the priests and Levites. In Deuteronomy 17:18, 19, one reads that the king, when he wanted the book of Law, had to apply to the priests of the tribe of Levi. The Law had to be read aloud to the people from time to time.

was divided into three parts, the Gersonites, the Cahathites and the Merarites. To these Levites were assigned thirty-five places as their dwellings and as means of livelihood they had, besides the produce of their herds, a tithe of the produce of all fields and gardens and of all cattle. They had, however, to pay a tenth of this tithe to the priests. They were summoned to take part at the sacrificial meals.

They were admitted to the holy service by means of a special dedication, called *taher* = cleansing. They were sprinkled with water of purification, prepared for the purpose; their hair was cut off, and they washed their clothes. Then they came to the place of the sanctuary, where the people were assembled, with two oxen destined for sacrifice. Here some men of the people, acting in the name of the nation, laid their hands upon the Levites, who on their part laid their hands on the oxen, which were then sacrificed, one being a burnt offering and the other a sin offering. After this ceremony, the Levites entered on their duties.

It is easy to see that the laying on of hands on the part of the community signified that the whole nation was really pledged to God's service and was ready to perform it, but the Levites were the representatives of the people and especially of the firstborn. The Levites on their side acknowledged that they, as sinners, were unworthy to serve the Lord, and deserved death. As, however, in that case there would be no ministers for the sanctuary, they allowed the oxen to die in their stead, and signified that these creatures were their representatives by laying their hands upon them.

The first dedication of the Levites in the wilderness was performed in the manner just described. It is uncertain whether this held good always, or was repeated subsequently. There is no record of a renewed dedication, and so probably the first dedication held good forever.

In the performance of their duties the Levites were absolutely subordinate to the priests, and were regarded as their assistants (Num. 8:26). They were forbidden to make sacrifice, and might not touch the furniture of the Holy Place, nor the altar of incense, under penalty of death (Num. 18: 3). During the wandering of the Israelites in the wilderness, their business was to keep guard over the Tabernacle, for which reason they were encamped nearest to it, the Gersonites on the west, the Cahathites on the south and the Merarites on the north (Num. 3:23, 29, 35), whilst Moses and Aaron and the priests were stationed on the east side near the entrance. The Levites had to erect the Tabernacle, and take it down when the march was resumed, and carry the parts of it, when it was taken to pieces, as well as the sacred furniture, which was all covered up. In Palestine they had to guard the Tabernacle, and later the Temple, to open and to close it. Every day sixteen Levites kept watch at the gates of the Temple (I Par. 26:12), and in the second Temple still more were employed because the spaces were so great and the gates so numerous.[30]

Moreover, the Levites were required to clean the Temple and everything connected with it, to prepare the showbread and the cakes used at sacrifices, to procure and look after all the accessories of worship (garments, grain, flour, salt, wine, oil and beasts for sacrifice) and to supply whatever was wanting. Further, they were bound to provide for the music in the Temple and to arrange for the singing. They assisted the priests in slaying and skinning the victims.

Besides serving in the Temple, the Levites acted as judges, and therefore they had to instruct the people in the Law and to punish transgressors in conformity with its precepts. According to I Par. 23:4, there were four distinct classes of Levites: (1) ministers of the priests; (2) overseers and judges; (3) porters, or doorkeepers; (4) singers and musicians. They were bound to devote themselves to their official duties between the ages of 25 and 50.[31]

Besides the Levites, there were other men employed in menial work in the Temple, such as cutting wood and carrying water. These were called *Nethinim* = given ones, bondmen (see Jos. 9:27; I Par. 9:2; I Esdras 2:43 and 70).

113. The Priests.—Only the descendants of Aaron, Moses' elder brother, belonging to the Cahath branch of the

[30] The ''officer of the temple'', mentioned in Acts 4:1, was probably the commander of the guard of Levites.

[31] Num. 8:24. In Num. 4:2 the age when a Levite could enter upon his duties is mentioned as thirty, but this passage refers to the removal of the Tabernacle during the wandering in the wilderness.

tribe of Levi, were chosen by God to be priests. Aaron had four sons, two of whom, Abin and Nadam, were slain for their carelessness in the service of God (Lev. 10:1), so only the two remaining sons, Eleasar and Ithamar, could pass on the priestly office to their descendants. Not every one belonging to Aaron's family was fit to be a priest; all were excluded who had any bodily defect, who were blind, lame, deaf, or suffering from permanent sores, etc. (Lev. 21:16). No fixed age is prescribed in the Law, but the age appointed for the priests no doubt was the same as that for the Levites. Thirteen of the Levite towns were assigned to the priests as their dwellings.

The maintenance of the priests was provided for by: (1) tithes, which the Levites had to give over to them from their tithes; (2) first fruits of field and garden produce; (3) money paid for the redemption of the firstborn, each of whom was redeemed for a sum to be fixed by the priest, but not exceeding 5 shekels; (4) the first male born of all clean beasts had to be sacrificed; the fat was burnt on the altar, but the rest of the carcass belonged to the priests (Num. 18:18); (5) the first male born of unclean beasts either had to be killed, or a clean beast, that could be sacrificed, was substituted for it, and the fifth of its value was paid in addition; (6) the skins of all the animals used for burnt offerings, and definite parts of those used in other sacrifices, belonged to the priests. Their sources of income were abundant; they had no taxes to pay and were free from military service. It was to their own interest to preserve a knowledge and the observance of the Law among the people; for thus only had they an assured income.

Apart from their sacred duties, the priests wore the ordinary dress of the people, but when engaged in these duties they wore special garments prescribed by law. These were: (1) a tunic [32] with narrow sleeves, reaching from the neck to the ankles, and made of white linen; (2) a head-covering,[33] made of byssus, in the shape

---

[32] כֻּתֹּנֶת, from כָּתַן, to spin, weave.

[33] מִגְבָּעָה, Ex. 28:40, and elsewhere. The word is connected with גְּבִיעַ, a cup, so the head-covering was probably cup shaped.

of an inverted flower-calyx, so that it was a kind of hat; (3) a loin-cloth, also of byssus,[34] probably a large cloth, such as was worn also by other people beneath the tunic for the sake of decency (in Exod. 28:42 it is mentioned as covering the middle of the body), as the ordinary garments reached only to the knees; (4) a colored girdle, of white, purple, crimson and dark blue threads, all interwoven. According to the Rabbis, this was 3 fingers in breadth and 32 cubits in length, so that it could be wound several times round the body. The priests wore no shoes, as the sacred places must be entered barefoot.

The priest's office consisted of the following duties: (1) Every morning and evening he had to put incense on the altar of incense, near the inner curtain in the Holy Place, and trim the lamps on the golden candlestick. The old showbread had to be removed and the fresh substituted on the table of proposition every Sabbath.[35] (2) In the Court of the Temple, the priests offered very many sacrifices on the great altar, where they kept the fire burning day and night. Every morning after the daily offering of incense, they blessed the people. (3) They were especially bound to uphold the Law of Moses, and therefore it was their duty to instruct the people in the Law and to attend to the administration of justice (Deut. 17:8; 19:17; 21:5); (4) among their extraordinary occupations were: (a) negotiating about first fruits and the firstborn; (b) blowing the silver trumpets at certain festivals; (c) examining lepers and pronouncing them clean, as well as inspecting houses and garments infected with leprosy; (d) releasing Nazirites from their vows; (e) performing the ceremony of the offering on behalf of women suspected of adultery.

Priests were required to be in a state of cleanness whenever they discharged any part of their office. As long as they were engaged in the sacred service they might not drink wine nor anything intoxicating (Lev. 10:9), and remained apart from their wives (Exod. 19:14). Even when not em-

---

[34] מִבְנְסֵי בַּר, covering of cleanness; it does not mean breeches or drawers.

[35] Descendants of Aaron, who were disqualified from the sacred service by some physical defect, might eat of the loaves of proposition or showbread, but only in the court, not entering the Holy Place.

ployed in their priestly duties, they were forbidden to touch
any corpses (Lev. 21:1), with the exception of those of their
nearest relatives (Lev. 10:6), nor might they wear mourning, for sin and its consequences are an abomination to God,
and therefore no reminder of it, such as mourning for the
dead would imply, could be tolerated in His priests. If, accidentally, a priest incurred legal defilement, he could not discharge any sacred duty, nor eat anything consecrated, until,
after the lapse of a definite time, he had been cleansed by
legal ceremonies. The priests were particularly bound to
lead pure and blameless lives, as the Law prescribed, and
the same obligation rested also upon their families, so
that a priest's daughter, who had fallen into immorality,
was required to be burned to death (Lev. 21:9). It seems,
however, that the priests often went astray, for the prophets
frequently complain of their setting the people a bad example; see Jer. 5:31; 6:13; Mich. 3:11.

114. The Highpriest.—The head of the priestly class
was the highpriest, who was always the firstborn of Aaron's
race, provided that he possessed the necessary physical and
mental qualifications. His exalted position conferred upon
him various prerogatives, so that he stood to the other priests
in the relation of a father to his sons (''Aaron and his
sons''); but it was his duty to live a life peculiarly pure and
blameless.

Over and above the usual priestly attire (tunic, loin-
cloth, girdle and head-covering) an official costume in keeping with his exalted dignity was given to the highpriest and
worn exclusively by him. If his head-covering be includeb,
this costume also consisted of four parts, *viz.*:

1. The *Meîl*,[36] a garment made of dark bluish purple, and
worn over the priest's tunic. It had an opening at the top,
so that it could be passed over the head. There were no
sleeves. On the lower edge it was ornamented with artificial
pomegranates made of yarn and twelve[37] golden bells ar-

---

[36] מְעִיל from מַעַל, upper; hence ''upper garment''.

[37] This is the number given in the apocryphal Gospel of Saint James.
The Rabbis say seventy-two, but this is plainly too large a number.

ranged alternately. It probably reached only to the knees, so that the white tunic could be seen below it.

2. *The Ephod,*[38] made of white linen skillfully interwoven with gold and colored threads, dark blue, dark red and bright red. It consisted of two squares of cloth, one covering the breast and the other the back. These two squares were fastened together and held in place by means of shoulderpieces of gold, on each of which was an onyx.[39] On the two precious stones were engraved the names of the twelve tribes of Israel, six on each. The lower part of the ephod was fastened to the body by means of a girdle of the same materials.

3. The *Ḥošen,*[40] or breastplate. This was a double square folded in half, so as to form a sort of pocket (not unlike the burse to contain the corporal). It measured half a cubit in each direction, and was made of the same material as the ephod. On the outer side were twelve precious stones set in gold, arranged in four rows, and bearing the names of the twelve tribes of Israel engraved upon them. At each corner of the *ḥošen* was a golden ring. To the rings at the two upper corners were attached little gold chains, having at their extremities golden clasps, by means of which they were fastened to the shoulder-pieces of the ephod, close to the onyx stones. Blue cords were passed through the rings at the two lower corners, and also through two other rings which were sewn on to the edge of the shoulder-pieces of the ephod below the arms. In this way the *ḥošen* was fastened to the ephod, both at the top and at the bottom, and so was drawn close to the breast and prevented from slipping out of place.

Inside the *ḥošen* the *Urim* and *Thummim* were placed.

---

[38] אֵפוֹד = dress. In every place where the word occurs, not excepting Judges 8: 27 and I Kings 21: 9, it has this meaning. It never means the figure of a deity, or a shrine in which to keep images.

[39] Heb. שֹׁהַם, perhaps the sea-green beryl. The word means in Arabic "pale". Sept., σμάραγδος, Vulg., *lapis onychinus;* ὄνυξ = finger nail.

[40] חֹשֶׁן from חָשַׁן, to cut off, secure, keep. The meaning is certainly "receptacle", and is correctly rendered δόχιον by the Sept.

What they were, is not explained, and the names do not help; they probably mean "light and right" or "clearness and truth"; Septuagint, δήλωσις καὶ ἀλήθεια; Vulgate, *doctrina et veritas*. The Jewish authors, Josephus and Philo and the Rabbis, are all at a loss as to the interpretation. It appears from Exod. 28:16, 30, and from Lev. 8:8 [41] that some solid thing is meant, which could be put into the breastplate and taken out again, and that this served as an instrument whereby the highpriest could ascertain God's will in matter of importance. One may be sure that the Septuagint translation δήλωσις and ἀλήθεια has some foundation. The words signify clearing away of doubt and recognition of the truth. The highpriest was believed to be inspired and capable of deciding upon the right course of action.

4. The *head-covering* worn by the high priest was, according to Josephus (*Ant.*, III, vii, 7) and Philo, the ordinary covering worn by the priests, with the addition of dark blue ribbon, to which a little gold plate was fastened, having engraved upon it the words "Holy to the Lord"—*qodeš la adonai*. The highpriest did not always wear his official dress. As a rule, when he had only ordinary business to transact, he dressed like the other priests, but the ribbon and plate on his head-covering always distinguished him from them.

Duties of the High Priest. The following duties were assigned exclusively to him: (1) To perform the important ceremonies on the great Day of Atonement. (2) To ascertain God's will by means of the *Urim* and *Thummim,* and to make it known. (3) In the administration of justice to give the final decision, from which there was no appeal. He seems to have presided at trials of important cases, and in the Synedrium. (4) To watch over everything connected with the worship of God, and over the Levites and Priests. He could, of course, discharge all the priestly functions.

Sanctity of the High Priest. Standing as he did near to

---

[41] The rational of judgment (*rationale judicii*) "shall be four square and doubled . . . thou shalt put in the rational of judgment doctrine and truth . . . the rational, on which was doctrine and truth".

God, and above the whole nation and the ordinary business
of life, the highpriest was strictly bound by the Law: (1)
to touch no corpse, not even that of his father or mother;
(2) at the death of his nearest relatives to show no outward
token of mourning and to omit none of his official duties;
(3) to take a virgin as his wife, not a dishonored woman,
or a widow, or a divorced person.

Tenure of Office. The highpriest retained his dignity
until his death, if he were not disabled by sickness or old
age, and so rendered incompetent to perform his sacred
duties. Occasionally two high priests are mentioned as holding office at the same time, but only one of these is to be
regarded as really acting as highpriest.

115. The Sanhedrin, and Jewish Sects.—During the closing period of the Jews' existence as a State, the Sanhedrin
(*Synedrium*), or Great Council of the Jews, was the chief
legislative body in both religious and political matters, having authority to decide on the most important questions in
the national life, and claiming also the right to pronounce
sentences of life and death. Our Saviour and the Apostles,
St. Stephen also and St. Paul, were all brought before this
tribunal, which was formed, on the lines laid down by Moses
(Exod. 18 : 25; Num. 11 : 16), of seventy of the chief priests,
elders and doctors of the law, and met under the presidency
of the high priest, generally in one of the side buildings of
the Temple, but occasionally in the high priest's house.

116. Mention is often made in the New Testament of
scribes, doctors and teachers of the law (γραμματαεῖς, νομικοί,
νομοδιδάσκαλοι); these persons were not connected with the
Temple worship in these capacities, but belonged for the most
part to the sect of the *Pharisees,* the upholders of the claims
and doctrines of orthodox Judaism. The name *Pharisee*
comes from *paraš,* to separate, and means "those set
apart", those who by their piety and wisdom are conspicuous
above the mass of the people. Their reputation was so great
that even the priests, who formed the hereditary aristocracy
of the nation, found it expedient to join this sect, in order
to retain their prestige, and the Council, or Synedrium, con-

sisted chiefly of Pharisees. They seem to have originated before the time of the Machabees, as they were already strong and influential under Jonathan Machabæus in 144 B.C. (Jos., *Ant.*, XIII, v, 9). Besides the Holy Scriptures they reverenced a particular tradition, which they ascribed to Moses, as the source of the Law; this developed later into the Talmud. The sect was at first worthy of high esteem, but it gradually degenerated, and at the time of our Lord the Pharisees appear as sanctimonious persons, full of uncharitableness, pride and avarice. There were, however, noble exceptions, such as Nicodemus (John 3) and Gamaliel (Acts 5:34). Inasmuch as they were the expounders and teachers of the Law, they received the honorable title of Rabbi = master (רַבִּי, from רַב, "much, great" = *magister*).

At the time of Christ there were two famous teachers with a numerous following, Shammai and Hillel. The former represented the strictest school of thought, especially with regard to divorce; the latter adhered to milder doctrines and practice.

117. In direct contrast to the stern Judaism of the Pharisees were the easy-going views of the party of the *Sadducees*, which had penetrated into Palestine from the west after the Greco-Persian wars. It is impossible not to recognize a connection between the Sadducees and the Epicurean philosophy. In origin and name this sect is generally derived from a certain Sadok, a disciple of Antigonus of Socho (died 264 B.C.). According to another account they called themselves Zaddikim = honest people. It is, however, most probable that they declared themselves to be Sadokides, *i.e.*, members of the high priest's party, for, from the time of David, the high priesthood remained hereditary in the family of Sadok. They accepted Holy Scripture, at least the Pentateuch, but no traditions. They believed in God, but not in angels; declared the soul to be material and mortal, and consequently rejected the doctrines of the resurrection of the body and of future rewards or punishments; moreover they denied the action of Divine Providence. This sect consisted chiefly of rich and powerful persons, for which reason it became influential in the Synedrium, and secured the high priesthood (Acts 23: 6), but it never won much esteem among the nation as a whole.

The *Essenes* are not mentioned in the Bible, but Josephus and Philo describe them as ascetics, who apparently had added to Judaism the tenets of heathen and especially of the Pythagorean philosophy. They formed a kind of religious order governed by definite rules and divided into four classes. They conceived of the Deity as the purest light, and the sun they regarded as His symbol. They honored Moses and his law; believed in the immortality of the soul; observed the Sabbath very strictly, but rejected the Jewish sacrificial worship. Their morality was based on love of God and man, and on self-control. For love of God they sought to lead pure lives and always to speak the truth; their love of man showed itself in good will, charitable deeds and community of property. They exercised self-control by despising wealth, honors and pleasures, and many refrained from marriage. They lived partly in settlements of their own near the Dead Sea, partly in the midst of other Jews in towns and villages, supporting themselves by the work of their hands or by agriculture. Their number did not exceed four thousand.

A fourth, and probably not numerous sect, was that of the *Herodians,* who are mentioned a few times in the New Testament. They were adherents of the Herodian royal family, and were therefore inclined to favor the Romans, and were hostile to the Jewish religion.

Art. 4: SACRED RITES AND LAWS

Texts: Lev. 1: 3-17; 3: 1-17; 7: 11-36; 14; Num. 9: 6-13; Lev. 15.

118. Ritual of Sacrifice.—The chief matter for sacrifice consisted of animals, oxen, sheep, goats, doves, since the shedding of blood has ever been associated with the expiation of guilt. In unbloody sacrifices, whether alone or in conjunction with some animal sacrifice, ears of grain, flour, bread, and incense were offered up, whilst wine and water were poured in libation about the altar. The sacrifices were divided into: (1) holocausts, in which the whole victim was consumed by fire; (2) peace offerings, in which some portions of the animal slain, after having been "waved" or "heaved" before the Lord, were consumed by the priests, and other portions eaten by the participants in a sacrificial feast; (3)

sin offerings, wherein the blood of the victim was carried into the Temple or Tabernacle, and its flesh burnt outside [42] the city or camp.

Whilst there were various distinguishing rites, animal sacrifices in general were performed after the following manner: the animal was brought into the Court of the Tabernacle or Temple (for it was forbidden, under pain of death, to offer sacrifices elsewhere). It was tied up to a ring fastened in the earth, and the person offering it laid his hands on its head. (This was omitted in the case of the Paschal lamb, and of pigeons.) The meaning of this ceremony was that the sin of the offerer passed over to the victim, that was to die in place of the sinful man. According to the Rabbis, a confession of sin accompanied the laying on of hands, the words being as follows:

"I have sinned, have acted amiss, have been rebellious, especially have I committed [43] . . . But I return to Thee full of repentance. May this [*i.e.,* the offering of the victim] be my expiation!"

Thus laden with the sin of the offerer, the victim was slain on the north side of the altar, generally by the person who offered it, but it might be done by the priest (II Par. 29:24). The priest caught the blood in a vessel, and, according to the kind of sacrifice intended, he sprinkled some of it either on the side of the altar, or on the horns, or on the altar of incense, or even towards the Kapporeth in the Holy of Holies. The rest of the blood was poured out on the ground near the altar of holocausts (Lev. 4:7). Then the victim was skinned and cut to pieces. Either all the flesh

[42] See on this subject Heb. 13:10–15, which is explained as follows: It was certainly no mere accident that Christ was crucified outside the city. He died as a sin offering. The Jews were forbidden to eat the flesh of the more important sin offerings; it had to be burnt outside the city. Therefore the author of this epistle calls upon the Jewish Christians thus: "Let us go forth to him without the camp, bearing his reproach"—let us separate ourselves from the Jews, let us share in His sacrifice, even if those who believe not despise.

[43] The confession of sins answers a need of human nature and has at all times appeared as accompanying true penance. Adam had to acknowledge his guilt and did so, but Cain refused (Gen. 3:11, 4:9). David says of himself, "Because I was silent my pain consumed me". He rightly perceived that sacrifice alone was not enough. *Si voluisses sacrificium, dedissem utique* (Ps. 50:18).

was laid upon the altar and burnt, or only some of the fat was consumed by the altar fire, and the rest of the flesh was cooked and eaten by the priests, or used by the offerer of the sacrifice for a sacrificial feast, or burnt outside the city or encampment.

When pigeons were offered, the priest killed them by breaking their necks, not by cutting off the heads (Lev. 1:15; 5:8).[44] Apparently a cut was then made in one place, and the blood was allowed to drip on the side of the altar. The wings were slightly torn and then the birds were thrown into the fire on the altar. Vegetable offerings were seldom made alone, but generally in conjunction with bloody sacrifices. The procedure was as follows: If the sacrifice belonged to the class of burnt offerings, the priest took only a small portion of the flour, cakes, etc., and burnt it with incense on the altar. The rest belonged to the priest, but had to be eaten unleavened in the court, after being prepared for food. If the offerer were himself a priest, the whole was burnt. If the sacrifice was a peace offering, one cake out of all that were brought was taken for the Lord and given to the priest; the rest was used by the offerer for a sacrificial feast.

119. Nazirites.—Every Israelite could consecrate himself exclusively to God, by vow, either for a definite period or for life. Persons bound by such a vow were called Nazirites, *i.e.*, "set apart" (נָזִיר from נָזַר to set apart). The obligations incurred by those thus consecrated were threefold: (1) they had to avoid all intoxicating drinks; (2) the hair of their head must be allowed to grow;[45] (3) they were forbidden to take any part in mourning for the dead.[46] If the vow was

---

[44] The Hebrew מָלַק means to break off; Septuagint, ἀποκνίζειν; Vulgate, *retorquere ad collum, ad pennulas*. It seems that the neck was not wrung, but violently bent backwards, so that the throat was separated inside from the body, remaining united to it only by the skin.

[45] According to I Cor. 11, long hair was a mark of a subordinate position and of dependence on another, hence it befitted women.

[46] Death suggests sin and is due to sin, but God is the Lord of Life, who will bestow eternal life on all that serve Him. Probably also some heathen superstitions were often connected with mourning for the dead, as a cultus of the dead was very common among the Gentiles, and whoever took part in it showed a tendency to heathenism.

temporary, it held good for thirty days, and when these expired the Nazirite had to make a threefold sacrifice: a sin offering, a burnt offering and a thank offering.[47] After making the thank offering, the Nazirite cut off the hair of his head and cast it into the fire on the altar. If a Nazirite broke his vow, by joining in lamentation for the dead, or in any other way, he had to offer two pigeons in reparation, and begin his time of consecration over again.

Nazirites were held in great respect. Saint John the Baptist and Saint James the Less, the Apostle, were Nazirites; even Saint Paul did not hesitate to become one for a time.

120. Marriage Laws.—God had originally instituted marriage as a monogamous union, but, after the Fall, even among the patriarchs, there were found men having one or more concubines besides their real wife. The Israelites as a rule had, however, mostly only one wife, for whom a sum of money was paid to her parents or relatives when the marriage took place; the practice of giving a dowry did not prevail. The position of women was not degraded, as with the Gentiles. Proverbs 31 shows how much liberty and independence a wise wife could enjoy in her household. There is no doubt that monogamous marriages were the rule.

If a married man died, leaving no son, his surviving brother was bound to marry the widow. This custom of levirate marriage exists also among some heathen nations. According to the Mosaic Law, the eldest son born of such a marriage took the dead man's name and was regarded as his legitimate son and heir. The object of this law was to secure as far as possible security of tenure and permanence to each family. If the brother-in-law were unwilling to comply with his obligation, the widow could summon him before a court of justice, and if he still refused, he had to put up with public reviling from the widow, but he was not forced to marry her (Gen. 38:8; Deut. 25:5; Matt. 22:24).

[47] A sin offering, because during the time of consecration some transgressions of the law might have occurred; a burnt offering, because the Nazirite wished to show especial honor to God; a thank offering, to express his gratitude for the successful completion of the period for which he had taken the vow.

As long as marriage was not a Sacrament, divorce could not altogether be forbidden. According to Deuteronomy 24: 1-4, it was permitted:

"If a man take a wife, and have her, and she find not favor in his eyes for some uncleanness, he shall write a bill of divorce, and shall give it in her hand, and send her out of his house. And when she is departed and marrieth another husband, and he also hateth her and hath given her a bill of divorce and hath sent her out of his house, or is dead, the former husband cannot take her again to wife".

The expression translated "some uncleanness" is in Hebrew *errath dabar,* literally "shame or disgrace of a thing", something arousing horror or disgust. The doctors of the law did not agree concerning the interpretation of this passage, and in Christ's time it was hotly discussed by the followers of Hillel and Shammai. The former thought that it meant any unpleasant fact, giving rise to dislike, such as want of skill in cooking on the woman's part. The latter believed that it referred only to indecencies and particularly to adultery. The first interpretation was the one commonly accepted, and the Saviour protested against this frivolous opinion when He declared adultery to be the sole ground for the dissolution of a marriage, and forbade re-marriage under His new law (Matt. 19: 3-12). Divorce must have been rare; there are very few allusions to it in the Old Testament, and the prophet Malachias (2:13) speaks very emphatically against it. The woman had not the same rights as the man, and therefore was not entitled to claim a divorce for herself.

Adultery, *i.e.,* intercourse with another man's wife or betrothed, was punished with death; both parties were stoned (Lev. 20:10; Deut. 22:22-24; John 8:5). This penalty was of course inflicted only if the case were brought before a judge. A husband might, in secret instances, adopt the line of action proposed by Joseph, "the just man", and put away his wife privately.

121. Circumcision.—Circumcision was imposed upon Abraham and his descendants, the Hebrew race, by God (Gen. 17) as an individual mark and reminder of their being the Chosen People. This obligation was binding not only upon all male descendants of Abraham, but also upon their slaves, as quasi-members of the community or family.

Circumcision was a painful operation, consisting in the removal of the foreskin by means of a sharp knife. Originally stone knives were used for the purpose (Exod. 4:25), but later on iron ones. As a rule this ceremony of purification was performed by the head of the household.

Precise instructions as to the manner of fulfilling the divine command are not given in the law. Some details have, however, come down to us by tradition, which was always an adjunct to the written law. The most important are as follows:

1. Any one can circumcise, but it is to be done by women only if no man is present.

2. A Gentile is not permitted to circumcise a descendant of Abraham, and such circumcision by a Gentile is invalid.

3. If an already circumcised Gentile embraces Judaism, a wound is made at the place of circumcision in order to bring out the blood of the Covenant.

4. A sick child or a proselyte is not circumcised until he has recovered his health. If a child dies before he is eight days old, circumcision is still performed on the dead body.

5. Circumcision is permissible even on the Sabbath (John 7:23).

The later Israelites generally performed circumcision in the synagogue, and united the naming of the child with it.

122. Proselytes.—In every age, but especially after the Captivity, members of other races, "strangers in the land", lived among the Israelites. They were called *gerim* = those added. Although every Gentile was regarded by the Israelites as unclean, these strangers were tolerated by the Mosaic law, but they had to pledge themselves to conform to some extent to the worship of the true God. According to tradition, they were especially bound to observe the seven Noachic commandments; *i.e.*, they had to refrain from (1) blaspheming the true God; (2) worshiping the heavenly bodies and false gods; (3) murder; (4) incest, *i.e.*, marriage with very near relatives; (5) robbery; (6) rebellion against authority; (7) eating blood and flesh containing blood.[48]

[48] These rules of late Jewish origin plainly received their name Noachic from the instructions given by God to Noe (Gen. 9:3), relating

If these strangers desired to attain to the full rights of Israel, they had to seek admission to the Mosaic Covenant by submitting to circumcision, and thereby pledge themselves to observe the whole Jewish law.

At the time of Christ (according to the Mishna and Gemara), the Proselytes of the Gate were distinguished from the Proselytes of Righteousness or of the Covenant. The former lived indeed within the gates of Jewish towns, but were only tolerated, the latter had acquired civil rights, observed all the precepts of the law, and were completely on a level with the Israelites. Sacrifice and baptism were required in their case, as well as circumcision.[49] This baptism is nowhere mentioned in Holy Scripture and seems to be a further development of the bath that preceded the performance of religious ceremonies. The whole ceremony expresses a desire for purification from sin and to be born again to a new life.

123. Music and Singing.—David was the chief musician among the Hebrews; he played the harp so beautifully that he was able to banish Saul's melancholy by means of it. He introduced music and singing into the sanctuary; 4000 Levites, with Asaph, Heman and Idithun at their head, had to supply it (I Par. 23:5; 25). Solomon and his successors maintained the music, but gradually the interest in it diminished, and Ezechias and Josias had to make new arrangements. During the Captivity it was no longer a joy to practice sacred music (Ps. 136), but it was not completely forgotten, for among those who returned home were 200 singers (I Esdras 2:65). Their piety caused David's music to be revived (I Esdras 3:10; II Esdras 12:27), and thenceforth, as long as the Temple existed, it was always kept up with joy.

The chief part of the music seems always to have been singing; instruments served only to support it; *i.e.,* to supply a prelude and an accompaniment, to make a transition from

to the killing of beasts and the eating of blood. That these particular rules have come down from Noe can not be proved.

[49] The baptism was complete immersion in running water in token of their new birth.

one key to another, and to fill up pauses when the singers rested. It is doubtful whether the Hebrews had melodies, strictly so called. It might be assumed that the singing resembled that somewhat high-pitched kind of recitative that is still heard in the synagogues when the Scriptures are read. This monotonous declamation could hardly, however, be called singing. The headings of the Psalms, too, show that different modes of singing were in use; for instance, in the Masoretic text the heading of the 8th Psalm is "according to the Gathitic tune", and that of the 21st Psalm is that it must be sung to "the hind of the dawn", *i.e.*, to the tune of a well-known song. It seems probable, therefore, that the songs possessed melody, but harmony was absent, *i.e.*, the union of high and deep voices singing together. Musical notation was unknown.[50]

The musical instruments mentioned in the Bible may be divided into stringed and wind instruments and instruments of percussion.[51]

(a) *Stringed Instruments.* Those in use among the Israelites were known as the *kinnor* and the *nebel*. The *kinnor* by its very name suggests a harp, lyre or guitar. It had six strings. The *nebel* was like the *kinnor*, but larger, with 10 or 12 strings. As *nebel* means skin, the sounding-board was probably uneven, or twisted. The instruments called in Daniel 3:5, etc., the *sabbeka* (סַבְּכָא, σαμβύκη) and *pesanter* (פְּסַנְתֵּרִין, ψαλτήριον) were something like the harp. They were used in Babylon.

(b) *Wind Instruments:* the bagpipe, or *ugab* (עוּגָב); the flute, *halil* (חָלִיל), made of reed or wood; the trumpet, *hazozera* (חֲצֹצְרָה), and the trombone, *šophar* (שׁוֹפָר); according to Josephus, the trumpet was a straight, thin tube of metal, about a cubit in length, with a bell-shaped mouthpiece. It is represented on the Arch of Titus. The trombone or horn (קֶרֶן) was probably originally an ox or a ram's horn, and was afterwards made of metal in the same shape.

[50] Dancing often accompanied the music, even at religious ceremonies. Even King David danced before the ark (II Kings 6:14). The two sexes never danced together except at the sacrifices to false gods.
[51] Bow instruments seem not to have been known.

(c) *Percussion Instruments:* the tambourine (תֹף, τύμπανον), a ring of wood or metal, with a skin stretched over it and bells attached to it;[52] cymbals (צְלְצְלִים)[53] two concave pieces of metal, giving a clear note when struck together; the *sistrum* (מְנַעְנְעִים)[54] an oval ring of metal, across which were four metal rods loosely attached to it; the instrument had a handle, by which it was shaken and swung; the triangle (שָׁלִישִׁים), made of steel, and attached to a string, by which it was held; it was struck with a little metal rod.

124. Legal Defilements.—In the Law of Moses certain natural conditions are said to constitute uncleanness in persons who have made a covenant with God, and directions are given for removing this defilement. The reason is that these conditions are due to sin and bear a resemblance to it. They fall into three classes: the defilement of death, the uncleanness of leprosy, and sexual uncleanness.

(1) A human corpse defiled the tent or house in which it lay, all open vessels in that house, and the people living in it or entering it, for the space of seven days. (2) In the same way contact with a corpse or bones or a grave made a man unclean for seven days. (3) The defilement of death was contagious, for every person and thing touched by the unclean person became unclean until the evening. (4) The dead body of an animal caused any one who touched it to be unclean until the evening.

For the removal of this uncleanness, persons and things had to be sprinkled, on the third and seventh days after contracting it, with water of purification specially prepared (from the red cow). Human beings were required, moreover, to take a bath on the seventh day, and to wash their clothes. For those who were unclean until the evening, including the man who performed the ceremony of sprinkling with the water of purification, and any one else who accidentally touched this water, it sufficed to take a bath and to wash their garments.

[52] It was held in the left hand and shaken in time, whilst the right hand struck the skin, perhaps with a little stick.

[53] In I Esdras. 3: 10, cymbals are called מְצִלְתַּיִם.

[54] Gk. σεῖστρον, Lat. *sistrum,* a sort of gong, used in Egypt chiefly in honor of Isis.

Leprosy rendered every person attacked by the disease unclean. If any one was suffering from a suspicious eruption, he had to show himself to a priest, and if the latter recognized his disease as true leprosy (according to the rules laid down in Lev. 13) and declared it to be such, he was bound forthwith to exclude the unhappy man from all intercourse with healthy people. The leper had to rend his garments (*i.e.*, tear them down a short distance over his breast), uncover his head, muffle up his chin, and cry to every one meeting him: ''Unclean, unclean!'' His dwelling could only be outside the camp or outside any inhabited place. It very rarely happened that any one recovered from leprosy; but when this occurred, he had again to allow himself to be examined by a priest, and if the latter judged him to be really free from the disease, the prescribed ceremonies had to be performed for his purification, and offerings made.

Besides human leprosy, the Mosaic law recognized a leprosy affecting houses and clothes (Lev. 14:33 *ss*. 13: 47 *ss*.).

(1) *Vir, qui patitur fluxum seminis, immundus erit.* A chronic morbid condition is meant. The uncleanness connected with it extended to the persons, furniture and utensils touched by the sick man. Persons so touched were unclean until the evening, and were obliged to wash their clothes and to bathe. Earthen utensils must be broken, wooden ones washed with water. For the ceremony of purification after recovery two pigeons were required as burnt and sin offerings (Lev. 15:2-15).

(2) *Coitus viri cum uxore ambo immundos reddit usque ad vesperam, ac se et vestimenta aqua lavabunt* (Lev. 15: 16-18).

(3) *Homo qui nocturno pollutus sit somnio, egredietur extra castra et non revertetur priusquam ad vesperam lavetur aqua* (Deut. 23:10, 11).

(4) A flow of blood in women caused uncleanness, as long as it lasted. When it was over, the woman had to present two pigeons as burnt and sin offerings (Lev. 15:25).

(5) Menstruation made a woman unclean for seven days.

Persons and things that she touched were unclean until the evening, and required purification in the way described. On the seventh day she had to bathe (Lev. 15:19).

(6) After childbirth (Lev. 12:6-8) a woman was unclean,—for seven days after the birth of a son, and for fourteen days after that of a daughter. Moreover, in the former case she had to remain at home for thirty-three days, and in the latter for sixty-six; *i.e.*, any considerable walks, and especially visits to the sanctuary, were forbidden. When the time of purification expired she had to present a lamb as a burnt offering and a pigeon as a sin offering. If she were poor, two pigeons sufficed.

The regulations regarding legal defilements had the same religious and symbolic basis as those in regard to choice of foods (Lev. 11; Deut. 14). Corruption, whether it make its appearance at the end of life, in sickness, or in sex activities, is symbolically related to sin, and calls to mind separation from God, who is true and ordered life. Now, Israel was the specially Chosen People. Hence its members were ever to appear in a condition of cleanliness conforming to its calling to holiness. These regulations, moreover, confessed a general inherited condition of natural unworthiness in regard to things divine on the part of man. They were a tacit acknowledgment of original sin. Similar practices have been and are in vogue in the higher systems of heathenism, as amongst the Hindus and Parsees.

Art. 5: CALENDAR AND FEASTS

Texts: Exod. 12; Lev. 23 and 25; Deut. 16:13.

125. Hebrew Year.—For their chronology the Jews used a solar year, but within the year itself the arrangement of time seems to have been governed rather by lunar months. The day was reckoned from sunset to sunset, perhaps because it is only after the sun has gone down that the crescent moon shows itself in the sky. (This division of time has been adopted by the Church, as festivals and days begin with first vespers and end with second vespers.) The natural day, the period of daylight, was divided at first only into morning, noon and evening; but later into twelve hours, which were

longer in summer than in winter. The night was divided
into three (Jud. 7:19), and afterwards into four watches,
called evening, midnight, cock-crow and morning.[55] The
week, a quarter of a lunar month, was based on the story of
Creation, as God created the world in six days and rested
on the seventh day. With the exception of the seventh, the
days had no particular names, they were called simply the
first, second, etc. The seventh was the Sabbath = rest.

The month (= moon) corresponds to the duration of
the moon's circuit round the earth. It lasted 29 or 30 days.[56]
According to the Talmud, whoever in or near Jerusalem
caught sight of the new moon was bound to notify the fact
to the priests in the Temple, who then declared the previous
month with its 29 days to be ended, and the 30th day to be
the first of the new month. If the sky was too cloudy for
the new moon to be seen, the month was ended with the 30th
day, and the following day was regarded as that of the new
moon. In very early times no special names were given to
the months, with the exception of the first, which was called
Abib (ear of corn), but during the Captivity the Babylonian
names came into use and are still retained by the Jews.
These names, the meaning of which is quite obscure, are as
follows: (1) *Nisan,* the spring month—the Pasch was kept
on the 14th of *Nisan;* (2) *Iyjar;* (3) *Sivan,*—Pentecost fell
on the 6th day of this month; (4) *Tammuts;* (5) *Ab;* (6)
Elul; (7) *Tišri,*—on the 1st fell the civil New Year's festival, on the 10th the Day of Atonement, on the 15th the
Feast of Tabernacles; (8) *Marĥešwan;* (9) *Kislew*—the
Feast of the Dedication of the Temple, that occurred in
winter, was celebrated on the 25th (John 10:22); (10)
Tebeth; (11) *Šebat;* (12) *Adar;* sometimes there was a thir-
teenth intercalary month, called *Veadar.*

As the Pasch had always to be celebrated at the beginning of
harvest (about April 1st), and Pentecost at the end of it, the lunar

---

[55] ὀψέ, μεσνύκτιον, ἀλεκτοροφωνία, πρωΐ (Mark 6:48; 13:35).

[56] Astronomically a lunar month consists of 29 days, 12 hours, 44
minutes and 3 seconds. For want of astronomical knowledge it was impossible to determine this precisely, and people had to reckon from the
moment when the new moon became visible.

year of 364 days had to be reconciled with the solar year of 365 days, as otherwise the festivals would have been celebrated at the wrong seasons. For this reason about every three years an inter-calary month was inserted. The beginning of the year was prob-ably reckoned thus: Towards the end of the 12th month *Adar,* the cornfields were surveyed to see if the barley would be ripe by the middle of the following month, so that the harvest could be begun with the ceremony of offering the first sheaf at the Pasch. If the corn seemed likely to be ripe, the new year began with the next month, but if not, the old year was lengthened by the month *Veadar.* After the Captivity, the decision whether the month should be inserted or not rested with the Synedrium, and the rule was observed that in the Sabbatical year there should never be 13 months.

The new year was originally reckoned as beginning in the spring, but after the Captivity it became the custom to begin the civil year with the first day of *Tišri,* in the autumn, whilst the religious year always began with the first day of *Nisan,* in the spring. For an agricultural people the be-ginning of seed-time seems the most appropriate date for the beginning of the year.[57]

126. The Sabbath.—Keeping certain days sacred to the Divinity was not peculiar to the Israelites. Already the Assyrians and Babylonians distinguished the 7th, 14th, 21st, and 28th days from the other days of the month, but with them they were rather days of penance and atonement. Among the Greeks and Romans all remembrance of the ob-servance of a day of rest seems to have died out, and they often ridiculed the Jews as idlers.[58] The institution of the Sabbath did not originate in the Mosaic law, as many people assume, but is to be referred to the history of creation. The hallowing of the seventh day was therefore no new thing imposed upon the Israelites on Sinai, but it had been almost forgotten, and consequently they are ordered to "Remember to keep holy the Sabbath day" (Exod. 20:8; see Exod. 12: 16, 16:22).

[57] The Jewish era, reckoning from the creation of man, only came into general use about the fifteenth century of the Christian era. The Jews say that 1656 years elapsed between the creation and the Deluge, and 3828 years between the creation and the destruction of Jerusalem by the Romans. According to them, the birth of Christ took place in the year 3760.

[58] Juvenal, *Sat.,* XIV, 105; Sen., in Aug., *De civ. Dei,* VI, 11.

The whole nation was required to rest from sunset of the sixth day to sunset of the seventh. According to tradition, the beginning and the end of the Sabbath [59] were made known by trumpet-blasts in every town in the country.

The observance of the seventh day had both a negative and a positive side; the former consisted in refraining from work, the latter in particular devotion to God and His law.

The law does not contain precise instructions regarding the kinds of work forbidden, but the general sense of the ordinance is quite clear from certain passages. In Exod. 35:3, it is forbidden to light a fire for the purpose of cooking.[60] In Num. 15:32, picking up sticks on the Sabbath was severely punished.[61] It seems, therefore, that every kind of bodily work, even the most trivial, must cease. Therefore the Jews believed all traveling and trading on the Sabbath to be prohibited.

All that the law enacts with regard to walking is that every man is to stay at home and not go forth out of his place (Exod. 16:29). The doctors of the law fixed two thousand cubits, about a quarter of an hour's walk, as the farthest point to which a man might go. In Acts 1:12 the distance of the Mount of Olives from Jerusalem is defined as a Sabbath day's journey. Even at the present day the Sabbath day's journey is marked out in Jewish communities by means of a string or wire. The Jews refused also to bear arms on the Sabbath, often to their own great disadvantage. But in later times they were less strict, and sometimes they availed themselves of the law regarding the Sabbath to practice some stratagem of war.

How rigorously the Pharisees observed the day of rest is seen in the New Testament. The Mishna, which contains a special treatise on Sabbath observances, names thirty-nine chief kinds of work (*aboth melakoth = patres operum*), each

---

[59] שַׁבָּת is an emphatic form of שָׁבַת, to rest. It designates a particular kind of quiet and rest.

[60] Food for the Sabbath was cooked on the preceding day; and lights were kindled before sunset on Friday evening.

[61] The offender had to be put to death. It seems likely, however, that he did not merely collect wood, but, in order to obtain it, either cut down a tree or exerted himself to break down bushes. This at least is the interpretation of the Samaritan Targum.

with many subsidiary occupations (*toledoth = generationes*), which were all prohibited on the Sabbath.[62]

The law contains no definite regulations for the positive observance of the Sabbath. In general, the Israelites regarded it as a duty to employ themselves reverently with God and His law. The daily sacrifice in the Temple was doubled [63] and fresh loaves of proposition (showbread) were provided. Prayers were held in the synagogues, and passages of the law and the prophets were read aloud and expounded. The Sabbath was regarded as a day of rejoicing (Is. 58:13; Judith 8:6; Luke 14:1). Cheerful meals were held in the houses, as far as this was possible without cooking on the day itself, and people wore their best garments.

127. New Moons.—The Hebrews kept each new moon as a religious festival. As the date could not be precisely fixed by means of astronomy, it was necessary to choose the day after the first appearance of the new moon; on the day when the moon changes it cannot be seen, owing to the proximity of the sun. In the Temple this day was celebrated by special sacrifices of several animals with the corresponding meat and drink offerings, in addition to the usual sacrifices (Num. 28:11). To increase the solemnity, trumpets were blown (Num. 10:10). The day was observed as a Sabbath, although this was not absolutely prescribed, and feasts took place. The new moon of the seventh month (1st of *Tišri*) received particular honor, like the seventh day of the week; it was called the day of the blowing of trumpets; and on it an extra sacrifice was offered, over and above those usually offered at the new moons (Num. 20:2). As after the Captivity the civil year began with the seventh new moon, this day is also called New Year's day.

The custom of honoring the new moons has been altogether lost under the new Covenant, perhaps because the Sun of Righteousness has arisen, and so the faint moonlight of the Old Covenant is bound to disappear. The change seems to rest upon instructions

[62] To carry the smallest burden, even a piece of broken crockery, or a needle or a false tooth, was enough to violate the commandment.

[63] "On the sabbath day you shall offer two lambs of a year old without blemish, and two tenths of flour" (Num. 28:9).

given by the Apostles. Just like the observance of the first instead of the last day of the week, the abolition of the new moon ceremonies marks the freedom of Christians from the Jewish law. St. Paul writes to this effect in Galatians 4: 10 and Colossians 2: 16, etc.

128. Sabbatical Year.—As men and beasts, after six days of work, had to dedicate the seventh to God and spend it in rest, so, after each six years of cultivation and fruit-bearing, the whole country was ordered to keep a year's Sabbath in God's honor, and to rest. During this seventh year no field might be cultivated or sown, no garden and no fruit tree might receive attention. Whatever grew without any action on the part of mankind was common property, belonging to all without distinction.

The Sabbatical year always began in the autumn, when the usual sowing did not take place.

As during the Sabbatical year no profit could be derived from the soil, it necessarily followed that no creditor could forcibly demand payment of debts during it. In the same way no taxes could be claimed by the government. According to Josephus,[64] even the pagan rulers of Palestine always remitted the taxes of the Jews in the Sabbatical year.

The Mosaic law (Deut. 31: 10-14) required that the law should be solemnly read aloud to the whole people by the Levites in the sanctuary on the Feast of Tabernacles in this year.

It is a mistake to suppose: (1) That as soon as the Sabbatical year began every debtor was absolutely released from payment, so that his creditor had thenceforth no claim upon him. The law states (Deut. 15: 2) only that in this year the creditor shall not raise his hand, nor oppress his neighbor therewith, *i.e.*, in this year he is not recklessly to claim his due, as his debtor can have no income. (2) That Hebrew slaves always obtained their freedom in the Sabbatical year. The law orders (Exod. 21: 2; Deut. 15: 12) them to be emancipated in the seventh year, *i.e.* not necessarily in the Sabbatical year, but in the seventh year of their service. Although slavery existed in Israel as well as in the rest of the ancient world, it was of a far milder type than among the heathen.

129. Jubilee Year.—After seven times seven years there followed one year (no doubt beginning in the autumn) of

[64] *Ant.*, XIV, x, 6.

particular rejoicing. This was called the Jubilee, *šenath hayobel*, because on the 10th of the month *Tišri*, on the Day of Atonement of the seventh Sabbatical year, it was proclaimed throughout the country with the sound of trumpets.

In this year the whole land rested, as in the Sabbatical year, and might not be cultivated. Thus in two successive years there was no agriculture, but the fertility of the soil was so great that provision could be made, and there was no reason to fear a famine. The rest affected only agriculture; cattle breeding and other business went on as usual.

In the year of jubilee all persons, who for any reason had been reduced to slavery, were set at liberty, if one of their relatives had not previously purchased their freedom. When a man was set free, all the members of his family acquired their freedom.[65]

All landed property that had passed into the possession of strangers reverted in the year of jubilee to the original owner or his descendants, without payment. This contributed greatly to the prevention of oppression and destitution among the people.

130. The Passover or Pasch.—The first and most important festival in the year was always the Pasch (Exod. 12),[66] celebrated on the 14th of *Nisan*. The feast itself and the seven days following it commemorated the delivery of the Israelites from Egypt. On the 10th day of the first month a male lamb, free from blemish, and one year old, was set aside for each family. On the 14th, about sunset (Deut. 16: 6),[67] the head of the household killed it. If any

---

[65] This applied only to the slaves who were Israelites, not to those who were Gentiles. The latter could be bequeathed by a man to his descendants (Lev. 25: 46). The law disapproved of the enslavement of people of the same race (Lev. 25: 42; John 8: 33).

[66] פַּסְחָא is the Aramaic name; the Hebrew is פֶּסַח; both signify "passing over, sparing".

[67] Exod. 12: 6, "between the two evenings". Various explanations are given of this expression; it probably means that the killing was to take place just at sunset. Before the sun went down, the evening belonged to the 14th, after sunset, to the 15th of *Nisan*. Each evening was divided into two parts, one belonging to the preceding, and the other to the following day. The modern Samaritans sacrifice on Mount Garizim, as soon as the sun has set.

family was too small to eat a whole lamb, two families might unite for the purpose. A bundle of hyssop was dipped into the blood as it streamed out, and some was smeared on the two doorposts and on the lintel of the house. No bone of the animal might be broken, nor was it cut up, but, after the skin and the entrails had been removed, it was roasted whole at the fire. When it was cooked through, it had to be eaten the same night, with unleavened bread and bitter herbs.[68] All the household took part in the meal; only the uncircumcised were excluded. As the ceremony commemorated the flight from Egypt, all present had to have their loins girt, shoes on their feet, and a staff in their hand.[69] It was incumbent on the head of the house to explain why the feast was held. What could not be consumed had to be burnt on the following morning.

When settled conditions prevailed in Palestine a change was made in the ceremony, and all full-grown males were required to attend in the sanctuary. The Paschal lambs were no longer sacrificed in each house, but were killed and eaten near the Tabernacle or Temple. Some of the blood was sprinkled on the altar and the fatty parts were burnt. Pilgrims visiting Jerusalem at the time of the festival received the necessary accommodation gratis from the inhabitants, but it was usual to present the hosts with the lambs' skins. As the number of strangers was very great, many spent the nights in the open air, and ate the lamb in tents.

The Pasch, like all the Old Covenant, though in a special degree, had a symbolical meaning. It represents the sacrifice of Christ, the true Paschal lamb, not one of whose bones was broken on the Cross, and whose blood brings forgiveness to mankind. His death and the sacrifice of the Holy Eucharist obtained thereby are means of salvation for all men. For this reason every one was sentenced to death who took no part in the celebration of the Pasch.

According to the Mishna (*Pesach* 10), the Paschal rites were performed as follows: In commemoration of God's promise in Exodus 6:6: "I am the Lord, who will bring you out from the

---

[68] *Merorim.* Apparently these might not be selected at will, but the wild lettuce is meant; for the Septuagint has πικρίδες, and the Vulgate *lactuca agrestis.*

[69] It was not until the institution of the Eucharist that Saint John leaned on our Lord's breast (John 13:25).

work-prison of the Egyptians, and will deliver you from bondage and redeem you with a high arm . . . and I will take you to myself for my people"—four cups of wine were brought in. After the first cup the roasted lamb with the unleavened bread and bitter herbs was carried in, whilst the 112th and 113th Psalms were sung (in the Heb., 113 and 114). The second cup of wine was now handed round. Then the son asked the father the meaning and significance of the Paschal ceremony (Exod. 12:26) and the father explained fully that it was held in remembrance of the delivery from Egypt and the sparing of the firstborn among the Israelites. The unleavened bread was next distributed and then the third cup, the "cup of blessing", was handed round; it was so called because meantime the blessing was pronounced over the food, which was now eaten. After the feast the fourth cup of wine was passed round, and at the close the 114th to 117th Psalms were sung. A fifth cup might be added; if so, Psalms 119 to 136 had to be sung.

Our Saviour appears to have instituted the Holy Eucharist after the fourth cup of wine, so that He made the optional fifth cup the "cup of blessing" of the New Covenant (I Cor. 10:6), *i.e.* the chalice of His Blood. Also the washing of the feet, which was the preparation for the Holy Eucharist, can not have taken place until after the fourth cup had been drunk, for St. John says (13:2): "When supper was done . . . he riseth from supper [ἐκ τοῦ δείπνου] and . . . girded himself", etc. In the same way St. Paul says (I Cor. 11:25) μετὰ τὸ δειπνῆσαι= *postquam cenavit.* The Paschal feast was therefore at an end; then followed the washing of the feet and the feast of the New Covenant, and that was concluded with singing psalms (Matt. 26:30).

The Paschal supper was not the whole of the festival, which lasted for an entire week. Connected with the Pasch was the seven days' feast of unleavened bread (*ḥag ḥammazzoth*) from the 15th to the 21st of *Nisan.* On the 15th and 21st people refrained from work and assembled in the sanctuary; the other days might be spent in work, provided the weekly Sabbath did not fall upon one of them.

"The first day shall be most solemn unto you and holy, you shall do no servile work therein, but you shall offer sacrifice in fire to the Lord seven days. And the seventh day shall be more solemn and more holy, and you shall do no servile work therein" (Lev. 23:7, 8). See Numbers 28:18. As only "servile work" is expressly forbidden, we may infer that these days were not required to be kept as Sabbaths. For this reason the bodies of Christ and the two thieves could be taken down from the crosses on this day (John 19:31).

On each of the seven days a special sacrifice was offered after the usual daily sacrifice (Num. 28:19-23). Only un-

leavened bread might be eaten during the whole period, and
after midday on the 14th no leaven might remain in the
houses. The festival was regarded as the beginning of the
harvest. Therefore on the 16th of *Nisan*, the second day,[70]
the beginning of the harvest was marked by the offering of
a sheaf of barley.[71] Before this offering was made, none of
the new harvest might be used.

131. Pentecost.—From the 16th of *Nisan*, on which the
harvest was opened by the offering of the first sheaf, seven
full weeks were reckoned, and another festival observed on
the 50th day. This was Pentecost, so called because it fell
on the 50th day ($\pi\epsilon\nu\tau\eta\kappa o\sigma\tau\acute{\eta}$ *sc.* $\acute{\eta}\mu\acute{\epsilon}\rho a$) after the beginning
of harvest. It was also called the Feast of Weeks (Exod.
34: 22; Deut. 16: 9), because seven weeks had to pass before
it might be celebrated. Another name was the Feast of the
Harvest (Exod. 23: 16), because as the harvest was then
over, it was regarded as a thanksgiving festival. In Numbers 28: 26 it is called the Feast of First Fruits, because two
loaves were then offered as the first bread baked from the
new harvest.

On this day: (*a*) all adult males were required to appear
in the sanctuary (Exod. 23: 16), and they were expected
to bring with them free-will offerings according to the abundance of the harvest. In later times this festival was largely
attended by foreign Jews, because it occurred at the most
favorable season (Acts 2: 9-11). (*b*) All work, except cooking, had to cease. (*c*) After the ordinary morning sacrifice,
there was another special offering of several beasts with the
accompanying meat and drink offerings (Num. 28: 26, etc.).
(*d*) Two loaves of wheaten flour were offered as the first
fruits of the harvest now just gathered in. These loaves

[70] Leviticus 23: 11, *mimmahorath haššabbat* = *altero die sabbati.*
The 15th was the first and chief day of the festival, on which people
refrained from all heavy work. Knobel and Hitzig regard the 15th as
the beginning of harvest.

[71] The law does not specify what kind of grain is to be offered, nor
does the Mishna; but there can be no doubt that barley was meant, as it
was the first to ripen. According to the Mishna it was not the sheaf
itself that was offered, but flour hastily ground from it, and of this an
ascara was placed on the altar.

were leavened, hence they might not be burnt on the altar, but were only "waved" and then eaten by the priests. Two lambs were sacrificed as a thank offering. The feast lasted, according to the law, only one day, but modern Jews have added another day.

In Holy Scripture this feast appears only as a harvest festival; but it can not be accidental that it coincides exactly with the season when the law was given on Sinai. We are therefore forced to assume that Pentecost had a double significance: it was the harvest thanksgiving, but it was at the same time a commemoration of the giving of the law, and Jewish and Christian tradition both lay more stress on the latter than on the former significance.

132. The Day of Atonement.—Each year on the 10th of *Tišri* (in September), Israel celebrated the Day of Atonement,[72] renewing a national reconciliation with Yahweh. All work was forbidden on this day, and the whole nation was required to fast, taking no food at all, from the evening of the 9th to the evening of the 10th of *Tišri*.

This was the day when the highpriest performed his chief functions. He was obliged to watch during the whole preceding night, so as not to become unclean according to the law. In the morning he bathed, and put on the simple white dress of a priest, distinguished from that of ordinary priests only by having a plain white girdle instead of a colored one (Lev. 14:4). In this attire, without the distinctive ornaments of his rank, he appeared as a penitent. For himself and his house, *i.e.*, for the entire priesthood, he brought a young bullock as a sin offering and a ram as a burnt offering; and from the people he received two he-goats, one to be a sin offering, the other to be turned loose into the desert, and also a ram to be a burnt offering. With these five beasts expiation was to be made for priests and people.

After the ordinary morning sacrifice, the ceremonial peculiar to the day began, and the highpriest, standing in the

---

[72] *Yom hakkippurim;* in the Mishna "the Great Day" or simply "the Day". The passages of the law relating to it are Lev. 16: 1–34, 23: 26–32; Num. 29: 7–11. Josephus refers to it (*Ant.*, III, x, 3).

Court of the Temple, before the sanctuary, cast lots for the two goats, to decide which should be dedicated to Yahweh and which to Asasel. The one on whom the lot fell "for the Lord" was destined to be slain as a sin offering; the other who received the lot "for Asasel" was to be forever removed from the abode of Israel.

The meaning of the name *Asasel* is uncertain; probably it signifies the chief devil. The name is an intensive form of *'asal* or *'asal*, to separate, connected with the Arabic *'azal*. The full form should be Asalsel; in the same way Babel is a shortened form of *Balbel*, and Golgotha of *Golgoltha*. The word denotes the wicked one, who, cut off from others, lives apart. The Arabs still believe that the desert is the devil's abode. See also Luke 11:24, where our Saviour speaks of the unclean spirit as being in the wilderness.

After casting these lots, the high priest made a confession of sins and then slew the bullock for himself and all the priests. He next took the censer, filled it with coals from the altar, and taking incense with him, passed through the Holy Place into the Holy of Holies, where he strewed the incense on the coals immediately, so that the cloud of smoke might rise up between him and the Lord, and he might not die. Then he came out again and, taking with him the bullock's blood, he re-entered the Holy of Holies, and with his finger sprinkled the blood once on the front of the *Kapporeth,* and seven times on the ground in front of the ark of the covenant. Then, coming out, he sacrificed in the Court the goat destined for Yahweh, as a sin offering on behalf of the people. He used its blood in the same way, going again into the Holy of Holies. By means of these sprinklings with blood, the Holy and Most Holy Places were purified from the defilements that the priests might have caused in the course of the year. The high priest now returned to the Court, and smeared the horns of the altar of holocausts with the mingled blood of the bullock and the goat, and sprinkled the blood seven times on the ground beside the altar. Thus both the altar and the Court were purified.

The high priest next proceeded to set the living goat, destined for Asasel, before him in the Court. He laid both his hands upon its head and pronounced a solemn confession of sin in the name of the people. A man stood ready to drive away the goat thus laden with sins into the desert, that it might die or be lost there. All the sins of Israel were believed to vanish with it.[73] The high priest returned to the sanctuary, took off the garments he had worn hitherto, bathed somewhere in the neighborhood, and put on all the attire belonging to his office. Then he went back to the Court, and offered the two rams, that still remained, as holocausts, one for himself and the priesthood, the other for the people. The flesh of the two sin offerings (the bullock and one goat) was carried, after the fat had been burnt on the altar, outside the camp or town, and was there destroyed by fire. Those who performed this duty, as well as the man who had taken the living goat into the wilderness, were required to wash their garments and to bathe before returning.

The ceremony called *Taschlich,* observed by the Jews in various countries, still contains a reminiscence of the Day of Atonement. Wherever the Jews live near running water (as, for instance, in Vienna), they are in the habit of praying beside it for forgiveness of sins, and after the prayer they throw a handkerchief into the water, or they put their hands into their pockets, as if to take out something which they then pretend to throw into the water. The sins of the preceding year are supposed to be carried away by the stream.

133. Feast of Tabernacles.—The Day of Atonement was penitential in character, but the Feast of Tabernacles (*hag hassukkoth*), celebrated five days later, was a joyful festival. It marked the completion of the gathering in of all the fruits, and lasted from the 15th to the 21st of *Tišri,* occurring thus exactly six months after the Pasch. Sabbath rest was observed on the first and eighth days, *i.e.,* the 15th and 22nd of *Tišri,* the latter being added to close the festival, but not being reckoned as actually part of it; the other days were not ordered to be kept as Sabbaths. All adult males again appeared in the sanctuary, and on each day solemn sacrifices were offered. On the first day booths of green boughs of trees were erected in the streets and open spaces, and also

---

[73] The man received instructions to throw the goat down somewhere if possible, that it might be sure to perish.

on the roofs and in the courtyards of the houses; and these
were occupied by the people throughout the festival, though
probably only occasionally. This custom commemorated the
dwelling of the ancient Israelites in tents after their departure from Egypt.

According to the Mishna (*Succah* III, 1, etc.) those participating
in the festival carried in their hands branches of citrons and palms.
Moreover a solemn libation of water was made each day. At the
time of the morning sacrifice a priest fetched water from the spring
of Siloë in a golden jug, and poured it and wine together into two
bowls or pipes near the altar. Music and singing accompanied this
ceremony. In the evening the court of the women was illuminated
in honor of the feast. It seems that our Saviour referred to these
customs when He said (John 7 and 8): "If any man thirst, let
him come to me", and "I am the light of the world". It is probable
that the libation of water had reference to the water from the rock,
and the illumination to the pillar of fire in the wilderness.

134. Festivals Instituted after the Captivity.—After the
return of the Jews from their Babylonian exile, several feasts
were added to those prescribed by the Mosaic law, and some
of those then introduced are still observed. The following
deserve particular mention:

(1) *The Feast of Purim.*—The name comes from the Persian word *pur,* plural *purim* = lots. The Persian governor,
Aman, had determined on the death of all the Jews in the
Persian Empire, and the 13th of *Adar* had been chosen by
lot as the day for this massacre. The murderous plan was
frustrated through Queen Esther and her kinsman, Mar-
docheus. In remembrance of this event, the Jews, first in
Persia, but afterwards also in Palestine and elsewhere, celebrated a festival on the 14th and 15th of *Adar,* keeping the
13th as a fast. The celebration consisted in reading the Book
of Esther aloud in the synagogues; joyful feasts were held
in the houses.

(2) *The Feast of the Dedication of the Temple* (τὰ ἐγκαίνια,
Encænia, John 10) was kept every year in commemoration
of the purification of the Temple from the idolatrous worship
of the Syrians, and its re-dedication by Judas Machabeus in 164 B.C. On the 25th of *Kislew* and on the following
seven days the houses in Jerusalem and other places were

illuminated; hence Josephus calls the feast φῶτα. There seems to have been no special ceremony in the Temple, but perhaps more sacrifices than usual were offered.

(3) *The Feast of Rejoicing of the Law.*—The reading of the Pentateuch having been concluded on the last day of the Feast of Tabernacles every year, it was begun again on the following day (23rd of *Tišri*).

(4) *The Feast of Wood Carrying* (ξυλοφορία or ἑορτὴ ξυλοφορίων) was, according to Josephus (*Bell. Jud.*, II, 17, 6), celebrated on the 14th of *Ab*, but the Talmud does not mention it. It appears that all who wished to do so carried wood to the Temple on this day for the maintenance of the fire on the altar of holocausts.

According to Nehemias 10:34, certain families were appointed by lot, at least in the period immediately after the Captivity, to supply wood, and the days on which they performed this duty were, for the persons concerned, days of rejoicing and honor.

(End of section adapted from Dr. Seisenberger.)

THIRD PART

SPECIAL INTRODUCTION TO THE OLD TESTAMENT

THE PENTATEUCH

Sicut pellem extendisti firmamentum libri tui, concordes utique sermones tuos, quos per mortalium ministerio superposuisti nobis. . . . Ibi est testimonium tuum, sapientiam præstans parvulis.

St. Augustine, Confessiones, XIII, 15.

SPECIAL INTRODUCTION TO THE OLD TESTAMENT

THE PENTATEUCH

PROLEGOMENA

135. The Bible and Jewish History.—Besides being the written Word of God, the Bible is also the literature of the Jewish nation. In fact, Hebrew history and the course of God's revelation are inextricably intertwined. Sacred Scripture, after beginning with the universal prologue of the hexaëmeron, gradually removes from its world-stage divers characters, till all attention is focussed upon the people of Israel. Thereafter the vicissitudes of this ethnic group, God's dealings therewith, and its own reactions to the influences of other nations with whom the Jews come into contact, occupy the historical Books almost exclusively, and are reflected in the prophetic and other writings. The ancient Jews were God's chosen people, and Holy Writ is concerned primarily with them alone, until, toward the close of the New Testament section, the word goes forth: "Teach ye *all* nations" (Matt. 28:19), and, with the Acts and Epistles, the stage of revelation becomes once more world-wide, and in the Apocalypse it is carried through to the very end when "time shall be no longer" (Apoc. 10:6),—as it opened with Genesis "in the beginning" (Gen. 1:1).

136. Sacred Scripture may be considered as the epic of the age-long paradoxical warfare of God's love against the powers of hatred and evil. Under another aspect it records the deliberate, unhurrying, but insistent chase whereby the Hound of Heaven pursues with His mercy the human soul or mankind, whilst the latter throughout the course of history seeks along every avenue in the universe of nature surcease

from that inward urge which impels it continually towards
its true rest and satisfaction, the supernatural life for which
it was originally created.   Hence the Bible is incidentally
also a record of the religious vagaries of mankind, showing
forth the influence of divers thought-movements that have
from time to time drawn mankind to one side or the other
out of the exact orbit of true religion,—which is naught else
but the cumulus of men's proper relationships to God.

Like other really great works of literature, then, the Bible
not only by gigantic synecdoche places the tiny nation of
the Jews for all mankind, but by an equally astounding
metonymy uses the same unit of the Hebrew people and its
vicissitudes to designate the brief but variegated span of
each individual man's own life.   In Sacred Scripture God,
the All-Author, has concurrently delineated not only the
history of the Jews, but the broad chronicles of the world,
and the private biography of every man; under the characters and periods of the Hebrew people He has wrought a
drama as universal as all human nature, and as particular
as the last and least person who reads the sacred text.

137. A correct appreciation, therefore, of the history
and function of the Jews as the Chosen People is of prime
importance for the proper understanding of Sacred Scripture.   Moreover, as every act of a drama is accompanied by
appropriate scenery, and the chief actors by their counterfoils, so the particular world-background of each period of
Jewish history must be taken into consideration, as well as
the peoples and movements to which Israel itself reacted.
Thus the great biblical drama of God and Man may be divided into seven great acts, each with several scenes and its
own special subsidiary actors and properties.

SYNOPSIS OF SACRED HISTORY

Factors and Movements

Towards God	Away from God	Books

I

Prologue: Creation

Towards God	Away from God	Books
Adam and Eve in Paradise	The Fall of man	Gen. 1–2
	Cain's fratricide	Gen. 3–4

Patriarchal World

Seth, the Patriarchs	Children of the world	Gen. 5–6

The Deluge

Saving of Noe and his family	Drowning of the impious	Gen. 7
Noachic sacrifice and precepts	Curse of Cham	Gen. 9, 10, 11
	Tower of Babel	

From Ancient Babylonian Culture to Palestine

Call of Abraham	Sodom and Gomorrha	Gen. 19
Isaac and Jacob	Ismael and Esau	
Joseph the Dreamer	Sold by his brethren	

II

Egypt and the Wilderness

Schooling of Israel into nation	Egyptian nature worship	Exodus 1
	Oppression of the Jews	
Moses and Aaron	Pharao and the magicians	

The Ten Plagues

Delivery of Jews from Egypt	Murmuring of Jews	Exodus
The Law from Sinai: Mosaic code	The Golden Calf	Leviticus
Elimination of unfit during the	Repeated murmuring	Numbers
forty years' wandering	Moabitic depravation	Deuteronomy

III

Palestine and the Kingdom

Conquest under Josue	Opposition of Canaanites	Josue
The Judges and Samuel	Syro-Phenician cults	Judges
David	Saul: the Philistines	Ruth
Solomon's building of the Temple	Division of the Kingdom	I & II Kings
Faithful Kings and Prophets like	Lapses into idolatry: Achaz and	Isaias
Ezechias and Elias.	Samaria: Athalia and unfaithful	III & IV Kings
	kings	Paralipomena
		Jeremias, Baruch

IV

Assyria and Babylon

Persian culture: the Captivity a	Laxity in observance of Mosaic	Esdras
		Nehemias
punishment and at same time	code	Tobias
the cure of idolatry	Persian persecution	Esther
Return under Esra and Nehemias	Opposition of Samaritans	Daniel
		Ezechiel

V

Hellenistic Palestine and Egypt

Sapiential studies in Jewish	Alexander's world conquest	Eccles.
thought	Hedonistic philosophy of the	Wisdom
Translation of the Scriptures	Greeks	Proverbs
The Machabean reformation	The Ptolemies in Egypt; persecu-	Ecclus.
Reaction from Hellenism	tion from Syrian Antioch	Machabees
Alliance with Rome	Apocalypses: Pharisaism	

Factors and Movements—Continued

Towards God	Away from God	Books
VI		
Climax: Christ, Messias and World Saviour		
Conception: Magi: Precursor	Birth in obscurity: Herod	Gospels of
Baptism: Public life	Opposition of Scribes and Phari-	Matthew,
Supernatural teaching: Miracles	sees ever increasing	Mark, Luke
Organization of Church in the		and John
Apostles and Disciples	Betrayal by Judas	
The Resurrection and Ascension	The death upon the Cross	
VII		
Kingdom of God in the World		
Apostles' preaching and writing to	Opposition of Judeo-Christians in-	Acts
world at large	sisting on ceremonial	
Spread of the Church	Hostility of heathenism	Epistles
Epilogue		
Perseverance of faithful	Persecution by the world	
Eventual victory of God	End of the World	Apocalypse

138. Spirit of the Old Testament.—Between the Ancient Covenant and the New Dispensation there is an abyss of modal difference in the view of the basic relationships between God and man. Thus the Old Testament represents rather the pursuit by the Hound of Heaven; the New, the capture of man, His much-beloved prey. From another standpoint, the Old Testament symbolizes man's erratic seeking of God; the New, his finding of the object of age-long search, the true pearl of great price (Matt. 13: 45-46). The Old Testament exemplifies the imperfect, childhood, inchoative, novitiate, training stage of mankind in religious attitude; the New Testament, on the other hand, shows forth the state of adult maturity, of possession, of perfection, of enjoyment, of love. Therefore also the two great divisions of the Sacred Scriptures are not to be judged by the same standards, as Christ Himself made clear in the Sermon on the Mount (see Matt. 5: 21-47), and as St. Paul insistently repeats: "Before the Faith came, we were kept under the Law shut up. . . . Wherefore the Law was our pedagogue in Christ. . . . But after the Faith is come, we are no longer under a pedagogue. . . . We also, when we were children, were serving under the elements of the world [childish natural observances]. . . . But now . . . how turn you again to the weak and needy elements? . . . Brethren, we are not children of the bondwoman [Agar], but of the free [Sarah], by the freedom wherewith Christ hath made us free" (Gal. 3-4).

The Mosaic ceremonial Code and the Commandments are not to be placed on a par with the Sermon on the Mount and the Evangelical Counsels. The former was for the imperfect in the "way of God" (Mark 12:14); the latter substituted and completed the former for the perfect (Matt. 5:17, 48; 19:21). The Ancient Covenant was a law of fear; it was given for "the spirit of fear" (II Tim. 1:7). But the New Dispensation is the law of love: "love is the fulfilling of the Law" (Rom. 13:10); for, "fear is not in charity, but perfect charity casteth out fear" (I John 4:18).

The perfection of man, then, is to love God fully. But perfection here below is attained only by gradually ascending through various stages of imperfection. Thus, before man could appreciate God adequately to love Him, he had to be trained by fear not to despise Him. Hence fittingly came the cataclysms and other terrific punishments recorded as meted out under the Old Covenant for even small offenses. The manifestation of Yahweh as the great God of power and justice, was a necessary preliminary to the coming of Christ, the God-Man of love and mercy.[1]

[1] "To Israel of old God's first great proclamation of Himself came in the form of the Moral Law. . . . They [the Jews] no doubt at first had little knowledge of what it meant; if they broke the Law, He punished them. . . . We, as we look back, can see that such punishments were the utmost mercy. They drove the people back into the path that led to God, they kept them in the school in which they were being educated in the knowledge of God and prepared for greater and still greater revelations. . . . A few hundred years of the discipline of the Law changed the irreverent familiarity of their peevish complaints [in the Wilderness] into the deep penitence of the *Miserere* and the spiritual yearning of the 41st Psalm. . . . In the burning fire of His Holiness they would begin to see the outlines of that other attribute which was to be the subject of another revelation. They were being prepared, they were preparing the world, for that revelation. It could not have been given earlier. They would not have understood it. To know Him as Love, without first knowing Him as Holy, would only have unfitted them from ever knowing Him. The moral training must come first. . . . Those long years of stern discipline, wrestling with the Law written on tables of stone, cold, stern, uncompromising, that would not yield, but merely condemned them if they did not obey,—did their work,

139. Messianic and Ecclesiastical Aspects of the Old Testament.—In reading the Old Testament text one must, moreover, recognize a distinction to be made in its interpretation according as one looks at the ancient pages from the standpoint *of the contemporary hagiographer* and his readers or hearers, or from the standpoint *of the later, fuller, New Testament revelation.* Thus besides the *historical meaning* or import of Old Testament personages and events as they appeared in the eyes of contemporaries, there must be admitted also, frequently at least, a *messianic meaning,* a wider, typical significance relative to the God-Man's personal advent. And at times this Messianic meaning may itself in turn expand into a still broader, *ecclesiastical* significance, illustrative of the mystical body of Christ, which is the Church, the Kingdom of God, "a greater and more perfect tabernacle not made with hands" (Heb. 9:11b), "living stones built up, a spiritual house, . . . a chosen generation, a kingly priesthood, a holy nation, a purchased people" (I Pet. 2:5, 9). For, according to the testimony of its own Divine Author, the historic happenings and characters of the Old Testament were really "a shadow of things to come" (Col. 2:17; Heb. 8:5; 10:1). Thus many events and persons, obscure perhaps in their own context, or details of such apparent irrelevance that one wonders why they had been selected for record, when studied from the perspective and in the stronger light of the New Dispensation, are seen in their broad outlines and with their contrasting shadows to be connotative each of a single phase, and to constitute an individual facet, of the great complete antitype which is Christ and the Church. Thus the text of the Old Testament may be said to resemble the miniature image in a photographic film. This indeed bears a correct representation

gave them the moral education which fitted them for the deeper spiritual knowledge. It was in very truth the Pedagogue to bring them to the revelation in Christ. And, as before the sun rises the dawn spreads upon the mountains, so, long before Christ had come, those who stood upon the mountains, who had climbed to the heights to which the Law led them, caught the first foretastes of the Love which was revealed in its fullness in Christ" (Maturin, *Self-Knowledge and Self-Discipline,* p. 297ss.; Longmans, Green, 1922).

when viewed in itself; but, if the light, instead of simply falling upon the face of the film, is made to pass through it and be modified by it, scenes much broader and more magnificent, yet corresponding withal to the tiny original, may be produced according as the light is projected and expanded upon more and more distant screens. In like manner again and again the historic original of the Old Testament may be projected upon the screen of the distant times of either the personal Messias or of His moral expansion in the Kingdom of God, the Church, to give greater and more varied aspects of divine revelation.

140. However, it is not implied hereby that the messianic or ecclesiastical applications of their messages were necessarily present in the consciousness of the hagiographers or their first readers. For, the Scripture itself says in regard to the Jews, that "even until this day, when Moses is read, the veil is upon their heart. . . . Their senses are made dull" and "the selfsame veil, in the reading of the Old Testament, remaineth not taken away. . . . But when they shall be converted to the Lord, the veil shall be taken away" (II Cor. 3:13-16; I Pet. 2:16). Hence the deepest significations of their own literature remained unperceived by the Jews at large; nay, even the Apostles did not grasp these great biblical meanings until Christ "opened their understanding that they might understand the Scriptures" (Luke 24:45). But, that messianic and ecclesiastical significations or senses were intended and laid in the text of Old Testament history by the Holy Ghost, its prime author, who "reacheth from end to end mightily, and ordereth all things sweetly" (Wis. 8:1), is not to be denied.

Art. 1: THE AUTHENTICITY OF THE PENTATEUCH

Text: Gen. 1-9.

141. Untraditional Views.—Whilst Jewish and Christian traditional history for almost three thousand years has concordantly and consistently attested that the Pentateuch,[1]

---

[1] Πέντε, five, and τεῦχος, utensil, tool, but in the Alexandrian period also book. The name is properly feminine = ἡ πεντάτευχος βίβλος, but

the collection of historic, prophetic, and legislative writings which form the opening group of the Bible, had for its hagiographic author Moses, national seer and liberator of the Jews from Egyptian thraldom, certain rationalistic critics, of the late 19th century particularly, have denied the objective reality of the traditional authorship and the sincerity of the apparent plan and object of the Pentateuch. Whilst no two hypotheses of such destructive criticism are in agreement on even essential points (such as the date and authorship of the hypothetical integrating parts of the composition), the substance of the untraditional or "divisive" view of the origin of the Pentateuch (soon extended to the whole Bible) may be summarized as follows:

The Untraditional view borrowed its method from the ingenious theory whereby Jean Astruc, a Jewish physician of Montpellier, strove (1753) to offset the attacks of freethinkers upon the Mosaic authorship of the Pentateuch. Astruc's starting-point is "the observation, long noted and variously explained, that through entire chapters or large portions of chapters [of Genesis and Exodus] [2] the name of the Deity appears consecutively either as 'God' (Elohim) or as 'the Lord' (Yhwh). . . . The novel explanation proposed by Astruc is that the change of appellation is the mark of divers writers".[3] Thereby the divers names of God are used as tests for determining the integrating writings, originally independent and disparate, but largely parallel in subject matter, which Moses is presumed to have used as sources, or to have combined in his composition.

is masculine in Latin, because *liber* is understood. The word *Pentateuch* occurs first in Origen (*Ad Joh.*, IV, 25), and in Latin first in Tertullian (*Adv. Marc.*, I, 10). The Hebrew name is *Thora* = law; in the New Testament it is ὁ νόμος. The names for the single books, Genesis, Exodus, Leviticus, Numbers and Deuteronomy, are taken from the Septuagint, and were given with reference to the contents; the Vulgate retained the Greek names, only rendering ἀριθμοί by Numeri.

[2] For example, "Yahweh" is used throughout Gen. 1 and 2: 1–3; from there to the close of the Gen. 4 (with the exceptions of 4: 25 and 3: 1–5, which with other "abnormalities" breed some very absurd divisions) is found either the composite "Yahweh-Elohim" or simply "Yahweh". Further on, the form "Elohim" was evidently preferred by the Chronicler; it exceptionally preponderates in Book II of the Psalms, and especially in Psalms 73–83. Contrast Ps. 13 (14) with Ps. 52 (53).

[3] This summary is largely adapted from *Max Margolis' The Hebrew Scriptures in the Making* (Philadelphia, 1922), pp. 38–47. This Jewish writer is not sympathetic with destructive theories, and shows conclusively that the Thora of the times of Josias (621 B.C.) and of Osee (8: 12) could not have been substantially different from the Pentateuch as arranged to-day.

Later critics, then, carrying this divisive process further than the first two chapters of Exodus, construed phenomena of compilation into the times of Moses himself,—whence it follows that the compiler of the Pentateuch must have been some one other than Moses. Operating with the aid of internal evidence (change of divine names, repetitions, contradictions, incongruities of sequence, differences of vocabulary and turns of speech), Wellhausen and his imitators to the present day, with more eloquence than acumen, have applied this imaginative text-mincing system to the whole Scripture, not even excluding the New Testament, apparently never reflecting that its very extensiveness would make plain its essential absurdity.

In this destructive hypothesis, *J* represents Yahwistic sources, *E*, Elohistic sources, each characterized by the use of the names *Yahweh* or *Elohim* respectively. *D* is roughly equivalent to Deuteronomy (chapters 12-26), presumed to have been written shortly before the incident of IV Kings 22: 8 (621 B.C.) in order to embody the program of the party of reformers by whom King Josias is asserted to have been won over to doing away with the country sanctuaries and restricting sacrificial worship to the Temple at Jerusalem. *P* is the symbol of the "Priestly Code", that is: Leviticus, and fragments of Genesis, Exodus, Numbers, and Josue. The *P* sections are supposed to be characterized by a dry, pedantic style, which gives attention chiefly to genealogies, lists of names, dates, etc. Whatever of narrative they contain is presumed to be but an artificial framework for giving the later ceremonial laws an atmosphere of antiquity. To this source is ascribed every element of systematic chronology and systematic religion in the Pentateuch. "In *P*'s picture of the Mosaic age, the minute description of the tabernacle, sacrifices, and other ceremonial institutions, and the systematic marshalling of the nation by tribes and families, and the unity of purpose and action which in consequence regulates its movements (Num. 1-4; 10: 11-28) are the most conspicuous features".[4] *P* is supposed to date from the 6th century, or the Babylonian exile.—Thus the final "redaction" of the complete Pentateuch would be brought down to times subsequent to Esdras.

142. Untenableness of the Untraditional Hypothesis.—The *J* and *E* sections can not be definitely ascribed to distinct authors on the strength of the use of the Divine names alone. For, (1) the cutting up of the text which this involves implies a practically impossible motley work of patches, which is incongruent with the work of any reasonable redactor. (2) Elsewhere in the Scriptures than the Pentateuch, where there can be absolutely no possibility of distinct and different underlying documents, the Divine names are arbitrarily varied, thus pointing to the redactional work of an editor. *Yahweh* is evidently substituted, according to the editor's taste, by *Elohim*. If *Yahweh* may thus come to be changed elsewhere, why not also in the Pentateuch? Particularly in the "Second Creation" section of Genesis no argument can be drawn from the

---

4 * Driver, *The Book of Genesis,* ed. 9, p. 23.

Divine names. For, here *Yahweh-Elohim* occur together 20 times up to the end of Gen. 3, and only sporadically elsewhere. Now, the occurrence of the two names linked, but without a pronominal suffix, is very generally considered an anomaly, and, when evidence points to the elimination of one of them, it is invariably *Yahweh* that is to be regarded as interpolated, because it is not found in Gen. 3:1, 3, 5, and because in Gen. 2:9, 21 the Septuagint and Old Latin agree in ousting it.

P's claim to separate authorship from the rest of the Pentateuch upon the basis of distinct vocabulary is most precarious. For, what is claimed to be distinct terminology in those sections is, in the main, a collection of words and expressions that had to be used by the very nature of the matter treated; the subjects could hardly have been spoken of or written about by any one without the use of these terms, which consequently are no criterion of authorship. Examples of *P*'s terminology are: "these are the generations"; "kind" (=species), found 10 times in Gen. 1, seven times in the Flood narrative, nine times in Lev. 9, and elsewhere in the Old Testament only in Deut. 14:13-18 and Ezech. 47:10 (which are certainly never considered *P* sections); "creep" and "creeping things". Moreover, the *P* section of Gen. 1-2 4*b* is certainly not homogeneous in style and character with the rest of *P*, and, within its own compass, the hexaëmeron section of *P* shows more difference from the rest of *P* than all the rest of *P* shows from *J*.

143. The Untraditional school generally identifies *D* with the book found in the Temple during the reign of Josias (IV Kings 22:8). This finding of the code which commanded a single sanctuary in Israel is supposed to have been but a trick or ruse of the reform party to give their pet hobby the authorization of antiquity. However, "the book was really found; it had actually been lost. . . . The find is brought in connection with the restoration of the Temple edifice. The writer clearly conveys the impression that the discovery was made during the process of repairs, when much rubbish was removed and ancient layers were uncovered; in other words, that the book was found secreted, not in an open place in one of the chambers, but in some spot in the Temple walls. A most plausible explanation . . . would be that Manasseh had the Temple copy consigned to its stone entombment on the occasion of alterations in the edifice. We possess a parallel in the case of Gamaliel the Elder. Shortly before the destruction of the Herodian Temple (which was far from completed when the soldiers of Titus set fire to it), he is said to have immured beneath a layer a copy of a *translation* of the Book of Job. In either instance the obvious aim was to withdraw the offensive volume from public use. Both Gamaliel and Manasseh shrank from off-hand destruction [of a Scripture writing]; the book might be left to destroy itself. But by the act of sequestration each plainly indicated the disfavor in which he held it,—Gamaliel because he discountenanced written translations; Manasseh for the reason that he had set aside the Thora in the form presented by the Temple copy. It was an early

case of *genizah,* tantamount to rejecting the Code and declaring it ineffective in the realm".[5]

In conclusion, no evidence has ever been brought to prove that the Thora of Josias contained only *D* or Deuteronomy. It could not have been different from the Thora of Osee (8:12), who confronts a people "swearing, lying, killing, stealing, and committing adultery", breaking all the commandments, yet scrupulous in presenting their sin-offerings. There is a multiplicity of sanctuaries; but "Ephraim hath multiplied altars—to sin". Lastly, the Thora of Josias could not have been different from that brought forth by Esdras at the return from the Captivity, which contained the whole Pentateuch, otherwise the Samaritans, bitterly hostile to the Jews, would never have received it as their only Scripture. Had the Thora as a compilation received its finishing touches from Esdras and his associates, the Samaritans would never have ceased upbraiding the Jews for tampering with the Sacred Scripture. The Samaritans themselves made but the slightest changes in the Pentateuch to adapt it to their own particular purpose, as, for instance, substituting Gerizim for Ebal in Deut. 27:4; and modifying Exod. 20:24 to read: "In *the* place where I *have caused* my name to be mentioned".

Untradition, whilst originally a mere opinion, an hypothesis, gradually hardens into a tradition of the critical school, unquestioned by its followers. True criticism bows before no mere opinion; it recognizes "no master but that tradition which, when all is said and done, is found to be based not on opinion but on fact. There is no other approach to antiquity except through tradition".[6]

144. Mosaic Authorship Maintained.—In contrast to the divers and clashing vagaries of the untraditional view, the Church has ever taught and consistently defended the proposition that the Pentateuch is substantially the work of the man and the time by whom and in which it purports to have been composed; that is, the Church insists upon the Mosaic authorship of the Pentateuch. For, upon this authenticity depends the trustworthiness, the credibility, of the whole narrative. Without a genuine Pentateuch there is no satisfactory key to the rest of Scripture; mankind will be quite at a loss for an adequate account of its origin and explanation of its present status; the whole history of the Jews will become an inexplicable enigma. In the Pentateuch alone are

[5] * Margolis, *Hebrew Scriptures in the Making,* p. 100.

[6] A fuller discussion of the Untraditional view, as well as interesting explanations of several difficulties, may be found in the collection of studies of Pentateuchal problems by several eminent Jesuits, entitled: *Moses and the Law* (London, 1922).

laid down reliable and satisfactory basic explanations of these phenomena, for "God made known His ways to Moses" (Ps. 102:7).

The Mosaic authenticity of the Pentateuch, however, does not necessarily imply that Moses personally either wrote or dictated each and every word and phrase thereof.[7] It does not preclude the possibility that Moses, having under the *afflatus* of inspiration conceived the contents of his work, afterwards entrusted the actual composition to one or more secretaries who recorded without substantial omission or addition what Moses had conceived and wished to have written. Moreover, it may congruently be admitted that Moses availed himself of traditional sources of information and even of written documents, incorporating them with more or less modification or correction, in his own work. Lastly, for the resolution of difficulties, besides theories like the above, one may legitimately invoke the presence of material error,[8] scribal emendations or interpolations of a later age, except in such passages as have ever been accepted by the Church as genuine. No such theory would impugn Moses' basic and principal authorship of the Pentateuch.

The *external* evidence witnessing to the Mosaic authorship of the Pentateuch is so abundant that it can only summarily be indicated here. Thus, outside the Pentateuch itself, there are at least 125 passages in Sacred Scripture that declare or assume Moses' authorship of the Thora.[9] Rabbinic lore shall be represented by this one passage which the Talmud cites from a source older than itself: "Moses wrote his own book and the section concerning Balaam [Num. 22:

---

[7] This paragraph reproduces the 2nd, 3rd, and 4th *responsa* of the decision of the Biblical Commission, of June 27, 1906 (*Acta Sanctæ Sedis.* 39, p. 377. See p. 239 below.

[8] See No. 15 above.

[9] Typical examples are: Jos. 8: 31; 23: 6; Judges 3: 4; I Kings 12: 6; III Kings 2: 3; 8: 53; IV Kings 14: 6; 23: 25; I Par. 22: 13; II Par. 25: 4; 33: 8; I Esdras 3: 2; II Esdras 1: 7; 8:1; Tob. 7: 14; Judith 8: 23; Ps. 76: 21; 104: 26; 105: 16; 23, 32; Ecclus. 24: 33; Is. 63: 11, 12; Jer. 15: 1; Baruch 2: 2; Dan. 9: 11, 13; Mich. 6:4; Mal. 4: 4; II Mach. 7: 30; Matt. 19: 7–8; Mark 12: 26; Luke 20: 28; John 1: 17; Acts 7: 40, 44; Rom. 10: 19; I Cor. 9: 9; II Cor. 3: 13, 15; Heb. 7: 14, etc. Christ Himself said to the Jews: "Did not Moses give you the Thora?" (John 7: 19).

2—25 : 9], and Job. Josue wrote his own book and [the last] eight verses of the Thora''.[10] The testimony of patristic antiquity need but be mentioned.

145. But all this external evidence, which is chiefly the base of the Church's tradition, is arbitrarily ruled out of court by purblind partisans of the untraditional, destructive school of biblical criticism, the suicidal absurdity of whose claims has been evinced above and may be graphically brought home by a glance at the ridiculous ''Rainbow Bible''. However, to acquiesce to their prejudiced preference for *internal* evidence, the following arguments have been summarized from internal (alone or in combination with extra-biblical and profane) evidence for the Mosaic authorship of the Pentateuch.

(1) *The text* of the Pentateuch itself repeatedly *claims Moses as its author* (Exod. 17: 14; 24: 4, 7; Deut. 4: 8; 17: 18): "And Moses wrote this Thora, and delivered it to the priests" (Deut. 31: 9); "After Moses had written the words of this Thora in a volume . . ." (Deut. 31: 24). Here it may be noted that Deuteronomy can not monopolize the title of Thora or Law, as it declares itself to be but a summary, repetition, expounding thereof (Deut. 1: 5). The name *thora*, moreover, may be applied also to any unit of the Jewish legislative system, even any formal decision of what is right or wrong, any "judgment", such as is given in Aggeus 2: 11-13.

(2) *The archaisms* and characteristic expressions of the Pentateuch are *inconsistent with* the Hebrew language of *the time of Josias* (621 B.C.), in which period the divisive critics would have its composition take place. Thus in 195 passages of the Pentateuch the masculine form of the third person singular of the personal pronoun, *hû'*, is found instead of the feminine form *hî'*. Similarly *na'ar* (= boy) is used 21 times for the proper later feminine form *na'arah* (= girl), which Masoretic tradition has everywhere affixed in the margin (Gen. 24: 14; 34:3, 12; Deut. 22: 15, etc.). Although the Masoretes have certainly eliminated many of the grammatical anomalies of the Pentateuch, yet sufficient traces remain to show that the original language of the Pentateuch was considerably more archaic and approached the primitive than did Hebrew of post-Davidic times. Not even Josue uses the archaisms of the Pentateuch. Other such characteristic expressions are *'abib* (= ear of grain; Exod. 9: 31; 13: 4; Deut. 16: 1); *kibšan* (= furnace; Gen. 19: 28; Exod. 9: 8); the expression: "to be gathered to one's people", with the word *'amâw* (Gen. 25: 8, 17; Num. 20: 25; Deut.

[10] *Baba Bathra*, 14b–15a.

32:50) in this sense is not to be found outside the Pentateuch. Already in Judges (2:10) it is found altered (see IV Kings 22:20; II Par. 34:28).

(3) The *author* of the Pentateuch *must have seen the Egypt recorded* in his pages. Thus in Gen. 13:10 the author says that the country about the Jordan was "like Egypt as one comes to Zoar" (Zar was an ancient Egyptian frontier fortress; later cities like Migdol and Taphnis are not mentioned). The taskmasters of Exod. 5:14, with their rods, may be seen on many a bas-relief and painting of ancient Egypt. The irrigation system characteristic of Egypt, whereby the Nile waters flowing through small ditches were stopped by the feet of the gardener so that they might overflow upon the surrounding plot of land (Deut. 11:10 Hebrew), was contrasted with the Providential rainfalls of Palestine. The bastinado is ordered to be inflicted on offenders (Deut. 25:2) after the manner still pictured in ancient Egyptian archeology. The only foreign words in the Pentateuch are Egyptian; thus the *thêbâh* of Exod. 2:5 (Gen. 6:14) is but a reproduction of the Egyptian *tba* = chest, box: the Hebrew of Exod. 5:12 is obscure because the author designated the swamp reeds by their Egyptian name of *qaš*.

(4) *The Egypt of the Pentateuch is not the Egypt of the times of the later Jewish kings.* The author of the Pentateuch knows Egypt only as a united empire, not divided into small principalities such as it is described by Isaias (19:2, 12-13, etc.). He senses no impending danger from Assyria (Is. 20:1, 4); in fact, the latter empire is not of world-importance in his time. Ethiopia, which dominated Egypt from before the time of Ezechias, is not mentioned in the earlier documents. Phithom and Rameses and Tanis (Exod. 1:11; Num. 13:23; Ps. 77:12), ancient Egyptian fortresses or cities, are mentioned to the exclusion of Memphis and Migdol and Taphnis (Jer. 44:1; Is. 19:13; Ezech. 30:13), well known at the time of the prophets.

(5) *At the time of the composition of the Pentateuch Israel was not yet in possession of Palestine.* In fact, the whole compilation may be considered as powerful propaganda brought to influence the descendants of Abraham to bring them to seize back as their proper heritage the Promised Land. Many ceremonial regulations in the Thora, on the other hand, have significance only for the nomadic life of the desert wandering, and none whatever for the fixed and stable dwelling in Palestine. Such were for example, the special functions assigned to certain groups of the Levites (Num. 3:17-38; 4:1-49), the Cahathites, the Gersonites, the Merarites; there were no such functions in the Temple service as arranged by David (I Par. 23-26).

In view of these and other facts, the theory that the Pentateuch should be a forgery out of whole cloth of post-Davidic age becomes an untenable absurdity. Many of its partisans advocate it undoubtedly because it would seem to dispense with the miracles and other wondrous works of God recorded in the Pentateuch: but to accomplish this elimination they themselves must assume that mere men successfully contrived and put over without ever a single betraying anachronism, on an unwilling and clever nation, a miracle of compilation and fabrication greater than the whole Ten Plagues of Egypt together, in short, the world's most magnificent and successful forgery. *Qui nimis probat, nihil probat.*

146. Redactions and Interpolations.—That a book of the antiquity of the Pentateuch, especially after over two thousand years' existence in manuscript form, should show traces of recension and interpolation, is not at all surprising. The Hebrew language itself underwent noticeable change from the time of the Pentateuch's composition till the tongue itself became practically dead some centuries before Christ; moreover, the mode of writing was revised entirely, probably from semi-ideographic and syllabic cuneiform to alphabetic. Scribal rewriting would include primarily revision of the language, such as the substitution of newer for archaic or obsolescent terms, but would likewise not exclude the insertion of notes, explanations, comments, and other proper editorial functions.

The hand of an early editor (Josue or Samuel, perhaps?) is seen in the closing chapters of Deuteronomy, first in the prefatory note to c. 33: "This is the blessing wherewith the man of God Moses, etc."; and then in the account of the death of Moses (c. 34). Even the great canticle of c. 32, although previously written by Moses, seems to have been appended later, as Moses' work concludes with Deut. 31:23. Other such prefatory or appended editorial notes seem to be Deut. 1:1-5a; 4:41-49; Gen. 36:31-39. Besides these, there are to be found quite a number of brief historical, archeological, and geographical notes which seem to have crept into the text from the margin, such as the recurrent remark that "the Canaanite was at that time in the land" (Gen. 12:6; 13:7); the value of the ancient *sekel* or *epha* (Exod. 16:

36; **Num.** 3:47; 18:16); comparisons with later times
marked by the expression "until this present day" (Deut.
3:14c); the note on the basalt sarcophagus (or perhaps traditionally named rock-formation) of Og, king of Basan
(Deut. 3:11b). As cases of interpolation Deut. 2:-10-12,
20-23; 3:13d; Gen. 36:31, etc., also are adduced. Even for
the passages cited the evidence for interpolation is not absolutely conclusive. If really interpolations, they are such
by accident; there is no indication of their having been inserted with intention to deceive.

Art. 2: OBJECT AND PLAN OF THE PENTATEUCH

Texts: Gen. 12-16, 37-41, 46-49; Exod. 1-7, 12-14, 19-21, 34, 40.

147. Instruction and Legislation for Chosen People.—
The immediate object of the Pentateuch was the instruction
of the Jews, the Chosen People, as to their supernatural
origin and destiny, and the accompanying promulgation of a
proportionate code of moral, social, and ceremonial conduct
for both the individual and the nation. The Pentateuch may
be considered as the Constitution of the ancient Jewish
people, with Genesis occupying the position of a preambu-
latory Bill of Rights or Declaration of Independence. Of
course, in the wider, ecclesiastical, sense according to which
the Chosen People were but a type prepicturing the great
kingdom of the adopted sons of God, the Pentateuch applies
in an analogous but sublimated manner to the ideals of all
mankind. It lays the primitive foundations for the com-
plexus of man's relationships to God, which is called religion.

148. The content of the Pentateuch is very variegated:
history, law, poetry, liturgy, are all combined in its volumes,
without that strict classification generally striven for by the
Aryan mind, but rather in the loose, almost haphazard, fashion of Oriental and especially Semitic compositions. However, the lack of systematic arrangement or treatment of
divers topics so apparent after the recording of the exodus
from Egypt (when the account becomes contemporary with

its author), may be but a reflection of the circumstances surrounding its composition,—the movement of the author-leader from encampment to encampment in the Wilderness, the occurrence of succeeding problems of most varied character day by day in the vicissitudes of that itinerant nation, the moments of respite and leisure more fitted for the writing of revelations received.   Thus the very irregularity of the Pentateuch bespeaks the authenticity of its composition.

Nevertheless the disparate elements of the Pentateuch are not thrown together planlessly: rather are they arranged toward a dominating unity of object: the revelation of man's fundamental relationship to God, in order that he may come to know, appreciate, and serve Him better.   And the uniform ordering of the divers constituents toward this one primary object again makes evident the work of a single composing mind.   In a narrower, more immediate sense, the Pentateuch may also be considered as propaganda establishing title to, and inducing the descendants of Abraham to reëstablish themselves in the Promised Land of Palestine.   To rekindle the national consciousness of the Jews, so ruthlessly crushed during the closing years of their dwelling in Egypt, to animate them in face of the hardships of the Wilderness, to encourage them for the conquest of Canaan,—these were secondary and immediate objects of the composition of the Pentateuch.

149. The Eliminative Plan, particularly of Genesis.—Two things are to be especially borne in mind in criticism of the style and arrangement of the Pentateuch: First, *it was not intended to be a book for popular reading.*   Rather was it to be the treasure of the priests, who were to read and ponder its contents, and from whose "mouth they shall seek the law" (Mal. 2:7): "And Moses wrote this law and delivered it to the priests the sons of Levi. . . . And he commanded them: . . . Thou shalt read the words of this law before all Israel, . . . that hearing they may learn, and fear the Lord your God, and keep and fulfill all the words of this law" (Deut. 31:9-13).   Second, as regards Genesis more particularly, *its handling of history is frankly not exhaustive, but rather restrictive, eliminative.*   **The Pentateuch begins**

with the width of the universe, and then gradually but swiftly, through masterful sketching of millennia of history, tapers down to the ethnographic pinpoint of the nation of the Jews. The contracting stages of this process may be sketched as follows:

ELIMINATIVE PLAN OF GENESIS

Preface (Hexaëmeron), Gen. 1:1; 2:3

Creation of the Universe, Heaven (= the Spiritual World) and *Earth*	Spiritual World (of Angels) eliminated
Formation of the Earth, and its Ornamentation with Flora, Fauna, and *Man*	

History of Adam, Gen. 2:4; 4:26

Detail of Man's Creation; Paradise and the Fall; Fratricide of Cain, *Seth*	Both Cain and Abel eliminated

History of Adam's Descendants, Gen. 5:1; 6:8

Seth's genealogy; the Patriarchs till *Noe*	All side issues of the patriarchal line eliminated, except where incidentally mentioned, Gen. 6:2

History of Noe and his Descendants, Gen. 6:9; 11:9

Noe and the Ark; the Deluge; Cham, Japhet, and *Sem*	Cham and Japhet eliminated, and all peoples outside the Semitic
The great Ethnographic Table	

History of the Semites, Gen. 11:10-26

The genealogy of *Sem's* descendants	Side lines of Sem's descendants also eliminated

History of Thare and Abraham, Gen. 11:27; 25:11

Call of Abraham; his life; birth of Ismael and *Isaac*	Lot eliminated, as also Ammonites and Moabites, and Ismael

History of Isaac, Gen. 25:19; 36

Account of Esau and *Jacob*	Esau eliminated

History of Jacob, Gen. 37:50

Jacob's sons, especially Juda and *Joseph*	Other sons of Jacob mentioned only in passing
History of Joseph; Descent of Israel into Egypt	

As may be noted from this outline, Genesis was composed upon a definite plan. Here genealogy forms the framework of history. Genesis is in fact a great *liber generationum*, a genealogical table having historical comment upon the outstanding vicissitudes of its chief personages interspersed.

150. Exodus.—The second book of the Pentateuch is closely linked to the first. Genesis had given the origins of the Jewish race and explained their presence in Egypt. The account now becomes contemporary, and shows Israel grievously oppressed beneath the yoke of unsympathetic Pharaos, and freed from that yoke by God's commissioned leader, Moses, to the terrors of stupendous calamities. The Book may be divided into three parts, of which the first (1-12:36) treats of the events preceding and preparatory to the exodus from Egypt; the second (12:37; 18), of the actual exodus until the arrival at Sinai; the third (19-40), of the promulgation of the Law at Sinai, and of the construction of the Tabernacle.

151. Leviticus.—Exodus in its closing section had determined the place of worship, and related the preparation of the necessary furnishings thereof. Leviticus (so named because its topics largely concern the specific Jewish priesthood) now proceeds further to regulate, first (1-11), sacrifices; second (12-22), ritual defilements; third (23-27), the Sabbath and feast days. These cultus regulations were promulgated during the first week of the second year of sojourn in the Wilderness (Num. 1:1 and 9:1, 3).

152. Numbers.—This book receives its name from the lists and registers of both military and hierarchic importance, which form a notable feature of its history, that covers about 38 years after the departure from Egypt. It does not enumerate all the details of this history, but records the principal events: first (1-10), preparations for leaving the camp at Sinai; second (11-19), various revolts, falls, murmurings, of the Jews during the Wilderness travels, and ordinances promulgated in the same period; third (20-36), the conquest of Palestine east of the Jordan, events and laws of the first ten months of the 40th year of the exodus. Numbers is, in turn, closely allied with the preceding book.

153. Deuteronomy.—This closing volume of the Pentateuch forms quite a distinct work, and is not closely attached to any one of the preceding Books. It purports to be a *résumé* of the Thora, an easily remembered summary of all the lessons and laws of the 40 years wandering in the Wilderness, to be emphatically impressed upon the mind of Israel now about to cross over the Jordan into its ancient heritage of the Promised Land. Differently from the other Books, instead of recitals of events and records of laws, Deuteronomy is made up chiefly of discourses or orations, preceded by short introductions. There may be distinguished three great discourses or sections: the first (1:6; 4:43) serving as an introduction to the book; the second (5-26), forming the main portion, being subdivisible into three thought groups (5-6:3 recalling the Decalogue, 6:4; 11, and 12-26, which is a summary of Mosaic legislation). This is followed by an historic conclusion and several appendices, such as the Canticle of Moses, and the account of his death.

Art. 3: MOSAIC COSMOGONY, OR THE HEXAËMERON

Texts: Lev. 1-3, 7-12, 16-17, 23-25.

154. Corrects the Heathen Mythical Corruptions.—The question of the world's beginning has ever piqued the mind of man, and even from most ancient times it has received divers answers. The original revelation, undoubtedly given Adam by God in this matter, in the course of ages became corrupted into the various myths and origin-legends.

An example of such legends (to be found in the primitive literature of most peoples) is given for the Teutonic group from the *Völuspa Edda:*

"Once was the age when Ymir lived.
There was nor sand nor sea nor smooth waves;
No earth was to be found, nor sky above,—
Yawning abyss alone, and grass nowhere,—

Till Bör's sons raised the spheres. . . .
The sun knew not where was his seat,
The moon knew not what power she had,
The stars knew not where was there place.
Then went the Councilors to the judgment-seats,
High-holy gods held council:
To the night and new moon gave they names,
Told Morning and Middle of the Day,
Under and Evening to set the times."

All of these myths and legends postulate, no matter how confusedly, a conscious creative Power. The absurdities with which the basic truth became entangled and by which it was obscured in these legends, early made philosophic minds, especially among the Greeks, reject them in favor of theories of an eternal matter combined with a blind law of necessity. Similar hypotheses have been produced by modern thought in its fearful flight from the Divine. And these latest imaginations of the unaided human mind in sketching the genesis of the universe and man are nigh as fantastic in the unreasonableness of their postulates as are the origin-myths of ancient heathenism.

A typical example of a modern cosmogony by a professor of biochemistry may be seen in the *Yale Review* of Jan. 1922, pp. 340-352 ("The Road of Evolution", by A. P. Matthews): "Let us imagine ourselves now at the beginning of the world. Out of chaos it takes form. From its flaming gases, its clouds and mists, the oceans condense. Lightnings flash without cessation in the heavens. . . . Rocks, sand, clay, water, vapors, air and fire. Out of these life is to arise. . . . The sun, then as now, shining on this atmosphere, produced in time every kind of chemical compound. Given time, energy, and matter, and all is possible. . . . Carbon, oxygen, nitrogen, hydrogen unite to make amino acids, which condense in the seas. . . . Slowly they condense to form every kind of complex compound: proteins appear, phosphoric acid compounds, fats, sugars; and at last, as a result of these complex molecules, emulsions are formed. A slime appears in the pools. . . . The universe is dividing into two parts, an individual, a slime, and all else. This is a living slime. . . . What is there in that colloidal foam, colorless and microscopic in size, and almost homogeneous, without visible differentiation in structure? Everything is in it: every-plant, every animal, you and I. . . . Outside of it shells will precipitate, sculptured as if by Phidias; within it, bones. . . . To an age of invertebrates, that is, of crabs, worms, and molluscs, there followed an age of fishes. . . . The amphibia arose because they won their freedom from the water. Some fishes had an air bladder which enabled them to change their specific gravity. A great discovery consisted in using this air bladder as a lung, so that it became possible to live on land as well as in the water. . . . Some amphibia, driven by adversity, succeeded in overcoming the limitation of water, and became able to live in dry places. They acquired a dry and scaly skin; they improved their circulation and nervous system, and won independence of aqueous control. And this great discovery gave the reptiles such an advantage that they dominated creation," etc., etc.—The chief difference between such an account and that, say, of the *Edda,* is that the latter is more poetical.

That, providentially, somewhere among the descendants of Adam and Eve the essentials of the true account of the origin of the world should have been preserved by tradition, is not at all improbable. That Moses utilized this tradition, crystallizing it in the Genesis prologue is a valid conjecture —borne out by the strikingly mnemonic arrangement of the hexaëmeron, as if it had been compiled specifically for the purpose of facilitating its impression upon the memory of childhood. That the biblical cosmogony, though not purporting to be a detailed scientific treatise, but only a summary in the simplest of popular language, outlines the substantial facts of the world's beginning, is vouched for by the infallible truthfulness of the Holy Spirit, the primary author of this account, as of all the rest of Sacred Scripture.

The Mosaic cosmogony is plainly designed to correct common false notions. It starts out with the clear distinction of a personal Divinity from the world, emphasizing next the deliberate freedom of this same Divinity in creation, and tracing to Its wisdom the order and systematic regularity of nature. Thus the terrible heathen bugaboo of an unfree, fate-ruled or merely arbitrary divinity governing the world is laid at the very outset. Fear of the power of an irresistible but blind Fate, of a mysterious, original, eternal Matter, of a dualistic, gloomy, Power of Evil, and many an allied error which lay oppressive as a nightmare upon the mind of mankind during the darkness of heathenism, is banished. On the base of the Mosaic cosmogony, man, instead of turning away with shuddering nausea from dimly visioned horrors of formless primeval slime, and hanging his head in shame at subconscious atavistic manifestations of hideous simian ancestry, may freely raise his face to high heaven where dwells a personal, living, just God who made him for great destinies, and proudly gaze about on a "good", fair world of which he himself is "the roof and crown". Thus the hexaëmeron stands out as the lofty portico to the whole magnificent temple of subsequent revelation.

155. Interpretation of the Hexaëmeron.—When reading the Mosaic cosmogony one should primarily keep in mind the comment of St. Thomas: *"Circa mundi principium aliquid est quod ad substantiam fidei pertinet, scilicet mundum incepisse creatum. . . . Quo autem modo et ordine factus sit, non pertinet ad fidem nisi per accidens, in quantum in Scriptura traditur, cuius veritatem diversa expositione sancti salvantes diversa tradiderunt"*.[11] Next, the key to proper understanding of the language of the hexaëmeron is the realization that in composing this section it was not the intention of the hagiographer to display in detail the interrelationship and make-up of the material world, or to explain the complete order of its coming into being in the technical terminology of a science textbook, but rather to give the Chosen People a popular but correct account in everyday speech that would be accommodated to the language and capacity of men of those times.[12] This principle has been well expressed in the words of Ruskin:[13]

"Now, with respect to this chapter, we must remember that it is intended for the instruction of all mankind, not for the learned reader only, and that therefore the most simple and natural interpretation is the likeliest in general to be the true one. . . . I would desire, therefore, to receive God's account of His own creation as under the ordinary limits of human knowledge and imagination it would be received by a simple-minded man. . . . By accepting the words in their simplest sense [Heavens = veil of clouds above the earth, in Gen. 1:8] we are thus led to apprehend the immediate presence of the Deity [in "He bowed down the heavens"] and His purpose of manifesting Himself as near whenever the storm-cloud stoops upon its course; while by our vague and inaccurate acceptance we remove the idea of His presence far from us, into a region which we can neither see nor know . . ., we refine and

[11] *In II Sent., dist.* 12, q. 1, a. 2, c.
[12] Biblical Commission June 30, 1909, n. VII. See Appendix.
[13] *Modern Painters*, Part V, c. vii, 2, 5, 6, 8 (Everyman's ed. vol. IV, p. 78ss.).

explain ourselves into dim and distant suspicion of an inactive God inhabiting inconceivable places and fading into the multitudinous formalisms of the laws of nature. . . .

"What space of time was in reality occupied by the 'day' of Genesis, is not, at present, of any importance for us to consider. By what furnaces of fire the adamant was melted, and by what wheels of earthquake it was torn, and by what teeth of glacier and weight of sea-waves it was engraved and finished into its perfect form, we may perhaps hereafter conjecture; but here, as in few words the work is summed up by the historian, so in few broad thoughts it should be comprehended by us; and as we read the mighty sentence: 'Let the dry land appear!' we should try to follow the finger of God, as it engraved upon the stone tables of the earth the letters and the laws of its everlasting form; as, gulf by gulf, the channels of the deep were ploughed; and, cape by cape, the lines were traced, with Divine foreknowledge, of the shores that were to limit the nations; and chain by chain, the mountain walls were lengthened forth, and their foundations fastened forever; and the compass was set upon the face of the depth, and the fields, and the highest part of the dust of the world were made; and the right hand of God first strewed the snow of Lebanon, and smoothed the slopes of Calvary".

156. Whilst the division of the description of creation into six "days" may well be a mnemonic aid, it is more evident still that there were successive stages or cycles of development in that work,—cycles which, even if overlapping or rather gradually passing from one to another, were nevertheless characterized by some outstanding feature which distinguished these divers step-like phases in the perfectioning of the world. Moreover, it is clear that the creation account is intended to depict a God-week, and thus to lay the foundation of Sabbath observance for the Jews: "For, in six days the Lord made heaven and earth, and the sea, and all things that are in them, and rested on the seventh day: therefore the Lord blessed the seventh day, and sanctified it" (Exod. 20:11). God is represented as laboring at the task of constructing the universe, by direct creation or mediate formation, during six periods, thereupon in the seventh period leaving the finished universe to carry on its own activity through the powers and laws wherewith He Himself had endowed it whilst it was a-building. Similarly man is to work six days at supplying the needs of material imperfection; on the seventh, however, he is to give himself over more especially to the influx of the Divine. But all this does not militate against interpreting the "day" periods of the hexaëmeron as cycles of thousands of years,—since already the Psalmist had declared that "a thousand years, in Thy sight, are as a yesterday which is past" (Ps. 89:4). In fact, the Hebrew term *yôm* has quite commonly also the wider, indefinite significance of a lengthy time period.[14]

157. Symmetrico-Logical Plan of Hexaëmeron.—That in the hexaëmeron events are arranged not so much according to the order of their occurence, in simple chronological sequence, as according to a definite artificial, logico-poetical scheme in the hagiographer's mind, must strike even a superficial reader. Thus the works of the cycles of creation are grouped according to distinctive phases of universe—construction, sometimes simultaneously going on, in a spreading triple arrangement of *creation, division,* and *equipment* (ornatio), as outlined in the accompanying diagram:

(1) "Heaven" is here certainly not to be taken in the same sense as in Gen. 1:8: "And God called the firmament 'Heaven'", or in Gen. 1:14, 15, 17, because the firmament or sky which is named 'heaven' is adduced as a specific work. Rather, the word "heaven" is to be taken as metonymically standing for the great world of immaterial creatures as contrasted with matter, the latter being represented by the term 'earth'. Thus St. Augustine opines that Moses "'cœli' nomine spiritualem vel intellectualem illam creaturam semper faciem Dei contemplantem (Matt. 18:10) significavit".[15] In this sense may be understood the Psalmist's: "By the word of the Lord were the heavens established" to which is subjoined as a parallel: "and all the army thereof by the spirit of His mouth" (Ps. 32:6). "Heaven" here would be more particularly the *cœlum cœli* considered as the place of the angels and of God. Compare the summary of the creation account in II Esdras 9:6: "Thou Thyself, O Lord alone, thou hast made heaven, and the heaven of heavens, and *all the host thereof,* . . . and the host of heaven adoreth Thee".[16] Note also the expression "angeli cœlorum" in Matt. 24:36; Mark 12:15; 13:32, etc. The IV Lateran Council states explicitly "[Deum] ab initio temporis utramque de nihilo condidisse creaturam, corporalem *et spiritualem"*.

[14] See Gen. 26:1; 47:8; II Kings 21:1; IV Kings 10:21; Job 15:10, etc.

[15] *Confess.,* XII, 17, *in principio.*

[16] The "Heaven of heavens" as the special seat of God and the angels may also be noted in Deut. 10:14; III Kings 8:27; II Par. 2:6; 6:14; Ps. 67:34; 113:16; 148:1; Ecclus. 16:17.

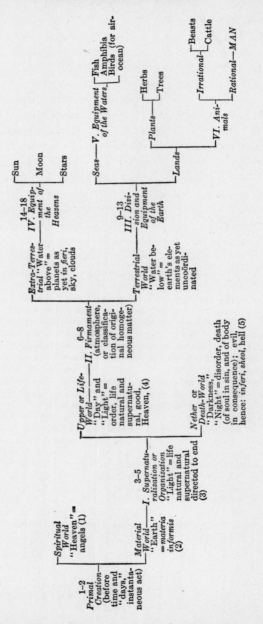

(2) This *materia informis* is, of course, not to be confused with the philosophical *materia prima*. In the words of St. Augustine, primitive homogeneous matter is so denominated relatively, "non privatione omnis formæ, sed comparatione formosiorum",[17] that is, the fair compounds into which it was ultimately to be developed. In this elemental initial stage matter was as yet undiversified, "totum prope nihil erat, quoniam adhuc omnino informe erat; iam tamen erat quod formari poterat".[18] The physical laws (as: attraction and repulsion, with their consectaries of motion, force, etc.) being not as yet operative (they presuppose heterogeneity), the condition of primitive matter is graphically described by the Scripture as *thóhû wabóhû*, "topsy-turvy", in a chaos of lawless confusion, *thehôm*, which is emphasized by the expression "darkness". Hence also "ista informitas terræ invisibilis et incompositæ nec ipsa in diebus numerata est. Ubi enim nulla species, nullus ordo, nec venit quidquam nec præterit; et ubi hoc non fit, non sunt utique dies nec vicissitudo spatiorum temporalium".[19] Nevertheless, over this lifeless chaos already broods the life-giving Spirit.

(3) The work of the First Day, expressed in terms of light, should likewise be interpreted in the broadest meanings of its terminology. For, this work can not be limited to the production of physical light and its distinction as against physical darkness, because such distinction and division is later given by the hagiographer as the characteristic of the Fourth Day, when the planets are described as set "to divide the day and the night, . . . to shine in the firmament of heaven, and to give light upon the earth, . . . and *to divide the light and the darkness*" (Gen. 1:14, 15, 18). The restriction to a significance of physical light production being thus excluded, what is the metonymic meaning of "light" terminology which will best bear out this passage? Now, "light", in its broader Scripture aspects denotes *order, activity, life*. And in this sense it may be applied to the lowest laws of the association of elements, the natural existence of plants, beasts, and men.[20] But more especially is "light" synonymous scripturally for the *supernatural order* and *life of grace* by which both angels and men (and, subsidiarily, even lower creatures, as man's life-means) are "made partakers of the Divine nature" (I Pet. 1:4). Thus of the penitent man it is said: "He hath delivered his soul from going into destruction, that it may *live and see the light*" (Job 33:28); the Wise Man says of the life of the just that "as a *shining light* it goeth forwards and increaseth even unto *perfect day*" (Prov. 4:18); and of the Logos it is said: "What was made in Him was *life*, and *the life was the light of men*" (John 1:3b-4). In this sense also is best made intelligible the obscure passage of II Cor.

[17] *Confess.*, XII, 5.
[18] *Ibid.*, 7.
[19] *Ibid.*, 9.
[20] The equivalence of "light" to "life", natural, or supernatural, may be seen in many passages of Scripture, such as Job 3:20; 12:22; 15:22; 18:5-6, 18, etc.

4 : 6 : "God who said, 'Out of darkness light shall shine', is He that hath shone into our hearts".

158. The work of the First Day, then, may well be thought of as, primarily, God's decreeing to elevate what had been created, to the supernatural order. Particularly would this have reference to the test of the angels,[21] and the fixed adherence of some of them by free choice to God, and the equally free aversion from Him by others,—which latter would constitute a *disorder* in God's universe, imply spiritual *death*, and bring about the punitive habitat of *evil*, *hell.* Hence God's forcible statement in Isaias (45 : 7) : "I form the light and create darkness; I make peace, and create evil".— For *matter*, the work of the First Day may be understood as the giving thereto of the basic laws and forces of the physical world, upon which is based the order constituting the life of the heterogeneous complexity whereby it reflects the multiple perfections of God. That coincidently with the beginning of the operation of the laws of matter, some kind of physical light also made its appearance, is not excluded.

(4) Had the divine decree, "Let there be light !" been applicable only in a physical sense and to the preëxistent *materia informis* alone, there would have been no occasion for a subsequent division of the "light" from the "darkness", for, matter can not resist the Divine Will. Such non-conformity is possible only to a free, hence intellectual, creature. In this connection it is to be noted that in Gen. 1 : 4 (differently from parallel passages of the hexaëmeron) it is stated exclusively that "God saw the light that it was good", not applying this adjective either to the division itself or to the counterdistinguished "darkness". There is here implied a note of censure for the "darkness", as though the latter were indeed beside God's antecedent and direct will in creating. One concludes, then, that the fact that *all* creation did not react obediently to the

[21] That the decreeing of the supernaturalization of the universe, and particularly the "trial" of the angels, is the topic of the First Day, is the opinion of St. Augustine: "Quod autem in primis conditionibus dixisti 'Fiat lux, et facta est lux,' non incongruenter hoc intelligo de creatura spirituali, quia erat iam qualiscumque vita quam illuminares. . . . Quid de Te promeruit inchoatio creaturæ spiritualis . . . nisi per idem Verbum converteretur ad idem a quo facta est; atque ab eo illuminata lux fieret. . . . Creato spiritui non id est vivere quod sapienter vivere, alioquin incommutabiliter saperet. Bonum autem illi est hærere Tibi semper, ne quod adeptus est conversione, aversione lumen ammittat, et relabatur in vitam tenebrosæ abysso similem" (*Confess.*, XII, 2, 3). "Defluxit angelus, defluxit anima hominis, et indicaverunt abyssum universæ spiritualis creaturæ in profundo tenebroso, nisi dixisses ab initio, 'Fiat lux', et facta esset lux;—et inhæreret Tibi omnis obediens intelligentia cœlestis civitatis tuæ. . . . Alioquin et ipsum cœlum cœli tenebrosa abyssus esset in se; nunc autem lux in Domino. . . . Beata creatura [angeli], quæ non novit aliud, cum esset ipsa aliud, nisi dono tuo, quod superfertur super omne mutabile mox ut facta est; attolleretur nullo intervallo temporis in ea vocatione qua dixisti, 'Fiat lux', et facta est lux. In nobis enim distinguitur tempore quod tenebræ fuimus, et lux efficimur (*ibid.*, 8, 10).

Fiat lux was due to deliberate refusal on the part of some of the earliest created intellectual beings (the angels) to conform to God's order of the universe. Thereupon followed a segregation of these rebellious elements, whose status relatively to all the rest of creation would of course be one of disorder and therefore comparable to the primeval *informitas* of matter; hence the appellation of "darkness".

This great primitive division of the universe into "light" and "darkness" is found reflected in the traditional cosmological systems of ancient peoples, who conceived the world to be arranged in a series of cosmic planes or spheres of life, occupied in their highest parts by divinities (or, with the Hebrews, by God and the angels), with men dwelling on the lowest stage. Opposed to these life- and light-filled "Upper Regions," the "Nether World", a region of death, darkness, and confusion, was thought of as existing either within or below the earth. Even ancient Hebrew eschatology had no clear concept of a beatific hereafter for the just; good and bad alike at death went down to dim *šeôl*, until the advent of the Messias. Dante's *Divina Commedia* with its circles and stages of Hell, Purgatory, and Heaven, is a Christian and modern reproduction of a cosmic system more ancient than the *ziggurat* or stage-towers of Babylonia, with their various terraces painted a distinctive emblematic color and dedicated to some planet-god according to the order of their spheres.

159. The "day" and "light" of Gen. 1: 4-5, then, in conformity with the usage of Hebrew philosophical and poetical writing, may be taken as metonymically representative of the life-planes of creation. Primarily the word will be synonymous with "heaven" as the abode of God, the good angels, and men who have persevered in their supernatural estate. Thus the dwelling place of the saints is described in the Apocalypse (21: 23-25) as a city that "hath no need of the sun, nor of the moon, to shine in it. For the glory of God *hath enlightened* it . . . there shall be *no night* there". St. Paul warns the faithful that "Satan himself transformeth himself into an *angel of light*" (II Cor. 11: 14). Again, the expressions "light" and "day" are used also to symbolize the supernatural life even inchoatively upon earth. Thus the just, as *"children of light"*, are contrasted with the wicked, as "children of this world" (Luke 16: 8); "For, what participation hath justice with injustice? Or what fellowship hath *light* with darkness? And what concord hath Christ with Belial? Or what part hath the faithful with the unbeliever?" (II Cor. 6: 14-15). For, you were heretofore darkness, but now *light* in the Lord. Walk then as children of the light" (Eph. 5: 8). "For, all you are the *children of light,* and *children of the day:* we are not of the night, or of darkness" (I Thess. 5: 5, 8). "Let us therefore cast off the works of darkness, and put on the *armour of light*" (Rom. 13: 12). "Light" and "day" as synonymous with natural *life* may be seen in Job 3: 20; 12: 22; 15: 22; 28: 5-6, 18.

(5) On the other hand, "night" and "darkness" are in poetical

and philosophic Scripture language synonymous with the "Nether World", "a land that is dark and covered with the mist of death, a land of misery and darkness where the shadow of death and no order, but everlasting horror dwelleth" (Job 10: 21-22). These terms designate a phase of the universe that is out of harmony with the primary decrees of God; hence they signify lack of supernatural life of grace, sin, evil, physical death as its consequence, and eventually hell as the habitat of fallen angels and impenitent sinners. There burns the gloomy "everlasting fire which was prepared for the devil and his angels" (Matt. 25: 41); there is the "exterior darkness [where] there shall be weeping and gnashing of teeth" (Matt. 8: 12). In Old Testament eschatology this "limbo" or šeôl is the dwelling place of all the departed indiscriminately, although there appears already early (in Job especially) the hope of an eventual delivery of the just therefrom.[22]

In conclusion it is not to be overlooked that each "day's" work is itself rhythmically divided into (a) the Divine command, (b) the execution thereof, (c) detail or division, (d) naming, calling good, or blessing. So, whether the "days" be considered as actual time periods, or merely a mnemonic aid, there can be scarce any doubt but that the hexaëmeron follows a subjective, artificial, logico-poetical plan of the hagiographer's, rather than the objective chronological course of events. And by this consideration many difficulties from geology are obviated.[23]

Art. 4: PARADISE AND THE FALL OF MAN

Texts: Num. 1: 1-4, 47-54; 3-6; 8-12.

160. The Two Creation Accounts.—Man was made "in the image and likeness" of God, that is: not only was there naturally in the tripartition of the human soul into being, knowing, and willing (each of which functions is nevertheless the whole soul) a reflection of the characteristic unity of Three Persons in One Divine Nature; but, man was raised

---

[22] Other passages in which "darkness" is equivalent to death, hell, or the powers of evil, are I Kings 2: 9; Tob. 4: 11; Job 3: 19; 17: 13; 18: 18; 20: 26; 38: 19; Ps. 87: 12-13; Eccles. 6: 4; Ecclus. 11: 16; 21: 11; Matt. 25: 30; Jude 1: 13, etc.

[23] For commentary on the hexaëmeron, consult Aquinas, *De Opere VI Dierum;* Lépicier, *L'Opera dei Sei Giorni;* Hummelauer, *Der Biblische Schöpfungsbericht;* and "The Days of Genesis" and "Genesis and Evolution", in *Moses and the Law* (London, 1922). See also the author's articles in *Homiletic and Pastoral Review* for May-August, 1924,

above the status which was his by nature into an adoptive
filiation to God, whereby he was graciously given participation in the very life of the Divinity. Hence a special account
is devoted to human origins, especially the supernatural
phases hereof. Gen. 2:4 *ss.* is not to be considered as a
doublet or mere repetition of Gen. 1-2:3. Rather, the account of universal creation is first given for its own sake,
and then summarized as a preliminary setting for the story
of First Estate [24] and Fall of man.

161. Paradise.—From the material organization of the
universe the Scripture proceeds to describe the *moral, spiritual formation* and vicissitudes of human kind. Man is shown
as originally placed in a special environment set apart [25]
from the rest of the material world, as befitting the dignity
of his supernatural state. This dwelling place, called Paradise, is not described as if it were an allegory or myth, but
is delineated as a real district to the east of Palestine. [26]

On account of the obscurities of ancient geographical conception
(perhaps also because of considerable prehistoric changes in the
earth's surface) it is difficult to identify the "rivers" named in
Gen. 2:10-14. Thus, for example, the ancients seem to have traced
rivers at times from mouth to source, contrary to the modern custom. The "river" of Gen. 2:10 may have been the *naru marratu*,
"Salt or Ocean River", of the Babylonian geographers, which was
practically the Persian Gulf. This branch of the ocean in prehistoric times seems to have extended considerably farther north-east
than at present, along the Tigris line perhaps as far as Kut-el-
Amâra, so that the Tigris and Euphrates had rather widely separated mouths. [27] The Phison, according to Josephus, is the Ganges;
according to Haneberg, [28] the Hyphasis or the Indus; according to
Vigouroux, the Rion of Armenia (Phase of the classics) flowing
westwardly into the Black Sea, or the Kur, arising near Kars, not
far from the western sources of the Euphrates, and through the

[24] " . . . who kept not their principality, but forsook their own
habitation" (Jude 1:6).

[25] Etymologically "paradise" has been derived from Sanskrit *pairi-
daêza*, a "hedging or heaping about", and also from *parâ*, "high up"
and *dêsa*, "land"; it is used as a common noun in Cant. 4:13; Eccles.
2:5; II Esdras 2:7. Eden, as a "place of pleasure", seems to have
some etymological connection with the Greek *hêdonê*.

[26] Gen. 2:8 (Hebrew): "towards the rising of the sun".

[27] See Father Legrain's map appended to his *Historical Fragments*
(vol. XIII, Publications of the Babylonian Section of the University of
Pennsylvania, 1922).

[28] *Geschichte der biblischen Offenbarung* (Ratisbon, 1863), pp. 16-19.

Araxe flowing into the Caspian. In the last case, Hevilath would
be Colchis, where the Argonauts sought the Golden Fleece. Sayce,[29]
however, would derive Phison from the Babylonian *Pišannu*, a "pipe
or artificial watercourse", as a name given to an irrigation canal and
tidal marsh stream which together with the Persian Gulf would
have enclosed the south-east and east of Babylon and Elam. In
that case, the reading *Havilah* is conjectured as a scribal error of
vav for *resh* (ו for ר), to be corrected to Harilah,—which might
allude to the Babylonian *Aralli* or "mountain of gold". The Gehon,
according to the Septuagint of Jer. 2:18 and Ecclus. 24:27, is
the Nile. According to Sayce, it would mean "an outburst of
water" and be identifiable with the *bitq*, "cleft or fissure in the
ground", which, according to an old Babylonian map, communicated
with the Ocean River and bounded or surrounded the Old Testament Cush or modern Arabia.

162. Adam was placed in the garden of Eden "to dress
and keep it" (Gen. 2:15), according to the ordinary version,
—although, with St. Augustine, it is possible to read also
that Adam was set in Paradise in order that God "might
develop and guard him".[30] If the former interpretation be
accepted, Adam's care of Eden can not be conceived as laborious and tiring, as such a process is later punitively imposed as an indication of the Fall (Gen. 3:17-19). In this
case one may have an explanation of the First Parents' relationship to Paradise in Ecclus. 17:7-9. This would seem
to imply that Adam and Eve were to *exercise their faculties
of intellect and will* in studying and contemplating the perfections of the Divine Nature as reflected in the beauty and
order of material creation about them, and in reaction to
be the living voice of appreciation and praise rising up ever
from the world to the Creator thereof. And thus, in fact,
man is soon seen to be exercising his reason in its perfection
of vocal expression by correctly estimating the character of
the objects about him, and giving them names accordingly
(Gen. 2:20).

But in this very process it becomes evident that man is
quite superior to all the rest of material creation, and that
the latter alone can not afford him full exercise of his highest, spiritual faculties. This can be brought about only by

[29] "The Land of Nod", in *Proc. of Soc. of Bibl. Archeology*, vol. 38,
p. 6, Jan. 19, 1916.
[30] See *Summa*, 1a, q. 102, a. 3.

interchange of acts of will and intellect, of knowing and loving, with another human creature that should be man's
counterpart or complement, that could adequately fulfill his
desire for equal companionship, and return his affection and
communication of knowledge. After this preface the Scripture goes on to narrate the creation of Woman, made (as the
Talmud significantly comments) not from the feet of man,
lest he despise her as an inferior, nor from his head, lest
she should arrogate to herself the dominion, but from his
side, from the part of the body which is generally clothed,
to indicate her equality with man, and at the same time to
intimate her characteristic of modesty. Through mutual
coöperation, then, is the human race to develop its perfection, and particularly through the inseparable association of
the sexes in marriage is the proper propagation of mankind
to be assured (Gen. 2:21-24). And, because man's highest
faculties, intellect and will, are still perfectly coördinated
with God, his lower, animal appetites—the strongest of which
(after the instinct of self-preservation) is that of sex or the
preservation of the species—remain entirely under the control and regimen of his reason. Adam and Eve, therefore,
needed not "be ashamed" at any uncontrollable manifestations of disorderly tendencies in their animal powers (Gen.
2:25).[31]

163. The Test and the Fall.—Man's relationship towards
the world and, so to speak, towards himself, his own kind, had
been perfectly established. There remained yet to be accomplished his own free acknowledgment and regulation of his
relationship to God—which was by nature that of creature,
but by gratuitous gift that of adopted child,[32] participant in
the supernatural life of the Divinity. Consequently, as man
was a free intellectual creature, endowed with adequate
knowledge of God and nature, with a will free to make choice
of the means to his happiness, he himself had to determine

[31] For a detailed study of the status of Adam and Eve, see Lépicier's
tract *De prima hominis formatione* (Lethielleux, Paris).

[32] "We are now the sons of God . . . Whosoever is born of God,
committeth not sin . . . In this the children of God are manifest, and
the children of the devil" (I John 3: 2, 9, 10).

the proper attitude of his relationship to God. As the angels had done at the very threshold of creation, so now man would have in the test to decide [33] whether he would in all things *conform to the order of the universe* as outlined by God, and thus finally deserve the encomium of "good",[34] which could not definitely be pronounced over him at his creation, because he had not then as yet fair opportunity to make his choice. This opportunity of self-expression, of distinct, independent, and unforeconditioned actuation of his personality towards God was given to man by God's prohibiting him from eating of the fruit of a particular tree in paradise,[35] whilst all the other fruits were freely granted him for his use. Other tests or commands could have been given; this was perhaps the simplest and most natural under the circumstances.

164. Another factor now enters upon the scene, a factor of disorder and of the "darkness" first appearing at the very beginning of creation (Gen. 1:4b). The evil nature of this unharmonious power is taken for granted, and is evidenced by his words and suggestions, which drive toward revolt against the ordinance of God. This Evil Power makes its appearance in the guise of a serpent, through whose body it places before man the argument of the Temptation.

The apocalyptic literature of the Jews, and the mythological traditions of other peoples, throw light on the association of a snake or dragon-monster with the personal Power of Evil. But, rather than lead back the Genesis narrative to a pagan myth, one should see in their basic concordance (when it is established) evi-

---

[33] "God made man from the beginning, and left him in the hand of his own counsel" (Ecclus. 15: 14).

[34] The encomium of "good" is pronounced over every work of the hexaëmeron (in Greek also after "firmament", Gen. 1: 8) except the segregation of evil ("darkness" of Gen. 1: 4–5) and the creation of man (Gen. 1: 27–30),—although in a generic manner it is applied to the creation as a whole, at the close (Gen. 1: 31).

[35] The appellation "tree of experience of good and evil" (Gen. 2: 17) is probably equivalent simply to "test-tree", and certainly implies no inherent virtue or quality of the tree itself; any fruit or paradise might have been chosen by God for man's trial. A primary allegorical sense in "tree of knowledge", "serpent", and eating of the forbidden fruit, to the exclusion of historical narrative, is here inadmissible, according to the constant teaching of the Church. See *Biblical Commission* of June 30th, 1909, in Appendix, p. 240. Consult also Schumacher on the *Historical Value of Genesis,* Chapter II, in the *Homiletic and Pastoral Review* (April–June, 1923).

dence for primitive facts and language which formed a common
tradition origin for both the correctly preserved Hebrew account
and the fantastically corrupted myths of other peoples.

The "serpent", *naḥaš*, as the personification of Evil, hostile to
God, is introduced in Genesis without any preliminary explanation,
thus showing that the terminology used by Moses and its real significance was familiar and clear to his readers.   Traces of this
traditional serpent **or** dragon-monster terminology as applied to
the Evil Powers and associated with the "darkness" and entire
Nether World of disorder and death, are not lacking elsewhere in
the Bible.   The clearest use thereof is found in the Apocalypse
(12: 9-10), where "that great dragon . . . that old serpent" is
identified with "the devil and Satan, who seduceth the whole world",
who "was cast unto the earth, and his angels were thrown down
with him".   In Isaias (27: 1) the serpent terminology shows also
the association with the "sea" or *tehóm-abyss* (= Nether World)
as the abode of death and the Powers of Evil: "In that day [of
the messianic conquest] Yahweh shall unsheathe His sharp and
great and mighty sword against the elusive dragon, the deceitful
serpent, and He shall finish off the *Thannin* (= devil-monster) in
the sea".   Likewise in Amos (9: 2-3) the inevitableness of the doom
of the wicked is expressed in these words: "Though they dig down
into hell, thence shall My hand snatch them, . . . though they hide
from My eyes in the depth of the sea, there shall I command the
Dragon (*nachaš*) to bite them".   Job also complains of his bitter
but undeserved suffering: "Am I Sea (= hell) or *Thannin* that
Thou shouldst set guards about me?" (Job. 7: 12).   Fragments
of these ideas may be recognized in the Babylonian Tiâmat legend
where this monstrous goddess representative of the primitive chaotic
abyss, is overcome by the light-demiurge Marduk, in the Seth-
Typhon-Horus myth, or the Ra-Apophi contest of Egypt, the
Python legends of the Greeks, and even in the world-encircling
(oceanic) Midgard-snake so hostile to the lightsome Loki.   All
these witness to the interpretation given to the First Day of the
hexaëmeron account of Nos. 157 and 159 above, and to its extra-
scriptural traditional diffusion among primitive peoples.

The predicates applied to the serpent (*e.g.*, "more
subtle than all the living-things of earth"),[36] the propositions enounced by him, and the curse uttered over him (Gen.
3: 14-15) are, of course, not to be considered as applying to
the snake, but rather to the invisible terrific personal Evil.

165. That man fell as he did, and by Satan's temptation,
may, in final analysis, have been by a most merciful dispensation of Providence.   Had man, like the angels, fallen by tak-

[36] Compare, on the astuteness of the Power of Evil, Christ's declaration: ''The children of this world are wiser than the children of light''
(Luke 16: 8).

ing his God-likeness for God-equality—instead of, as was
actually the case, improperly striving for God-equality—the
Redemption, as with the fallen angels, might never have
taken place.

By the Fall, man's harmony with the universe as established by God became disrupted. This jarred the harmony
previously existing within man's own being between his animal and his spiritual elements. In his own body appeared
the uncontrollable manifestations of carnal desires not in
accord with the dictates of reason,—which were thenceforth
to be a reminding stigma of the loss of original righteousness, order, justice,[37]—and therefore Adam and Eve were
ashamed "when they perceived themselves to be naked"
(Gen. 3:7, 10). For the woman in particular, her chief
function as man's "helpmate" (Gen. 2:20) in the propagation of the human race, intended to be her crown of joy,
would henceforth be steeped in bitter pain in its accomplishment (Gen. 3:16). The external world, likewise, no longer
would in every respect harmonize with man's life; "thorns
and thistles" it would offer him in return for his labor (Gen.
3:18-19). Lastly, man was driven from paradise, the special
environment of the high estate he had forfeited, and made
to dwell unprivileged in the common plane of the world.

Man had sought by misuse of nature to become like to
God: henceforth the enjoyment of nature would be so poi-
soned for him that thereby he would often forget, doubt, or
deny his Creator. Because man had sought in nature that
which God alone could give, therefore the pain and sorrow
which nature henceforth would so frequently inflict upon
man, would in last analysis be a blessing in disguise, as tending to make him return to God. As false enjoyment brought
on the Fall, so suffering became the keynote of Redemption.

[37] "Peccatum originale per se est habitualis aversio a Deo fine
supernaturali, unde privat iustitia, seu, quod idem est, caritate et gratia,
quatenus convertunt hominem ad finem supernaturalem scil. Deum"
(Suarez, *De vitiis et peccatis,* disp. 16, dub. 3, n. 56); "Fecit igitur
persona [Adami] peccatricem naturam [humanam] quia cum Adam
peccavit, homo peccavit . . . facit natura personas peccatrices. Sic
spoliavit persona naturam bono iustitiæ in Adam, et natura egens facta
omnes personas quas ipsa de se procreat, eadem egestate peccatrices et
iniustas facit" (St. Anselm, *De conceptu virginali,* c. 23).

166. Protoevangel.—Fallen mankind was not to be hopeless as were the fallen angels. The alliance so deceitfully foisted upon Eve by the devil was not to persist forever. "I will put enmities between thee [the serpent] and the woman," says God, "between thy descendants and hers" (Gen. 3:15). Thus, at the very dusk of the Fall, the position of the Mother to come is emphasized in the promise of a restoration of man to conformity with God. As by Eve the feminine sex had been disgraced in the Fall, so in the Mother of the Redeemer would it once more be glorified.[38] As Eve had made a mockery of her title of "mother of the living" (Gen. 3:20) by becoming the cause of death to all men, so was the highest verity of that title to be restored in Mary, the *Mother of the Redeemer* (who was indeed "the way, the truth, and the life"), and, at the same time, spiritually, adoptively, by Christ's efficacious testament upon the Cross (John 19:26-27), the *Mother of the Redeemed*, "the rest of her seed" (Apoc. 12:17), who, unlike the seed of the serpent, "keep the commandments of God" (Apoc. 12:17) and consequently "have life and have it more abundantly" (John 10:10).

This first messianic prophecy strikes a theme which shall be rung again and again throughout Old Testament history: the association of a woman with the Redeemer to come, for the re-creation of mankind, analogously as Eve had been associated with Adam as his "helpmate" (Gen. 2:20) in the primal creation, and as coöperatrix unto destruction in the Fall. Henceforward the expression "woman" *par excellence*, becomes the formal title of the co-redemptrix in the language of Israel's seers,[39]—until the day when she herself is exhorted thereby to intimate coöperation in the opening of the messianic mission at Cana of Galilee, and again is appealed to therewith at the close of that same messianic work, when, beneath the Cross, the "tree" bearing the fruit which im-

---

[38] That "woman" in Gen. 3:15 does not have reference to Eve personally is clear from both the context of that same verse and from the malediction uttered in Gen. 3:16 upon her, which is incompatible with the rôle of victrix.

[39] Thus the texts: "Behold a *virgin* shall conceive and bear a son" (Is. 7:14); "The Lord hath created a new thing upon the earth: a *woman* shall compass a man" (Jer. 31:22).

parts true God-likeness, she indeed "cried travailing in birth and was in pain to be delivered" (Apoc. 12:2) of "the rest of her seed" (Apoc. 12:17), against which, in accordance with the protoevangel, "the serpent-dragon" continues to "make war" as he is "angry against the woman." Thus in the end her image merges with that of the Church, the living organization of the head and members of the mystical "body of Christ" (Eph. 4:12; Col. 1:18), as the latter Himself bore the lineaments of Mary,—who finally stands forth as the "woman in heaven . . . clothed with the sun, having the moon [of earthly corruption and changeableness] under her feet, and on her head a crown of twelve stars" (Apoc. 12:1).

This prominence of the Woman in the protoevangel has perhaps influenced the exegetic translation of the Vulgate which has "ipsa conteret caput tuum" in Gen. 3:15, instead of the neuter which the Hebrew text grammatically demands.[40] The sense, of course, is not thereby substantially changed; only the opposition as between the Serpent and the Woman is sharpened.

As to the significance of "thou shalt 'lie in wait for' her heel", it can not be established from the verb alone, sûf (=go after, or lie in ambush for, with gaping mouth) which is the same just previously translated by "shall crush". The meaning is: that these two opposing world-forces, the Serpent and his "seed", spiritual followers, sequaces, will scheme and wrestle in warfare against the Woman and her "seed", which implies both the personal Christ and the spiritual children of whom Christ is the "elder brother". The relative efficiency of this bitter age-long contest is to be judged from the injury to be inflicted (according to the prophecy) which is on the head of the Serpent, hence fatal; on the heel of the Woman's seed, hence painful but not destructive.[41] Mary suffered indeed beneath the Cross, and the Church and the faithful suffer each day from the assaults of diabolic persecution, yet never is such injury effective unto death.

[40] St. Jerome favored the reading ipse, which was also that of the Old Latin and the Septuagint. Melchior Canus says: "Cum enim apud Hebræos neutro genere ad semen referatur, interpres rem significatam perpendens, in masculino genere transtulit ipse. Quod imperiti non intelligentes, vitiumque scriptoris existimantes, substituerunt ipsa" (Locis theol., II, xv). But the expression, even if it is "infidèle à la lettre du texte, est cependant conforme à son esprit".

[41] The quality of venomousness (implying fatal results with the slightest wound, and often associated with all snakes) is here not taken into consideration. It must be remembered that in the mind of the hagiographer "serpent" here as the personification of evil stands for Dragon-monster, "leviathan", Thannin, with which venomousness was not predicated as a characteristic.

Art. 5: THE DELUGE

Texts: Num. 19-20; 22-25; 35-36.

167. Antediluvian Characteristics.—After Cain's fratricide, when, as a "weakling and an outcast",[42] he with his undoubtedly already numerous clan [43] left the first district of man's habitation to establish a separate community in a new region,[44] there becomes already evident in the human race a division into a group which strives to conform to God's order of the universe, the "children of God" (Gen. 6:2), and into another group whose members give uncontrolled rein to their natural desires, without regard to their first supernatural end, thus being typically "seed of the serpent". Of the former group a line of outstanding persons is recorded in Gen. 5. These apparently, with their families and associates, strove for the right and even by exhortation tried to convert to the supernatural life-attitude those who had rejected it.[45] However, in the course of time even the "sons

[42] Thus Sayce would interpret the mysterious *na'wanad* of Gen. 4:14, basing it upon an Assyrian original, *nu'u û nidu*. Cain in fact did not become a "vagabond", for he established a community and one of his descendants was an artificer in bronze and iron (Gen. 4:22). But he was indeed an "outcast" from mankind's original habitation.

[43] It is only reasonable to assume that at the time of Abel's death there were also other living brothers and sisters of Cain, even in considerable number, and probably themselves having children, since Adam was then already 230 (Gen. 5:3 Greek) years old. Their vengeance, then, Cain might have to fear. Again, the longevity of the first descendants of Adam, as recorded in the Scripture, may very well be presumed to have been paralleled by a corresponding prolificness; in fact, the fertility of the antediluvians is attested by the late dates in their lives at which children were still brought into the world (Gen. 5). This would be in accord with the wise providence of God to assure the rapid multiplication of mankind. Hence there is no need of postulating a preadamite race to people the earth.

[44] This "land of *Nôd*" (Hebrew), *Naïd* (Greek), according to Sayce (*Proceedings of Soc. Bibl. Archeol.*, vol. 38, p. 6, Jan. 19, 1916) would be the Sumerian name of Dilmun (modern Dailem or Dilem, north of Bushire), alias Guggirinna, near the Persian Gulf. Etymologically *Nidu* would very comfortably mean "that [place which is] at the end [of the world], hence "No-man's-land". This would explain Cain's calling himself an outcast "from the land" (Gen. 4:14).

[45] Thus Noe is called "the preacher of justice" (II Pet. 2:5).

of God" began to be corrupted with the vices of the earthly group, having become acquainted with them through inter-marriage.

Thereupon the moral depravation of mankind seems to have become almost cataclysmic. The bodies of the ante-diluvians seem in their constitution to have been still fresh with the pristine vigor of paradise (perhaps of the "tree of life"), hence their animal passions would be most violent. Especially then, upon the conjunction of those of the stock of Seth,—perhaps by its previous virtuous life even more vigorous,—unbridled lust ran riot upon the earth. The animal and vegetative faculties of men being their chief care and interest, developed their physique far beyond the normal, so that "giants were upon the earth in those days" (Gen. 6:4; Bar. 3:26; Wis. 14:6; Ecclus. 16:8). Glorying in their physical might and absorbed in the pursuit of bodily pleasure, these men were soon so sunk in the flesh that no exhortation, no spiritual warning, nothing in short could stop the course of headlong corruption of the human race, and bring man once more to a realization of his basic rela-tionship to God, but some great physical catastrophe.

168. Deluge Legends.—The biblical account of a great flood destroying all mankind is echoed in the folk-lore of almost all peoples, witnessing thus to a universal tradition going back to an event which would be the common source of both biblical and extra-biblical tradition. There is space here only for reference to the several cuneiform tablet ac-counts from Babylon, Niniveh and Nippur which so wonder-fully confirm (and have thrown considerable light upon) the history of Gen. 6-8. The longest of these accounts is con-tained in the Gilgamesh epic, discovered in the library of King Ashurbânapal (668-626) at Nineveh, and is itself a copy of a Babylonian original that may go back to 1700 B.C. In this version Ut-napishtim corresponds to Noe. Through the advice of Ea he is saved when the gods decide to destroy all mankind by a great flood:

Line 20: "Thou son of Ubartutu, man from Shurippak,
    21: Construct a house, build a ship (= make a house-boat)

27: Bring seed of life of every kind into the ship
28: The ship which thou shalt build
29: Let its form be long
30: Its breadth and height shall correspond
31: Roof it over like the nether waters".

Then follows a description of the building of the deluge-boat, concluding:

Line 61: "I saw cracks, and repaired them
    62: Six measures of bitumen I spread over the outside
    63: Three measures of bitumen I spread on the inside
    79: All that I had living I brought together
    80: All things I brought into the ship, my man-servants and maids
    81: The beasts of the field, the animals of the lands
    89: Into the ship I went and shut the door
   121: Six days and six nights (passed by)
   122: Raged wind, rain, storm upon all things
   123: On the seventh day the storm calmed, the flood decreased
   140: I sent out a pigeon, and she flew here and there
   141: There was no resting place, she turned back
   142: I sent out a swallow, she flew here and there
   143: There was no resting place, she turned back
   144: I sent out a raven, and he flew away
   145: The raven flew and saw the corpses on the water
   146: It ate, it waded, it wandered, and did not return

The fragments conclude with a description of the sacrifice which Ut-naptishim afterwards offers, about which the gods "gather like flies", etc.

The oldest cuneiform deluge account, according to its discoverer, Hilprecht, was written before the time of Rîm-Sin of Larsa, or about 2100 B.C., bringing it more than 600 years before the time generally assigned to Moses, and "even some time before the Patriarch Abraham rescued Lot from the hands of Amraphel [Hammurabi] of Shinar and Chedor-laomer of Elam" [46] (Gen. 14). Furthermore, on account of its age, which brings it so much closer to the source of primitive tradition, it is interesting to note that this fragment shows "a much greater resemblance to the Biblical Deluge Story than any other fragment yet published".[47] In Hil-

[46] See *Researches and Treatises of the Babylonian Expedition of the University of Pennsylvania*, vol. V, fasc. 1, edited by H. V. Hilprecht (Philadelphia, 1910).
[47] *Ibid.*, p. 34.

precht's own translation it reads as follows, the portions in
parentheses being supplied on conjecture or from the context:

Line 1: . . . . "thee
       2: . . (the confines of heaven and earth) I will loosen
       3: . . (a deluge I will make, and) it shall sweep away all
          men together
       4: . . (but thou seek l)ife before the deluge cometh forth
       5: . . (For, over all living beings,) as many as there are, I
          will bring overthrow, destruction, annihilation
       6: . . Build a great ship and
       7: . . total height shall be its structure
       8: . . it shall be a house-boat carrying what has been saved
          of life
       9: . . with a strong deck cover (it)
    10: . . (The ship) which thou shalt make
    11: . . (into it br)ing the beasts of the field, the birds of
          heaven
    12: . . (and creeping things, two of everything) instead of
          a number
    13: . . and the family
    14: . . and" . . . .

Of particular value, for one instance alone, in these accounts are the etymological indications that the ark (written
in the biblical text by *thebah,* an Egyptian loan-word designating a box or chest which can be closed with a cover or
lid) was not so much a ship in the ordinary acceptation as
a *magur* (a Sumerian loan-word), a deluge- or house-boat,
strongly roofed over, for shelter against the pouring rain.
Hence the *tsihar* of Gen. 6:16 should be translated rather
as a "covering, hatch, or roof" than as a "window" (see
8:13). The obscure Hebrew expression *mîni* is explainable
as a Babylonian loan-word (from *mînu, manû* = to count
or number), to be translated in 6:19 by "two for its number" in the sense of "two as representative for a number".

Mini has long been emphasized by destructive criticism as an
important identification word of **P** (= Priests' Code), or the section of the Pentateuch imagined and then asserted to have been
composed even a century later than the time of King Josias (621).
And now Assyriology makes it an expression characteristic of the
times preceding Hammurabi!

169. Extent of the Deluge.—The language of the deluge
account in Genesis was long interpreted as implying that the

punitive flood covered the entire globe, and that all men and beasts, besides those in the ark, perished therein. In consequence there could be raised such absurd difficulties as to how all the fauna species living upon the earth at present, together with sufficient feed for their sustenance, could have been collected and contained within the ark; how afterwards the islands would once more be populated with their characteristic beasts; whence the enormous quantity of water requisite for such a flood, would come in such short time, etc.

But such exegesis was faulty insofar as it unconsciously gave a modern extent and conception to the ideas underlying the terms of the Genesis account. For this, for its primary literal or historical sense, must be read in the light of men's knowledge (specifically here, geographic) at the time of its composition. Perhaps, as a record of pre-Mosaic tradition, it should be interpreted in the light of the world-concept of the first postdiluvians, approaching rather that of ancient Sumer and Akkad. In any case, the *kol-ha'arets* (= "whole earth") of Gen. 7:3, and similar expressions, may just as well be translated as "the land or country" or the "whole world inhabited by humans". The geographic concepts and interests of both Moses' contemporaries and their ancestors would be limited to the territory or portion of the world they were acquainted with—and how small this was is familiar to students of archeology, and evidenced by fragmentary antique maps.

The Deluge, then, need not have submerged the whole globe as at present known and denominated "the earth". Men, especially as being of "one tongue and the same speech" (Gen. 11:1), would not yet have left the first seats of mankind, perhaps the great alluvial basin of the Tigris and Euphrates, or the southwestern steppes of Asia, bordering upon the Caspian Sea. Hence a seismic depression of the comparatively small district of land occupied by the antediluvians could wipe out of existence the whole human race through a flood caused by inrushing ocean waters and torrential rains. Noe, then, would have been obliged to save with himself in the ark specimens of only such species of animals as he had been acquainted with, and as would be desirable for the restocking of the land which had been denuded of animal life by the Deluge. Such a collection could be accommodated without extreme difficulty in a house-boat of several stages, about 450 feet long, 75 feet broad, and 45 feet high. The fauna, of course, of the rest of the world would remain unmolested.

However, whilst a mere relative universality of the Deluge, considered geographically, is quite consonant with the biblical narrative, the Scripture clearly insists upon the fact that *all mankind* with the exception of Noe and his family, were destroyed. Thus Gen. 9:19 states that from the sons of Noe came all the inhabitants of earth. And the text of I Pet. 3:20c has always been interpreted by the Church as implying that only eight human beings were saved from the Deluge.

Art. 6: ISRAEL IN EGYPT

Texts: Deut. 1-3; 22-25; 31-34.

170. From the Deluge until Abraham.—After the Deluge the descendants of Noe once more fell away quickly from the order of God, this time rather in the direction of pride, their presumption crystallizing in the building of the Tower of Babel, by which they foolhardily expected to save themselves in case of another world-flood. But God would not suffer men to coöperate without let unto their own destruction. Therefore, by varying their speech, He divided and grouped them into opposing nations, so that their self-seeking and pride of one could not but check and oppose that of another (Gen. 11). With the great ethnographic table of Gen. 10, Sacred Scripture thereupon leaves the history of peoples and their turmoils, to concentrate exclusively upon the vicissitudes of the descendants of Sem, the eldest son of Noe.

From Sem the hagiographer simply traces a genealogical line down through the subsequent period, without giving other details, just as he had previously enumerated the emi-

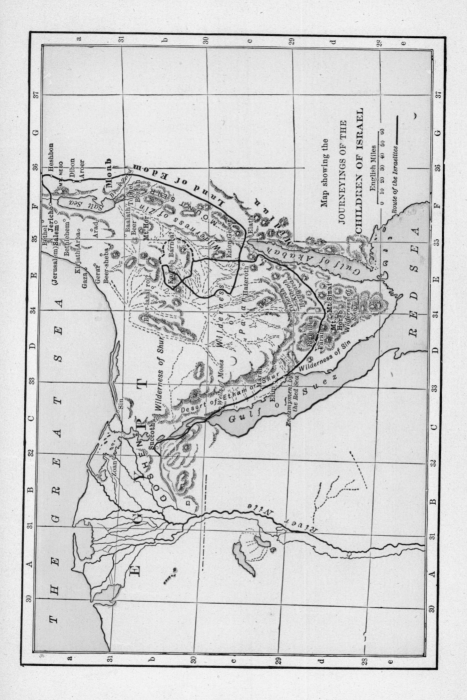

Map showing the
JOURNEYINGS OF THE
CHILDREN OF ISRAEL

English Miles
0 10 20 30 40 50 60

Route of the Israelites

THE GREAT SEA

RED SEA

Gulf of Arabah

Gulf of Suez

Land of Edom

MOUNT SEIR

Moab

Wilderness of Zin

Wilderness of Paran

Wilderness of Sin

Wilderness of Shur

EGYPT

GOSHEN

River Nile

Heshbon
Dibon
Aroer
MT NEBO
Salt Sea
Bethel
Jericho
Salem
(Jerusalem)
Bethlehem
Kirjath-Arba
Gaza
Gerar
Beer-sheba
Arad
Baalath
Bene-jaakan
Beeroth
Mt Hor
Kadesh Barnea
Ezion-geber
Elath
Hazeroth
Mt Mt Sinai
Horeb
Wilderness of Sin
Elim
Marah
Sin
Zoan
Succoth
Desert of Etham or Shur
Encampment by the Red Sea

nent personages of the "children of God" from Seth, son
of Adam, to Noe (compare Gen. 5 with 11:10-32). This
Semitic group evidently increased and multiplied for centuries in the fertile river basin watered by the Tigris and
Euphrates. For there archeology has found evidence, including dynastic lists, "for more than 2000 years of history
before the foundation of the first Babylonian empire",[48]
that of Hammurabi (1958–1928 B.C.), contemporary of Abraham.[49] In the northern portion of this region, Mesopotamia,
are found the most ancient Akkadian city-communities, Kiš
(Babylon), Upi, Akkad, Isin, inhabited by a Semitic race;[50]
in the southern portion, extending about 150 miles from
Nippur to Eridu (then on the sea), are located the Sumerian
city-communities, Uruk, Ur, Adab, Hamazi, Larsa, and others,
inhabited largely by a non-Semitic people, the Sumerians,
with Semites as a strong minority. "The first known kingdom was the Semitic kingdom of Kiš", but during this long
stretch of chronology eleven royal cities had in turn the honor
of controlling the land between present Bagdad and the sea.

[48] Léon Legrain, *Historical Fragments,* p. 5 (Babylonian Section of
University of Pennsylvania, 1922).

[49] The identification of Hammurabi, the great Babylonian lawgiver,
with the Amraphel of Gen. 14 is practically established. As for the
difference in the spelling (consisting in the additions of the final "1"),
it is to be accounted for, according to Sayce (*Expository Times,* Oct.,
1912, p. 37; see also Drum in *Ecclesiastical Review,* vol. 48, p. 352), on
the theory that the scribe who first transliterated the names of Gen.
14:1 from the ancient syllabic (cuneiform) script into the Phenician
alphabetic, aspirated very naturally "p" to "ph"; and, as "pi" and
"pil" are represented by the same syllabary sign, he closed with the
Hebrew "-el" for "-il". Arioch would be Eriaku, of Larsa (Heb.
Ellasar) in Sumer (according to Pilter in *Proceedings of Soc. of Bibl.
Archeology,* vol. 37, p. 177), or Rîm Sin (to be read Rîm-Aku) of Larsa
(according to Hilprecht in *Researches and Treatises of Babylonian Expedition of University of Pennsylvania,* 1910, vol. V, fasc. 1, p. 8, note 3).
Chodorlahomor would be Kudur-mabuk (Kudurlagamar), king of Emut-
bal (= Elam), probably leader and instigator of the expedition, as he
was at the time in control of the Tigris-Euphrates basin, and of the west,
i.e., Syria. Thadel (Tidal) has been conjectured to be of Guti (Goths)
origin. Hammurabi did not remain long an ally vassal of Elam, but
defeated his associates, to take the title of "King of Babylon, of
Sumer and Akkad, and of the four quarters of the compass".

[50] For further information on ancient Babylonian history, consult
Father Legrain's *Le Temps des rois d'Ur* (Paris, Champion, 1912) and
Empreintes des cachets elamites (Paris, Leroux, 1921); also L. W.
King's *History of Sumer and Akkad* (London, Chatto, 1910), and a new
history of Sumer by St. Langdon, of Oxford.

Although Akkad was really the older group, yet "all civilization, art, religion looked toward the Sumerian south as its cradle",[51] as might well be expected from the principle that the older and monogenous communities would be more conservative, the newer, with their heterogeneity of race, more alert, radical, prone to change and improvement. Both countries were later united, with Babylon as the capital of the new empire.[52]

171. With Abraham, the last member of the genealogy of Gen. 11 : 10-32, Sacred Scripture again enters into details. Service of God had been corrupted in the meantime so far that even Thare, Abraham's father, was not free from idolatry (Jos. 24 : 2). Nevertheless, of the ancestors of the Jews it is written (Judith 5 : 7-9) : "They would not follow the gods of their fathers, who were in the land of the Chaldeans. Wherefore, forsaking the ceremonies of their fathers, which consisted in the worship of many gods, they worshipped one God of Heaven,—who also commanded them to depart from thence, and to dwell in Charan". Abraham was originally of Ur,[53] in southern Sumer. Together with his father and other relatives he migrated northwest to Haran (Charan), identified with Carræ,[54] not far south of Edessa, on the Belilk, an affluent of the Euphrates. Thence, after the death of Thare, Abraham, upon God's order, moved into the land of Canaan, where God promised to make of his stock "a great nation".

172. Israel in Palestine.—The third generation of the family of Abraham, under Jacob, is seen to have grown to a considerable clan in Palestine. But their activity is confined

---

[51] Legrain, *op. cit.*, p. 6.

[52] Legrain, *op. cit.*, p. 6.

[53] The city of Ur gave name to three dynasties of Babylonian rulers, the third beginning with Ur-Engur (2304 B.C.) and ending with Ibi-Sin. It was the seat of the great moon-god Sin, who is represented on seal-cylinders as seated, wearing the turban, and having a long, dark, lapis-lazuli beard. Deified kings are sometimes represented in like manner. Dungi was the name of the great temple mount of this city, whose site is now occupied by Muqajjar, *i.e.*, "the bitumined city" (Pilter, in *Proceedings of Soc. of Bibl. Archeol.*, vol. 37, p. 176, note 7).

[54] Where Crassus lost the great battle against the Parthians, south of Edessa, west of Nisibis, in the upper reaches of Mesopotamia.

chiefly to pastoral pursuits. Their Amorrhite neighbors no doubt consisted of similar bands. As all were herdsmen with large flocks, they seem to have led a rather isolated, independent life in frequently moved encampments.

Had things been permitted to continue thus, Israel would no doubt have developed into self-sufficient, brave, but nomadic tribes, like the modern Bedawin. They would have remained forever semi-civilized, without any but the rudest arts, and above all lacking that culture which makes an ethnic group self-subsistent in its thought treasures, and keeps it from being swayed at will by the contact influence of neighboring peoples.

Israel was thus set down on the highroad between the two most cultured and powerful nations of antiquity, Babylon and Egypt. But it had as yet no art, no literature, no culture, not even a national consciousness. It was but a child, and as a child it would have to go to school, and the school which God chose for the training of His own nation, was the most solemn-minded and perhaps the most highly civilized of antiquity, Egypt.

Joseph, Jacob's youngest son, sold by his brethren as a slave into Egypt, afterwards made the Pharaoh's prime minister, was destined to prepare a place for his people. At his invitation, then, Jacob and his entire tribe, to the number of sixty-eight men, besides women and children, took up their residence in the fertile grazing district of Gessen (Goshen), near Heliopolis.

173. Israel in Egypt.—Israel's entry into Egypt most probably took place during the rule of a Hyksos dynasty,— whilst that alien, semi-civilized, Semitic group was lording it over the people of the Pharaohs, the enervating influence of whose refinement and high civilization made them succumb to the onslaught of these rude but sturdy Shepherd Kings from Asia. How distasteful and despised was the government of these uncouth aliens may be judged from Joseph's word of explanation and caution to his brethren when he assigns them their land, removed from the cities: "The Egyptians have all shepherds in abomination" (Gen. 46:34). On the other hand, the ruler of Egypt, feeling himself isolated from a conquered nation which despised his favorite pastoral antecedents, would eagerly welcome immigrants from his own homeland, and be delighted to entrust to them, as experienced cattle and sheep men, the royal herds. Hence his words, when Israel's occupation is announced: "Make them dwell in the best place, and give them the land of Gessen. And if thou knowest industrious men among them, set them over my flocks" (Gen. 47: 6).

174. It is difficult to determine with closer approximation the time of Israel's arrival in Egypt. It seems most probable that it took place during the reign of the Hyksos, the XVIth dynasty, who came into power about 1600 B.C. As from the entry of Abraham into Palestine to the arrival of Jacob in Egypt there elapsed 215 years, and Abraham was contemporary with the great Hammurabi, to whom Legrain assigns the new, low dates of 1958 and 1928,[55] no anachronism results. The duration of Israel's stay in Egypt is likewise involved in obscurity. Moses apparently sets it down as 430 years (Exod. 12: 40), but here the Septuagint and the Samaritan Pentateuch as well as Josephus[56] would include in this figure the 215 years previously spent in Palestine, which latter acceptation is also that of St. Paul (Gal. 3: 17). The shorter period, then, of 215 years for the Egyptian stay would seem preferable, as harmonizing better with the transitory purpose of Israel's providential presence, and with the statement that "in the *fourth* generation" (Gen. 15: 16) the Israelites should return to Palestine, which statement is itself borne out by the actual enumeration of generations (Levi Caath Amram Moses in Exod. 6:16-20; Levi Caath Isaar Core in Exod. 6:16-21 and Num. 16: 1; Levi Caath Oziel Mizael in Exod. 6: 16-22 and Lev. 10: 4; Ruben Phallu Eliab Dathan in Num. 26: 5-9), and by the fact that Josue's generation is considered the fifth (see Jos. 7: 1 and Gen. 38: 30).

175. Enslavement and Training.—Thus Israel at first lived segregated in a kind of pastoral ghetto on the border of Egypt and Arabia, and there multiplied under the protection of the Shepherd Kings. But later "there arose a new king over Egypt, that knew not Joseph" (Exod. 1: 8), that is: did not recognize the privileged status of these foreigners from Asia. This seems to point to the rise of a new dynasty which had overthrown the Hyksos usurpers. Was it Ahmosis, or the later Amenophis IV[57] who marked the transition

55 Legrain, *op. cit.*, p. 13.
56 *Ant.*, II, xv, 2.
57 Breasted (*Ancient Records*, I, p. 43) places Amenophis IV in 1375–1350, and Luckenbill makes him a contemporary of Burna-Buriaš.

point? Early Egyptian chronology is too uncertain as yet to give a definite answer. At any rate, for Israel a period of servitude began.

The long pent-up dislike of the Egyptians for everything connected with the Hyksos was vented also upon the latter's *protégés*, the Hebrews. The Shepherd Kings had destroyed many of the monuments and public works of Egypt. These had to be rebuilt, and nothing was more natural than that the now enslaved descendants of Jacob should be employed at the menial labors of the task.

176. In this manner was Israel forced to come into intimate contact with the monumental arts and works which constitued the glory of ancient Egyptian culture. These loosely grouped clans were made to feel first of all, and in only too painful a manner, the efficiency of a closely knit, systematic government. Next, they had to become acquainted with other avocations than the wandering care of cattle, for they were conscripted for "all field labors" (Exod. 1:14 Greek),—and Egypt was renowned for irrigation and intensive agriculture. Lastly, coöperating as they did in the restoration and building works of the XVIIIth dynasty, the alert and imitative genius of the Hebrew could not but assimilate of the arts and sciences of mathematics, mechanics, architecture, which have made Egyptian construction and ornamentation a marvel even to modern times. The subsequent building of the Tabernacle and its appurtenances in the Wilderness may be considered the masterpiece of Israel's bitter apprenticeship in Egypt.

177. There was of course an obvious danger that the Hebrews, being thus brought at every step under the influence of their Egyptian masters' solemn worship of the dead and of animals, might be led to corrupt their own divinely entrusted tradition and service of God. But this danger was providentially neutralized by the very *tyranny of the oppression* which forced this contact, so long at least as its duration was not sufficient to break the spirit of the oppressed. Moreover, these harsh measures employed to cow and extinguish a people accustomed to the freedom of nomadic pastoral life would, according to a principle universally recognized in history, serve but to *rouse a national consciousness*. The fiery blasts of persecution which fell upon the descendants of Jacob in the furnace of their oppression in Egypt served in the last analysis but to weld its loosely aggregated elements into one united people. Israel graduated from a family, a clan of tribes, into a nation. And this newly aroused national consciousness would make the sons of Abraham, Isaac, and Jacob cling most tenaciously to the ancestral traditions which formed their only hope, pride, and consolation, and make them look with indifference upon the polytheistic necrolatry of their masters, and with disgust upon their animal cult, termed "the abominations of the Egyptians" (Gen. 8:26).

Had Israel settled down amid ease and plenty in the land of Egypt, no leader would ever have succeeded in advocating a return to Palestine. But, under the actual condition of grievous servitude, Moses appeared as a liberator, "and the people believed" (Exod. 4:31) and were ready to follow his guidance, especially after the stupendous prodigies of the Ten Plagues had once more raised their spirit to that admirable trust in God which ever afterwards characterized the Jews. Thus was brought about the united transmigration of a new nation of over 600,000 men from Egypt through the Wilderness to its promised seat in Palestine.

The time of the Exodus (which would practically coincide with that of the composition of the Pentateuch) has not been definitely determined. Chevalier (in Moigno, *Splendeurs de la foi*, II, p. 46*) and Vigouroux would place the oppression largely during the long reign (60 years) of the great Ramses II (Sesostris), whose mummy may be viewed now in the museum at Gizeh, Cairo. His harsh and tyrannical character and his ambitious building undertakings are familiar to Egyptologists. Dying in 1365, he was succeeded by his son Amenophis Menephtha, who reigned about 54 years. According to Moigno, then, the Exodus would have taken place in April (Egyptian) of 1340. But recent studies incline towards placing the Exodus further back in history. Thus Lattey (in *Moses and the Law*, p. 69), basing himself upon the date 973 for the beginning of the building of Solomon's Temple, by adding on the 480 years of III Kings 6:1, obtains 1453 "as roughly the date of the Exodus". Hontheim likewise places it in the XVIIIth dynasty, under Amenhotep II (1472-1446, according to Breasted 1448-1420), in 1449.

APPENDIX

DECISIONS OF THE BIBLICAL COMMISSION

De Mosaica Authentia Pentateuchi

Propositis sequentibus dubiis Consilium Pontificium pro studiis de re biblica provehendis respondendum censuit prout sequitur:

I—Utrum argumenta a criticis congesta ad impugnandam authentiam Mosaicam sacrorum Librorum, qui Pentateuchi nomine designantur, tanti sint ponderis, ut posthabitis quampluribus testimoniis utriusque Testamenti collective sumptis, perpetua consensione populi Iudaici, Ecclesiæ quoque constanti traditione necnon indiciis internis quæ ex ipso textu eruuntur, ius tribuant affirmandi hos libros non Moysen habere auctorem, sed ex fontibus maxime ex parte ætate Mosaica posterioribus fuisse confectos? *Resp.* Negative.

II—Utrum Mosaica authentia Pentateuchi talem necessario postulet redactionem totius operis, ut prorsus tenendum sit Moysen omnia et singula manu sua scripsisse vel amanuensibus dictasse; an etiam eorum hypothesis permitti possit qui existimant eum opus ipsum a se sub divinæ inspirationis afflatu conceptum alteri vel pluribus scribendum commisisse, ita tamen ut sensa sua fideliter redderent, nihil contra suam voluntatem scriberent, nihil omitterent; ac tandem opus hac ratione confectum, ab eodem Moyse principe inspiratoque auctore probatum, ipsiusmet nomine vulgaretur? *Resp.* Negative ad primam partem, affirmative ad secundam.

III—Utrum absque præiudicio Mosaicæ authentiæ Pentateuchi concedi possit Moysen ad suum conficiendum opus fontes adhibuisse, scripta videlicet documenta vel orales traditiones, ex quibus, secundum peculiarem scopum sibi propositum et sub divinæ inspirationis afflatu, nonnulla hausit eaque ad verbum vel quoad sententiam contracta vel amplificata, ipsi operi inseruerit? *Resp.* Affirmative.

IV—Utrum, salva substantialiter Mosaica authentia et integritate Pentateuchi, admitti possit tam longo sæculorum decursu nonnullas ei modificationes obvenisse, uti: additamenta post Moysi mortem vel ab auctore inspirato apposita, vel glossas et interpolationes textui interiectas; vocabula quædam et formas e sermone antiquiato in sermonem recentiorem translatas; mendosas demum lectiones vitia amanuensium adscribendas, de quibus fas sit ad normas artis criticæ disquirere et iudicare? *Resp.* Affirmative, salvo Ecclesiæ iudicio.

—Die autem 27 Iunii 1906 . . . Sanctissimus prædicta Responsa adprobavit ac publici iuris fieri mandavit (*Acta Sanctæ Sedis,* vol. XXXIX (1906), p. 377).

De Charactere Historico Trium Priorum Capitum Geneseos

I—Utrum varia systemata exegetica, quæ ad excludendum sensum litteralem historicum trium priorum capitum libri Geneseos excogitata et scientiæ fuco propugnata sunt, solido fundamento fulciantur? *Resp.* Negative.

II—Utrum non obstantibus indole et forma historica libri Geneseos, peculiari trium priorum capitum inter se et cum sequentibus capitibus nexu, multiplici testimonio Scripturarum tum veteris tum novi Testamenti, unanimi fere sanctorum Patrum sententia ac traditionali sensu, quem, et israëlitico etiam populo transmissum, semper tenuit Ecclesia, doceri possit, prædicta tria capita Geneseos continere non rerum vere gesiarum narrationes, quæ scilicet obiectivæ realitati et historicæ veritati respondeant; sed vel fabulosa ex veterum populorum mythologiis et cosmogoniis deprompta et ab auctore sacro, expurgato quovis polytheismi errore, doctrinæ monotheisticæ accomodata; vel allegorias et symbola, fundamento obiectivæ realitatis destituta, sub historiæ specie ad religiosas et philosophicas veritates inculcandas proposita; vel tandem legendas ex parte historicas et ex parte fictitias ad animorum instructionem et ædificationem libere compositas? *Resp.* Negative ad utramque partem.

III—Utrum speciatim sensus litteralis historicus vocari in dubium possit, ubi agitur de factis in eisdem capitibus ennarratis, quæ christianæ religionis fundamenta attingunt: uti sunt, inter cætera, rerum universarum creatio a Deo facta in initio temporis; peculiaris creatio hominis; formatio primæ mulieris ex primo homine; generis humani unitas; originalis protoparentum felicitas in statu iustitiæ, integritatis et immortalitatis; præceptum a Deo homini datum ad eius obedientiam probandam; divini præcepti, diabolo sub serpentis specie suasore, transgressio; protoparentum deiectio ab illo primævo innocentiæ statu; necnon Reparatoris futuri promissio? *Resp.* Negative.

IV—Utrum in interpretandis illis horum capitis locis, quos Patres et Doctores diverso modo intellexerunt, quin certi quippiam definitique tradiderint, liceat, salvo Ecclesiæ iudicio servataque fidei analogia, eam quam quisque prudenter probaverit, sequi tuerique sententiam? *Resp.* Affirmative.

V—Utrum omnia et singula, verba videlicet et phrases, quæ in prædictis capitibus occurrunt, semper et necessario accipienda sint sensu proprio, ita ut ab eo discedere nunquam liceat, etiam cum locutiones ipse manifesto appareant improprie, seu metaphorice vel anthromoporphice, usurpatæ, et sensum proprium vel ratio tenere prohibeat vel necessitas cogat dimittere? *Resp.* Negative.

VI—Utrum, præsupposito litterali et historico sensu, nonnullorum locorum eorumdem capitum interpretatio allegorica et prophetica, præfulgente sanctorum Patrum et Ecclesiæ ipsius exemplo, adhiberi sapienter et utiliter possit? *Resp.* Affirmative.

VII—Utrum, cum in conscribendo primo Geneseos capite non fuerit sacri auctoris mens intimam adspectabilium rerum constitutionem ordinemque creationis completum scientifico more docere; sed potius suæ genti tradere notitiam popularem, prout communis sermo per ea ferebat tempora, sensibus et captui hominum accomodatam, sit in horum interpretatione adamussim semperque investiganda scientifici sermonis proprietas? *Resp.* Negative.

VIII—Utrum in illa sex dierum denominatione atque distinctione, de quibus in Geneseos capite primo, sumi possit vox Yôm (dies), sive proprio pro die naturali, sive sensu improprio pro quodam temporis spatio, deque huiusmodi quæstione libere inter exegetas disceptare liceat? *Resp.* Affimative. Die autem 30 Iunii 1909 . . . Sanctissimus prædicta Responsa rata habuit ac publici iuris fieri mandavit (*Acta Apostolicæ Sedis*, vol. I, p. 567).

FOURTH PART

THE HISTORICAL BOOKS

Omnis Scriptura Sacra eo spiritu debet legi quo facta est. Quærere potius debemus utilitatem in Scripturis quam sublimitatem sermonis. . . . Curiositas nostra sæpe nos impedit in lectione Scripturarum. Si vis profectum haurire, lege humiliter, simpliciter, et fideliter.

De Imitatione Christi, I, 5.

THE HISTORICAL BOOKS

JOSUE, JUDGES, RUTH, I-II KINGS (SAMUEL), III-
IV KINGS, I-II PARALIPOMENON (CHRONICLES),
TOBIAS, JUDITH, ESTHER, I-II ESDRAS (ES-
DRAS-NEHEMIAS), I-II MACHABEES

PROLEGOMENON

178. General Character of the Historical Books.—As the
Pentateuch outlines the relationship of the universe, and of
man more particularly, to God, tapering down to a narrative
of the vicissitudes of the Hebrew race,—as the Chosen People
typical of all mankind,—so the Historical Books continue the
account of Israel's career, assuming always the Mosaic revelation of the Hebrews' special position before God and the
rest of the world, and ever and anon looking forward to the
perfect idealization of the House of Jacob in the future messianic Kingdom.

Thus the Historical Books are not concerned with the
world at large except insofar as the latter impinges upon
and affects the Hebrews, for whom an attitude of separate-
ness, aloofness, from the Gentile world is continually postulated and prescribed, just as that world itself is generally
pictured as hostile, inimical to the characteristic culture of
the Hebrews. Nevertheless, from time to time (as in the
Book of Ruth) there occur indications that non-Hebrews too
are not entirely excluded from and may be brought to share
in the unique intimate relationship to God accorded primarily
to the descendants of Abraham.

179. The progress of Hebrew history may be described
as a continual pendulum movement, as that nation with its
leaders culturally and religiously swings toward or away from

God. The factors bringing about this movement are almost the only ones chronicled: this may be considered the hagiographers' principle in choice of subject matter. These factors are: idolatrous or naturalistic influence of contact with Syro-Phenician, Assyro-Babylonian, Hellenistic and Roman religious and cultural forms; on the other, the encouragement of the supernatural intervention of God for His people by miracle and prophecy, as well as His clear chastisement of their withdrawals from Him. Hence world-events and movements which do not directly serve to illustrate the relationship of Israel with God are passed over in silence by the sacred chronicler, or only alluded to in passing. God's dealings with the Hebrews and their reaction thereto make up the substance of the Old Testament Historical Books.

180. As for the literary form, it varies in the different Books according to the personal predilection, plan, or character of the respective hagiographer. Whilst generally simple and natural, the style is now brief, condensed, now broad and diffuse; repetitions are numerous; transitions from one subject to another go frequently unmarked, are made without apparent connection,—as is commonly the case with Oriental, and particularly with Semitic, writers. Above all, the historic account is, almost without exception,[1] kept entirely objective and impersonal. The hagiographers note persons and deeds without expressing judgment as to their moral value in particular, being content to remark the general conformity or non-conformity of events and subjects to the divine order or the Mosaic law. Thus the mere fact that Sacred Scripture records evil acts done by some great biblical persons is not to be interpreted as an approval or even toleration of all the acts of such persons.

---

[1] About the only exception to this rule is the Second Book of Machabees, whose author praises or blames deeds and men, after the manner of Greek historians.

Art. 1: THE BOOK OF JOSUE

Texts: Jos. 1-5; 9-10; 13, 23-24.

181. The Author and Date.—The author of the Book of Josue is not known for certain, but Jewish tradition [2] has named Josue himself, who figures so prominently, even if unobtrusively, in the contents. That the author was contemporary with the events he records is indicated by occasional lapses from the impersonal, objective, style, into the first person: "... until *we* had crossed", "... the land which He had sworn to their forefathers to give unto *us*" (Jos. 5:1, 6 Hebrew). Moreover, the Book of Josue seems to have been composed long before Davidic times, as Bethlehem is not mentioned in the list of towns belonging to the tribe of Juda; the Jebusites are spoken of (15:63) as still in control of Jerusalem; Sidon is still called "the great" (11:8), a title which it lost at its destruction by the Philistines during the time of the Judges, after which Tyre acquired the preponderance of power. Lastly, as an argument for the composition of the work by Josue himself, it may be noted that throughout the book in all the accounts of events wherein Josue was the master-mind and leading spirit, there is not one word of praise [3] given to that great hero. Rather he seems to wish to efface his personal share as much as possible. [4]

182. Object and Chief Contents.—To the Pentateuch the Book of Josue bears much the same relationship that the Acts of the Apostles has to the four Gospels: Josue shows forth the fulfilling of the prophecies and promises of Moses, as Acts manifests the realization of the great prophecies and promises of Christ. The thesis of the Book may be said to be: trust, believe, confide in God, for He is the faithful ful-

[2] "Joshua wrote his own book and [the last] eight verses of the Thora", *Baba bathra*, 14b. Abarbanel ascribes the redaction to Samuel.

[3] Note on the contrary how Josue is praised by the Son of Sirach (Ecclus. 46: 1–10).

[4] Only in the account of his death, added by a subsequent hand, is Josue called "the servant of the Lord" (Jos. 24: 29).

filler of His promises. Josue himself is represented as continually acting upon this principle. No wonder, then, that
he is one of the few persons of the Old Dispensation to whom
the Holy Spirit never addresses a word of reproach.

According to subject matter the Book of Josue falls into
two chief parts: 1st, the Conquest of Palestine (1-12) ; 2nd,
the Distribution of the Promised Land (13-21). To this body
of the Book is added a supplement containing: (1) Various
Events and Meetings of the Tribes beyond the Jordan (chap.
22) ; (2) the Exhortation to Israel before Josue's death
(chap. 23) ; (3) Josue's Farewell and Final Exhortation (24:
1-24) ; (4) the Renewal of the Alliance of Israel with God
(24: 25-28) ; (5) the Account of the Death of Josue and
Eleazar (24: 29-33).

In the text of Josue as in that of the Pentateuch, there may be
traced certain glosses and additions emanating from some later
editorial hand. Such is the expression repeatedly occurring: "until
this present day" (Josue 4: 9; 5: 9; 6: 25; 7: 26, etc., about fourteen times). But the addition of this gloss is certainly previous
to the eighth year of David's reign, when that monarch cast the
Jebusites out of Jerusalem. So the prophet Samuel may have given
the final redaction to the Book of Josue.[5]

183. Miraculous Hailstorm at Battle of Gabaon.—As the
Israelitic invasion of Palestine under the leadership of Josue
proceeded victoriously, the native clans and towns were terrified and determined to form an alliance in opposition. One
group, however, the Gabaonites, being only about fifteen miles
distant from Josue's headquarters at Galgala, near Jericho,
judged it more advisable to make peace betimes. Hence, by
a clever ruse whereby they gave the impression of having

---

[5] Haneberg (*Geschichte der biblischen Offenbarung*, 3rd ed., p. 203)
mentions a curious extra-biblical reference to Josue's conquest of
Canaan (also known as Phenicia), given in Procopius' account of Beli-
sarius' wars against the Vandals in Africa (*Bell. Vandal.*, II, 10).
According to this historian, some of the Canaanites vanquished by Josue
fled to Africa and there built a fort in a Numidian city later known as
Tigisis. Here were to be found two pillars (στῆλαι) of white stone
"having sculptured upon them in Phenician language and Phenician
letters the following: 'We are they who fled from the face of the
Josue, the Robber, the son of Nave' (Ἰησοῦ τοῦ λῃστοῦ υἱοῦ Ναυῆ)'. This
Numidian city has been conjectured to be Tidjes of the Ibn Haukal,
southeast of Constantina, in eastern Algeria.

journeyed from a distant land outside Canaan, they tricked
Israel into a treaty of protection (ch. 9). The other chief-
tains of Canaan were enraged at this defection of an important town from their confederation. Therefore the other
five "kings" of southern Canaan laid siege to Gabaon. But
the Gabaonites managed to get a message through to Josue
acquainting Israel's leader with their plight and begging his
assistance.

184. By a forced march during the night Josue's soldiers
succeeded in surprising and thus routing the Canaanite be-
siegers of Gabaon. Josue himself, however, wished not only
to relieve Gabaon but at the same time to strike a decisive
blow at the Canaanite league at this the very beginning of
its functioning. But his men had already been wearied by
the long night-march from Galgala. To their weariness was
now superadded the oppressing [6] heat of the July sun blazing
down at high noon ("in the midst of heaven" Jos. 10:13c)
upon the slopes of Gabaon. With the enemy already seeking safety in full flight,[7] it was practically impossible for
Josue's men in their exhausted condition to pursue them.
At this crisis, seeing the fruits of victory in danger of slipping from his hands because of the oppressing heat of the
sun, Josue "cried to the Lord . . . and said: 'Cease [shin-
ing], O sun, upon Gabaon, and thou, O moon, over the vale
of Ajalon!' And the sun did cease and the moon desist
[from shining] till the people revenged themselves of their
enemies, as it is recorded in the Book of the Just. So the
sun ceased [shining] in the midst of heaven, yet hasted not
to go down during the whole day" (Jos. 10:12-13). As
this incident was later summarized: "Did not the sun with-

---

[6] Abbot Kleber translates the Hebrew of Ecclus. 46: 5b: " . . .
during its [the sun's] oppressing", thus obtaining a direct reference to
the heat of the event. But in that case there is difficulty in placing the
ἐχθροὺς of the Greek, whose presence is vouched for also by the Vulgate
inimicos. The Douay version unfortunately here mistranslates. Vigouroux has, much better: "en attaquant les ennemis de toutes parts".

[7] There is absolutely no indication in the text that on this occasion
the Israelites were at any time in danger of being vanquished by the
besieging Amorrhites. The Greek of Ecclus. 46: 5b would seem to mean
that Josue "called upon the All-Powerful Most High whilst they [the
Israelites] were hard pressing their enemies".

draw whilst in its fervor,[8] and the one day become [through the intervening darkness] like unto two''? (Ecclus. 46: 5, combining Hebrew, Greek, and Latin). For, whilst the Canaanites ''were fleeing from the face of the children of Israel down the slope of Beth-Horon, the Lord hurled great hailstones upon them from heaven, and many more were slain by the hailstones than were killed by the swords of the children of Israel'' (Jos. 10: 11).

What occurred? At Josue's prayer miraculously the heated summer air was filled with storm clouds so dense and dark that both sun and moon were blotted from the sky, as if night had come, thus affording welcome relief to Josue's wearied men. At the same time great hailstones descended out of the black clouds upon the fleeing Amorrhites, no doubt throwing them into a still greater panic of terror and confusion, so that they may have even slain each other by mistake.

185. Older interpretations of this account in Josue, which supposed a lengthening of the daylight period, implying an arrest of the earth's diurnal motion, were induced by inaccurate translations of the verbs *damam* and *'amad* in Jos. 10: 12-13, Ecclus 46: 4, and Hab. 3: 11-12. Thus the Douay has in these places "Move not", "stood still". In reality these two verbs have the basic sense of "to cease from action in general", not only "to stop onward motion".[9] The characteristic action of the sun and the moon is "to shine". Hence applied to these heavenly bodies these verbs would signify "to stop shining". This is most naturally accomplished by an obscuring screen of dense clouds,—and a violent summer hailstorm is a feature of the Scripture narrative. That the verbs used do not signify here "to cease (apparent) diurnal motion" is made evident from the text of Habacuc, where the word *'amad, steterunt,* is paral-

[8] Because the Vulgate translates what is now in the Septuagint and Hebrew ''hand'' (χειρ and *yad* יד) by *in iracundia*, it may be suspected that the Greek text used by St. Jerome had a word equivalent to some derivative of *zûd,* זוד or זד, which terms have the meaning of boiling with heat or raging, and whose initial letter might easily be misread for that of *yad.* On such an hypothesis is based the translation of Ecclus. 46: 5 given in the text. There would be a direct reference to the ''oppressing heat'' of the sun on this occasion.

[9] *Damam* denotes primarily ''to be silent, quiet'', secondarily ''to cease, leave off'', and only in the last place ''to stand still''. The other verb, *'amad,* used in parallel with the above, in Gen. 29: 35; 30: 9; IV Kings 13: 18; Jon. 1: 15 has the general meaning of ''to cease from any action''. In Ecclus. 46: 4 *'amad* is translated into Greek by ''Did not the sun step back, withdraw?''

leled in the other hemistich by *yehalekû, ibunt,* πορεύσονται, "they shall go",—where the latter verb has the meaning of "to go out, quit", as in Ps. 77:39; Job 7:9; 19:10; 14:20. Hab. 3:11-12 may be paraphrased as follows:

> "At the coruscation of Thine arrows the sun and the moon
> ceased shining in their sky-dwellings;
> They were put out by the effulgence of Thy dazzling spear."

In Jos. 10:13c the Hebrew "and" is to be translated as an adversative conjunction, and the sentence is to be taken as an explanation declaring that though the darkness of the storm cloud was like that of night, nevertheless the sun had not really set, the oncoming of night had not been hastened, but rather that "one day", through the intervening period of darkness, "was made into two" (Ecclus. 46:5b). The "so *long* a day" of Jos. 10:14a is only "such a day" in the original. The "then" of 10:12 does not refer to the time subsequent to the storm, but to the time of the previous battle and flight.[10]

Art. 2: THE BOOK OF JUDGES

Texts: Jud. 1:4-5, 6-7, 11, 14-15, 20-21.

186. Date, Plan and Author.—This Book could not have been written before Samuel's victory over the Philistines indicated in I Kings 7:1-14, because the body of the composition closes with the death of Samson, Jud. 16:21.[11] Moreover, it seems not to antedate Saul's coming to the throne, unless the recurrent phrase in the appendices, "In those days there was no king in Israel" (Jud. 17:6; 18:1, 31; 21:24) are to be taken as editorial glosses. On the other hand, the Jebusites are recorded expressly (1:21) as still inhabiting a section of the later Jerusalem together with the tribe of Benjamin: they were definitely evicted only by David (II Kings 5:6-7).[12]

187. The Book of Judges begins with: (*A*) an Introduc-

[10] The substance of the explanation just given must be accredited to Abbot Kleber's excellent article on "Josue's Miracle" in the *Ecclesiastical Review* of May, 1917, pp. 477–488.

[11] The Philistine oppression lasted 40 years (Jud. 13:1).

[12] The expression in Jud. 18:30: *gelôth haárets* (= taking away of the land), "until the day of their captivity", is probably to be read *gelôth haarôn* (= the taking away of the Ark).

tion, which itself comprises two parallel parts. The first
of these (1-2:5) sketches the political and military vicissitudes of the Hebrews relatively to the Canaanites, who had
not been expelled from their ancient seats by Josue's campaigns: the second (2:6—3:7) shows forth the religious aspects of the Hebrews' early history in Canaan. They are
represented as vacillating ever between fidelity to God and
the worship of idols, prospering when faithful, chastised
when apostatizing. Next comes (B) the History of the
Judges (3:8—16:31). There are thirteen of these outstanding local leaders or dictators (or fourteen, counting Abimelech, who attempted to usurp the royal power at Sichem),
but details are given of the lives of only seven. Hence this
portion of the Book may be divided into seven sections: (1)
Othoniel (3:8-11); (2) Aod and Samgar (3:12-31); (3)
Debbora and Barac (4—5); (4) Gedeon (6—8:32); (5)
Abimelech, Thola, and Jaïr (8:33—10:5); (6) Jephte,
Abesan, Ahialon, and Abdon (10:6—12:15); (7) Samson
(13—16). At the end are two Appendices (17—18 and 19—
21), which chronologically should have a place at the beginning of the Book, for their events belong to, or shortly after,
Josue's time. The author or compiler of Judges is unknown,
although the Talmud mentions Samuel.

188. Characteristics of the Judges' Period.—With the
entry into Palestine after the Exodus Israel entered upon
an entirely new phase of its existence. The Hebrews were
now powerful enough to wage vigorous and victorious war
upon the local clans, the cup of whose abominations before
God was now full.

For, the inhabitants of Canaan were devotees of the ancient orgiastic Phenician cults of Baal, Thammuz and Astarte, the Syrian Venus. Bloody sacrifices, even of human
beings, of children, with self-mutilation [13] were therein united
to the most unnatural lusts. And these unspeakable rites
were carried out in green groves and on hill tops with much

---

[13] Note, for example, the acts of the priests of Baal on Mount Carmel: ''So they cried with a loud voice, and cut themselves *after their
manner* with knives and lancets, till they were all covered with blood''
(III Kings 18: 28).

splendor of processions under the encouragement of a numerous priesthood. As it was in origin a worship of secret and mysterious powers of Nature, particularly in her death and revivification from season to season, there were intimately connected with such cult superstitious observance and veneration of all changes and happenings in the sky, the earth, the animals and plants. The curiosity and idleness of man were catered to by magic formulæ and sorceries that would seem to give control over hidden terrestrial and celestial forces. All these things combined to attract the Israelites from the ascetic, cold, pure worship of the spiritual, unimageable, strict Yahweh to the sensuous, easy, and varied service of Baal, Moloch, and Astarte.

189. Two reasons, then, were there to justify God's command of a war of extermination upon the Canaanites: "Thou shalt suffer none at all to live, but shalt kill them with the edge of the sword . . . lest they teach you to do all the abominations which they have done to their gods" (Deut. 20:16-18). The inhabitants of the land which had been promised to Israel as its own peculiar possession were to be eradicated root and branch, both in punishment of their sins, which cried to heaven for vengeance, and to preserve the Hebrews from contamination. For, the experience of history shows that so terrific is the contagion of such immoral beliefs and practices that the only safe prophylaxis (as for their concomitant diseases) is destruction of the subjects.

190. Unfortunately for the Hebrews, through false mercy and through deceit, God's command of extermination was not carried out in full strictness,[14] and the deplorable results were not slow in making themselves manifest, as Josue had foretold: "But if you will embrace the errors of these nations that dwell among you, and make marriages with them, and join friendships, know ye for a certainty that the Lord God will not destroy them before your face, but they shall be a pit, and a snare in your way, and a stumbling block at your side, and stakes in your eyes" (Jos. 23:12-13).

---

[14] See, for examples, Jud. 1:21, 24–33. "After Israel was grown strong, he made them tributaries, and would not destroy them".

For, when God, because Israel had already been unfaithful to His covenant, did "not destroy the nations which Josue left when he died" (Jud. 2:20-21), but "left them that He might try Israel by them, whether they would hear the commandments of God", "the children of Israel dwelt in the midst of the Canaanite . . . and they took their daughters to wives, and they gave their own daughters to their sons, and they served their gods, and they did evil in the sight of the Lord, and served Baalim and Astaroth" (Jud. 3:4-7). Instead, then, of keeping their own internal unity—so well established during the Egyptian oppression and during the wandering in the Wilderness—and taking full advantage of the terror which their first advent had inspired, the Israelitic tribes sought rather each his own advantage, Ruben dwelling "between the borders" that he might hear the bleatings of his own flocks, Galaad resting beyond the Jordan, and Dan applying himself to ships, Aser dwelling on the sea shore and abiding in the havens (Jud. 5:16-17). Quarrels and dissensions arose among the conquerors, so that the hardly subdued Canaanites took a fresh lease on life, and in many cases even turned the tables against their invaders. Moreover, during the 400-year period of the Judges there were also invasions by other peoples, Mesopotamians (Jud. 3:8), Moabites from the east, Philistines from the west. The last especially long held a hostile and generally victorious position in relation to Israel. Small wonder, then, that in these periods "the paths rested, and they that went on them walked through by-ways" (Jud. 5:6).

191. The Judges.—During these troublous ages, after the Mosaic high council (Jud. 21:16; compare Exod. 18:21-26) had ceased to function (probably during the first generation in Canaan, when "every one did what was good in his opinion", Jud. 21:25), God from time to time [15] and in

[15] The chronology of Judges is inextricably confused, unless one assumes the legitimate hypothesis that their magistracies were at times contemporary. This is made all the more probable by the fact that the Judges were dictatorlike liberators, having no dynastic claim to ruling power, effecting no systematic organization of government, and rising to authority in divers sections of Palestine, to sway certain tribes or groups.

divers places raised up extraordinary men to be for a season leaders and magistrates for His people. These men, as a product of their times, were not always without fault or defect: frequently violent, crude, sometimes insensible to the finer duties of morality, they nevertheless fitted that turbulent, unsettled war-filled age, having with military faults also the great military virtues of courage, prompt decision, strict discipline, to which, above all, they joined the supernaturalizing virtue of faith, whereby, as St. Paul eulogizes them, they "conquered kingdoms, wrought justice, obtained promises, stopped the mouths of lions" (Heb. 11:31).

Art. 3: THE BOOK OF RUTH

Text: Ruth 1-4.

192. Object and Contents.—This charming pastoral idyl appears as a welcome relief between the struggles and disturbances of Judges and the wars of David, the ancestry of whom it is its object to trace. However, the genealogy given in Ruth 4:18-22 must be considered as giving only the salient members, for it counts only ten persons from Phares, son of Juda, to David, which is certainly too few for an interval of from six to eight centuries. In itself the Book may be considered as another appendix to Judges, during whose time its action takes place. The author and time of composition are unknown, although the fact that the genealogy closes with David may date it subsequent to that king's death.

The events related are apparently merely a matter of family history—how a young widow from the land of Moab became the wife of Boöz, a wealthy land owner of Bethlehem, who, according to Josephus,[16] lived under the magistracy of Heli, after Samson's death. But a providential motive may have been to call the attention of the Jews to the fact that God did not absolutely reject the Gentiles from the messianic promises, that from the simple trustfulness of a Moabite woman who had forsaken the errors of her people, rose the

16 *Ant.*, V, ix, 1.

family of David, from whom the Saviour of the whole world would one day spring.

193. Simple Charm of Account.—Critics are unanimous in extolling the touching naïveté of this history. Its simple composition is yet so artistic that some have been tempted to class it as fiction. Its style and construction make an ideal short-story. Thus does Vigouroux summarize his opinion:

It is a touching idyl of matchless freshness, of charming grace-fulness, of delicate reticence of touch,—a work of exquisite art. A professional fictionist could not have imagined characters more harmonious and better chosen. What a dignified figure is that of Booz, a man of faith, filled with the realization of God, so that the idea of Him is present in all details of life! How diligent and care-ful he is in the cultivation of his fields, how thoughtful of the wel-fare of his servants, beloved by all, respecting the rights of others and observing the Law even in his love for Ruth, his kinswoman! What a sympathy-evoking figure, too, is that of the young Moabitess, so generously devoted to her mother-in-law and to the memory of her husband, so simple in her modesty, so great in her patient sup-port of poverty, so docile in following the advice of Noëmi! That stranger, adopted by the people of Yahweh and destined because of her virtues to become an ancestress of the Messias, is also for us, Gentiles, who like her have been called from error to the truth, a guarantee of our vocation to the Faith.

Art. 4: FIRST AND SECOND BOOKS OF KINGS

Texts: I Kings 1-2; 7-9; 14-16; II Kings 1-3; 5-7; 21-22.

194. Plan, Date and Style.—These two Books were orig-inally one, the division into two parts being first made by the Septuagint, whence it passed to the Vulgate, and now is to be found even in the Hebrew. The reason for separation was simply convenience in writing and handling; the con-tents, making too bulky a roll originally, were put into two rolls or "books". In the Hebrew original (as in the non-Catholic versions) the First and Second Books of Kings are entitled "the Books of Samuel", taking their name from the great judge-prophet with whose life they open, and to whom Jewish tradition ascribed (but without adequate foundation) the authorship of the first part. The name "Kings" was given to these two Books also by the Septuagint interpreters, who combined them with the following two Books of Kings [17] to form a complete history of the royal power in Israel from its beginning to the Captivity.

195. In outline the First and Second Books of Kings fall into three parts: (*A*) Childhood and Judgeship of Samuel (I Kings 1-12); (*B*) History of Saul's Reign (I Kings 13-31); (*C*) History of David's Reign (II Kings 1-24). The last three chapters are in the nature of supplements. In style the hagiographer is writing the biographies of the three chief personages rather than history. He is rather diffuse and given to recording details. But in places he abridges in the form of annals. His language, moreover, whilst free from the archaisms of the Pentateuch and the provincialisms of Judges, still belongs to the golden age of Hebrew literature, showing practically no aramaicisms. In these Books we find for the first time the appellation: "God of Armies (Sabaoth)", so frequently used in Isaias, Jeremias, and the Minor Prophets.

196. The author of I and II Kings is unknown, although the Gemara of Babylon ascribes the authorship of I Kings 1-24 to Samuel, and of the rest to the prophets Gad and Nathan.[18] The date of composition would seem to be shortly after the death of Solomon, during the reign of Roboam. For, the distinction made between Juda and Israel (I Kings 11:8; 17:52; II Kings 3:10; 24:1) began to be introduced during the lifetime of David (II Kings 2:9-10; 5:1-5, etc.). Moreover, the death of David is assumed in II Kings 5:5. And lastly, the expression that "Siceleg belongeth to the *kings of*

---

[17] The title is all that I and II Kings has in common with III and IV Kings. The two hagiographers differ clearly in plan, style, and language. The historian of III and IV Kings loves citations and references, and makes direct quotations from the Pentateuch, whilst the author of I and II Kings, though acquainted with the Pentateuch (see I Kings 12:6, 8), does not make quotations.

[18] This opinion is based on I Par. 29:29: "Now the acts of king David first and last are written in the book of Samuel the Seer, and in the Book of Nathan the Prophet, and in the book of Gad the Seer". But that these compositions are not identical with I and II Kings is evident when one notes that events recorded were not written down by eyewitnesses or contemporaries (I Kings 7:15; 9:9; 27:6). Some canonical Books of Kings may be referred to in II Mach. 2:13.

Juda unto this day'' (I Kings 27 : 6) makes it appear that the secession of the ten northern tribes had already taken place, as under Roboam.[19]

197. Samuel.—The 10th century before Christ found the Hebrew nation at a very low ebb of national existence. It had borne the yoke of the Philistines for a hundred years. General economic conditions and social conditions may be surmised from the statement that was true even as late as Saul's time: ''Now there was no smith to be found in all the land of Israel; for the Philistines had taken this precaution, lest the Hebrews should make them swords or spears. So all Israel went down to the Philistines, to sharpen every man his ploughshare and his sickle and his ax and his spade'' (I Kings 13 : 19-20).

And religious conditions were much on a par with the rest. Heli is highpriest and judge; though without gross faults, he is nevertheless unspiritual, material, content with the mere external observance of forms without sincere striving for the realization of religion also in the interior soul-life. Hence his policy of *laissez-faire,* aggravated by his purblind indulgence of his sons, who sacrilegiously took advantage of the trust of the pious in the sanctuary (I Kings 2 : 12 *ss.*).

198. At this time a pious mother, Anna, of the tribe of Levi, obtained from God a privileged child, the future prophet Samuel. During his youth came the final disgrace of the capture of the ark by the Philistines. Its miraculous return, not to Silo in the land of Ephraim but to Gabaa, of the tribe of Benjamin (I Kings 7 1), prognosticated, even if perhaps it did not help to effect, a shifting of the ruling power towards the south, towards the tribe of Juda. Shortly after, whilst Samuel was offering sacrifice the Philistines were utterly defeated by the Hebrews, after they had publicly acknowledged their defection from Yahweh, and put away their Baalim and Astaroth (I Kings 7 : 3-13) at that prophet-judge's exhortation. Sincere and unalloyed service of the

[19] Several additions which the Septuagint has to II Kings 8 : 7 and 14:27, mention Roboam.

true God was ever Samuel's message to Israel. On this principle he traveled about from place to place and tribe to tribe, conciliating differences and revivifying the worship of Yahweh by frequent sacrifices.[20] Such was his success in restoring the ancient unity and spirit that he dreamt of organizing Israel into a formal theocracy ruled by the chief priest during his tenure of office. But Samuel's ideal could not be realized in a people still too merged in the material to appreciate their high spiritual function as a nation. They desired a king not directly of God's choice, but of their own selection. And thus came Saul, reigning by the authority and under the tutelage of Samuel.

199. Prophetic Communities.—Besides these labors, Samuel must be accredited with the founding of the religious order or collections of ascetic communities which the Scripture designates as the "schools of prophets" (I Kings 10: 5-10). These groups had a head (I Kings 19: 20) called father (I Kings 10: 12) or master (IV Kings 2: 3), and probably formally anointed to that office, as was Eliseus (III Kings 19: 16; Is. 61: 1; Ps. 104: 15). They applied themselves to the praises of God (I Kings 19: 20-24; I Par. 25: 1-6) and probably to the study of the Law. They were originally gathered about Samuel himself at Rama, the *nayôth* (I Kings 19: 19; 20: 1) being perhaps rudely constructed wooden huts (see IV Kings 6: 1-4) for their dwelling like those of the later Egyptian monks. The word "prophet" in this connection did not necessarily mean one who foretold the future, but designated one who followed the ascetic or religious life of these communities. There are but passing allusions to these "schools of the prophets" in Holy Writ, but they continued in existence long after Samuel's time (see IV Kings 2: 3, 5; 4: 38; 6: 1-2; III Kings 18: 4, etc.).

200. Saul.—The reign of Saul falls into two widely different divisions: the first and glorious section, in which he carries out the will of God and governs with a realization of his dependence upon and responsibility to Yahweh (I Kings 9-11; 13: 1-5, 15-23; 14); the second and decadent portion, in which, trusting to his own natural powers, he would rule Israel as the kings of the Gentiles "lorded it over them",

---

[20] This practice of sacrifice in divers places may seem to have been against the letter of the Mosaic legislation (Lev. 17: 4; Deut. 12: 5), but again it may have been legalized by the bringing along of the ark, which, especially after leaving Silo, had as yet no fixed location in Israel.

making even religion but an instrument for his own aggrandizement. God's spiritual ideal of an Israelitic kingdom that would be permeated with the idea of its high function as the Chosen Race elevated and preserved in that dignity by Yahweh could not come to perfect realization in such a material-minded man as Saul, who in the end took refuge in the very superstitions which he had formerly abolished (I Kings 23:7 ss.).

201. David.—Anointed by Samuel as King of Israel even during the lifetime of Saul, David first spent seven long years in the bitter but practical school of persecution and exile. Nevertheless "all Israel and Juda loved David" (I Kings 18:16), even though his position might at times have been open to suspicion, as when he had gathered about him "all that were in distress and oppressed with debt or that had a grudge" (I Kings 22:2), and put his family under the protection of the King of Moab. David manifested his religious disposition by frequent communication with the high priest, by whom indeed he was favored with consultations of Yahweh through the ephod. Moreover, the affectionate friendship for Jonathan [21] and the regard always given to the regal dignity of Saul show forth a deep and generous character, whilst the numerous poetic compositions of the "sweet singer of Israel" breathe a spirituality and realization of God in all phases of life that has not been matched elsewhere in literature.

When at Saul's death he ascended the throne of Juda at the age of 30 years, David's first work was to gain control of Jerusalem (whose citadel was then in the possession of the Jebusites), make it the capital, and bring the ark thither. Thereupon God made with him the great messianic covenant (Ps. 88:4, 5, 27, 28, 30, 36):

> "I have sworn to David my Servant:
> Thy House I will establish forever,
> And I will build up thy throne
> Unto generation and generation. . . .

[21] See Drum's translation and comment on the "Song of the Bow", David's dirge-song over Jonathan and Saul (II Kings 1: 18–27), in the *Homiletic and Pastoral Review*, Oct., 1921, pp. 15–18.

> I will make him my firstborn,
> High above the kings of the earth.
> I will make His house to endure forevermore,
> And his throne as the days of heaven".

David's activity was at first primarily external. He not only threw off the yoke of the Philistines, but also made tributaries of a number of neighboring peoples. His strengthening of the national consciousness of Israel by religious unity and practice brought on a storm of attack from the surrounding nations, who dreaded being absorbed into the new theocracy. Of this David himself wrote (Ps. 2):

> "Why have the Gentiles raged
> and nations devised vain imaginings?
> The kings of earth have assembled together
> and its princes have leagued
> Against God and against the lord,
> His consecrated one.
> They said: 'Let us break their bonds
> and cast off the yoke of their suzerainty'.
> But He who dwelleth in the skies hath mocked at them
> and the Lord hath smiled in derision at their schemings.
> For I have been set by Him as king over Sion, His holy hill."

Thus did David, differently from Saul, consider his kingship vicarious for God's over the Chosen People.

Not all the acts of David recorded by Holy Writ are to be considered approved. The Scripture itself lays sharp censure upon the incident of Bethsabee and Urias. His cruelty to the vanquished in war (II Kings 8:2 and 12:31 [22]) and vengeance upon Joab (III Kings 2:5) must, however, be judged also in the light of the customs of his rude times, and of the pitiless character and treachery of his and Israel's enemies.

[22] In this account the Hebrew reading should perhaps be the same in I Par. 20:3, *vayašem* (= he set or placed) instead of *vayašar*. Taking into consideration the Septuagint and the obscurity of the passages, the meaning would seem to be: "and leading away their people, he set them at [making] saws and iron-shod threshing wains and iron axes, and made them go into the brick-kilns". It must be remembered that the Ammonites had the advantage of the Hebrews in arts, and that Israel must have been lamentably short of iron tools (see I Kings 13:19-20, in No. 197 above). David forced these people to use their skill and industry for the arming and upbuilding of his kingdom.

202. Of equal import with the external victories were for the national life of Israel the internal activities and reforms, chiefly towards centralization, brought about by King David. The greatest act in this regard was the bringing of the Ark of the Covenant into Jerusalem,[23] thus making that city the center both of government and of worship. Connected with this was the reorganization of the priesthood and Divine service generally, the division of duty in the twenty-four orders of priests and levites, which immensely augmented the dignity and splendor of religious practice. Part of this same reorganization was the appointment of 6000 men of the tribe of Levi as judges and officials, of 4000 as a guard for the sanctuary, and of 4000 more to take care of the liturgical music and chant (I Par. 23:3 *ss.*). Thus the knowledge and observance of the law was given a stable basis, whose essentials were not changed even in subsequent régimes.

Lastly, this whole official body was permeated with the life and vigor of the sincerity and spirituality of the poet-king's psalmody. If he who makes the songs of a nation controls its spirit, then Israel was indeed fortunate. God Himself by the mouth of David gave the Hebrew people the hymns that expressed most beautifully its essential function and dignity. The Psalms interpreted for each individual the deep spiritual import of the apparently harsh ascetic code of the revelation on Sinai. They formed in man's heart the counterpart of the great principles of Mosaic legislation; they made the remote, stern, cold, ideal glow and flow in the fervent aspirations, yearnings, and thanksgivings of practical life. Through his Psalms David has reigned not only temporarily from the sea to the Euphrates, but in all ages even more gloriously in the world-wide Kingdom of God, of which his earthly reign was but a type, the Church, which has made his hymns her chant both in suffering and in victory.

[23] See Ps. 67: *Exurgat Deus,* composed for this occasion, and not for the victorious return from an East Jordan expedition in Machabean times. Ephraim no longer had any national significance for the Jews of that late date.

Art. 5: THIRD AND FOURTH BOOKS OF KINGS

Texts: III Kings 1-9; 12-13; 17-19; IV Kings 2-4; 16-18; 20, 25.

203. Name, Plan, Object, Date.—Like I and II Kings these two Books are in reality one, having been separated for convenience' sake into two volumes by the Septuagint and Vulgate.[24] This was the Book originally bearing the title of "Kings", since it dealt with the history of the rulers of both Israel and Juda from the time of David until the Captivity, roughly from 1050 (the accession of Solomon) until 588 (the destruction of the Temple). Whilst this Book begins where the previous one left off, it is quite distinct in plan, style, and language from I and II Kings, clearly showing different authorship. The author of III and IV Kings is rather an annalist, inclined to brevity; he makes much use of previous documents, coördinating them for his purpose; he notes uniformly the beginning, the characteristics, and the end of each reign, using stock phrases to describe the death and burial of the various kings. He evaluates the deeds of the latter according to their conformity with the law of Moses. He is very careful to mark the chronological sequence and relationship. His language, lastly, is marked by neologisms and aramaicisms which belong to the later and inferior periods of Hebrew literature.

204. However, the author of III and IV Kings, as that of the preceding Book, is unknown. Its composition has been ascribed to the prophet Jeremias by the Talmud and ancient commentators. The conjecture is not improbably correct: certain similarities of ideas and language may be traced between this Book and Jeremias' prophecies;[25] thus, for ex-

---

[24] See No. 194 above.

[25] The events recorded in III and IV Kings are very frequently such as Jeremias had personal knowledge of. The hagiographer's account closes just when Jeremias himself was borne off to Egypt. Only the last four verses (IV Kings 25: 27-30) relative to Jechonias are of subsequent date, and might have been added later. The following list of

ample, the conclusion of IV Kings 24:18;—25 has many parallels with that of Jer. 52. The date of this Book must be placed after the beginning of the Captivity.

205. III and IV Kings falls into three sections: (*A*) The Reign of Solomon (III Kings 1-11); (*B*) The History of the Separated Kingdoms of Juda and Israel (III Kings 12-22; IV Kings 1-17); (*C*) The History of the Kingdom of Juda after the ruin of Israel until the Captivity (IV Kings 18-25). For the Northern Kingdom there is intercalated a lengthy excursus or series of episodes showing the wondrous activity of the great Elias (III Kings 17-20; IV Kings 1-2:18). The object of III and IV Kings would seem to be to show the fulfillment of God's promise to David: "When thy days shall be fulfilled and thou shalt sleep with thy fathers, I will raise up thy seed after thee, . . . and will establish his kingdom. He shall build a house to my name. . . . If he commit any iniquity, I will correct him with the rod of men. . . . But my mercy I will not take away from him, as I took it from Saul" (II Kings 7:11-16). Consequently the hagiographer's account continually shows how the kings who adhered to Yahweh were rewarded for their fidelity, whilst the unfaithful and wicked ones were punished for their sins, but not entirely rejected. The sins of Solomon are chastised in his son Roboam, who loses the people of ten tribes, yet retains Jerusalem; the Northern Kingdom expiates its persistent idolatry in a banishment from which it never returns; Juda also satisfies the Divine vengeance in the Captivity of Babylon.

206. Chronology and Sources.—Whilst the hagiographer of III and IV Kings very carefully incorporated an elaborate system of chronological references and cross-references in his

passages may be noted in studying the parallels between III and IV Kings and the works of Jeremias:

Material Parallels		*Stylistic Parallels*	
III Kings 9:8-9	Jer. 22:8	III Kings 9:8	Jer. 22:8
IV Kings 17:13-14	Jer. 7:13-24	IV Kings 17:14	Jer. 7:26
IV Kings 21:12	Jer. 19:3	IV Kings 24-25	Jer. 52
IV Kings 25:3	Jer. 38:9	III Kings 2:4	Jer. 22:17
IV Kings 25:1-7	Jer. 39:1-7	IV Kings 21:12	Jer. 19:3

original work, unfortunately the very abundance of his data
has led to so many material errors [26] in the course of transmission in succeeding ages, that at present the restoration of the strict chronology of this Book has become
practically an insuperable task, decried indeed by St. Jerome
himself as a waste of time.[27]   This is not surprising when one
realizes that the more carefully calculated year-dates are
given in a work, the more numbers written, each correlated
with all the others, the greater are the chances of error in
reading and copying, and once even a single mistake has thus
crept into the text, the whole system fails, and generally subsequent attempts at emendation by mathematics or conjecture
will only make the confusion worse.   And precisely this has
happened in III and IV Kings perhaps more frequently than
elsewhere in the Sacred Scripture.

It must be remembered that originally the dates of Scripture
were not written out in full, but indicated by cuneiform or Hebrew
letter-numerals. Several of the latter could easily be confused with
each other. Then, if there was an apparent discrepancy, there was
always a great temptation for a clever scribe to calculate a (to him)
more congruous figure from other data given. It is noteworthy,
however, that where Assyrian chronology (preserved unchanged in
clay tablets of contemporaries) disagrees with the artificial suppu-
tations of biblical commentators, it nevertheless synchronizes with
absolute data of the Bible; for example, that Manahem, King of
Israel, was a contemporary of Teglathphilasar III; Oseë, of Israel,
of Salmanasar IV; Ezechias of Juda, of Sargon and Sennacherib;
Achab of Israel, of Salmanasar II.[28]

207. The author himself indicates the three chief sources
of his information: the "Acts of the Reign of Solomon"
(III Kings 11:41); the "Acts of the Kings of Juda" (III

---

[26] See No. 15 above.

[27] "Tantam annorum reperies dissonantiam, et numerum inter Iudam
et Israël, id est inter regnum utrumque, confusum, ut huiuscemodi
hærere quæstionibus non tam studiosi quam otiosi hominis esse videatur"
(*Epist.* 52, ad Vitalem; P. L., 22: 675-676).

[28] See Pinches, *The Old Testament in the Light of the Historical
Records of Assyria and Babylonia;* Deimel, *Veteris testamenti chrono-
logia.*—For the chronology of III and IV Kings as adopted in this
volume, especially on pp. 271-274, the author is gratefully indebted to
the computations of fr. B. Gissler, O.S.M., who recognizes the presence
of island-like consistent synchronistic groups of dates in these Books,
as against Šanda who rejects all the synchronisms, in his *Bücher der
Könige,* II, p. 410 (Münster 1912).

Kings 14: 29; 15: 7, 23, etc.) ; and the "Acts of the Kings of
Israel" (III Kings 14: 19; IV Kings 1: 18, etc.). It would
seem that from the time of King David onwards the annals
of each king were officially chronicled (see I Par. 27: 24).
They must have been quite detailed, as the hagiographer fre-
quently refers to them for fuller information. Those of the
Kings of Israel were brought down as far as Phaceë (IV
Kings 15: 31); those of Juda, to Joachim (IV Kings 24: 5).

208. The Elias Cycle.—Unexpectedly, suddenly, without
introduction or foregoing announcement, as was characteristic
of his appearances in life, there looms up in III Kings 17,
one of the mightiest and most mysterious figures of the Old
Testament, Elias the Thesbite. The providential reason of
his advent is indicated a few verses previously:

"Now Achab the son of Amri reigned over Israel . . . In Samaria
two and twenty years . . . and did evil in the sight of the Lord
above all that were before him. Nor was it enough for him to
walk in the sins of Jeroboam . . . but he took also to wife Jezabel
daughter of Ethbaal king of the Sidonians. . . . And he set up an
altar for Baal in the temple of Baal which he had built in Samaria,
and he planted a grove [dedicated to Astarte]. And Achab did
more to provoke the Lord the God of Israel than all the kings of
Israel that were before him" (III Kings 16: 29-33).

It was as a moral counterweight to that weak and evilly influenced ruler of the at that time flourishing Northern
Kingdom, that God raised up Elias, and it is against the
troublous and lurid background of that reign that the great
Converter's activities must be viewed.

209. A little over half a century had passed since the
fatal division of the Hebrew nation after Solomon's death,
a division which, on the side of the rebels, had quickly added,
to secession, schism (III Kings 12: 28-33). During this
period the two parts of the now separated nation had been
almost continually in a state of violent repulsion, expressed
in their internecine wars. Whilst at this time also the religious and moral conditions of both kingdoms were practically
parallel in their decadence, nevertheless the rebel Northern
Kingdom was, by its origin and subsequent vicissitudes, fore-
doomed to wander entirely from the way of the Hebrews'
God-given law. For, it was at this time the greater and more

powerful, and, by its rebellion from the theocratic ruler, had already manifested in how little esteem it held the Mosaic observances, one of the most pronounced of which was the principle of non-communication with heathen peoples. Consequently it was open to alliances with the neighboring Gentiles, alliances always fraught with an infiltration of the cults of those idolatrous peoples.

With the accession of Achab to the throne of Israel, the relations between that kingdom and Juda were to enter into a new and most critical phase. For, a *rapprochement* was about to take place between the two divisions that had so long been mutually bitterly hostile, and this was to be made more effective by intermarriage between the reigning dynasties.[29] At the same time Israel was about to confirm its alienation from Yahweh's religion by the introduction of the vilest, most unnatural cults of the hideous Phenician degradations of worship, after Achab married Jezabel,[30] daughter of Ethbaal (Ithobal I), king of Sidon and priest of Astarte.

210. Thus, for the sake of the kingdom of Israel itself, and perhaps even more for the nearby Juda, did God then raise up Elias. Of the latter's origin nothing definite is known, although the Septuagint (III Kings 17:1) and Josephus mention a Thisbon in Galaad, east of the Jordan, as his native town.[31] His surname of Thesbite, however, is perhaps not so much a patronymic as a popularly given title to indicate his function and office, for the Septuagint has "the Thesbite" wherever the Hebrew text now has the title of "the prophet". According to the etymology of the word, then, Elias was popularly designated as "the one who turns, the one who makes to return", in short, "the Converter". And it may be noted that the expressions "return to God,

---

[29] "But Josaphat the son of Asa began to reign over Juda in the fourth year of the reign of Achab king of Israel . . . and had peace with the king of Israel" (III Kings 22:41-45); "Now Josaphat was rich and very glorious, and was joined by affinity to Achab" (II Par. 18:1).

[30] According to Menas, Jezabel (Isobel) was a great-aunt of Dido, foundress of Carthage. See also Josephus, *Ant.*, VIII, xiii, 1.

[31] The Greek of Tobias also speaks of a Thisbe in northern Galilee (Tob. 1:2).

be converted'' form the keynote of Elias' exhortations (for example, III Kings 18: 36 Greek). It was his life-work, as is indicated in Ecclus. 48: 19b and Luke 1: 16, to turn back the apostate kingdom of Israel to the religion of its ancestors, thus bringing about a religious, if not a political union, with the co-national kingdom of Juda.

For this purpose God had superadded great miraculous powers to this prophet's naturally ascetic, stern character.[32] For, not by oratorical exhortations or by statements of doctrine (as with the later prophets of Juda) but only by wonderful and terrible works, dire chastisements, could the people of Israel be once more converted, turned back, since their forefathers' keen religious sense had been dulled by continual contact with the grossest paganism.

However, in turning back and saving his nation from the abyss of destruction, Elias did not succeed. For, though the Lord had exhorted Israel ''by the hand of all the prophets and seers, saying: 'Return from your wicked ways and keep my precepts which I commanded your fathers', . . . they hearkened not, but hardened their necks . . . and they followed the Gentiles which were round about them. . . . And the Lord was exceedingly wroth with Israel, and removed them from His sight. . . . And Israel was carried out from its land to Assyria'' (IV Kings 17: 13, 15, 18, 23). However, as did his latter antitype, John the Baptist (Luke 1: 17), Elias effected that at least ''a remnant'' of Israel was turned back to God, and tradition maintains that, as the forerunner of the Judgment-advent of Christ (note the

---

[32] After that wonder-piled Carmel day, when Jezabel swore a threat of death against Elias which probably she could not have carried out, the fierce fires of that prophet's zeal seem strangely to have burnt down, leaving nothing but the ashes of mere humanity (III Kings 19: 1 ss.). And in the record of his subsequent panic-stricken flight there are indications that perhaps, in that day's wondrous works, a trace of the human, of self-reliance, a momentary forgetfulness of the divine origin and purpose of his charismatic powers, may have crept into this great man's soul. Thus one might imagine as rather superfluous the previous racing in ecstatic power before Achab's swift chariot (III Kings 18: 41-46). Be that as it may, the subsequent humiliating lesson did not escape the keen ascetic sense of Elias. ''It is enough for me, O Lord,'' he cried, ''take away my life, for, I am not better than my fathers!''

"written unto the season of judgments" of Ecclus. 48:10a and also Mal. 4:5-6), he shall return to earth [33] to convert the last remnant of the Jews to the God of their fathers.

Art. 6: FIRST AND SECOND BOOKS OF PARALIPOMENON

Texts: I Par. 9-11:25; 23-24:6; 29; II Par. 1-2; 9-10; 34-36:22.

211. Name, Date, and Author.—In Hebrew this Book is known as *Dibre Hayâmim,* that is "the Acts of the Days", or Chronicles, which name is given it also by the King James version. Paralipomena, Παραλειπόμενα, that is "things left over" or "supplements" is the title given by the Septuagint, which has been retained in the Douay-Challoner version. Of course, the division of the original Book into two volumes (as with I-II Kings and III-IV Kings) was made simply for convenience in handling. Even now the Book is not complete, the end having been cut off in the middle of a sentence, —which may be found continued in I Esd. 1:3b.[34]

Whether or not the decree of Cyrus putting an end to the Babylonian Captivity (II Par. 36:22) be considered part of Paralipomena, it is nevertheless clear that the Book was composed after the Captivity, since it gives the full genealogy [35] of Zorobabel, chief of the restoration (I Par. 3:19-21). That the time of composition antedates the Seleucid domination of Israel, is shown by the use *darics* or coins of the Persian regime (I Par. 29:7 Hebrew): for the Alexandrian conquest introduced *talents* and *drachmas.*

Jewish tradition assigns the authorship of the Paralipomena to Esdras (Ezra), and the correctness of this opinion

[33] There is no indication in the context of II Par. 21:12 that the letter from Elias originated after the latter had already been removed from the earth, even though the chronology of present figures in Kings would seem to make this a conclusion. Had the latter been the case, the extraordinary character of such a message would surely have been noted.

[34] See introduction to I Esdras, below.

[35] This genealogy, however, is continued on even beyond Zorobabel; it is generally admitted that certain later names have been added to this list subsequently.

is confirmed from internal evidence. The author of Paralipomena exhibits the same fondness for describing levitical and liturgical matters, for compiling genealogies, and for certain characteristic stock phrases, such as *kemišpat*, "according to the Law" (I Par. 23:31 Hebrew; II Par. 35:13; I Esd. 3:4); *hithyahes*, "to be accounted, numbered, or inscribed" (I Par. 5:1, 7, 17), and liturgical formulas as in I Par. 16:34, 41; II Par. 7:6 and I Esd. 3:11.

212. The Contents and Object.—The first part of the Paralipomena (I Par. 1-9) is made up exclusively of genealogies, drawn largely from the Pentateuch and other previous historical records. The second part (I Par. 10-29) contains the history of David and many emumerations and details in connection with his reorganizing the levitical service before the ark. The third part (II Par. 1-36:21) contains summary annals of the reigns of the kings of Juda from the time of David until the Captivity. The writer is always careful to indicate at the close of each section the source of his information. In many cases these were the same sources used by the author of III-IV Kings; this would explain the verbal similarity observable in so many parallel passages of the two works.

213. Whilst the author of Paralipomena has omitted many facts reported in the Books of Kings, he has likewise recorded others not previously mentioned. He is particularly concerned to give prominence to everything connected with the cultus of the Mosaic law; under that aspect, where Kings give the political phase of Israel's vicissitudes, Paralipomena give the religious side.[36] The hagiographer's object was clearly to show how God rewarded with prosperity the observance of the law, and punished idolatry and other unfaithfulness with adversity. He shows the gradual withdrawal of Israel from its Divine Ruler, climaxing in the chastisement of the Captivity. Hence also the account of Paralipomena is not so impersonal and objective as that of Kings.

[36] Compare, for example, in the account of the raising of Joas to the throne (IV Kings 11), the prominent part played by the Levites, according to II Par. 23.

214.—SUMMARY OF THE HISTORY OF JUDA AND ISRAEL
FROM SOLOMON TO THE CAPTIVITY

JUDA			ISRAEL
Roboam (18 years), Solomon's son, foolishly advocates royal absolutism, thus alienating ten Northern tribes (III Kings 12: 1–24; II Par. 10). Sesac of Egypt pillages Temple (III Kings 14: 25–26). Roboam allows Phenician phallic cults (III Kings 15: 13; II Par. 12).	929	929	*Jeroboam I* (21 years), made king over the ten Northern tribes, establishes idolatry at Dan and Bethel; tries to combine Apis-cult and worship of Yahweh. Ahias is prophet in Silo (III Kings 14: 2). Jeroboam at first dwells in Sichem, then in Phanuel, lastly in Thersa. There is continual war between Juda and Israel. Prophesies of the fall of Jeroboam's altars and dynasty (II Par. 12: 15; III Kings 14: 2 *ss*.).
Abia (3 years), victorious against Jeroboam (II Par. 13), unfaithful to God.	912		
Asa (41 years), destroys idolatry, has many years of no actual warfare (II Par. 14: 1; see also 15: 19), but there is a continual state of hostility between Juda and Israel.	910		
		909	*Nadab* (2 years), slain during siege of Gebbethon (III Kings 15: 25–28).
Asa ousts his grandmother Maacha from her phallic grove; bribes Benadad I to break his alliance with Israel; overcomes Zara, the Ethiopian invader (II Par. 14: 9). Has quite a religious reunion at Jerusalem. Reproved by Hanani for trusting rather to alliance with Benadad (II Par. 15–16).		908	*Baasa* (24 years) had to give up building Rama (III Kings 15: 17, 21); has league with Benadad of Syria.
		885	*Ela* (2 years). *Zambri,* 7 days (III Kings 16: 9–15).
		884	*Amri* (12 years) is for some years opposed by the rival Thebni. After 6 years at Thersa he builds Samaria (III Kings 16: 16–28).
Josaphat (25 years, including regency) has the Law taught.	870	873	*Achab* (20 years) marries Jezabel: the Elias cycle (III Kings 17–21); persecution of those faithful to Mosaic law. Benadad I besieges Samaria, but has to raise the siege; returns following year; is again and worse defeated, but spared (III Kings 20).
An alliance is effected between Juda and Israel against Damascus (II Par. 18).			
Josaphat appoints judges, takes away the groves; overcomes the coalition of Ammonites, Moabites and Syrians (II Par. 19–20).			Death of Achab in battle against Syria whilst aided by Josaphat (III Kings 22).

SUMMARY OF THE HISTORY OF JUDA AND ISRAEL
FROM SOLOMON TO THE CAPTIVITY—*Continued*

JUDA		ISRAEL
Makes alliance with Ochozias, loses his navy at Asiongaber; Joram his son begins co-regency. Eliseus reverences Josaphat (IV Kings 3: 14).	854	*Ochozias* (reigns 2 years), wicked, insults Elias (IV Kings 1).
Joram (reigns 5 years), married to Athalia, daughter of Achab.	846	853 *Joram* (reigns 12 years) removes Baalim; makes alliance with Josaphat and Edom against Mesa (IV Kings 3), king of Moab. Eliseus cycle (IV Kings 3–8: 15).
Ochozias (1 year), ally with Joram of Israel against Hazael of Syria (IV Kings 8: 25–29).	843 842	Wounded at Ramoth, Joram goes to Jezrahel for cure, where he is visited by Ochozias, during which visit both are slain.
Athalia seizes government for 7 years, assassinating all stock of Ochozias but the boy Joas (IV Kings 11). Joiada high-priest	842 842	*Jehu* (reigns 29 years) seizes throne after double regicide: ousts Baal worship (IV Kings 10). Hazael ravages Israel, which loses the East-Jordan territory.
Joas (reigns 40 years), under direction of Joiada repairs Temple (IV Kings 12: 1–21); buys off Hazael. After death of Joiada, however, idolatry is begun again (II Par. 24: 17–27).	836	814 *Joachaz* (17 years) afflicted by Hazael and Benadad his son (IV Kings 13: 1–8).
Amasias (29 years) vanquished Edom in battle of Saltpits: offers league to Joas, but is rejected by Joas, who breaks wall of Jerusalem (IV Kings 14: 1–20). Revolt against Amasias, who is killed at Lachis.	797	798 *Joas* (16 years) consults Eliseus during that prophet's last illness. Rovers from Moab invade Israel: Hazael afflicts Israel: dies (IV Kings 13:22–25). Joas recovers from Benadad cities captured by Hazael. Prophet Jonas?
Ozias (33 years) also called Azarias (IV Kings 15: 1–7) fostered husbandry and was successful against Philistines, fortified Jerusalem (II Par. 26): Joathan co-regent, as Ozias is struck with leprosy for presuming to offer sacrifice.	769	783 *Jeroboam II* (41 years) widens the borders of Israel (IV Kings 14: 23–29). The prophet Osee (1: 4) fulminates the divine threatenings against Israel. The prophet Amos likewise exhorts Israel to return and foretells its desolation.
	743 743 743	*Zacharias* reigns 6 months in Samaria. *Sellum* reigns 1 month, to be supplanted by *Manahem* (6 years), who

SUMMARY OF THE HISTORY OF JUDA AND ISRAEL
FROM SOLOMON TO THE CAPTIVITY—*Continued*

JUDA			ISRAEL
			buys off Phul of the Assyrians (IV Kings 15: 8–22).
Joathan (2 years) does much building: overcomes Ammonites. Still there is idolatry.	737	738 737	*Phaceia* (2 years) is slain by *Phaceë* (6 years), under whom Assyrian deportations begin. Phaceë allies himself with
Achaz (16 years) practices idolatry and is once overcome by Phaceë and Rasin. Isaias foretells (Is. 7: 3–8) delivery of Jerusalem and downfall of Israel. Achaz bribes Teglathphilesar to go against Israel (II Par. 28; IV Kings 16).	736	732	Rasin of Syria and besieges Jerusalem. Teglathphilesar captures Damascus and deports Israelites from Galilee. *Oseë* (12 years) refuses tribute to Assyrians; allies himself with Sua of Egypt (IV Kings 17: 4). The prophet
Ezechias (29 years), faithful, cleanses the Temple; invites all Hebrews to great Pasch (II Par. 29: 3 *ss*.). Juda has to suffer much in the Assyrian campaigns against Egypt (Sargon's in Is. 20?).	721		Nahum active. Salmanasar captures Samaria and carries off Israel into captivity from which there is no return (IV Kings 18: 10–11).

Sennacherib comes up against Jerusalem, which, according to the prophecy of Isaias, is wondrously delivered (IV Kings 18–19; II Par. 32). Later Berodach Baladan of Babylon makes offers of friendship (IV Kings 20: 12; Is. 39: 1). He had usurped Babel from the Assyrian suzerain.

Manasses (54 years): during his minority Sobna and Eliacim **693** seem to have been regents (see IV Kings 18: 18; Is. 22: 20 *ss*.). Manasses acts as an apostate, restoring idol-worship: endeavors to destroy the good his father had accomplished: persecutes the warning prophets (II Par. 33: 18). He is carried off to Babylon captive by the invading Assyrians; there he suffers a complete change of mind. On his return to Juda he endeavors to make good the evil he had done.

The events of the Book of Judith may have occurred at this time.

Amon (2 years) follows the wickedness of Manasses; assas- **640** sinated.

Josias (31 years) coöperates with the prophet Jeremias; destroys **639** idolatry (II Par. 34: 3 *ss*.; IV Kings 23: 15). Whilst the Temple is repaired a copy of the Law is found. General religious revival (IV Kings 22: 8–11; II Par. 34: 14–21).

This coincides largely with the destruction of Ninive and the rise **612** of the neo-Babylonian kingdom, alongside the Median. Jews suffer from wars between Egypt and Babylonia: Josias slain

SUMMARY OF THE HISTORY OF JUDA AND ISRAEL
FROM SOLOMON TO THE CAPTIVITY—*Continued*

during encounter with Nechao of Egypt at Mageddo (IV Kings 23: 29).

Joachaz (3 months): Nechao places Juda under tribute and holds Joachaz at Rebla (IV Kings 23: 33.) **609**

Eliakim (Joakim, 11 years) is placed upon the throne by Nechao. At this time Nabuchodonosor makes a campaign against Phenicia and subjects Juda; carries Joakim captive to Babylon (II Par. 36: 5–8), together with noble youths (among whom is Daniel) and part of the Temple vessels (Dan. 1: 1; Jer. 22, 25, 36). **608**

Joachin (Jechonias, 3 months and 10 days) is quickly borne off to Babylon, together with artificers and nobles to the number of 10,000 (IV Kings 24: 12–16; II Par. 36: 9–10). **598**

Sedecias (11 years) is made king by Nabuchodonosor instead of his nephew Joachin. He pays no attention to the warnings of Jeremias (Jer. 37: 1–2), who is cast into prison. He makes a visit to Babylon (Jer. 51: 59). In his ninth year Sedecias revolts against Nabuchodonosor who besieges Jerusalem until the fourth month of the eleventh year, when the city fell. Sedecias was captured and blinded, and some of the remaining Jews were deported, whilst the Temple was despoiled and wrecked (Jer. 52; IV Kings 25; II Par. 36: 10–21). **597**

587

215. The Assyrian and Babylonian Exiles.—The deportation of the Israelites to foreign lands has for the history of revelation a momentum much broader than its primary punitive aspect. For an inevitable consequence of this scattering of Hebrews amongst alien peoples would be to bring to the latter some knowledge at least of the truths originally revealed by God but which had become corrupted almost beyond recognition in the traditions of the world outside Jewry.

In this connection it is well to remember that not all the inhabitants of the Northern Kingdom of the Ten Tribes were given to idolatry. Thus in III Kings 19: 18 Yahweh assures Elias that there were left "seven thousand men in Israel whose knees have not been bowed before Baal". Even at the time of Ezechias men from the districts of Aser, Manasses, and Zabulon attended the Pasch at the invitation of the king of Juda (II Par. 30: 1-18). Hence even the exulants of the Northern Kingdom, which were scattered and lost, never to return, could bring knowledge of the true God to the seats of their exile.

216. Just whither the armies of Teglathphilesar III (745-727) and Salmanasar IV (727-722) bore away the inhabitants of Samaria and its surrounding country, has never been definitely ascertained, as the places named in I Par. 5:26 and IV Kings 17:3-6 have not since been identified with certainty. But the districts about the sources of the Tigris and Euphrates would seem to have first received the exiles, whence the latter migrated in time north to the Black Sea, the Crimea, and southern Russia, and east even to Mongolia. Median cities like Ecbatana, Rages, and Ninive formed centers of colonization. There were communities of Hebrews also in Elam (I Esd. 2:7, 31; 10:2, 26; II Esd. 7:12, 30) and in Susa (Esth. 4:16).

217. As the inhabitants of the Northern Kingdom had been carried off by the Assyrians, so, not quite 150 years later were the dwellers in Jerusalem and Judea removed by Baylonian armies in long-threatened chastisement of unfaithfulness. This deportation did not take place all at one fell swoop, but extended over a period of 20 years. First of all, during the reign of Joachin (606), Nabuchodonosor (Nebukadnezar) at the opening of his reign took away a number of nobles, especially youths who might be trained as pages and thus become attached to the national culture of the Babylonians (Jer. 25:1; 52:2, 8; IV Kings 24:8; II Par. 36:8-9; Dan. 1:1). Daniel and his companions were among those deported, Daniel himself being but a boy of twelve or fourteen. On this occasion many of the golden vessels and utensils of the Temple were also removed. Seven years later 10,000 able Hebrews, among them many artisans and King Jechonias (Joachin) himself together with the prophet Ezechiel, were carried off (599). This was the most extensive draft (IV Kings 24:14; Jer. 52:2). The last deportation took place after the capture of Jerusalem and the destruction of Solomon's Temple, in the 11th year of King Sedecias (587; see II Par. 36:19-20).

That the Judean exiles gravitated toward the centers already colonized in those regions by their brethren of the Northern Kingdom over a century previously is highly probable. This would explain the flourishing and well-organized Jewish colony in or near Babylon at a time when Daniel was still a youth (Dan. 13). The details of life in these two exiles are reflected in the Books of Tobias, Esther, Baruch, and the prophetic records of Daniel and Ezechiel.

218. Providential Function of the Babylonian Captivity. —For the Jews themselves the great effect of the deportation and captivity was the final and absolute relinquishment of idolatry, into which this people had again fallen since its delivery from Egypt. In the fires of the tribulations and temptations of the *diaspora* the dross of Jewry was burnt away and absorbed in the general slag of heathendom, leaving behind only "a remnant" (Is. 10: 20-21) indeed, but that the pure gold of faithful and zealous souls,—"the consumption abridged shall overflow with justice" (Is. 10: 22).

Moreover, the religion of the Hebrews was thus brought into intimate contact with the world at large. At the opening of the 6th century B.C. the kernel of Yahweh's people was situated at Babylon, whilst numerous Jewish colonies were scattered all through Media even to the Hindukush, and a special settlement of refugees (to be later so important for the history of revelation) was establishing itself in Egypt. Thus the Jews were in excellent position to note and participate in the great world-happenings which marked the 6th century before Christ. The mighty wars and changes of culture which had shaken all Asia during two long generations may be summed up at the time of Cyrus in the following total: in the leading position of the world the Semitic Assyrians and the hybrid Babylonians have been replaced by an Aryan (Indo-germanic) people, the Persians, who are masters of Asia. At the same time Greek influence has become strengthened in Egypt, that great center of Chamitic culture. Japhet now dwells in the tents of Sem (Gen. 9: 27), according to the prophecy of Noe: and more and more is Chanaan reduced to the position of "a servant of servants unto his brethren" (Gen. 9:25). This signifies a great advance in religious history: nothing less than the overthrow and destruction of the crude, sensual, naturalistic false worship which had always persisted among Chanaanitish races, and through them had infected even the Jews. Of course, these orgiastic cults were not abolished entirely, continuing their mysteries in isolated temples and sanctuaries, but their dominant position was occupied by nobler religious concepts and practices.

Originally the Hebrew nation had been chosen for this task, but it had after a manner failed, and so Providence made use of the mighty political hammer of the Persians to deal the first blows at an ancient cultural structure which would finally fall into utter ruin under the martial and intellectual conquests of Alexander and Hellenism, leaving the ground unencumbered for the building up of the great world-edifice of Christ.

Broadly speaking, the age just before Cyrus was marked by the stirring of new spiritual breezes in the musty glooms of antique heathenism: in Bactria, Zoroaster arises; in India, Buddha; in China, Confucius and Lao-tse; in Greece, the beginnings of philosophy under Pythagoras. And the seed of Jacob, scattered in the colonies of the *diaspora* throughout all civilized nations, was forced into a broader view and execution of its providential function of being the instrument for bringing true knowledge of God to the world.

Art. 7: THE BOOK OF TOBIAS

Texts: Tob. 1-6, 7-14.

219. Original Text and Versions.—Whether the Book of Tobias was originally written in Hebrew (which is more probable) or in Aramaic, is uncertain. The present-day MSS. of the text fall into four groups: (*A*) the Greek of the Vatican and Alexandrine and of the Codex *Veneto-Marcianus* (all uncials), the Syriac of Tob. 1-7: 9, the Armenian version, and the Hebrew of Fagius [37]; (B) the Sinaiticus, the Old Latin, and the Hebrew of Sebastian Münster [38]; (C) the Ferrara MS. (Holmes 106, reproduced in the Holmes-Pearson edition), with which may be grouped also the other minuscules 44 and 107, and the Syriac of Tob. 7: 10;—14; (D) the Vulgate. These groups are distinguished by additions or suppressions, and by variants in the proper names and numbers. Whilst the account of the Sinaiticus and Old Latin seems to be preferable for literalness, the Vatican or ordinary Greek seems based on an esthetically better redaction. Neither the Hebrew nor the Aramaic [39] texts can be considered originals.

220. The Vulgate version was made in one day from an Aramaic MS., St. Jerome, having read the Book with a Rabbi, dictating his translation to a secretary. And from the text it would appear that his version was not so much a translation as a summarizing. The first person, in which the senior Tobias speaks in the Greek versions, was changed to the third; almost everything of the Achior (Ahikar) [40] sections (Greek 1: 20-22; 2: 10; 11: 17; 14: 10 ss) was eliminated, whilst the moral and dogmatic passages seem to have been accentuated in a later tone. The condensation characteristic of the Vulgate version here may be surmised from the translation of some *plus* passages in the Greek, as given below.[41]

---

[37] This is a translation from the Greek (Isny, 1542).

[38] Brought out at Basle (1542); found also in the London Polyglot.

[39] See Neubauer, *The Book of Tobit*, a Chaldee text from a unique MS. in the Bodleian library, with other rabbinical texts, English translations, and the Itala (Oxford, 1878).

[40] There exists an ancient oriental romance concerning Ahikar the Sage, whose details seem to identify that personage with the character in Tobias. Rendel Harris, in collaboration with F. C. Conybeare and Mrs. Agnes Smith, has edited *The Story of Ahicar, from the Syriac, Arabic, Armenian, Ethiopic, Greek, and Slavonic versions* (London, 1898). At the beginning of LaFontaine's *Fables* may be found some of Ahikar's adventures. The author of this romance seized upon the person of the ancient and probably renowned Assyrian prime minister for the nucleus of his tales.

[41] This translation combines the texts of both the Vatican and the Sinaitic MSS. (B and Aleph).

"And he [Sennacherib] seized all my possessions, and left me naught that was not confiscated to the royal treasury, except Anna my wife, and my son Tobias. And fifty days did not pass before two of his sons slew him, and themselves fled to the mountains of Ararat[h]. And his son Sacherdonos [Assarhaddon] reigned in his stead. And he placed Achiachar [Acheichar], the [son of] Anaël [Antaël], the son of my brother, over all the income of his kingdom and over all the disbursements.

"Thereupon Achiachar pleaded for me, and I returned to Ninive. For, Achiachar was chief cup-bearer, and was [set] over the seal-ring and over the income and disbursements, by Sennacherim, king of the Assyrians. And Sachardon set him up as second [in the kingdom]. Now, he was my cousin-german, and of my family (Tob. 1:20 Greek).

"And, when I returned to my home and was restored to my wife Anna and to Tobias my son, on the festival of Pentecost, which is the Feast of Seven Weeks, there was prepared for me a fine dinner, and I reclined to eat. And a table was set before me, and I noted many viands. Whereupon I said to Tobias my son: 'Child, go, and if thou findest any of our poor brethren among the captives of Ninive who is mindful in his whole heart of the Lord, bring him in and let him eat together with me. And lo! I shall wait, my son, until thou returnest' (Tob. 2:1-2 Greek).

"And Tobias went to seek out some poor man of our brethren. And being come back he said: 'Father'! And I said to him: 'Here I am, my child'. And he answering said: 'Father, lo! one of our people has been slain, and was thrown down in the market-place where he was strangled'.

"And, leaping up, I left my dinner before I had tasted thereof, and bore him away from the public square, and put him in one of the buildings until the sun had gone down, that I might bury him" (Tob. 2:3-4 Greek).

221. The Author and Time.—According to the Greek text of Tob. 12:20, Tobit [42] and his son were ordered by the angel Raphael to record in a book the dealings of God in their regard; then Tob. 13:1 (Greek) states that Tobit wrote down his canticle. It may be assumed that Tobit and Tobias left memoirs which an editor later compiled into the Book of Tobias, of which the canonical Tobias is a substantial summary. Tobit himself, of the tribe of Nephthali, was one of the faithful Hebrews of the Northern Kingdom who was borne away into Assyrian captivity in one of the early depor-

---

[42] The Greek texts consistently name the elder Tobias Τωβὶς or Τωβείθ and his son Τωβίας. The father's name would seem to be but a shortened form of the son's, both radically signifying "Yahweh [is my] good".

tations of the great Sargon (714-705), or of his father, Sal-
manassar IV. In his old age he could have become acquainted
with the prophecies of Jonas and Nahum against Ninive, as
is suggested in the Greek of Tob. 14: 6-7, 10-13 (Greek 4, 8).

222. Its Canonicity and Historicity.—The Book of Tobias
is of the number of those called deuterocanonical, not
being included in the present Jewish canon (nor in Protestant editions of Bibles). But, its own content shows
that it was a kind of practical life-manual for the Jews
in exile, and the very divergences so notable in the texts
which have come down to the present time, witness to wide-
spread and common use, at least among the exulants. Perhaps this fact in itself militated against Tobias' reception into
the Pharisaic canon as compiled about a century after Christ.
For, other sacred Books also which had been composed
outside Palestine were then either rejected altogether (as
Ecclesiasticus) or drastically edited (as Daniel and Esther).
Most of all probably this Book's conciliatory attitude toward
the Gentiles, its patent declaration of a messianic missionary
function of the Jews brought about through the exile, and
lastly its plain confession of Israel's sin and failure before
Yahweh (Tob. 13: 3-5), were repugnant to the chauvinistic
and proud Pharisees. Hence their refusal to recognize this,
together with similar broader-visioned works, as inspired.[43]

223. Modern rationalistic scripturists would consider
Tobias as a pious and instructive fiction, without claim to
historic value. But the internal evidence of the Book vouches
for its historicity. Tobias' genealogy and place of origin are
given at length; historic and geographic details are carefully noted, and chronological bearings marked. The angel-
ology and demonology of the Book concord exactly with the
developments made along these lines during the exilic period.

[43] That the primitive Church considered the Book of Tobias undoubtedly canonic, is evidenced by the numerous scenes therefrom
pictured in the catacombs and upon early Christian sarcophagi: the boy
Tobias bearing a travelers' staff and accompanied by an angel clothed
in a long tunic; the dog running up and caressing an old man seated
in a doorway (Tob. 11: 9); the fish (Tob. 6: 2-9) is almost invariably
featured, probably because it was considered a type of Christ, and on
account of the punning association.

The Asmodeus incidents (Tob. 3:8; 6:17; 8:3), whether the name be considered derived from the Hebrew *šamad* "to destroy", or from the Persian *azmûden* "to tempt", need in no wise to be traced to the Zend-Avesta,[44] as the name could be applied quite generically to demons. The treatment of this phase, far from being fabulous or extravagant, is most restrained and matter-of-fact, where an Oriental fictionist would have given broad leeway to the imagination. The apparent anachronisms raised from the names of Assyrian kings are plainly due to copyists' mistakes. Even if in Tob. 1:2 Salmanasar or Sargon be the true reading, it is known that Teglathphilesar III did not lead the entire tribe of Nephthali into captivity, so that his successors in subsequent invasions could still deport others.

224. Theme, Plan, and Lessons.—For its first Jewish readers the keynote of this Book was given in Tobias' canticle (13:3-8):

> "Give glory to God, ye children of Israel, because He hath scattered you among the Gentiles who know Him not
> In order that you might declare His wonderful works, and make them know that there is no other almighty God besides Him.
>
> He hath chastised us for our iniquities, and He will save us for His mercy's sake."

A new, broad vista is hereby opened in the field of revelation. To the Jews it is made clear that the knowledge of the true God is not to be confined narrowly and selfishly to themselves, but that in the end salvation is to be shared with the Gentiles. This doctrine had before been implicitly inculcated by the sending of the prophet Jonas to Ninive: now it is here explicitly declared, as a precaution against the later narrow Pharisaic attitude, which could see in the Gentiles only subjects of judgment and destruction, to be visited upon them by an entirely earthly messianic empire of the Jews.

In full accord with this major theme is the revealed advice of the angel Raphael (Tob. 12:8-13), which stresses, not

---

[44] "When the ancient hell-serpent with two feet, this unclean Aschmogh, finds itself in a human form, how many then shall be defiled with Hamrid and Pitrid." *Vendidad*, Fargad V.

ceremonial but, moral righteousness, and the efficacy, not of many beeves and fatlings in holocausts but, of alms, prayer, fasting, and other good works before God. The Temple was soon to be a thing of the past, but the deepest significances of the Temple worship, of the whole ceremonial code, their real spiritual import, were more than ever to be impressed upon the hearts of the Chosen People, now crushed and made humbly receptive under the yoke of the Captivity. No wonder then, that the exiles chose for the expression of their souls' deepest yearning the psalm *Miserere,* which has as its concluding verse (Ps. 50:19):

> "A sacrifice to God is an afflicted spirit:
> a contrite and humbled heart, O Lord, Thou wilt not despise."

Finally, in this connection, it may be noted that the problem of evil is here (as in Job,[45] where it is treated at length) given the more generous and consoling interpretation: its infliction is not always punitive: "Because thou wast *acceptable* to God, it was necessary that temptation should prove thee" (Tob. 12:13).

225. The Book of Tobias may easily be divided into the following six sections: (*A*) the Virtues and Trials of Tobias Senior (1-3:6); (*B*) the Virtues and Trials of Sara (3:7-23); (*C*) Journey of Tobias Junior to Media (3:24; 6:9); (*D*) his Marriage to Sara (6:10; 9); (*E*) his Return to Ninive (10-11); (*F*) conclusion: the Revelation of Raphael and the Canticle of Tobias (12-14:1). As an epilogue is added Tobias' dying discourse, as well as chronological data concerning him and his son, probably supplied by one of the grandchildren.

In the form of simple narrative recording the doings and sufferings of everyday characters are inculcated lessons of domestic virtue more effectively perhaps here than anywhere else in the Sacred Scriptures. The family life of the Tobiases, father and son, and of Sara the bride, and not least

---

[45] However, the Vulgate's reference to Job in 2:15 has nothing to correspond therewith in the Greek text, and should perhaps be considered an insertion of St. Jerome's in his summarizing or paraphrasing.

of Anna, the typical housewife and mother, with its routine vicissitudes of difficulties, sorrows, and joys, all carried on under the ever-present realization of God's care and government, charmingly pictures an ideal to be followed by all in domestic conduct. Tobias Senior is sketched as zealous for religion (1:5-7, 12), honored for his uprightness (1:13), generous and kind towards others (1:19-20), yet keen in business (4:21-22), fearless for justice, honest to a scruple, patient in adversity, ever trustful of God. The younger Tobias is a model of filial piety, and together with Sara an exemplar of how to contract a marital union pleasing to God. Almsgiving is again and again recommended (1:16-17; 2:1-2; 4:7-12, etc.); the great Golden Rule is given for the first time in a negative form (4:16; see Matt. 7:12); prayer is shown as ever drawing down the blessing of God on important affairs (4:20; 6:18, etc.), and flight from sin is insisted upon as avoidance of the only real evil (4:23). The whole Book, like that of Job, is a justification of the dispositions of Divine Providence, but whilst Job is more a formal thesis of theoretic discussion, in Tobias the problem is solved by picturization of the incidents of an average man's life.

Art. 8: FIRST AND SECOND BOOKS OF ESDRAS

Texts: I Esd. 1-2:2; 3-7; 9-10:16; II Esd. 1-2; 4-7:5; 8-9:6.

226. Relationship to Paralipomena, and Structure.—The present I Esdras is a combination of the concluding part of the Chronicler's levitical history of Israel (I-II Par. 36:21 and I Esd. 1-6) with the personal memoirs of Esdras (I Esd. 7—10), with which latter were also grouped the memoirs of Nehemias (II Esdras). The identity of the author of I Esd. 7-10 (who, speaking in "I" and "we", calls himself the priest Esdras [Ezra] of the Achaemenid period) with the writer of I-II Par. and I Esd. 1-6 is unmistakable. As the "Chronicler" he planned and wrote, with careful consultation of documents—he was a "skillful scribe in the Law of Moses" (I Esd. 7:6)—a summary his-

tory of the Hebrews from the earliest times, in order both
to reawaken the religious zeal and national consciousness of
those who returned from the Babylonian captivity, and to
establish the unmixed legitimacy of the survivors and descendants of the Southern Kingdom or Judea, as against any
claim which the hybrid rabble dwelling in the former seats
of the Northern Kingdom or Israel might have to sharing
in the restoration of the Temple and the Hebrew nation.

This history, conceived and undoubtedly composed as a
unit, was for convenience' sake or other reasons subjected
to rather arbitrary divisions at the hands of subsequent
editors. These divisions were probably made first into "volumes" simply for facility [46] in handling the Book. The first
division (fortunately quite logical) was made as between I
and II Paralipomenon, I Par. opening with genealogical summaries beginning with Adam, and closing with the death of
David, and II Par. opening with the reign of Solomon and
going down briefly through the annals of the decadence, until
the destruction of the Southern Kingdom in the Captivity
at Babylon. The third volume, then, containing the history
of the restoration, would logically be divided off at the decree
of Cyrus (II Par. 36: 22-23) permitting the return, and be
continued down to the writer's own childhood.[47] Thus the

[46] A single roll of parchment containing the Chronicler's whole history would certainly have been unwieldy.

[47] In this matter some interesting studies and conjectural restorations
have been made by *C. C. Torrey in The American Journal of Semitic
Languages and Literatures (Chicago University Press), Jan., April, Oct.,
1907, and April 1908. Between I Esd. 1: 11 and 2: 1 he would insert
III Esd. 4: 47b-5: 6, as follows:

"And Cyrus the king wrote for him [Sassabasar] letters to all the
satraps and governors and captains and deputies, commanding them to
aid him and all those who were going up with him to build Jerusalem.
And he wrote letters to all the governors in the province Beyond the
River, and to those in Lebanon, commanding them to bring cedar wood
from Lebanon to Jerusalem, and to aid him in building the city. And
concerning the freedom of all the Jews who went up from his kingdom
to Judea, he wrote that no ruler, deputy, governor, or satrap, should
forcibly enter their doors; that all the territory they should possess
should be free from tribute; and that the Edomites should relinquish
the villages of the Jews which they had seized. For the building of the
temple he ordered twenty talents to be given yearly until it should be
finished; and for offering the whole burnt sacrifices upon the altar day
by day, according as they had commandment to offer them, ten other

restoration or third and concluding part of the Chronicler's
history would comprise (as it is now to be seen) I Esd. 1-6
(with perhaps some lost fragments in the apocryphal III
Esdras).

There is a break of 50-odd years between I Esd. 6:22, the end
of the Chronicler's history, and I Esd. 7:1, the introduction to
Esdras' personal memoirs. The Chronicler would not consider events
occurring within his own life time as history. In the Hebrew
arrangement, Ezra-Nehemia immediately precede Chronicles (I-II
Par.), which may suggest that the former Book was considered as
a kind of introduction to the latter, or rather that it was composed
previously.

This third section, when compared with the other two (I
and II Paralipomenon, containing 29 and 36 chapters respectively) would be rather small. For contents-reasons also
it would be but natural that the personal memoirs of Esdras
(I Esd. 7—10) should be appended to the Chronicler's own
work, especially since they constituted a valuable document
continuing and supplementing the restoration history. They
would be related to it somewhat as the Acts of the Apostles
are to St. Luke's own Gospel in the New Testament writings.
With equal fittingness could a second appendix be made of
the similar memoirs of Nehemias, Esdras' associate (II Esdras, 13 chapters). The resulting volume would not only resemble in size the other two volumes of the Chronicler's account (I and II Par.), but would contain all the historical information available in the Sacred Writings on the third or
restoration phase of Israel's history.

talents yearly. For all those who went up from Babylonia to build the
city he commanded that freedom should be given both to them and to
their children. To all the priests that went up he commanded to give
the wages, and the priests' garments in which they minister. And to
the Levites he ordered to give their portions, until the day when the
house should be finished and Jerusalem builded. And he commanded that
all those guarding the city should be given allotments and fees. . . .
After this there were chosen to go up the chief men of the families, with
their wives . . . And Cyrus sent with them a thousand horsemen, to
bring them to Jerusalem in safety. . . . And these are the names of
the men who went up . . . Of the priests, the sons of Phineas and
Aaron, Jeshua, son of Jozadak, son of Seraiah; and there rose with
him Zerubbabel, son of Shealtiel . . . in the second year of the reign
of Cyrus king of Persia, in the month Nisan, on the first day of the
month.''

That I Esd. 1-6 was originally conjoined with Paralipomena is plainly evidenced by the identity of the opening verses of I Esdras (1:1-3b) with the closing verses of II Paralipomenon (36:22-23), which latter, moreover, break off the Book abruptly in the very middle of a sentence. Similar testimony is offered by the apocryphal III Esdras, which begins with the last two chapters of II Par. and continues right on through I Esdras, and adds the Esdras sections (II Esdras 8-10) of Nehemias.

227. Aramaic Section and Documents of I Esdras.—

Whilst in I Esdras both the history and the Esdras memoirs are written in the Chronicler's Hebrew, certain sections (as in Daniel) are given in Aramaic, which was the language of official and common intercourse in Western Asia during the Achaemenid regime. The main Aramaic portion comprises mostly documents quoted by the author, but the brief intermediate verses are also written in the same language.[48] These documents are the following: *A* (1:2-4): decree of Cyrus ordering the return of the Jews; *B* (4:8-16) letter of Reum and Samsai to Artaxerxes I Longimanus,[49] urging the Persian king to stop the building of Jerusalem, and likewise *C* (4:17-22) that king's reply ordering cessation of work.

Probably because of an early scribal transposition this whole Artaxerxes (I Longimanus, 465-425) correspondence (I Esd. 4:8-23) is out of place, as chronologically it should come after the Darius (I Hystaspis, 521-485) correspondence of the following chapter (I Esd. 5:6-13). The Chronicler is still recording the building of the second Temple, of which not a word is said in the Artaxerxes correspondence, the latter being concerned only about the fortification of Jerusalem, which came much later. Chronologically, then, this section should be placed somewhere after the arrival of Esdras in Jerusalem (458 B.C.) and before that of Nehemias (445 B.C.). There it would explain the ruined condition of the walls of Jerusalem complained of in II Esd. 1:3; 2:3, 13 (compare I Esd. 4:21-23). In the Darius correspondence (I Esd. 5:7-6:12) the Transflumen officials are courteous and cautious; in

[48] This method of writing in either Aramaic or Hebrew is paralleled in Daniel (2:4-7:28) where, after beginning with an Aramaic quotation, the author himself continues his narrative in that language. It must be remembered that at the time the two tongues were scarcely more than dialectally differentiated.

[49] In this document the name of Artaxerxes is spelled with a double *Šin*, *'Arthachšaštha*, whilst elsewhere it is always written with a *Šin*, *'Arthachšasstha*. In I Esd. 6:14d, where it is likewise written with a *Šin*, it is apparently a gloss.

the Artaxerxes correspondence the Samaritan informers boldly misrepresent the reconstruction of Jerusalem as a secretly rebellious fortification, thus throwing suspicion on the work for which Esdras had been authorized by Artaxerxes.

D (I Esd. 5 : 7-17) : letter of Palestinian officials to Darius I Hystaspis, inquiring about the authorization for the rebuilding of the Temple; *E* (6 : 3-5) : memorandum of the decree of Cyrus [50] regarding the building of the Temple; *F* (6 : 6-12) : part (the opening is missing) of the letter of Darius Hystaspis in reply to the above-mentioned Palestinian officials, permitting the resumption of Temple construction. The last Aramaic document contains *G* (7 : 12-26) Esdras' credentials from Artaxerxes Longimanus appointing him religious head in Palestine. The longest uninterrupted Aramaic portion is from 4 : 7 to 6 : 18.

The authenticity of the Aramaic documents in I Esdras has been a favorite object of attack by rationalistic criticism.[51] But the Church's constant defense of their substantial authenticity has been remarkably confirmed by the papyrus discoveries at Elefantine [52] in Egypt. These papyrus fragments, many of them Aramaic documents from the Persian epoch of the 5th century B.C., not only show that the Esdras documents are formally such, but otherwise also confirm the data of Esdras-Nehemias in many important points, even as regards the names of persons, such as Sanballat, satrap of Samaria at the time of Nehemias, and Hanani, the latter's brother. In short, "these documents [the Elefantine papyri], resurrected from the rubbish, agree in contents and wording in such detail with the documents contained in the Book of Ezra, that there can be no doubt as to the genuineness of the latter. More than that: therein appear

---

[50] This memorandum seems to contain the latter part of the decree of Cyrus given in I Esd. 1 : 2-4, going into detail about the Temple construction. This is insinuated by the fact that I Esd. 1 : 7-10 records the actual carrying out of the orders recorded as given in 6 : 5.

[51] See, for example, * Torrey's ''Aramaic Portions of Ezra'' in *The American Journal of Semitic Languages and Literatures* (Chicago University Press), April, 1908.

[52] The name Elefantine designated an island in the Nile, opposite Assuan, the ancient Syene. It may have been in ancient days a marketing center for ivory from the interior. During the Persian period it was colonized by a garrison consisting in the main of Jewish mercenaries, who also had erected a temple to Yahweh there. From the rubbish heaps of this old Semitic settlement have been rescued numerous papyrus fragments and ostraka with writing in Aramaic and Greek. These have been published by E. Sachau, *Aramäische Papyrus und Ostraka* (with phototypes, Leipzig, 1911); A. Ungnad, *Aramäische Papyrus aus Elefantine* (Leipzig, 1911); W. Staerk, *Alte und neue aramäische Papyri übersetzt und erklärt* (Bonn, 1912).

in part the same personages who occur in the biblical account, so that concerning these people and their times we have information which is thoroughly authentic and at the same time entirely independent of the Old Testament, and in all minutiæ confirms and supplements the picture drawn by the latter".[53]

228. The Return of the Exulants.—In October 539 B.C.[54] Cyrus, king of the conquering Medes and Persians, victoriously entered Babylon, whose defense was in charge of Baltassar (Dan. 5:30), associate in the kingdom with his absent father Nabunaid. And although, after all, the condition of the Jews in the Babylonian exile colonies had not been one of dire oppression (some indeed had attained positions of wealth and prestige there, as witness the lives of Daniel, and Susanna), the exulants nevertheless seem to have welcomed the change of masters, probably considering the downfall of the Babylonian dynasty rightful retribution for the destruction of Jerusalem and the deportation of its people, whilst at the same time they recalled the liberation prophecy of Isaias (44:28; 25:1) which, according to Josephus, they brought to the attention of their new sovereign.

At any rate, the exiled Jews immediately appear as standing in the good graces of Cyrus. Perhaps this was due to the latter's respect for a monotheistic religion whose God he may have identified with Ahuramazda (Ormuzd) of the Zoroastrianism which he himself professed. Cyrus' favorable attitude toward the Jews is paralleled by recorded acts of his in regard to other subject peoples, whose good will he strove to conciliate, especially when their religious sentiments had been outraged by the high-handed procedure of Babylonian kings. Thus the gods of Akkad, brought to Babylon by Nabunaid, were returned to their cultus towns by Cyrus, by whom also an Apollo sanctuary in Magnesia seems to have been declared free of imposts and taxes.[55]

[53] *Meyer, *Der Papyrusfund von Elefantine* (Leipzig, 1912), p. 4.
[54] The first year of the new dynasty would, however, be dated from the spring New Year's feast of the following year (538 B.C.), when the new king seized the hands of Marduk and thereby formally assumed the rule over that god's country of Babylonia. Cyrus himself did not remain at Babylon, but left there in charge a certain Ugbara (Gabryas), who in Dan. 5:31 is called Darius the Mede.
[55] See Nikel, *Biblische Zeitfragen*, Series VIII, n. 5-6, p. 4-5.

229. Work of Esdras and Nehemias.—At the very beginning of the Jewish restoration, a certain Sassabasar,[56] a "prince of Juda", was appointed to be *pecha* or governor of Judea as vice-gerent of the Persian king. The leadership of the returning Jews was divided between Zorobabel (Zerubbabel), a scion of the Davidic line, and the high priest Josue. Under these the foundations of a new Temple were laid,—for the younger generation an occasion for rejoicing, but for the older folk, who had seen the irreplaceable glory of the Solomonic Temple, a cause of tears (I Esd. 3:11-13).

But the jealous intrigues of the hybrid Samaritans, whose proffered coöperation had been scornfully rejected by the strict Jews, soon brought to a stop the work so enthusiastically begun. During the rest of Cyrus' reign, and during the tumultuous times of his immediate successor Cambyses and of the pretendant Smerdis, that is, for over 15 years, the restoration of the Temple was at a standstill. With the accession of the great Darius I Hystaspis (521-485), at the encouragement of the prophets Aggeus and Zachary, the work was resumed. After some more difficulties with the Palestinian authorities, which were successfully overcome by showing the earlier authorization from Cyrus, the Temple was finally completed in the sixth year of Darius I Hystaspis, 515 B.C. With its dedication and the celebration of the next passover closes the Chronicler's history of Israel (I Esd. 6:15-22).

There follows a period of 50 odd years for which no record of the vicissitudes of the Jews is found in Holy Writ except that in Babylonia the Jewess Esther became the favorite of Xerxes I (*Ahašweroš*, Assuerus, 485-465), during whose reign the Samaritans brought accusations against the Jews (I Esd. 4:6). During this time there seems to have been a relapse from the great enthusiasm of the returned Jews which amid such difficulties had finally accomplished the restoration of the Temple. Perhaps the death of Zorobabel and the high priest Josue, as well as of the prophets Aggeus and Zacharias (I Esd. 5:1), left the people without energetic leaders capable of stimulating zeal for the observance of the Law. Jerusalem's walls were not rebuilt, and its ruined streets were vacant

---

[56] *Sešbatsar*, Greek Σαναβασαρ, probably corrupted from Σασαβασαρ by change of σ for ν. It has been conjectured that this man may be identical with Šenatsar, son of Jechonias, of I Par. 3:18.

of houses (II Esd. 7:4). After the strenuous efforts and really notable achievements of the early restoration, a time of spiritual decadence followed.

230. The day of prophecy was almost over. God's revealed lessons to His people had almost all been given: they were now to be conned and assimilated into their spiritual being. As the Law, comprising in this word the whole of previous revelation, had been given and recorded, it was now the season to turn to its study and practice. Therefore did Yahweh raise up "a ready scribe in the Law of Moses" (I Esd. 7:6) to bring about the spiritual reformation of His returned people.

In the seventh year of Artaxerxes I Longimanus (458), the priest Esdras set out from Babylonia to Judea at the head of a large caravan of returning Jews, bringing new blood and encouragement to the homeland. His object is plain from the credentials he bore from Artaxerxes, which authorized him "to visit Judea and Jerusalem according to the Law of thy God", to "appoint judges and magistrates . . . for them who know the Law of thy God" (I Esd. 7:14, 25), and to teach the ignorant.

Upon his arrival in Jerusalem Esdras delivered to the Temple the rich donations which he had received not only from the Jews still at Babylon, but even from king Artaxerxes. The local Jews Esdras found to be rude, ignorant, careless, much corrupted by their intermarriages with Samaritans and Gentiles, so much so that he rent his clothes and tore his hair upon seeing the deplorable condition of things (I Esd. 9:3-4). In a general assembly of the people which Esdras then convoked, a resolution was passed to get rid of these foreign women and their offspring (I Esd. 10:1-12). Other abuses too, especially in regard to Sabbath observance, were soon after corrected. With a list of those who put away strange wives the memoirs of Esdras close rather abruptly.[57]

[57] Basing himself upon the text arrangement of the apocryphal III Esdras, Torrey would have II Esd. 8-10 (which features Esdras' work in cooperation with Nehemias) fit in after I Esd. 8. But these sections are thus grouped in III Esdras only in order to bring together all infor-

Of the work of Esdras during the next thirteen years there is no record in the Scripture. Esdras would seem to have been too busy educating and reforming to continue his memoirs. From the Artaxerxes correspondence (preserved extra-chronologically in I Esd. 4: 6-23) it would seem that his presence, aside from being of spiritual benefit, had roused the Jews also toward attempting to restore the walls of Jerusalem. But the hatred of the Samaritans (probably freshly enkindled by the Jews' action in casting off foreign wives) made them send to Artaxerxes Longimanus a letter which misrepresented the work of restoration as a fortification for rebellion. The king was influenced by these calumnies and ordered the work to be stopped. The Samaritans saw to the execution of this order so effectively that only the ruins of the attempted walls remained (II Esdras 2: 13-14).

231. But, besides the spiritual and interior renovation of the returned Jews so well striven for by Esdras, there was a corresponding social and economic one to be brought about. Jerusalem about the Temple was not forever to lie in ruins. For this work of the political, exterior renovation of Israel Divine Providence made use of Nehemias,[58] cupbearer to Artaxerxes Longimanus (II Esd. 2: 1-4). Appointed governor of Judea (II Esd. 5: 14), he came to Jerusalem (445 B.C.) under royal convoy, and immediately set about the building up of the walls.

Nehemias being a close favorite of the king, the Samaritans did not dare attempt to calumniate him to Artaxerxes (as they had probably done with Esdras). But their head, the cunning Sanballat, governor of Samaria, made use of threats of violence and tricks of all kinds in order to frustrate the purpose of Nehemias, even bribing men to speak as false prophets against the work of Jerusalem's restoration (II Esd. 6: 12). But no opposition availed against the wise tenacity of Nehemias. For the twelve years of his term as royal vice-gerent over Judea he unselfishly fostered the welfare of his compatriots (II Esd. 5: 14). Besides offsetting the hostility of the Samaritans, he had to fight against interior enemies, such as food storage and profiteering, by his own

mation from whatever source regarding Esdras. They can not be proved to have been written by the same person who wrote the memoirs of Esdras.

[58] Nehemias was not of the tribe of Levi, not a priest, therefore, as some might conclude from II Mach. 1: 18, 21 and I Esd. 10: 20.

good example. In matters of religious welfare and the training of the people in the observance of the Law, he relied
upon the valiant coöperation of Esdras. Probably shortly
before Nehemias' return to Babylon, at a Feast of Tabernacles, after Esdras (II Esd. 9:6 Greek) had recalled at
length the ancient history of God's dealings with His Chosen
People, the whole Jewish community once more drew up and
signed a formal covenant with Yahweh (II Esd. 10:1-31 =
the signatures; 10:32-39 = the covenant). After Nehemias'
return to Babylon (II Esd. 13:6 = 433 B.C.)[59] various abuses,
the worst being due to the high priest's being related by
affinity to Sanballat, again crept into the life of the community. These Nehemias remedied at a second visit to
Jerusalem.

232. Author of II Esdras.—The main portion of this
Book is certainly formed by the memoirs of Nehemias, an
account of the latter's efforts for the full restoration of Israel,
written by himself in the first person. But, together with
these are found other documents, such as census and genealogical lists, and the covenant with Yahweh. It is not unlikely, therefore, that the final compilation of the Book was
made by Esdras, as Jewish tradition and the constant combination of I and II Esdras seem to indicate. There are also
to be noted certain glosses due to a later editor: thus II Esd.
12:10-11 and 22-23 are inserted to bring the hierarchial lists
down to the time of Alexander the Great.

Josephus[60] makes Sanballat, who is a contemporary of Esdras
and Nehemias, live under Darius III Codomanus (336-330) and
intrigue with the conquering Alexander the Great. This is but
another of that historian's chronological errors. For, aside from
the biblical account, the Elefantine papyri show Sanballat as satrap
of Samaria in 407, under the successor of Artaxerxes I Hystaspis,
Darius II Mnemon.[61] For, when the Yahweh temple of the Egyp-

---

[59] Nikel, however, would have Nehemias make a stay of only somewhat over two months in Jerusalem, and then return to the king, to
return again as governor in the 32nd year of Artaxerxes. See *Biblische
Zeitfragen*, Series VIII, p. 186.
[60] *Ant.*, XI, vii, viii, 6.
[61] The following is the full table of the Achaemenid dynasty, beginning with the taking of Babylon. Before that Cyrus had begun to reign

tian Jewish mercenary colony at Syene was destroyed, the inhabitants wrote to Jerusalem asking for assistance in the rebuilding. But the Jews of the homeland, not acknowledging the legitimacy of such a temple, refused, whereupon the colonists of Elefantine turned to the sons of Sanballat of Samaria.[62] The governor of Judea, Bagoas (Bagohi), to whom they turned for help, may have been the *pecha* succeeding Nehemias: the high priest Johanan mentioned as Bagoas' contemporary is to be identified with the grandson of Eliasib (II Esd. 12:22-23 and 10-11), whose name is twice spelled Jonathan in those glosses.[63]

Art. 9: THE BOOK OF ESTHER

Texts: Esth. 1-2; 3-7; 8-9; 10:4-11.

233. The Text and Date.—The present Hebrew text represents a carefully edited and abbreviated version of the Book of Esther, in which the name of God does not once occur. From this Hebrew text are derived Esth. 1—10:3 of the Vulgate. The rest of the Book in that version is composed of various *plus* fragments preserved in the Greek (and Old Latin), which fragments St. Jerome gathered into a (deuterocanonical) appendix at the end of his Latin translation of the Hebrew.

To parallel the Greek version, these fragments should be inserted in the present Latin as follows: 11:1 = Greek title;

over the Medes and Persians in 559. Assignments are correct within a year or so:
Cyrus: 538-529 (Return of Jews decreed; Temple foundations); Cambyses: 529-522; Pseudo-Smerdis: 522; Darius I Hystaspis: 521-485 (Temple is finished); Xerxes I: 485-465 (Esther as favorite); Artaxerxes I Longimanus (Esdras and Nehemias authorized); Xerxes II and Sogdianus: 425; Darius II Nothus: 425-405; Artaxerxes II Mnemon: 405-359; Artaxerxes III Ochus: 359-338; Arses: 338-336; Darius III Codomanus 336-330.

[62] Nikel, *Biblische Zeitfragen*, Series VIII, nn. 5-6, pp. 13-14.

[63] Through the misplacing of the Artaxerxes correspondence in I Esd. 4:8-23, Haneberg and Torrey have both been misled into construing Artaxeres I Longimanus into an enemy of the Jews (as having stopped the Temple building, which, according to them, is supposed to have been completed under Darius II Nothus), whilst Artaxerxes II Mnemon is taken to be the patron of Esdras and Nehemias. Thus the whole dating of the memoirs of Esdras and Nehemias would be brought a century later. But the presence of Zorobabel, Josue, and others of the early return at the dedication of the Temple, forms an anachronism which Haneberg tries to avoid by assuming a Zorobabel II and Josue II.

11: 2-12: 6 = Greek beginning of the Book, to 1: 1; 13: 1-7 = Greek after 3: 13; 15: 1-3 = Greek, after 4: 8; 13: 8-14: 19 = Greek, after 4: 17; 15: 4-19 = Greek 5: 1-2; 16: 1-24 = Greek, after 8: 12; 10: 4-13 = Greek, after 10: 3.

The present Hebrew text should probably be considered as but an extract or summary of an earlier longer Hebrew or Aramaic text, which is still represented by the Greek translations. Perhaps when the feast of Purim began to degenerate into a mere secular saturnalia or carnival,[64] the present deuterocanonical portions, with their references to God, were deleted out of reverence in the synagogue reading.

234. The authorship of the original Esther account might be ascribed to Mardochai himself (see 9: 20), but 9: 31 shows that at least the end is not from his hand. The author must certainly have been close to the time of the events he relates, as he can give precise details as to the arrangement of the royal palace and park in Susa, and knows the names and stations of royal officers. Allusions to Juda and Jerusalem are practically absent, which would seem to place the writer outside the homeland of the Jews. The date of the composition of the original can not, of course, be placed before 485, the time of the accession of Xerxes I, nor later than the destruction of the Persian kingdom, for there is no indication in the Book that the writer knew of the conquests of Alexander the Great.

The expression *Macedo* in Esth. 16: 10 and 9: 24 is, of course, due to the Greek translator, who used it as the best equivalent for the *hâgagi* of the original. Instead of being referred to Agag, king of the Amalecites,[65] this word should probably be taken as representing

[64] The feast of Purim would fall some time in February. Rejoicing and feasting even to drunkeness seem to have been allowed by Jewish tradition: ''On the feast of Purim one should eat, drink, and make merry to such an extent that he can not distinguish between 'Perish Aman!' and 'Live Mardochai!'. . . Rab and Rabbi Sira treated each other on the feast of Purim. Rab got up and [in drunken fit] slew R. Sira. Then he prayed mercy for him, so that he came back to life'' (Sheeloth de Rab Achia in Haneberg, *Geschichte der bibl. Offenbarung*, p. 496).

[65] The masoretic text would seem to be trying to emphasize a descent of Aman from Agag, king of Amalec, at the time of Saul (see I Kings 15: 8 ss), as contrasted with Mardochai, who is supposed to be descended from the same Cis stock as Saul. But, according to Oppert (*Com-*

gâgi (= Γωγαῖος found in some Lucian MSS.), and as meaning
"Gagean, man of Gog" (Ez. 38:2; 39:1; note Greek of Num.
24:7), which would have the generic sense of "northern barbarian
or heathen". . . . Now, a Macedonian was such a "northern barbarian" to the Greeks.[66] The *Bugæus* of Esth. 12:6 is not to be
read Βουγαῖος as a *nomen gentilicium*, but as the Homeric term of
reproach βουγαῖος a braggart, one who boasts like a bull.

235. Historicity and Difficulties.—Rationalistic scripturists generally make the Book of Esther a fabulous legend
compiled for the feast of Purim, or an account of the Seleucid
persecution era projected back into, or expressed in terms of,
the Achaemenid period. But, the historic detail is too abundant and too free from anachronisms to admit of such an
hypothesis. Thus, what is said of Assuerus[67] in Esther is
confirmed remarkably by the accounts of Xerxes I given by
extra-biblical historians, who furnish many other examples
of his characteristic vanity, capricious humor, sensuality, and
cruel rages.

Thus, when a storm broke up the bridge of boats which had
been constructed across the Hellespont for the passage of his hordes
into Greece, he had the engineer of the work put to death and the
sea itself scourged and chains thrown therein.[68] At the battle of
Thermopylæ he had his Median soldiers placed in the first ranks,
to assure their death, whilst he himself seems usually to have assisted
at battles seated upon his throne (note Esth. 15:9).

The great feast, lasting about half a year (Esth. 1:4)
which Xerxes gave in the "third year of his reign" for all
the grandees of his empire in order "that he might show the
riches of the glory of his kingdom and the greatness and
boasting of his power" (Esth. 1:4), has its extraordinary

mentaire historique et philologique du livre d'Esther, p. 13), the Khorsa-
bad inscriptions would show that there was in fact a part of Media
called Agag.

[66] See Paul Haupt* "Critical Notes on Esther", in *The American
Journal of Semitic Languages and Literatures* (Chicago, Jan., 1908), pp.
123-124.

[67] Assuerus = *Ahašweroš*, Hebrew = Old Persian *Khšayârša*-Greek
Xerxes. The deuterocanonical fragments of the appendix, and the
Greek version consistently call this king Artaxerxes, the translator
having been deceived by the prosthetic *aleph* of the Hebrew.

[68] For Xerxes' life and deeds see particularly Herodotus, V, 18, VII,
8, 9, 35, 37-39, 97, 98, VIII, 65, 69, IX, 108, 110; Plutarch, *Themistocles*,
XIII.

length explained by the time it would take for the officials invited thereto, to come successively from divers distant parts of the Persian empire. Its real purpose was perhaps the following: to sound sentiment, estimate resources, and remotely prepare for the great but eventually disastrous invasion of Greece, which actually took place later (480).[69] On his return therefrom it is also known that he plunged into debauchery to drown the bitterness of the memory of defeat. This might coincide with the great harem selection which eventually brought Esther, Mardochai's cousin, into such fortunate power as the king's favorite (479 or 478).

Mardochai's name is most probably a Babylonian theophorous appellation, derived from the god Marduk. With such a name it is quite impossible to assume that Mardochai himself had been carried away into captivity under Jechonias (599 B.C.). Rather, the genealogy of Esth. 2:5-6 is elliptical (as is so frequently the case with biblical genealogies): Jair (living about 600 B.C.) is Mardochai's father; Semei (about 1000) and Cis, Saul's father (about 1050) are but two of Mardochai's most notable ancestors. The Targum inserts between Semei and Cis the name of Semei's father, Gera.

236. The massacre of Persian subjects to the number of 15,000 (Esth. 9:6, 16 Greek) by the Jews becomes quite explicable on closer study of the circumstances. Undoubtedly (as has been invariably the case wherever Jews have risen by numbers or affluence to prominent position in a nation) Aman was not the only man in all Persia who hated the now rich and influential descendants of the original captives. But he had special reasons. He bore a private grudge against the Jew Mardochai, whom, however, he could not ruin directly or openly, as the latter also stood in the good graces of Xerxes. But, as a wise man hides a pebble upon a beach and a leaf in a forest, so Aman took advantage of his position to plan and threaten a nation-wide pogrom against the hated race, expecting thus successfully to hide in the ruin of a people his private vengeance upon his rival. To achieve his nefarious end, Aman deceived Xerxes into granting him

[69] Herodotus relates that, after having conquered Egypt, Xerxes took four years to prepare for the campaign against Greece (VII, 8).

a blanket authorization for one of the irrevocable "decrees of the Medes and Persians" (Esth. 3:8-15), upon which he issued the order for a pogrom to take place eleven months from its date. Combining cupidity with cleverness, Aman's intention was probably thus to force the Jews through fear to sell, or to dispose of their property otherwise, cheaply but legally to himself and his friends (instead of having it confiscated directly to the royal treasury), in order to save their lives by fleeing the country before the fatal day arrived.

Esther at the same time, taking her own life into her hands, reveals the wicked plot against her people to the king. But, what could be done, as the fatal decree, once issued, was practically irrevocable? [70] A new decree was issued, authorizing the Jews to offer armed resistance to any attacks made upon them. By this it was to be expected that the effect of Aman's orders would be for the greater part nullified.[71] The Persian authorities were not to interfere should the Jews defend themselves. Hence the permission granted by Aman's decree was of no more value than the pound of flesh which Portia would have allowed Shylock to cut from the body of Antonio.

The Jews, then, did prepare themselves for the fatal day, and, when their enemies attacked them (a great number of them perhaps ignorant of the second counteracting decree), they were not able to prevail against the forewarned and forearmed Jews, and thus were slain by the Jews in self-defense.[72] The gibbeting of Aman's sons and the second massacre in Susa were measures necessarily taken to prevent subsequent anti-Jewish outbreaks, which were to be expected

[70] Compare Dan. 6:8: "What is decreed by the Medes and Persians can not be altered", and "The law of the Medes and Persians is: that no decree which the king hath made, may be altered" (Dan. 6:15). See however in the deuterocanonical sections Esth. 16:9, 17.

[71] By parallel, had the former Russian authorities permitted the Jews to bear arms or organize in resistance against the mobs which attacked them, many deplorable pogroms would never have taken place.

[72] In this sense are to be interpreted all the passages referring to the killing by the Jews of their enemies. They had received permission (Esth. 9:2) "to lay hands on those who would attempt to do them harm"; they were allowed forcibly to resist a forcible attack upon their persons or property.

when on the following day the disappointed fury of the populace should break out anew against the Jews thought surely then to be defenseless. But the bodies of Aman's sons would be a warning.

237. The Feast of Purim.—The Book of Esther is undeniably connected with the feast of Purim, a fast followed by a day of rejoicing on the 14th Adar (end of February).[73] But the etymology of *Purim* as being equivalent to "lots" offers some difficulties. For, there is no Persian word for "lot" itself from which *p(h)ur* could well be derived. Perhaps the term is to be referred to some word allied with (Hebrew) *parûr* = boiling pot, or *pûrah* = vat or wine press (Assyrian, *pûru* = urn), having in mind a vessel from or into which lots were cast (Esth. 9:26; 3:7). Haupt thinks it more tenable that *purim* would refer to the *manoth*, "portions" or presents of food (mentioned also in Esth. 9:22; II Esd. 8:10, 12) which the people exchanged, perhaps more especially on occasion of the Spring New Year.[74] The word might then be traced to the Vedic *pûrtu*, an indication of which is preserved in the Lucian Greek's φουρδι, where the ordinary Greek has φ(ρ)ουραι (by haplography ΦΟΥΡΑΙ for ΦΟΥΡΔΙ). In any case, it is well known that the Persians frequently appealed to the casting of lots.

The 13th Adar was especially considered a *dies ater*, hence most auspicious for a massacre of the Jews. If the feast of Purim could be definitely connected with the Persian Spring festival *Naurôz*, itself derived from the Babylonian New Year's feast, then *Purim* would become equivalent to Latin *strennæ* (French *étrennes*) = New Year's gifts, and the meaning of the Greek received text would be an allusion to the "watching in" of the New Year.

238. The keynote of the feast of Purim for the Jews

[73] See Esth. 9:28 and I Mach. 15:37, where it is called "Mardochai's day", and combined with Nicanor's day.

[74] But, another and broader sense is suggested in Mardochai's prayer (Esth. 13:15-17): "O God of Abraham, have mercy on Thy people, because our enemies . . . are resolved to destroy Thine *inheritance* (κληρονομίαν). Despise not Thy *portion* (μερίδα) . . . be merciful to thy *lot* (κλήρῳ) and innheritance (Latin: *sorti et funiculo tuo*)." See also Esth. 10:10-11.

would seem to be the celebration of their future messianic (in the Pharisaic, materialistic acceptation) delivery from the yoke of the Gentiles, the day when they would indeed have their vengeance upon the *Goyim,* when there would finally come forth from the urn of providential destiny the "lot" of the day of eventual triumph for the people of Israel. And on this basis the spiritual sense of the theme of this Book might be applied to the eventual victory of the Kingdom of God (the spiritualized Kingdom of Israel) through Christ (Mardochai) and Mary (Esther), over the Antichrist and all the world's machinations for its destruction

Art. 10: THE BOOK OF JUDITH

Texts: Judith 1-4; 5-6; 8-11.

239. Text.—The Vulgate presents of this Book a version which is rather a summary or a paraphrase made in haste, as St. Jerome notes in his prologue,[75] from an Aramaic text now lost. That the original was written in either Hebrew or Aramaic is shown by the very character of the versions, which lack the usual Greek connective particles and include many characteristic Semitisms. Even the mistranslations of the Greek witness to this. Thus in Judith 3:9 (Greek) the translator evidently read משׂור *masôr* "a saw" instead of מישׁור *mišôr,* "a plain".

The Vulgate and the Greek both have expansions, each over the other. Thus, for example, the Greek concludes Judith 1:12 as follows:[76]

And Nabuchodonosor was angered exceedingly against all that land. And he swore by his throne and by his kingdom that he would punish all the confines of Cilicia, Damascus, and Syria, de-

[75] "Sepositis occupationibus quibus vehementer arctabar, huic [libro] unam lucubratiunculam dedi, magis sensum a sensu quam ex verbo verbum transferens. Multorum codicum varietatem vitiosissimam amputavi, sola ea quae intelligentia integra in verbis chaldaeis invenire potui, latinis expressi."

[76] This translation combines the text of both B (Vaticanus) and P3 (Parisiensis 609).

stroying [them] with his sword, and all the inhabitants of the land
of Moab, and the sons of Ammon, and all Judea, and all those
in Egypt, till one comes upon the boundaries of the two seas. And
he stood prepared with his forces against Arphaxad in the seventeenth year. And he overcame him in war, and defeated the forces
of Arphaxad and all his cavalry and all his chariots, and he became
master of his cities. He came even to Ecbatana, where he seized
the towers and sacked the bazaars, and put its commander into
disgrace. And he captured Arphaxad in the mountains of Ragau,
and he shot him down with javelins, and utterly destroyed him even
to this day. And he himself and all his companions and an exceeding great multitude of men of war, were conquered. And he was
there taking things easy and feasting, both he himself and his army,
for about 120 days.

240. Date.—Scripturists so far have not been of accord
as to the precise period of Jewish history to which the events
recorded in Judith are to be assigned. Two conjectures will
be stated here, representative of the two more probable and
reliable groups of opinion.

The greater number of Catholic exegetes incline to place
the events of Judith in the time either of the absence of
Manasses (699-644) of Juda in Babylon, or of the minority
of Josias (642-609).[77] In that case the Assyrian king mentioned might be Assurbanipal (668-626),[78] who made an expedition against the Arabians. Arphaxad, king of the Medes,
would then be the corrupted name of Phraortes or Apraartes
(*Frawarti*), who reigned 647-625. In his inscriptions Assurbanipal records having vanquished the Medes, after which
he endeavored to reëstablish control over Western Asia which
had revolted. In 648-647 he waged a successful war against
his brother, Samaššumukin of Babylon, who had assembled
a strong alliance against him.

Against the above view militate the following difficulties. The
times seem more reminiscent of the period of Esdras and Nehemias,
"for, they had recently come up from the captivity, and but a
short time before the whole people of Judea had been gathered

[77] For Manasses, see II Par. 33: 11. Josias was but eight years old
when he came to the throne (IV Kings 22: 1); Helcias was high priest
then.
[78] There never was any Assyrian king named Nabuchodonosor. Probably for a difficult or illegible name the copyist substituted that of the
traditional archenemy of the Jews, the king of Babylon who reigned
from 604 to 561 and captured Jerusalem in 586.

together, and the utensils and the altar and the Temple had been sanctified" (Judith 4:3 Greek). Such a return before 538 is unknown. This is confirmed by the conclusion of Achior's speech, which can scarcely be interpreted as of the Northern Kingdom deportation alone: "When they departed from the way He had marked out for them, they were utterly beaten in many wars, and were led away captive into a land not their own, and the Temple of their God was reduced to its foundation. . . . And now having turned back to their God, they have come up again from the dispersion into which they were scattered, and they have rebuilt Jerusalem, where is their holy place" (Judith 5:18-19 Greek).[79] Lastly, the closing statement of the Book, that "there was no one disturbing the children of Israel in the days of Judith, and after her death for many days" (Judith 16:30), demands a lengthy period of peace that can scarcely be verified in the first hypothesis.

Basing themselves upon the proper names Holofernes and Bagoas (Vulgate: *Vagao,* Judith 12:10), some have placed the siege of Bethulia in the time of Artaxerxes III Ochus (359-338). A certain Orophernes and a Bagaos [80] are recorded as in the service of this king. During his reign, moreover, according to Eusebius, an expedition was made against certain rebellious Jews, Jericho was destroyed, and a number of Jews were deported to Hyrcania on the south shore of the Caspian Sea.

Lastly Nikel [81] suggests as a fit setting for the Judith history the early part of the reign of Darius I Hystaspis (521-485), so friendly towards the Jews. When he ascended the throne there was rebellion of vassal states in the Persian empire. Among the opponents of Darius in these wars were Phravartiš of Media (who might be identical with Arphaxad) and a certain Aracha (who likewise might be identifiable with the Arioch, king of the Elamites, of Judith 1:6). In this wide-scattered revolt Darius could not be everywhere personally directing his campaigns, and might reasonably be expected to entrust the command of a punitive expedition

---

[79] Vulgate: ''Plurimi eorum captivi abducti sunt in terram non suam. Nuper autem reversi ad Dominum Deum suum, ex dispersione qua dispersi fuerant, adunati sunt, et ascenderunt montana hæc omnia, et iterum possident Ierusalem, ubi sunt sancta eorum'' (Judith 5:22-23).

[80] Diodorus, XXXI, 19. A Bagoas is likewise mentioned by Josephus (*Ant.*, XI, vii, 1) as governor of Judea under Artaxerxes II Mnemon (404-361), and alluded to in the Elefantine papyri as Bagohi.

[81] *Biblische Zeitfragen*, Series VIII, pp. 220-221.

into Syria and northern Palestine to a subordinate general
(Holophernes). The troops beleaguering Bethulia were of
Persian and Median nationality (Judith 16:11). In about
two years after Darius' accession to the throne the Persian
empire was again pacified, and the Jews enjoyed undisturbed
tranquillity for a long time till the reign of Artaxerxes III
Ochus (359-338).

241. Historicity.—That the author of the original text of
Judith intended to record a history of actual events, and not
simply to point a consoling or encouraging tale in the form
of history, seems clear from the following. He gives exact
data on history, geography (Judith 1:6-8; 2:12-17; 3:1;
14, etc.), chronology (Judith 1:5; 8:4; 16:28), and the
genealogy of Judith (8:1). Ancient Jewish prayers for the
first and second sabbath of the feast of the Dedication contain a *résumé* of the Book of Judith, and there would have
been no sense in thanking God for a mere imaginary deliverance. The Book itself mentions the institution of a feast
in memory of its heroine (16:31). Ancient *Midrašim* re-
count the same events independently of the biblical history.[82]

Art. 11: HELLENISM AND THE JEWS

Texts: Dan. 11:1-35; I Mach. 1:1-5, 12-16; II Mach. 4:13-15.

242. Political Vicissitudes.—In apocalyptic vision already Daniel (8:3-10, 20-26) had foreseen the destruction of
the Medo-Persian empire, represented by the two-horned ram
which is overthrown by the "he-goat from the West" having
the "notable horn", that is, the short-lived Macedonian empire having Alexander the Great as its first head, to be replaced by the various succession states into which it was partitioned by Alexander's generals upon their leader's death
in Nabuchodonosor's palace at Babylon in 324. Thus Syria

---

[82] In the *Proc. of the Soc. of Biblical Archeology* (March, 1894, vol.
XVI, pp. 161-163), Gaster has published an abridged account of the life
of Judith which he found in an old Hebrew MS., where Holophernes has
become Seleucus and Bethulia, Jerusalem. Consult also Montfaucon,
La Vérité de l'histoire de Judith (Paris, 1690).

and Mesopotamia came under the rule of Seleucus I (306-281) and his successors of the Seleucid dynasty, with a capital at Antioch. Ptolemy I Soter (died 285) set up his throne in brilliant Alexandria, ruling Egypt and soon bringing under the sway of the Ptolemaic dynasty Phenicia, Palestine, Cœlosyria, and Cyrene in North Africa.

243. Thus the Jews of the Babylonian *diaspora* fell under the government of the Seleucids, those of Palestine and of the Egyptian dispersion, under that of the Ptolemies, until 198, when Palestine was wrested from Egypt by the Seleucids. The kernel of the Jewish nation continued to dwell in Palestine, looked up to as the homeland by the numerous and influential colonists in both Babylon and Alexandria. The rule of the Ptolemies was well disposed towards the descendants of Jacob. The Jews formed autonomous communities having special privileges and exemptions within the Egyptian state, although they were denied full citizenship. They erected synagogues and even a temple (at Leontopolis), and during this period their Sacred Books were translated into Greek.

244. Hellenistic Thought Characteristics. — Hellenism may be formulated briefly as Greek philosophy plus Alexander's campaigns. It was the intellectual precipitate remaining after the violent religious, cultural, and political ebullition which set in when, through the medium of the Macedonian conquest, the sharp acid of Hellenic thought was first poured into the alkaline passivity of the Oriental peoples. Philosophy, now in its second, popular stage, was discussed in the *agorá* of every considerable town from the Black Sea to the Cyrenaica. For Greek deserters, traders, colonists, scattered far and wide along the broad paths of Alexander's armies. By thus coming into intimate contact with the despised *bárbaroi* the Greeks began to appreciate their institutions and to examine and assimilate their doctrines. The old Attic reserve and self-sufficiency had been permanently battered down. The opening of the Greek language to non-Greek words is the significant parallel of the opening of the Greek mind to non-Greek thought. Hence, in the philosophico-theological plane, *syncretism* was the dominant note of Hellenism. And this tendency, with its inherent consequences for good as well as for evil, it communicated to all minds it infected. The Greeks became true *spermológoi*,[83] flitting "seed-pickers" of ideas in the market-places of the world's thought, gathering scraps of knowledge and belief from all nations. In adopting and assimilating foreign religious elements, to harmonize them with their own philosophic principles, they employed the help of *allegorism,* a medium found useful early in expounding popularly current Greek myths.[84] In the political and social plane, Hellenism rather encouraged *individualism,* consciousness of personal responsibility and value, as contrasted with blind mass-action fostered by Oriental despotism.

245. A natural consectary of this liberalism in matters of theory was *hedonism* in practical life,—a policy of expediency, usefulness, pleasure, in the acceptation and treatment of material facts concerning which there could be no abstract disputes. Hence also the gymnasia with their classes of *epheboi* were community institutions, social centers in every country touched by Hellenism.[85] In short, Hellenism, a world-culture phase growing out of Greek philosophy's impinging on other thought-systems through the original medium of Alexander's campaigns, had for its outstanding feature, syncretism, and had for good effects chiefly a destruction of gross pagan superstitions, and a liberalizing, broadening, of men's outlook upon the world and God. Its bad effects were: sapping of religious sincerity, indifference, materialism.[86]

[83] Note how the epithet was later so contemptuously applied to St. Paul by the Epicurean and Stoic philosophers of Athens: "What is this seed-picker trying to tell us?" (Acts 17: 18).

[84] For example, the tale of the companions of Ulysses turned to swine by Circe was allegorically explained as the soul degraded by giving way to animal passions. By this anti-anthropomorphizing tendency the old gods were treated as concretizations, symbols, of virtues, vices, etc.

[85] This importance attached to the care of the body was in the beginning controlled by traces of the ancient Spartan asceticism, but later degenerated into luxury in its worst phases, enervated by Oriental influences absorbed through syncretism.

[86] On this whole matter, see Simon, "Hellenism and the Jews" in the *American Catholic Quarterly Review,* April, 1920, pp. 243-254.

246. Effects of Hellenism on the Jews.—In Palestine itself the seed of Hellenism sown by Alexander's invasion lay latent for a long time, but the leaves of its growth finally made their appearance in favorable season, after Palestine passed from Ptolemaic to Seleucid suzerainty. Under Antiochus IV (175-163 B.C.) the younger generation of the Jews, the more radical element, partly to cater to the government, partly through plain Hellenistic corruption, suddenly wished to hellenize all Jewish life. With the king's authority to back them, Greek customs were forciby introduced, Greek dress was adopted, a gymnasium for bodily training and luxury in Greek style was erected near the Temple itself, and the ancient Law and traditions were despised to such an extent that even the physical sign of Hebrew nationality was obliterated by surgical operation (I Mach. 1: 12-16; II Mach. 4: 12).

247. But, interesting as are the politico-social changes consequent upon the importation of Hellenism into Palestine, they are exceeded in importance by the fundamental changes thereby wrought in the traditional mentality of Jewry. These changes consisted chiefly in a broadening of intellectual outlook and religious interpretation. Hebrew thought, so characteristically Semitic in its synthetizing tendency, now became acquainted with Aryan analysis, as taught by its unrivaled exponents, the Greek philosophers. The treasure of divine revelation for the first time was studied with the aid of exact philosophic terminology, and thus entirely new aspects of the Scriptures revealed themselves. The weapons were forged and the battleground prepared for the age-long war to be waged between the wisdom of God and the wisdom of the world.

248. In proportion as the concept of God, through removal of anthropomorphisms, became more transcendent, it was also more and more universalized. Yahweh, God of Israel, is now insistently proclaimed as "Ruler of the Universe" (II Mach. 7: 9; see also 7: 35-38; 14: 35). Moreover, having at last been definitely cured of tendencies to idolatry, polytheism, in the Captivity, the Jews were in fit mental attitude for a more advanced and explicit revelation of the Deity's pluripersonal life. Hellenism, as involving the Platonic idea doctrine, became a way-breaker for the concept of the

Trinity. Hence the revelation developments of God's life in Himself, found in the Books of Ecclesiasticus and Wisdom.

At this time also the soteriological ideas latent in revelation came more and more to the forefront in Hebrew thought. The messianic kingdom began to be conceived as having not only a national but also a universal scope.[87] Again, a most notable change is found to have been wrought at this time in the domain of ideas relative to the whole economy of relations of man to God. Witness the remarkable insistence of Ecclesiasticus and Wisdom on free-will and the responsibility of the individual. Ritual is not so much emphasized; sacrifices, the Temple itself, seem to become subordinated to the *opus operantis,* the personal conduct of the individual. At the same time stoicism and hedonism were forcefully combated.

249. Hellenism Preluded Christianity.—Indeed, Hellenism was the fitting intellectual dawn to precede the rising of the Sun of Justice, Jesus Christ, the Logos, the divine *Sophía* incarnate. By it the world was prepared for the full pouring forth of dazzling final revelation. Hellenism had long ago battered down or weakened pagan myths. Its syncretic character made men's minds receptive of new doctrines. Its keen analytic philosophy furnished the technical aid which enabled reason better to grasp the sublimities and subtleties of Christ's teaching, and its cosmopolitanism assured the ready reception of the Good Tidings. Not without providential cause was the ancient Noachic prophecy now fulfilled, that Japhet should dwell in the tents of Sem (Gen. 9:27) and, in the Kingdom of Heaven, be "enlarged" so as to spread over the whole earth a glorious dominion, surpassing in extent and duration Alexander's world-empire. Therefore was it ordained that, after a manner, the spear-points of Macedonian phalanges should open the ways of the world to Christianity.

[87] An extreme and false development of the messianic idea, brought about in sub-Machabean times in the reaction from the evils of the Hellenic invasion, and responsible for many narrow, earthly-theocratic misconceptions regarding the Messias' nature and function, was the *apocalyptic* movement, an endeavor to revive the courage of the disconsolate faithful ground under the heels of the *goyim,* by painting glittering visions of messianic liberation and material world-conquest.

Art. 12: THE BOOKS OF MACHABEES

Texts: I Mach. 1-2; 3-4; 15-16; II Mach. 1-3; 9-10; 15.

250. Summary of the Jews' History after Esdras.—As previously noted,[1] the Chronicler's accounts bring post-exilic Jewish history in the Sacred Scriptures well up into the period of Persian overlordship, till about the time of Darius II Nothus (425-405). But there is no direct record in the Bible of the destruction of the Achaemenid kingdom about a century later by Alexander the Great (333), nor of the subsequent partitioning of the Macedonian's empire by his generals into divers succession states (I Mach. 1: 9-10), whereby Palestine was at first allotted to the Ptolemies, the Lagi dynasty of Egypt, under whose mild rule thousands of Jews flourished in the colonies of Alexandria and Leontopolis (On), where the Septuagint version and several of the Old Testament "deuterocanonical" Books originated. Neither does inspired history relate how Palestine, with Cœlosyria, later became a dependency of the Seleucids of Syria, with their capital at Antioch, after Antiochus III (the Great), at the battle of Paneas (198) near the sources of the Jordan, was victorious over the general of his feeble Egyptian rival, Ptolemy V Epiphanes.

The Jews of Palestine evidently expected greater benefits from the energetic Seleucid regime (which also had already granted special privileges to those of the Hebrew race within its domain) than from the now weak Lagi. They gave the Syrian troops friendly welcome, and in return received valuable religious privileges. The Temple personnel was declared tax exempt, and the Syrian treasury, in continuation of the old Persian custom (III Esdras 4: 52; I Esdras 6: 9-10), probably followed also by the Lagi,[2] contributed towards the cultus expenses (II Mach. 3: 2-3). The other inhabitants of

[1] See above, Nos. 188-189, and 239-240.
[2] Josephus, *Ant.*, XII, ii, 5-11.

Jerusalem were likewise favored in the matter of taxes,—so that the beginnings of Syrian suzerainty over Palestine, under Antiochus III (the Great, 223-187) and Seleucus IV Philopator (187-175), were on the whole rather auspicious for the Jews.

251. The following is a conspectus [3] of the rulers of Egypt, of the Jews themselves, and of Syria, after the breakup of the Macedonian empire, which almost immediately succeeded the conquest of Persia (333).

EGYPT Under the Lagi	THE JEWS Under High Priests	SYRIA Under the Seleucids
Ptolemy I Lagos, 323-284	Onias I, 321–310	Seleucus I Nicator, 312–281
	Simon I "the just", 310–291 (*see* Ecclus. 50: 1–22)	
Ptolemy II Philadelphus, 286–247 (*Pentateuch translated into Greek?*)	Eleazar, 291–276	Antiochus I Soter, 281–262
	Manasses, 276–251	
Ptolemy III Euergetes, 247–222	Onias II, 251–219	Antiochus II Theos, 262–247
		Seleucus II Callisthenes, 247–227
		Seleucus III Ceraunos, 227–223
Ptolemy IV Philopator, 222–205	Simon II, 219–199	Antiochus III "the Great", 223–187, *seizes Palestine from Egypt* in 198
Ptolemy V Epiphanes, 204–180	Onias III, 199–175 (*see* II Mach. 3:1)	
Ptolemy VI Philometor, 180–145, *had* Physcon *as associate after* 171	Jason, 175–172	Seleucus IV Philopator, 187–175 (*beginning of history of II Mach.*)
		Antiochus IV Epiphanes, 175-164 (*beginning of history of I Mach.*)

[3] Adapted from table on pp. 397-398 of Father Pope's *Catholic Student's 'Aids' to the Bible,* vol. I. The chapter on Machabees therein gives most useful information and summaries (2nd ed., 1918).

EGYPT Under the Lagi	THE JEWS Under High Priests	SYRIA Under the Seleucids
Ptolemy VII (IX) Euergetes II or Physcon, 146–117 (but was ruling with Ptolemy VI from 170 whilst Philometor was in the hands of Antiochus)	Menelaus, 172–163 HASMONEANS Judas Machabeus, 166–161	Antiochus V Eupator, 164–162 Demetrius I Soter, (son of Seleucus IV), 162–152
Jewish schismatic temple founded at On in Egypt by refugee priest, Onias IV	Jonathan, 161–143 Simon, 143–136	Alexander Balas (son of Antiochus IV), 152–145 Demetrius II Nicator, 147–142 Antiochus VI (son of Balas), 144–143 Trypho, his general, usurps the throne, 144–143 Antiochus VII Sidetes (son of Demetrius I), 143–131
Ecclesiasticus translated into Greek in Egypt Ptolemy VIII (X) Lathyrus, 117–81	John Hyrcanus, 135–106	Demetrius II (for the second time), 130–126
	Aristobulus I, 106–105, Alexander Janneus, 105–78; his widow Alexandra (Salome), 78–69; her sons, Hyrcanus II and Aristobulus II, dispute sucession. Pompey conquers Aristobulus, and Roman domination begins about 63, under Idumean kings, Antipas and Herod the Great (40)	Antiochus Dionysius

252. Title, Relationship, and Object.—Whilst bearing the same name, the Books of First and Second Machabees have scarcely anything in common but the fact that both concurrently cover the period of a dozen years of Jewish history, from about 175 to 162, which was marked by the reaction of a faithful group of the Jews under the leadership of the Hasmonean family (otherwise known as the Machabees) against the oppression of the Seleucid kings. II Machabees treats only of the chief of these liberators, Judas Machabeus.

The name of Machabee comes from the surname given Judas, the eldest son of Mathathias, in I Mach. 3:1. It is commonly interpreted as there signifying "the Hammerer" (as "Charles *Martel*"), as if derived from *maqaba* (see Judg. 4:21), although the Rabbis write *makabi*. The family itself is called Hasmonean, from the genealogy of Josephus, who makes Mathathias the "son of John, of Simeon the Hasmonean, a priest of the course of Joarib".[4]

The two Books of Machabees are not related as consecutive volumes, being quite independent each of the other. I Machabees is simple history covering the wars waged by the three sons of Mathathias, namely, Judas, Jonathan, and Simon, during the period from 176 to 133 B.C. It starts from the first year of Antiochus IV Epiphanes. II Machabees begins a trifle earlier than I Machabees, namely, with the last year of Seleucus IV Philopator (177). Treating of the exploits of Judas Machabeus only, it closes much sooner than the history of I Machabees, about 162 B.C. I Machabees, with its simple language, confines itself rather to the narration of the natural factors operative in the events narrated, without much reflection or commentary. II Machabees, on the other hand, with its rather oratorical style, looks upon its history from the prophetic viewpoint, reflectively, and is concerned about emphasizing the supernatural direction and intervention. It also lays stress upon the glorification of the Jerusalem Temple,—probably in opposition to the schismatical

---

[4] Josephus, *Ant.* XII, vi, 1. In Eusebius, *Hist. eccl.*, the original title of I Mach. has been preserved in a Greek transliteration: Τὰ Μακκαβαϊκὰ ἅπερ ἐπιγέγραπται Σαρβὴθ Σαρβανὴ ἔλ, which might be read as ''Sceptre of the Princes of the Sons of God''.

Temple erected during that period near Leontopolis, at Onion in Egypt, by the refugee priest Onias IV.[5]

253. Language and Date of I Machabees.—The orignal text of I Machabees, written in either Hebrew or Aramaic, was seen by St. Jerome, but has since become lost. The present Greek translation is very ancient, having been used already by Josephus (about A.D. 93) in the composition of the 12th and 13th books of his *Jewish Antiquities*. It is preserved in the *Codex Alexandrinus* (A) and in the *Sinaiticus* (א), but lacking in the *Vaticanus* (B); hence it is not known from what MSS. the received text of the Sixtine Greek Bible was derived.

The Latin translation in the Vulgate was not made by St. Jerome, but is that of the Old Latin version. It embodies a number of slight changes, omissions and additions, as compared with the present Greek, none, however, of great import. Especially has it inserted the words *Deus* and *Dominus* which, according to the best MSS., are quite wanting in the Greek. However, the word "Heaven", which frequently replaces those expressions in the original Greek, may have been substituted by an editor for the ineffable Yahweh, thus eliminating the Divine Name, as in Esther.

254. Of the author of I Machabees nothing is known except, as may be gathered from internal evidence, that he was a devout Jew, reverencing the Sacred Books (I Mach. 1:59-60; 3:48; 12:9, etc.) and the feasts and solemnities, and glorying in the victories of his national heroes as constituting a triumph of righteousness over iniquity. The characteristic Pharisaic thought tendency of separation from everything Gentile, of opposition to Hellenistic innovations, already becomes manifest in this Book, although the author shows also the influence of Hellenism in his succinct, sober style, as well as in his approving, even hopeful, attitude

[5] "Now as to Onias [IV], the son of the High Priest [Onias III], who was left a child when his father died, when he saw that the King [Antiochus IV Epiphanes] had slain his uncle Menelaus and had given the high priesthood to Alcimus, who was not of the High Priest stock . . . he fled to Ptolemy [VI Philometor], King of Egypt. And finding that he was held in great esteem by him and his wife Cleopatra, he asked and obtained a place in the Heliopolitan Nome, and there he built a temple like that at Jerusalem." Josephus, *Ant.*, XII, ix, 7; see *ibid.*, XIII, iii, 1-3, and *Wars of the Jews*, VII, x, 2-4.

towards the Jews' alliances with the Romans and the Spartans.[6]

In fact, in this unchauvinistic, liberal attitude of the author of I Machabees towards the Greeks and the Romans, one may see a reason for the exclusion of this Book from the later Pharisaic canon of Jamnia, now followed by Protestants. For, nothing could be more distasteful to the Pharisaic Jewish authorities after the destruction of Jerusalem, than to have one of their Sacred Books remind them that the much-hated Roman oppressors had at one time been deliberately patronized by the Synagogue. Another reason for its exclusion is probably the late date of its composition.[7] For, I Mach, 16: 23-24. referring to the annals of John Hyrcanus' pontificate (135-104), indicates that the author wrote his book not so very long after the death of Simon Machabeus. The composition may be conjectured as having taken place between 100 and 70 B.C. After 70, and especially after 64 (when Pompey captured Jerusalem), the Romans, having in their turn become aggressive and oppressive, surely would not have been mentioned in the amicable manner of I Mach. 8 and 12.

255. Chronology of the Machabees.—The author of I Machabees especially, as befits an historian, is careful and exact in his dates and other chronological references. Like the compiler of II Machabees, he follows the new Hellenistic Seleucid era in his reckoning but—differently from II Machabees—he begins this era, not (as the Greeks did) on Oct. 1st, 312 B.C., the date of the accession of Seleucus I to the throne, but (after the Hebrew manner) from the preceding Nisan or April (which marked the beginning of the post-exilic Jewish civil year). Compared with the Greek computation, then, his dates are about six months too soon. Hence synchronous references in II Machabees may be found placed a year later, apparently, since the compiler of the latter work accepted the system of the completely hellenized Jason of Cyrene, whose books he utilized as sources. Compare I Mach. 7: 1 and

---

[6] See I Mach. 8 and 12: 1-23.
[7] See close of citation from Josephus in No. 19 above.

II Mach. 14:4; I Mach. 6:16 and II Mach. 11:21; 33; I Mach. 6:20 and II Mach. 13:1.

256. Author, Object, and Date of II Machabees.—The author of II Machabees is also unknown. In his preface (II Mach. 2:23, 27) he frankly states that his work is but a summary of the five books of a certain Jason (probably Josue hellenized) of Cyrene, concerning whom there is an equal lack of information. The compiler of II Machabees wrote in Greek, and his style is redolent of Hellenism, having even a formal introduction and conclusion (II Mach. 15:38-40). The writer is elaborate and reflective in his accounts.

The Pharisaic tendency is much more marked than in I Machabees, special emphasis being laid on the resurrection of the dead (II Mach, 7:9, 14, 23, 29; 14:46) and the existence of angels (II Mach. 3:25-26; 5:2-3; 11:18).[8] The compiler has likewise greatly at heart the sacredness of the Jerusalem Temple, glorifying it with many encomiums, picturing foreigners as revering it, and recounting incidents that tend to bring it honor. Indeed, the pivotal points of his narrative seem to be the two feasts instituted by Judas Machabeus in memory of his purification of the Temple, and of his victory over Nicanor, who had desecrated the sacred edifice.

257. All this was of great importance in his time. For, amid the turmoil and persecutions rampant in Palestine under Antiochus IV Epiphanes, there was danger that the Jews of the prosperous and more peaceful colonies in Egypt would neglect the legal offerings and pilgrimages to the Jerusalem Temple prescribed by the Law, and might even transfer their cult to the schismatic temple erected near Leontopolis. In fact, one may conceive II Machabees as counter-propaganda to the efforts of the renegade Onias IV, who built his temple, "not out of a pious disposition, but because he had a mind to contend with the Jews at Jerusalem. . . .

---

[8] Compare Acts 23:18, where St. Luke remarks that "the Sadducees say that there is no resurrection, neither angel nor spirit; but the Pharisees confess both" as basic tenets of their sect. See also for characteristic differences of Pharisees and Sadducees, Josephus, *Ant.*, XIII, x, 6, and *Wars of the Jews*, II, ix, 14.

He thought that by building this temple he would draw away a great number of them to himself.'' [9] This propaganda purpose may explain the author's writing in Greek, and the prefaced letters inviting the hellenized Egyptian Jews to the Temple festivals at Jerusalem. Accordingly it might also be conjectured that the date of the Book's composition should be assigned to a time when the Leontopolis temple might threaten to rival Jerusalem's, perhaps after 145 B.C. and certainly before 123 B.C., the date of the first prefixed letter of the Book.

II Machabees likewise is a "deuterocanonical" work, not being listed in the present official Jewish canon,—followed by Protestant versions. It is, however, referred to by St. Paul in Hebrews 11: 35 (compare II Mach. 6: 19, 28). Philo (20 B.C.-50 A.D.) likewise seems to base portions of his tract *Quod omnis probus liber* on II Mach. 6-7, which sections also seem to have been known to Josephus. [10]

258. The Two Letters Prefixed to II Machabees.—Prefixed to the author's foreword to II Machabees, are two letters from the Palestinian Jews to their brethren in Egypt. Both are concerned about inviting the latter to join in celebrating the Feast of the Dedication or rather Purification of the Temple. The first letter is quite short (II Mach. 1: 1-10a), it alludes to a previous similar letter written in 142 B.C., and is itself dated 123 B.C. Both the Greek and the Vulgate texts are now so divided that the latter date is connected with the following letter; the ancients, however, regularly dated their letters at the close.

The second prefixed letter, rather lengthy (II Mach. 1: 10b—2: 19), is undated. It purports to be sent by the Jerusalem Jews, the Sanhedrin, and a certain Judas, who is not to be indentified with the Machabee. [11] The letter is addressed

[9] Josephus, *Wars of the Jews*, VII, x, 2-4.
[10] Josephus, *Ant.*, XII, v, 4; *Contra Apion*, I, 8; *Wars of the Jews*, I, i, 2. The extreme Pharisaic clique dominating the synod at Jamnia might be expected to reject II Machabees from the canon, not only because of its recent date, but also because it was written in Greek—a language considered incompatible with inspiration.
[11] It has been conjectured that this man might be Judas the Essene, who was head of a prophetic school at Jerusalem about 107-105 (Josephus, *Ant.*, XIII, xi, 2, and *Wars* I, iii, 5).

primarily to an Aristobulus, "preceptor of King Ptolemy".
It is uncertain whether this man may be identical with the
Peripatetic philosopher and Jewish counselor of the same
name who dedicated an allegorical commentary on Genesis
to Ptolemy (Philometor, 181-146?), and in fragments
of whose writings is found for the first time the term
Logos in the sense of the personal Word of God.[12] The Antiochus of II Mach. 1:11-16 can not well be Antiochus VII
Sidetes[13] (143-131), but is probably Antiochus III the Great
(203-187), of whom profane authors[14] record that, having
been obliged to pay tribute of 15,000 talents to the Romans,
he attacked the temple of Bel in Elymais, and was slain by
the populace of that town, who arose to defend their gods.[15]
Some commentators, however, prefer to have this incident
refer to Antiochus IV Epiphanes, noting that "the leader"
who was killed might have been a general and not necessarily
the king himself.

Whether these two letters (II Mach. 1-2:19) should be considered
an integral part of II Machabees within the purview of the Tri-
dentine decree on the canon, and consequently inspired, is not clear.
They would seem to be as distinct from the Book to which they
are now prefixed, as is the translator's prologue from Ecclesiasticus,—that prologue certainly not being inspired. And even if
these letters must be considered an integral part of II Machabees,
they are nevertheless a *citatio explicita*, and consequently, whilst
inspiration would assure the correctness of the hagiographer's quotation, it would not necessarily imply a divine guarantee of the
veracity of the propositions quoted.

[12] Εἰς δὲ Λόγον θεῖον βλέψας τούτῳ προσέδρευε 'Ιθύνων κραδίης νοερὸν κύτος, εὖ
δ' ἐπίβαινε Ατραπιτοῦ, μοῦνον δ' ἐσόρα κόσμοιο ἄνακτα (τυπωτήν).

[13] As a note in the Douay-Challoner version asserts.

[14] Diodorus of Sicily, XXIX, 15; Strabo, XVI, i, 18; Justin, xxii, 2.

[15] Nanea, Nanâ, was a moon-goddess whose image, with its crescent
moon has been preserved on two Indo-Scythian coins (Vigouroux,
Manuel biblique, I, 247). Assurbanipal mentions also a statue of Nanâ
which had originally been brought from Assyria to Elam. Bel or Baal
is, of course, the moon-god. It is not surprising that the worship of the
two divinities should be conjoined, or perhaps confused.

FIFTH PART

THE PROPHETICAL BOOKS

Quanquam tam divina quam humana, tam spiritualia quam corporalia, prophetiæ lumini subesse certum sit, propriissime tamen ad ipsam pertinet futurorum eventuum revelatio.

Aquinas, 2a 2æ, q. 171, a. 3.

THE PROPHETICAL BOOKS

ISAIAS, JEREMIAS, BARUCH, EZECHIEL, DANIEL;
OSEE, JOEL, AMOS, ABDIAS, JONAS, MICHEAS,
NAHUM, HABACUC, SOPHONIAS, AGGEUS, ZACH-
ARIAS, MALACHIAS

PROLEGOMENA

259. Nature and Function of the Prophets.—In the widest scriptural sense, a prophet is a person to whom God reveals a message to be communicated to men. The prophet is
thus primarily a προφήτης (=πρό+φημί) or "one who speaks
for or in place of [God]", a Divine interpreter, corresponding closely to the Hebrew *nâbi'*. In this broad sense all
hagiographers are prophets, and the grace of prophecy is
coextensive with inspiration. Under this aspect the Hebrew
canon classes the Historical Books following the Pentateuch
(Josue, Judges, Samuel, etc.) with the Prophets.

But usage has restricted the signification of *prophecy* to
the foretelling of future events whose eventuality is known
to God alone. Hence the prophet, from acting in this special
function, is frequently called *ro'êh* or "seer". But, rarely
is the prophet's activity confined to prediction. Reproaching
the evil-doer, threatening the obstinate, exhorting the negligent, arousing the dormant, consoling the afflicted,—all these
are comprised in the prophet's work. His rôle is quite distinct from that of the priest. The latter is chiefly concerned
with the ordinary routine of life, which largely treads the
road of precedent. The prophet, on the other hand, deals
rather with emergencies, acute evils or dangers, critical sit-
uations; and his message, rooted in attendant circumstances,

is generally novel, startling, always forceful. Soberness might mark the priest in his teaching and application of the Law. But the prophet frequently walked in a trance when he received his visions and auditions. The hand of God rests heavily upon him; the Spirit of the Lord bears him hither and thither; he not only speaks his message, but acts it out (Osee 7:9). As the priest was the ordinary minister of the Law, of religion and patriotism, among the Chosen People, so the prophet was God's extraordinary minister, adviser, guardian, reformer, in the Jewish theocracy.

260. Unlike the priests, the prophets were not chosen from any special class or tribe. Isaias and probably Daniel belonged to the royal stock; Jeremias and Ezechiel were priests; Amos was a herdsman. Men called prophets are frequently found acting as scribes or annalists about the kings' courts. Whilst the nature of the "Schools of Prophets" is not quite clear, they seem to have been groups or communities of men who lived a separate ascetic life which served to prepare them for their office. Of course, to have a real prophet, the Divine *missio* had to be superadded to the mere technique or bodily preparation for the prophetic function. From these schools, but lacking the supernatural authorization, seem to have come the "false prophets" so often denounced in the writings of Scripture (see Jer. 23).

The prophet's mission had a double phase, according as it pertained to the present or to the future. For his contemporaries the prophet, by his exhortations or threats, had to safeguard the Mosaic religion in its integrity and keep alive in the people the hope of the Messias to come.[1] For the future generations it was the object of prophecy to give an unmistakably supernatural proof of the divine character of the Messias and of the Kingdom of God He was to establish. And, as Israel's vicissitudes were types of those of the Kingdom of God, so the prophets' burning words are valid and applicable in their widest and deepest sense to the Church and its members in its own history.

261. Obscurity of the Prophecies.—Undeniably fraught with special difficulties is the understanding of the prophets'

---

[1] For an exhaustive treatment of the Messianic prophecies, see Maas, *Christ in Type and Prophecy*, two vols.

messages. Some of this obscurity is due, of course, to the many allusions to places, persons, customs, events, and proverbs now unknown,—which may be cleared up by the progress of biblical philology and archeology. But the prophecies of their very nature could scarcely ever be more than mere sketches and bold outlines, never fully detailed paintings of the future events. For, such detail would have been practically useless and generally unintelligible to the prophet's audience. The point was the clear emphasis of the essential verities which were to warn or to encourage, to terrify or to console, the primary recipients of the prophecy,—not, to satisfy the meticulously comparing curiosity of later skeptics who might check up the fulfillment with the prediction. Again, as St. John Chrysostom notes, by veiling the harsh outlines of bitter truths which had to be proclaimed, God spared His messengers too great danger of injury at the hands of powerful kings or even of smugly contented people changed to raging mobs. Again, the abolition of the Mosaic code could not well be too definitely foretold, lest that system should be looked down upon in disrespect by those who were still bound to its observance.

262. Times of the Prophets.—The prophets and their messages are to be seen in correct relief only against their own historical background. In this matter their present arrangement in the Bible may be misleading to the careless reader, as there the Prophetical Books are divided into the Major and the Minor Prophets and classified, not with first regard to chronological sequence or subject matter, but simply for a pleasing order according to the size of their writings,— somewhat as St. Paul's Epistle to the Romans is placed at the head of his works, even though some of the following letters, antedate it.

The table here given attempts to give the chronological order of the Prophets, with approximate dates for at least those hagiographers who name the rulers under whom they prophesied. The names of those whose times are quite uncertain, are printed in italics. The three large divisions indicate the three great historic periods of prophetic activity, namely: (*A*) the Assyrian Group (about 890-700); (*B*) the Babylonian and Exilic Group (about 630-586); (*C*) the Restoration or Persian Group (about 520-423). The reader can himself look up the details of each prophet's times and environment and historical vicissitudes in the part on *Historical Books,* and elsewhere.

DATE (Approximate)	PROPHETS	RULERS Contemporary	ADDRESSEES Of the Prophecies
800	*Abdias*	*Azarias and Jeroboam II?*	Edom
800	*Joel*	*As above*	Juda
800	*Jonas*	*Scarcely IV Kings, 14: 25?*	Ninive
800–750	Amos	Azarias and Jeroboam	Against Israel
790–720	Osee	Azarias, Joatham, Achaz, Ezechias, Jeroboam II	Against Israel
750–720	Micheas	Joatham, A c h a z , Ezech	Against Israel and Juda
759–699	ISAIAS	Azarias, Joatham, Achaz, and Ezechias	Syria, Assyria, Babylonia
640	*Nahum*	*Manasses-Josias?*	Against Ninive
640–609	*Habacuc*	*As above?*	Against Babylonians
640–623	Sophonias	Josias	Against Jerusalem
628–585	JEREMIAS	Josias, Joachim, Jechonias, Sedecias	Upon Jerusalem; against Egypt and Babylonia
583	Baruch	Sedecias	Exhortation to Captives
595–574	EZECHIEL	Joachin	To the Captives
604–534	DANIEL	Jechonias, Nabuchodonosor II, Darius	Of the World Empires, encouraging Captives
519	Aggeus	Darius I Hystaspis	Zorobabel and Josue, leaders of the Returned
519	Zacharias	Darius I Hystaspis	Encouragement of the Returned, f u t u r e glorious
433–423	*Malachias*		To the Jerusalem Priests

Art. 1: THE BOOK OF ISAIAS

Texts: Is. 1-4; 7-9; 11-14; 36-39; 40-42; 45, 53, 63.

263. The Author.—Whilst he is not the earliest of the writing prophets, Isaias has his collected discourses and narratives placed at the head of the Prophetical Books in every canon, probably on account both of the importance of the content and the sublimity of the language of his writings. Being himself traditionally of royal stock (nephew of Amasias by his father Amos,—the latter not to be confused with the prophet of similar name in the versions), his style reflects a cultured personality familiar with the refinements of court life in Juda's splendid capital of Jerusalem at the period of its greatest economic prosperity. Isaias was active in his prophetic function during the reigns of Ozias (769), Joatham (736), Achaz (736-721), and Ezechias (721-693). His earliest dated prophecy (Is. 6:1) falls in the year of Ozias' (Azarias) death; the latest dated one (Is. 36-39) is from the 14th year of Ezechias (707). The annals of Ozias' reign, which he also wrote (II Par. 26:22; 32:32), probably as court scribe, are now lost. According to rabbinic and Christian tradition, Isaias lived to a ripe old age, some time into the reign of Manasses (693-639). It would seem that when this king outgrew the tutelage of the high priest Eliacim [2] (see Is. 22:20 ss), he persecuted the prophets (IV Kings 21:16; Jer. 2:30)—who may have been living in community —and that on this occasion the venerable Isaias was martyred with a saw.[3] Tradition placed his tomb at Paneas in Galilee or Basan, whence his remains are said to have been transported to Constantinople under the emperor Theodosius II (A.D. 442).

264. Political Situation in Isaias' Time.—Isaias' long lifetime was coincident with the most prosperous and at the same time the most critical period of the Davidic dynasty.

---

[2] This man is identified by some with the Joachim of Judith 15:9.
[3] Some understand Heb. 11:37: "they were cut asunder", to allude to this. See also Josephus *Ant.*, X, x, 1, and the apocryphal *Ascension of Isaias.*

His kingdom was placed midway between the two world-powers of that age, Egypt and Assyria, both striving in their struggle for domination to subjugate or at least ally the smaller border states. When not directly conquered, these smaller states (Babylonia, Damascus or Syria, Sidon-Tyre, Juda, Israel or Samaria, Edom, Philistines, Arabs, Urartu, etc.) sought to maintain their independence either by leagues among themselves, or under the protectorate of one or the other of the two great Powers. Assyria, the younger, was the more feared; and with reason, for it was the more mighty, and the sculptures of its time attest the cruelty of its iron yoke. Assyria, acting on the principle of *divide et impera,* would naturally also instigate and foster internecine warfare among the smaller governments. And, should any one of its vassal states secede from alliance or, what came to the same thing, fail in paying its tribute, the terrible armies of the Assyrians swept down in swift retribution, plundering, massacring, destroying the very trees so necessary in Palestinian countries,[4] and carrying kings and even their peoples off into captivity.

This condition of international affairs strongly influenced also the internal politics of countries like Juda and Israel. Their inhabitants naturally divided into parties which were either pro-Egypt or pro-Assyria. The effects of these divisions may be seen in the revolutions and assassinations disturbing the government of the Northern Kingdom more especially. In Juda a faithful minority (of which Isaias was the mouthpiece) ventured to stand for non-entanglement with either Egypt or any other country, trusting in God's promises of protection of His theocratic kingdom as against Assyria or any aggressor.

265. Thus Isaias was a contemporary of Teglathphilesar IV (or III, 745-727), Salmanasar IV (726-722), the great Sargon (724-705), Sennacherib (or Sanherib, 704-681), and probably also of Assarhadon (680-669). Teglathphilesar IV (III)—who, as king of Babylon, 728-727, bore also the name Pulu or Phul—was the first known Ninivite ruler to invade the homeland of the Jews. Achaz, king of Juda, dreading

---

[4] The crime of cutting down fruit trees, such as palms, was distinctly forbidden in the international law of the Jews. See Deut. 20: 19.

the effects of the league of Rasin of Damascus and Phacee of Israel against himself, sought to assure his throne by voluntary submission to Teglathphilesar. Isaias, who clearly foresaw the fatal consequences of this timid policy, which would open a pathway for the Assyrian, upbraided the king for his want of confidence in God, the Jews' divine Protector, offering at the same time choice of a miraculous sign to confirm the king's faith. When the material-minded Achaz cynically rejected supernatural aid, the prophet uttered the great punitive "Virgin Prophecy" (Is. 7:14), whereby the Davidic dynasty, which had now formally rejected God, was definitely excluded (as such, *i.e.*, in the male line) from direct participation in the advent of the Messias (see Is. 7, and IV Kings 16:7).

266. Osee, last king of Israel, endeavoring to cast off the heavy load of Assyrian tribute, sought to establish an alliance with Sua (Šabaka) of the 25th (Ethiopian) dynasty of Egypt,—which was itself weakened by the dissensions of the Dodekarchy. The result, however, was the destruction of Samaria (721), and the deportation of the inhabitants of the Northern Kingdom into the Assyrian captivity, whence they never returned. Unfortunately, despite the disastrous issue of Osee's pro-Egyptian policy, the same was more or less favored also by the kings of Juda during the period of the great duel between the Nile country and the land of the Tigris and Euphrates. Isaias continually inveighed against this tendency, insisting that "Egypt is man and not God" (Is. 31:3),—as indeed it proved to be for Juda also a "broken staff of a reed, upon which if a man lean, it will go into his hand and pierce it" (Is. 36:6). Already then did the great prophet foresee the rise of the at his time military impotent Babylonian kingdom, which in 607, under Nabopolassar, would achieve its own definite independence, absorb Assyria, and wage successful war against Egypt and its allies.

267. But even Babylonia was not to be trusted by God's Chosen People. Hence, when King Ezechias, in a prideful mood, showed the early ambassadors of the Chaldean, Merodach-Baladan (703), his full treasure house, Isaias takes oc-

casion to point out the foolishness of this exposure of Jerusalem to Babylonian cupidity, foretelling that in the days to
come what had been "laid up in store . . . shall be carried
away into Babylon; there shall not anything be left" (Is.
39:6). This embassy and the prophecy connected therewith
is the great dividing point of Isaias' work. The Babylonian
Captivity briefly announced in the chapter just quoted, is
thereupon considered by the prophet as an accomplished fact,
and the rest of his writing is taken up with the "Book of
Consolation" (chapters 40-66), addressed to the future suf-
ferers in the great Captivity, cheering and heartening them
with clear promises of redemption and eventual return.

268. Plan and Content.—The Book of Isaias is not a
single homogeneous work comparable, *e.g.*, to Job, which was
poured forth at one heat into its present form. Rather is it
a collection of divers discourses pronounced on various occasions during the prophet's long period of activity, gathered
later in all probability by the author himself, and arranged
with some prose or historical introductions or narratives
(as Is. 7:1-12; 36-37, 39) that serve to make the import of
some of the speeches clearer to posterity. The actual arrangement seems to be partially according to subject matter,
and partially chronological.

In broad outlines the themes of this Book are the following:
(*A*) Only insofar as man's will is at one with God's, has he true
life and permanent happiness; the apparent prosperity of any
material-minded people only serves to cloak basic social injustices
which will eventuate in economic disaster, to whose coming a luxury
loving nation is blinded. (*B*) The invasions of earthly armies are
not to be dreaded by a people which clings to God,—whilst apostasy
from Him brings in train rejection and dire punishment. (*C*) Not
utterly, however, is Jacob's people to be cut off; hence the opposing
nations (which are God's punitive ministers) need not exult in their
victories; they themselves shall in turn come to utter destruction,
whilst a remnant at least of Jacob shall be saved, to form eventually
the nucleus of the true world-wide Kingdom of God. (*D*) This salvation shall be wrought by a personal Servant of Yahweh, through
whose sufferings the sorrows of all God's people shall be healed.
(*E*) The earthly theocracy of the Jews shall be replaced by an unearthly, spiritual Kingdom, into which all peoples of the world
shall be united.

269. Speaking by and large, the Isaic prophecies may be divided into two major groups: (*A*) the Assyrian series (1—37) concerned chiefly with contemporary evils, consisting of both internal corruption (1—6) and external aggression by Assyria and its allies (7—37) ; enmeshed with all these are their messianic counterfoils: (*B*) the Babylonian series (38—66), concerned chiefly with the eventualities of the Babylonian Captivity and their messianic expansions. The first group, concluding with the record of its actual conclusion, the destruction of the Assyrian (Is. 37 : 36-37), may be considered as an historical retrospect. The second group is a purely prophetical prospect assuring a similarly favorable eventuation of the future Babylonian danger. The recorded accomplishment of the main point of the first series of prophecies and denunciations becomes logically the guarantee of credibility for the second, greater one—as the miracle of Elizabeth's conception serves as a sign for the preservation of Mary's virginity (Luke 1 : 36).

The division of the two major sections of Isaias is generally made between chapters 39 and 40. But chapter 39, at least, is the logical introduction to the whole "Book of Consolation," since it alone announces the fact-basis of the latter, the Babylonian Captivity, which is thereupon assumed as a *res acta*. The reception of Merodach-Baladan's embassy by Ezechias is the turning point.—It is immaterial that actually Ezechias' illness and the Chaldean embassy probably preceded the rout of Sennacherib (related in c. 37) by about 14 years (compare IV Kings 38:13; Is. 36:1; II Par. 32:1). The prophet inverts the chronological order so as to bring into relief the point of his whole Book: "Trust in God! As He has brought to naught the assaults of your enemies in the past, so also will He save this people in the future."

270. Within the first great Isaic cycle may be distinguished: (*a*) the introduction to the whole work, and reformatory discourses against the internal corruption of Juda, during the times of Ozias and Joatham (1—6); (*b*) prophecies of Achaz' time, indirectly against Assyria, relating typically to the future Messias (7—12); (*c*) prophecies against non-Assyrian nations, foretelling their destruction, though they are presently instruments of God's wrath against Juda and

Israel [5] (13—27); (d) prophecies and happenings under Ezechias, concerned chiefly with the Assyrian invasion (28—37). Within the second great cycle may be distinguished: (a) the historical introduction, of Ezechias' illness and the Chaldean embassy (38—39); (b) the "Book of Consolation", a whole, symmetrically subdivided into three groups of nine discourses each, as follows: I = 40; 41; 42—43:13; 43:14—44:5; 44:6-23; 44:24—45; 46; 47; 48; II = 49; 50; 51; 52: 1-12; 52:13—53; 54; 55; 56:1-8; 56:9—57; III = 58; 59; 60; 61; 62; 63:1-6; 63:7—64; 65; 66.

Throughout the second cycle of Isaias the theme is "Redemption". But this has a two-fold phase in the prophet's mind. The primary and local one is material, from the Babylonian Captivity, by means of an earthly and temporal redeemer, Cyrus, divinely chosen and named even before his birth (Is. 44:28—45:3). The secondary but universal one, in the remote future, is a spiritual redemption from the thraldom of sin, accomplished through an unearthly, Divine Redeemer, the "Servant of Yahweh",[6] Christ, the Anointed of God.

271. Authenticity and Integrity.—Whilst Jewish and Christian tradition agree in ascribing the authorship of the whole Book named after him to the one prophet, Isaias, the Talmud would have his writings edited by "Ezechias and his company".[7] The after-Christian school of biblical criticism—chiefly in order to eliminate verified prophecy, considered by them a priori impossible—would have the Book of Consolation composed by an unknown Deutero-Isaias, and some even proceed to trace therein the handiwork of a Trito-Isaias. Only internal evidence has been advanced for these opinions,[8] and the value of their arguments has been greatly

[5] These denunciations of alien peoples were, it may be assumed, intended rather for home consumption, to dissuade the Jews from entangling alliances.

[6] However, the theocratic king of the Jews, and that people itself, and Cyrus also, are sometimes spoken of as the "Servant of Yahweh", in an inchoative, typical sense.

[7] Baba bathra, 15a.

[8] Rejected by the Church as untenable. See decree of Biblical Commission of June 28, 1908, in Acta Sanctœ Sedis, XLI, p. 613.

exaggerated. Thus the difference of vocabulary (as judged by *hapax legomena*) between the Book of Consolation and the rest of Isaias, is not greater than between other portions of even the admittedly Isaic sections. Whatever difference exists in style and language is easily explainable by the underlying diversity of subject matter and purpose.

That the "Book of Consolation" was written by the same author as the rest of Isaias, and that it really antedates the Babylonian Captivity, is evinced from the following. The author of Ecclus. 48:25-28 states that Isaias "with a great spirit saw the things that are to come to pass at last, *and comforted the mourners in Sion*". The pre-exilic prophet Sophonias (2:14) applies to Ninive the words of Isaias in 34:11, 13-14 against Babylon, and continues to borrow (Soph. 2:15) from the "Book of Consolation" the words of Is. 47:8, 10. In the original the wording is identical. Jeremias (5:22; 46:7) cites Is. 51:15. Nahum, also pre-exilic, quotes (Nah. 1:15) Is. 52:7 and alludes to 52:1. Compare also Nah. 3:7 and Is. 51:19. In the New Testament Is. 40:3-4, for example, is expressly attributed to that prophet in Matt. 3:3; Mark 1:2; Luke 3:4; John 1:23. A comparison of Cyrus decree in II Par. 36:23 and I Esd. 1:2-4 with Is. 44:27-28; 45:1-3 will indicate that the decree could well have been formulated upon the prophecy, as Josephus claims. Internal evidence that the "Book of Consolation" is really pre-exilic may be found to the punning allusions to the name of Ezechias (= Yahweh's strength) and of his queen, Haphsiba (= my delight—IV Kings 21:1), to be found in Is. 41:6, 7, 9; 42:6; 45:1; 56:2, 4, 6; 62:4-5, as in Is. 35:4.

272. Present Interest and Applications.—Of all the Prophetical Books, that of Isaias should most appeal to the reader of the present day, not only because of the force and elegance of this prophet's diction—citations from which might brighten up the dullest sermon—but more still because his messages to ancient Israel and its neighbors find parallel application to the Church and the world at all times. This secondary sense, in fact, lies immediately beneath the surface of the letter, easily to be recognized by even the casual student. And indeed it was said to Isaias: "Too small a thing were it for thee to be My servant to raise up only the tribes of Jacob and to convert the dregs of Israel; nay, I have made thee a light to the Gentiles and [a means of] My salvation even to the farthest parts of the earth" (Is. 49:6). This is the key to the modern appreciation of Isaias. Fleshly

Israel was but a type of the spiritual Israel, whose members are to be gathered from all nations of the earth.

The scathing denunciations of the internal corruption of Jerusalem's kingdom are seen admirably to apply to the luke-warmness, lack of faith, material-mindedness, greed, luxury, and kindred sins of negligent members of the Church, born to the faith as the descendants of Abraham were born to the promises, but similarly falling short of their high voca-tion, largely through contact with an irreligious world, as the Jews were corrupted by neighboring heathen peoples. Well might be addressed to oppressors of labor, usurers, ex-tortionate landlords, monopolizing capitalists the fearless in-vective:

> "Woe to you that join house to house
> And lay field unto field,
> Till there is left no more room" (Is. 5:8).

> "You have devoured the vineyard,
> And the spoil of the poor is in your house.
> Why do you tread under foot my people,
> And grind down the faces of the poor?" (Is. 3:14-15).

Venal judges, grafting public officials, might again be made to reflect and fear by the excoriating directness of such pas-sages as:

> "Thy princes are faithless, companions of thieves;
> They all love bribes; they run after rewards.
> They render not right to the fatherless;
> The widow's cause cometh not in to them" (Is. 1:23).

> "Woe to them that make wicked laws; and when they write,
> write injustice,
> To oppress the poor in judgment, and do violence to the
> lowly of My people,
> That widows might be their prey, and that they might rob
> the fatherless!" (Is. 10:1-2).

And to the senseless multiplication of trivial legislation, the continual compromise of principle with expediency, the hes-itating, vacillating, patching public policy of to-day might be particularly applied the caustic irony of the prophet's

mocking message to the wealth-drunk rulers of the Northern
Kingdom:

ki tsav latsav, tsav latsav;
qav laqav, qav laqav;
zèyr šam, zèyr šam!

"For it is: 'Law upon law, law upon law;
Rule upon rule, rule upon rule;
A little bit here, a little bit there' "! (Is. 28: 1-10).

On the other hand, most instructive is the picture of the
Church, the Mystical Body of Christ, suffering calumny and
oppression unjustly from her many persecutors, to accomplish in the end the salvation of her children. And most
consoling is the whole message of encouragement and tenderness, fore-telling eventual triumph, with which that same
Church is addressed as dwelling during time in the captivity
of the unbelieving, idolatrous world. Lastly, besides these
wide, universal senses, each individual Christian,—as a Servant of God and a miniature of Christ and the Church,—may
easily read abundant personal application in his own life
and environment, of the words of the prophet whom the
Jews called by excellence *Menahem,* "the Consoler".

APPENDIX

DECISIONS OF THE BIBLICAL COMMISSION

De libri Isaiæ indole et auctore

Propositis sequentibus dubiis Commissio Pontificia de Re Biblica
sequenti modo respondit:

I.—Utrum doceri possit, vaticinia quae leguntur in libro Isaiæ,—
et passim in scripturis,—non esse veri nominis vaticinia, sed vel
narrationes post eventum confictas, vel, si ante eventum prænuntia-
tum quidpiam agnosci opus sit, id prophetam non ex supernaturali
Dei futurorum præscii revelatione, sed ex his quæ iam contigerunt,
felici quadam sagacitate vel naturalis ingenii acumine, coniiciendo
prænuntiasse? *Resp.* Negative.

II.—Utrum sententia quæ tenet, Isaiam ceterosque prophetas vaticinia non edidisse nisi de his quæ in continenti vel post non grande

temporis spatium eventura erant conciliari possit cum vaticiniis, imprimis messianicis et eschatologicis, ab iisdem prophetis de longinquo certo editis, necnon cum communi Sanctorum Patrum sententia concorditer asserentium, prophetas ea quoque prædixisse quæ post multa sæcula essent implenda? *Resp.* Negative.

III.—Utrum admitti possit, prophetas non modo tamquam correctores pravitatis humani divinique verbi in profectum audientium præcones, verum etiam tamquam prænuntios eventuum futurorum, constanter alloqui debuisse auditores non quidam futuros sed præsentes et sibi æquales, ita ut ab ipsis plane intelligi potuerint; proindeque secundam partem libri Isaiæ (40-66), in qua vates non Iudæos Isaiæ æquales, sed Iudæos in exilio babylonico lugentes veluti inter ipsos vivens alloquitur et solatur, non posse ipsum Isaiam iamdiu emortuum auctorem habere, sed oportere eam ignoto cuidam vati inter exules viventi assignare? *Resp.* Negative.

IV.—Utrum, ad impugnandam identitatem auctoris libri Isaiæ, argumentum philologicum, ex lingua stiloque desumptum, tale sit censendum, ut virum gravem, criticæ artis et hebraicæ linguæ peritum, cogat in eodem libro pluralitatem auctorum agnoscere? *Resp.* Negative.

V.—Utrum solida prostent argumenta, etiam cumulative sumpta, ad evincendum Isaiæ librum non ipsi soli Isaiæ, sed duobus, imo pluribus auctoribus esse tribuendum? *Resp.* Negative.

Die autem 28 Iunii 1908 Ssmus prædicta responsa rata habuit ac publici iuris fieri mandavit.[8a]

Art. 2: THE BOOK OF JEREMIAS; THE LAMENTATIONS

Texts: Jer. 1-3; 23-25; 46-49; 26-29; Lam. 1-2.

273. Jeremias' Life and Background.—The writings of Jeremias give more autobiographical details regarding his own work, sufferings, and sentiments, than do those of the other prophets. He came of the priestly clan of Anathoth, a small town a short distance north of Jerusalem. His childhood may have remembered the cruelties of the reigns of Manasses and Amon, kings of Juda (693-638). As a youth he was contemporary with Josias' (638-608) great attempt to restore Mosaism to its primitive purity (II Par. 34—35). Probably at that time, too, began his friendship with the family of Nerias, son of Maasias, then governor of Jerusalem

[8a] *Acta Sanctæ Sedis*, XLI, p. 613. English text in Pope, *Catholic Student's Aids to the Bible*, vol. I, p. 178.

(II Par. 34:8), who coöperated with Helcias the highpriest and Saphan in forwarding Josias' reforms. At any rate the two sons of Nerias, Baruch and Saraïas, later became Jeremias' disciples, the former being his secretary (Jer. 36:4; 51:59).

Jeremias was familiar with the Scriptures, and had studied particularly the oracles of Isaias and Micheas, whose words he sometimes textually reproduces (see Jer. 23:5-6; 33:15 and Is. 4:2; 11:2; Jer. 10:3-5 and Is. 40:19-20; Jer. 26:18 and Mich. 3:12). A reflection of the finding of an ancient volume of Deuteronomy during the Temple repairs of Josias (II Par. 34:14 ss) may be seen in the thought tenor and even phraseology on Jer. 7:4; 32:34; see Jer. 2:6 and Deut. 32:10; Jer. 2:15 and Deut. 28:49; Jer. 7:3 and Deut. 28:26. Comparisons may also be made with other scriptural writers: Jer. 14:10 and Os. 8:13; Jer. 10:25 and Ps. 78:6; Jer. 10:13 and Ps. 134:7; Jer. 49:7-16 and Abdias 1-8.

274. Jeremias' vocation to the prophetic office came in 627 B.C., when he was about twenty (Jer. 1:6; 16:2), and he continued his arduous function amid much suffering and persecution, at first by neighbors (Jer. 11:21) and even relatives (Jer. 12:6) and later by the inhabitants of Jerusalem and by its rulers (Jer. 37—38), for more than forty years, till the fall of the capital of Juda (588), and even perhaps in the subsequent forced exile in Egypt. During his time the pro-Assyrian party of Isaias' day was replaced by a pro-Babylonian faction. The old pro-Egyptian party acquired fresh impetus after the fall of Ninive (606) and urged alliance with Pharao Nechao. As Isaias had done earlier, so now Jeremias opposed this human-reliance policy (Jer. 2:18, 26). And the pious Josias did in fact oppose even by force the passage of Nechao's army into Asia, but lost his life in the great battle of Mageddo (II Par. 35:20-25).

The immediately succeeding ruler, Joachaz or Sellum (608: IV Kings 23:33), deposed by Nechao after three months, is mentioned in Jer. 22:11-12. With his successor, Joakim (Eliakim), Egypt became master in Juda (Jer. 35: 18-19). The prophet soon brought storms of indignation upon his head by announcing that Egypt would be power-

less to protect Jerusalem against Nabuchodonosor (604-561).[9]
And in fact about four years later the army of Nechao was
vanquished at Charcamis (Karkemiš), and this victory of
Nabuchodonosor ruined the expectations of the Egyptian
party in Palestine. Babylonian soldiers soon made their
appearance even in the south, so that the nomad Rechabites
(IV Kings 10:15-23) had to flee into fortified Jerusalem
(Jer. 35).

At this imminent crisis Jeremias published through
Baruch all the divine oracles of warning which he had received. King Joakim (608-598) burnt the volume indig-
nantly (Jer. 36), and Jeremias and his companion were
forced into hiding. The prophet rewrote his messages (Jer.
45) and received the revelation that the beforestanding Babylonian captivity would last seventy years (Jer. 25:8-12).
Soon Nabuchodonosor besieged and took Jerusalem, and
carried off the cream of the inhabitants (including Daniel
and his companions) in the first Judean deportation, which
marked the beginning of the great Captivity (598-597).
Jechonias (Joakin) reigned but three months, and was led
away captive to Babylon (Jer. 22:24-30; IV Kings 24:16-
18; Ez. 1:2).

275. Sedecias was put upon the throne. Only the dregs
of Jewry were left in Palestine. Their chastisement, too,
was announced by the prophet. A temporary resurgence of
strength in Egypt under Hofra and Amasis roused new hopes
at Jerusalem, even the king (who sometimes secretly consulted the prophet) dallying with the idea of revolt. Jeremias vainly combated these illusions (Jer. 27—28). The approach of an Egyptian army and the retirement of the Babylonian forces made the prophet's position precarious. He
tried to hide at Anathoth, but was seized, accused of high
treason, and imprisoned (Jer. 37). Even from far off Babylon false prophets (Jer. 29) incited the Judean authorities
to violence against him. Jeremias was thrown into a slimy
pit to perish (Jer. 38), but was rescued thence by an Ethiopian intimate of the king, remaining, however, in durance

[9] See Jer. 46:2.

until the Babylonian armies once more besieged and this time destroyed the city and the Temple and dragged King Sedecias and his courtiers into captivity (588).

Jeremias also was at first taken along in chains, but was later set free at Rama and given his choice of Babylon or Jerusalem as residence. At Babylon honors awaited him, but the prophet preferred to return to chant his Lamentations upon the smoking ruins of the city he so loved. There he was favored by Godolias, the vice-gerent set up by Nabuchodonosor (Jer. 39). The foolish assassination of this really well-meaning official by the fanatic Ismahel brought terror of retribution upon the poor remaining refugees. Jeremias was consulted as to what should now be done. He answered in God's name: "If you will be quiet and remain in this land, I will build you up. But if you say . . . : 'We will go down into the land of Egypt,' . . . the sword which you fear shall overtake you there" (Jer. 42).

But, despite this warning, the terrified Jews fled to Egypt, bearing with them Jeremias. Even there the prophet was not silent. At Daphne he once again vigorously insists that Nabuchodonosor shall set up his throne in the very city of his companions' refuge (Jer. 43—44). According to a Christian tradition Jeremias was stoned to death at Daphne by Jews who resented his continual remonstrances. According to Jewish tradition he was taken to Baby.... .y Nabuchodonosor when the latter invaded Egypt, a... died there.

276. Religious Momentum.—It would seem that the magnificent reforms inaugurated under Josias were more external than sincere, more the king's than the people's, more apparent than real in their moral effects. The truth was that God could still complain in the words of Isaias (29:13): "This people draw near Me with their mouth and with their lips glorify Me, but their heart is far from Me". Far removed, indeed, was the heart of this now wealthy nation from the stern ideals of ancient Deuteronomy. Jeremias' painful task it was to dispel the illusions based upon such false assurances. Therefore the keynote of his message is: sin and its punish-

10 Epiphan., *De vita et obitu prophetarum.*

ment, and a calling to repentance. Moreover, his own life in relation to his contemporaries was a living prophecy of the sufferings and opposition that were to be endured by the future Messias,—who also was to call the Jews of His time to sincere, heartfelt repentance, to the sublimated, spiritual observance of the Mosaic Code in the new Kingdom of God, and who was to counteract the false hopes of an earthly messianic kingdom, and to announce the coming destruction of Jerusalem by the Romans,—against whom the Jews of that period would have had Christ lead them in revolt (John 6:15). Therefore also the Church, especially in commemorations of the sufferings and Passion of Christ, has used of the Saviour many of the words which Jeremias had applied to himself.

The unpopularity of Jeremias during his lifetime was made up for by the devotion the Jews paid him after his death. For, then he became the greatest of the writing prophets. His Book, according to the Babylonian Talmud, was ranked even ahead of Isaias. He came to be considered Jewry's special patron with God (II Mach. 15:14). Even in New Testament times people expressed their high hopes of Christ by saying that he might be Jeremias come to life again (Matt. 16:14).

277. Textual Arrangement.—Although Jeremias himself made two collections of his utterances (Jer. 36:4, 18, 32), none of the present arrangements seem due to him. Chronological system is quite lacking,—which would hardly befit the methodical presumed author of III and IV Kings. Perhaps the very confusion of the pages of this long work reflects the troublous conditions of its times and author. Baruch may have prepared an edition for the Jews in the Captivity. The Septuagint version may have as its base a shorter, hurried, edition, made in Egypt about the time of the prophet's death. The arrangement of the Greek—according to which the "Prophecies against the Nations" (Jer. 46—51) are placed between verses 13 and 15 of Jer. 25,—is probably to be preferred, as paralleling the central position of similar groups in Is. 13—28 and Ez. 25—32. In Jer. 27:1 ss one should probably read (with several Hebrew MSS. and the Syriac) Sedecias instead of "Joakim", to conform with vv.

12 and 20. Besides the difference of arrangement, the Greek shows a considerably briefer text, nearly every verse having been cut down. Both editions are authentic, and both are quoted in the New Testament, the Greek (Jer. 31:32) in Heb. 8:9, the Hebrew (Jer. 31:15) in Matt. 2:18.

278. The Lamentations.—In the Vulgate and Greek the *Threni* are immediately joined to the Book of Jeremias, of which they were considered an integral part. Hence also they are not enumerated separately in the old canon lists. For liturgical reasons the Hebrew Bibles place them among the Third Group or Hagiographa. The Lamentations form a suite of five elegies bewailing the destruction of Jerusalem and its Temple by Nabuchodonosor.

Their form is highly artificial, probably as a mnemonic aid. Four are acrostics, the first word of each verse beginning with a corresponding letter of the Hebrew alphabet, thus giving twenty-two verses to each poem. The third elegy is triply alphabetic; and in chapters 2, 3, and 5 *phe* precedes *àyin*. The fifth elegy, whilst also having twenty-two verses, is not acrostic. There is also to be noted in the original the very frequent appearance of similarly sounding terminations, *-nu, anu, enu, inu*, giving an effect of slowly and dully pulsating rime.

With poignant sadness, tender pity, tearful sorrow these songs (reminiscent of chapters 30-31 of Jeremias' prophecies) grieve over the culpable loss of so many gracious gifts of God to the Jewish nation, weep for the destruction of its glory, the humiliation of its people. The silent solitude of the erstwhile so populous and busy city forms the opening theme. Jerusalem is pictured as a widow bowed down in voiceless weeping, seated among the scattered ruins of her former delightful home, whence her husband and children have been torn by the cruel conqueror, who has left her alone, covered with shame, to lament her bitter loss. At times there come shuddering memories of the horrors of the siege, and ever and again returns the deep sob of sorrow at the realization of guilt.[11] So long as sin and suffering mark

[11] Fully to appreciate the infinite plaintiveness of these elegies one should hear them rendered in the Florentine chant by solemn monastic voices amidst the dim darkness of some high-vaulted cloister choir before the bare stripped altars of Good Friday eve.

the course of men's lives, so long shall the Lamentations be
the loftiest expression of sorrow and repentance, molded as
they have been by God Himself to aid mankind in expressing
its loss of Him.

Art. 3: THE BOOK OF BARUCH

Texts: Bar. 1-3: 9-38; 5-6.

279. Text and Canonicity.—As Lamentations, so also this
Book was of old generally considered integral with Jeremias,[12]—whose letter to the Captives is appended, and whose
secretary the author of its greater part was. Hence also the
name Baruch does not appear in the older canonical lists.
The Vulgate text of this Book is not by St. Jerome, but is
taken from the Old Latin, which itself was a translation from
the Greek.

That Baruch was originally composed in Hebrew or Aramaic, is to be concluded from the Semiticisms with which it
abounds (Bar. 1: 2, 8, 15, 22; 2: 4, 9, 18, 19, 25; 3: 8; 4: 37).
Moreover the Greek lacks those characteristic thought and
language forms which conspicuously mark Books written in
the Hellenistic period, such as Wisdom and II Machabees. In
the prefaced letter of the Babylonian Jews it is requested
that the accompanying Book "be read in the Temple" (Bar.
1: 14), where the Semitic tongue alone might be used. Finally, Theodotion had a Semitic original from which he
made his Greek translation.

The new Hebrew canon (followed also by Protestants in their
versions) does not include Baruch. The reason is probably to be
sought in the fact that the Book was composed on non-Palestinian
soil, to which the Pharisees denied the possibility of the presence
of the *charisma* of inspiration; but Baruch's excision might equally
be due to the prominence of its sentiments of humble acknowledgment of Israel's guilt, and its broad interpretation of God's spiritual
Temple and Kingdom (Bar. 3: 24-25; 4: 1). Such ideas would be

---

[12] In the Septuagint edition the first five chapters of Baruch follow
immediately upon the prophecies of Jeremias; then come the Lamentations; then, the sixth chapter of Baruch or Letter of Jeremias.

quite repugnant to the principles of the proud, chauvinistic Pharisaic clique which "reformed" and narrowed to its own limitations the ancient Jewish Scripture canon, at the notorious synod of Jabneh (also Jebniah and Jamnia, about A.D. 90) in which the segregation of the "Apocrypha" was the work of Phariseeism triumphant.[13]

280. Composition and Date.—The Book of Baruch is not a homogeneous whole. First comes an introduction (Bar. 1:1-9) which was written later than the main portion. Then comes a covering letter from the exiles composed in all likelihood by Baruch himself (Bar. 1:10-14). This letter itself introduces the first section of Baruch's original "book" (Bar. 1:15—5:9). The latter falls into two quite distinct parts, notably differentiated even by their style, namely: (A) the Confession of the Exiles (Bar. 1:15—3:8), and (B) a Discourse of Baruch which in magnificent rhetoric calls upon Israel to broaden its mind to receive the new and wider concepts of God's world-economy (Bar. 3:9—4:8), consoles the Captives somewhat after the manner of Isaias' Second Part (Bar. 4:9-29), and finally utters the promise of a return (Bar. 4:30—5). To all this is appended a Letter of Jeremias (Bar. 6), showing the Exiles, in language often dripping with sarcasm, the emptiness of Babylonian idolatry. Its description of the ritual and deities tallies well with the archeological discoveries of the Neo-Babylonian kingdom.

The "book of the commandments of God, and the law, that is forever" of Bar. 4:1, refers neither to the Thora nor to Baruch's own composition, but is a figurative allusion to the personal Wisdom spoken of Bar. 3:28-37. The latter contains perhaps the earliest expression of the later so famous Memra or Logos idea.

281. The final redaction of the whole of Baruch must have taken place quite some time after Nabuchodonosor's destruction of Jerusalem and its Temple. For, the Exiles have already settled down in their colonies to regular life and business; they have their regular assembly place for prayer besides the running water of a canal; they can even afford to succor the refugees left behind in Palestine. They are recon-

[13] See * Margolis, *The Scriptures in the Making* (Philadelphia, 1922), pp. 87-90.

ciled to their foreign rulers (Bar. 1:11). Above all, they have suffered an entire change of heart, showing that the bitter medicine of the Exile is already producing its providential cure.[14]

Anachronistic difficulties have been pointed out: thus in Bar. 1:10, 14 the Temple would seem to be still standing; according to Bar. 2:26 it is already destroyed. Haneberg conjectures that the Exiles' letter was written before the destruction of Jerusalem. But it seems more plausible to understand the first passages as referring simply to the temporary altar and services held on the Temple grounds (see Jer. 41:5 and I Esd. 2:68; 3:2-3).—It is not at all improbable that Baruch visited Babylon at least the first time as a member of the embassy sent by Sedecias in his fourth year to that city (Jer. 51:61). Baruch's brother Saraïas is mentioned as a member of that embassy.

Art. 4: THE BOOK OF EZECHIEL

Texts: Ez. 1-3, 15; 4.5; 25-27; 33; 40.

282. The Author and His Times.—Ezechiel was of priestly extraction, consequently in his youth familiar with the Temple and its liturgy, for which he must have evinced great interest, to judge especially by the great concluding spiritual Temple vision of his prophecies (Ez. 40—47). As a young man he, with many others of the higher classes, including King Jechonias, was borne away in Nabuchodonosor's first deportation (598) of the inhabitants of Juda, eleven years before the destruction of Jerusalem and its Temple. In Babylonia he settled down in a Jewish colony at Tell-Abib, on one of the great irrigation canals, called Chobar (Kebar). There he received his call to the prophetic office in the stupendous Chariot Vision of 593. He carried out his divinely imposed task for at least twenty-one years (his last dated vision is of 571: Ez. 29:17), his messages burdened with the "glory" and allusions to the omniscience, omnipotence, and

[14] Perhaps the National Confession of Bar. 1:15—3:8 should be looked upon as the crystallized effect of Baruch's great Discourse, recorded in Bar. 3:9—5:9.

omnipresence of God,—new and broader themes of revelation to Jewish hearts and ears.

283. Juda, in Ezechiel's time, is a vassal state of Nabuchodonosor II, with its rightful king at Babylon in captivity, and Sedecias, a creature of the invader, ruling at Jerusalem. As long as that city and its magnificent Temple stood, even after the first deportation, an extravagant and foolish optimism prevailed in Juda (Ez. 8:12; 9:9), whilst in the colonies of Babylonia there was profound depression (Ez. 12:27; 20:49; 33:10, 24, 30-33). Ezechiel's mission was: to show that God is equally faithful in keeping His threats as in fulfilling His promises,—even though the threats be only for a time, but the promises for all eternity. For seven years, then, in far-off Babylonia the prophet awaits the divinely assured doom of his home city. As its time approaches he undergoes by mystic compassion in his own body the woes and miseries of his compatriots in the homeland. During the days of the siege he lies hungry before a great Babylonian brick upon which he has drawn the plan of Jerusalem (Ez. 4:1-10): every attack of the enemy and every loss of his people he feels in acute sympathy, and afterwards, when the flight and banishment begin, he is commanded significantly to remove his mean furniture from his hut before the eyes of astounded onlookers (Ez. 12:3).

284. Symbolic Actions: "Chariot Vision".—This graphically enacted symbolism is one of the characteristics of Ezechiel. Mystic deeds rather than words are often employed by him to set forth his messages (Ez. 4:9-17;[15] 5:1-4; 24:18-27; 37:16-20). Hence it is but congruent that his teaching is frequently found veiled in symbolic or parabolic vision (prophecies against Tyre, Ez. 26-28; the Sword of God's Wrath, Ez. 21, etc.), wherefore his own companions said of him: "Doth not this man speak by parables?" (Ez. 20:49).

[15] Where wood and other combustibles are scarce, dung dried in flat cakes against the wall, is frequently used in the Orient for fuel. The prophet is commanded to bake his bread beneath such cakes, to show forth the penury of fuel and food at Jerusalem, but a concession is made to his natural repugnance.

Perhaps the most magnificent and mysterious of these is the great "Chariot Vision" (Ez. 1 : 4—3 : 14) with which the Book opens.[16] Ezechiel beholds in the stellar spaces a wondrous chariot or triumphal car of which cherubim form the living, seeing wheels. Upon it God is enthroned in human appearance. Lightnings and sparks and lamps emphasize its dazzling coruscations. Coals of fire amidst the wheels show forth the stored up wrath of Yahweh (Ez. 10 : 2). According to this vision, God manifests Himself incarnate, ruling supreme over all kingdoms of beings, but in such manner that these are subject to Him in living order and free activity of service. Greater honor no creature can command than that it bear up the Creator in free coöperation, that all powers and beings of the universe, inanimate, vegetable, animal, human, angelic, harmoniously work together for the one supreme object, the showing forth of God's glory in the unified diversity of operations which is the key to the world's beauty. Thus in all the manifold activities of nature, opposite as they may seem, there is no real clashing, no conflict, no contradiction, but all things ever move forward in their respective planes to carry out the stupendous plans of an All-wise Providence. Of course, the perfect fulfillment of this vision will take place only in "the end", when Christ "shall have delivered up the Kingdom to God and the Father . . . for He must reign . . . that God may be all in all" (I Cor. 15 : 23-28), but the basis of this is already laid in the Incarnation.

The material prototypes of Ezechiel's cherubim were the great sculptured *kirub*, statues or *reliefs*, which decorated the temples and palaces of Babylonia. These were mighty stone images having the body of a powerful bull or lion, the wings of an eagle, and the bearded head of a man. They were frequently set in pairs facing each other along avenues or colonnades. Symbolically the human head represented the intellectual, spiritual, elements of the world; the lion's body, the brute strength of metals and all inanimate matter; the bull's form, the animal kingdom; the eagle's wings,

[16] According to the Rabbis this section of Ezechiel, as well as the whole of Canticles, was not to be read by the student before the age of thirty. The "Chariot Vision" was considered by them to be somehow on a par with the opening chapter of Genesis, the former showing forth the end and eventuation of the universe, as the latter told of its beginnings.

the vegetable kingdom so dependent upon swift light. At times also these four characteristic forms stood for the four quarters of the earth, in short, for the whole world. They appear again in strikingly parallel context in the imagery of the Apocalypse (4: 6-9), and later were applied to the four evangelists.

285. Vision of the Temple Idolatry.—Discord and evil is injected into the divinely ordained progress of the universe only by the dissension of free-willed creatures,—who would, at least implicitly, worship other gods. For, idolatry of passions is only more refined and not less unreasonable and wicked than idolatry of images. The secret sources of such discord, both for Juda and for all mankind, are revealed in the first Jerusalem or Temple Vision (Ez. 8-10). There, in the great Court of the People, opposite the Altar of Holocausts, at the door that leads into the Temple from the north, the prophet beholds the idol of jealousy, God's rival, Baal (Ez. 8: 3),—symbol of the coarse sensual cult of the common herd who spiritually were still steeped in ancient heathenism. In the wider sense, hinted at by the Septuagint version's στήλη τοῦ κτωμένου this might also represent the cult of business, of money-making, of being entirely absorbed by the cares of this world.[17]

Next, in a secret chamber over the eastern entrance of the Temple (Ez. 8: 7-12) the prophet sees the ancients, leaders, counselors, of Israel, practicing the higher animal worship of Egypt,—fit symbol of the more refined cultus of ambition and power secretly, often unconsciously, indulged in by proud, ambitious statesmen and others of superior intellectual capacity. Then, in subsidiary buildings on the north side of the Temple, Ezechiel are shown Temple women worshiping Thammuz (Ez. 8: 13),—symbol of the cult of vanity, estheticism, and sentimentality to which the higher groups of the feminine gender are prone. Lastly, inside the sanctuary itself, before the Holy of Holies, the prophet beholds priests with backs turned to the Holy Place, mysteriously worshiping

---

[17] Compare the warning against absorption in mundane cares, given in the Sermon on the Mount (Matt. 6: 24-32), and concluding with the dictum: ''For, after all these things do the *heathens* seek''.

the rising sun (Ez. 8:16),—symbol of the most refined, esoteric, attenuated, astral cult of those who adore empty metaphysical phantasies and far-off scientific speculations of their own minds, whilst deliberately and insultingly turning away from the greatest source of all knowledge and wisdom, and truth.

286. The Vision of Gog and Magog.—Exceedingly difficult, because still in the future, is the broadest interpretation of the Vision of Gog and Magog (Ez. 38-39). It seems to refer to a great eschatological conflict between the powers of Evil, elsewhere grouped under Antichrist, and the Church, typified by united and restored Israel. Part of these evil forces designated by Roš, Thubal, and Mosoch, might allude to Slavic peoples, whilst Magog has been taken to signify Mongol or Tartar nations. Their eventual destruction is described in hyperbolic metaphor.

The primary reference of this vision may, of course, be to the Scythian invasion of Asia Minor in 630 B.C. Gog and Magog may be identical. Of the former St. Jerome says that the Jews understood thereby "gentes Scythicas immanes et innumerabiles quæ trans Caucasum montem et paludem Mæotidem et prope Caspium mare ad Indiam usque tendantur". Magog is sometimes represented as the territory of Gog. Driven from their seats in the Caucasus mountains by the Massagetes, these wild hordes, mounted on horseback and armed with bows, took Sardes and defied Cyaxares in Media, then turned towards Egypt, where Psammeticus bought them off, so that returning the pillaged temple at Ascalon. Their name, like that of Hun or Goth in modern history, became a symbol for terror amongst the Jews, in whose memory their dread might still be alive in Ezechiel's time. In the Apocalypse they typify the eschatological "terror from the North".

287. The Vision of the Temple Rebuilt.—Just as in the Apocalypse the destruction of Gog and Magog (Apoc. 20: 7 *ss*) is followed by the description of the glorious New Jerusalem, so in Ezechiel the horrors of the conflict at Armageddon are followed by the limning of the fair ideals of the Temple Rebuilt (Ez. 40 *ss*). The compass of this vision can scarcely be limited to encouragement towards raising the Jewish Temple anew after the Captivity. This is evident by the repetition of its salient traits in the Apocalypse (11:1 *ss*) of St. John, who had absorbed and gives the deepest interpretation of many of Ezechiel's parables, especially in their eschatological phases. The "living water" of Ez. 47, which issuing from the rebuilt Temple makes the desert fruitful and sweetens even the Dead Sea, is to be compared with the "river of water of life" of the Apocalypse (22:1-2), more particularly in the light of Christ's own declarations in John 4:13-14 and 7:37-39. Such a fountain was Christianity, bursting forth from the Temple on the day of Simeon's recognition of the Saviour, and growing ever greater as it spread abroad over the deserts of mankind's ignorance, till it sweetened even the most bitter waters of the Dead Sea of the world's sinful misery.

Art. 5: THE BOOK OF DANIEL

Texts: Dan. 1-2; 5-6; 8-9; 13.

288. Daniel's Person and Function.—Even before the deportation which carried off Ezechiel, Daniel, as a boy of the royal stock, was borne away to Babylon (about 606 B.C.) and there educated at the court of Nabuchodonosor II. Whilst still a young man he was endowed with the prophetic *charisma* on the occasion of the trial of the virtuous Susanna (Dan. 13:45). Already under Nabuchodonosor Daniel rose to high position at court. Under that king's successors in Babylon, Evil-Merodach and Nergal-sar-usur (Neriglissar), he seems to have been in retirement, to emerge again into prominence at court in the last few years before the Babylonian dynasty succumbed to the Medo-Persian (538). The new government also held the expounder of visions in high esteem, and "Daniel prospered in the reign of Darius and in the reign of Cyrus the Persian" (Dan. 6:3, 28). His tomb was later pointed out near Susa.

Difficulties are encountered in identifying in profane history the rulers met with in Daniel's Book under the names of "Baltassar" (Dan. 5:1, 30; 7:1; 8:1) and "Darius the Mede" (Dan. 5:31; 6:1; 9:1; 11:1). Baltassar, "under whom Babylon was taken when he had reigned seventeen years",[18] was, according to Josephus, "of the posterity of Nebuchadnezzar", that is, either a son (Bar. 1: 11) or a grandson. By Josephus he is identified with Nabûnâ'id (Nabonidus). But the annals of Nabûnâ'id record the capture of Babylon, and a cylinder of the same ruler gives a prayer for his son Belshezzar, who has actual charge of the troops.[19] It is noteworthy that the text of Dan. 5: 7, 29: ". . . he shall be the *third* man in the kingdom", indicates that Baltassar himself occupied a *second* highest position. He was a weak and effeminate prince, probably much under the influence of the queen-dowager (Dan. 5: 10).—Darius the Mede, "son of Assuerus" (Dan. 9: 1), according to Josephus a "son of Astyages" the last king of the Medes and a "kinsman" of Cyrus, was associated with the latter at the head of the Medan forces in the campaign against Babylon. By some he is called Cyaxares II. According to Xenophon,[20] Cyrus left the administration of the captured city to a certain Gobryas (Ugbara), who was on that account considered its king.

Being of noble birth and having been educated in Babylonian court circles, Daniel will not be found so intimately in contact with the common folk of Jewry. His writings are not messages of exhortation, denunciation, or comfort, addressed directly to the people, as were those of most the other prophets. Rather are they apocalyptic visions referring to events of future history, especially of the pre-messianic and messianic times. Indeed, rather than a prophet of the older type, Daniel is an apocalyptic seer, disclosing the remote future by means of symbols, without direct reference to his own times and the immediate future. He never speaks of the person of God, or announces ''Thus saith the Lord''. His visions do not directly teach the lessons of faith, hope, trust, repentance of sin, which are so character-

[18] Josephus, *Ant.*, X, xi, 4. See also the quotation from Berosus in Josephus, *Contra Apion*, n. 20.

[19] Bêl-šar-usur was the oldest son of Nabonidus, and probably his co-regent. Nabonidus inscriptions having reference to him may be found in Langdon, *Neubabylonische Königsinschriften;* Weissbach, *Die Keilinschriften der Achämeniden,* p. 22 ff.; Roger, *Cuneiform Parallels to the Old Testament; Clay, Miscellaneous Inscriptions,* n. 45; Langdon, *Oxford Editions of Cuneiform Texts,* vol. I. The whole Nabonidus-Baltassar problem is discussed by Roger, *History of Babylonia and Assyria,* 6th ed.; Hall, *Ancient History of the Near East;* Driver, *Cuneiform Research,* p. 24; *Goucher College Cuneiform Inscriptions,* vol. I, p. 34; Dougherty, in *Journal of the American Oriental Society,* vol. 42 (1922), p. 303. For these references the writer is indebted to Dr. D. Luckenbill of the University of Chicago.

[20] *Cyrop.*, VIII, v, 15-33. See also Herodotus, I, 191.

istic of Isaias, Jeremias, and Ezechiel. Rather the import of most of his pages seems to have been primarily the instruction and warning of the Babylonian and Medo-Persian masters of the exiles, than of the Jews themselves. In truth he is as much a prophet for the Gentiles as for the Jews.

The absence of the usual prophetic characteristics may have been a reason for the removal of this Book by the later Jews from the prophetic group into the Hagiographa or third section of the Scriptures. Moreover, the broadness of world-outlook and the prominence accorded the Gentiles, as well as the predicted doom of the Jews, may have motived the compilers of the Pharasaic canon in this arrangement. The ancient true Jewish canon classed Daniel with the prophetic Books, giving him the position immediately after Ezechiel, as is witnessed to by the Septuagint.

In Daniel ripens the lesson which had gradually been inculcated by Providence in the bitter school of the exile,— the expansion of the messianic idea to world-wide comprehension. For this seer not only Jerusalem and Juda, but the whole world in its historic course, is the field of God's manifestation of Himself: "I am a great King, . . . and My name is dreadful among the Gentiles" (Mal. 1:14). Daniel almost ruthlessly sweeps aside (*e.g.*, Dan. 9:27) the earlier popular notions of a material glorification of the kingdom of Israel in the messianic age. He is the prophet of the Universal Divine Majesty, and fortells a world-wide messianic empire to be erected upon the ruins of the Jewish, Babylonian, Medo-Persian, Macedonian, and Roman kingdoms of earth.

289. Date and Authenticity.—"It has never been a point of Catholic doctrine that the Book of Daniel was actually written by him, nor even that it was written in the 6th century B.C. It has, however, ever been a point of doctrine that it was predictive of the future".[21] Hence its date may not be brought down later than the events predicted therein as future. Later editing and compilation is suggested by the very condition of the text, of which, as with Jeremias and Esther,

[21] Pope, *Catholic Student's Aids to the Bible,* p. 363 (London, 1918).

there seems to have been current a longer and a shorter redaction.

Rationalistic criticism, primarily on the principle of an *a priori* denial of real prophecy and miracles, would have the composition of the Book of Daniel take place during the Seleucid or Machabean period, so that the prophecies of the Greek and Roman world-developments and especially the symbolic but detailed description of the reign of Antiochus Epiphanes (175-164) might be explained as reminiscences of past events. Arguments adduced for this late date are: (*a*) the silence of the author of Ecclesiasticus in his catalogue of seers (Ecclus. 49); (*b*) the subordinate position assigned to the "Chaldeans" as soothsayers and magi; (*c*) the long sections written in the Western Aramaic dialect; (*d*) the frequent occurrence of Persian, and even of Greek, terms in the vocabulary; (*e*) the confusion in regard to "Baltassar" and "Darius the Mede".

The existence of the historical Daniel at the time purported in the Book is vouched for by Ez. 14:14-20, where also he is already celebrated as a man illumined by God (Ez. 28:3). The author of I Machabees (composed not later than 70 B.C.) mentions Daniel and alludes to incidents recorded in his Book (I Mach. 2:59-60). In the New Testament Matt. 24:15, Mark 13:14, Heb. 11:33 testify to Daniel's authenticity.

The Jewish canon admitted Daniel, although the Talmud ascribes the editing of the Book to "the Men of the Great Synagogue",—of which the prophet himself was reputed a member. The omission of Daniel's name from the catalogue of Ecclus. 49 is not fatal, as that list does not pretend to exhaustiveness, and the author's principle in compiling it is not clear. The intimate details of the customs, regulations, history and religion of the Neo-Babylonian empire, given in the Book of Daniel and confirmed by archeological discoveries, point towards the acquaintance of a contemporary person. The admixture of Persian words in the vocabulary supports this. As for the few Greek words (if indeed they be such, and not simply derivatives from a common Aryan source) in Dan. 3:5, 7, 10, they are technical terms which may have been imported through Phrygian musicians with the musical instruments they designate. Moreover, it is now established that items of Hellenic thought and culture and language were known outside of Greece long before the Persian period.

The Greek punning in Dan. 13 : 54-55 and 58-59, σχῖνον — σχίσει and πρίνον — πρίσαι, could be a happy reproduction of a similar play of words in Hebrew or Aramaic,—the Greek names of the trees being chosen to accommodate the pun. Thus the σχῖνον could be paralleled by the tsari "the balsam tree", and tsarah, "to split or crack" or tsôr in the sense of "cut". Even the Latin translator made a like attempt in the first case with schinus—scindet.

290. Literary Characteristics.—Whilst Ezechiel, also an exilic prophet, has occasional Aramaisms, in Daniel, as in Esdras, whole sections are written in that dialect. Aramaic was at that period a *lingua franca* for Eastern Asia and even Egypt. The Tell-el-Amarna correspondence is practically all in Aramaic, and even the banking documents of Murashu Sons excavated at Nippur bear notes in Aramaic on the back.

The portions of Daniel which would have peculiar interest only for Jews, such as the incident of Daniel's observance of the Mosaic košer food regulations (Dan. 1-2 : 4a) and the closing sections containing the great apocalyptic prophecies whose primary term is the Messias and His time, are written in Hebrew, the consecrated language of the Jewish Scriptures.

But the historic sections (Dan. 2 : 4b—3 : 23 ; 3 : 91—6 : 28), comprising Nabuchodonosor's Dream of the Statue, the incident of the Three Youths in the Fiery Furnace, whose sequel is an edict of toleration; the long Manifesto of Nabuchodonosor regarding his lycanthrophy, which was foretold by Daniel; the Feast of Baltassar, are written in Aramaic. These sections would have a special interest for all nationalities groaning beneath the yoke of Babylonia, and thus these peoples could read of the humiliation of their conquerors, note that even the Babylonian kings had to bow before the God of the Jews, and thus they themselves might gather hope from the predicted ruin of their overlords.

As for the deuterocanonical portions of Daniel (the Canticle of the Three Youths, Dan. 3 : 24-90, and chapters 13-14), only their Greek translation by Theodotion is preserved in the Bibles. However, in the ''Chronicles of Jerahmeel''

Gaster found an Aramaic text of the Canticle of the Three
Youths, and of the Bel incident.[22]   The Septuagint had a
translation of the deuterocanonical portions of Daniel, but
for that Theodotion's version was early substituted.   "Hoc
cur acciderit, nescio", says St. Jerome, and adds, anent the
Septuagint text: "Hoc unum affirmare possum: quod multum
a veritate discordet, et recto iudicio repudiatus sit".[23]

Chronological order is almost entirely absent in the Book
of Daniel as it has come down to the present time.   The writer
varies from the first to the third person in his narrative, using
the first by preference when the matter related would have
to be accepted upon his sole authority.

291. Apocalytic Prophecies.—The First Vision, of the
Four Beasts, covers largely the same ground as the Dream of
the Statue in Dan. 2.   But here the Babylonian empire is
symbolized by a winged lion; the Medo-Persian, by a bear
with triple denture (= the kingdoms of Lydia, Egypt, and
Babylon); the Greco-Macedonian, by a swift-leaping leopard
with four wings (= the four succession lines of Antigonus,
Ptolemy, Lysimachus, and Cassandra); the Roman, by the
terrific fourth monster with ten horns standing for the great
rulers of the Roman system.   The eleventh horn, which destroys three of the others, is generally taken as emblematic
of the Antichrist (II Thess. 1).   Relative to the Roman empire
in this vision, Cardinal Newman comments well: "As, then,
the ten horns belonged to the fourth beast, and were not
separate from it, so the kingdoms into which the Roman empire was to be divided, are but the continuation and termi-
nation of that empire itself,—which lasts on and in some
sense lives in the view of prophecy. . . . Consequently we
have not yet seen the end of the Roman empire".[24]

The Second Vision (Dan. 8), of the Ram and the He-

22 See Gaster, *The Chronicles of Jerahmeel* (London, 1899) and *Proceedings of the Society of Biblical Archeology*, XVI, pp. 312-317 (1894);
XVII, pp. 75-94 (1895).
23 The Septuagint text has been published after the *Codex Chisianus*
by De Magistris in *Daniel secundum Septuaginta* (Rome, 1772).
24 Newman, "Patristical Idea of the Antichrist", in *Discussions and
Arguments* (1879).

Goat, by *emboîtement* develops a phase of the preceding revelation. The Medo-Persian empire is symbolized by the two-horned ram; the Macedonian, by the one-horned he-goat. His original single horn is Alexander the Great, who destroyed the Persian empire. The four succeeding horns stand for the four succession kingdoms of Macedon in the West, Syria in the East, Egypt in the South, and Thrace in the North. The fifth horn is Antiochus IV Epiphanes, who made sacrifice to cease at Jerusalem. The 2300 days, or six and one-half lunar years, may be counted from 143 of the Seleucid era, when Antiochus became master of Jerusalem (I Mach. 1:21), to 149, when he died.

The Third Vision (Dan. 9), of the Seventy Year-Weeks, by another *emboîtement*, develops more specifically the time-phase of the messianic prophecies of Dan. 2 and 7. From the consideration of Jeremias' seventy years of the Baby-lonian Captivity (Jer. 25:11-12; 29:10), the drawing to a close, the seer's mind is directed toward a more universal, spiritual deliverance, to take place with the advent of the Messias, and practically coincidently with the utter destruction of the earthly Jewish commonwealth, all of which was to come about in the course of seventy year-weeks. The essentials of this prophecy may be shown in the following amplifying paraphrase:

"Seventy year-weeks have been set for thy people and for thy Holy City, whereupon their transgression shall be concluded, their sin finished, and their wickedness consummated. Then shall ever-lasting Justice be brought [to the earth], vision and prophecy be fulfilled, when the Holy One shall be anointed [= formally open His Messianic career at His baptism].

"Know thou, therefore, and note well: From the promulgation of the edict to rebuild Jerusalem unto the Prince Messias there will run seven year-weeks [of the restoration], wherein the squares [of Jerusalem] shall once more be populated; and sixty-two year-weeks, when the divine decrees shall be poured out in full.

"For, after the sixty-two year-weeks the Messias shall be slain, without there being any cause against Him. Whereupon a future leader and nation [= Roman legions under Titus] shall destroy the city and the sanctuary, and that war shall last until destruction be complete, and the decreed devastation shall all have come to pass.

"Furthermore [the Messias] shall make a firm covenant with

many [even of the Jews] during a year-week [= evangelization by Christ and His apostles in Judea], and in the middle of that year-week [the efficacy of Jewish] sacrifice and victim shall cease,—whereupon the abominations of the devastators shall reach their limit, and the decreed destructions shall be poured forth even unto utter ruin" (Dan. 9: 24-27). . . .

"But the Kingdom [of God] with all its magnificence and power, extending under every sky, shall be given to the people of the Saints of the Most High,—which Kingdom is an everlasting reign, and all rulers shall serve and obey it" (Dan. 7: 27).

The Fourth Vision, of the Seleucid Kings, develops particular phases of the Second Vision, having reference to the Machabean times. Dan. 10 forms the introduction; Dan. 11 and 12, the body. The characterization of the person and persecutions of Antiochus IV Epiphanes is especially marked. And as this king is scripturally typical of the Antichrist, Dan. 12 is particularly susceptible to eschatological interpretation. Indeed, Daniel's visions are practically the groundwork of St. John's revelations in the Apocalypse.

Art. 6: THE TWELVE MINOR PROPHETS

Texts: Selections from each Prophet.

292. Osee.—In the Hebrew Bibles the writings of the prophets Osee, Joel, Abdias, Jonas, Micheas, Nahum, Habacuc, Sophonias, Aggeus, Zacharias, and Malachias, are grouped together as one book or roll, immediately following upon the Book of Ezechiel. The order of their arrangement, which is certainly not chronological, varies greatly in the different Greek MSS. Osee is generally placed first. Scarcely anything is known of his person and life, except that he was active during at least the latter part of the reign of Jeroboam II of Israel (783-743, Gissler) and during at least the first part of that of Ezechias of Juda (721-693, Gissler), which would include the turbulent revolutionary period of Menahen, Phaceia and Phaceë in Israel. He seems to have been a subject of the apostate Northern Kingdom, to whose inhabitants the bulk of his exhortations is addressed. The kingdom of

Juda is, however, also mentioned (Os. 4:15; 5:5; 10-14, etc.)[25] but never the Temple or Jerusalem.

Whilst the Book of Osee may have been written out in one draft, it nevertheless probably embodies a series of prophetic oracles uttered at divers periods during the prophet's life. Whilst economically in Osee's time the status of Israel was prosperous, politically and morally its condition at the time of Jeroboam II was most deplorable. Its inhabitants, alienated from the center of Mosaic religious life by the great schism and calf-worship, had forgotten Yahweh as the "giver of all good gifts" had enriched their land with "corn and wine and oil, and multiplied her silver and gold, which they . . . used in the service of Baalim" (Os. 2:8). In short, Israel, wedded of old to Yahweh by the covenant made with Abraham and renewed under Moses, as a faithless bride had abandoned her one true Bridegroom, to espouse herself to many false gods. She had turned from her Divine Lover to follow the glittering but hollow seductions of the *Baalim,* the petty idols of her time. Instead of, like Amos, inveighing directly against the social evils of his period, Osee points out their common source: the irreligion of princes and people, of rich and poor alike. It is the supreme sin of infidelity to the Creator that he so vividly describes as "fornication against God".[26]

Hence comes Osee's recurrent use of adultery metaphors and symbols. As God's representative he is divinely commanded to enter into marriage with harlots. The first of these, whom he seems to have divorced as unfaithful, may have typified Israel, which God cast off in the Assyrian captivity, never to receive back as an earthly commonwealth.

[25] In Os. 11:12 the Septuagint, oppositely from the Hebrew, but probably more correctly, groups Juda with Ephraim in a common guilt.
[26] "Such was the folly of our statesmen who assembled to make peace and excluded from their councils the Prince of Peace, following after the lure of their own worldly prudence, diplomacy, ambition, and dreams of national aggrandizement. Such, no less, is the folly of those in our own day who seek for social reconstruction, but build up their elaborate systems without God or religion. . . . For, every social structure that is not established upon God is resting on the sand" (Husslein, "Osee and Micheas as Social Teachers", in *Homiletic and Pastoral Review,* Sept., 1923).

The second he is commanded to keep apart for many days,
languishing for her husband; she typifies Juda, for a time in
punitive exile far from the Temple and its sacrifices (Os.
3 : 4 and 2 : 10-15). Yet even Israel, apparently utterly cast
off, shall, in the messianic age, when she shall call God " 'My
husband,' and she shall call Me no more *'Baali'* ", be received
again in the great gathering of the Gentiles to the Church:

> "And I will say to that which was not My people:
>   'Thou art My people!'
> And they shall say:
>   'Thou art my God' ".

> And I will espouse thee to Me forever,
> And I will espouse thee to Me in justice and judgment,
> And in mercy and in commiserations.
> And I will espouse thee to Me in faith,
> And thou shalt know that I am Yahweh" (Os. 2 : 14-24).

293. Joel.—Perhaps the oldest Book of the Minor Prophets, if not of all the prophetic writers, is that of Joel, which
bears no definite indications of date. Vigouroux and many
other weighty authorities place it early in the reign of Joas
(836-797, Gissler). In Joel's time the Temple is still standing and its service is organized. The enemies of Yahweh's
people are, not the Northern Kingdom or Assyria, but Tyre
and Sidon and the Philistines (Joel 3 : 4), the Egyptians and
the Edomites (Joel 3 : 19). Now, it is known that against
the latter Ozias (769-736, Gissler) waged successful campaigns (II Par. 26 : 6-8).

Joel is quoted in Amos 1 : 2 (Joel 3 : 16) and Amos 9 : 15 (Joel
3 : 18): in Amos 4 : 9 that prophet may refer to the failure of the
locust plague to bring about a permanent repentance. Jer. 25 : 30
may be quoting either Joel 3 : 16 or Amos 1 : 2. The "Great Day
of the Lord" of Is. 13 : 6, 10; Soph. 1 : 14-15; Mal. 4 : 1, 5, may
be allusions to Joel 1 ; 15; 2 : 10-11.

Almost every verse of this Book shows the work of a master of literary art: vividness, freshness, and clearness make
his style almost classic. Here are joined the vigor of Micheas
with the tenderness of Jeremias and the colorful brilliancy
of Nahum.

A devastating plague of locusts, graphically described in Joel 1—2:10, gave occasion to this prophecy. Joel draws therefrom a lesson of repentance from the sins which have merited such chastisement (Joel 2:12-17), and promises thereafter a restoration of that which had been lost (Joel 2: 18-27). Then, from that local and temporal rain (Joel 3:23) which again will make Israel's fields to bear bountifully, the prophet raises the minds of his contemporaries to the time when God will send His universal spiritual rain of grace upon the world in the messianic age (Joel 3:28). Having in mind also the injuries which the Jews have suffered through the incursions of Gentile nations (types of the injustices ever inflicted upon the Church by the world), the prophet's vision leaps to the eschatological future and describes the "Great Day of the Lord" when all wrongs shall at last be righted,—not omitting, however, the earlier punishments with which the Gentile nations and the world, who have afflicted God's Chosen People, both in the Old Dispenstation and in the New, will be visited even in their own times.

The "Greeks" of Joel 3:6 are not the people of classical Athens, but *Yavan*, already mentioned in Gen. 10:2 and in the inscriptions of Sargon (721-705), from which "Ionian" is probably derived.— The words of the original of Joel 3:1 contain no reference to a past Captivity, but mean simply: "I shall change the destiny of Juda and Jerusalem".

294. Amos.—From the barren heights of Thecue, between Hebron and Bethlehem, Amos (Am'ots) came. His biography and credentials, as given to the contemptuous hierarch of Bethel, are brief and blunt: "I was neither a prophet nor a member of the Prophetic Schools, but a herdsman and a dresser of wild-figs. But Yahweh took me whilst I was following the flock, and said to me: 'Go, prophesy to My people Israel'" (Amos 7:14). This was in the days of the reign of Jeroboam II (783-743, Gissler) and of Ozias of Juda (769-736, Gissler). In connection with the earthquake mentioned in Amos 1:1, it is remarkable that Josephus [27] speaks of such an occurrence happening at the time Ozias usurped sacerdotal functions (II Par. 26:6-19; see also Zach. 14:5).

[27] Josephus, *Ant.*, IX, x, 4.

Something of ancient Solomonic splendor had at this period been attained by Israel and its capital Samaria,—a great metropolis, with lavish riches and bitter poverty, financial magnates and numerous proletariat. But it was to Bethel, then the religious center of the Northern Kingdom—where the golden calves had been set up from the first by Jeroboam I, and where now the cult of Yahweh was blended with superstitious abominations—that Amos was sent. Having gained the confidence of his hearers by foretelling God's judgments that should fall upon the surrounding nations (Amos 1:3—2:3), and not omitting to confess the shortcomings of neighboring Juda (Amos 2:4-5), he directs his denunciations against the social evils of Israel (Amos 3:6 ss).

Financially and commercially successful Israel is personified under the figure of a greedy, grasping, usurious capitalist (Amos 2:6-8). Its people are invited to look down from the surrounding mountains upon the luxury purveying shops, the slave-driving factories, and the great storehouses of Samaria, swollen with unjustly produced goods (Amos 3:9-10). The basic rottenness and wrongness of such a materialistic social system can not be permanently concealed beneath the glittering trappings and tinsel of exterior convention and culture: "Behold", says Yahweh, "I will skreak under you as a wain skreaketh that is laden down with hay" (Amos 2:13). And, after the present threats, God continues: "I will strike the winter houses and the summer villas, and the ivory-trimmed palaces shall perish" (Amos 3:15).[28]

The prophet next condemns the luxurious women and the impurity which are the inseparable concomitants of wealth acquired without regard to social justice and disposed of without a sense of stewardship under God (Amos 4 and 6:3-7). Bribery and graft and the subversion of the processes of justice are likewise excoriated (Amos 5:12). Small wonder then that Amasias, the exquisite hierophant of Jeroboam's sanctuary, when confronted with this outspoken fig-pricker, denounces the prophet to his king as a dangerous revolution-

[28] See Husslein, "Amos, the Herdsman of Thecua", in *Homiletic and Pastoral Review*, July, 1923, pp. 1019-1026.

ist, and, unable to deny the truth of the accusations, tells Amos: "Go, flee away into the land of Juda, and eat bread there, and prophesy there!" (Amos 7: 16-17).

Of the five visions with which the Book closes (Amos 7-9) the first four form a gradually intensified series of denunciations of Israel's wickedness, and announcements of coming punishment. The fifth, which is independent, begins in the same key, but concludes with the merciful promise of Redemption, when the Divine Mason shall once more take up His trowel to "rebuild it (= Israel) as in the days of old" (Amos 9: 11). Then shall be at hand the blessed messianic season, "when the plowman shall overtake the reaper, and the treader of grapes, him that soweth the corn" (Amos 9: 13).

295. Abdias.—Whilst direct evidence concerning the person and times of Abdias is absent from his short oracle, the consensus of responsible critics is that he antedates Jeremias, who quotes Abdias (1: 1-9) in his own prophecy against the Idumeans (Jer. 19: 7, 9-10, 14-17, 22). The Edomites are upbraided for having rejoiced at the evils which befell the Jews at an earlier date (Ez. 25: 12; Ps. 136: 7), probably through the attack by Arabian and Philistine forces at the time of Joram (846-843, Gissler), when the Edomites themselves threw off the yoke of tribute to the king of Juda (II Par. 21: 8-10, 16-17; IV Kings 8: 20-22). In punishment for this perfidious attitude toward their "brother Jacob" (Abdias 1: 10)—the Edomites were descendants of Esau—they are not to be in position to repeat this traitorous hostility in the day when another calamity, in all probability the destruction of Jerusalem and the Babylonian Captivity, shall befall Juda (Abdias 1: 12-14). Joel (2: 32; see also Heb. 3: 5) seems to have imitated Abdias (1: 17), as the latter himself (Abdias 1: 4, 18, etc.), the prophecies of Balaam (Num. 24: 8, 21).

But if the calamity of Abdias 1: 11 be taken for the (later) destruction of Jerusalem by Nabuchodonosor II, then the punishment of the Edomites will be found realized in their conquest in Machabean times by John Hyrcanus (I Mach. 5: 3), who made of

Idumea a Jewish province. Consequently there were no sons of
Esau on Mount Seir to rejoice at the final destruction of Jerusalem
by the Romans.

296. Jonas.—Generally this prophet is taken to be identical with the Jonas mentioned (IV Kings 14: 25) as active
in the reign of Jeroboam II of Israel (783-743, Gissler), whose
military successes he predicts.[29] It may be noted that the
reign of Ramman-nirari III (812-783) fairly coincides with
a period of luxury and decay in Assyria.

In the Book of Jonas may be found one of the earliest
clear indications of the fact that not only the Jews but the
Gentiles also were to be included in the dispensations of God's
mercy. Jonas himself was a striking exponent of the narrow,
rigoristic, literal, unspiritual concept of Judaism, which later
evolved the Pharisee. Having the Jew's deep distaste for
the Gentile, and especially for the Assyrian, who was associated with so much evil and humiliation for Juda, Jonas
refused to obey the divine command to go and preach penance
to Ninive. Perhaps he hoped by this refusal to bring down
the more quickly Yahweh's vengeance upon the hated city
and nation. It would also seem that he imagined to escape
the impelling force of the prophetic *afflatus* by fleeing far
from the boundaries of the Holy Land,—according to a theory
plainly held in later Jewry.[30] But Yahweh utilizes this very

[29] Šanda, in *Bücher der Könige*, II, p. 172 (Münster, 1912) finds
the identification unacceptable because the Book speaks of a "king of
Ninive" (Jonas 3: 6), whereas since the time of Aššurnaçirpal (885-
860) the royal residence was at Kalhi (Gen. 10: 11), about 20 km.
south of Ninive. Permanently Ninive became a royal residence only
under Sennacherib (705-681). The difficulty raised is, however, not
insuperable. Jonas 3: 6-9 does not state that the king dwelt in Ninive
itself: indeed the length of time it takes for the rumor of Jonas to reach
the king, and the previous uncommanded action of the Ninivites themselves (Jonas 3: 5) might be taken as indications of the king's distant
residence.—Note that the Septuagint makes the period of grace allowed
but three days, instead of forty.

[30] "All ground upon which non-Israelites dwell, makes unclean",
was an axiom of the Talmudists (*Šabbath*, 16A). Even the air above a
pagan country was deemed to cause ritual uncleanness. Only in the
Holy Land will the Šekinah, the manifest presence of God, come down.
Hence the Targum Jonathan notes that Ezechiel was prophetically endowed before he left Palestine, although a Talmudist (in *Sohar* I, 84)
cleverly theorizes that the canal Kebar, at which Ezechiel received his
inspirations, was connected with one of the rivers of Paradise, and thus
in times of need, might have the privilege of ritual holiness.

flight to expedite the prophet's mission. For, miraculously
he is in three days brought probably near Alexandretta,
whence the greater part of the rest of his journey could be
easily made by floating down the Tigris to Ninive in one of
the round bitumined wicker boats still in use on that river.

Arrived in the great Assyrian metropolis the prophet,
apparently to his own deep satisfaction, announces its proximate doom. But all Ninive, even to the beasts, does penance
in sackcloth and fasting. Thereupon God's mercy spares the
city,—to the rigoristic prophet's great disgust, since he evidently expected that now Israel's haughty enemy would
surely be destroyed. Jonas had not yet grasped the significance of his mission,—the revelation to the Jews of the *universality* of God's redemptive plan. The Book closes suddenly with this being made unmistakably plain by a striking
object lesson,—leaving the reflective reader to absorb the
truth of the world-wide expansion of men's salvation.

And with this moral of the Book is intimately connected
Jonas' miraculous preservation in the maw of a sea monster,[31]
as Christ Himself pointed out (Matt. 12:39-41). In the
process of bringing salvation to the Ninivites Jonas dwells
three days "in the womb of Šeol" (Jonas 2:3). Thus also
Christ, plunged in the sea of suffering in His passion and
received into Šeol at His death, in the process of mankind's
salvation, could have applied to Himself the words of the
prophet's canticle:

> "Thou hast cast me forth into the sea
>   so that the flood compassed me
> And all Thy billows and waves
>   did pour about me.

[31] Popular language has generally designated this sea monster as a
whale—and the presence of such an animal in the Mediterranean has
been scoffed at as absurd. But Haupt ("Assyrische Name des Potwals",
in *American Journal of Semitic Languages and Literatures*, April,
1907, vol. 23, pp. 253-263, Chicago) concludes from etymological reasons
that the sea beast of the Book of Jonas (which of course he considers
fiction, and assigns to the Machabean period) was probably a cachalot
or sperm whale, known to the Assyrians under the name of *nâxiru*, "the
blower or squirter". Aššurnâçirpal records as a notable feat that
Tiglathphilesar I (about 1100 B.C.) on a sea voyage off Arvad killed one
of these beasts. In the mighty maw of a cachalot a man could find room.
Commentators propose the white shark, known to Hollanders as the
Jonas-Haay.

It seemed I was forever banished
    out of the sight of Thine eyes,
Yet was I again to behold
    Thy sacred Temple" (Jonas 2: 4-5).

297. Micheas.—Whilst Osee was denouncing the sins of the Northern Kingdom, the same mission was being fulfilled in Juda by Isaias and Micheas, the latter being active under kings Joathan, Achaz, and Ezechias (736-693, Gissler). "Money, money, money; greed, greed, greed, that was the tale of Samaria and Jerusalem before the wrath of God smote them even unto final destruction. From wealth easily and unjustly accumulated by means of extortion, graft, and every other evil practice, there sprang . . . luxury and voluptuousness. And the root of all . . . was the irreligion of high and low. But the more powerful were also the more responsible for these conditions. Priests and prophets alike had gone the common way, satisfied with a lavish outward observance of religious ceremonies". Most of all Micheas, a veritable tribune of the common folk, arraigned the princes and magnates of Juda for their insatiable avarice and greed. As veritable ghouls he depicts them (Mich. 5: 1-3) despoiling and flaying the people, living on the flesh of the poor, cracking open their very bones and feeding on the marrow of them.

However, "king and people did penance, for on this occasion the prophet's message was spoken in the days of the great and God-fearing ruler Ezechias. So God's punishment was stayed for a time". But the last chapter of Micheas, which may summarize the preaching of many years, admits that there has been no lasting fruit. The Jews have failed religiously, morally, socially, and must go down to a destruction that is not far off. Nevertheless their enemies may not exult overmuch. God will eventually have mercy on a faithful remnant. There is left the great messianic hope, through whose realization Jew and Gentile will be joined in the great future Kingdom of God, the Church.[32]

The prophecy designating Bethlehem as the Messias' birth

[32] Quotations are from Husslein's "Osee and Micheas as Social Teachers" in *Homiletic and Pastoral Review*, Sept., 1923, pp. 1281-1283.

place (Mich. 5:2-3) and differs in verbal form from its citation in the Gospels (Matt. 2:6; John 7:42):

> "And thou Bethlehem Ephrata,
>   altho too small to be numbered among the towns-of-
>   thousand of Juda
> Nevertheless out of thee shall come forth to Me
>   He that is to be the Ruler of Israel—
> Whose (original) going forth is from the beginning,
>   even from the days of old.
> They (the Jews) will be given up, therefore, by Him
>   until the season when the Woman travailing gives birth,
> When a remnant of His brethren (by flesh) shall be converted
>   to (true) children of Israel".

298. Nahum.—The prophet Nahum is concerned exclusively with the eventual destruction of the terrible Assyrian power. He writes after the fall of the Northern
Kingdom, and the invasion of Sennacherib. His prophecy
must have been uttered between 666 (or 662) B.C., when
Assurbanipal took Thebes (Nahum 3:8: No Amon), and 606,
when Ninive fell. His style is quite artificial, rhetorical. All
the glory of ancient Ninive, with its sumptuous chariots, its
magnificent military displays of soldiers in gleaming accoutre-
ments, has been crystallized in his taunt-song. A "com-
forter", as his name signifies, was Nahum to his countrymen,
as, against a popular fear, he assured them that the destruction of Assyria would be final:

> "Why do you imagine against God?
> He will make an utter end,
> Nor shall such affliction arise again.
> Although as thorns they cling together
> And are overfilled with wine,
> Still as dry stubble shall they be consumed" (Nahum 1:9-10).

299. Habacuc.—That the author of this Book is identical
with the man of the same name who brought food to Daniel
in the lions' den at Babylon (Dan. 14:32-38) is scarcely
probable. Only from indirect internal evidence may one
conjecture the date of this prophecy. The chief indication
is that the Neo-Babylonian empire is hardly known and not
feared. Hence the writer's time must be previous to the

rise of the Chaldean power. Meroch-Baladan (721-709), the would-be ally of Ezechias (721-693, Gissler) is the first Babylonian ruler to whom much attention is given in the Scriptures. An invasion of Juda by the Babylonian forces is pronounced in the offing. Such an invasion actually took place during the reign of Ezechias' successor, Manasses (693-639). Habacuc himself (Greek Αμβακούμ), to judge from the technical instructions marked in his canticle (*selah*, Hab. 3:9, 13; *šigyonôth*, 3:1 3:19 "for the chief musician, to the accompaniment of stringed instruments") was a Levite in the Temple choir. He also shows himself familiar with the Psalms.

Habacuc's prophecy proper is in the form of a dialogue between God and the prophet. The latter asks first (Hab. 1:2-4): Why is sin and injustice tolerated in Juda?—to which Yahweh replies that it will be punished through the instrumentality of Babylon. Thereupon the prophet asks again (Hab. 1:12—2:1): Why at the hands of the Chaldeans, who are themselves more wicked than the Jews? Yahweh replies (Hab. 2:2-20): For the Jews, eventual redemption is in store: they must believe and trust in God; and Babylon in its own turn will be punished for its greed and violence. This retribution is announced in five Woes (Hab. 2:6-20) consisting of an equal number of strophes of three verses each, naming a crime and threatening its penalty.

The closing chapter is a canticle in which the prophet implores God's mercy on Juda, acknowledges His power and justice, and expresses his confidence therein. The language of this canticle gives it a place among the most sublime passages of Scripture.

The Vulgate translation of this Book falls short of its usual excellence; hence the obscurity of the Douay in many passages.— In Hab. 3:2 the Septuagint, instead of "in the midst of the years", has "between two beasts it shall be made known", which may have connection with the traditional ox and ass at the manger of Bethlehem.—Besides the regular Septuagint version, the *Codex Barberinus* gives an anonymous Greek translation made by a Jew.[33]

[33] See *Max Margolis, "Character of the Anonymous Greek Version of Habakkuk, Chapter 3" in *American Journal of Semitic Languages and Literatures*, Oct., 1907, vol. 24, pp. 76-85 (Chicago).

300. Sophonias.—The genealogy of this prophet traces him, in the fourth generation, to an Ezechias, who may be the king of that name. But Sophonias himself is active under Josias (638-608, Gissler), probably very early in that king's reign, since the Baal cult was still flourishing (Soph. 1:4-5) and Ninive was not yet destroyed by the Medo-Scythian forces (Soph. 2:13).[34]

Sophonias starts from oracles against the Chosen People, then proceeds to predictions against the Gentiles, and finishes with words of comfort for both. He foresees clearly the great "day of wrath" (Soph. 1:15) which shall come upon Jerusalem for its sins,—a prediction also admitting of eschatologic expansion.[35] The name of the invader who is to bring destruction upon the nations, including Assur, is not mentioned. But the Scythians (alluded to in Ez. 38-39) may be meant. Their hordes began a scourge-like wandering into Eastern Asia, and even as far as Egypt, about this time,—a trace of their presence in Palestine being the name Scythopolis given to Bethsan, below the Sea of Galilee.

In Soph. 3:18 the Vulgate *nugæ* is mistranslated "triflers" (*hommes légers*, Glaire) by the Douay. St. Jerome used this word in the archaic Plautan sense of "mourners" or "sorrowful", justified by the Hebrew word *nûgey*, which has also the double meaning of "the removed" and "the afflicted".

301. Aggeus.—With Aggeus is associated Zacharias,[36] both of these prophets having as the main object of their mission the rebuilding of the Temple in the restoration period following immediately upon the Babylonian Captivity. Aggeus begins to prophesy shortly before, during the reign of Darius I Hystaspis, in August, 520 B.C. His messages of encouragement are addressed primarily to Zorobabel as the

---

[34] This Book exemplifies the precariousness of date conjectures deduced from internal evidence only. Soph. 2:7; 3:20 has reference to a captivity, and Soph. 3:10 to a dispersion. Yet it is undeniable that the Book itself was written prior to the great Captivity.

[35] Thomas of Celano took the opening words of his *Dies Iræ* from this passage of Sophonias.

[36] See Esdras 5:1-2. Note that according to the Septuagint, these two prophets are collaborators of Psalms 137, 145-148; according to Vulgate, of Psalms 111, 145; according to Syriac, of Psalms 125-126, 145-148.

civil "head of the captives", and Josue or Jesus, the high priest. These were the first post-exilic leaders of Jewry, representatives of the royal and levitical stock respectively. Hence they were also typical of the combined kingly and priestly aspects of the Messias.

The Jews who had returned from the Babylonian exile with Cyrus' decree (II Par. 36 : 23—Esd. 1 : 1-4) authorizing them to restore their ancient Temple, had scarcely erected a temporary altar and laid out the foundations, when the turbulent years of Cambyses and the Pseudo-Smerdis (529-522) in the Persian monarchy, were taken advantage of by the renegade Samaritans to block by their intrigues the chief work. Moreover, the limited means of the returned exiles made it impossible for them to reconstruct the Temple upon the magnificent scale of Solomon's structure (Esd. 3 : 12). Discouragement therefore cooled the enthusiasm of the builders.

Aggeus is called to stir up once more the energy and interest of his compatriots. He does this by assuring them that this Temple, like the Solomonic, shall be the dwelling-place of Yahweh's presence, of His "Spirit", despite the lack of the ark and of the tables of the Law. Moreover, "the latter glory" of this house shall be "greater than its first" (Ag. 2 : 10) under Solomon, because the Messias, the "Desired of all nations",[37] shall one day walk therein.

Again, it would seem that the crops and harvests of the first years of the restoration had been poor; that no success had attended the attempts made at economic rehabilitation (Ag. 1 : 6, 9-11; 2 : 17-18). This is interpreted as a punishment for the selfishness of the returned exiles, in devoting all their energy and means to their own comfort,[38] whilst the greater, national work of rebuilding the Temple was given but

[37] The Hebrew text reads in the plural, "venient", but the sense is equivalent, as the desires of all nations are concentrated in the Messias, who alone shall fulfill them. The Septuagint and the Greek Fathers understand this passage, not of the person of the Messias, but of the Gentiles to be converted: "Venient electa omnium gentium".

[38] In Ag. 1 : 4 the Jews are reproached for dwelling in "tiled houses" whilst the Temple is bare.—Note that Ag. 2 : 1 belongs with Ag. 1 : 14 as its date, as the King James version has correctly divided.

scant consideration. God now promises abundance at the next harvest if the latter work be seriously furthered.—Lastly (Ag. 3:21-24) in a special oracle the hands of Zorobabel, uncrowned and unthroned but nevertheless the legitimate prince of David's royal house, are strengthened by God's promise that He will preserve and keep the Davidic stock, not indeed in regal pomp and royal power (for, that had been forfeited by the infidelity of so many kings of Juda) but at least hidden in the midst of the nation, as a signet or seal ring would be kept cherished and safe in its jewel case by its owner.

302. Zacharias.—The Book of Zacharias, Aggeus' associate in post-exilic restoration work, is longer and much more brilliant in style, being replete with apocalyptic visions and symbols, which offer many difficulties. Zacharias himself, called to the prophetic office as a young man (Zach. 2:4), was the son or grandson of a certain Addo (Iddo, Adaia) of priestly stock, who came up with Zorobabel's caravan from Babylon to Jerusalem (Neh. 12:1, 4, 14; Esd. 5:1; 6:4). That he is the prophet "slain between the Temple and the altar" (Matt. 23:35)[39] is improbable. According to the dates given in his Book he was active from November 520 to December 518 (Zach. 1:1, 7; 7:1).

Whilst the authenticity of Zach. 1-8 is unquestioned, many critics adjudge the second part of the Book (Zach. 9-14) to some other writer, preferably pre-exilic, perhaps of the time of Isaias.[40] Arguments adduced for this position are the

---

[39] It has been conjectured that in Matt. 23:35 "son of Barachias" is a later insertion, as it is absent in the parallel citation in Luke 11:51. It has also been conjectured, on the basis of the hypothesis that Zach. 9-14 is to be ascribed to a pre-exilic writer (who might be identifiable with the "Zacharias, son of Barachias" of Is. 8:2), that an editor-copyist, having the works of two Zacharias' before, mistakenly fused the authors in Zach. 1:1. See Steuernagel, *Einleitung in das Alte Testament*, (Tübingen, 1912), pp. 640, 645.

[40] *Moulton, in *Literary Study of the Bible* (Boston, 1905), p. 470, assuming that "Malachi" is the subject-title of an anonymous prophecy, theorizes that when " 'Malachi' came to be read as a personal name, like the names of the prophets from Isaiah to Zechariah, it was natural that the intervening prophecies, without author's name to cover them, should attach themselves to the preceding book of Zechariah". The Jeremias reference in Matt. 27:9 he explains by the theory that there "the whole Roll of Prophets is cited by the longest prophecy, that of Jeremiah, as the whole Book of Psalms is cited by the name of its chief contributor, David".

following: (*a*) The style of the second part is quite different from that of the first. (*b*) Whilst the disputed section is quoted several times in the New Testament, Matt. 21: 4-5; John 12: 15 (Zach. 9: 9); John 19: 37 (Zach. 12: 10); Matt. 26: 31; Mark 14: 27 (Zach. 13: 7), the citations are uniformly anonymous, except in Matt. 27: 9-10 (Zach. 12: 10) where the passage alluded to is ascribed to Jeremias. (*c*) The nations, Egypt, Assyria (Zach. 10: 10-11), Phenicia, Philistia, Syria (Zach. 9: 1-8) are represented in their pre-exilic powerful condition: Juda and Ephraim, as distinct and existing national entities (Zach. 10: 6-9).

In explanation of these apparent anachronisms it may be said: (*a*) The style of Zach. 9-14 is different from that of the previous portion because the subject matter, instead of being a narration in large part of apocalyptic visions and symbols, consists of prophetic discourses, in which the author imitates the standardized terminology of the earlier prophets. (*b*) Critics would not consider ascribing Zach. 9—14 to Jeremias on the strength of Matt. 27: 9.

It has been plausibly conjectured that in Matt. 27: 9 the word "Jeremias" is a gloss inserted from a marginal allusion to Jer. 32: 6-7. However, it is to be noted that the citation in Matt. 27: 9-10 is not verbal, and very loose. It seems designedly compiled thus in order to allude both to the Zacharian "thirty silver pieces", the casting thereof into the Temple, and the "potter" (= "statuary"), and the Jeremian public buying of a field with the (to Jewish readers so significant) name of "field of Hanam-El (= "for nothing-God"). The key for explanation is found in Matt. 27: 4, where Judas says: "I have sinned in betraying innocent blood" (*dame-hinam* = "blood shed for nothing, or innocently": see III Kings 2: 4). This connection of *haqal-dam'a*, "the field of blood," with name of the Jeremian field would be appreciated by St. Matthew's first readers, keenly familiar with the symbolism of Scriptural acts and names.

(*c*) The pre-exilic peoples mentioned in the second part of Zacharias, were still in existence at that prophet's time, although shorn of much of their ancient prestige and power. Above all it is to be noted that Greece, which rose to prominence only in post-exilic times, is mentioned among them (Zach. 9: 13: *Yawan*). Moreover, the names of these nations, adopted from the usage of pre-exilic writers, are probably used rather as symbols, conformably to apocalyptic usage, as "Babylon" in I Pet. 5:3 and Apoc. 16:19 *ss.*

303. The Book of Zacharias opens with a series of nine visions or symbols, which seem to refer to the providential protection God ever had and still was to have over the Jews as the depositories of His revelation and promises, and likewise to the duties devolving upon the Chosen People from this favored position. Messianic features are naturally emphasized. The Jewish priesthood, whose corruption had been a great contributing cause to the national ruin of Jewry,[41] shall have its shabby garments of iniquity replaced by the clean vestments of renewed perfection (Zach. 3:1-8). The diadem which had been taken away from the House of David in Sedecias (Ez. 21:25-26), is now conferred in a manner on the levitical line—prognosticating the civil authority to be henceforth exercised in large measure by the highpriest, and especially typifying the union of the royal and the sacerdotal powers in the Messias, the *Tsemah,* "Bud" (Vulgate: *Oriens*). Similar ideas are expressed in Zach. 6:9-15, where crowns are ordered made from the gifts of certain wealthy Jews from Babylon, to be bestowed upon the highpriest, to show God's appreciation of these donations. They are thereupon to be preserved as a memorial,[42] as in fact given to the Messias and His Temple, of which the present Temple and highpriest are a sign.

Next Zacharias resolves a difficulty proposed regarding the obligation of continuing to observe the penitential fasts instituted in connection with the destruction of Jerusalem. The prophet takes advantage of the occasion to remind the people of the denunciation of Isaias (58:3 *ss*): that such external ceremonial observances are valueless unless accompanied by charity and fasting from sin. This is followed (Zach. 8) by a discourse against the common Jewish fault of religious snobbishness, which would exclude the Gentiles from participation

[41] See Is. 28:7; Jer. 2:8; 5:31; 8:10; Os. 5:1; Mich. 3:11; Soph. 3:4, etc.

[42] Instead of "to Hem the son of Sophonias" one should read "to the kindness of the son of Sophonias" in Zach. 6:14.

in the divine benefits. The new Temple is not to be erected for purposes of Pharisaic self-glorification. Hence God says: "I will save My people from the land of the east and from the land of the going down of the sun. I bring them hither, and they shall dwell in the midst of Jerusalem, and be My people" (Zach. 8 : 7, 22).

The ninth chapter outlines the preliminaries to the coming of the universal Messianic Kingdom, and some of its early consequences. Alexander's armies, destroying what is left of Israel's ancient enemies, overthrow at the same time the remains of gross heathen superstitions by the introduction of Hellenism, which shall open the way to Christianity, whose leader in contrast with the mighty Macedonian shall come "lowly, riding upon an ass" (Zach. 9 : 9). Peace and not war shall be the method of His conquest; and His emissaries in their turn shall vanquish the wisdom of Greece.

The thought sequence and signification of the following chapters (Zach. 10-14) is very difficult and obscure. The literary structure probably contains *emboîtements,* "envelop-arrangements" or enclosures which have not yet been definitely distinguished. Portions of the discourse appear applicable to the Machabean period and the persecutions of Antiochus. Other portions, even by the autexegesis of Scripture, are Messianic. Others again seem to fit the unhappy lot of the Jews under irresponsible highpriests and pseudo-Messias' at, and subsequent to, the final destruction of Jerusalem by the Romans. Others again seem to have reference to the age-long wars of the world against the Church, in which the Jews are allies of the former (Zach. 12 : 2; 14 : 14). Much of the content of these final chapters of Zacharias is, if not primarily at least secondarily, eschatologic, and has reference to vicissitudes of both Jewry and the Church about the end of time.—The Hebrew people were intimately connected with the beginnings of Christianity. The Apostles were Jews, most of them from Galilee (Zach. 9 : 13: Ephraim), and the Jewish colonies of the *diaspora* served as channels of their preaching to the Gentiles. Thereafter, however, the Jews have kept themselves strictly separate from the Church, the new Kingdom of Israel. That this attitude of absolute non-participation shall continue to the very end of time, is improbable, in view of the Divine promises so often iterated to Jacob's sons. Jewry still has an eschatological rôle to play—which may be broadly sketched in the closing chapters of the prophecy of Zacharias.

304. Malachias.—Whilst the canonicity of the last Book of the Minor Prophets is unquestioned, as likewise its integrity, it has not yet been definitely determined whether the author's name was really Malachy, or the prophecy is to be considered anonymous, with that word representing a subject-title. For, the word *mal'aki* (=‘‘my messenger’’) given as a proper name, Malachias, in the Vulgate, does not so well conform to the Hebrew usages of name-formation. However, the argument from the Septuagint, which has in Mal. 1:1: ‘‘by the hand of *His* messenger’’, is not conclusive. For the Greek translator read *mal'akô*, probably by the easy and common confusion of ' with). *Mal'aki* might therefore be an anomalous abbreviated form for *Mal'akyah* (=‘‘God's messenger’’), as suggested by the Septuagint title Μαλαχίας. The Targum Jonathan names Esdras as the author.

Whilst no direct indications of the writer's period and person are given in the Book, indirect evidence points to the time of Nehemias (about 450–430 B.C.) as the date of composition. For, a ‘‘governor’’ is mentioned (Mal. 1:8); the Temple reconstruction is finished (Mal. 1:10; 3:1), various abuses, especially mixed marriages and slackness in tithing, so strongly deprecated by Nehemias on his second visit to Jerusalem (Neh. 13), are censured.

The literary form is largely that of dialogue, in the sequence of a complaint by Yahweh, an interposed objection by the people, and an answering discourse by God or the prophet. In the poem the special love Yahweh has ever shown Jacob's children is emphasized by sharp contrast with the lot of the descendants of Esau (Mal. 1:2-3):

> ‘‘‘I have favored you,’ saith Yahweh, and yet you say: ‘In what hast Thou favored us?’

'Was not Esau Jacob's brother?' saith Yahweh, 'and nevertheless I gave Jacob preference over Esau, and left the latter bleak mountains for his share and reptiles of the desert for his heritage' ".

On account, then, of this special love the Jews' service of their God should similarly be animated by special fervor. The sons of Jacob, gathered about their rebuilt sanctuary, should enter into the spirit of the Deuteronomic legislation. It is true that the Old Testament cultus is but approximative, imperfect, but by faithful observance of its prescriptions the nation should perfect itself for the reception of the perfect cultus of the New Law.

The social evil of divorce had "covered the altar of the Lord with tears" of wives cast off in favor of heathen women. Against this wrong are uttered some of the most forcible words of the prophecy (Mal. 2:13-16):

"And this moreover you have done:
You have covered the altar of the Lord with tears, with weeping and lamentation, so that I no more regard your sacrifice, nor accept it at your hand.

And you have said: 'Why not?'
Because the Lord hath been witness between thee and the spouse of thy youth, against whom thou hast been unfaithful, although she was thy partner and thy covenanted wife.
Did He not make (her) one (with man) and a life-complement to him? And why 'one', unless that godly seed was desired?
Keep, therefore, to your own life(-mate), and be thou not unfaithful to the wife of thy youth.
For, He hateth a divorcing man, saith the Lord God of Israel, and He protects from injustice the cast-off wife.
Keep, therefore, to your life(-mate), and be not unfaithful".

To those who cynically complain: What's the use of being good? there is no justice in the world; it is rather the unscrupulous that seem to enjoy God's favor—the prophet answers that the present is a time of preparation for the coming of the Dispensation of Righteousness, when "the Sun of Justice shall arise with healing in His wings" (Mal. 3:2). The two groups, Mal. 2:17-3:12, and Mal. 3:13-4:6, are best considered as parallel treatments of practically the same topics. In the first, however, the "preparatory messenger" (John the Baptist, who is to be clearly distinguished from the "Angel of the Testament") is put at the beginning; in the second, at the end. The advent of the "preparatory messenger" and of the "Angel of the Testament" admits also of eschatological expansion, crystallized in the tradition of the return of Elias before the last judgment.

Of direct Divine interference in the national life of the Jews by God through His prophets there shall henceforth be none, until the Precursor shall come "in the spirit and power of Elias" (Luke 1:17) shortly before the coming of the Messias into this very Temple. Therefore it behooves Moses' disciples meanwhile to study and observe the Law already given for their guidance, until the "coming of the great and dreadful Day of the Lord".

SIXTH PART

THE POETICAL BOOKS

L'Ecriture se trouve répandue partout dans les offices de l'Eglise. . . . Quand on ne l'entend pas, on la respire; dans les faits contingents qui ne sont ni doctrinalement, ni historiquement de son domaine, on voit que l'Eglise profite de tout, d'une analogie de fait, d'une similitude de métaphores ou de circonstances, parfois d'une simple indentité de noms, pour faire à l'Ecriture des emprunts et mettre au moins sa teinte, son reflet lointain, son arome, sur ces choses d'un ordre bien différent.

E. Cormier, O.P., Lettre à un Etudiant en Ecriture-Sainte, p. 27.

THE POETICAL BOOKS

JOB, PSALMS, CANTICLE OF CANTICLES

PROLEGOMENA

305. Parallelism in Hebrew Poetry.—In all literature poetry is distinguished from prose by a more brilliant and picturesque style conjoined to a more harmonious or at least artificial or unusual use of words. In this respect Oriental poets differ from those of the West chiefly by greater boldness, vivacity, by a richer profusion of metaphor, by more daring and strikingly colored hyperbole. But Hebrew poetry, as Oriental in general, is widely divergent in structure or form from that to which the European or American mind is accustomed. It rarely tends to rime or alliteration. Its meters are not quantitative nor strictly accentual. Above all, in common with other Semitic tongues, it has as its outstanding characteristic, parallelism.

As rime is essentially a balancing of sounds, so parallelism may be described as a balancing of thoughts. This may be by similarity, contrast, or simply extension. The variety possible in this system is almost infinite, far greater indeed than that of rime or rhythm in Western poetry. As in the latter riming words mark the end of a line, so the line in Hebrew verse is determined by the *termini* of the thought. And as with rime there goes a certain measurement of lines in Western poetry, so in Hebrew the balanced lines may not vary greatly from each other in length. Of course, frequently a thought but elliptically indicated by a few syllables in Hebrew, may require many words for its expression in English.

As the lines are related to each other within a verse by

parallelism, so the strophes themselves are often interconnected by a higher echo of the same. This sometimes eventuates into a regular pendulum movement of thought cadences. All this is of invaluable assistance in determining the sense and sometimes even the text-reading in obscure passages. For, a careful student will note how the lines or strophes balance each other, and thus the difficult portions are frequently explained in parallel clearer lines or strophes.

Although intentional rime, assonance, or alliteration are practically absent from Hebrew poetry,[1] nevertheless the rhythmical sequence of thought is generally also reflected in a rhythmical pulsation of sounds in the language. But the principles of this rhythm (if ever conscious in the writers) have not yet been certainly determined, although many scholars have made various essays. At any rate, it is now widely admitted that in Hebrew verse the metrical balance of the connected lines in a distich or stanza is not due to an exact equality or other mathematical relationship of the number of syllables. It is determined rather by the number of stresses, accent-beats, or cadences.[2]

Despite the fact that neither the Greek translators of the Sacred Scriptures nor their Latin successors took any particular pains to give a *poetic* rendering of the Hebrew originals, nevertheless the characteristic of parallelism is markedly preserved in the Greek and Latin prose translations. This Oriental note is one reason for the natural charm felt by most readers of the poetical Books of the Bible. And, although found in similar productions of ancient Sumer, Akkad, and Babylonia, still amongst the Jews did the literary characteristic of parallelism reach its most perfect development. It seems quite inimitable by Western minds in original composition.

---

[1] But there are cases like that of Is. 28: 1-10 (see No. 268 above).

[2] In a translation given below (No. 322) may be seen an attempt to reproduce in English an original meter of three—two stress-accents. The hemistichs here and elsewhere printed on separate lines with indentation because of space limitations, should of course be written in full across the page, with something like a cesural pause indication between the parts.

The Masoretic editors gave their peculiarly poetic pointing to only three Books: Job, Psalms, and Proverbs.[3] But it is undeniable that other Books, such as Canticles and many of the Prophets, as well as scattered sections elsewhere in the Old Testament, are written in verse. Hence the grouping here made of Job, Psalms, and Canticles, is not to be considered comprehensive but rather as made on the basis of more striking exemplification of poetical form and content.

Art. 1: THE BOOK OF JOB

Texts: Job 1-4; 11-12; 18-19; 26-28; 32; 38; 40-42.

306. Content and Literary Form.—The solution of the most ancient and basic difficulty that has at all times intrigued the mind of man, is the object of the Book of Job. It is a study of the problem of evil, a disquisition on the reason of suffering, an attempt to solve the riddles of sin, pain, and punishment. And yet, in the language of Chesterton, "if the word pessimist means anything at all, then emphatically Job is not a pessimist. . . . Job does not in any sense look on life in a gloomy way. If wishing to be happy, and being quite ready to be happy, constitute an optimist, Job is an optimist. He is a perplexed optimist; he is an exasperated optimist; he is an outraged and insulted optimist. He wishes the universe to justify itself, not because he wishes it to be caught out, but because he really wishes it to be justified. He is anxious to be convinced, that is, he thinks God could convince him. . . . He shakes the pillars of the world and strikes insanely at the heavens; he lashes the stars: but it is not to silence them; it is to make them speak."[4]

"Here in this Book the question is really asked whether God invariably punishes vice with terrestrial punishment, and rewards virtue with terrestrial prosperity. If the Jews had answered that question wrongly they might have lost all their after influence in

[3] That in English versions of the Sacred Scriptures the verse portions were typographically distinguished from the plain prose, is a highly desirable improvement, already found in several Continental editions.

[4] Quotations from G. K. Chesterton's introduction to an edition of the Book of Job by Palmer and Hayward (London).

human history. They might have sunk even down to the level of
modern well educated society. . . . If prosperity is regarded as
the reward of virtue, it will be regarded as the symptom of virtue.
Men will leave off the heavy task of making good men successful.
They will adopt the easier task of making successful men good.
. . . The Book of Job is chiefly remarkable . . . for the fact that
it does not end in a way that is conventionally satisfactory.   Job
is not told that his misfortunes were due to his sins or a part of
any plan for his improvement.   But in the prologue we see Job tor-
mented, not because he was the worst of men, but because he was
the best.   Here is the very darkest and strangest of paradoxes: and
it is by all human testimony the most reassuring.   I need not suggest what a high and strange history awaited this paradox of the
best man in the worst fortune.   I need not say that in the freest
and most philosophical sense there is one Old Testament figure who
is truly a type: or say what is prefigured in the wounds of Job''.

307. Whilst not falling strictly under the classical form,
the Book of Job nevertheless approaches the drama, being for
the most part a progressive series of discourses exchanged in
debate style between Job and the Friends.   The background
is supplied by a prose prologue of patriarchal simplicity (Job
1-2) wherein also the action is initiated by the allegorical
dialogue between God and Satan.   A brief epilogue (Job 42),
likewise in prose, gives the *dénouement,* and adds historical
notes of the chief actor, besides satisfying the conventional
taste of the author's contemporaries.   It is true, the prime
problem treated is not solved; the mystery of the presence of
evil in God's creation still remains a mystery.   But the reason
for this is indicated: man's mind can not grasp the complete
nature of God, and hence can not plumb the deepest abysses
of His providential plans.   But it is also indicated that man
has evidence sufficient even in the plane of nature's course
and arrangement, to justify his placing utter trust in the
Divinity, no matter what vicissitudes may befall, since the
Almighty easily controls all powers of nature, "playing in the
world" (Prov. 8:31).   This trust in God is the practical
conclusion.

308. Language and Plan.—The Hebrew of the Book of
Job is most difficult.   This may possibly be due to intentional
archaism; it is certainly not diminished by frequent sententious expressions incorporating obscure folk-phrases:

"I hold my life in my teeth" (Job 13:14), meaning: to be at the point of death;[5] "Contempt to him who suffereth misfortune; a kick to those who have lost their footing!" (Job 12:4a-5); "As a man inviting friends to a portion, whilst his children are weeping out their eyes" (Job 17:5).

Language and thought, in the primeval sweep and surge of their gigantic power and brilliance bespeak the work of perhaps the greatest literary genius of all times. The style could scarcely be called didactic, since the profound argumentation of the discourses is expressed in a broad, unhesitating flow of varied and colorful metaphor with ever and anon rhapsodic outbursts of hot lyric passion or ecstaticly clear contemplations of God's marvels in the universe. With all its mixture of epic, lyric, didactic, and dramatic elements, the Book of Job is a unified and finished work of art, woven of fresh, picturesque speech, pulsating with mighty human feeling, subdued nevertheless by a divinely majestic dignity, rounded to perfection on every side.

309. The structure of Job is symmetrical, balanced. First of all, by the incidents related in the prologue, and by the plot laid in heaven in the altercation between God and Satan, the drama is set in motion and its general purport made clear to the audience. At the outset the author's whole thesis is, as it were, preproved by this glimpse behind the earthly scenes, showing evil and suffering to be by God's free permission, and not necessarily conjoined to moral guilt. The action thereupon shifts to earth and is focused in a close-up of Job and the Three Friends, who occupy the stage for the main part of the drama.

"These people of the East have adopted a stationary life; absorbed in higher thoughts, they are content to sit still and let the world go by, as swift posts between great empires hurry past them, or the caravans of Tema stay a night in their neighborhood, passing to and from the desert. In their thoughts they are familiar with the whole range of the larger world. They speak of kings and counsellors, and judges and priests; of solitary sepulchral piles where the great lie with their buried gold; Egypt, under the name Rahab, is a byword with them. They have marked the lessons of nations in their rise and fall. They know of cities, the abode of the prosperous wicked, who cover their faces with fatness and have collops of

---

[5] Arabic parallel: "He has his life between his jaws".

fat on their flanks; the place also of prisons, slaves, and taskmasters. They talk familiarly of the gold of Ophir and the topaz of Ethiopia; and can picture every detail of the miner's venture into the earth. War they know: the casting up of military roads and encampments, the warrior with his thick bosses of bucklers, his iron weapon and bow of brass. . . . They know also the robber bands whose god is their strong right hand, breaking upon the prosperous out of their lairs in ruined and desolate cities. Their knowledge extends even to the outcasts of mankind, savages gaunt with want and famine, gnawing the dry ground in the gloom of wasteness and desolation. Of all these extremes they are content only to know; they have themselves attained the golden mean of restful serenity, as far from the glitter of life as from its stains." [6]

The Friends and Elihu are subordinate figures, serving in their divers mentalities as fit foils for the great central tragedian, Job. Their business is to argue the positions which the latter aims to refute.[7] Thus the Three Friends particularly are exponents of hidebound conservatism, holding tenaciously to a purely punitive theory of suffering, each supporting his case in his characteristic manner, and all united in imputing sinful guilt to Job. Eliphaz, an ancient graybeard, is stately and formal, with perhaps a wider range of thought than the others, as befitted a wise Themanite. Baldad is less original, more brusque and blunt, blustering rapidly to practical conclusions. Sophar, younger than the other two, and representing the narrow, prejudiced type, is at times almost violent in his invective. All three bring their arguments for the old material theory of retributive justice consummated on earth. Job, although shaken time and again, in his retorts shows the inadequacy of their explanations, and stubbornly persists in his protestations of innocence.

Job's own position, it may be noted, varies in the progress of the drama. Previous to its opening he was perfect in his resignation (Job 2:10). But, when on the arrival of the Friends he first removed his eyes from God to consider his own misery, he began to fall short, to grow impatient, and to wish for death (Job 3). Next he complains that God seems to put justice and wickedness on the same footing of helpless-

---

[6] Moulton, in Introduction to * Modern Readers' Bible, p. 8.
[7] Hence it follows that many opinions advanced in the Book of Job, especially by the Friends, are not thereby to be taken as having divine approval.

ness before Him. Against Eliphaz he maintains, not indeed that he is entirely sinless, but that his sins are disproportioned to this total ruin (Job 6-7). Next he appeals to God against his oppressing friends (Job 10, 16). Growing exasperated at their insistence that he is guilty, he warns them that they in turn lay themselves open to punishment, according to their own theory (Job 27). Finally he takes a solemn oath of clearance, and adjures God Himself to vindicate his right-eousness. And in this process of reasoning and of wrestling with difficulties, although he falls into faults for which he is later reproved, nevertheless Job gradually rises and brings himself and his audience to a broader conception of God and of His rule of the world. The unfolding of the progress going on in the mind of Job constitutes the main action of the drama.

310. Elihu Section.—The entrance of the unannounced person of Elihu, when the Friends apparently have been silenced and Job himself is exhausted, seems anomalous, until one reflects that in the Friends only antiquity and hoary tradition have had their say. There still remains to be heard in the matter of the mystery of evil and suffering the newest theory of the contemporary generation, although it be more loquacious than thoughtful, and even inclined to irreverent scoffing at antiquity. Perhaps in the turgid mass of impetu-ous Elihu's youthful verbosity may be found some new prin-ciples which, although not all-sufficient, yet will throw their light farther into the fathomless abyss of an age-old human mystery. "Ex ore infantium . . ." And such indeed seems to have been the plan of the Book's author.

Elihu starts out with a long-winded introduction (Job 32). He is as full of words as a skin is of fermenting wine (Job 32:19). In youthful haste and carelessness he wanders from the point now and then; with youthful irreverence he neglects conventional forms of politeness, challenging directly his opponents in the debate; and with youthful conceit and cocksureness he upbraids almost equally both Job and the Friends. But his rambling discourse, whilst exaggerated in some of its claims, becomes a supplementary confutation of the Friends and in the end approaches closely to Job's own final position.

Elihu really offers a new solution: a *Läuterungstheorie,* according to which the purpose of man's suffering is not necessarily punitive; it may be purification. Temporal evils are not signs of utter rejection; they may be indications of God's love, insofar as they warn a sinner to repentance. Towards the end Elihu admits that, in any case, God is all-wise and all-powerful, and therefore man need not presume full comprehension of His plans. When Elihu's verbose eloquence is finally drowned by the bursting of the thunderstorm whose gradual approach he himself had already noted during his speech,[8] there is no chance for either Job or the Friends to reply. But it is to be noted that in the sequel God does not censure the position of Elihu, as he does that of the Friends (Job 42: 7).

311. The Divine Intervention.—A climax of unearthly literary beauty is reached by the simplest means in God's discourse, or the Divine Intervention Section (Job 38-41). The storm which, during Elihu's harangue, had been indicated as brewing on the horizon and then approaching with chilly blasts, now is represented as bursting in majestic fury over the heads of the cowering disputants. And out of the murk amid rolling peals of thunder flash the lightning-like, swift, direct, and iterated interrogations of God:

> "Hast thou ever given orders to the morn?
>   or shown the dawn of day its place?—
> When it lays hold of the wings of earth
>   and shakes from the sky the gleaming stars,
> Turning it red as sealing wax,
>   and making it stand robed in a garment?
>
> *   *   *
>
> Canst thou tie the girdle of the Pleiades?
>   or loose the belt of Orion?
> Canst thou lead forth in their season the constellations?
>   or guide the Bear with her cubs?
> Knowest thou the laws of the heavens?
>   and canst thou direct their rule over earth?"

8 See No. 310 below.

To respond to Job's adjuring challenge in the Oath of Clearance would seem to be impossible without a lowering of God. For, His intervention has really been called for presumptuously.

> "Wouldst thou consider void My judgment?
>   or condemn Me only that thou mayest seem justified?"
> (Job 40: 8)

But marvelously does the inspired writer avoid the difficulty. Not one word does God utter of His providential dispositions in regard to Job (already known to the audience); He does not even mention the allegorical wager with Satan; He disdains to touch upon the speculative questions so broadly broached in the previous discussions. But, by a series of apparently simple questions He manifests Himself as All-wise and as the Supreme Ruler, whilst man, like a child, is put in his place.

With the delicate sarcasm of the queries regarding the constitution of the world and the government of the universe, God takes up the thread of the discussion where Job and Elihu had left off. He enunciates by insinuation the principle that absolute wisdom is to be found in the Divinity alone, and that man, because of his finite intellect, can never fully grasp the mystery of God's rule. Job, dumbfounded, realizes his presumption and the unreasonableness of his challenging complaint: in humble submission he acknowledges his fault.

In the sequel to the Divine Intervention it becomes clear that no one of the parties to this typical Oriental disputation was entirely right in his contention. Theoretically the problem of evil and the mystery of suffering remains as before. But Job's original and final practical positions in the face of it, are confirmed as best. Moreover, the Divine Intervention has widened the view of the question still more, by showing that the Good and the Sublime—which men admire and love—are equally as inexplicable as the Evil, which they hate and fear. It intimates also that behind all the apparent *Wilkür* and chance of the universe is ever to be glimpsed, at least darkly as seen through the glass of mortal mind, a great Law of fitness, justice, and order.

312. Outline of Composition.—The symmetrical arrangement of Job may be seen at a glance from the following schematic outline. It is to be borne in mind, however, that in several parts, especially from chapter 28 on, the actual original arrangement of the text is still a matter of considerable discussion.[9] One may note, moreover, that in the Third Cycle of the speeches, the monotonously regular triple sequence of the actors is skillfully tapered off. Baldad closes very briefly as if he had exhausted argument. And Sophar (whose turn would normally come next) does not even open his mouth, as if he had been confuted, or realized the futility of further discussion.[10] The literary balance is nevertheless preserved, as Job's own speech is twice extended in a final apostrophe.

FIRST SCENE
(Job 1-3)
Prologue
Historical Introduction: the Altercation in Heaven: Job's Affliction: the Arrival of the Friends: Job's Complaint

SECOND SCENE
(4-31)
The Disputation between Job and the Friends

Cycle I	Cycle II	Cycle III
1: Eliphaz	1: Eliphaz	1: Eliphaz
Job	Job	Job
2: Baldad	2: Baldad	2: Baldad
Job	Job	Job (26: 1-14)
3: Sophar	3: Sophar	3: Job's Oath of
Job	Job	Clearing

[9] An excellent analysis of chapters 25-28 of Job may be seen in *Revue Biblique* for April, 1924 (pp. 186-200), by M. A. Régnier.

[10] The text of the Greek version is considerably shorter than that of the Hebrew original. There seems to have been deliberate editorial excision or shortening in order better to accommodate the Book better to the Hellenic mind and style. St. Jerome, in the *Preface* to his second Latin version, made from the Hebrew, remarks: "If you take away the portions marked with asterisks (= the plus of the Hebrew over the Greek) you will cut away the larger part of the Book—I am speaking only of the text the Greeks have. But as to that which the Latins have, previous to the publication of my recent translation, with *obeli* and asterisks, practically seven or eight hundred verses were wanting. . . . This (namely the present Vulgate) translation follows no one ancient interpreter, but you will find in it now the very words, now the sense, of either the Hebrew or the Arabic, or sometimes even of the Syriac. For, even the Hebrews grant that there is an indirectness and elusiveness about the Book.''

THIRD SCENE
(32-37)
The Elihu Section
Introduction (32:-33:11); First Argumentation (34-35);
Second Argumentation

FOURTH SCENE
(38-41)
The Divine Intervention
Divers Queries from Nature: the Behemoth: the Leviathan

FIFTH SCENE
(42)
Epilogue
Sequel of the Drama   Historical Conclusion

313. Historicity and Date.—As in every drama, the figures of the Book of Job are of course but puppets expressing the thoughts of the author. The elaborate artificial language and arrangement show this most clearly. Nevertheless, that the chief character at least is not purely fictitious, but based, together with the main vicissitudes, upon historical fact, is undeniable. The suffering Job is spoken of as a real personage in Ez. 14:14, 20; Tob. 2:12; James 5:1.[11] He is evidently not a Jew. He is not recorded as being acquainted with any of the vicissitudes of Jewish history subsequent to Abraham, although he knows of the Creation, the fall of man, the giants, the deluge, and Sodom's destruction. The *qesitah* of Job 42:11 is mentioned elsewhere only in Gen. 33:19 and Josue 24:32, and seems to denote the very ancient unminted money shaped to represent a sheep.

To whom belongs the glory of the authorship of Job is quite unknown. Old Jewish tradition held that Moses composed the Book whilst in Arabia with his father-in-law Jethro.

---

[11] A Greek addition to Job 42:17 makes Job a descendant of Esau, and identifies him with the Jobab of Gen. 36:33. The Talmudists in one place (*Baba bathra*, f. 15) deny the historical character of Job; elsewhere they make him a contemporary of Moses.

In new Tell-el-Amarna tablets is mentioned a certain Aiab, kinglet of Bihilim (probably the ancient Pella). He writes of having received a letter from the Pharao. He seems to have been entrusted with the duty of conducting to the North the caravans sent out for trading by Egypt's ruler. During an absence from home a ''prince of Ha-zu-ra'' seized three towns of his. See *Revue biblique*, Jan., 1924, pp. 9-10.

The conjecture of Christian commentators, who note that the language belongs to the golden age of Hebrew, runs in favor of Solomon's time or shortly thereafter. Parallels to the Book of Proverbs are pointed out, especially the Logos idea: thus Job 28 and 15:7 may be compared with Prov. 8:22-31. The rather rare Aramaisms can no longer be urged for a very late origin, as it is now established that, through commerce and war, Aramaic was widely known at a much earlier period than has hitherto been assumed. Whoever the author was, and at whatever time he lived, he was familiar with the environment of a desert sheik's life: desert scenery (Job 4:10-11; 6:5; 8:10-11; 9:26, etc.); Bedawin tribes (Job 24:2-13; 30:1-8); desert animals (Job 28:39; 42:5); the description of the working of the mines (Job 28:1-11). But he is also acquainted with the life of the cities (Job 29:7; 24:12; 31:21), and he has seen the ships of the sea (Job 9:26). The oppression of workmen by taskmasters, and the Egyptian custom of burying a wealthy man's gold with his body, are also alluded to.

314. Authenticity of Elihu Section.—The authenticity of the Elihu Section (Job 32-37) is generally denied by divisive critics. Budde and Cornill, however, defend it. Difficulties pointed out are: (a) the appearance of Elihu is unprovided for in the prologue, nor is he considered in the epilogue, nor elsewhere outside his own cycle of speeches; (b) according to Kautzsch, there are 31 Aramaisms traceable in this section— an abnormally large number in comparison to the 53 found in all the rest of Job; (c) the Divine Intervention (Job 38) connects directly with Job's last speech (Job 31).

In explanation the following considerations offer themselves. The essentially dramatic character of the Book is to be kept in mind—and not all the characters of a play appear on the stage in the first scene. Elihu may be pictured as a young man of Job's own clan, who with other onlookers stood back of the circle of venerable disputants gathered about the refuse-heap upon which sat the stricken central figure. Only the deference due guests and seniors has restrained his eager tongue. He is a gawky youth, an unimportant villager: as part of the normal environment he is taken for granted and not introduced. He has no right to interrupt illustrious strangers and his own headman. After the outburst of his speech he steps back again unnoticed into the ranks of the bystanders. And thus is emphasized the disdain with which his new liberal theories are received by the sages of his time.

Again, the author of Job cleverly indicates the character of his puppets in their style of speech. Very properly then would he have Elihu use "up-to-date" and current vulgar terms—and Aramaisms are marks of modernity in Hebrew—rather than have such appear frequently on the lips of the more sedate and solemn actors of his play. Lastly, properly does God's sarcastic discourse refer directly back to Job's closing speech, wherein the latter had formally adjured the Divine Intervention. Elihu had not called for a theophany. But, the introductory "stage-directions" of God's discourse show that the Elihu Section always immediately preceded. For, that storm which is represented as bursting in Job 38:1 (admittedly original and authentic) has in the Elihu section been carefully noted as gathering on the horizon (Job 36: 27-30), as muttering preliminary distant peals of thunder (Job 37:1-9), as finally enveloping the group of speakers with murk of mist and dust so that "now they see not the light" and as drowning their voices with the terrific din of its bursting noise (Job 37:19-22). Those who would tear out the Elihu Section, must excise also the introductory verses of the Divine Intervention (Job 38:1; 40:1).

Art. 2: THE PSALMS

Texts: Ps. 2; 40; 67; 92; 126-127; 147

315. Spirit and Themes.—The Book of Psalms forms the counterpart of the Thora and the Prophets. In the latter God speaks to His people; in the Psalms, Israel—the original and the antitypical—speaks to its God. Sumerians and Babylonians and Egyptians had poems that admired and described the Divine: but songs giving the reaction of man's heart to the supernatural, Psalms, belong to the Hebrews alone.

The basic note of the Psalter is a desire of oneness with God, of conformity to His decreed order of the universe. The various states of the human soul relative to this oneness with the Divine afford the most diversified themes for the Psalms. The highest of these is, of course, the state of mystical union, to which Ps. 44: *Eructavit cor meum,* perhaps corresponds. To this may be joined a few hymns contemplating the attributes and functions of God. At the opposite pole, corresponding to various phases of the actual state of disunion with God by sin or other evil, are the penitential and imprecatory Psalms. The penitential Psalms correspond more closely with the lack of harmony through personal delinquency; they express horror at the realization of deliberate separation from God, contrition for guilt, desire of amendment. In the imprecatory Psalms the singer is ranged on the side of God and identifies the latter's cause with his own: most emphatically therefore can he deprecate and denounce all mundane discord with God's plans. Those who attack the psalmist, or those who oppress the Chosen People of old, are but types of those who persecuted the Chosen One of God whilst He was upon earth in the flesh, figures of all the powers of evil opposed to God's spiritual Kingdom and harassing Christ's mystical Body, the Church, in all ages. Beside these Psalms may be placed other chants celebrating the triumphs of God and good over evil, either as recorded in history or as promised for the future.

316. The messianic Psalms, picturing the God-man and His redemptive function, show the means by which the gap made between the Divinity and the world by sin, is eventually closed and the original oneness of man with God is reëstablished. Moreover, it is to be noted that, even in Psalms not strictly to be termed messianic, the speaker or man placed face to face with God is frequently personified as the ideal Servant of Yahweh, the Messias, as the destined representative mankind before its heavenly Father. Thus the psalmist often speaks in the name of Christ, or at least in terms that may readily be placed in the Saviour's mouth.

The development of these themes in the Psalms is very rarely abstract; rather it is usually conjoined to concrete incidents of personal life or of history. The most common concretization is the true Israelite's reverence and love for the Law, the Thora, as the embodiment of the Divine Will with which man's will strives ever to be at one. Nevertheless, even the most personal Psalms by sublimation are generalized from the individual to mankind. The psalmist speaks ever not only in his own name but in the name of all humanity. This universality of conception is all the more striking since the Hebrew language itself only stubbornly admits of expressing generalizations or abstract ideas. But here the genius of the author overcomes marvelously the handicaps of his material. And thus, whilst their concreteness gives most interesting vivacity and color, the universality of the Psalms, embracing the most basic facts and world-wide principles, sounding the chords of every sentiment of the human heart, makes them as effective in expressing man's aspirations and fears, desires and dreads, in the ultimate cycle of the world's existence as in the days of their composition.

317. Collection and Text.—The Book of Psalms is frequently called the Psalter of David, because that "sweet singer of Israel" (II Kings 23 : 1) is the author of the greater part of its content,—from seventy-three to eighty-six Psalms, according to various opinions, being traceable to him. Many of the Psalms, however, are anonymous; others are ascribed to various authors, such as Moses, Solomon, Asaph, Eman, Ethan, and the prophet Jeremias.

The Psalter as now constituted is in fact Israel's liturgical hymnal. Possibly in imitation of the Pentateuch, it is at present divided into five books: I = Ps. 1-40; II = Ps. 41-71; II = Ps. 72-88; IV = Ps. 89-105; V = Ps. 106-150. This and other features indicate that the Psalter was not collected by a single editor who brought together a number of individual hymns scattered among the people, but rather that it grew gradually and for the most part by the putting

together of small preëxisting collections of poems.   Thus
Ps. 13 of Book I is to be seen again with slight modifications
as Ps. 52 in Book II.   Similarly Ps. 39:14 *ss* reappears as
Ps. 69 in Book II.   And Ps. 107 of Book V is only a combination of Ps. 56:8-12 and Ps. 59:7-14 in Book II.   Moreover,
the variations in the use of the Divine names, *Yahweh* and
Elohim manifest the hands of divers redactors editing groups
of Psalms.   The collector of Book II seems to have had strong
prejudice against using *Yahweh,* employing instead reduplications of *Elohim* in a manner unparalleled elsewhere in the
Old Testament.   On the other hand in Book IV only *Yahweh*
occurs, and Book V also has *Yahweh* generally.   Psalms having *Yahweh* in Book I, have this term changed to *Elohim*
when they reappear in Book II.   The gradual growth of the
Psalter from preëxisting smaller collections is further witnessed by the deliminability of smaller groups yet, such as
the Asaphite Psalms (Ps. 49; 72-82), the "sons of Core"
collection (Ps. 41-48; 83-88), the *maskil* Psalms (Ps. 51-
54), the Hallel groups (Ps. 104-106; 110-118; 134-135,
145-150).   But many poems of the Psalter are also outside
the obvious groups, and seem to have been incorporated
singly by editors in their collections.

318. How the text of the Hebrew Psalter fared in its
transmission through various editorial hands may be seen
from the double recensions of the same Psalms.[12]   Thus the
poem which appears as Ps. 17 is found also in II Kings 22,
"and it can readily be seen by comparing the two texts, that
the primitive text . . . has suffered so much corruption that
it can not be completely recovered".   Through their constant liturgical and popular use the Psalms were more liable
to textual changes and additions than other parts of the
Hebrew Bible.   Directors of the Temple choirs would put in
their annotations, or would modify an older hymn to suit

---

[12] Incidentally these divergent, though both admittedly inspired recensions, seem to militate against the view that the very words also of
the Sacred Scripture are the direct product of inspiration, whilst in
these same cases true inspiration for the different recensions is well
safeguarded on the theory that inspiration extends primarily to the
propositions or the substance of the text.

later circumstances. Thus Ps. 50: *Miserere,* undoubtedly
Davidic, is adapted to the use of the Exiles by the addition
of the closing verses, 20-21, which in their hope of a restoration of the Temple sacrifices, scarcely seem to harmonize with
the spiritual sentiments just expressed in verses 18-19.

319. Time of Composition.—The period during which the
poems collected in the Psalter were composed extended over
at least six or seven centuries, from the time of David to
some date after the return from the Exile (538 B.C.). The
doxologies at the close of the Books are generally considered
to be notes added by the editors to mark the end of their
respective collections. Now, the doxology at the close of Book
IV (Ps. 105:48) is quoted in I Par. 16:36. Hence it would
seem that already about 300 B.C. the Psalm collections existed
practically in their present form.

It is true that the Psalms only vaguely show linguistic
features by which the earlier ones might be distinguished
from the later. Redactors would naturally have smoothed
out such irregularities. Even Psalms embodying Aramaic
forms and words can not thereby alone be marked as late.
For, such peculiarities may be due to editorial hands, and
moreover what modern scholars regard as later forms or
borrowings from the Aramaic, "may be really echoes of
popular speech, and very ancient, appearing to be modern
only because we know so little of the popular speech of Israel
in any period." [13]

It was quite a fad with divisive critics to assign many Psalms
to the Machabean age (167-63 B.C.). Examination of the cases
adduced, however, shows that such judgments are not backed up by
objective evidence, or that certain elements of evidence are exaggerated whilst others are neglected. Haupt,[14] for example, makes
Ps. 67: *Exurgat Deus* (admittedly one of the most difficult of the
whole Psalter) a chant composed to celebrate the return of Judas
Machabeus in triumph from his victorious sally into the East Jordan
region in 165 B.C. (I Mac. 5:54-65). He does not realize that the
content of the Psalm will fit equally well if not better with some

[13] Boylan, *The Psalms,* p. xvii (Herder, 1920). Much of the matter
here embodied has been borrowed from this work, which is one of the
best and most accessible of modern books on this topic.

[14] Paul Haupt, in *American Journal of Semitic Languages and Literatures,* April, 1907, pp. 221-225 (University of Chicago Press).

Davidic expedition,—say, that against the Syrians and the Ammonites (II Kings 10-12; I Par. 19-20). Above all, the fact escapes Haupt's attention that in Machabean times Israel was composed of the tribes of Juda and Benjamin alone,—whilst Ps. 67: 28 specifically associates "principes Zabulon, principes Nephtali" with the former in the triumphal cortège, which is clearly an indication of pre-Solomonic origin.

320. Vulgate Version of the Psalms.—The Latin version of the Psalms in most common use is not from the Hebrew, and is not a translation of St. Jerome's. In 383, at the request of Pope Damasus, St. Jerome made a revision of the Old Latin Psalter (itself a translation of the Septuagint version) to bring it into better conformity with the then current Greek text. This revision was the original *Psalterium Romanum.* A second revision of the Old Latin Psalter made by the same saint in 392 on the basis of the Hexaplaric Septuagint is called the *Psalterium Gallicanum,* because of being first adopted in the Church of Gaul. This edition, as St. Jerome himself testifies, again quickly became corrupted with the old errors. Finally, about 393, St. Jerome made a fresh Latin version of the Psalms directly from the Hebrew text, his *Psalterium iuxta Hebræos.* Although superior in many respects to the other editions, this version was never officially adopted in the Church,[15] because of the tenacity with which the popular mind clung to the old text, so familiar to it through the liturgy.

The text at present read in the Vulgate and in the Breviary [16] is that of the *Psalterium Gallicanum.* Hence it is a literal translation in the idiom of post-classic or Vulgar Latin, of a Greek Psalter which itself was an almost verbally literal version of the Hebrew Psalms, with all consequent shortcomings.

Thus peculiarities of the Vulgate Psalter may be traced to the Hebrew originals, the Greek translation, and to the character of the

[15] Report has it that with the publication of restoration of the Hieronymian translation texts (now being made by the Benedictine commission at Rome), St. Jerome's *Psalterium iuxta Hebræos* may be put into the Vulgate.

[16] The invitatory Ps. 94 in the Breviary is, however, from the *Psalterium Romanum;* its Gallican form may be read in the third nocturne of the Epiphany matins.

Vulgar Latin idiom itself. From the Hebrew many Semitisms have come over. Thus the feminine is sometimes used for the neuter: "Unam petii a Domino et hanc requiram" (Ps. 26:4); "Haec facta est mihi" (Ps. 118:56; 108:27). The comparative is expressed by *a* and *ex* with the ablative: "Mirabilis facta est scientia tua ex me" (Ps. 138:6; 92:3, 4). In oaths *si* is used in the sense of 'surely not', and *si non* in the sense of 'surely'—probably because of an implied imprecation: 'May such and such happen to me if (or, if not) . . .': "Si introibunt in requiem meam" (Ps. 94:11; 88:36). Abstract nouns in the genitive are frequently used as adjectives: "virga directionis" = just scepter (Ps. 44:7); "sacrificium iustitiæ" = a due sacrifice (Ps. 4:6; 77:54).

Traceable primarily to the Greek translators is the frequent defective reproduction of Hebrew verbal forms. The only two tenses of Hebrew, the perfect and imperfect, do not express so much the time at which the action takes place, as the degree of completeness of that action. The time element has generally to be determined by the context. Hence in such complicated poetical texts as the Psalms, with their subtle *nuances* of emotional moods, the translators seem to have worked mechanically, usually making the Greek aorist represent the Hebrew perfect, and the Greek future the Hebrew imperfect. This of course was slavishly reproduced in the Old Latin. Hence tenses are thrown together in a confusing manner in the same passage (Ps. 6:7). Thus in Ps. 118:97 *dilexi* = *diligo;* in Ps. 8:4 *videbo* = *video*, etc.

Finally, Vulgar Latin generally had a tendency to set up new word-formations with sonorous endings, to form new verbs from nouns and adjectives, to employ new compounds. Where classical Latin would use simple verbs, the Vulgar age used compound: *abire* for *ire* (Ps. 1:1); *retribuere* for *tribuere* (Ps. 118:17). Deponents are used as passives: *consolari* (Ps. 76:3 = permit oneself to be comforted). Transitive verbs are used intransitively, and contrariwise: *emigrare*=*expellere* (Ps. 51:7); *convertere* = *retroire* (Ps. 9:4). *Contra* = *coram* (Ps. 50:5); *nimis* = *valde* (Ps. 111:1); *paulo minus* = *propemodum* (Ps. 93:17), etc., etc.[17]

321. Psalm Titles.—With the exception of a small number (34 in the Hebrew; 20 in the Vulgate) the Psalms have each prefixed a superscription or title, indicating either the author, the historic occasion of composition, the time or tune of the chant, or some other liturgical notation. Whilst not part of the inspired text, these titles are most valuable as recording ancient traditions concerning their respective Psalms, and their authenticity for the most part is not lightly

---

[17] Vigouroux, in the *Manuel biblique*, II, pp. 348-355, and also in vol. IV of the *Bible polyglotte* has given a list of both difficult Latin words and of obscure expressions in the titles, of the Vulgate Psalms.

to be called into question.[18]   The very fact that not all the
Psalms have titles prefixed, makes for a presumption in favor
of those on hand, by indicating critical discrimination on the
part of the annotators.   Again, their very diversity, brevity,
and obscurity are guaranties of high antiquity.   Many of
them were already unintelligible to the Septuagint translators; nevertheless these dared not change their enigmatic
phrasing.

Many of the most obscure phrases in the titles seem to be
technical musical or liturgical terms.   Thus *in finem* (Ps. 4:
1, etc.) is now generally taken to be equivalent to 'for the
choir director' (I Par. 15:21).   Sometimes the names seem
to indicate the instruments to be used or the melodies to be
followed when the respective Psalms were chanted.   Thus
in Ps. 44:1 *pro iis qui commutabuntur* might be read 'to the
tune of The Lilies'; *pro arcanis* and *pro occultis* (Ps. 45:1;
9:1) is perhaps to be taken as 'for the virgins', *i.e.*, for
soprano or high voices, perhaps of boys' choir.

322. Translation and Commentary of Psalm 22.—This
Psalm is here chosen for its combined brevity and beauty
as the base of a sample exegetic study.[19]   It is a delicately
wrought cameo of inspired poetry, whose color tones though
few and simple are rich and warm.   Rhetorically it is made
up of two extended metaphors taken from ordinary scenes
of Semitic life: that of the solicitous shepherd tending his
flock (strophes I-III); and that of a generous host giving
hospitality to a fugitive stranger (strophe IV).   It climaxes
to fervent apostrophe (strophe V), and ends with a fitly
grateful reflexive conclusion.   Metrically the Psalm is built
up of half-line couplets, each pair forming a strophe.   Each
couplet has three rhythmical stresses or beats in the first half-
line, and two in the second (as Ps. 109 and Jonas 2:2-10).
The parallelism is chiefly synthetic, dividing the composition
into rhythmically and logically complementary portions, al-

[18] See Replies II and III in Decision of the Biblical Commission
given below.   Of course, a few of these inscriptions have been proved
inaccurate, and have been rejected.

[19] Reproduced from the author's article in *Ecclesiastical Review* of
July, 1916, pp. 1-10, with permission of the latter's publishers.

though between the couplets themselves one can hear also the finer thought-cadences of synonymic parallelism like faint musical overtones.

A HARP-SONG BY DAVID

I The Eternal being my shepherd, I shall not want,
　　for in lush-grassed pastures He will make me lie down;
Beside tranquil waters will He bring me;
　　He will refresh my soul.

II Along level pathways will He lead me,
　　according to His name.
Yea, though I enter a death gloomy valley,
　　no harm need I fear!

III　　　　　　*　　　*　　　*
　　For Thou art with me:
Thy staff, Thy shepherd's crook,
　　will make me feel secure.

IV Thou hast spread a table before me
　　to spite my harassers;
Thou hast perfumed my head with ointment,
　　my goblet overfloweth ever.

V Truly Thy good things and favors pursue me
　　all the days of my life!—
So Yahweh's House shall be my home
　　for many a day!

The object of the Psalm is to acknowledge and praise the care and generosity of Divine Providence toward the psalmist, or toward mankind in general. Although one might see in v. 5a an allusion to the incidents related in I Kings 25:25, or II Kings 16:1; 17:27, yet the whole tone of the Psalm seems to point to a spontaneous outpouring of David's soul in his more reminiscent old age, at some time after the ark had been brought into the "City of David",[20] when his people were in peace and plenty.

[20] *Beth Yahweh* in verse 6 does not necessarily mean the Temple, but is also used to designate the Tabernacle or sacred tent of the Exodus and early sojourn in the Promised Land (Exod. 23:19; Josue 6:24; I Kings 1:7, in which last place the Vulgate also has "templum Domini"). In the *qeri* is given *sok*, which is properly "wattled hut".

Strophe I: "The Eternal" is a paraphrase probably coming nearest to conveying the idea at the root of *Yahweh,* the proper name of God as the Divinity of the Hebrews.—*Dešê* means the first tender green sprouts in which flocks delight.—*Rabats,* "lie down", is used specifically of quadrupeds; the Greek has κατεσκήνωσεи from idea of encampment.—"Tranquil waters": the reference may be either to noon encampment for rest, or to the quiet, smooth flow of a stream.—"Refresh": literally *"restore, bring back",* like to *"recreation".*—"My soul": Semitism for "me".

Strophe II: *Tsedek* means "straight" primarily in the physical sense; the Greek and Vulgate have given the secondary, ethical signification, to point an allegory.—"Valley of the shadow of death" may refer to the *šeol* with its unknown terrors, but certainly takes its sense from the idea of a deep, dark cañon, lonely and terrible, with chasms and wild beasts threatening death.

Strophe III: According to Bickell and Vigouroux the first hemistich of this strophe has been lost. And in fact the hemistich with which the strophe now begins, *ki-'atháh'imadyí,* has only two rythmical cadences, instead of the three which it should have in the metrical scheme adhered to quite faithfully throughout the rest of the poem. The parallelic balance may be saved by assuming there was lost a three-stressed line containing perhaps an idea like: No wolves shall set upon me, or: I shall not perish in the pits. Such an hypothesis would also dispense with the many hard-wrought explanations of the following line.[21] For, a cudgel was the ordinary weapon of shepherds for warding off the attacks of wild beasts.

Strophe IV: To attempt to carry the sheep metaphor over into this section entails absurdity, as sheep are not fed at tables nor anointed with perfumes.—In verse V the Hebrew has: "My cup (is) an abundant potion". The Greek adds ὡς κράτιστον the *quam præclarus est* of the Vulgate. It would seem that the Septuagint interpreter, not knowing well what to do with the short and obscure phrase *koçi rewayah,* thought to obtain a clearer meaning by connecting it with the first two words of the following hemistich, *'ak tôb* (instead of *tûb*), thus obtaining an interjectional predicate complement, "Most excellent!"

Strophe V: Calmet calls attention to the Oriental custom of food being sent from the royal table to favorites of the king (II Kings 11:8; Dan. 1:5).

With the Fathers this Psalm may be interpreted mystically as picturing God's tender and bountiful care for His chosen souls, the members of His Church, compared by Christ Himself to a flock and a sheepfold of which He Himself is

[21] Examples of such are: that the sheep somehow are consoled by chastisement with the rod or that the latter supports them.—If Oriental shepherds staves were really curved at the top, and this crook used in extricating sheep that had fallen into crevices or thorns, the second suggestion given might be applicable.

the Good Shepherd. Thus the fair downs are the Church; their fresh green grass, the doctrines of true faith or the Sacred Scriptures, which nourish the soul after it has been brought out of the barren, dreary wilderness of sin or unbelief. There, too, man's will is strengthened ''lest it faint in the way'' by the quiet cool waters of graces that flow so silently and refreshingly into the soul. Along straight though perhaps narrow paths does the Divine Shepherd guide man's life by His wholesome laws and counsels,—which are, after all, sweet and light, ''according to His name''. And even when life's road leads through some gloomy, danger-fraught valley of despondency, wherein men or demons threaten temporal or eternal welfare like so many fierce wolves or silent, deadly serpents, can not one still put all confidence in the shepherd's staff of God's providential power, wherewith eventually the threatening assailants will be put to flight?

The rich table, the inebriating chalice, have ever been understood of the sacramental feast of the Eucharist, whereat poor sinners are admitted to the Divine intimacy and, although dust-covered from the fight, are strengthened again for life's battle against their spiritual enemies by partaking of the Good Shepherd's own Body and Blood. The oil or perfume symbolism is, of course, readily applicable to the Holy Ghost and His fortifying function in various sacramental unctions. The concluding apostrophe of gratitude expresses the sentiments of every Christian reflecting on God's dealings in his own regard.

APPENDIX

DECISIONS OF THE BIBLICAL COMMISSION

De Auctoribus et de Tempore compositionis Psalmorum [21a]

I. Utrum appellationes *Psalmi David, Hymni David, Liber psalmorum David, Psalterium Davidicum,* in antiquis collectionibus et in Conciliis ipsis usurpatæ ad designandum Veteris Testamenti Librum CL psalmorum; sicut etiam plurium Patrum et Doctorum sententia, qui tenuerunt omnes prorsus Psalterii psalmos uni **David**

[21a] *Acta Apostolicæ Sedis,* II (1910), p. 294.

esse adscribendos, tantam vim habeant, ut psalterii totius unicus
auctor David haberi deabeat?

Resp. Negative.

II. Utrum ex concordantia textus hebraici cum græco textu alex-
andrino aliisque vetustis versionibus argui iure possit, titulos
psalmorum hebraico textum præfixos antiquiores esse versione sic
dicta LXX virorum; ac proinde si non directe ab auctoribus ipsis
psalmorum, a vetusta saltem iudaica traditione derivasse?

Resp. Affirmative.

III. Utrum prædicti psalmorum tituli, iudaicæ traditionis testes,
quando nulla ratio gravis est contra eorum genuinitatem, prudenter
possint in dubium revocari?

Resp. Negative.

IV. Utrum, si considerentur Sacræ Scripturæ haud infrequentia
testimonia circa naturalem Davidis peritiam, Spiritus Sancti charis-
mate illustratam in componendis carminibus religiosis, institutiones
ab ipso conditæ de cantu psalmorum liturgico, attributiones psalmorum ipsi factæ tum in Veteri Testamento, tum in Novo, tum in
ipsis inscriptionibus, quæ psalmis ab antiquo præfixæ sunt; insuper
consensus Iudæorum, Patrum et Doctorum Ecclesiæ, prudenter
denegari possit præcipuum Psalterii carminum Davidem esse auctorem vel contra affirmari pauca dumtaxat eidem regio Psalti carmina
esse tribuenda?

Resp. Negative ad utramque partem.

V. Utrum in specie denegari possit davidica origo eorum psalmorum, qui in Veteri vel Novo Testamento diserte sub Davidis nomine
citantur, inter quos præ ceteris recensendi veniunt psalmus II *Quare
fremuerunt gentes;* ps. XV *Conserva me Domine,* ps. XVII *Diligam
te, Domine, fortitudo mea;* ps. XXXI *Beati quorum remissæ sunt
iniquitates;* ps. LXVIII *Salvum me fac, Deus;* ps. CIX *Dixit Dominus Domino meo?*

Resp. Negative.

VI. Utrum sententia eorum admitti possit qui tenent, inter
psalterii psalmos nonnullos esse sive Davidis sive aliorum auctorum,
qui propter rationes liturgicas et musicales, oscitantiam amanuensium aliasve incompertas causas in plures fuerint divisi vel in unum
coniuncti; itemque alios esse psalmos, uti *Miserere mei, Deus,* qui
ut melius aptarentur circumstantiis historicis vel solemnitatibus
populi iudaici, leviter fuerint retractati vel modificati, subtractione
aut additione unius alteriusve versiculi, salva tamen totius textus
sacri inspiratione?

Resp. Affirmative ad utramque partem.

VII. Utrum sententia eorum inter recentiores scriptores, qui indiciis dumtaxat internis innixi vel minus recta sacri textus interpretatione demonstrare conati sunt non paucos esse psalmos post tempora
Esdræ et Nehemiæ, quinimo ævo Machabæorum compositos, proba-
biliter sustineri possit?

Resp. Negative.

VIII. Utrum ex multiplici sacrorum Librorum Novi Testamenti
testimonio et unanimi Patrum consensu, fatentibus etiam iudaicæ

gentis scriptoribus, plures agnoscendi sint psalmi prophetici et messianici, qui futuri Liberatoris adventum, regnum, sacerdotium, passionem, mortem et resurrectionem vaticinati sunt; ac proinde reiicienda prorsus eorum sententia sit, qui indolem psalmorum propheticam ac messianicam pervertentes, eadem de Christo oracula ad futuram tantum sortem populi electi prænuntiandam coarctant?

Resp. Affirmative ad utramque partem.

Die autem I Maii 1910, in audientia utrique Rm̄o Consultori ab actis benigne concessa, Sanctissimus **prædicta responsa rata habuit** ac publici iuris fieri mandavit.

Art. 3: THE CANTICLE OF CANTICLES

Texts: Cant. 1-2: 7; 4-5, 8.

323. Literary Outline.—Whilst dramatic in form, the Song of Songs has none of the regular order and balance of the Book of Job. It is rather a *canticum dramatis* or *Wechselsang,* a group of passionate yet delicate love idyls strung on the thread of the action of a typical Oriental wedding feast. The persons in whose mouths the dialogue and songs are placed, seem to be the following: the Bridegroom, represented now as a shepherd, now as King Solomon himself; the Bride, likewise represented as a shepherdess or rustic lass, and again as a queen-bride, called Sulamitess—probably the feminine form of Solomon as his counterpart; a chorus of women, the "daughters of Jerusalem"; and there are indications also of a chorus of men, who might be called the "brothers of the Bride" (Can. 8:8). Many of the lyrics are best considered as reminiscences recounting on the wedding day the incidents of the previous courtship.

Possibly the whole action may best be conceived as follows: King Solomon, visiting his vineyard upon Mt. Libanus, comes by surprise upon the Sulamite maiden, who flees from him. He visits her, disguised as a shepherd, and thus wins her love. Then he comes in state to her rustic home, to claim her as his queen. The poem opens at the wedding in the royal palace. The Bridegroom with a whole wedding procession has gone to fetch the Bride. Then, at the door of the palace, at the Bride's words: "Draw me!" (Cant. 1:3), the

Groom lifts her over the threshold in token of marriage. The chorus follows in: "We run after the . . . ". The Bride announces her entry. The chorus rejoices with her. The Bride deprecates her rustic appearance, as compared with the brilliant beauty of the ladies of the court (Cant. 1:4). Then begins a dialogue of reciprocal praise by the Bridegroom and the Bride (Cant. 1:7—2:6), concluding with a refrain parenthetically addressed to the chorus (Cant. 2:7; 3:5; 8:4).

The next cycle opens with reminiscences of the first springtime visit of the Groom (Cant. 2:8). The "brothers of the Bride" interject an obscure comment (Cant. 2:15). Then comes a mutual pledging of love, which appears again and again as a refrain (Cant. 2:16-17; 6:2; 8:14). The Bridesmaids describe the pomp of the royal escort of the King bringing his Bride to his own city (Cant. 3:6-11). Then comes a repetition of his proposal by the Bridegroom (Cant. 4:1-15). The Bride announces her acceptance (Cant. 4:16—5:1). An invitation to all to feast closes this part (Cant. 5:1d).

Next, perhaps during the feasting, the Bride recounts a dream of a visit of her Lover (Cant. 5:2), and, at the query of the chorus (Cant. 5:9), proceeds to describe his beauty at length (Cant. 5:10-16). Thereupon the Bridegroom chants an elogium of the Bride (Cant. 6:3 ss) recalling the surprise of his escort at their first sight of her (Cant. 6:8b-9). The Bride interrupts to tell how she had gone afield that morn, and had been frightened at seeing the King's military cortège (Cant. 6:10-11). The members of the latter, at her precipitate flight, had cried to stop her (Cant. 6:12). The Bridegroom then asks the chorus for a description of the Bride as she dances, and this the "daughters of Jerusalem" give (Cant. 7:1b-5). He breaks in on their elogium (Cant. 7:6-9a), and the Bride in turn interrupts him, taking his own closing metaphor out of his mouth (Cant. 7:9b).

A fresh cycle of dialogue and song begins (Cant. 7:11) with the Bride's invitation to a return to her girlhood home: perhaps this is connected with the wedding party's adjournment to the palace garden. At an aside refrain from the Bridegroom (Cant. 8:4), the chorus answers with comment on the fairness of the Bride leaning upon her Lover's arm. The Bridegroom resumes (Cant. 8:5b ss) with a renewal of his vows of love. The "brothers of the Bride" intervene to tell how in her childhood they had been worried about her future: "If she be a wall", steadfast in chastity and virtue, they resolved to honor and exalt her: if, however, like a portal, she should show herself open and accessible to seductions, they would guard and enclose her jealously (Cant. 8:8-9).

The Bride can now retort that she has indeed been a wall, a veritable fortress of virtue. Hence also she has become Solomon's consort. For her brothers, who had so faithfully kept her hitherto, she would also speak. Solomon had a vineyard near Mt. Libanus which he had let out at a rental of a thousand pieces of silver. Similarly, the vineyard of her own person, which she has kept herself, and which has now become Solomon's, she now hands over to him freely, but asks a double tithe as reward for those who watched over her childhood. Finally, in a brief epilogue, the Bride pleads with the Bridegroom to end the ceremony, so that, far from distracting guests, she alone may hear his voice and undisturbed enjoy the bliss of his love (Cant. 8:14):

> "Run to me, O my Beloved,
>   swiftly as the roe or the hart
>   upon the perfumed mountains!"

The freedom of the language of Canticles, which uses as its rhetorical base the theme of love as between man and woman, must not be judged by the puritanical standards of decadent European literature. Nay, in this matter the direct frankness of the ancient Orient, with its innocent, candid recognition of the fairest aspects of what are, after all, divinely given functions of human nature, is preferable to that later Western prudery which too often affects a glossy reticence of words only to cover real nastiness of thought. The language of Canticles indeed does not abuse or debase sexual love, but rather glorifies and sublimates it, by delicately utilizing its phases to describe, in its purest, white-hot, incandescence, the *caritas* uniting God and man.—Nevertheless, since this language is liable to be misunderstood by persons entirely ignorant of the final mystical aspects of Divine love, the reading of this Book, especially without directive commentary, is not advisable for the rude and immature.[22]

324. Thought Content.—The Canticle of Canticles is patently an allegory.[23] The very extravagance of its language demonstrates that not the primary literal significance, but the secondary or symbolical one, is that which the writer intends to be conveyed to the reader. The words and acts of perfect human love are used to express the sublimest aspects of Divine love in the state of mystical union between the human soul either personally, or collectively in the Church, and God. As by marriage human individuals, although naturally distinct, become conjoined in highest and most intimate and insepar- able relationship—"and they shall be two in one flesh" (Eph. 5:31)—so the terminology of conjugal love is fittingly used to express the consummation of the union between God and intelligent creatures, by which the latter become insofar as creatures can, "partakers of the Divine Nature" (II Pet. 1:4). Other Books of the Sacred Scriptures treat mainly of various preparatory stages of Divine love or *caritas:* Canticles treats of its final and highest earthly phase, mystical union or marriage.

The symbolic use of marital love to express relationship between God and man is not uncommon elsewhere in Sacred Scripture. The Prophets particularly use its negative or adverse phase, adultery, unfaithfulness, to express the absence or imperfection of man's love for God (Os. 1:3; 2:21; Jer. 2:2; 5:7; 23:14; Ez. *passim*). In the New Testament Christ often is compared to the Bridegroom (Matt. 9:15; 25:1; Mark 2:19; John 3:29, the Parable of the Ten Virgins, and of the Marriage Feast) and the Church, to the Bride (Eph. 5:25ss), to be united inseparably to Him in the Mar- riage of the Lamb (Apoc. 19:7, 9; 21:9; 22:17).

325. Keys to Symbolism.—It must be remembered that the allegory of Canticles may be consistently interpreted not

---

[22] The ancient rabbis did not permit the reading of this Book to persons under the age of thirty.

[23] The most venerable Jewish exegetical school interpreted Canticles as an allegory, as may be noted in the Targum *Hašir*. Solomon was taken as a figure of God, and the Bride, of the Synagogue. About the time of the Synod of Jabneh (Jamnia, A.D. 90) the rigoristic and materialistic school of Šammai strove to have this and the Books of Job and Ecclesiastes excluded from the Canon.

only in one but in several sense planes.   The Bridegroom represents God wooing mankind to Himself with an everlasting, persistent love.

> "I am True Love that false was never:
> My Spouse, man's soul, I loved her thus;
> Because she would in nowise discover
> I left My Kingdom glorious.
> I purveyed for her a palace precious;
> She flieth, I follow, I sought her so.
> I suffered this pain piteous
> *Quia amore langueo.*

> "I crowned her with bliss, and she Me with thorn;
> I led her to chamber, and she Me to die;
> I brought her to worship, and she Me to scorn;
> I did her reverence, and she Me villany.—
> To love that loveth is no mastery.
> Her hate made never My love her foe.
> Ask Me no question why
> *Quia amore langueo.*[24]

The Bride may be read to stand for either (*a*) the collective society of those who love God, namely the Church, or (*b*) for the soul of each individual man:

> "Ah, fondest, blindest, weakest,
> I am He whom thou seekest!
> Thou dravest Love from thee, who dravest Me".[25]

The royal palace at Jerusalem represents the final state of mystical union in this life, or the beatitude of Heaven in eternity.   Mt. Lebanon, or the original home of the Bride, is earth, the habitation of mankind, or man's fallen estate. The "daughters of Jerusalem" may be interpreted as the good angels, who have ever dwelt in God's glorious presence, are witnesses of His wooing of mankind, and are called upon to rejoice at the return of man to God (Luke 15:7).   And, according to Gietman,[26] "Mater autem Sponsi . . . non est alia nisi cœlestis Ierusalem.   Nunc igitur Sponsa non iam

---

[24] From a medieval English MS. ascribed to Richard Rolle, or Lydgate, according to a version by Mary E. Segar, in *Catholic World* of March, 1918, pp. 786-788.

[25] From Francis Thompson's *Hound of Heaven.*

[26] *In Ecclesiasten et Cant. Canticorum*, pp. 531-532.

rogavit (Cant. 8:5)[27] ut secum in domo matris suæ, *i.e.*, terrestris Ierusalem, habitaret, sed ut in domum Sponsi ipsa induceretur''. The vicissitudes of earthly lovers' mutual seeking and fleeing, losing and finding, longing and satisfaction are types of parallel but sublimated vicissitudes in the relationship between God and the soul, in each man's earthly life, who too can say:

> "I fled Him, down the nights and down the days,
> I fled Him, down the arches of the years. . . ."
> but "Fear wist not to evade as Love wist to pursue".

Again, it may be God who seems to flee and elude the yearning of the soul (Cant. 5:6), only to draw it on to more intense affection.—As Solomon went from Jerusalem to Lebanon to visit his vineyard, so God left His heaven to come upon earth to visit the vineyard of the human race which He had planted and let out to the prophets and teachers of old as keepers. There He found the soul, the object of His quest, darkened indeed by the hot rays of human passion (Cant. 1:5), nevertheless fair in the eyes of Divine Love. Thus it came about "ut *Dilectus* Patris *in hortum* Ecclesiæ *descenderet*, ibique *meteret myrrham* acerbarum passionum *cum aromatibus* odoriferarum virtutum cœlestemque doctrinam tanta suavitate prædicaret, ut videretur comedere *favum cum melle;* tum in ara crucis pendens amarum mortis *vinum* biberet, spe tamen resurrectionis tanquam dulci *lactis* poculo temperatum; demum omnes ad sui consortium invitaret: *Comedite, amici, et bibite, et inebriamini, carissimi*".[28]

326. Author and Authenticity.—Jewish and Christian tradition, as well as the title, ascribe the authorship of Canticles to Solomon. The thought and language bear out this ascription, as they fit well in the mouth of that brilliant monarch, or at least his times. The frequent allusions to plants,

---

[27] This obscure verse reads as follows in the Greek:
  "Under the apple tree I waked thee;
  There thy mother travailed with thee,
  There did labor she that bore thee."
See article by H. Schumacher on this verse, in *Homiletic and Pastoral Review*, Jan., 1924, pp. 345-348.
[28] Lépicier, *De incarnatione*, I, p. 2.

trees, and animals, is conformable to what is recorded else-where of Solomon (III Kings 4:33): "He treated about trees from the cedar that is in Libanus, unto the hyssop that cometh out of the wall: and he discoursed of beasts and of fowls and of creeping things and of fishes". The rhetorical comparisons to ivory, marble, and precious metals, and the references to perfumes and spices are to be expected in a king whose navy "went with the navy of Hiram by sea to Tharsis, and brought from thence gold and silver and ele-phants' teeth and apes and peacocks" (III Kings 10:22), so that "he made silver to be as plentiful in Jerusalem as stones, and cedars to be as common as sycamores which grow in the plains" (III Kings 10:27). Similarities have been noted in style between this Book and Proverbs,—likewise ascribed to Solomon. Any Aramaic terms occurring are easily explain-able by the lively commerce, even literary, with outside peoples which occurred during Solomon's time, when "they came from all nations to hear the wisdom of Solomon, and from all the kings of the earth, who heard of his wisdom" (III Kings 4:34). Besides Jerusalem, Thirsa is indeed men-tioned as a fair city (Cant. 6:3a Hebrew), but not as the capital of Samaria, which it later became.

SEVENTH PART

THE SAPIENTIAL BOOKS

Entro v' è l'alta mente u sì profondo
Saper fu messo, che, se il vero è vero,
A veder tanto non surse il secondo.
Dante, Paradiso, X, 112.

THE SAPIENTIAL BOOKS

PROVERBS, ECCLESIASTES, WISDOM, ECCLESIASTICUS

PROLEGOMENA

327. Wisdom, *hokmah,* in the common Scriptural sense, is the term applied to the human mind's reflective recognition of the order of the universe, of the consequences to be drawn from revealed or philosophic principles, and their practical application to the concrete affairs of life. As such it is presumably built upon experience and shrewd observation, and hence is looked for in persons of riper years, the "elders". These are able to cite precedent; the accumulated knowledge of generations is in their keeping. They have the lore "which wise men have told from their fathers, and have not hid it" (Job 15:18). Hence they know beforehand what the issue of an act or of a conduct series will be. But the young, inexperienced, heedless of peril, thoughtless of consequences, may say: "We are but of yesterday, and know nothing", and will do well to "inquire" of the former generation "that which the fathers searched out" (Job 8:8-9).

The answer is generally given in the form of a *mašal,* which, whether brief or lengthy, is considered as the concentrated essence of many and multifarious experiences and observations, gathered in the alembic of a sagacious intellect and distilled over the fire of life's sufferings. This traditional lore, in its primitive and most characteristic stage, is set forth under the form of wise saws or maxims, pithy, sententious, replete with wit and humor, indulging in genial banter or biting sarcasm, with a bent for detecting likenesses and contrasts,—in short, proverbs. But the *mašal* may also be expanded from an enigmatic, paradoxical gnome contained in a sentence or two, to a parable, a didactic essay or poem, or even a speculative discourse on most abstruse questions. Nevertheless its usual tendency is utilitarian, practical.

However, in final analysis, the wise man realizes that the design of God's universe is greater than the human mind and can not be included comprehensively in the latter. Hence he goes on to show that over and beyond all human science and wisdom, there is a Wisdom Divine—God's own knowledge of Himself and of all things else, whereby also the world was planned, and to whom alone the full plan of the universe is clear as to its architect. That this Divine Wisdom is expressed in a Personality, is already glimpsed. The assimilation of man's wisdom to this uncreated One, by practically taking God's complete viewpoint of the universe, is taught to be the ideal consummation of human wisdom.

328. There are not wanting indications that among the Jews (as also amongst other ancient peoples) there was a kind of caste or gild of *ḥakyim* or "wise men", distinct from priests and prophets (Is. 29:14; Jer. 18:18; Ecclus. 39:1ss). Perhaps these may be considered ancient academicians. Some of them seem to have been judges (Ecclus. 38:38); others, official counselors, as in Egypt (Gen. 41:8; Is. 19:11-12) or Babylonia (Jer. 50:35; 51:57). In David's time Chusai and Achitophel held some such position (II Kings 16:15-17:15). And of the latter indeed it was said: "Now the counsel of Achitophel which he gave in those days, was as if a man should consult God" (II Kings 16:23).

Art. 1: THE BOOK OF PROVERBS

Texts: Prov. 1-2; 8-9; 10; 22; 25; 30-31.

329. Analysis of Arrangement.—The Book of Proverbs opens with its title and a short preface (Prov. 1:1-6) which outlines the purpose of the whole work. Its motto or theme is given in Prov. 1:7: "The fear of the Lord is the beginning of wisdom". Then comes a longer general introduction (Prov. 1:8—9:18, sometimes called the "first book"). This treats of wisdom as a whole, rather than of its particular aspects, which are considered in the maxims proper. Its sub-divisions are uncertain. False wisdom is warned against under the figure of the Strange or Foolish Woman (Prov. 2: 16 ss). True wisdom is declared the supreme prize of God (Prov. 3: 11-20). Prov. 5: 1-20 may be taken literally as an exhortation against adultery, or perhaps better still symbolically as a warning against false wisdom—seductive paganism or worldly prudence as opposed to the true religious principles of God's own people (compare Prov. 6: 20—7: 1-27; 9: 13-18). Solomon may have had in mind how he was brought to idolatry through his foreign concubines (III Kings 11: 1-10). This part closes with a monologue of true Wisdom declaring her nature (Prov. 8—9), which is even Divine, insofar as the design of the universe and its true order is personified in God's knowledge.

The first collection of maxims is comprised in Prov. 10-24. Up to Prov. 22: 17 these form a generally disconnected series, having however (as far as Prov. 15), a striking uniformity of structure, insofar as the gnomic sentences are expressed in distichs of marked antithetic parallelism. With Prov. 22: 17 begin the "words of the sages", perhaps so called because they originated with the ancient ḥakim but were collected by Solomon. They are precepts on prudence and justice, developed more at length than the preceding maxims.

The second collection of gnomic sayings is comprised in Prov. 25-29. It is a supplement made under King Ezechias (about 725 B.C.), and is sometimes called the "book of the people", in contradistinction to the first collection, called the "book of youth". In this supplement antithetic parallelism is much rarer: allegory appears more frequently (Prov. 25: 11 ss). The comparisons at times are mere juxtapositions; the style is looser. In several groups a single word is repeated as a key (Prov. 25: 8-10; 26: 3-12, 13-16).

To the main collections are added three [29] short appendices. To the first of these is prefixed the name of Agûr, son of

---

[29] Steuernagel considers the "Words of the Sages" (Prov. 22: 17 ss) also as an appendix.

Yakeh (Prov. 30 : 1-39). Many of its maxims are in the riddle-like number form found also in the Prophets. The second appendix is ascribed to Lamuel, and contains the advice given him by his mother. The Book closes with an alphabetic acrostic sonnet in praise of the ideal housewife (Prov. 31 : 10-31) : it is one of the most charming compositions of Sacred Writ.

330. Authors and Text.—The general superscription and also the titles prefixed to the assimilated parts show that Solomon is to be considered the author of the major portion at least of Proverbs—which conforms to what is told of this gifted king elsewhere (III Kings 4 : 32) : "Solomon also spoke three thousand parables (*mešalim*), and his poems were a thousand and five". This conclusion receives confirmation from the general uniformity of style, and the use of certain favorite words, such as *qereth* "town", and *haderé batén* "*intima viscera*" throughout (Prov. 8 : 3; 9 : 3, 14; 11 : 11, and Prov. 18 : 8; 20 : 27, 30; 26 : 22; 7 : 27).

It is not to be said, however, that the Book of Proverbs as now it presents itself, dates from Solomon's time and hand. For, first of all it is to be noted that III Kings 4 : 32 does not state that Solomon *wrote* his proverbs, but only that he spoke them. They were probably recorded in writing at divers time by some secretary (III Kings 4 : 3), which also would explain numerous real reduplications. Like the Psalms, then, Proverbs grew gradually from several collections of maxims, most of which were of Solomonic origin or at least compilation. For, the *ḥakim* not only uttered their own sententious sayings, but gathered also those of others: "The wise man will seek out the wisdom of all the ancients. . . . He will keep the sayings of renowned men. . . . He will search out the hidden meanings of proverbs" (Ecclus. 39 : 1-13).

Whether the appendices of Prov. 30—31 are also traceable to Solomon may be questioned, although the Greek and Vulgate versions have translated the prefixed names as common nouns, and older commentators preferred seeing in these but pseudonyms of Solomon himself. The title of the first appendix should probably be read: "Sayings of Agûr, son of Yakeh, the Massaite [by הַמַשָּׂאִי for common noun הַמַשָּׂא], to Ithiel and Ukal". That of the second might be: "Sayings of Lamuel, King of Massa [by connecting *melek-massa*], which his mother taught him". Massa was a descendant of Ismahel (Gen. 25:4; I Par. 1:30), and a district about Mount Seir may have been named after him, as Duma (another of Ismahel's sons) gave his name to Idumea. Otherwise the territory is unidentified. In both these places the Greek and Vulgate translated *massa* in the sense of "burden" or message, so frequent in the Prophets. The elogium of the Valiant Housewife is anonymous, although, from its position one might conjecture that it was a tribute from Lamuel to his mother.

There are notable variations in the text of Proverbs as between the Hebrew and the Greek. The chief of these are explained by Steuernagel [30] as follows: besides the introductory section (the same in both Hebrew and Greek) there were originally three main collections and three appendices. In the Hebrew the three main collections are given first, then, the three appendices. In the Greek the appendices are joined separately to each of the main collections. Certain readings of the Greek are good, but generally the Hebrew text is better.

The Vulgate version of this Book, together with that of Ecclesiastes and Canticles, was made by St. Jerome in three days. He seems to have used a Hebrew text different from and anterior to that of the Masoretes. His translation embodies some additions apparently from the Greek (Prov. 10:4; 12:11, 13; 15:5, 27, etc.) and others of his own (Prov. 14:21; 18:6). Here and there he paraphrased the original with a thought more familiar to the Latins. Thus the "Sicut qui mittit lapidem in acervum Mercurii" of Prov. 26:8 alludes to the heathens' custom of passersby throwing a pebble at the foot of that god's statue,—whilst the original has: "As tying a stone to the sling. . . ." Both are figures of an utterly useless act.

---

[30] * C. Steuernagel, *Einleitung ins Alte Testament*, p. 676 (Tübingen, 1912).

Art. 2: THE BOOK OF ECCLESIASTES

Texts: Eccles. 1-2; 4; 8; 11-12.

331. Synopsis of Content.—Ecclesiastes is written in the form of a rambling discourse or meditative study. It has not the logical methodic rigor of a dissertation. Nevertheless one can trace a general plan, according to which the Book would be made up of a prologue, four main sections, and an epilogue. The prologue (Eccles. 1:2-11) sets forth the theme of the work: "Vanity of vanities . . . and all is vanity"—which sentence is also repeated at the beginning of the epilogue. The closing sentence of the prologue: "There is no remembrance of former things", summing up the pointlessness of life when considered apart from God, finds its answering counterpart at the close of the epilogue: "All things that are done, God will bring into judgment" (Eccles. 12:14), where the basically Divine purpose and sanction of life are declared.

The first section (Eccles. 1:12—2:26) shows the vanity of life by depicting the inconclusiveness of human wisdom (Eccles. 1:12-18) and the lack of satisfaction in the enjoyment of earthly goods and pleasures (Eccles. 2:1-11) even when these are used in moderation (Eccles. 2:12-26). Thus wisdom, riches, and pleasure, which appear to be the greatest earthly goods, are shown to be but vanity. The author confesses the attempts he has made to find real happiness outside of God—somewhat as Thompson poetically describes a similar vagrant search after happiness, in the *Hound of Heaven.*

The second section (Eccles. 3-5) shows that man is not the master of his own life, which is so dependent upon the vicissitudes sent by Providence. The happenings of existence are fixed and ordered as by fate. Man must submit and try to make the best of them. In revering God, trusting His Divine Providence, and fulfilling one's duties, lies true wisdom. The conclusion is that one must resign himself patiently to unavoidable evils, and make use of the good things that God gives.

The third section (Eccles. 6—8:15) shows that happiness does not consist in the acquisition of riches or reputation. Many are the paradoxes of life. Moderation is the best rule. Life is too vast a riddle to be solved by any man. The apparent happiness of the wicked is not to be trusted; it is safer to rely on the justice of God.

The fourth section (Eccles. 8:16—12:7) is largely a summing up of the thoughts and experiences of the three preceding ones. It is impossible for human wisdom to sound the depths of God's work (Eccles. 8:16-17); the virtuous as well as the wicked are all alike under divine Providence, whose will is unsearchable (Eccles. 9:1-6). Man must ever labor because he does not know which of his efforts will be crowned with success (Eccles. 11:3-8). Nevertheless, since all this is after all not satisfactory to the human soul as a rule of conduct, Qoheleth concludes definitely that the thought of the judgment to come should be the final practical rule of life (Eccles. 11:9-10). Man, therefore, should live from his youth to his old age in the fear of God and of the Last Judgment, wherein all the paradoxes of life shall be made clear (Eccles. 12:1-7).

The epilogue (Eccles. 12:8-14) contains the solution of the problem stated in the prologue. All man's efforts to obtain complete and real happiness upon earth are vain. The experience of Solomon, the wisest of men, who had tried everything, is proof thereof (Eccles. 12:8-10). The Sacred Books, which teach man true wisdom, lead him also to real happiness. They inform him that there exists a just Judge who on the great day of Judgment will render every man according to his works. The rule of life, then, is to revere God and keep His commandments, that is to say, to practice religion faithfully (Eccles. 12:11-14). It is God and the thought of God and the supernatural that alone give the solution to the problem of human life. Although in Ecclesiastes God is not represented as intervening personally, as in the Book of Job (with which the present has much subject matter in common), it is none the less He who solves the problem, as in Job.

328. Apparent Skepticism and Materialism.—Not a few difficulties may be raised in Ecclesiastes from the views of life and the world which the author seems to state. For example, the accusation of skepticism may be drawn from several passages (Eccles. 1:2, 8-18; 3:9-11; 6:8 and above all 8:16-17). But Qoheleth can not be accused of holding materialism *ex professo*, since he formally distinguishes the soul from the body in several passages, especially in Eccles. 12:7. But he does at times seem to deny the existence of a hereafter, or at least to doubt it (Eccles. 3:19-21): "The death of man and of beasts is one, and the condition of them both is equal: as man dieth, so they also die: all things breathe alike, and man hath nothing more than the beasts. . . . Who knoweth that the spirit of the children of Adam is sent upward, and if the spirit of the beasts is sent downward?"

In explanation of these and other statements contained in Ecclesiastes which are in apparent contradiction with revealed truth or sound philosophy, it has been suggested that the Book is in the form of a dramatic dialogue, with one person raising objections against true doctrine, and another giving their solution in statements of correct principles, or that a redactor later added corrections to the unmitigated pessimism and cynicism of the original author. But such theories are scarcely verifiable in Ecclesiastes, since there is no marked distinction of persons or of argumentation.

Perhaps the most feasible theory for explaining the apparent contradictions and the alleged skepticism, materialism, fatalism, and epicureanism of Qoheleth, is the following: that the author of Ecclesiastes is realistically portraying the vicissitudes of the unaided human intellect searching for truth in the face of the world-riddle. Thus he makes evident the errors into which man is prone to fall when, basing himself on human wisdom alone and leaving aside altogether the supernatural, he attempts to evolve a satisfactory explanation of life upon the earth. Such a person is continually running into blind alleys of mystery and despair. On the one hand the soul glimpses the highest ideals and truths, and becomes enthusiastic for virtue; on the other it is so impressed with the naked reality of crass material things that, despite all ideals, it tends to consider the latter as the sum of attainable verity, and thus is easily brought to doubt the existence of any absolute truth or right or of a finally purposeful scheme of life. Thus the contradictions and various false conclusions placed in the text of Ecclesiastes, are but vivid reflections or graphic representations of the false conclusions which every only-naturally thinking man comes to at times when observing the course of the world about him, and of the contradictions which he inevitably finds between the theory of reflective truth and the facts of practical life. Divers errors, which were to be specifically proposed later in the writings of numerous heathen philosophers, are here found conjoinedly prestated together with their corrections. And these errors and contradictions are no more to be imputed to the hagiographer's personal belief (nor to be alleged against the inspiration of Ecclesiastes) than are the imperfect or false theories on the problem of evil and suffering which the author of Job puts in the mouths of the three friends.

329. As against the allegation that Qoheleth denies the immortality of the soul and retribution in a future life, the following passages from the same Book may be adduced: "I saw under the sun [= here below] in the place of judgment wickedness, and in the place of justice iniquity. But I said in my heart [= I was convinced]: 'God shall judge both the just and the wicked, and a time shall come for everything, and (there shall be a judgment) upon every deed *there*' "— and this last word, *šam* in the Hebrew, undoubtedly here designates the future life. Again (Eccles. 12:14): "And all things that are done God will bring unto judgment, even every secret thing, whether it be good or evil", and this is the concluding sentence of the Book (see also Eccles. 9:9). As regards Eccles. 3:21, the sense of the original is the following: Who understands the nature of the soul of man, which aspires on high towards heaven, or of the soul of beasts, which turns below towards earthly things alone? The previous verses (Eccles. 3:19-20) are to be understood of the physical life only. Qoheleth compares man with the beasts under one aspect only: both have to die. In Eccles. 9:4-5, 10, the author's credence is unmistakably implied in his closing words: ". . . for neither work nor reason nor wisdom nor knowledge shall be in hell [= *šeol*, the place of the soul after death] whither thou goest".

The lack of uniformity and order in the form and alignment of the ideas in this Book serves only to bring out more forcibly, even if unconsciously, the truth which the author wishes primarily to impress: namely, the inexplicability and futility of life without God. He himself has tried everything, and nothing has satisfied him; he passes insensibly from one subject to another because nothing is capable of fixing and holding him: even utmost human wisdom of itself alone is unsatisfactory, for "the words of thinkers are like ox-goads and nails deeply driven in" (Eccles. 12:11) and torturing the mind. Nay, "much study is an affliction of the flesh".

330. Author and Language.—The title Ecclesiastes (Hebrew *Qoheleth*) assumed by the writer, signifies: He who speaks to the assembly, or the Preacher. It is a symbolic pseudonym used to express the author's function of instructing the people.[31] Whilst, of course, the figure of Solomon might be only a literary artifice assumed by a writer of a latter time (as in the Book of Wisdom), nevertheless Jewish and Christian tradition has been unanimous in ascribing the authorship of Ecclesiastes to King Solomon himself. This is confirmed by such passages as: "I, Qoheleth, was king over Israel in Jerusalem" (Eccles. 1:12); "I attained greater and more wisdom than all others who were before me over Jerusalem" (Eccles. 1:16); "I undertook great works. . . . I heaped together for myself silver and gold, and the wealth of kings and provinces, . . . And I surpassed in riches all who were before me at Jerusalem" (Eccles. 2:4-10). The high degree of culture presupposed by this Book (Eccles. 3:21; 4:17) quite befits the Solomonic period, and even the phrase "And all things obey money" (Eccles. 10:19) may well be expected to be congruent of that time. The statement, likewise, that "of the making of books there is no end" (Eccles. 12:12),

[31] Some, basing themselves on Eccles. 12:9, 13, suppose that Solomon assembled his people at the close of his life as he had once done at the dedication of the Temple (III Kings 8:55-66) and addressed to them a discourse largely preserved in this Book.

by its implication of literary activity, better befits the golden age of Hebrew national life than a later one of political and religious poverty.

Against Solomonic authorship are alleged: (*a*) Aramaisms, such as *medinah* = province (Eccles. 2:8; 3:7), *šalat* = to rule (Eccles. 2:19; 5:18), *šilton* = ruler or sultan, etc.; (*b*) Persian and other foreign words unknown to ancient Hebrew, such as *pardes* = garden, paradise (Eccles. 2:5) and *pithgan* = decree (Eccles. 8:11), in which some critics see the Greek word φθέγμα ; (*c*) philosophic and abstract expressions not met elsewhere in Hebrew writings, such as *yeš* = being (Eccles. 2:21; 8:14) and *sikluth* = foolishness (Eccles. 1:17; 2:3).—As regards the first difficulty, even if all the words so claimed are really Aramaic, it is now known that their sporadic appearance is not an indication of late Hebrew. For these and the other not strictly Hebrew terms (of the second difficulty also) would readily be imported with the strange merchandise of peacocks and ivory and monkeys and horses and sandalwood brought into Solomon's kingdom from Tyre and Egypt and even by the fleet from far-off Ophir. As for the last difficulty, Solomon could certainly have coined words to express his new ideas, just as St. Paul did later in the Epistles.—It must be admitted, however, that the argument against post-Solomonic authorship, on the basis of language and thought, is not absolutely conclusive.

Art. 3: THE BOOK OF WISDOM

Texts: Wis. 1-2; 7; 10; 16-17; 19.

331. Author and Date.—The Greek text of this Book bears the title of "Wisdom of *Solomon*", but that king is not its author. It was mistakenly attributed to him probably because the unknown hagiographer, by a common Oriental literary artifice, in Wis. 7—9 speaks in the person of Solomon, who already in antiquity had become proverbial for both his wisdom and his wealth. The Vulgate, based upon the Old Latin, omits his name.

Although indications that the writer of Wisdom was conversant with Proverbs and Ecclesiastes are not wanting, yet internal evidence does not support a theory of Solomonic authorship. For, the original language of the Book is Hellenistic Greek; the writer lived outside of Palestine, and had some knowledge of Greek philosophic schools, like the Stoics (Wis. 8:7: the four cardinal virtues) and the Epicureans

(Wis. 2:1-6, 8); he seems familiar with the work of idol factories (Wis. 15:4-9). Moreover the writer cites the Old Testament according to the Greek translation: compare the original of Is. 3:10 and 44:20 with the citations in Wis. 2:12 and 15:10 (see also Wis. 6:8; 11:4; 12:8; 16:22; 19:20).

Similarly one may deduce from internal evidence that the author was a Jew, and wrote primarily for Jews, for, his Book is filled with biblical allusions which would be intelligible only to the latter. Thus he speaks of Noe and Lot without mentioning their names (Wis. 10:4, 6) and praises the Hebrew people and the Law as only a Jew could (Wis. 3:8; 12:7).—In all probability the Book was composed in Egypt, at Alexandria, the luxurious capital of the Ptolemies. It contains evident allusions to Egyptian animal and idol worship (Wis. 12:24; 15:18-19), and the polemics of Wis. 16-19 are best understood as designed to show the superiority of the Jews' religion over the native cultus of Egypt.—The date of the composition may be conjectured to be between 150–130 B.C., since the author cites the Septuagint translation of the Pentateuch and Isaias, and the trials and persecutions of the Jews alluded to in Wis. 2:10-20; 3:1-6 may belong in the reign of Ptolemy VII Physcon (170–117 B.C.), or, if one may credit the apocryphal III Mach. 2, in that of Ptolemy Philopater (225–222 B.C.).

332. Background and Object.—With the spread of Greek philosophy consequent upon Alexander's campaigns, crass heathenism received its death-blow amongst the cultured classes of antiquity. But the skepticism this destruction primarily engendered was quickly to be followed by the rise of new world-views and theories of life. These soon crystallized into the two opposed philosophic schools of the Stoics and the Epicureans.

The district of Cyrene, bordering on the kingdom of the Ptolemies in northern Africa, and harboring numerous colonies of refugee Jews, was the homeland of both Epicurus and Carneades. These Jews could scarcely avoid reacting to the thought influences brought to bear upon them by their environment. The luxurious principles of the Epicureans would promptly be found in direct contradiction to the asceticism of the Thora, whilst the skepticism of the new systems would challenge also the closed clique of the Hebrews for answers to its numerous queries and for solutions of its doubts and difficulties.

At this period the popular teachings of Epicurus had enwrapped northern Africa, and especially Egypt with its wealthy and cultured capital of Alexandria, in an atmosphere of effeminate luxury. Eating and drinking became fine arts —not to speak of the prominence accorded to tne even lower lines of sensuality. Elegance in dress and ornament, magnificence in festivals, licence in the theatres and baths, in short, refined, systematic debauchery was the order of the day not only in Africa, but in most of the centres of the new Hellenistic culture clustered about the Mediterranean, Corinth, Tarentum, Massilia, Miletus, and even the Sicilian cities. And lust, as is well known, goes hand in hand with cruelty, with persecution of those who oppose it.

In this vicious atmosphere, and in order to combat its false philosophic principles, the Book of Wisdom was written. Therein the carnal-minded rake is opposed to the "just man" who subdues his appetites through the consideration of higher, supernatural principles. Divine wisdom revealed to the Jews is shown to be superior to the merely earthly wisdom of the Greek philosophic schools. The present is not the be-all, nor death the end-all, of existence (Wis. 1: 12-16), contrary to both the voluptuousness and the despair of the Epicurean. God made man to be like to Himself; death and sin are the fruits of diabolical disorder (Wis. 2: 22-25). The future life is ever to be borne in mind as the directive norm for the present (Wis. 1: 15-16; 3: 1-8; 6: 19-21). The author's aim is to present, in contrast with the false teachings of his period, a picture of that practical and true wisdom which shall lead man to union with God and harmony with God's order of the universe: "She is an infinite treasure to men, which they that use become the friends of God" (Wis. 7: 14).

333. Arrangement and Content.—The plan of this Book is not very clear. However, it may roughly be divided into two large sections. The first (Wis. 1-9) opens with an exhortation to the acquisition of real wisdom (Wis. 1-2), addressed particularly to princes. It gives a theoretic outline of the characteristics, intellectual and moral, of true wisdom. As against the pantheistic poverty of the Greeks this Book emphasizes the free will and personal responsibility of man, corresponding to the personal and free nature of God. Not satisfied with presenting the idea of God as a spiritual Being (which had been the zenith of Greek philosophy), Wisdom goes on to indicate the mystery of a plural personality in the Godhead (Wis. 7—9), thus developing the indications of Job. 28 and Prov. 8, and laying the foundations of the *Logos* teaching of the New Testament (John 1: 1-14; Col. 1: 15, 17; Heb. 1, 4: 12). From the unsearchable depths of the Divinity His personal Wisdom emerges as an omnipotent, willing, and understanding Being. A glimpse is granted into the ever-active, ever-blissful life of God in the eternity before the world began.

Having given the speculative aspect of wisdom, the author in the second part (Wis. 10-19) proceeds to its practical execution in historical exposition, taken from the providential preservation of God's chosen people, the Jews. Wisdom both saves and punishes, as may be seen in the history of the patriarchs (Wis. 10-11: 4), and in the punishments which befell both the Egyptians (Wis. 11: 5-27) and the Canaanites (Wis. 12: 1-18). The absurdity of idolatry, whether of the powers of nature (Wis. 13: 1-9), or of graven images (Wis. 13: 10—14: 13), or in apotheosizing ancestor worship (Wis. 14: 14-21) is brought out, sometimes with lurking sarcasm. Thereupon the author returns to the Egyptian plagues, contrasting the condition of God's faithful servants with that of the worshippers of idols, and showing how the very powers which the Egyptians revered were in the end turned to their own destruction (Wis. 15: 18—19: 5).

334. Canonicity and Language.—The Book of Wisdom was excluded from the Pharisaic canon probably because of having been composed in a foreign tongue and land. Hence it is also not found in Protestant Bibles. But St. Paul referred to it in the Epistle to the Hebrews for the establishment of dogmatic truth (compare Heb. 1:1 with Wis. 7:22; Heb. 1:3 with Wis. 7:26 in Greek; Heb. 4:12 with Wis. 18:22 and 1:6). Hence that Apostle and his contemporaries must have considered this an inspired work. Other Pauline allusions to Wisdom may be seen in Rom. 1:20-32 (Wis. 13: 1-9); Rom. 1:20-21 (Wis. 15:7); Rom. 9:22 (Wis. 12:18-20); I Thes. 5:8; Eph. 6:13-17 (Wis. 5:17-19).

335. Whilst the characteristic parallelism of Semitic authorship may be noted throughout the Book, and especially in the first part, still the writer is at ease with Greek. Compound words and adjectives are found frequently. He can handle gracefully even Greek alliterations and puns (Wis. 1:1, 8, 10; 6:22; 7:13; 16:5). Contrary to the genius of Hebrew the style at times is diffuse, sentences being filled with adjectival elements (Wis. 7:22-23).—The translation in the Vulgate is that of the Old Latin. It uses many popular expressions, such as *nimietas, partibus* for *partim, providentiœ* in the plural, etc. Now and then the translator has kept in the Latin the gender of the Greek word (Wis. 1:7: *spiritus* πνεῦμα . . . *hoc*), and the Greek singular verb form after a neuter plural subject.[32] The crude popular Latin *continens* of Wis. 8:21 should be represented in English by "And as I knew that I could not otherwise *possess* it, unless God gave it. . . ."

Art. 4: THE BOOK OF ECCLESIASTICUS

Texts: Prologue; Ecclus. 1; 6; 19; 38; 48;; 50-51.

335. Title, Author, and Date.—In the Vulgate this Book has its name of *Ecclesiasticus* (*scil. liber*) or "Church Book" probably from its having been read in the liturgical assemblies

---

[32] A similar mistranslation may be seen in the Vulgate of I Cor. 2:14: "Animalis autem homo non percipit ea quæ sunt Spiritus Dei: stultitia enim est [instead of *sunt*] illi et non potest intelligere; quia spiritualiter examinatur [instead of *examinantur*]".

of the early Christians, even when with some there was still question of its full canonicity.[33] It seems to have been in vogue especially for the instruction of catechumens. The Greek version bears the title of "Wisdom of Sirach". The Hebrew calls the author "Simon son of Josue son of Eleazar son of Sirach". Little is known of the author besides his name, which is given in the titles, in the prologue of his grandson's translation, and in the colophon (Ecclus. 50:29). It is clear that he was a diligent Scripture student, as the prologue notes, and that he was especially conversant with the Solomonic writings, which his own imitates. According to Ecclus. 34:12-13 he seems to have travelled considerably and undergone perils or persecutions of enemies (see also Ecclus. 51:3-7). It has been conjectured that he was a physician, from the praise of that profession in Ecclus. 38:1-15.

336. As to the time of the Book's composition there are two opinions, depending on whether the highpriest Simon ben Onias eulogized in Ecclus. 50:1-21 (whom the author had seen officiating), is taken to be Simon ben Onias I "the Just", who lived under Ptolemy I Lagus (305–284 B.C.), or Simon ben Onias II, who was highpriest when Ptolemy IV Philopater I (222–204 B.C.) tried to enter the Temple by force.[34] The grandson's statement in the prologue that he came into Egypt during the reign of a Ptolemy Euergetes, does not clear up the matter. For, there were two Kings also of that title, and it is not certain which one is referred to: Ptolemy III Euergetes I (247–222 B.C.), or Ptolemy VII Physcon (Euergetes II, after 170, and again 146–130 B.C.). Vigouroux [35] and Haneberg [36] favor the earlier highpriest and king and consequently date the composition of Ecclesiasticus about 280 B.C. and its translation about 230 B.C. Pope,[37]

---

[33] "Alia Sapientia, quæ dicitur filii Sirach . . . apud Latinos hoc ipso generali vocabulo Ecclesiasticus appellatur, quo vocabulo non auctor libelli sed Scripturæ qualitas cognominata est" (Rufinus, *Comm. in Symb.*, 38, in Migne 21: 374).

[34] See the apocryphal III Machabees 1: 2.

[35] *Manuel biblique*, II, p. 556 (Paris, 1906).

[36] *Geschichte der biblischen Offenbarung*, p. 486 (Ratisbon, 1863).

[37] *Catholic Student's Aids to Bible*, I, p. 316 (London, 1918).

Hudal,[38] and *Steuernagel [39] prefer to see in the names the
later personages, and consequently place the composition and
translation about 180 B.C. and 120 B.C. respectively.

The highpriest Simon the Just was indeed a remarkable man (lived
310-291 B.C.) and a real protector of his people. This can hardly
be said truthfully of Simon II, who took the part of the "sons of
Tobias" who furthered pagan ideas. Moreover, Ptolemy Physcon
claimed indeed the name of Euergetes (the well-doer), but the
Alexandrians called him rather Kakergetes (the evil-doer) or simply
Physcon (the fat-belly), and the monuments likewise do not accord
him the more flattering title. On the other hand only this latter
Ptolemy Physcon reigned sufficiently long for a man to come into
Egypt in the 38th year of his rule—as the clause in the prologue
is now generally interpreted, instead of "in the 38th year [of the
writer's age] at the period of King Euergetes". Ptolemy III
Euergetes I reigned but 25 years—The word $\pi\acute{\alpha}\pi\pi\sigma\varsigma$ used by the
translator to denote his relationship to the author, whilst ordinarily
meaning "grandfather", might also designate a remoter forbear.

337. Original Language and Versions.—As its prologue
states, Ecclesiasticus was composed in Hebrew. But, with
the exception of a few passages quoted in the Talmud, the
Hebrew text was lost until the end of the 19th century. In
1896 Mrs. Agnes Smith-Lewis and Margaret D. Gibson found
several fragments of the Hebrew text written on paper, in
a monastery of Mt. Sinai. Various unnoticed fragments were
subsequently found in European libraries. And Dr. Schech-
ter discovered larger portions in the *genizah* of an old Cairo
synagogue.

The *genizah* (from *ganaz* = to store away, cover up, hide) was
a room or treasure-place attached to a synagogue, where Scripture
manuscripts which had outserved their usefulness were reverently
laid to molder away. Books esteemed heretical by the Jews were
burnt outright. Hence the fact that certain writings are found
in the *genizah* witnesses to the canonic esteem these were held in by
the early Jews.

The combination of all these pieces has restored almost
two-thirds of the Hebrew text of Ecclesiasticus, from Ecclus.

[38] *Einleitung in die hl. Bücher des A. T'es*, p. 152 (Leipzig, 1920).
[39] *Einleitung in das A. T.*, p. 794 (Tübingen, 1912).

3:8 on.[40]   The restored text offers a considerable *plus* over the Greek and Latin. Yet it has been conclusively demonstrated that this text is not a retranslation from the Syriac version, which was itself made from the Hebrew.[41]

338. The Greek text differs considerably in the various codices; all of them agree in passing directly from Ecclus. 30:34 to 33:13b and then resuming the omitted passage—thus showing that they were all derived from one archetype. The Old Latin version found in the Vulgate was made from the Greek, and was not translated but only revised by St. Jerome. It differs considerably from the Greek, Syriac and Hebrew texts (having additions all its own, like Ecclus. 18:32 and 30:24). However, it has not the misplacement noted above as characteristic of the present Greek text.

339. Canonicity.—Because it did not appear in the Hebrew Scriptures of the 16th century, Protestants excluded Ecclesiasticus from their versions. But it was only after Christ's time, at the Synod of Jabneh (A.D. 90), when the broader-minded Gamaliel was deposed and the truly Pharisaic Eleazar ben Azariah was made head of the school, that the Jews threw out Ecclesiasticus from the canon by the dictum: "Ben Sira and all the books written from that time on do not defile the hands".

In rabbinic phraseology "all the Holy Scriptures defile the hands", that is to say, after handling one of the *canonical* Books a person must wash his hands. This peculiar custom becomes intelligible when it is noted that on the Day of Atonement the high priest washed his body, not only when he put on the sacred vestments, but also when he put them off (Lev. 16:4, 23-24). The transition from the holy to the common is marked by an ablution, as if contact with the former left behind an aura of consecration which due reverence demanded be removed before any unhallowed thing was again touched.

That, despite the decree of Jabneh, Ecclesiasticus continued to be considered Scripture by the body of the Jews

---

[40] The restored Hebrew text (without vowel-points) and a translation with notes is published as an appendix to vol. V of Vigouroux' *Sainte bible polyglotte* (Paris, 1904).

[41] See Aloys Fuchs, *Das Plus des Hebräischen Textes . . . gegenüber der Griechischen Übersetzung*, in *Biblische Studien* (Herder, 1907).

for a long time after, is shown by the citations thereof in the Talmud and Midrashim,[42] and by its being stored away in the *genizah.*[43]

Whilst there are no explicit quotations from Ecclesiasticus in the New Testament writings, still not infrequently the language of the later hagiographers reflects an esteeming familiarity with the earlier Book. Especially in the Epistle of St. James, that first Bishop of the Jerusalem community "shows himself a deep student of Ecclesiasticus, the thought of which he frequently echoes" [44] Compare, especially in the Greek texts, Ecclus. 5:13 with James 1:19; Ecclus. 19:4-17 and 28:14-30 with James 3:1-3; Ecclus. 1:33 with James 1:5-8, etc. Besides these passages, I Tim. 6:9 seems to allude to Ecclus. 11:10; Luke 12:19 to Ecclus. 11:18-19; Luke 16:19, to Ecclus. 29:15.

According to *Nestle, "early Christian writers made such extensive use of Wisdom, Sirach, and Baruch, that they appear more familiar with them than with several Books of the New Testament".[45] As an example of use of Ecclesiasticus by the Apostolic Fathers, it may be noted that Ecclus. 4:31 is quoted in the *Epistle of Barnabas* (XIX, 20), in the *Didache* (III), and in the *Apostolic Constitutions* (VII, 11).

340. Language and Contents.—The style of the Vulgate version of this Book is difficult and frequently very obscure, because the translator, clinging closely to the Greek, did not conform to the usage of classical Latin. Moreover, whilst Ecclesiasticus must be pronounced a single work and not a compilation, yet it lacks coherence and unity of sequence. It is rather a collection of varied reflections, like the *Pensées* of Pascal. The author himself perhaps realized and referred tc this when he wrote: "I awaked last of all, and as one that gathereth after the grapegatherers . . . and as one that gathereth grapes have I filled the winepress" (Ecclus. 33:

---

[42] Ecclus. 6:6 in *Sanhedrim* 100b and *Yebamoth* 63b; Ecclus. 13:15 in *Baba Kama* 92b; Ecclus. 13:25 in *Berešith Rabba* 64b.

[43] Compare No. 337 above. See also Drum's article in *Ecclesiastical Review* for March, 1918, pp. 336-339.

[44] Moulton, *Literary Study of the Bible*, p. 327 (Boston, 1905).

[45] In *Dictionary of the Bible*, art. "Sirach."

16-17). The greater part of the Book is a heterogeneous conglomerate of sententious reflections directed to the guidance of practical life. The form is generally not so gnomic as that of Proverbs. Semitic parallelism is characteristically present throughout. But very often the individual *mešalim* or maxims are expanded into brief essays, and these are separated by disconnected proverb clusters.

341. Broadly divided, Ecclesiasticus falls into two parts of unequal length. Of these the first (Ecclus. 1—42:14) contains a medley of precepts on life conduct, moral maxims suitable for divers states and occasions. A series of important virtues is enumerated, and the reader is exhorted to their practice. In similar manner common passions and sins are recounted, and men are warned against them by the painting of their evil consequences. This first section abounds in advice relative to the proper conduct of domestic and civil affairs. It exhorts to calmness of mind, to contentment with one's lot, and gives prudent rules for dealing with superiors or those of higher station. Above all it vaunts the benefits of wisdom, invites to its recognition and pursuit, and declares the Divine origin of the orderly world-plan, personified in the Logos or *Sophía,* which "came out of the mouth of the Most High" (Ecclus. 24:5).

The second section (Ecclus. 42:15—51:38) has for its object the praise of the Creator in His works, and especially in the saints of the Ancient Dispensation, who are held up as models. The recounting of the latter's history serves as a practical confirmation to the theoretic moralities of the first part. The doxology to the Creator is a veritable summary of natural theology, wherein the hagiographer expounds the divine attributes whilst describing the wonders of the visible world. It closes with an allusion to the marvels of the unseen universe (Ecclus. 43:36-37; compare Ps. 18). The Book ends with a prayer of thanksgiving for all the helps and good things which the author has received, and especially for the gift of wisdom; others also are exhorted to share therein.

342. Ecclesiasticus has always been considered by the Church as one of the first Scriptural works for reading and meditation by the young.   Already in sub-Apostolic times it was used as a kind of hand-book for the instruction of cate-chumens—the milk wherewith they were nourished before partaking of the meat of the Apostolic and prophetic writings. For, the maxims and lessons of Ecclesiasticus serve admir-ably to form not only the mind but the heart also; they inspire high ideals, strengthen against the temptations of the passions, and impress true and solid principles to guide man in the present life and make him worthy of that to come—"which in His times He shall show who is the Blessed and only Mighty, the King of kings and Lord of lords, who alone hath immortality and inhabiteth light inaccessible, whom no man hath seen nor can see, to whom be honor and empire everlasting.   Amen" (I Tim. 6:15-16).

Vetus Testamentum in Novo patet:
Novum Testamentum in Vetere latet.
(Medieval axiom)

APPENDIX

A DIGEST OF THE ENCYCLICAL "SPIRITUS PARACLITUS" OF POPE BENEDICT XV

By the REV. WALTER DRUM, S.J.[1]

In this Encyclical, of September 15, 1920, Pope Benedict XV does honor to St. Jerome, the defender of Holy Writ, and adds an important contribution to the sum of papal documents on the Bible.

A brief anlaysis of the Encyclical here follows:
Introduction: The life of St. Jerome.

I. *Doctrinal Part:* St. Jerome on the Divine dignity and absolute truth of Scripture.
1. St. Jerome on inspiration.
2. St. Jerome on Biblical inerrancy.
   A. No distinction between primary and secondary elements in the Bible.
   B. No distinction of relative truth from absolute truth in the Bible.
3. St. Jerome on historical truth in the Bible.

II. *Practical Counsels.*
1. St. Jerome on the love of the Bible.
2. St. Jerome on the virtues necessary for Bible study.
3. St. Jerome's charge to study Scripture.
   A. To the faithful.
   B. To the clergy.
4. St. Jerome on the purpose of Biblical knowledge.
   A. Spiritual food.
   B. Spiritual delights.

[1] *Reprinted from The Homiletic and Pastoral Review, January, 1921.*

This lengthy Encyclical takes up thirty-seven pages quarto, as it is promulgated in *Acta Apostolicæ Sedis*. We shall give a digest of its content, rather detailed in the important doctrinal section, somewhat cursory in the practical part. Quotations are from the Holy Father, unless either the text or foot-notes indicate some other author. Even when we use no quotation marks, our digest contains only the thoughts of the Encyclical. Our own comments will be found in the foot-notes; and they will be very few.

In his teaching on Biblical interpretation, Pope Benedict XV leaves no loophole of escape for *l'école large*. Members of this school may no longer appeal to their misconception of *Providentissimus Deus*. The Apostolic See has now explicitly condemned their theory that God intended by inspiration to teach only *primary* or *religious* truths of the Bible. They cannot now teach that the historical parts of the Bible contain errors, which have been called relative truths—that is, notions in conformity with erroneous popular traditions of the times. And the absurdity may no more be foisted upon the laity that John the Mystic so merges the discourses of Jesus into Johannine thought-forms, as to make it impossible to determine with certainty what words are of Jesus and what are of John. For this timely defense of the absolute historical worth of the Biblical narrative, scholars will ever be grateful to the Sovereign Pontiff. He has driven another stake deep down in the Llanos Estacados—in the Staked Plains of Biblical interpretations—wherein a few Catholic writers have recently lost their way.

I. INTRODUCTION: THE LIFE OF ST. JEROME

Fathers of the Church, who wrote about the same time as St. Jerome, deemed him to be "a man signally Catholic and most skilled in Holy Writ,"[2] "the teacher of Catholics,"[3]

[2] Sulpitius Severus (early fifth century), *Dialogi inter Gallum et Posthumianum habiti*, 1, 7.
[3] Cassianus (early fifth century), *Libri septem de Incarnatione*, 7, 26.

"a model in morals and leader of the world."[4] He was born[5] at Stridon, "on the confines of Dalmatia and Pannonia,"[6] baptized at Rome,[7] "nourished from childhood on Catholic milk,"[8] and educated at Rome in Latin and Greek literature. While yet a mere lad, he attempted the interpretation of Abdias;[9] and began so to love the Bible as to contemn "all the rewards this world might offer."[10] Later on[11] he again set out for the East to acquire still greater knowledge of Sacred Scripture.[12] "I did not teach myself, as some presume; but frequently gave ear to, and was a follower of, Apollinarius of Laodicea, at Antioch. Yet, while he taught me Holy Writ, I never admitted his heretical ideas in regard to its meaning."[13]

St. Jerome then led an eremitical life[14] in the desert of Chalcis, southwest of Antioch, toiling most zestfully at Hebrew and Aramaic, under the direction of a converted Jew.[15] Heretics drove him from this solitude back to Antioch, where he was ordained priest. He then betook himself to Constantinople; and here, for nearly three years, was guided by his friend and master, St. Gregory of Nazianzus, Bishop of Constantinople. The literary results of this stay were the Latin translation of Origen's *Homilies on the Prophets* and of Eusebius' *Chronicon*, and the interpretation of Isaias' *Vision of the Seraphim*. He then returned to Rome, and was often employed by Pope Damasus in ecclesiastical affairs.[16] The study of the Bible, however, was not set aside;[17] manuscripts thereof were critically studied and copied;[18] and classes in Biblical exegesis were conducted for both men and women.[19]

---

[4] St. Prosper of Aquitaine (early fifth century), *Carmen de Ingratis*, v. 57.

[5] A. D. 340-342.

[6] *De Viris Illustribus*, 135.

[7] *Epistolæ*, 15, 1, 1; 16, 2, 1.

[8] *Epistolæ*, 82, 2, 2.

[9] *In Abdiam Præfatio*.

[14] From 374 to 379.

[15] *Epistolæ*, 125, 12.

[16] From 382 to August, 385, cf. *Epistolæ*, 123, 9 (10); 127, 7, 1.

[17] *Epistolæ*, 127, 7, 1.

[18] *Epistolæ*, 36, 1; 32, 1.

[19] *Epistolæ*, 45, 2; 126, 3; 127, 7.

[10] *In Matthæum*, 13, 44.

[11] About 372.

[12] *Epistolæ*, 22, 30, 1.

[13] *Epistolæ*, 84, 3, 1.

Moreover, at the wish of the Pope, the revision of the Old Latin version of the New Testament was begun during this period.[20]

After the death of his great patron, Pope Damasus, St. Jerome went the way of his yearnings, and established a religious community nigh to the crib at Bethlehem.[21] He was still a student, and happy to learn of others:

My head was becoming hoary with gray hair; it bespoke the master, rather than the pupil. Yet I went to Alexandria; I heard Didymus. I thank him for much. That which I knew not, I learned; that which I knew, I lost not—even though he taught the opposite. Folk thought I had completed my education. Whereas, oh, the toil and the cost to me to have Baranina as my preceptor at night in Jerusalem and Bethlehem! He feared the Jews and was another Nicodemus to me.[22]

Vast were his labors now. Many codices, and his own copies of others, were collated with manuscripts provided by synagogues and the library that Origenes and Eusebius had collected at Cæsarea. He traversed Palestine in quest of Biblical knowledge, and conferred with the most learned of the Hebrews.[23] The letters of St. Paul were interpreted. Latin Biblical readings were corrected according to the wit. ness of Greek manuscripts. Most of the O. T. books were again translated from the Hebrew original into Latin.[24] Lectures in exegesis were daily given. Many letters were written in defense of Catholic unity and doctrine.

[20] In 383, the Gospels were revised. In 384, the *Roman Psalter*, a revision according to the LXX, together with the Vulgate editions of Job and the Epistles of St. Paul, were completed. These dates are controverted.

[21] Damasus died on December 11, 384. Bitter enemies then were more open and violent in their opposition to Jerome. This opposition seems to have had to do with his departure from Rome in August, 385. He stayed a spell in Antioch, Alexandria, and Jerusalem, and reached Bethlehem in 386.

[22] *Epistolæ*, 84, 3, 1 f.

[23] *Ad Domnionem et Rogatianum in I Paral. Præfatio.*

[24] Between 386 and 390 was done the Gallican Psalter, a revision which the Vulgate now contains—this is a revision of the Old Latin Psalms according to the text of the Hexapla of Origen; and parts of the Old Testament were revised according to the LXX. From 390 to 405, the Old Testament was translated from the Hebrew into the Latin.

II. DOCTRINAL: ST. JEROME ON THE DIVINE DIGNITY AND ABSOLUTE TRUTH OF SCRIPTURE

1. St. Jerome on Inspiration

From the writings of the great doctor, it is clear that with the universal Catholic Church he firmly and constantly held that "the Sacred Books, written under the inspiration of the Holy Spirit, have God as Author, and as such were given to the Church." [25] "He asserted that the books of Holy Writ were composed while the Holy Spirit inspired, or suggested, or insinuated, or even dictated,—yea, were written and edited by the Holy Ghost."

"On the other hand, he has no doubt but each sacred writer, according to his own nature and ability, acted as a free agent in giving ear to God inspiring." God's authorship is common to all the books; but their language and style are characteristic of each sacred writer. What they write, "are the Lord's words, not theirs. What He says by their mouth, the Lord utters as if by an instrument." [26] How does God effect this?

By actual graces, He illuminates the reason to see the truth that is to be given to men; He moves the will to write that which the reason dictates, and is ever present, in an especial manner, until the book is completed. Hence the knowledge of Scripture is "a precious treasure" [27] and "a choice pearl"; [28] in the Bible are found the riches of Christ, [29] and "the silver wherewith the House of God is bedecked." [30]

The appeal to the authority of Holy Writ is final. Helvidius had denied the perpetual virginity of Mary. Jerome wrote: "As we do not deny that which is written; so we

25 Vatican Council, Section III, *Constitution on Faith*, chapter 2.
26 *Tract. de Psalmis*, 88.
27 *In Matthæum*, 13, 44; *Tract. de Ps.*, 77.
28 *In Matthæum*, 13, 45 ff.
29 *Quæst. in Gen.*, Præf.
30 *In Agg.*, 2, 1 ff.; *in Gal.*, 2, 10, etc.

reject that which is not written. We believe that God was born of a Virgin, because that is what we read. We do not believe that Mary married after this birth, because we do not read that." [31]

2. St. Jerome on Biblical Inerrancy

There is no false statement in Sacred Scripture. Jerome "is not so blunt in mind nor such a country lout as to deem any of the Lord's words to need correction, or not to be inspired." [32] "There is nothing in the Gospels that does not shine and illumine the world with its light. And so, even what are looked upon as of no importance and mere commonplaces, flash with the majesty of the Holy Spirit." [33] "The Scripture cannot lie." [34] "It is wrong to say that Scripture lies," [35] or even to admit in its words an error of a name. [36] One passage of Holy Writ cannot contradict another. [37] "Though the Bible may seem to have contrary statements, both are true." [38] To accuse the sacred writers of the smallest error "smacks of the wicked Celsus, Porphyrus, and Julian." [39]

St. Augustine, too, believed in the absolute inerrancy of Holy Writ. He wrote to St. Jerome that, if he found therein anything that seemed contrary to the truth, he concluded that either the codex was defective, or the translator erred, or he himself failed to understand. [40]

Leo XIII, in *Providentissimus Deus*, taught that error was as necessarily excluded from the inspired word of God as from God Himself. And yet, despite the fact that this teaching "leaves no room for doubt or backsliding, it . . . harrows our very soul that, even among clerics and teachers of sacred studies, they have not been wanting who have proudly flaunted their own judgment, and either openly rejected or

---

[31] *Adversus Helvidium*, 19.
[32] *Epistolæ*, 27, 1, 1 f.
[33] *In Exod.*, 1, 15, ff.
[34] *In Jeremiam*, 31, 35, ff.
[39] *Epistolæ*, 57, 9, 1.
[35] *In Nahum*, 1, 9.
[36] *Epistolæ*, 57, 7, 4.
[37] *Epistolæ*, 18, 7, 4; 46, 6, 2.
[38] *Epistolæ*, 36, 11, 2.
[40] St. Augustine to St. Jerome, *Epistolæ S. Hieronymi*, 116, 3.

covertly opposed the *magisterium* of the Church in this matter.''

A. Primary and Secondary Elements in the Bible. These recent writers distinguish between a *primary,* or religious, and a *secondary,* or profane, element in Scripture. ''They profess to extend inspiration to every sentence—yes, to every word of the Bible; and yet they restrict and narrow down its effects—especially inerrancy and absolute truth—to the *primary* or religious element.'' God teaches only religious truths, and leaves the rest to the imbecility of the sacred writer! No wonder, then, that the Bible contains error in matters physical and historical! And some go so far as to claim that this opinion is within the bounds set by Leo XIII, ''since he declared that the sacred writer speaks of things of nature according to their outward appearances, which are at times deceiving.''

Against these writers, Leo XIII allows no error in the Divine Word because of such outward appearances. ''He teaches that inspiration extends, without any preference or distinction, to all parts of the Bible; and that no error can enter into the inspired text.''

B. Absolute and Relative Truth. They also err from the teaching of the Church, ''who deem that historical statements in Scripture rely not on the *absolute,* but on what they call the *relative* truth of the facts—that is, on the common opinion of the times.'' Nor do they hesitate to appeal to Leo XIII, ''because he said that the principles laid down about things of nature could be applied to history.'' As the sacred writers spoke of physical phenomena according to appearances, so they narrated historical events according to the common opinion of the times and the false witness of others, without indicating the sources or making these statements their own.

''Why should we refute at length an opinion so harmful to our predecessor, so false and full of error?'' There is no comparison of things of nature with history. Physical statements have to do with that which appears to the senses; they must agree with the phenomena or appearances. Historical statements have to do with the facts; they must agree with the facts. "The principal rule of history is this, that the written facts must agree with the facts as they actually took place."

As to the teaching of Leo XIII in *Providentissimus Deus,* it is directly against the admission of any error whatever into the sacred text: "Utterly impossible were it either to restrict inspiration to only certain parts of Sacred Scripture, or to grant that the sacred writer erred."

If Leo XIII says that in interpreting historical statements we may apply the same principles as in the exegesis of physical phenomena, "he lays down no general rule to this effect; but only bids that we proceed in like manner to refute the errors of adversaries, and to defend from their attacks the historical worth of Sacred Scripture."

3. St. Jerome on Historical Truth in the Bible

These seekers after novelties think even to back their theory by the authority of the Doctor of Stridon, as if he made it his rule in history to defend the worth of the Bible, "not according to what took place, but according to what at that time was thought to have taken place." [41]

This is to twist the words of St. Jerome away from their meaning. He does not say that, "in narrating historical facts, the sacred writer was ignorant of the truth and fell in with the opinion of the people; but that, in naming persons and things, he followed the current way of speaking." Thus the evangelist speaks of St. Joseph as the father of Jesus; and his whole narrative leaves no doubt as to the meaning of the term. St. Jerome's real teaching in this matter is that, unless we believe in the historical worth of the Scriptures, we give up the belief in God Himself:

This is what I say. A man believes in God the Creator. He cannot believe that, unless he first believes those things to be true which are written of the saints. . . . Unless a man believes this and all the rest that is written of the saints, he cannot believe in the God of the saints. [42]

[41] *In Jeremiam,* 23, 15 ff.; *in Matthæum,* 14, 8; *Adversus Helvidium,* 4.
[42] *In Philemonem,* 4.

Other maligners Sacred Scripture has. "Were he alive, St. Jerome would fire at them the shafts of his piercing words. For they set aside the interpretation and judgment of the Church; they fly to cover of what they call implicit citations and narratives in the guise of history; they vaunt it that there are in the Sacred Books certain forms of literature, with which the entire and perfect truth of the Divine Word cannot be made to dovetail; or they express such views on the origin of the Bible that its very authority totters or utterly tumbles down."

In interpreting the Gospels, these writers "lessen the human, and destroy the Divine trustworthiness thereof. They deem that what things our Lord Jesus Christ said and did, have not reached us entire and unchanged by the witness of those who exactly wrote up that which they themselves saw and heard; but (especially in the case of the Fourth Gospel) have partly come from the evangelists—who evolved out of their own consciousness and superadded many of these facts— and have partly accrued from the narrative of the faithful of a later age. Thus it comes to pass that waters, which sprang from two sources, now flow in the same channel in such wise as not to be distinguishable from each other with any degree of certainty.

"Not so did Jerome, Augustine, and the other Doctors of the Church understand the historical trustworthiness of the Gospels. Of this trustworthiness 'he, who actually saw, hath borne witness; and his witness may be relied upon. Yea, he knoweth that he speaketh truth, so that ye also may believe.' " [43] The teaching of Jerome on the inerrancy of Scripture is the very teaching of Christ Himself.

III. PRACTICAL COUNSELS

1. St. Jerome on the Love of the Bible

St. Jerome had a most ardent love for the Bible. That is why he studied it so accurately. To his scientific knowledge it is due that "the Vulgate version, done by our Doctor of

[43] John 19: 35.

the Church, is admitted by the consent of all unbiased judges to be far superior to other ancient versions. For it seems more accurately and more elegantly than they to render the original text." This Vulgate, "if God most graciously grant Us life therefor, We hope to see corrected and restored according to the witness of manuscripts. From this arduous and painstaking task, which Our predecessor of happy memory, Pius X, wisely entrusted to the Benedictine brethren, We do not in the least doubt but new aid to the understanding of Scripture will result."

2. St. Jerome on the Virtues Necessary for Bible Study

St. Jerome's way of Biblical study was that of solitude, diligence, and humility. He fled the vanities and inanities of this world, so as the more readily to apply his mind to hard mental work. And, the more effectively to do that work, he put on Christ, who was "meek and lowly of heart." [44]

At the outset, pride prevented St. Augustine from understanding Scripture:

It seemed to me not to be worth comparing with the dignity of Tullius. My pride turned away from its style; my wit failed to reach its meaning. It was a something that children might esteem more and more. But I chafed at being a child; and, with overweening arrogance, rated myself full grown. [45]

In like manner, St. Jerome was at first so distracted by the delights of profane literature that he failed to learn the lowly Christ in the lowliness of Scripture:

And so, wretch that I was, I fasted, when about to read Tullius. After long watches by night, after the tears which the memory of my past sins aroused from the deepest depths of emotion, I took up Plautus to read. If at times, in an afterthought, I began to read the Prophets, their rude language palled on me; and, because I saw not the light with blinded eyes, I laid the blame on the sun and not on the eyes. [46]

However, he soon so loved the foolishness of Christ as to be a living proof that lowliness of mind helps to the right understanding of the Bible.

[44] Matthew 11: 29.
[45] *Confessions*, iii, 5; cf. also viii, 12.
[46] *Epistolæ*, 22, 30, 2; Encyclical, *Acta Ap. Sed.* (1920), p. 401.

By this lowliness of mind he was convinced that, "in interpreting Holy Writ, we always need the Holy Spirit." [47] He begs prayers for guidance and grace, and humbly relies on that which has been handed down by the Fathers, who wrote before him. "He so entrusts himself to the authority of his forebears as to say that he has learned 'whatsoever he has learned, not by himself—that is, by presumption, the worst of teachers—but from the illustrious men of the Church.' [48] He confesses that he 'never trusted in his own powers in regard to Holy Writ.' [49] And to Theophilus, Bishop of Alexandria, he makes known this norm, whereby he regulated his life and sacred studies: 'Know thou that there is nothing more timehonored for us than to stand by the rights of a Christian; not to change the boundaries, set by the Fathers; and ever to remember the Roman faith, proclaimed by the Apostolic lips.' [50] . . . Always following this rule of faith in the study of Scripture, he refutes a certain false interpretation of the sacred text by one only argument: 'The Church of God does not accept that!' " [51]

That humble, absolute, unreserved trust in the Church as his rule of faith, made Jerome fearless against the foe: "I have never spared heretics. I have done all in my power to make the foes of the Church to be my foes." [52] To Rufinus he wrote: "I cannot agree with you in regard to one thing, —that I spare heretics, and so proclaim that I am not a Catholic." [53]

"If ever before, Venerable Brothers, certainly to-day, when not a few boldly carp at the authority and power of God revealing and of the Church teaching, all Christians, cleric and lay, should be quickened by the spirit of the great Doctor. . . . Therefore it behooves that ye by all means raise up many and most fit defenders of the holy cause, that

---

[47] *In Michæam*, 1, 10, 15.
[48] *Epistolæ*, 108, 26, 2.
[49] *Ad Domnionem et Rogatianum in I Paral.*, Præfatio.
[50] *Epistolæ*, 63, 2.
[51] *In Daniel*, 3, 37; Encyclical, *Acta Ap. Sed.*, p. 403.
[52] *Dialogus contra Pelagianos*, Prologus 2.
[53] *In Michæam*, 1, 10 ff.

they may not only battle against those who deny there is a
supernatural order and admit no such thing as Divine revelation and inspiration; but may also take issue with those who
hanker after profane novelties, dare to interpret Sacred Scripture as if it were merely a human book, throw over opinions
that have been accepted in the Church from venerable antiquity, or so neglect her *magisterium* as to make little of, or
to pass by in silence, or treacherously and rashly to distort
to their own way of thinking, the Constitutions of the Apostolic See and the decrees of the Pontifical Biblical Commission. May all Catholics follow the golden rule of the holy
Doctor; and, giving ear to their Mother, abide in all modesty
within the ancient boundaries set by the Fathers and ratified
by the Church.''

3. ST. JEROME'S CHARGE TO STUDY SCRIPTURE

A. To the Faithful. So long as the soul be made ready
by piety and humility, St. Jerome charges all to read the
Bible daily: ''Let the mind be daily fed by Divine reading.'' [54] ''Day and night we should read the Scripture, and
meditate on the Lord's law, so that, as skilled money-changers,
we may know which coin is genuine and which is counter-
feit.'' [55]

Most especially are the Gospels and Acts to be daily read
by all the faithful. To this end, the Society of St. Jerome
is spreading these books far and wide, so that no Christian
family be without them. It is most desirable that there be
in every diocese branches of this Society of St. Jerome.

B. To the Clergy. St. Jerome charges priests, even more
than the faithful, to study Scripture; since ''they are Divinely
called to preach the Divine Word.'' To Rusticus he writes:
''Let the Book never be out of thy hand or thy sight.'' [56] To
Nepotianus: ''Often read the Divine Scriptures; let the
sacred reading never be set aside.'' [57]

[54] *In Titum*, 3, 9.
[55] *In Ephesios*, 4, 31.
[56] *Epistolæ*, 125, 7, 3; 11, 1; Encyclical, *ibid.*, p. 406.
[57] *Epistolæ*, 52, 7, 1.

Priests should nowadays study the Bible after the manner prescribed by Leo XIII in *Providentissimus Deus*. This Catholic way of Biblical study will be the better followed, if priests attend the Biblical Institute which Pius X "established to the great gain of Holy Church—as has been clearly proven by the experience of the past ten years." Hence, "it is desirable, Venerable Brothers, that, under your direction and auspices, select members of both the secular and regular clergy gather from all parts of the world, to devote themselves to Biblical study in Our Institute."

4. St. Jerome on the Purpose of Biblical Knowledge

A. Spiritual Food. The first purpose of a knowledge of Sacred Scripture is the food whereby the life of the spirit is sustained. St. Jerome "was wont in Biblical study to eat the bread of heaven and the celestial manna, which held within itself all delights." [58] How can we do without that food? How can we break unto others the bread of doctrine, unless we are ourselves sated therewith? Leo XIII wrote in *Providentissimus Deus:* "It is most desirable and necessary that the use of Scripture inflow into the study of theology, and be wellnigh its very soul." That is why the study of the Bible is of the greatest moment to those who preach the Divine Word. "Let the very language of the priest be seasoned by the reading of the Scriptures." [59]

The rules, which Jerome wishes observed in the use of Scripture, are especially worth while to preachers. First is to be found out just what the sacred writer meant to say.[60] Thereafter, the allegorical interpretation may be given, if it have the authority of many Fathers and commentators. "We do not deny that Jerome and some Latin Fathers, in imitation of the Greeks that went before them, at first yielded unduly, perhaps, to allegorical interpretations." But love of Scripture and indefatigable toil led Jerome more and more to insist on the literal meaning.

[58] P. 408.
[59] *Epistolæ*, 52, 8, 1; Encyclical, *ibid.*, p. 409.
[60] *In Matthæum*, 25, 13.

"Hence, we should first fix our mind on the literal interpretation." [61] Even when Jerome interpreted allegorically, he presupposed the literal meaning of the Bible as a foundation: "We do not deny the historical fact; but we prefer its spiritual interpretation." [62] He warns that, "while we seek spiritual riches, we should not seem to contemn the poverty of historical facts." [63] Such mystical interpretations as neglect the historical sense are condemned by him: "The prophetic promises should not be rated mere words, meaningless terms that contain only a figurative sense. Let them be understood to be builded on solid ground, and to be founded on history. Then they may uphold a spiritual interpretation." [64] The allegorical meaning of a passage may be given, "so long as it is derived from the literal and is approved of by the authority of many." [65] "There is great danger, when one preaches in the Church, lest perchance by a false interpretation the Gospel of Christ become a gospel of man." [66] The chief aim of the preacher should be to give to the faithful the simple truth of the inspired text; and not to disport his own empty eloquence.[67]

B. Spiritual Delights. In the study of Scripture Jerome found the greatest spiritual delights. He wrote to Paula: "I ask thee, what is more hallowed than this hallowed study? What is sweeter than this pleasure? . . . Let others have their wealth, drink, gems, dazzle by their silks, delight in popular applause, and fail to reach the end of their riches in the merry-go-round of pleasures. Our delight is day and night to meditate on the law of God, to knock at the door as yet unopened, to beg bread of the Trinity, and, following the Lord, to trample upon the surging sea of worldly pleasure." [68]

Loyalty to the Church was a great delight which Jerome got by Scripture study. "In the Holy Writ of each Testa-

---

[61] *Acta Ap. Sed.*, p. 410.
[62] *In Marcum*, 9, 1-7; cf. *In Ezechielem*, 40, 24-27.
[63] *In Eccle.*, 2:24 ff.
[64] *In Amos*, 9, 6.
[65] *Acta Ap. Sed.*, p. 412.
[66] *In Galatas*, 1, 11 ff.
[67] *Acta Ap. Sed.*, p. 413.
[68] *Epistolæ*, 30, 13; Encyclical, ibid., p. 414.

ment, he was wont everywhere to find the praises of the Church set forth." Are not almost all the holy women of the Old Testament types of the Spouse of Christ? Do not the priesthood, sacrifices and solemnities of the Old Law foreshadow the glory of the New? [69]

A strong personal love of Jesus Christ also came from Jerome's study of the Bible. "Since the Head cannot be separated from His mystic Body, zeal for the Church is necessarily joined to a love of Christ; and this love is the chiefest and sweetest fruit of a knowledge of Scripture." He wrote: "Ignorance of Scripture is ignorance of Christ." [70] To him even Old Testament study was a means to knowledge and love of our Lord. "I do not belittle the Law and the Prophets; rather I praise them in that they preach Christ. I so read the Law and the Prophets, as not to abide in the Law and the Prophets, but through the Law and the Prophets to come unto Christ." [71] From this strong personal love of Jesus sprang Jerome's spirit of prayer, love of the Cross, ardent devotion to the Holy Eucharist, and reverence for the Mother of God. [72]

"Jerome still cries out! He cries out what is the dignity of Scripture, what is its entire and historical trustworthiness, what a precious harvest may be reaped from reading and meditation therein." [73]

[69] *Acta Ap. Sed.*, pp. 414-418.
[70] *In Isaiam*, Prologue; cf. *Tract. de Psalmis*, 77.
[71] *Tract. in Marcum*, 9, 1-7.
[72] *Acta Ap. Sed.*, p. 420.
[73] *Acta Ap. Sed.*, pp. 421-22.

INDEX OF SUBJECTS, PROPER NAMES, PLACES, ETC.

The Spelling of Biblical Names follows the usage of the Vulgate and Douay-Challoner versions.
The numbers refer to pages of this volume.

INDEX OF SCRIPTURE PASSAGES

Quoted, Commented, or Referred to.

Order and Nomenclature is that of the Vulgate and Douay-Challoner versions.
The bold figures indicate pages in this volume.

OLD TESTAMENT

New Testament

COMPARATIVE LIST OF THE TITLES OF BIBLICAL BOOKS

For the convenience of converts or others accustomed to the King James (English Protestant) version spelling and nomenclature, the following list gives the titles of the Old Testament Books according to the King James version, opposite their corresponding form in the Douay-Challoner version commonly used by English-speaking Catholics. There are also slight differences to be noted in the division and numeration of chapters and verses in some of the Books. Those of the Psalms are stated in the article of that name in this volume.

The New Testament titles are the same in both versions, with the exception that the Apocalypse is called "Revelation" in the King James.

DOUAY-CHALLONER	KING JAMES	DOUAY-CHALLONER	KING JAMES
Genesis	Genesis	Ecclesiastes	Ecclesiastes
Exodus	Exodus	Canticle of	Song of
Leviticus	Leviticus	Canticles	Solomon
Numbers	Numbers	Wisdom	*lacking*
Deuteronomy	Deuteronomy	Ecclesiasticus	*lacking*
Josue	Joshua	Isaias	Isaiah
Judges	Judges	Jeremias	Jeremiah
Ruth	Ruth	Lamentations	Lamentations
I Kings	I Samuel	Baruch	*lacking*
II Kings	II Samuel	Ezechiel	Ezekiel
III Kings	I Kings	Daniel	Daniel
IV Kings	II Kings	Osee	Hosea
I Paralipome-non	I Chronicles	Joel	Joel
		Amos	Amos
II Paralipome-non	II Chronicles	Abdias	Obadiah
		Jonas	Jonas
I Esdras	Ezra	Micheas	Micah
II Esdras (*Nehemias*)	Nehemiah	Nahum	Nahum
		Habacuc	Habakuk
Tobias	*lacking*	Sophonias	Zephaniah
Judith	*lacking*	Aggeus	Haggai
Esther	Esther	Zacharias	Zechariah
Job	Job	Malachias	Malachi
Psalms	Psalms	I Machabees	*lacking*
Proverbs	Proverbs	II Machabees	*lacking*